THE PICTURE HISTORY OF THE BOSTON RED SOX

GEORGE SULLIVAN

THE PICTURE HISTORY
OF THE
BOSTON RED SOX

1980 EDITION

THE BOBBS-MERRILL COMPANY, INC.

INDIANAPOLIS / NEW YORK

Grateful acknowledgment is made for permission to quote from the following books:

The Glory of Their Times by Lawrence S. Ritter. Copyright © 1966 by Lawrence S. Ritter. Reprinted by permission of the author.

My Turn At Bat: The Story of My Life. Copyright © 1969 by Ted Williams and John Underwood. Reprinted by permission of Simon & Schuster, a Division of Gulf & Western Corporation.

The Babe Ruth Story by Babe Ruth as told to Bob Considine. Copyright, 1948, by George Herman Ruth. Reprinted by permission of the publisher, E. P. Dutton.

My Greatest Day in Baseball as told to John P. Carmichael, copyright 1945, 1950, 1951, © 1963, 1968 by Grosset & Dunlap, Inc. Used by permission of Grosset & Dunlap, Inc.

Unless otherwise noted, the photographs in this book are from the Boston Red Sox, Northeastern University's World Series Room, the Boston Public Library or the private collections of Smokey Joe Wood, Bob Remer and the author.

Library of Congress Cataloging in Publication Data

Sullivan, George, 1927-
    The picture history of the Boston Red Sox.
      1. Boston.   Baseball club (American League)—History. I. Title.
GV875.B62S9 1980 796.357'6409744'61 80-690
ISBN 0-672-52653-0

Designed by Helen Barrow
First printing

For my mother and father,
who passed on to me, among other appreciations,
a love of baseball in general
and the Red Sox in particular;
for Lisa, George and Sean,
who may carry that torch on to a future generation; and
for Betty,
who shared most of my Red Sox years,
from Fenway Park to Sarasota and Winter Haven,
as well as around the American League—sometimes in person,
always in spirit.

ACKNOWLEDGMENTS

Over the past quarter century, I have written countless words about the Red Sox. But those stories and columns were sprints compared to the marathon of compiling the roller-coaster history of that team in words and pictures.

Many along the route deserve credit for assists.

The Red Sox organization could not have been more cooperative. Particular thanks go to Vice President for Public Relations Bill Crowley, Publicity Director/Statistician Dick Bresciani, Promotions Director Jim Healey and to Mary Jane Ryan, the public relations department's all-league executive secretary.

George Collins and his *Boston Globe* library team also deserve special recognition—no clipping was too elusive, no microfilm too remote. And the *Globe*'s help in locating and providing photographs was always generous. Those results can be appreciated throughout the book in the artistry of chief sports photographer Frank O'Brien and the parade of *Globe* camera people who have captured the sports scene on film over the decades.

A wealth of photographs was also provided by the Red Sox, much of it the product of team photographer Jerry Buckley's skilled lens.

Dick Raphael, whose work often decorates *Sports Illustrated*, also brightens this book with his color genius.

Other important artwork was provided by Jack Grinold, Northeastern's all-pro director of sports information who oversees that university's unique World Series Room, and the late Frank Moloney of the Boston Public Library.

Smokey Joe Wood and son Bob contributed some notable pictures from their family collection. So did longtime newspaper colleague Bob Remer.

And John Fredrickson was both patient and fearless in risking pneumonia and frostbite while shooting rolls of film of the author at Fenway Park one harsh March afternoon.

The Boston Public Library and the Boston University libraries were important to my research. So were the writings of Harold Kaese, the late and gifted *Boston Globe* columnist, sports historian and friend. Also helpful were the writings of some other pretty fair baseball historians: Fred Lieb, Ed Walton, Henry Berry, Larry Ritter and Donald Honig.

Kevin Dupont, Bob Duffy and David Cataneo helped in a variety of ways, all important. (They have also made their old journalism professor proud as I admire their sportswriting for the Boston *Herald American* and *Boston Globe*.)

Gene Rachlis and Kevin Connors of Bobbs-Merrill, designer Helen Barrow and literary agent Bill Berger once again proved their reputations as heavy hitters.

Mary Sullivan Ford was more than an all-star typist; she was, as she's been for 45 years, an inspiration to me, and surely belongs in the Big Sister Hall of Fame.

And finally, I am grateful to those who have been so patient all these many months—wife Betty and children Lisa, George and Sean, who shared their husband and father with a marathon he had to run.

GEORGE SULLIVAN
Belmont, Massachusetts
April 1980

CONTENTS

A section of color photographs follows page 128.

FENWAY PARK
Constructed 1912
Rebuilt 1934

Posted distances to fences:

	Feet	Meters
Left field	315	96
Left-center field	379	115.5
Center field	390	118.9
Right-center field	420	128
Right field	380	115.8
Right-field line	302	92

Height of fences:

Left-field wall*	37	11.3
Center-field wall	17	5.2
Bull pen fences	5	1.5
Right-field fence	3-5	.9-1.5

*Screen extends 23 feet/7 meters above wall, making total height of 60 feet/18.3 meters.

Seating capacity:

Roof boxes	594
Field-level boxes	13,250
Reserved Grandstand	12,274
Bleachers	7,418
TOTAL	33,536

Record crowds: 46,995 (August 19, 1934, doubleheader vs. Tigers)
46,766 (August 12, 1934, doubleheader vs. Yankees)
Post-war and single-game record: 36,388 (April 22, 1978, vs. Indians)
Night-game record: 36,228 (June 28, 1949, vs. Yankees)
Opening Day record: 35,343 (April 14, 1969, vs. Orioles)
Record season attendance: 2,320,643 (1978)
Home attendance has exceeded two million three times, one million 23 other times.

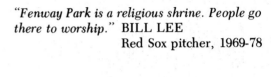

1
FENWAY

"Fenway Park is a religious shrine. People go there to worship." BILL LEE
Red Sox pitcher, 1969-78

FENWAY PARK'S OFFICIAL GROUND RULES

Foul poles, screen poles and screen on top of left-field fence are outside of playing field.

Ball going through scoreboard, either on the bound or fly: 2 Bases.

Fly ball striking left-center-field wall to right of line behind flagpole: Home Run.

Fly ball striking wall or flagpole and bounding into bleachers: Home Run.

Fly ball striking line or right of same on wall in right center: Home Run.

Fly ball striking wall left of line and bounding into bull pen: Home Run.

Ball sticking in bull pen screen: 2 Bases.

Batted or thrown ball remaining behind or under canvas or in cylinder: 2 Bases.

Ball striking bevel on the wall between the foul pole in left field and the corner back of the flagpole, and bounding into stands or out of park: 2 Bases.

Ball striking top of scoreboard, also ladder below top of wall and bounding out of the park: 2 Bases.

Above. Fenway Park in the late twenties. Note overflow crowd
perched on Duffy's Cliff in front of the left-field wall.

Below. Fenway Park on Opening Day 1934 after it had been
reconstructed the previous winter by new owner Tom Yawkey.

WASHINGTON vs RED SOX

Photo by
F.A. GEORGE
J.H. ARMSTRONG
126 Dartmouth St.
BOSTON

Fenway Park's entrance has changed little since 1912, when the ball park was built.

It is the last of a kind, a precious antique from another era. It is the major leagues' only remaining single-deck stadium and its grass is real.

Fenway Park is a snug, intimate bandbox where fans feel they can reach out and touch their heroes—and know that their taunts will be heard by the villains.

As Roger Angell wrote in *The New Yorker* reviewing the 1975 World Series, 50,000 fans *watched* the games at Cincinnati while 35,000 *participated* in the games at Fenway.

Along with its coziness and charm, there are other distinctive characteristics that contribute to Fenway's rare atmosphere. Its perimeters resemble part of a jigsaw puzzle, a succession of walls and barriers jutting in and out at odd angles, designed not by a mad architect, but to conform to the property's peculiar real-estate boundaries.

And the most unlikely contour of all is *The Wall*, alias the *Green Monster*. The 37-foot-tall fence in left field is baseball's Lorelei, luring right-hand hitters (even some left-hand hitters) with its beauty and apparent accessibility less than the posted 315 feet away—only to ruin many who have fallen for it. The Wall is baseball's most notorious landmark, a beckoning target staring batters in the face.

Has there ever been a right-handed fan—even those with increasing waistlines and decreasing eyesight—who isn't convinced he could stand at the plate and tattoo The Wall? It's a fantasy of any Fenway fan who has ever gripped a Louisville Slugger.

It's small wonder that rookies drool when they see The Wall for the first time, a temptation even weak hitters can't resist. It kindles a twinkle in the eye of banjo hitters, instant mental spinach to make them feel like sluggers. And ruined are those hitters so mesmerized that they've altered their stance and swing, their batter's box equilibrium and normal concentration destroyed.

The Wall has disturbed an entire team's concentration—the Red Sox building lineups around it. They have loaded up with a parade of right-hand hitters like Cronin, Foxx, Doerr, Tabor, DiMaggio, York, Stephens, Dropo, Jensen, Malzone, Stuart, Petrocelli, Conigliaro, Scott, Fisk and Rice. (Yet, curiously, the 13 league batting crowns worn by Red Sox hitters since 1941 all have been won by left-hand batters hitting to spacious right field. Ted Williams won six, Carl Yastrzemski three, Pete Runnels two, Fred Lynn one and Billy Goodman one.)

By shaping a lineup with right-hand power for Friendly Fenway, and some years proving almost unbeatable there, the Red Sox have invited disaster on the road, sometimes collapsing when confronted by stadiums with normal dimensions.

Right-hand hitters have cursed The Wall for another reason. While it has accounted for the world's shortest home runs this side of the old Polo Grounds, some of the longest singles also have rattled off it, the tall Wall abbreviating some liners before they could get fully airborne, drives that would be homers elsewhere. And while Red Sox hitters usually can squeeze doubles out of such shots, visitors often have been held to

View from the left-field roof.

singles by the superb retrieves of Williams and Yastrzemski, versed in The Wall's every dent and carom.

Most pitchers hate working at Fenway, too—especially southpaws. It is not coincidence that no Red Sox left-hander has won 20 games in more than 25 years (Mel Parnell the last in 1953). Not only does disaster lurk little more than 300 feet away, but pitchers loathe the closeness of the stands. While that proximity helps make Fenway so chummy, it also means most foul flies are unplayable, swallowed up by the stands to provide batters new life and pitchers more headaches.

So runs are cheap there; and that contributes to Fenway's allure because most fans love slugfests. Few leave a 7-0 game in the fifth inning, or even a 9-3 game in the eighth, in an effort to beat traffic. Those who do often tune in their car radios to learn the game somehow has been tied.

There is a temptation to try to beat the crush, though, because traffic congestion and lack of parking are among Fenway's shortcomings. Built in 1912 long before the boom of the horseless carriage, it is surrounded by narrow streets which congeal traffic and limit parking.

Fenway's basic construction also contributes to another blemish: girders and posts that obstruct view. Also, seating is squeezed, which heightens the park's intimacy but is hard on kneecaps and eardrums. And as the majors' tiniest stadium, its limited seating requires customers to purchase tickets well in advance.

For those who like contrived hysteria, there are no fireworks except on the field. And while a giant scoreboard with 8,640 light bulbs was installed in 1976 as a concession to the electronic age, it refuses to exhort the team to *"charge!"* or the fans to *"cheer!"* And the organ music is too conservative for some tastes, shunning ruffles and flourishes.

Whatever its flaws, New Englanders love Fenway and regard it as a landmark such as the Old North Church, Bunker Hill Monument and Old Ironsides. They prove it by flocking to Fenway in record numbers, averaging upward of 1.8 million the last 13 seasons in a park that seats only 33,538. They also spend well over a million dollars a year on concessions.

What fans get for their money is often throbbing excitement, drama heightened by some very odd bounces off Fenway's jigsaw and lopsided boundaries, particularly The Wall.

"It's the most interesting ball park in baseball in which to watch a game," notes Yastrzemski, who has played in nearly 1,500 games there, more than any other person. "You never know what's going to happen. Anything can happen there—and often does."

The Wall is closer than the posted 315 feet.

Random Fenway Facts:

The new stadium was named by Red Sox owner John I. Taylor, who said with indisputable logic: "It's in the Fenway section (of Boston), isn't it? Then call it Fenway Park."

First game at Fenway: April 9, 1912. Red Sox defeated Harvard, 2-0, in an open-house exhibition game to showcase the new park.

First official game: April 20, 1912, after rainouts the previous two days. Red Sox defeated the New York Highlanders, 7-6, in 11 innings to delight 27,000. Tris Speaker drove in Steve Yerkes with the winning run, but the story was pushed off the front pages of Boston journals by news of the Titanic's sinking.

FIRST OFFICIAL GAME AT FENWAY PARK
Saturday, April 20, 1912

RED SOX	AB	R	H	O	A	E
Hooper, rf	5	0	0	3	0	0
Yerkes, 2b	6	3	5	4	2	2
Speaker, cf	6	0	3	2	0	0
Stahl, 1b	6	0	1	8	1	2
L. Gardner, 3b	6	1	2	2	2	0
Lewis, lf	4	1	1	4	1	0
Wagner, ss	5	1	1	4	3	1
Nunamaker, c	4	0	0	5	2	0
bEngle	1	0	0	0	0	0
Carrigan, c	0	0	0	0	1	0
O'Brien, p	1	0	0	0	0	1
aHenriksen	0	0	0	0	0	0
Hall, p	3	1	1	1	3	1
TOTALS	47	7	14	33	15	7

HIGHLANDERS*	AB	R	H	O	A	E
Zinn, lf	5	1	0	3	0	0
Wolter, rf	3	1	0	1	0	0
Kauff, cf	1	1	0	0	0	0
Chase, 1b	4	0	2	13	0	0
Hartzell, ss	5	1	1	2	2	0
Daniels, cf, rf	5	1	0	3	0	0
Dolan, 3b	3	1	1	0	0	2
E. Gardner, 2b	5	0	1	1	2	0
Street, c	4	0	1	9	3	0
Caldwell, p	2	0	1	0	1	0
Quinn, p	2	0	0	0	4	0
Vaughn, p	0	0	0	0	0	0
TOTALS	39	6	7	32*	12	2

```
Red Sox        100  301  010  01  —  7
Highlanders*   302  000  010  00  —  6
```

aWalked for O'Brien in fourth. bGrounded out for Nunamaker in 10th. *Two out when winning run scored. Two-base hits — Yerkes 2, Speaker, Stahl, Hall. Runs batted in — Speaker 3, Henriksen, Hooper, Yerkes, Stahl, Hartzell, Daniels, E. Gardner, Dolan, Caldwell, Chase. Sacrifice hits — Wolter, Chase, Vaughn. Stolen bases — Daniels 2, Wolter, Chase. Hits — off O'Brien, 4 in 4 innings; off Hall, 3 in 7 innings; off Caldwell, 5 in 3⅓ innings; off Quinn, 6 in 4⅓ innings; off Vaughn, 3 in 3 innings. Bases on balls — off O'Brien 4, Hall 3, Caldwell 2, Quinn 3, Vaughn 1. Struck out — by O'Brien 4, Hall 2, Quinn 3, Vaughn 2, Caldwell 1. Wild pitch — O'Brien. Balk — O'Brien. Hit by pitcher — by O'Brien 2, Quinn 1. Passed ball — Street. Umpires — Connolly (plate) and Hart (bases). Time 3:20. Attendance — 27,000.

*Highlanders changed their name to Yankees the following year (1913).

General manager Eddie Collins (left) and Tom Yawkey oversee rebuilding of Fenway in 1934. Note the skeleton of the new left-field wall in background. The old wooden fence was replaced by a taller one of sheet metal and steel.

Dedication game: May 17, 1912. White Sox spoiled the party, 5-2, as American League President Ban Johnson orchestrated the champagne uncorking.

First Fenway fire: May 8, 1926. The bleachers along the left-field foul line burned down and weren't replaced, affording fielders the opportunity to chase foul flies behind the third-base grandstand.

First Sunday game at Fenway: July 3, 1932, as the Yankees damned the Sox, 13-2. Sunday baseball in Boston had been approved three years earlier, but not at Fenway because of its proximity to a church. So the Red Sox had to play their Sunday games at Braves Field until the law was amended to allow them to play seven days a week at Fenway.

Second Fenway fire: January 5, 1934. A four-alarm blaze, taking five hours to control, destroyed virtually all the construction in progress to rehabilitate the park by new owner T. A. Yawkey.

New Fenway opened: April 17, 1934. Joe Cronin's Senators defeated the Red Sox, 6-5, in another 11-inning inaugural. The reconstruction, variously estimated between 750,000 and two million Depression dollars, was completed for the season opener despite the fire. The grandstand was enlarged from the left-field wall in a V around to right field, and the wooden center-field stands were replaced by concrete bleachers. Other notable alterations: (1) "Duffy's Cliff," a treacherous ten-foot embankment in front of the left-field wall, was greatly reduced, although not completely leveled; and (2) the tall wooden fence in left was replaced by an even taller one of sheet metal and steel.

Biggest baseball crowds at Fenway: 46,995 for a Tigers doubleheader on August 19, 1934, and—a week earlier—46,766 to say goodbye to Babe Ruth at a Yankees doubleheader on August 12, 1934. They will never be equaled under Fenway's current dimensions. More stringent fire laws and league rules after World War II prohibited overcrowding that was permitted in the thirties. Fenway's current seating capacity of 33,536 could change, though. There are plans to double-deck the grandstand between first and third bases in the early eighties, and a rooftop restaurant may be built along the left-field line.

Other changes:

1936: A 23½-foot-tall screen was draped above the 37-foot left-field wall to save the windows on Lansdowne Street.

1940: Bull pens were constructed in front of the bleachers in right-center and right fields, affording Ted Williams a slightly closer target after he'd hit 31 homers as a rookie (including a record 14 into the distant right-field seats). The area was promptly dubbed "Williamsburg," but ironically Ted's home-and-away output dropped to 23 in 1940.

Workmen put finishing touches on Fenway reconstruction in 1934.

"Williamsburg" was constructed for the 1940 season, affording prodigy Ted Williams a closer target in right field. The old bull pen (behind dotted line on left) was replaced by the growing grandstand, and fenced-in bull pens were constructed in front of the bleachers in right and right-center fields.

1946: Sky-view seats were built alongside the press box to accommodate the national press covering the All-Star Game, and would come in handy for the World Series media that fall. Except for "national" attractions, those added rooftop skyviews are utilized as premium seats for the public.

1947: Arc lights were installed, the third last team among the then 16 major league clubs to do so. The Red Sox defeated the White Sox, 5-3, in Fenway's first night game on June 13.

1947: Green paint replaced advertisements covering the left-field wall. No more Calvert owl ("Be wise"), Gem Blades ("Avoid 5 o'clock shadow"), Lifebuoy ("The Red Sox use it") and Vimms ("Get that Vimms feeling").

1948: Red Sox games were first televised at Fenway.

1949: TV-radio perch was built atop the screen behind home plate.

1949: Ball boy was installed in foul territory along right-field line to shag foul balls.

1952: Visitors clubhouse was relocated beneath the third-base stands and connected directly to the third-base dugout. Thus the inconvenient, and sometimes combustible, practice of both teams using the same tunnel to adjacent clubhouses beneath the first-base stands was eliminated.

1959: Organ was installed, and John Kiley is still at the keyboard.

1960: Electric cart to taxi relief pitchers from bull pen to mound was introduced, and Al Forester is still behind the wheel. (Southpaw Luis Arroyo was his first customer, the Yankees' last passenger for awhile. Manager Casey Stengel thereafter forbade his pitchers to accept rides, ordering them to take the long stroll so they could mull what awaited them.)

1976: Scoreboard costing $1.5 million was constructed behind center-field bleachers. It is 40 feet wide and 24 feet high, flashes 8,640 light bulbs and is equipped to show both film and videotape, including instant replay. Traditionalists protested, labeling it creeping Finleyism

View from the bleachers.

Bat Day at Fenway.

that would destroy Fenway's charm. Similar anxiety was heard decades earlier when the Red Sox introduced an electronic public-address system, replacing the lungs of Wolfie Jacobs and others who used a megaphone to herald the batteries and other tidings up and down the foul lines.

Also 1976: Left-field wall was resurfaced, left-field scoreboard abbreviated, more padding added to the outfield walls. Also, the retaining wall backing the bleachers was extended and the press box was enlarged, glassed-in and air-conditioned.

○

The Wall isn't 315 feet (96 meters) from home plate as advertised.

After staring at it for 32 seasons and *knowing* it couldn't possibly be that far away—you can reach out and touch the Green Monster, can't you?—I finally measured it.

It was done on the spur of the moment a day or two before the 1975 Red Sox-A's championship series. I had a coconspirator—equally curious Art Keefe, former Red Sox statistician and Milwaukee Brewers public relations director, now a real estate tycoon.

We used a yardstick and used it hurriedly (but reasonably carefully) so as not to be discovered—not the most scientific method or circumstances in measuring such distance.

The result of our Woodward-Bernstein caper? The distance measured something like 309 feet 5 inches, as I recall.

Even allowing some leeway for error because of our less than computer-precise measuring—leaving a 12-inch latitude, say—that still would leave a distance considerably short of the 315 feet posted.

Now how's that for a scoop?

The Wall haunts pitchers—including Luis Tiant, who watches a Yankee homer soar over it to tie a game in the ninth inning . . . and he gets the message from a billboard looming over the fence. *(Boston Globe)*

All this isn't to suggest that the Red Sox are intentionally deceiving the baseball world.

The original Wall built in 1912 allegedly measured 320 feet from the plate. The discrepancy probably occurred after the 1933 season, when new owner Tom Yawkey overhauled his park. Renovations included honing Duffy's Cliff in left field and rebuilding The Wall, refacing it and making it thicker to house a built-in scoreboard and its operator.

The press announced it would result in The Wall being eight feet closer to the plate, from 320 to 312. Somehow it ended up 315—either because of some faulty mathematics or, more likely, there was no wish to stir those who felt that even 320 feet was scandalously short enough.

○

When The Wall was resurfaced after the 1975 season, its old facing benefited children's cancer research.

The green sheet metal was cut into thousands of 2½x4½-inch rectangles and mounted on polished wood—"authentic piece of the old left-field wall" souvenirs.

They were snapped up by Fenway aficionados for a contribution to the Jimmy Fund, the charity backed by the Red Sox for more than 25 years.

○

Fenway Park has housed other teams besides the landlord Red Sox.

The "Miracle Braves" authored history at Fenway by sweeping the 1914 World Series there while Braves Field was under construction. And there was talk—particularly in the thirties and to a lesser extent in the forties and early fifties—about the Braves selling less attractive Braves field and moving into more intimate Fenway. But Tom Yawkey had no wish to share his playpen, so didn't encourage the move.

(And the thought lingers: Rookie Henry Aaron joined the Braves the year after the team left Boston. How many more home runs would he have hit shooting at Fenway's left-field wall half his games?)

Three current pro football teams called Fenway home before heading to greener (dollarwise) pastures.

The Boston Redskins played there four years before moving in 1937 to Washington, where they would be led by a rookie quarterback named Sammy Baugh. The Boston Yanks played there 1944-48 before hitting the road for New York, Dallas and ultimately Baltimore, where they were rechristened the Colts. And the Boston Patriots played there 1963-68 before eventually traveling halfway to Providence and settling in a town called Foxboro, where they'd be renamed the New England Patriots.

The Boston College bowl teams and Harry Agganis-quarterbacked Boston University teams also played their home games there.

Thus some memorable football as well as baseball has been seen at Fenway.

○

When Fenway Park was resodded after the 1967 "Impossible Dream" season, a fitting use was found for the old-but-still-good bluegrass from the left-field area.

It was shipped to suburban Lynnfield—a new lawn for the Yastrzemski home, where Carl could still patrol it.

JIM LONBORG: "If a pitcher makes a mistake at Fenway, he can get hurt a lot quicker there than any other ball park."

ELSTON HOWARD: "My first big-league game was at Fenway in April 1955, and I'll never forget it for a number of reasons.

"When I came out of the runway and saw The Wall my eyes darn near popped out of my head. I mean, they really *popped.* I couldn't wait to get a bat and get a piece of it.

"And luckily I did. Willard Nixon was the Red Sox starter, and I went four for five—including one over The Wall and one off The Wall.

"But what I'll always remember beyond all that was when I came to bat for the first time the fans gave me a standing ovation. Not just an ovation, a *standing* ovation. I couldn't believe it.

"Boston quickly became my favorite city on the road. It has everything—terrific fans, nice ball park and unique city that reminds me of Europe.

"So I always looked forward to playing there. And so I guess it was fitting I ended my playing career there with the Red Sox."

BILLY MARTIN: "I'll never forget my first look at Fenway Park. It was my first day with the Yankees—Opening Day 1950. We were losing, 9-0, and Casey put me in.

"The first time up I doubled off the left-field wall for one run. Later that same inning I singled with bases loaded for two more. Two hits in the same inning my first two times up in the big leagues.

"And we won—15-10, I think."

Martin would.be involved in a lot more Fenway combustion both as player and manager, off the field as well as on, with teammate and foe alike. On May 24, 1952, Player Martin swapped punches with Jimmy Piersall of the Red Sox in the runway connecting the Boston bench and clubhouse, out of sight of the fans. And on June 18, 1977, a national TV audience watched Manager Martin apparently trying to fight superstar Reggie Jackson in the third-base dugout. The pair were having words after Martin pulled Jackson from right field in the middle of an inning against the Red Sox.

MICKEY MANTLE: "A nightmare series at Fenway got me sent back to the minors in 1951, my rookie year.

"Walt Masterson struck me out five times, and the water cooler took a pounding from me each time I went back to the dugout. And I got picked off by Bill Wight, a left-hander with a fine move to first base. That killed a bases-loaded rally and happened right after a clubhouse meeting in which Stengel had warned us about not getting picked off.

"That was my last time in a Yankee uniform for awhile. We moved on to Detoit, and before our first game there, Casey called me in and said he was sending me down.

"My first game as a Yankee had been against the Red Sox, too— Opening Day at New York that season. I was 19, up from Class C and scared. I don't recall too many details about that day, but I'll never forget the first ball hit to me in right field. Ted Williams lifted one of his skyrockets and I didn't think it would ever come down, but I caught it."

WHITEY FORD: "Fenway Park has special meaning to me. I joined the Yankees there in July 1950. I took the night train to Boston and pitched my first day in a Yankee uniform.

"We were losing something like 11-2, so Casey wasn't taking too much

Because the Red Sox traditionally have loaded up with power hitters who don't rely on speed, the Fenway baselines have long been doctored to slow enemy sprinters. The dirt is allegedly so soft and loose that Rod Carew, among others, compares it to running in sand.

Youngsters Jackie Jensen (left) and Mickey Mantle teamed in the outfield with Joe DiMaggio when the Yankees came to Boston in April 1951.

of a chance bringing me in to relieve Tommy Byrne. Vern Stephens was on third base, Walt Dropo on first, and Bobby Doerr was the batter.

"He singled for a run, and that was just the start. I gave them something like seven hits, six walks and five runs—even a wild pitch—in about five innings. There were a couple of shots off The Wall, and I think Stephens may have put one over it.

"I wasn't so hot that day, and part of the reason was that I was tipping my pitches. Their first-base coach kept hollering to the batters, and Tommy Henrich came over and said, 'That guy is calling every pitch you throw.'

"The next day Jim Turner put me under the microscope out in the bull pen trying to find out how I was tipping off the pitches. Then he discovered I was twisting my elbow whenever I threw a curve.

"I didn't pitch a lot at Fenway under Casey, and I guess a lot of people felt I was ducking it. It is a tough park for left-handers. Still, I wanted to pitch there but Casey wouldn't let me. But I pitched more up there when Ralph Houk became manager, and I liked that.

"While that big wall can give a lefty fits, you have to remember it also is going to mean some runs for your team, too. That means you'll have some runs to work on. So it can balance out."

JOE DiMAGGIO: "Fenway fans gave me an ovation I'll never forget, one of my greatest thrills.

"It was the last day of the 1948 season, the day after the Red Sox had eliminated the Yankees. To tie for first place and force a playoff, Boston had to beat us again and hope Cleveland lost to Detroit. So the full house at Fenway was watching two games that Sunday—one on the field and one on the scoreboard.

"My family was in the stands and were rooting for the Red Sox. They knew I couldn't play in the World Series, but Dom had a chance.

"I doubled home a run in the first inning, but the Sox rocked Bob Porterfield for five in the third. In the fifth I hit one off The Wall and we cut the margin to 5-4. The crowd was going crazy.

"I had charley horses in both legs and the one in my right leg hurt like fury. But I wanted to stay in, to win on the last day.

"We didn't. They beat us, 10-5. And I didn't last all the way. Bucky Harris sent Steve Souchock to run for me in the ninth after I got my fourth hit, a single. I turned and started for the dugout. I guess I was limping pretty badly.

"I'll never forget that crowd. It was standing and roaring—like one man. I tipped my hat but it didn't stop. I looked up at the stands and never saw a more wonderful sight. There were more than 30,000 people giving an ovation to a guy who had tried to beat them.

"They were still yelling when I disappeared into the dugout; they didn't stop for another three or four minutes.

"Dom and I had a reunion after it was over.

" 'That was the greatest tribute a crowd here ever gave a ball player,' he said. 'Everybody is talking about it.'

" 'I guess you felt like cutting my throat when I hit that one off The Wall in the fifth,' I said.

" 'No,' Dom said. 'Don't ever tell Joe McCarthy, but I felt like applauding too.' "

DICK RADATZ: "Boston isn't an easy town to play in.

"The fans are tremendous but can be rough, too. They turned on me quickly when things began going bad for me. It was a complete flip-flop

Joe DiMaggio was in his last season, Mickey Mantle in his first when the Yankees came to Boston in April 1951—the future Hall of Famers conversing in the Hotel Kenmore lobby before the 19-year-old rookie Mantle saw Fenway Park for the first time a half-hour later.

by them. The press really murdered me, too. All this shouldn't have bothered me, but it did. I guess it was because I wasn't used to it.

"Overall, though, the fans and newspapers were damn good to me."

JACKIE JENSEN: "Fenway fans were rough on me during my first couple of years in Boston. But that's part of the game—as long as they don't get too personal.

"I have too many fond memories of Boston to let that be spoiled by some boos. There's no better baseball town. New England fans are unique. A Fenway crowd has the voice of *one*. I've never seen—or heard—that anywhere else."

THE FANS

Wes Ferrell thumbed his nose at them.

Jackie Jensen had to be restrained from climbing into the right-field stands after one during pregame warmups.

Ted Williams spat at them and gave them a nasty salute. He also had a special message for some of them in the left-field stands, replying to their insults by spraying that area with line drives (proving among other things that he could hit to the opposite field with power and precision when the spirit moved him).

Don Buddin was reduced to tears by their taunts, once weeping in the dugout before responding with a game-winning home run.

Carl Yastrzemski tried the silent treatment on them, once trotting to his left-field position with wads of cotton stuffed in his ears.

Reggie Smith jawed with them regularly—both from the outfield and the on-deck circle. One pushed him too far during batting practice, so

Gene Mack's cartoons—including this masterpiece on Fenway Park and its history—spiced the pages of the *Boston Globe* and *Sporting News* for four decades. This one was drawn in 1949 and now graces the Baseball Hall of Fame. *(Boston Globe)*

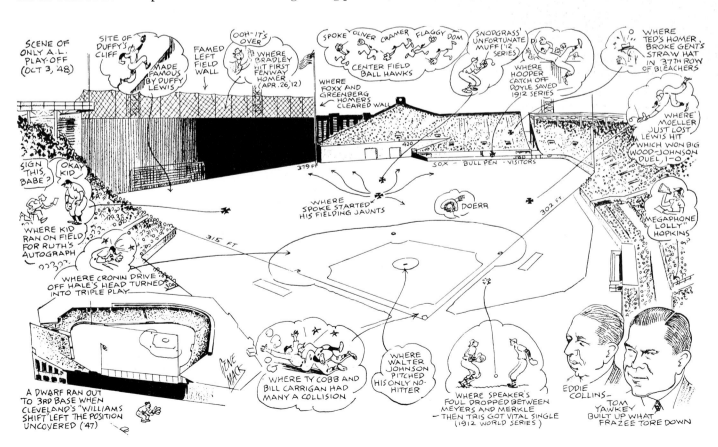

Hundreds of fans took a rare opportunity to inspect The Wall after the Red Sox defeated the Twins on the final day of the 1967 season, climaxing the Impossible Dream.

Smith hurled his cap and then his jersey into the box-seat area and told the heckler to put them on if he could do better.

Jimmy Piersall joked with them. So did Maury McDermott, making exaggerated tips of his cap to them.

Another comedian, Dick Stuart, communicated directly. After hitting a homer in the nightcap of a doubleheader, Stu sent a note to one who had been jeering him through a hitless opener: "Dear Red Sox fan: Have another drink on me. D. Stuart."

Fenway fans—they're a rare species, some of the world's best . . . and a few of the worst.

They have vented their wrath mostly on opposing players.

Ty Cobb so enraged them when he threw his bat at pitcher Carl Mays during a crucial 1915 series featuring high spikes and low-bridge pitches that a squad of police was needed to escort Cobb safely from the field.

Under bombardment from the bleachers in 1970, Indians center fielder Ted Uhlaender had to retreat to the dugout. There was talk of a forfeit, but order was restored after eight minutes.

Cal Hubbard *did* forfeit a 1939 game to the Yankees when fans littered the field to protest a stalling contest, but the umpire later was overruled by the league president.

Fenway spectators have thrown a miscellany of objects. Ted Williams was hit by a cooked hotdog in the forties. When Sammy White was ejected from a game in the fifties, one fan showed his dissatisfaction by throwing three box seats onto the field. And one night in 1967, a smoke bomb was tossed into left field, interrupting a game for ten minutes.

And on Caddy Day in 1949, youngsters stopped the game by showering right field with hundreds of golf balls—which players alternately ducked and stuffed into their caps and gloves for future use.

Fenway fans also hurl words, some of them ugly and profane.

They chanted vulgarly at Reggie Jackson during the 1978 playoff game. He answered during his next at-bat—homering for what proved to be the division-winning run.

Two of Jackson's Yankee predecessors received death threats warning them not to show up at Fenway: Phil Rizzuto in 1950, Mickey Mantle in 1953.

In marked contrast, three other Yankees—Babe Ruth, Joe DiMaggio and Elston Howard—all said that perhaps their most memorable ovation came at Fenway. Ruth pointed to his last visit there as a player in 1934, DiMaggio to the final day of the 1948 season and Howard to his first big league at-bat in 1955.

Some others recall it less fondly.

A pitcher mowing down the Red Sox one day in 1949 suddenly lost his efficiency when a loudmouth began reminding him every other minute of a paternity suit pending in the courts. As he departed for an early shower, the incensed hurler shook his fist at his tormentor.

Another antagonized right-hander, Bo Belinsky, used his pitching hand in a more graphic gesture.

The fans even turn on each other at times—and not just drunks and/or rowdies. A front-row occupant nearly needed asylum after he interfered with a Red Sox fielder in search of a foul pop during a crucial game.

Scorers haven't escaped the fans' anger either. While Ted Williams was again challenging .400 in 1957, he lined a smash off Harvey Kuenn's glove. More than 30,000 nearly rioted when it was ruled an error (it was later changed to a hit).

Fenway fans *did* riot to delay the seventh game of the 1912 World Series, a dark day in the park's history. Management blundered and oversold Fenway, including the left-field seats of the Royal Rooters, that song-singing, banner-toting group of boosters who not only flocked to home games but also traveled to many road games by the trainload.

Their regular seats taken, hundreds of Rooters staged a protest march around the field with their bands playing, refusing to leave the field until seats were provided. They finally were routed by police on foot and horseback, and herded off the field in what became a stampede that trampled down the cyclone fence in center field.

Most fan invasions at Fenway come one at a time, though—a girl wanting to pin a kiss on her favorite Red Sox hero, a one-too-many imbiber wanting to slide across home plate on national television.

The most entertaining invasion came in 1946, when a midget popped out of the third-base stands while Ted Williams was batting against the new Boudreau Shift.

A vaudevillian, the midget scooted toward third base, scooped up Mike Higgins's glove lying near the coaching box (gloves were left on the field in those days) and began pounding its pocket with his fist as he took a position at third base, the only "defender" on the infield's left side.

And when the third-base coach boosted him back into the stands, the midget climbed atop the visitors dugout and put up his dukes in a fighting pose as the crowd roared.

That's Fenway.

Red Sox fans will find a way to see their team even when the game is sold out. Top, Boston's finest join a woman in watching 1903 World Series action through a knothole. Center, fans nest atop a building behind the right-field stands to see a 1946 World Series game. Bottom, rooters cluster on a billboard beyond the left-field wall to watch a 1975 World Series game. *(Boston Globe)*

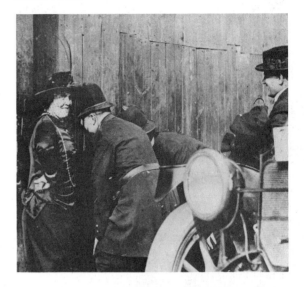

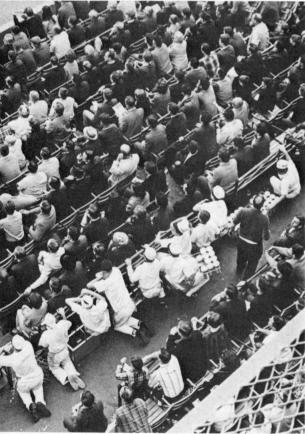

Fenway employees often get caught up in the game, like the usher at top and vendors at bottom.

The pigeon is Fenway Park's national bird, journalist Harold Kaese once suggested.

Pigeons have played a memorable role in the history of Fenway, where they once abounded in the eaves of the grandstand roof. They have changed the course of games. They have gotten Ted Williams in trouble. And they have soiled the clothing of more than one customer, which some contend is a good-luck sign.

However, pigeons didn't help Red Sox luck on at least two occasions in 1945. One got in the way of Hal Peck's throw after the Athletics outfielder had chased down Skeeter Newsome's hit in the right-field corner. There are two versions of what happened next. One is that the throw was wild and, after striking the bird, the ball deflected into the hands of the second baseman who tagged out Newsome. The other says Newsome was safe. There also are two versions of the bird's fate. One says it was killed by the throw; the other says it crashed on the grass, sat up, shook off a few loose feathers and flew away.

In another game with the A's that season, Sox center fielder Tom McBride chased a pigeon he mistook for Sam Chapman's line drive.

Pigeons have gotten in the way of batted baseballs, too. Shortstop Billy Hunter of the Browns nailed one during batting practice in 1953. The bird plunged to the Fenway outfield, shook out the cobwebs, looked around, then took off.

Willie Horton apparently mortally wounded a pigeon with a sky-high foul pop in 1974. The bird was carted off by a groundskeeper and put in the runway next to the Tiger bench for disposal after the game. But when the groundskeeper returned, the pigeon was gone.

Scores of other pigeons couldn't walk away. Considered nuisances, they were shot on the wing by Williams, who'd take up residence in one of the bull pens with a rifle and pick off 50, 60, 70 at a sitting. Sometimes he was joined by Tom Yawkey. When a newspaper once reported Ted's hobby, the Humane Society wasn't amused and protested.

Williams stopped—at least for awhile. He had proven years earlier that he didn't need pigeons for target practice anyway. That time, apparently fresh out of birds, Ted turned his sights on the left-field scoreboard and shot out over $400 worth of lights.

o

How do you describe Red Sox fans? Devoted. Patient. Long-suffering. And perhaps a little masochistic, always coming back for more frustration after having their hearts broken. They have even been accused of having a death wish.

Their numbers are legion, stretching coast to coast. There is so much rooting for the Red Sox at some road games that you wonder which is the visiting team.

Red Sox fans also are a diverse group.

John Fitzgerald Kennedy was brought up a Red Sox fan on both sides of his family. His mother's father was John F. Fitzgerald, the legendary "Honey Fitz," who was mayor of Boston and a leader of the fanatical Royal Rooters in the Sox's early decades. And JFK's father, financier and ambassador Joseph P. Kennedy, considered buying the team just before Tom Yawkey did.

Kennedy kept informed on the Red Sox while in the White House.

So did Grace Coolidge when she was First Lady. After leaving the White House, she kept box seats at Fenway for years.

Speaker of the House Thomas P. "Tip" O'Neill has been going to Fenway regularly for 60 seasons. The first game he saw there was Walter Johnson's no-hitter in 1920. He witnessed Ted Lyons's no-hitter there six years later, too.

Henry Kissinger and son (left) and Tip O'Neill (right) flank baseball Commissioner Bowie Kuhn at the second game of the 1975 World Series at Fenway. *(Boston Globe)*

Lifelong Red Sox fan Frankie "Crazy Guggenheim" Fontaine trades hats with Ted Williams.

Ted Williams blasted former President Truman along with other politicians and the Marine Corps during a 1957 outburst. But HST said he didn't mind, a predictable reaction for a guy who had his very own Red Sox cap—presented by then Massachusetts Governor Foster Furcolo (right).

The Kennedy Clan always has been Red Sox rooters, including patriarch Joseph P. Kennedy, who once considered purchasing the team. He is with Ted and Joan Kennedy and Dave Powers (right), longtime aide to President Kennedy.

Former Speaker of the House John W. McCormack also is an enthusiastic Red Sox follower, dating back to Huntington Avenue Grounds days.

Yale President A. Bartlett Giomatti was once presented a Red Sox jacket and cap, and can be seen strolling the campus with a transistor to his ear listening to Sox games.

Comedian Frankie "Crazy Guggenheim" Fontaine was a Sox diehard. So is author John Updike (who once wrote, "Fenway Park is a lyric little bandbox of a park"). And singer Jerry Vale, too.

The list is endless.

Bob Hope makes a hit with his Red Sox audience (left to right): Jimmy Piersall, Mike Fornieles, Ted Lepcio and Jackie Jensen.

2
ALL THE SEASONS

THE FIRST DECADE

The Boston Americans raided the Boston Nationals for ace third baseman Jimmy Collins (left), who would also serve as the new team's first manager and captain.

The Pilgrims' biggest coup was in luring the star battery of pitcher Cy Young (far right) and catcher Lou Criger (center) from the St. Louis Cardinals. *(Boston Public Library)*

March 15, 1901

The upstart Boston Americans have thumbed their noses at the entrenched Boston Nationals.

The new American League declared war in January, when founder Ban Johnson changed his mind and decided to invade Boston and put a team in a 25-year National League stronghold.

And now the Boston Americans have fired the first salvo in that war by brazenly raiding the Boston Nationals for the services of Jimmy Collins, not only a local hero but also baseball's greatest third baseman.

The 28-year-old Collins, who will manage and captain the new Americans as well as play the hot corner, is a gem of a fielder who is quick as a cat and packs plenty of power for his 5-foot-7½, 160 pounds.

The price of Collins's jump is $4,000, and that sum is guaranteed him even if his old team is able to legally block him from playing with the new club or if the Americans don't get off the ground. The $4,000 is a lot more than Collins was paid by the stingy Beaneaters, who have had a $2,400 salary lid despite their monopoly on the town and winning two pennants the last four seasons.

Getting Collins is a feather in the cap of owner Charles W. Somers, the midwestern moneyman who not only owns the Boston Americans but has pieces of the Cleveland, Chicago and Philadelphia franchises in the new circuit which he also serves as vice president.

Pilfering Collins shows Somers means business in Boston, and is a giant step in proving to Hub fans that this team is fact not fancy.

Somers has been aided in organizing his Boston team by Philadelphia's Connie Mack and Milwaukee's Hughie Duffy, natives of Massachusetts and Rhode Island respectively.

It was Mack who signed the lease last January for the Americans' new ballyard being built on Huntington Avenue. And it's likely that Duffy, who played the last nine years for the Beaneaters and once hit .438 for them and was their captain, is the gent who talked his old mate Collins into jumping to the Americans. Jimmy denies that, but it's probably true.

Collins says he's no deserter. "I like to play baseball, but this is a business to me and I can't be governed by sentiment," he told reporters. "I'm looking out for James J. Collins."

Collins is the final skipper to be hired in the new circuit, joining the

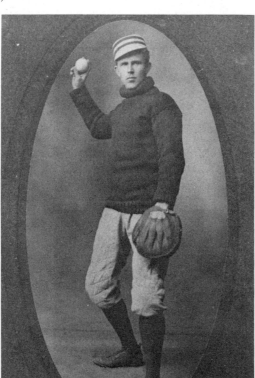

likes of Mack, Duffy, John McGraw and Clark Griffith. Jimmy will soon lead the club to preseason practice in Charlottesville, Virginia.

The raids were just beginning.

The Boston Americans' biggest coup was in luring Cy Young from the Cardinals for $3,500. He had averaged 28 victories for 10 seasons and gave the new team instant respectability. Although soon to be 34, Young was still in his prime—and would prove it by averaging 30 wins the next four seasons in helping establish the franchise. And for good measure, Young was accompanied from St. Louis by his faithful batterymate, Lou Criger.

And the Americans continued to jolt the rival Beaneaters by enticing Chick Stahl, Buck Freeman and Parson Lewis to follow Collins's path.

But wealthy Beaneater owner Arthur W. Soden professed: "Only one club will survive this battle in Boston, and that will be the same old National League club."

Most Boston baseball followers disagreed. Discouraged by the Nationals' skinflint reputation and shabby ball park, many fans deserted to the new game in town. Part of the attraction undoubtedly were stars such as Young and Collins; the love-of-underdog instinct and desire to be on the ground floor of something new were likely part of it, too.

Whatever the reasons, the Boston Americans outdrew the Boston Nationals from the start. And although the Braves would again have their glory days, particularly while winning the 1914 and 1948 pennants, by spring 1953 they were gone—headed for Atlanta via Milwaukee.

The first Boston Americans squad gathered for a team picture in 1901. In front row are (left to right) Ossee Schreckengost, Lou Criger, Larry McLean, Jimmy Collins, Cy Young and Chick Stahl. Second-row identification is incomplete, with only Freddy Parent (second left), Hobe Ferris (fourth left) and Buck Freeman (far right) certain. In back row are (left to right) Fred Mitchell, Harry Kane (he never played a game for Boston) and Tommy Dowd.

The Pilgrims' original infield in 1901 (left to right): third baseman Jimmy Collins, shortstop Freddy Parent, second baseman Hobe Ferris and first baseman Buck Freeman.

The Huntington Avenue Grounds was often filled to capacity.

CONNIE MACK: "Jimmy Collins was one of the fastest men ever to step on a baseball diamond. He could hit to all fields and threw the ball like a jet-propelled rocket. I rate him among the greatest players I ever saw, the greatest third baseman."

April 26, 1901

The Boston Americans made their debut today at Baltimore, but it was a sad day for New Englanders.

John McGraw's scrappy Orioles rolled over the Pilgrims, 10-6, as Ironman Joe McGinnity scattered nine hits. Boston scored five runs in the last two innings, after the game was lost.

Player-manager Jimmy Collins, batting cleanup and playing third base, and catcher Lou Criger led Pilgrim hitters with a double and single each.

The Orioles cuffed Win Kellum for 11 hits, including three by Bill Keister and two triples by Turkey Mike Donlin, in the one-hour, 45-minute contest.

The Pilgrims, who have been training this month at Charlottesville, Virginia, won't return home for two more weeks. They'll continue on to Philadelphia and Washington and return for another series in Baltimore before raising the curtain in Boston on May 8.

The Pilgrims had a disastrous 2-7 trip, and as the team stumbled home Collins advised: "We are too anxious. Everybody is trying too hard, and we are beating ourselves. I know we have a better team than we've shown." Nearly 80 years later, managers' dialogue has changed little.

○

The Pilgrim-Oriole opener was the roots of what quickly became—and has remained—one of baseball's great rivalries: Red Sox vs. Yankees. The Orioles (purchased for $18,000) would move to New York in 1903 and become the Highlanders. And in 1913, the Highlanders changed their name to the Yankees.

○

Boston's Larry McLean authored American League history during the Pilgrims' opener at Baltimore. The 19-year-old reserve catcher-first baseman doubled while batting for pitcher Win Kellum in the ninth inning—the league's first pinch hit.

McLean went on to further distinction as a catcher for the Reds and Giants. But perhaps the most memorable achievement by the fun-loving 6-foot-5, 228-pounder was breaking a rocking chair over a pal's head on a St. Louis hotel veranda one night—then swan-diving into a two-foot fountain pool.

McLean was shot and killed in a Boston saloon brawl in 1921.

May 8, 1901

A joyful crowd of 11,500 overflowed the Huntington Avenue Grounds today to welcome the American League to Boston.

The Pilgrims rewarded their loyal supporters by pulverizing Connie Mack's Athletics, 12-4, behind Cy Young. Young yielded 11 hits, but most after Boston had a safe lead.

Player-manager Jimmy Collins was presented a bouquet before the opening pitch, and his team quickly responded to all the home cheering.

The Pilgrims totaled four runs in the first inning and scored in each of the first five innings to breeze to victory. Mack left Bill Bernhard in for all 19 Boston hits—including a homer, triple and single by first baseman Buck Freeman. Even Young joined the slugfest with a triple and single—and stole a base.

The only sour note was that Boston center fielder Chick Stahl broke a rib.

The big crowd was pleasantly surprised to find the Pilgrims' new home ready. It's been less than two months since the March 12 groundbreaking. The little grandstand seats 2,600 and the bleachers hold another 6,500 for a 25-cent admission charge. With both grandstand and bleachers filled, another 2,500 or so stood behind ropes in the outfield.

The crowd far outnumbered that attending the National League game at the nearby South End Grounds, where the Beaneaters were edging defending champ Brooklyn, 7-6, in 12 innings. That contest drew about 2,000 paid—plus some 3,500 high school boys allowed in free today.

Crowd noises could be heard between the two ballyards, separated by the New Haven Railroad tracks. The new park is located on the trolley line at the corner of Huntington and Rogers Avenues, the old carnival lot across the street from where Buffalo Bill's Wild West Show and the Barnum and Bailey Circus play when in Boston.

The Boston Globe *headlined: "American League Men Given Royal Welcome by 11,500 Rooters."*

Properly inspired by hometown enthusiasm, the Pilgrims went on to a successful season as Cy Young easily led the majors with 33 victories and Freeman hit .346. Playing hustling baseball (to outdraw the established Boston Nationals), they were in the pennant race all season before finishing second, four games behind pitcher-manager Clark Griffith's Chicago White Sox.

That pennant fever was so heated in late August, when only percentage points separated the two teams, that uptight Boston fans were ready to tar and feather umpire Pongo Joe Cantillon after a game in which two

When all the seats were taken, fans were allowed to ring the outfield behind ropes. Note trolley wires and advertisements outside fence along Huntington Avenue.

Fans leave the ball park toward Huntington Avenue, where they could board trolley cars.

crucial calls had gone against the town team. But Chick Stahl and Ted Lewis fought their way through the mob to rescue Cantillon (only one umpire worked games in those days).

It was the first recorded demonstration in the passionate history of Red Sox fans.

◇ ◇
◇

April 20, 1903

The Pilgrims opened their season this morning by vexing strikeout star Rube Waddell and the defending champion Athletics, 9-4, at the Huntington Avenue Grounds.

And the plucky Pilgrims did it by bunting the visitors blind—to the amusement of 8,376 Patriots Day fans.

Manager-third baseman Jimmy Collins ordered the strategy because (1) Waddell probably hasn't been up before noon for years, and (2) Waddell supposedly was on a tear around town last night.

"Boys, the Rube has just come off a tremendous bender," Collins reportedly told his players before the game. "We're going to bunt the hell out of him—run his arse all over the park."

They did, and soon Waddell's tongue was hanging out and he kept looking over to Connie Mack on the visitors bench with pleading eyes. But the 26-year-old southpaw got no sympathy from his mates. "Get in there and pitch, you yellow so-and-so," his own first baseman, Harry Davis, kept barking.

By game's end poor Rube was in a state of near collapse.

The Philadelphians got revenge in the afternoon game by beating Cy Young, 10-7, to disappoint the big crowd of 27,658.

October 1, 1903

The Pilgrims were handed a 7-3 licking by the Pirates today in the first "modern" World Series game.

A crowd of 16,242 packed the Huntington Avenue Grounds and saw Cy Young take a 12-hit pasting while Pittsburgh's Deacon Phillippe was holding Boston to six hits. Buck Freeman was the only Pilgrim with any luck against Phillippe. The right fielder tripled, singled and scored twice.

Little Tommy Leach led the visitors with two triples and two singles. Jimmy Sebring, who had only four homers all year, hit the first World Series circuit clout and drove in four runs.

The Pittsburghers also got help from some shoddy Boston fielding—catcher Lou Criger and second baseman Hobe Ferris made two errors each—as the Pirates took a 1-0 advantage in the best-of-nine World Championships.

"Well, that's only one game," said skipper-third baseman Jimmy Collins, whose Pilgrims finished the regular season with a fat 14½-game advantage over the runner-up Athletics. "We've rid ourselves of a lot of bad baseball, and Cy won't give us another game like that one again."

Hopefully, Collins is right. The American League's honor is at stake in the uneasy peace between the rival leagues, and much bitterness remains despite the truce.

Many feel the only reason the old National League agreed to meet the young American League in a World Series was so they could vanquish the Americans, humiliating them so as to end all talk of equality once and for all.

The Pirates are big favorites, but there is plenty of Pilgrim money around in Boston.

Some $10,000 has been wagered in the lobby of the Hotel Vendome, where the Pirates are staying in town. The Pittsburgh players have been taking a lot of needling there by fans. Most of it has been good-natured, but some has gotten testy—especially when some Pirates have spit

tobacco juice at fans in the lobby and promised to wipe out the "junior league" Boston club.

Don't count on it, Pittsburghers. "When a team has pitching such as I have," said Collins, "it is bound to win a lot of games." Young led the staff this season with a 28-9 record, Long Tom Hughes was 21-7 and Big Bill Dinneen 21-11.

The Pirates have their share of fireballers. Phillippe, Sam Leever, Irvin "Kaiser" Wilhelm and Ed Doheny combined for six consecutive shutouts this season en route to the National League title by 6½ games over the Giants.

Doheny, from Andover, Mass., will not appear in the Series. He went berserk near season's end, almost killed a faith-cure doctor and male nurse with a cast-iron stove rest, and now is in an asylum.

Dinneen will face Leever in Game 2 tomorrow.

Big Bill more than met the task, holding the Pirates to three hits in squaring the Series at a victory apiece. But Pittsburgh countered with Phillippe the next two games, rolling to a 3-1 Series advantage.

Forced to defend the American League's honor at Pittsburgh's Exposition Park after Game 3, the Pilgrims captured Games 5, 6 and 7 there to return to Boston with a surprising 4-3 Series advantage.

o

Customers at today's first World Series game were greeted by an amazing sight—some of their Pilgrim heroes manning the ticket booths and selling ducats.

Among those literally pitching in was the great Cy Young, today's hurler.

The crowd of 16,242 was so unexpectedly large that extra help had to be recruited in a hurry, and some players volunteered.

Play is about to begin in the first World Series game ever. Note crowd clustered around diamond for close-up look at infield practice.

Cy Young manned a ticket booth for the opening game of the 1903 Series.

The loyal Royal Rooters and their band serenaded with "Tessie" and other songs throughout the first World Series, and some Pirates credited them with winning the Series for Boston.

Bill Dinneen was the pitching hero of the first World Series, winning three games including the deciding eighth game.

The next time you go to Fenway, look closely at the person behind the ticket window. Could it be Carl Yastrzemski? Or Jim Rice? Or Fred Lynn?

CY YOUNG: "Brass bands were all over the place. Men came in long-tailed coats and high hats or derbies. The ladies were bedecked in their ankle-length skirts and picture hats. The bands played all the tunes of the times—'Dixie,' 'Wait Till the Sun Shines, Nellie' and all the rest.

"It was fine, just fine."

TOMMY LEACH: "That was probably the wildest World Series ever played. Arguing all the time between the teams, between the players and the umpires, and especially between the players and the fans. That's the truth. The fans were *part* of the game in those days. They'd pour right onto the field and argue with the players and the umpires. Was sort of hard to keep the game going sometimes.

"I think those Boston fans actually won that Series for the Red Sox. We beat them three out of the first four games, and then they started singing that damn 'Tessie' song, the Red Sox fans did. They called themselves the Royal Rooters.

"In the fifth game the Royal Rooters started singing 'Tessie' for no particular reason at all, and the Red Sox won. They must have figured it was a good-luck charm, because from then on you could hardly play ball they were singing 'Tessie' so damn loud. Sort of got on your nerves after awhile. And before we knew what happened, we'd lost the World Series."

October 13, 1903

The National Leaguers no longer can sneer at the American League. The mighty Pilgrims are baseball champions of the world!

Big Bill Dinneen hurled the Pilgrims to the first World Series title today by shackling the Pirates with a four-hit gem for a 3-0 triumph at the Huntington Avenue Grounds.

Dinneen and his mates were immediately swept off their feet and carried around the field by many of the 7,455 celebrants who were thrilled by the club's fifth victory against three losses. They paraded their heroes behind a band while adults sang and children screamed, and the players were kept long after the final out, receiving the fans' handshakes for hours.

But the gala occasion didn't provide merriment for all. The Pittsburgh club's carriages were trapped for an hour on Huntington Avenue by the delirious legions.

And that didn't improve the temper of Fred Clarke, the Pirates skipper-left fielder. "How the devil is a man going to win with only one pitcher?" he demanded after seeing his ace Deacon Phillippe allow eight hits while making his fifth Series start, absorbing his second loss against three wins.

Dinneen was only slightly less busy, chalking up his third victory and second shutout against one defeat in four Series starts.

"This thing has gone far enough," the 27-year-old right-hander said. "I want to get home to Syracuse. I got a lot of things I want to do. Let's get this done with."

His teammates staked him with more than enough runs on a pair in the fourth built around Candy LaChance's triple. And just to make sure, the Bostonians added a final tally in the sixth.

Things were just warming up, though.

Clarke, his humor fading as he saw the National League's honor doing the same, thought Dinneen was throwing at his skull in the seventh. So the Pittsburgh leader pushed a bunt down the first-base line hoping to use Big Bill's back as a rug to trample his spikes on.

But first sacker LaChance knows that old trick and how to handle it. He hollered off the pitcher, scooped up the trickler and fired the baseball into Clarke's back as he scooted toward first base.

That did it. Players from both sides swarmed onto the diamond and the fans got into the act by breaking through the ropes in center field, where they had been standing ten deep. It took the beleaguered umpires, Tommy Connolly and Hank O'Day, half an hour to restore order.

Soon the game was over, the final out coming with a resounding roar as Dinneen fanned Honus Wagner, the great Pittsburgh shortstop and National League batting champ (.355), who must wear the goat's horns for batting only .214 in the Series.

Instead of destroying the American League as many National Leaguers hoped, the upset victory helped solidify the young league.

The Pirates' feelings were salved by drawing bigger shares than the winning Bostonians. Because of Pittsburgh owner Barney Dreyfuss's generosity, each Pirate received $1,316.25. The Pilgrims, who had threatened not to play unless owner Henry J. Killilea gave them most of the gate receipts, received $1,182 apiece and full salary through October 15, their contracts having expired September 30.

The inequity drew national attention, with Killilea branded a skinflint. So, early the following April, he sold the club to General Charles H. Taylor, owner, publisher and editor of the Boston Globe. *The General was looking for an outlet to occupy his son John I. Taylor, described in the journals of the day (if not in the* Globe) *as something of a playboy and rather wild sportsman.*

May 5, 1904

Cy (for *Cyclone*) Young today pitched a perfect game—the first since 1880—as the Pilgrims skunked the Athletics, 3-0, at the Huntington Avenue Grounds.

A crowd of 10,267 watched Young outpitch Rube Waddell. Just four days ago, in the opener of the five-game series, Waddell had one-hit Boston—retiring 27 batters in a row after Patsy Dougherty's leadoff bunt single.

The 27-year-old Waddell reportedly told the 37-year-old Young before today's match: "I'll give you the same thing I gave (Jesse) Tannehill the other day."

Young let his right arm do his talking, allowing only six balls to be hit to the outfield during the 83-minute masterpiece.

The closest Philadelphia came to a hit was Monte Cross's pop to short right in the third inning—caught by Buck Freeman after a long sprint. Fred Parent and Chick Stahl also made nice plays on a couple of scare bids by Ollie Pickering.

"I had good speed and good stuff," said Young, who fanned eight.

Meanwhile, the Pilgrims solved Waddell for ten hits, including a pair each by Jimmy Collins and Candy LaChance.

Fifteen weeks later, on August 17, Tannehill pitched the franchise's second no-hitter while defeating the White Sox, 6-0, at Chicago.

Cy Young (far left) and Candy LaChance (far right) flank the Boston bench during 1903 World Series action. It was Candy who triggered a ruckus in the final game when he intentionally fired the ball into a Pittsburgh runner's back.

The third game of the first World Series attracted 18,801 paid admissions. Yet the *Boston Globe*'s baseball editor reported there were 23,000 fans inside the Huntington Avenue Grounds. This photo explains the discrepancy.

Player-manager Jimmy Collins raises the first World Championship flag on Opening Day 1904.

In the 75 years since, only 12 more Red Sox pitchers have tossed no-hitters—attributable to both the lively ball and Fenway Park's chummy left-field wall. Only ten no-hitters have occurred at Fenway—six by Boston pitchers, four by opponents.

LARRY GARDNER: "Let me tell you about Cy Young.

"One of the first games I played in, maybe *the* first, was against the New York Highlanders. They had that guy who could 'hit 'em where they ain't'—you remember, Willie Keeler. He knew I was a green country boy and he bunted me to death.

"I was very discouraged, thought they were going to send me home, really down in the mouth. Cy came over and said, 'Come on, Larry, let's go have a couple.'

"A lot of people thought Cy didn't drink, but that's crazy. Cy drank plenty, but never the night before he was going to pitch.

"We went over to the Hotel Putnam on Huntington Avenue. That's where most of the players used to go in those days. Cy ordered some rye whisky called Cascade—how he loved that Cascade. Then he told me not to worry, everyone's nervous at first; I'd be all right.

"Well, that sure picked me up. Imagine drinking whisky with Cy Young and being told you were going to make it!"

October 10, 1904

Bring on the National League champion New York Giants! The Pilgrims are ready and eager to defend their World Championship.

The Boston Americans won their second pennant in a row today, clinching it with a 3-2 thriller over the runner-up Highlanders in the first game of the schedule-ending doubleheader at New York.

Boston's winning run scored when New York ace spitballer Jack Chesbro uncorked a wild pitch—probably a wet one—with two out in the ninth inning.

The big crowd of 28,540, which stood 15 deep around the outfield at Hilltop Park on upper Broadway, cried out in anguish as the pitch flew over the catcher's head and the Boston runner danced across the plate.

The Pilgrims needed only a victory in either game to clinch, so their ten-inning 1-0 loss in the nightcap meant nothing.

The Boston and New York teams had swapped the league lead back and forth the past few days. Three days ago, Clark Griffith's Highlanders, featuring Chesbro and .343-hitting Wee Willie Keeler, won at Boston, 3-2, to take a half-game lead. The next day the Pilgrims swept New York, 13-2 and 1-0, to regain the top and set up today's duel between Chesbro and Bill Dinneen.

Going into the game Dinneen was 22-14, Chesbro 41-11. Chesbro, the ornery right-hander from western Massachusetts, had almost single-handedly kept New York in the race, completing all but three of his 51 starts and winning 14 in a row.

Happy Jack was pitching his third game in four days when the Pilgrims did him in by breaking a 2-2 tie in the ninth.

Lou Criger beat out an infield hit, advanced to third on a bunt and groundout. He scored when Chesbro's 2-2 serve to Fred Parent soared over catcher Red Kleinow's head.

Dinneen easily retired New York in the last of the inning for the pennant, the Pilgrims' first under new owner John I. Taylor. Hundreds of Royal Rooters down from Boston, band and all, celebrated with a torchlight parade down Broadway tonight.

The Royal Rooters accompanied their heroes to New York for the season's final game to decide the 1904 pennant. That's Bill Dinneen (capless), who would outpitch the mighty Jack Chesbro, speaking with a New York police officer, and second baseman Hobe Ferris (with cap at jaunty angle).

The team's sights now are set on the other New York team, Mugsy McGraw's Giants. While breezing to their pennant, the National Leaguers have been saying for weeks that they won't play the American League winner because the junior circuit is inferior. But surely the Giants will relent and serve public interest—particularly since it'd be Boston they'd be facing, not their rival New York franchise.

The Highlanders, renamed Yankees, would twice gain revenge on the Pilgrims, renamed Red Sox, decades later in similar season-end show-downs.

The Red Sox went into New York in 1949 needing a victory in either of the season's last two games for the pennant. The Yankees won both—and the flag. And in 1978, after the rivals had ended in a tie for first, the Yankees came to Boston for a one-game, winner-take-all playoff. The Red Sox lost it and the A.L. East title.

The Pilgrims posed for a victory photo after winning the 1904 pennant at New York.

October 12, 1904

"We don't play minor leaguers!"

That's the official response from the National League and its yellow champion, the New York Giants, in response to the Pilgrims' challenge to meet in a World Series. Thus there won't be a meeting between the rival league winners this autumn—and maybe never again.

The insulting snub has outraged the Boston players. Upon their joyful return from New York, they were celebrating their new pennant at a party given for them at the Hotel Putnam by John I. Taylor. To a man, they called the great John J. McGraw and his Giants "dirty cowards."

The Pilgrims also claimed the world title by default.

They had been looking forward to defending their World Championship against the Giants and their great pitchers, Ironman Joe McGinnity (35-8) and Christy Mathewson (33-12).

N.L. President Harry Pulliam backs the Giants, saying last year's Series was strictly a voluntary agreement between the Pittsburgh and Boston clubs.

Owner John Tomlinson Brush is doing most of the talking for his Giants, but some believe that "Little Napoleon" McGraw is at the root of the decision. He and A.L. President Ban Johnson have been feuding for years, and the bad feeling intensified last year when the two leagues made peace and allowed the Orioles, McGraw's old team, to move to New York and become the Highlanders, thus invading the Giants' domain.

Seeing his stronghold threatened, Brush has continued a private war despite the truce, and says the N.L. should not lower itself by playing an unworthy, inferior league. He says his club is "content to rest on its laurels."

His players aren't. They're not taking kindly to losing the opportunity to pick up about $1,500 per man. They appealed to Brush to let them play Boston, but the owner turned a deaf ear to their pleas.

The furious Pilgrims say Brush's stated reasons are hogwash, that the real reason he refuses is because he's afraid to let his Giants play them—fearing the same embarrassing fate as the Pirates last fall.

The Sporting News *made it "official" by declaring the Boston Americans the "World Champions by default."*

The Giants remained adamant in their refusal, despite an uproar around the country. But the lambasting had its effect, and the World Series resumed the next season—and has continued each year since.

Former world heavyweight champion John L. Sullivan, the "Boston Strongboy," regularly attended games at the Huntington Avenue Grounds, sometimes visiting player-manager Jimmy Collins on the bench. Fifty years later the Red Sox would number among their fans another heavyweight champ, Rocky Marciano.

With a month to go in the 1906 season, Chick Stahl succeeded suspended Jimmy Collins as player-manager of the last-place Pilgrims. Stahl would manage the club only 18 games, committing suicide the following March as the team barnstormed its way home to Boston from spring training.

May 25, 1906

It was a long time coming, but the drought is over!

The Pilgrims' losing binge ended at 20 today when Jesse Tannehill conquered the White Sox, 3-0, as catcher Bob Peterson singled home all three runs.

It sparked a celebration at the Huntington Avenue Grounds, where the last 19 setbacks in the awful string were suffered. When second sacker Hobe Ferris tossed out the last Chicago man, the air was rent by a grand and joyful yell from the 3,055 attending.

Thus Pittsburgh's record of 23 consecutive losses still stands, but our boys made a noble bid—and at least have the American League record.

The Red Sox still have it, although now they share it with the 1916 and 1943 Athletics.

And the 19 consecutive losses at home remains the major league record. Next most by any big league team is 14—by the 1926 Red Sox.

September 1, 1906

Pity poor Joe Harris.

The hapless pitcher can't pick up a victory to save his soul. The Pilgrim right-hander chucked 24 valiant innings today at the Huntington Avenue Grounds—and lost! What a heartbreaker!

The Athletics scored three runs in the 24th canto to beat him, 4-1, in the longest game in major league history, outlasting the 20-inning match between the same teams last year, also won by Philadelphia, when Cy Young was the victim.

The visitors gathered 16 singles today, the home team 15 in the four-hour, 40-minute endurance contest witnessed by 18,084.

Harris, the 24-year-old local product from nearby Melrose, was out-dueled by Jack Coombs, the rookie right-hander from Colby College in Maine.

Poor Joe's record is now a sorry 2-21, and the sad Pilgrims are mired deeper in the cellar.

Philly scored a run in the third frame, the Pilgrims got one in the sixth, and after that it was all goose eggs on the scoreboard through the 23rd inning. It was getting dark, and both teams requested the game be stopped. Umpire Tim Hurst replied "no."

So Connie Mack's plucky Quakers quickly put a stop to it in their own way in the top of the 24th. Former Pilgrim Ossee Schreckengost batted in Topsy Hartsel with the winning run. Adding insult, Socks Seybold and Danny Murphy followed with hits for a couple of extra runs.

"Never mind, Joe, that game made you," consoled Chick Stahl, who recently replaced Jimmy Collins as Pilgrim manager. "Keep pitching like that and you'll stay in the league a long time."

After going 0-6 the next year for a 3-29 career mark, Harris was released to Providence at mid-season, never to return to the majors.

o

Nearly 75 years later, that 24-inning marathon is still in the record book. It remained the major league mark only 14 years—until the Braves and Dodgers played a 26-inning 1-1 tie in Boston in 1920. But it still is tied for the longest in American League history.

April 11, 1907

The Boston Americans have opened the season with a new nickname—the *Red Sox.*

Perhaps trying to improve the team's image after last season's last-place disaster, owner John I. Taylor has chosen the new moniker now that the Boston Nationals have discarded the red hosiery they've always worn.

"From now on we'll wear red stockings and I'm grabbing that name Red Sox," Taylor says.

The name is borrowed from the powerful Boston Red Stockings of the 1870s and 1880s, forerunners of the Boston Nationals. The Nationals have let the name Red Stockings fall into disuse, instead going by such appellations as Beaneaters, Rustlers and now Doves.

But they kept wearing red stockings until this year, when manager Fred Tenney abandoned them, saying he fears the red dye may cause infection in spike wounds, and have switched to white hose. It's also possible the Nationals' new owners want a new look for their club.

Whatever the reason, Taylor was quick to seize the opportunity and is delighted with his club's new nickname. So the team that's been known as the Somersets (after original owner Charles W. Somers), Plymouth Rocks, Speed Boys, Puritans, but mostly Pilgrims, now will have foes seeing red.

Hooray for the *Red Sox*!

The name soon won favor with fans and spread quickly throughout New England—and nationally. With the possible exception of the Yankees, no baseball team has more fans spread throughout the country.

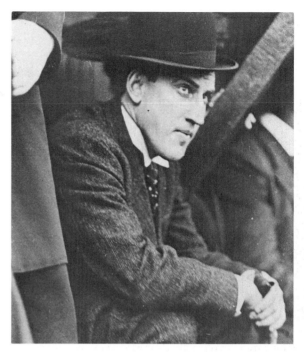

Owner John I. Taylor changed the team's name to the Red Sox. He also would name its new home Fenway Park.

June 30, 1908

Forty-one-year-old Cy Young pitched a no-hitter today, facing only 27 Highlanders during the Red Sox's 8-0 victory at New York.

Only one Highlander reached base—Harry Niles on a walk—and he was quickly gunned down by Lou Criger while trying to steal.

It was Young's third no-hitter, his second for Boston. Cy also chipped in with three of the Sox's 13 hits, knocking in four runs and scoring another.

The near-perfect game—part of his last 20-victory season—tied a bow on Young's eight years with the Red Sox, and he and favorite catcher Criger were dealt to Cleveland at season's end. Left behind were such statistics as 190 victories (including 39 shutouts) of his incredible 511 career wins, and 276 complete games in 298 starts.

Cy Young (right) and loyal battery mate Lou Criger teamed for their second Red Sox no-hitter in 1908 before being traded as a package to Cleveland at season's end. (Looking on here is "Nuff Ced" McGreevey, a leader of the Royal Rooters.)

July 19, 1909

The Red Sox's faces were the color of their stockings today at Cleveland as they fell victim to the first unassisted triple play in major league history.

In the second inning, Heinie Wagner and Jake Stahl beat out infield hits off former mate Cy Young. And with Wagner and Stahl running on a 3-2 pitch, Amby McConnell lashed a liner past Young's right ear.

Shortstop Neal Ball speared the drive near second base, stepped on the bag to erase Wagner and took just a step or two to tag out Stahl.

The crowd of 10,000 greeted the historic gem with stunned silence, then erupted in pandemonium.

Rubbing it in, minutes later Ball added to his heroics by hitting an inside-the-park homer against the still-numb Sox, who never did recover, losing, 6-1.

THE SECOND DECADE

Stuffy McInnis, a Greater Boston product starring for the Athletics, sparked one of the greatest rhubarbs in Boston sports history when he smacked a warm-up pitch for a homer. He later played on four Red Sox teams, including the 1918 World Champions.

Smokey Joe Wood is the youngest Red Sox pitcher to throw a no-hitter.

June 27, 1911

Athletics star Stuffy McInnis hit the most controversial home run in Red Sox history today, an inside-the-park wallop while some Boston fielders had their backs to the plate.

The homer was hit on a warm-up pitch, igniting a near riot at the Huntington Avenue Grounds during the 7-3 Sox loss.

Between-innings warm-up tosses are illegal this season, banned by American League President Ban Johnson in an effort to speed up games.

Noting that there was plenty of time before his fielders would be in place for the start of the eighth inning, Red Sox pitcher Ed Karger began lobbing the ball to rookie catcher Les Nunamaker, filling in for injured veteran Bill Carrigan.

McInnis, first baseman of the A's famed "$100,000 Infield," jumped into the batter's box and drilled the second warm-up pitch over second base. It rolled to deep center field—unoccupied because Tris Speaker hadn't reached his position after making the final out in the seventh inning.

No one chased the ball.

"Run!" Philadelphia teammates hollered to McInnis—and he did, scooting around the bases unchallenged.

One of the greatest rhubarbs in Boston sports history followed when umpire Ben Egan allowed the homer.

July 29, 1911

If you don't succeed at first, try again. That's what Smokey Joe Wood did today, and it earned him a no-hitter over the Browns at the Huntington Avenue Grounds.

The 21-year-old right-hander nearly had a no-hitter the last time he faced the Browns, on the team's last trip to St. Louis. But with two out in the ninth inning, Burt Shotton spoiled it with a single.

There was no stopping Smokey Joe today, though, as he struck out 12, walked two and hit one batter while coasting to a 5-0 victory.

At 21, Wood was the youngest Red Sox pitcher to throw a no-hitter.

April 26, 1912

Light-hitting Hugh Bradley slammed Fenway Park's first home run today, clearing the high left-field wall only six days after the ballyard opened.

The reserve first baseman's homer surprised experts who had predicted it would be years before a batter lifted the dead ball over the tall barrier in left.

Bradley was an unlikely candidate to accomplish the feat. It proved the only home run of his .190-hitting season. In fact, he would total only two homers during his five big league seasons.

September 6, 1912

Smokey Joe Wood bested Walter Johnson, 1-0, as the Red Sox squeezed by the Senators today in what will go down in baseball history as one of the classic pitching match-ups of all time.

A Friday afternoon crowd of nearly 30,000 jammed Fenway Park for the duel between the two fireballers who lead the majors in strikeouts.

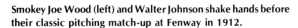

Wood chalked up his 14th consecutive win, closing in on the 16-straight-victory record set by Johnson last month.

The crowd overflowed the stands. More than 3,000 were perched on Duffy's Cliff, behind ropes strung in front of the left-field wall. Many hundreds more were jammed along the foul lines in front of the grandstand between first and third base, so both teams abandoned their dugouts, moving their benches next to the foul lines in front of the crowd.

The throng was treated to a masterpiece duel as advertised.

Wood allowed six hits while striking out nine. Johnson gave up five hits while fanning five.

The game's only run came with two out in the sixth inning on back-to-back doubles by Tris Speaker and Duffy Lewis.

Both doubles were to the opposite field. The left-hand-hitting Speaker drilled a liner over third that disappeared into the crowd roped off in left for a ground-rule double. The right-hand-hitting Lewis followed with a fly down the right-field line that glanced off the glove of the lunging right fielder who had made a long run from right center. Speaker scored easily.

The thriller was one of sixty-four 1-0 verdicts Johnson would be involved in during his Hall of Fame career, one of twenty-six he lost.

"Can I throw harder than Joe Wood?" the Big Train was quoted during that 1912 season as Wood carved a 34-5 record and added three more victories in the World Series. "Listen, my friend, there's no man alive who can throw harder than Smokey Joe Wood."

Smokey Joe Wood (left) and Walter Johnson shake hands before their classic pitching match-up at Fenway in 1912.

SMOKEY JOE WOOD: "That duel with Walter Johnson sticks out more than any other game I ever played at Fenway. I could never forget it.

"It was on a Friday. My regular pitching turn was scheduled to come on Saturday, but they moved it up a day so that Walter and I could face each other. Walter had already won 16 in a row, and his streak had ended. I had won 13 in a row, and they challenged our manager, Jake Stahl, to pitch me against Walter, so Walter could stop my streak himself. Jake agreed, and to match us against each other he moved me up in the rotation.

"The newspapers publicized us like prizefighters: giving statistics comparing our height, weight, biceps, triceps, arm span and whatnot. The Champion, Walter Johnson, versus the Challenger, Joe Wood.

"That was the only game I ever remember at Fenway Park, or anywhere else for that matter, where the fans were sitting practically along the first-base and third-base lines. Instead of sitting back where the bench usually is, we were sitting on chairs right up against the foul lines, and the fans were right behind us. The overflow had been packed between the grandstand and the foul lines, as well as out in the outfield behind ropes.

"In fact, the fans were put on the field an hour before the game started, and it was so crowded down there I hardly had room to warm up.

"Well, Boston won, but not because I was pitching. We had better players than Washington. Johnson was the greatest pitcher who ever lived. If he'd ever had a good ball club behind him, what records he would have set."

Spitballer Buck O'Brien (left) was the Red Sox starter in the Fenway opener April 20, 1912, when the Red Sox outlasted the Yankees, 7-6, in 11 innings. Six days later, Hugh Bradley (right) hit Fenway's first homer—clearing the left-field wall.

HARRY HOOPER: "That was probably the most exciting game I ever saw. After that, Joe won two more games to tie Johnson's record at 16, and then he lost the next time out on an error that let a couple of unearned runs score in the eighth or ninth inning. So now they both hold the record.

"I've seen a lot of great pitching in my lifetime, but I've never seen anything to compare with Smokey Joe Wood in 1912. He won 34 games that year, 10 of them shutouts, and 16 of those wins were in a row.

"The tension on Joe was just terrific all that season. First the 16 straight, and then the World Series. I still remember talking to him before one of the Series games and suddenly realizing that he couldn't speak. Couldn't say a word. The strain had started to get too much for him. Well, what can you expect? I think he was only about 22 when all this was happening. Mighty young to be under such pressure for so many months.

"But he still won three games in that 1912 World Series.

"After that wonderful season, Joe Wood never pitched successfully again. He hurt his arm and never was able to really throw that hummer any more, the way he did in 1912. Joe kept trying to come back as a pitcher but never could do it. He had a lot of guts, though. He couldn't pitch any more, so he turned himself into an outfielder and became a good one. He could always hit. He played for Cleveland in the 1920 World Series as an outfielder.

"I think he's the only man besides Babe Ruth who was in one World Series as a pitcher and another as an outfielder."

John F. "Honey Fitz" Fitzgerald, Red Sox fanatic and Mayor of Boston, threw out the first pitch of a 1912 World Series game at Fenway. At far right is his daughter Rose, whose son John F. Kennedy would become president.

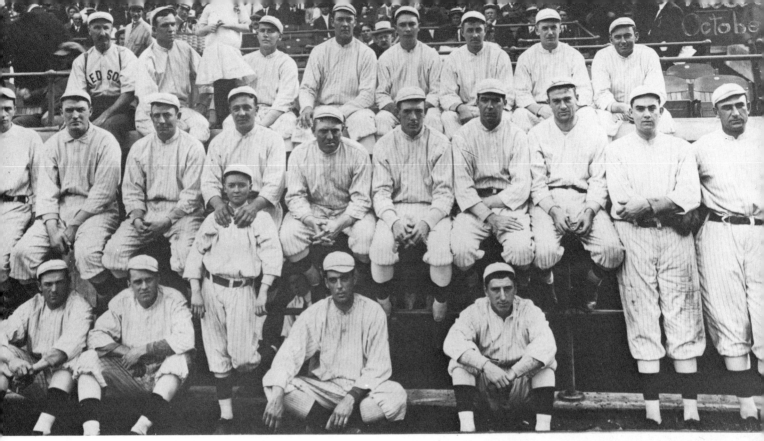

October 10, 1912

Seein' ain't always believin'.

The Red Sox lost a 2-1 heartbreaker to the Giants today in a World Series game that many of the 34,624 leaving Fenway Park thought the home boys had won, 3-2.

Confused? So were the spectators.

The game started at 3 p.m., and by the ninth inning the field was in semidarkness with a heavy mist rolling in from the harbor. Rube Marquard was blanking the Hose, 2-0, all set to even the Series at a victory apiece.

But the Red Sox finally got something going in the final frame, scoring once and putting runners on second and third with two out. Hick Cady then jabbed a streaker to right as the two Boston runners dashed across the dish.

But outfielder Josh Devore snared the ball in the gloaming, never broke stride and sprinted for the clubhouse with the final out tucked in his glove.

Most fans didn't see the catch and thought the ball had pierced the outfield for a 3-2 Boston victory, and much cheering followed.

There will probably be some barroom skirmishes tonight over which team won and which team lost—and about who has to pay up on bets.

October 16, 1912

The Red Sox are World Champions today thanks to the generosity of the Giants. John McGraw's New Yorkers committed two tenth-inning blunders that enabled the Red Sox to gain a 3-2 triumph at Fenway Park to take the World Series, four games to three, with another ending in a tie.

The Sox played brilliantly at times, particularly a miracle catch by Harry Hooper to prevent a homer. But it was sheer luck that tipped the scales in Boston's favor at the end. Not only did the Giants muff a creampuff fly to center, but they allowed a lazy foul pop-up to drop—two crucial boners that let the Sox tally twice and overcome New York's lead in the extra inning.

The Red Sox 1912 World Champions (left to right): front row, Heinie Wagner, Hugh Bedient, mascot Jerry McCarthy, Larry Pape and Marty Krug; middle row, Harry Hooper, Bill Carrigan, Steve Yerkes, Olaf Henriksen, Clyde Engle, Les Nunamaker, Charley Hall, Larry Gardner, Ray Collins and Jake Stahl; back row, trainer Joe Quirk, Tris Speaker (girl with head missing is Smokey Joe Wood's little sister Zoe), Joe Wood, Hick Cady, Pinch Thomas, Buck O'Brien, Hugh Bradley and Duffy Lewis.

Smokey Joe Wood (left) was the winning pitcher in the final game of the 1912 World Series, Christy Mathewson the loser.

It was a thriller, but only 17,034 saw it—half the size of the previous Fenway crowds. Many Bostonians boycotted the tilt to protest the shoddy treatment of the Royal Rooters. That loyal band of fan-atics had their regular seats sold out from under them in yesterday's sellout (in more ways than one), and when they paraded 300 strong around the field in protest, they were routed off the field by mounted police acting like Cossacks.

It was a public disgrace and left fans in a nasty mood. Some were so disgruntled that there was bitter talk that this Series was prearranged and fixed. But no schemer could have concocted what happened in this tumultuous finale.

The foes were locked 1-1 after regulation, and extra innings wouldn't have been necessary if Hooper hadn't made his game-saving catch in the sixth inning to steal a homer from Larry Doyle. Harry galloped back to the temporary bleachers in right center, leaping high above the low railing and balancing his back upon the front-row spectators. While almost horizontal, Hooper snared the ball just before it could disappear into the crowd, then himself tumbled into the stands with his circus catch.

Now it was the tenth inning, and two of baseball's top hurlers were dueling—starter Christy Mathewson (23-12) having scattered seven hits for New York, Smokey Joe Wood (34-5 including ten shutouts) in relief for Boston. Wood had replaced Hugh Bedient; the rookie pitched brilliantly before going out for pinch hitter Olaf Henriksen, who doubled home Boston's tying tally in the seventh.

It looked like curtains for the Red Sox when the Giants nicked Wood for a run in the tenth. And Smokey Joe hurt his pitching hand while knocking down a hot smash and throwing out Chief Meyers to retire the side.

Wood, a solid .290 hitter, couldn't continue, so Clyde Engle batted for him and hoisted a soft fly to center. Fred Snodgrass had to move only 10–20 feet, waving off the left fielder and tapping his glove as he camped under the ball—only to drop it for a two-base muff! Snodgrass then atoned for his misplay by making a slick catch of Hooper's drive, cheating Harry of a sure triple.

Mathewson walked Steve Yerkes to put Red Sox runners on first and second with one out as Boston's best hitter, Tris Speaker, stepped to the plate (.383 during the regular schedule, .300 in the Series).

Perhaps too eager, Spoke lofted a foul pop down the first-base line. The wind had been playing tricks with pop-ups, and first baseman Fred Merkle seemed a little slow starting for the ball. As the ball drifted toward the coaching box, somebody was yelling "Chief, Chief, Chief!" for catcher Meyers. But whether it was Mathewson hollering, or Speaker, or somebody on the Red Sox bench trying to create chaos isn't clear.

Whichever, confusion reigned, and when Merkle saw the on-charging Meyers wasn't going to reach the ball, Fred made a last-second lunge. But it was too late as the ball dropped among the triangle of Merkle, Meyers and Mathewson. The threesome walked back to the mound arguing.

Taking advantage of the reprieve, Speaker stung the next pitch for a single to tie the score. On the throw to the plate, both runners moved up, so McGraw ordered Duffy Lewis passed to set up a force at the plate. Larry Gardner then came through with a deep fly to right, and Yerkes raced across the dish with the run that won the game—and the Series. And 17,034 sounded like 117,034, in a roar that made Fenway tremble.

Sadly, there was no Royal Rooter band to zigzag a procession around the field. But the crowd did mob the Boston bench, where they gave hearty three cheers for all the Red Sox heroes, and for the "best player on the Giants, Snodgrass!"

There was further celebration in the Boston clubhouse—none of the Sox happier than Wood, who becomes one of the few pitchers ever to win three games in a World Series. In contrast, the visitors' locker room was glum.

Mathewson was outwardly calm. He consoled Snodgrass, then joined a game of bridge. Snodgrass took it hard. "I don't know why I dropped it," he lamented. "I just dropped it."

"Snodgrass didn't lose the game," snapped McGraw. "It was lost when Merkle didn't catch Speaker's foul. We were yelling at him from the bench that it was his ball, but the crowd made so much noise he couldn't hear us. But he should have caught it without anybody yelling at him."

McGraw's opinion wasn't unanimous. The New York press disagreed on both counts. The Times *bannered: "Sox Champions on Muffed Fly; Snodgrass Drops Easy Ball, Costing Teammates $29,514." And the* Herald Tribune *headlined the blame on "Damaging Error by Snodgrass and Blunder by Meyers."*

Snodgrass never lived down his error, forever after haunted by his "$30,000 muff," that figure being the difference between the teams' purses.

Proving once again that nothing succeeds like success, Boston fans forgot their anger the next day in the flush of victory. With manager Jake Stahl and Mayor John F. Fitzgerald riding together in the lead, a huge parade was staged at noon from Fenway to Faneuil Hall. There, "Honey Fitz" declared the Red Sox the "greatest club ever" (and clearly the luckiest), while Sox president Jim McAleer made a public apology to the Royal Rooters to soothe their hurt.

The victory parade was led by Mayor "Honey Fitz" Fitzgerald, standing in front seat. Seated in the back are player-manager Jake Stahl (left) and pitching hero Joe Wood (with hat and bow tie).

HARRY HOOPER: "Well, Spoke (Speaker) hit a little pop foul over near first base, and old Chief Meyers took off after it. He didn't have a chance, but Matty (Mathewson) kept calling for him to take it. If he'd called for Merkle, it would have been an easy out. Or Matty could have taken it himself...

"Spoke went back to the batter's box and yelled to Mathewson, 'Well, you just called the wrong man. It's gonna cost you the ball game.'"

FRED SNODGRASS: "For over half a century I've had to live with the fact that I dropped a ball in a World Series—'Oh yes, you're the guy that dropped that fly ball, aren't you?'—and for years and years, whenever I'd be introduced to somebody, they'd start to say something and then stop, you know, afraid of hurting my feelings."

October 5, 1913

Baseball's premier outfield of Tris Speaker, Duffy Lewis and Harry Hooper closed the season today with 84 assists, the most ever gathered by an outfield trio.

The Red Sox threesome also can hit—Speaker finishing third in the league at .365 (not to mention 46 stolen bases), Lewis adding .298 (and second in the league with 90 RBIs) and Hooper .288.

So don't blame them that the team didn't repeat as World Champions, finishing a distant fourth.

How great were Speaker, Lewis and Hooper?

They totaled 455 assists during their six years as a unit, 1910–15—an average of 76 per season. Speaker alone had 35 assists twice—in 1909 and 1912—each tying the American League record that still stands.

And those figures, of course, are only the tip of the iceberg—numbering the victims who challenged the Red Sox outfield's arms. There is no way of calculating how many thousands of baserunners were intimidated by the trio and didn't even try for an extra base.

Neither do these figures reflect the scores of potential hits denied by the trio's spectacular catches and by Speaker playing so shallow.

DUFFY LEWIS: "Speaker and I didn't speak to each other for awhile, but it certainly wasn't any feud as has been suggested. I'll tell you what happened.

"Leslie Mann, Joe Wood and I had our heads shaved in St. Louis as a gag. When we got back to Boston and were on the field practicing, Speaker said he was going to take my cap off.

"'You do and I'll hit you with a bat,' I said.

"Speaker grabbed my cap and I heaved the bat, hitting him on the shins so hard they had to carry him off the field. We didn't talk for three months, except to say 'Take it' or 'I've got it' on fly balls.

"But after that we became friends again. We were friends as long as he lived."

BUCK O'BRIEN: "Speaker played the shallowest center field of anybody. He could go back for a fly ball better than any outfielder. More than once he came in to second base to catch a runner off the bag.

"Believe me, he was a pitcher's best friend."

Baseball's legendary outfield (left to right): Duffy Lewis, Tris Speaker and Harry Hooper.

TY COBB: "I never let Speaker know how much I admired him—the great underlying respect—until we became teammates (with the 1928 Athletics) at the end of our careers. But from the moment he came into the league in 1907, I knew the mark of greatness was upon him."

July 11, 1914

Southpaw George "Babe" Ruth made his big league debut today at Fenway Park as the Red Sox defeated the Cleveland Naps, 4-3.

The 19-year-old rookie got the victory but wasn't around for the finish. He was lifted for pinch-hitter Duffy Lewis in a Sox rally in the seventh inning. Lewis's single set up the winning run.

The brash Ruth was acquired three days ago for $2,900 from the International League powerhouse Baltimore Orioles, one of the greatest teams ever assembled.

Outgoing and full of laughter, Ruth already is controversial among his Red Sox teammates for his rambunctious, crude and profane ways. He is on probation from St. Mary's Industrial School in Baltimore.

Ruth rooms with another pitcher, Ernie Shore, who was obtained in the same Baltimore deal that cost Boston $8,000 in all for three players.

Ruth and Shore would not last as roomies. Shore soon called player-manager Bill Carrigan to announce he was returning to his North Carolina home.

"Mr. Carrigan, I can't live with that man Ruth," Shore said.

"I thought you two were friends," Carrigan said.

"We are," Shore replied, "but there's a place where friendship stops. A man wants some privacy in the bathroom. Just this morning I told him he was using my toothbrush, and he said: 'That's okay. I'm not particular.'"

HARRY HOOPER: "Babe Ruth joined us in the middle of 1914, a 19-year-old kid. He had never been anywhere, didn't know anything about manners or how to behave among people—just a big overgrown pea.

"George was six-foot-two and weighed 198 pounds, all of it muscle. He had a slim waist, huge biceps, no self-discipline, and not much education—not so very different from a lot of other 19-year-old would-be ballplayers. Except for two things: he could eat more than anyone else, and he could hit a baseball further.

"Lord, he ate too much. He'd stop along the road when we were traveling and order half a dozen hot dogs and as many bottles of soda pop, stuff them in, one after the other, give a few big belches, and then roar, 'OK, boys, let's go.' That would hold Babe a couple of hours, and then he'd be at it again.

"He was such a rube that he got more than his share of teasing, some of it not too pleasant. 'The Big Baboon' some of them used to call him behind his back, and then a few got up enough nerve to ridicule him to his face. This started to get under his skin, and when they didn't let up he finally challenged the whole club. Nobody was so dumb as to take him up on it, so that put an end to that.

"You know, I saw it all happen, from beginning to end. But sometimes I still can't believe what I saw: a 19-year-old kid, crude and poorly educated, only lightly brushed by the social veneer we call civilization, gradually transformed into the idol of American youth and the symbol of baseball the world over—a man loved by more people and with an

Babe Ruth was removed for a pinch hitter in his Red Sox debut, but was the winning pitcher.

intensity of feeling that perhaps has never been equaled before or since.

"I saw a man transformed from a human being into something pretty close to a god. If somebody predicted that back on the Boston Red Sox in 1914, he would have been thrown into a lunatic asylum."

BABE RUTH: "When I joined the Red Sox I got some rough treatment. Someone must have told them I was a fresh kid who didn't have much respect for big baseball reputations, and some of the old guys let me have it.

"I suppose I did talk back, but not because I was fresh. I just wanted to show them I was as good as any of the other pitchers Bill Carrigan had.

"But the thing the older players most resented was that I insisted on taking batting practice. One day I came to the park and found that all my bats had been neatly sawed in two."

September 22, 1914

Ray Collins today became only the eighth major league pitcher since the turn of the century to hurl two complete-game triumphs in one day.

The Red Sox southpaw caged the Tigers, 5-3 and 5-0, at Detroit. The second game was called because of darkness after eight innings, but is considered a complete game.

Collins, zeroing in on his second straight 20-victory season, got stronger as the day progressed. The University of Vermont product allowed only four hits in the nightcap after scattering 12 safeties in the opener.

October 13, 1914

A World Series was won for Boston at Fenway Park today—by the Braves, not the Red Sox.

The Miracle Braves of Hank Gowdy and Rabbit Maranville concluded their four-game sweep of Connie Mack's mighty Athletics, climaxing the Boston Nationals' spectacular climb from last place in mid-July to the world title.

The Braves borrowed Fenway because their South End Grounds ballyard is inadequate to handle a World Series crowd.

Returning the compliment, the Braves let the Red Sox use their new and bigger (40,000-plus) park for the 1915 World Series.

So, in what had great potential for an Abbott & Costello routine, the Braves used the Red Sox's home for the 1914 World Series and the 1915 Red Sox used the Braves' home for the 1915 World Series. Got that?

May 6, 1915

George "Babe" Ruth hit his first major league home run today, a prodigious clout into the upper deck of the Polo Grounds off veteran Yankee right-hander Jack Warhop.

The homer by Slugger Ruth couldn't save Pitcher Ruth, however. The Yankees edged the 20-year-old southpaw in the 13th inning, 4-3.

But it was Ruth's wallop—the game's only homer—that had the crowd of about 5,000 talking as they left the Polo Grounds, the home the Giants share with the Yankees.

Ruth, in his first full big league season, has a classic stroke. He swings with no apparent effort—even though he wields a bat weighing about three pounds—grasping it at the end, his right pinky finger curled under the knob.

Vermonter Ray Collins pitched two complete-game victories over the Tigers in one day.

Boston players tell of colossal swats by Ruth during spring training at Hot Springs, Arkansas. Some feel his bat should be in the lineup every day. But how could he crack baseball's best outfield of Tris Speaker, Harry Hooper and Duffy Lewis?

Ruth, of course, would hit 713 more home runs. One of his four that year cleared the right-field bleachers at St. Louis for the longest homer ever recorded at Sportsman's Park. The Babe batted .315 that season, including ten pinch-hitting appearances. Although striking out 23 times in 92 at-bats, more than half his hits were for extra bases. And with his picture-book swing, he even looked good striking out.

Ruth also blossomed as a pitcher that season with an 18-6 record and 2.44 ERA. His effectiveness had grown after learning not to stick out his tongue when throwing a curve, a habit that had tipped off enemy batters.

October 8, 1915

The Red Sox got off on the wrong foot in the World Series opener today, suffering a 3-1 loss to the Phillies at Philadelphia.

That doesn't augur well for Bill Carrigan's boys. In the last nine World Series, the first-game victor has gone on to capture the World Championship eight times.

"We lost one, so what of it?" grumbled the Red Sox manager. "We've got lots of others to win, and to hell with what the first-game winners did in the past!"

It was no shame losing this one, for the Sox were beaten by 31-game winner Grover Cleveland Alexander, who bested Ernie Shore to tickle the 19,343 at little Baker Bowl. And Shore really outpitched Alex the Great—Shore surrendering five singles, Alexander eight hits.

But the Phillies broke a 1-1 tie in the eighth inning without benefit of a ball being hit out of the soggy infield—so soaked by several days of rain that it was set afire with gasoline before the game to try to dry it out.

"It was a crime for Ernie to lose that game," Carrigan said. "But we can't play into that kind of luck again."

The Red Sox almost got out of their bad luck in the ninth inning. With Olaf Henriksen on first base and one out, Carrigan sent up a pinch-hitter for Shore—Babe Ruth, the hardest-hitting pitcher in the business.

"Pick up your stick, Babe, here's your chance," the manager said, placing the 20-year-old sophomore in his first World Series game. "Pick out a good ball and hit it."

Ruth did exactly that, getting a good piece of the ball and cracking a hard grounder that first baseman Fred Luderus stabbed nicely.

One out later, the Philadelphia fans were hoisting their heroes—including manager Pat Moran of Fitchburg, Mass.—up on their shoulders and parading them around their bandbox park.

The crowd had no way of knowing they had witnessed history in the final inning—the World Series debut of baseball's greatest hero. George Herman Ruth would play in ten World Series—three with the Red Sox—and accumulate 15 homers and a .326 average.

This would be Ruth's only appearance in his first Series, though. Babe had an 18-8 record that season, and pleaded daily with Carrigan during the Series: "What about me, Bill? What does a guy have to do to get a chance to pitch a World Series game for your club?" But with Rube Foster (two victories), Dutch Leonard and Shore pitching so well, Carrigan kept putting Ruth off and promising, "You'll get your crack."

It's probable that that "crack" would have come in the sixth game of the Series—except that a sixth game wasn't necessary.

The 1915 World Champion Red Sox were reunited in 1961 at Fenway Park. Ray Collins (front) is joined at home plate by (left to right) Bill Carrigan, Hugh Bedient, Joe Wood, Larry Gardner, Duffy Lewis, Steve Yerkes, Olaf Henriksen and Harry Hooper.

George Foster was the Red Sox pitching hero of the 1915 World Series, beating the Phillies twice. *(National Baseball Hall of Fame)*

BABE RUTH: "The 1915 Red Sox World's Champions were baseball's greatest defensive team of all time.

"We weren't too much of a scoring club and Tris Speaker was our only .300 hitter. About all our pitchers would ask for would be two or three runs, and very often one would be enough. I don't recall how many low-scoring games we won that season, but we won plenty. Winning those three straight 2-1 games in the World Series seemed natural.

"Many years later, Ty Cobb and I were discussing the Tiger and Red Sox clubs of 1915 and our many fights during the red-hot season. Ty said: 'On defense I don't believe that club (Red Sox) ever had an equal. You'd get off to a 2-1 lead and hold on like grim death. Time after time we'd think we had a rally going in the late innings only to have Scottie or Gardner come up with great stops, or Spoke, Duffy or Hooper pull one of their circus catches in the outfield.' "

October 9, 1915

President Woodrow Wilson was among the 20,306 at Philadelphia's Baker Bowl who watched the Red Sox even the World Series at one game apiece today with a 2-1 squeaker over the Phillies.

Wilson, the first U.S. President ever to attend a World Series, threw out the first pitch. The Sox now would like to bring him to Boston as their good-luck charm for the next two games of the Series.

But even the President himself couldn't outshine George "Rube" Foster today. Not only did the stubby right-hander quell the Phillies on just three hits with no walks and eight strikeouts, but he also produced a double and two singles in the ten-hit Boston attack.

Fittingly, the short-in-height (5-foot-7) but big-in-heart Foster won his own game by driving home the winning run in the ninth inning with his third hit, a two-out single that registered Larry Gardner from second.

The Phillies had a few scares left in the last of the ninth. Foster hit Milt Stock with a pitch, but umpire Cy Rigler braved the wrath of the homefolk by ruling that, because Stock hadn't tried to get out of the pitch's way, he wouldn't allow him first base. That sparked a furious rhubarb.

Order was finally restored, and two outs later Dode Paskert stroked a screecher that appeared ticketed for the temporary bleachers in center. But Tris Speaker galloped back and lunged desperately at the last instant to snare the ball just before it went into the customers' laps.

"We got into our stride in that second game at Philadelphia," Red Sox manager Bill Carrigan said before Game 3 at brand new Braves Field, borrowed by the Sox because it seated more than Fenway. "If I say so myself, the Red Sox can play ball as few clubs can, and I haven't the slightest doubt we'll take the Series."

Carrigan was correct. Dutch Leonard three-hit the Phils that day before 42,300 as the Sox won that game and the two that followed—like their previous victory, all by one run.

Joining the Boston pitchers in the headlines were Duffy Lewis and Harry Hooper, lionized for their clutch hitting and fielding. Lewis batted .444, Hooper .350, and along with Speaker made some electrifying catches in the outfield. What's more, in the 5-4 finale at Philadelphia, Lewis hit one homer and Hooper belted two—Hooper's pair bouncing into the temporary seats in center field, making them ground-rule home runs.

DUFFY LEWIS: "We were behind 4-2 in the eighth inning of the last game, with a man on base, when I hit a home run high up in the left-field stands. Then in the ninth, Hooper bounced his second homer into the stands in center and we won.

"He and I, we had a hell of a Series."

April 12, 1916

The baseball world was astonished today when the Red Sox peddled Tris Speaker to the Indians for 50,000 simoleons and two obscure players.

Getting rid of the 28-year-old hero of the past seven seasons simply doesn't make sense, and infuriated most Red Sox players and put their loyal fans in a state of revolt. It makes a mockery of tomorrow's usually gala Opening Day, which was expected to be especially festive this year because the World Championship flag will be hoisted.

The deal is dumb. Not only does it strip Boston of one of baseball's two greatest players (only Detroit's Ty Cobb is in the same class) and the man who revolutionized outfielding, but it breaks up the dream outfield of Speaker, Harry Hooper and Duffy Lewis.

Some say the deal was made because Speaker and manager Bill "Rough" Carrigan are not friendly. That's cockeyed. True, the two aren't pals; but Rough wouldn't trade the Kaiser himself if it would help our Sox win.

No, the nonsensical deal must be the result of two old evils: greed and stubbornness, both on the part of Joe Lannin.

The Red Sox owner has been trying to chop Speaker's stipend to about half the $18,000 he's gotten each of the past two seasons to keep him out of the embrace of the Federal League. When that outlaw circuit folded last winter to end the costly war, all the American and National league teams began carving salaries back to what they were before the Feds came along two years ago.

Thus Lannin wanted Speaker to cut back to about the $9,000 he got in 1913. The owner maintained that the Texan has been slipping—falling from 1912's high of .383 to .365 to .338 to .322.

Tristram, of course, would have none of it. He wouldn't take a nickel less than $15,000.

His friend Joe Wood also refused to ink a pact, balking at being slashed to $5,000. Smokey Joe, 34-5 only a few years ago and 9-3 and 15-5 the last two seasons despite an arm ache, wouldn't report for such an "awfully measly sum." And Lannin lashed back that $5,000 was fitting for Wood's "measly number of victories" the last two years.

Whereas Wood wouldn't report to spring training, Speaker agreed to drill with the team at Hot Springs, Arkansas, and played in the exhibitions on a pay-per-game arrangement. He played in yesterday's pre-season finale at Brooklyn, homering in the ninth inning to beat Rube Marquard.

Speaker was supposed to huddle with Lannin after the game, but the owner supposedly said to the star as he came off the field: "You win. Your terms are OK. We'll sign tomorrow in Boston." So Speaker is as stunned and confused as everyone else. But one thing is clear: for the sake of about $5,000, Lannin has denied his World Champs and the dazed New England fans the services of one of the greatest players who ever lived.

No more will we see Tris in a Red Sox uniform making one game-winning grab after another . . . or sneaking in from his daringly shallow center-field slot and taking throws from the catcher to nab snoozing runners off second base . . . or making unassisted double plays by catching drives off his shoetops and outracing runners on second back to the

Tris Speaker takes batting practice before a 1915 World Series game at Braves Field.

Duffy Lewis batted .444 to lead Red Sox hitters in the 1915 World Series.

The trade of Tris Speaker shocked Red Sox players and fans.

Smokey Joe Wood remained at home with his wife during his holdout.

Bill Carrigan was a master at blocking the plate. He earned his nickname "Rough."

bag . . . or even being the pivot man on double-play grounders.

Instead, he'll be doing all those things for Cleveland—and in his place, Lannin can pile those 50,000 silver dollars in center field for the Red Sox.

By the time the fuss subsided, Lannin could pile only 40,000 silver dollars. While Speaker's mother in Texas cried that her boy couldn't be bought and sold "like a longhorn steer," her shrewd son said he wouldn't report to Cleveland unless he got $10,000 of the purchase price. The outraged Lannin finally relented when league president Ban Johnson stepped in and guaranteed payment; thus Speaker got the money that the Sox owner was trying to cut him all along—plus interest.

The prematurely white-haired "Gray Eagle" added another insult by leading the league in hitting at .386, breaking Cobb's nine-year hold on the batting crown.

Speaker was joined in Cleveland the next season by his buddy Smokey Joe, and Wood became an outfielder and a good one—batting .298 during the five seasons of his second career. And when Wood and player-manager Speaker led Cleveland to the 1920 pennant, Smokey Joe joined Babe Ruth as the only players ever to appear in the World Series as both pitchers and outfielders.

○

Luckily for Lannin, the Red Sox retained their World Championship in 1916 without Speaker, softening the furor but not eliminating it.

Further balm was added a few years later when one of the two "obscure" players obtained along with cash for Speaker blossomed into one of the league's best pitchers. Sad Sam Jones averaged 16 victories per season 1918–21, including 23 for the fifth-place 1921 club.

In fact, he was "too good"—so impressive that the Yankees coveted him. So naturally Harry Frazee packed him off to New York.

◇◇◇

BILL CARRIGAN: "I had nothing to do with the deal. It was Lannin's idea. He never told me why. He owned the club and didn't have to give reasons.

"Anybody who thinks I suggested the trade doesn't know me. My only goal as a manager was to win. I might hate a player's guts, but if he could help us win games I wanted him. If I were to get rid of a player because he and I didn't see eye-to-eye, I'd be cutting off my nose to spite my face.

"It was never any secret that Speaker wasn't one of my favorite persons, and neither was I one of his. But I recognized his talent and was delighted to have him on our side. I hated to lose him.

"I never did find out why Lannin made the deal, but I suspected at the time that he suddenly found himself in need of money to carry on his hotel business and figured there was no easier way to raise $50,000 than by cashing in on Spoke."

◇◇◇

BABE RUTH: "Spoke was something extra special. Only those who played with or against him really appreciated what a great player he was.

"In my Red Sox pitching days I would hear the crack of the bat and say, 'There goes the ball game.' But Tris would turn his back to the plate, race far out to the fences and at the last moment make a diving catch. Not once but a thousand times.

"He was more than a great outfielder; he actually was a fifth infielder. Tris would play close and get many balls in short center or right field and occasionally throw a runner out at first. Maybe with the present lively ball Tris couldn't play that way. But he could still go out for them, and with the modern ball his great hitting would be much greater.

"Tris was a great base runner, not quite up to Cobb, but ahead of most of the others. It just happened that when Speaker was in his prime so was Cobb, and Ty was such a competitor in both hitting and running that he would let no one finish ahead of him. In fact, when Cobb won 11 batting championships in 12 years, the only one who broke through on him was Tris Speaker."

Just before his death in 1948, Ruth picked Speaker as the center fielder on his all-time team.

BABE RUTH: "My 'feud' with Tris Speaker? We never really had a scrap, and Tris and I later became good friends.

"There were two cliques on that 1915 club. Speaker and Joe Wood were the heads of one and I guess Bill Carrigan and Heinie Wagner headed the other. I was on Carrigan's side.

"Speaker and Wood were inseparable. They roomed together and always went to the same places. Wood and I had a little friction on the field one day. The pitchers were warming up, and a ball thrown by Wood got away from his catcher. It came toward me, but instead of stopping it I bowed my legs and let the ball go through.

"It didn't amount to much, but Joe yelled something at me and I yelled something back. At first it was only rough kidding, but pretty soon we were calling each other some riper names. Wood finally said he would take a crack at me and I said, 'Let's go to the clubhouse and settle it right now.'

"We did start for the clubhouse, but by that time Carrigan got word of it and pushed us in opposite directions. The crazy incident did leave some bad feeling, and as Speaker was Joe's pal, naturally he was on Wood's side."

LARRY GARDNER: "I don't think anyone was better at blocking the plate than Bill Carrigan. Boy, was he tough!

"I remember one time we were playing Detroit. George Moriarty, their third baseman, and Bill were actually good friends. Moriarty got on first and yelled to Bill: 'Hey, you Irish S.O.B., I'm going to come around the bases and knock you on your arse.'

"Well, sure enough, George made his way around and came tearing into the plate. It was Moriarty, not Bill, that was knocked over. Bill walked over to George and let go with a hunk of tobacco juice. 'And how do you like that, you Irish S.O.B.?' "

BABE RUTH: "One reason I rate Bill Carrigan the best manager I ever played under was the way he kept the Red Sox up front after we lost Tris Speaker, our great center fielder and best hitter, just before the opening of the 1916 season.

"We all felt Speaker's sale had pulled the rug from under us. Some of us were talking it over and feeling sorry for ourselves when Carrigan overheard the conversation.

" 'All right, we lost Speaker,' he barked. 'But we're still a tight ball club. We've got good pitching, good fielding and we'll hit well enough. If you guys stop your moaning and get down to business we can win that pennant again.'

"And we did."

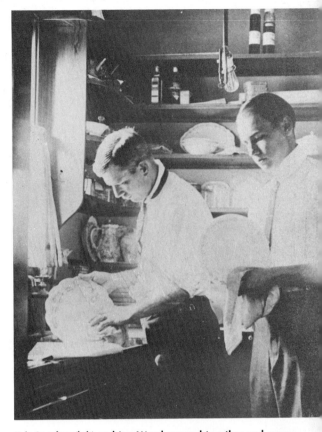

Tris Speaker (left) and Joe Wood roomed together and were inseparable. They led one faction of the team that was divided off the field.

Dutch Leonard pitched the Red Sox's second no-hitter of the season.

August 30, 1916

Hubert "Dutch" Leonard pitched the Red Sox's second no-hitter of the season today at Fenway Park, whitewashing the St. Louis Browns, 4-0.

And credit catcher-manager Bill Carrigan with an assist. Leonard was knocked out of the box in the first inning of yesterday's doubleheader opener with the Browns, so Carrigan figured Dutch was plenty rested and sent him back against George Sisler & Friends today.

The strategy worked—the chunky southpaw had a perfect game until the eighth inning when Hank Severeid walked. Grove Hartley also got a pass in the ninth.

Other than that, Leonard, who struck out three, had the Browns popping up all day, and the Sox defense was tested only three times.

Leonard's masterpiece matches that of teammate George "Rube" Foster on June 21.

October 9, 1916

Babe Ruth finally got his long-awaited chance to pitch a World Series game today and made the most of it—and how!

Ruth toiled 14 innings in hurling the Red Sox to a 2-1 victory over the Robins before 41,373 at Braves Field in the longest World Series game ever. The triumph was the second in as many outings for the heavily favored locals in the best-of-seven joust with the Brooklyns, mostly castoffs from other teams.

With darkness fast shrouding the diamond, the umpires had decided to call the game if the home team hadn't scored in the 14th frame. The game would have been played over from scratch tomorrow, bringing in another $100,000 or more in gate receipts.

So when pinch-hitter Del Gainor doubled home pinch-runner Mike McNally, the hit was worth $100,000 in lost revenue. It dissolved the knot tied early in the game—Brooklyn scoring a run in the first inning, Boston one in the third. The game's third batter, Hi Myers, bounced a Ruth offering that hopped over center fielder Tilly Walker's head for an inside-the-park homer. The Sox tied it when Deacon Scott tripled and scored on Ruth's infield out.

Babe and rival southpaw Sherry Smith then matched goose egg for goose egg until the 14th in a grand duel. Smith allowed only seven hits while taking the loss. Ruth spaced just six hits in carding the victory.

"I told you I could take care of those National League so-and-so's," the beaming Ruth yelled to manager Bill Carrigan.

Babe also took care of American League so-and-sos pretty handily this season with a league-leading 1.75 ERA and 23-12 record.

Ruth wasn't fully satisfied today, though. He bemoaned his failure to get a shutout. "Damn that bounce," he said of Myers's homer. "It should have been a single."

There's a consolation prize for brash Babe. A shutout would have given him only nine untainted innings. This way he achieved 13 straight scoreless frames—13⅓ to be exact.

And that was just the beginning. He'd stretch that string to 29⅔ innings into the 1918 World Series, a record that stood until 1961 when surpassed by another pretty fair southpaw, Whitey Ford.

o

That 14-inning game is still the longest in World Series history.

October 12, 1916

The Red Sox gained another World Championship today but lost a popular manager.

Bill "Rough" Carrigan said farewell to each of his players after they had beaten Brooklyn, 4-1, before the biggest crowd ever to see a baseball game: 42,620.

Police had to turn away another 20,000 from Braves Field on this Columbus Day holiday as New Englanders looked to baseball to escape all the war news from Europe—and, a lot closer to home, headlines of the sinkings of foreign ships by German U-boats lurking off Nantucket and Block Island.

Carrigan, the 33-year-old pride of Holy Cross and Lewiston, Maine, announced late in the schedule that he would quit at season's end and go into banking back in Lewiston. But few believed it, especially after the second straight pennant in his three and a half years as skipper-catcher. But the big guy is sticking to his guns, although some skeptics still think it's a ploy to squeeze a bigger salary out of owner Joe Lannin.

"Goodby, Bill. Good luck!" echoed around the clubhouse as Carrigan went from one locker to another shaking hands with his boys.

Well, no luck was needed today as Carrigan and his boys polished off Uncle Wilbert Robinson's Brooks in easy fashion, four games to one. Portsider Ernie Shore limited the visitors to three hits and one tarnished run in chalking up his second victory of the Series.

The Robins scored first without benefit of a hit in the second, parlaying a walk, a sacrifice and Hick Cady's passed ball. But the Sox tied it at 1-1 in the bottom of that inning, went ahead with two more runs in the third and iced it with a final run in the fifth.

The sloppy Brooks again graciously contributed three errors to total 13 for the Series, enough to send the frantic Robinson screaming back to his Hudson, Massachusetts, hometown. And two of today's allotment were made by shortstop Ivan Olson. That gives him four for the Series, and he's taken a terrific roasting from the Boston bench.

"When in doubt, hit it to Ivy!" was the chant, and it made the poor fellow so frantic that he challenged the whole Sox team to fight. They just laughed at that, and he got more upset. The more upset he got, the worse his fielding got.

Meanwhile, Duffy Lewis had two more hits to elevate his average to .353, the team's top regular for the second World Series in a row. Casey Stengel had one of Brooklyn's three hits, ballooning his average to .364, best on both teams.

The victory was followed by the customary spectator celebration, the fans swarming onto the field and locking arms for a parade behind the band around the diamond. As the parade passed the dugout to begin a second lap, the marchers collared Lannin and Brooks' owner Charley Ebbets and put them at the head of the victory dance.

Six months ago, when he sold Tris Speaker, they would have been marching Lannin to the gallows.

They would curse Lannin again. That December he sold the team to a New York theatrical man named Harry Frazee, a name that would be despised above all others in Red Sox history.

○

Carrigan was serious about retiring and stayed that way ten years. He was coaxed back in 1927 to resurrect the team that Frazee had wrecked, but could work no miracles. After three last-place finishes, "Rough" rushed back to his Lewiston bank when the stock market crashed.

Carrigan and Mike Higgins are the only two managers to have two tours at the Red Sox helm.

Duffy Lewis was the left fielder of the 1915 Red Sox World Champions, labeled baseball's greatest defensive team ever by Babe Ruth and Ty Cobb among others. Named in Lewis's honor was "Duffy's Cliff," a steep embankment in front of Fenway's left-field wall. It was treacherous terrain for most left fielders, but not Lewis, who negotiated it like a mountain goat.

Bill Carrigan retired and went home to Lewiston, Maine.

Jumping Joe Dugan's debut at Fenway was memorable.

JUMPING JOE DUGAN: "My first professional games were played at Fenway Park, where I joined the Athletics directly from Holy Cross. It was 1917, during World War I, and the Red Sox were defending world champs.

"I wasn't supposed to play, but Whitey Witt sprained an ankle and there I was, facing a couple of pitchers named Carl Mays and Ernie Shore in a doubleheader. They'd knock you down and then throw that big curve ball.

"I went 0-for-8 and wanted to catch the next bus back to Worcester.

"The next day it was Dutch Leonard, and his curve ball was coming in by way of Kenmore Square. I went 0-for-4. The last day it was Babe Ruth pitching for the Red Sox, and I was 0-for-16 leaving town.

"How's that for a start, brother?"

The slow start blossomed into a memorable career. Dugan played five seasons for Connie Mack's Athletics before joining the Red Sox in 1922. But after a half-season, Frazee sold him to the Yankees, where Jumping Joe gained fame as (1) one of Babe Ruth's closest pals, and (2) a three-time .300 hitter who batted seventh in Murderers' Row.

○

Now 82, Dugan sits in the press room on the roof of Fenway Park and nibbles at his lunch.

"They talk about this player or that player being the greatest who ever lived. But there can be no question about it. It's that man," he says, nodding to a portrait of Babe Ruth hanging above the bar. "There was nobody like him, no one even close.

"Ty Cobb? Tris Speaker? Willie Mays? Could they pitch?

"The Babe could do it all."

June 23, 1917

Ernie Shore pitched a perfect no-reach game at Fenway Park today in a game he didn't start.

Babe Ruth was the Red Sox starting pitcher in the opener of a doubleheader against the Senators. When umpire Brick Owen called a fourth ball on leadoff batter Eddie Foster, the irate Ruth stormed the plate.

"Can't you see, you blind bat?" Ruth roared.

"Get back to your position, you big ape," the umpire allegedly ordered.

After some saltier dialogue, Ruth threw a punch, hitting the umpire's neck.

Shore, recently reinstated from a league suspension following a brawl with the White Sox, hurriedly warmed up.

Foster promptly was thrown out trying to steal, and Shore retired the next 26 batters in order. Thus all 27 Washington batters were erased with Shore on the mound as the Red Sox won, 4-0.

So Shore is credited with the only perfect game ever pitched at Fenway, and one of only nine in the 100-year-plus history of major league baseball.

Bostonians feared Ruth would be banned for the season for his assault on the umpire. But American League President Ban Johnson was lenient, letting Ruth off with a week's suspension and a $100 fine.

BABE RUTH: "It wasn't a love tap. I really socked him—right on the jaw.

"Three of the four balls should have been strikes. I growled at some of the early balls, but when he called the fourth one I just went crazy.

"I rushed up to the plate and said, 'If you'd go to bed at night, you so-and-so, you could keep your eyes open long enough in the daytime to see when a ball goes over the plate.'

"Brick could dish it out, too. 'Shut up, you lout,' he said, 'or I'll throw you out of the game.'

" 'Throw me out and I'll punch you right on the jaw,' I bellowed.

"Brick looked at me coldly. 'You're out of this game right now,' he said with a big jerk of his thumb.

"I hauled off and hit him, but good."

ERNIE SHORE: "I was sitting on the bench and Jack Barry, our manager and second baseman, came running over and said, 'Shore, go in there and stall around until I can get somebody warmed up.'

"He never intended to have me finish the game. What he wanted me to do was go out on the mound and try to kill as much time as I could while he got somebody else ready in the bull pen.

"But there wasn't much stalling I could do, because when a pitcher was thrown out of a game, the next man was entitled to just five warm-up pitches.

"I took my warm-ups and then started pitching to the next batter. Well, on my very first pitch, the fellow Ruth had walked tried to steal and was thrown out. I threw two more pitches and retired the side.

"When I came back to the bench Barry said to me, 'Do you want to finish this game, Ernie?' My ball was breaking very sharply and he had seen that.

" 'Sure,' I said.

" 'Okay,' he said. 'Go down to the bull pen and warm up.'

"So I did that and came back for the second inning. From then on I don't think I could have worked easier if I'd been sitting in a rocking chair. I don't believe I threw 75 pitches that whole game, if I threw that many. They just kept hitting it right at somebody. They didn't hit but one ball hard and that was in the ninth inning. John Henry, the catcher, lined one on the nose, but right at Duffy Lewis in left field.

Ernie Shore hurled the only perfect game ever pitched at Fenway—in a game he didn't start. *(National Baseball Hall of Fame)*

"That was the second out in the ninth. Then Clark Griffith, who was managing Washington, sent a fellow named Mike Menosky in to bat for the pitcher. Griffith was a hard loser, a very hard loser. He didn't want to see me complete that perfect game. So he had Menosky drag a bunt, just to try to break it up.

"Menosky could run, too. He was fast. He dragged a pretty good bunt past me, but Jack Barry came in and made a wonderful one-hand stab of the ball, scooped it up and got him at first. That was a good sharp ending to the game."

June 3, 1918

Hubert "Dutch" Leonard today became only the sixth major league pitcher since the turn of the century to pitch two no-hitters.

The Red Sox southpaw blanked the Tigers, 5-0, at Detroit. He walked only one, Bobby Veach, while striking out four.

Babe Ruth, playing center field today, socked a home run to provide fellow pitcher Leonard with all the offense he needed.

Today's feat matches the 26-year-old Ohioan's no-hitter against the Browns two years ago.

Thus Leonard goes into the record books again—for his "bookends" no-hitters as well as his 1.01 ERA in 1914.

More than 60 years later, that 1.01 ERA remains the major league record, likely never to be surpassed in the lively ball era.

And only 12 more pitchers have joined the exclusive double no-hitter fraternity whose membership now totals just 18—two of them Red Soxers, Leonard and Cy Young.

August 30, 1918

Carl Mays boosted the Red Sox to within one game of the pennant today when he pitched them to victory in *both* ends of a doubleheader triumph over the Athletics at Fenway Park.

The submarining right-hander posted his 20th and 21st wins of this war-abbreviated season by allowing Connie Mack's Athletics only one run in the ironman stint. Mays shut them out in the opener, despite allowing nine hits, while coasting to a 12-0 victory before limiting them to four hits in the 4-1 nightcap.

The Red Sox can clinch their third pennant in four years tomorrow and finally eliminate the Indians, who have been snapping at their heels. Cleveland's two leading hitters are Red Sox refugees, Tris Speaker (.318) and sore-armed pitcher-turned-outfielder Joe Wood (.296).

Trailing by two games, Cleveland's slim hopes have been all but shattered by the loss of Speaker. He was suspended for the remainder of the season for assaulting umpire Tom Connolly at home plate two days ago.

Mays joined Ray Collins as the only Red Sox pitchers to sweep complete doubleheaders. Just 20 major leaguers have achieved the feat since 1900, none since 1926. The Red Sox were the victims of the last one—by Cleveland's Dutch Levsen at Fenway Park. He didn't strike out anyone, but allowed only four hits in each game, winning 6-1 and 5-1.

Bobo Newsom failed in an attempt at the double sweep in 1937 at Fenway, beating the A's 6-2 before they chased him in the third inning of the nightcap. And Chicago knuckle-baller Wilbur Wood, a onetime Red Sox bonus boy, planned to try it against his former team in 1971 at White Sox Park; but after losing the first game, there was no need to pitch in the second.

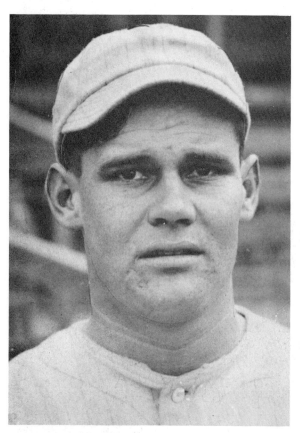

Dutch Leonard's 1.01 ERA remains the major league record.

September 5, 1918

Babe Ruth is still serving goose eggs. He fed nine of them to the Cubs today in a classic duel of southpaws against Hippo Vaughn, as the Red Sox won a 1-0 corker in the World Series opener at Chicago.

The only run came in the fourth inning when Dave Shean walked, sprinted to third on George Whiteman's single and scored on Stuffy McInnis's single. Those were two of only five hits off Vaughn, who was 22-10 during the shortened season.

Ruth spaced six hits while walking one and hitting a batter, all eight Chicago runners stranded by Babe to stretch his scoreless-inning skein (started in the '16 Series) to 22⅓ innings now—and creeping closer to Christy Mathewson's record of 28.

Babe was a surprise starter. After winning a total of 47 games the past two years, he was only 13-7 this season. That's because he played 95 games in the outfield to take advantage of his big bat and help patch the lineup now depleted of a number of stars, such as manager-second baseman Jack Barry, Duffy Lewis and Dutch Leonard who are in the Armed Forces. Playing mostly left field, National Guardsman Ruth batted .300 and tied for the majors homer title with 11.

Babe is still looking for his first-ever World Series hit after being thwarted in three trips today. Cubs manager Fred Mitchell plans to start southpaws every game in an effort to shackle Ruth's power—interesting strategy by the old Boston and Cambridge boy who was a member of the original Boston Americans back in 1901.

He got away with it today in what was a pip of a game, one that deserved a bigger audience. It drew only 19,274, reflecting the wartime apathy that grips our nation. That small gathering made unnecessary the Cubs' shift to Comiskey Park, which is far bigger than their usual home on Chicago's South Side. There were a lot of empty seats.

But it's lucky there's a World Series at all. The regular season was ordered concluded on Labor Day under the government's Work-or-Fight order, and the league winners were given special dispensation to play the Series. Because of travel restrictions, the first three games are being played in Chicago, the remainder in Fenway Park. The Red Sox won't borrow Braves Field, as they did in 1915 and 1916, because the crowds aren't expected to be that big.

Ruth broke Mathewson's record in Game 4, pitching 7⅓ more scoreless innings to total 29⅔ before finally allowing a run. And he might never have been scored upon, except for an incident the previous day on the long train ride from Chicago.

Some say it was horseplay; others say it was a genuine brawl. Whichever, Ruth swung at teammate Walt Kinney. The fringe southpaw ducked, and Babe's left fist slammed into the steel wall, the index finger swelling to three times its normal size.

Thus Ruth was pitching under a major and painful handicap the next day in going for the record, unable to grip the ball as usual or snap a curveball. Because of the disadvantage, Ruth said he was "lucky to get that far" before being scored upon—topping Mathewson's record by one inning for the mark which pleased Ruth more than any other in his career.

The game also was notable for Ruth for another reason. He was greatly relieved to finally get his first World Series hit, a triple that drove in two runs in his 3-2 victory. Babe needn't have fretted; he'd get 41 more World Series hits before he was through.

BABE RUTH: "The teams exchanged a lot of rough talk in the 1918 Series, with accomplished jockeys on both benches.

Babe Ruth set a World Series pitching record.
(National Baseball Hall of Fame)

"At one time the exchanges between Heinie Wagner and Jim Vaughn became so hot that Heinie charged the Cub bench to get at the big left-hander. They really let Heinie have it. His face was well bruised and he was covered with blood, mud and water when the umpires pulled him out of the brawl.

"I tried to get in the scrap but Ed Barrow held me back and said, 'I want you to pitch in this Series, Babe, not fight.' "

◇ ◇
◇

September 10, 1918

The Red Sox were drubbed by the Cubs, 3-0, today at Fenway Park in a World Series game that nearly wasn't played.

A sitdown strike by both teams protesting their paltry Series shares delayed the tilt an hour. A band serenaded the crowd of 24,694 with "Over There" and other favorites, but the fans' mood began turning ugly, and hundreds of extra coppers were rushed to the scene as a precaution against a riot that thankfully never developed.

The gladiators are disgruntled because they're playing the Series for peanuts—probably for less than $1,000 per winning player, about $500 per losing player. There are four reasons for the skinny shares, mostly war-related:

(1) Series ticket prices are the same as during the regular schedule, not raised for the Series as is usual. (2) The Series isn't drawing well, averaging less than 23,000 the first four games. (3) Part of the purse will be donated to war charities. (4) For the first time, the teams finishing second, third and fourth in both leagues will take a bite of the Series pie.

Boston's Harry Hooper and Chicago's Les Mann were named by their teammates to air the players' grievances to the National Commission. That is baseball's three-man governing board—American League President Ban Johnson, National League President John Heydler and Cincinnati club owner Gary Hermann.

The commission turned a deaf ear to the two player representatives during a meeting this morning at the Copley Plaza Hotel. When Hooper and Mann reported this stalemate to their mates at Fenway, both clubs decided not to play.

Meanwhile, Johnson and Hermann apparently decided to celebrate their victory and got tipsy. The situation that greeted them at Fenway should have sobered them up. The commissioners met with Hooper and Mann in the umpires room, and about a dozen reporters squeezed their way into the huddle.

The players asked that the plan to include all first-division teams in the payoff be abandoned until after the war, when the shares would be bigger. The commissioners said no. The players then asked that $1,500 winning shares and $1,000 losing shares be guaranteed. The commissioners said no.

In desperation, Hooper asked that all proceeds—every penny, including the leagues' and owners' shares—be donated to the Red Cross. Again, the commissioners turned thumbs down.

The two players were further frustrated trying to debate with two men who were making little sense, only one commissioner sober. At one point Johnson broke down and wept like a baby. He kept talking about league loyalty while pleading with Hooper to play.

Finally, the players said the teams would play, under the condition that no action would be taken against the strikers. For a change, the commissioners agreed.

Former Mayor John F. Fitzgerald was chosen to announce the news to the crowd, which he did with great relish. "The players have agreed to play for the sake of the public and the wounded soldiers in the stands," Honey Fitz shouted.

Harry Hooper aired the Red Sox players' grievances.

Ed Barrow's Bostonians might as well have taken the remainder of the day off. Hippo Vaughn dazzled them with a five-hitter to shut them out and outduel Sad Sam Jones, who yielded only seven hits. That narrows the Red Sox lead in the Series to three victories to two.

The mini-strike turned off fans, and only 15,238 showed up the next day to see the Red Sox wrap up this unhappy World Series on Carl Mays's second victory, a three-hitter. The score was 2-1, meaning all four victories by the Sox (who made only one error the entire Series) had come by one-run margins, just as had happened in the 1916 Series.

It marked the Red Sox's fifth World Championship in the 15 World Series so far, and they haven't won another since. It was also the last World Series game at Fenway Park for 28 years.

o

Technically, each Red Sox player received $1,102.51 (the smallest winning share in history), each Cub $671.09. And war deductions reportedly further shrank shares to $890 for each winner, $535 for each loser.

Worse, in one of the worst black eyes in baseball history, the National Commission went back on its promise not to penalize the players for their one-hour strike. Because of the players' "disgraceful actions," the Red Sox were denied their coveted World Champions emblems, a diamond lapel pin. Many members of that team went to their graves embittered by that flagrant injustice, and it haunts those still living.

"To this day, baseball owes all those fellows a debt," Harry Hooper said before his death.

MRS. BABE RUTH: "Home runs didn't provide Babe with his biggest thrill in baseball. The 29 consecutive scoreless innings he pitched in World Series competition for the Red Sox was the exploit he cherished most."

BABE RUTH: "I didn't turn from pitcher to outfielder overnight as some people seem to think. It was a gradual sort of thing, and I guess the old German Kaiser deserves an assist in my conversion. 1918 was one of those makeshift wartime seasons when a manager had to make the best of the material he had left.

"So one day Ed Barrow called me to his room. 'Babe,' he said, 'everyone knows you're a big fellow, healthy and strong. Why can't you take your turn in the box and still play the outfield on days when you're not pitching?'

"I didn't have to think about it very long. 'I'll try, Ed, and see how it goes,' I said."

TY COBB: "Babe Ruth probably gave me more trouble than any other left-hand pitcher. He would have been the greatest left-hander of the generation if he hadn't moved to the outfield."

September 24, 1919

Babe Ruth set a major league record today that many predict will stand for decades as he swatted his 28th home run of the season.

As if to mark the occasion, it was a mammoth blow off Yankee right-hander Bob Shawkey that is believed the longest ever hit at the Polo Grounds. The ball soared over the roof of the double-decked right-field stands and landed in adjacent Manhattan Field, where a small boy retrieved it and disappeared with the trophy.

American League President Ban Johnson wept and pleaded with Harry Hooper for the Red Sox to play the game.

Babe Ruth shattered every home-run record in the book as he hit an astronomical 29 homers for the 1919 Red Sox.
(National Baseball Hall of Fame)

Ruth's round tripper No. 28 surpassed all home run records dating back to, well, Abner Doubleday.

Ruth has been forced to shatter one homer record after another this season—as fast as statisticians discovered them. Earlier, the Red Sox slugger had broken the "modern" records—first Socks Seybold's American League mark of 16 set in 1902, then Gavvy Cravath's major league standard of 24 set in 1915. When someone pointed out that Buck Freeman had hit 25 for the old Washington club in 1899, Babe beat that.

Finally, record searchers dug up Ned Williamson's 27 for the Chicago White Stockings in 1884. That ignited a great debate.

Most argued that Williamson's mark isn't comparable today because the rules were so different in the 1880s. For instance, batters could call for tailor-made pitches of their liking, and many pitchers still served the ball underhand. But Ruth didn't complain about having another target to shoot for and set his sights on Williamson's mark.

Babe tied it four days ago, appropriately while being given an "appreciation day" by a Knights of Columbus Council during which Babe and Mrs. Ruth were showered with gifts, including a diamond ring.

The crowd of 31,000 taxed Fenway Park beyond capacity for the doubleheader against the White Sox, and the overflow of more than 5,000 was allowed to occupy part of the outfield behind ropes.

Ruth's record-knotting homer came in the ninth inning of the opener with the score tied and two out—a storybook setting—and the crowd in a frenzy clamoring for the record wallop that would also win the game.

Chicago pitcher Lefty Williams was determined not to have the record tied at his expense. Hoping to neutralize the slugger's power, he fed Babe an outside fastball he couldn't pull—and Ruth rammed it to the "wrong" field, over the tall left-field fence and through a window in a building across Lansdowne Street.

Fenway erupted in a mighty roar heard across the Charles River in Cambridge, as Babe tiptoed around the bases in his home-run trot. While he doffed his hat several times crossing the plate as teammates and bat boys patted him on the back, the crowd continued to howl until it stopped from sheer exhaustion.

The big crowd cost its hero the record-busting homer in the nightcap. With the score tied in the fifth inning, Ruth's drive into the right-field bleachers bounced back among the fans on the field. Base umpire Billy Evans saw the customers on the field scrambling for the ball and ruled it a two-base hit under the day's temporary ground rules.

An uproar followed, and state Guardsmen—on patrol per order of Governor Calvin Coolidge in place of the striking Boston police—passed a petition through the crowd in right field, witnessing that the ball had landed in the 50-cent bleachers, legitimate homer territory.

A Guard sergeant brought the signed petition onto the field to Evans, and this dialogue followed:

Umpire: "You are, as I understand it, to protect the public and me. It would be well for you to attend to your police duties and leave the umpiring to me."

Sergeant: "You can't talk to me like that."

Umpire: "Well, I am talking. You hear me, don't you? If you attend to your duties and let me attend to mine, we will get along very nicely."

At this stage a commissioned officer intervened and the game continued.

Ruth scored the winning run minutes later, giving the Red Sox a sweep of the twin bill.

Afterward, Boston baseball writer Johnny Drohan asked Ruth what owner Harry Frazee had given him for packing Fenway.

"A cigar," Babe replied honestly.

Everyone thought it was funny—except Frazee.

July 1, 19
Sore-ar
birthday
Bother
form desp
in Washir
Johnson
man Buc
inning. B
top of tha
Johnson
The dang
Judge sta
took Judg
Hoope

*It was
and a pai
week afte*

April 18,
The R
baseball
Sox help
them cha
And it
it possibl
in the ga
the para
The p
bandmas
lowed. T
Frank C
their re
Yankees
The cc
majestic
Babe Ru
right-fie
The n
biggest
42,620—
pitch to
Fraze
taking th
stars: R
Deacon
Bosto
up in a
Ehml
third, th
two sing
and two
Befor
home ru
On a
which t
Series. '

Ruth finished the season with 29 home runs, considered an astronomical total. He would nearly double that number to 54 the following season—but not for the Red Sox.

◇◇◇

BABE RUTH: "During my last season in Boston I had one unhappy experience, and the effects always remained with me.

"I came up with a very sore throat and our trainer tried to cure it. I guess the treatment was right out of that book 'Kill or Cure.' He got a big swab of cloth, put a lot of nitrate of silver on it, and reached deep into my throat.

"I know physicians use nitrate of silver in treating a sore throat condition, but it should never be applied by one who is not a skilled doctor.

"I started to strangle. Barrow, who was nearby, heard my gurgling gasps and quickly saw I was in a bad way. He started to take me to a hospital but decided I needed immediate help, so he rushed me to a drugstore near Fenway Park.

"I had another spasm in the drugstore, but the druggist succeeded in relieving my condition.

"Barrow fired the trainer on the spot, but it was a week before I could swallow solid food with any comfort. And I believe my husky voice came mostly from the change that nitrate of silver made in my throat."

January 3, 1920

Shock! Outrage! Disgust!

These are just some of the reactions to today's stunning news that George Herman Ruth, the greatest player in all baseball and the darling of New England, has been sold to the Yankees.

There is a terrible stench to it all—a joke that surely isn't funny.

This is the fourth Red Sox star shipped to New York by owner Harry Frazee, who is selling the Hose down the river—the Hudson River. This time it's believed Frazee pocketed about $125,000—by far the most ever paid for an athlete—although nobody is telling the price.

"No, I can't give exact figures, but it's a pretty check," Yankee boss Jake Ruppert said in Gotham. "No, no players are involved—strictly a cash deal."

Cash can't fill the Babe's spikes, but greenbacks are all Frazee has eyes for these days. He's having serious financial shorts.

Frazee bought the Red Sox three years ago on a shoestring and still owes former owners Joe Lannin and John I. Taylor on outstanding notes they want to collect. Also, Harry's theatrical enterprises have been doing poorly, producing one flop after another. A lot of good all those show posters he plastered around Fenway Park did him!

Frazee has fallen a long way from when he bought the club after the 1916 World Series and said, "Nothing is too good for Boston fans."

Hah! He is showing his true colors now. He may *like* baseball, but he *loves* the theater. Make no mistake about his priorities as he sacrifices one for the other.

In the process he's gotten into the clutches of his drinking crony, Colonel Ruppert. The Yankees' offices are only two doors down 42nd Street from the Frazee Theater, where Harry has his office. And that's where Red Sox manager Ed Barrow rushed yesterday to plead with Frazee not to make this infamous deal, which Barrow knows will cripple the team and outrage every New Englander.

Count the Babe himself among those shocked and unhappy. "My heart is in Boston," he said sadly from his farm in Sudbury.

Harry Frazee became the No. 1 villain in Red Sox history by selling a galaxy of stars to . . .

. . . Yankee owner Jake Ruppert, who knew a bargain when he saw one.

by pickling a drive ten rows deep into the right-field seats as the crowd let loose with the biggest roar in baseball history.

And the Babe loved it, beaming as he followed Dugan and Whitey Witt around the bases with his short, quick steps. As he rounded third, the big fellow doffed his cap, waving it at arm's length to the delirious audience the remainder of the route home.

That glorious smash was the game winner as Shawkey pitched his finest game ever, spacing three Boston hits—a triple by Norm McMillan and singles by Ehmke and George Burns. Burns's single in the second inning was the first hit made in the new stadium. (And moments later he became the first victim thrown out trying to steal.)

So the Yankees won, 4-1; a hard loss for Ehmke, who allowed only seven hits—one of them a classic.

Ehmke would pitch a more notable game at the new stadium later in the season.

July 7, 1923

The Red Sox were victims of an "Indian Massacre" today at Cleveland.

The Indians ambushed reliever Lefty O'Doul for 13 runs in the sixth inning—count 'em, 13 runs in one inning—during a 27-3 scalping of the feeble Sox who seem headed for their second straight last-place finish.

O'Doul walked six while facing 16 batters in the nightmare inning, as manager Frank Chance showed no mercy and left the southpaw in to absorb the full pasting.

Chance is upset by O'Doul's performance off the field. The manager has warned the second-line pitcher several times about breaking the midnight curfew and recently fined him $200. Chance considers O'Doul a gay blade, and was irritated this morning when he observed the slick San Franciscan admiring himself in the mirror of the hotel barber shop after a haircut, shampoo, shine and manicure.

As the Indians teed off on O'Doul in the sixth, Chance reportedly scowled: "I'm going to leave that looking-glass so-and-so out there if it takes him all day to get 'em out!"

It nearly did.

O'Doul was released soon after setting his record, which still stands as the most runs ever allowed in one inning by a Red Sox pitcher. It took him five years to work himself back from the minors at age 31. When he did, it was as an outfielder, *and he played seven more years and won two National League batting championships—hitting .398 in 1929 and .368 in 1932.*

September 7, 1923

Howard Ehmke got a big assist from Lady Luck while twirling a no-hitter today as the Red Sox thrashed the Athletics, 4-0, at Philadelphia.

The no-hitter was saved when rival pitcher Slim Harriss was declared out for neglecting to touch first base after ripping a "double" to center in the sixth inning. Harriss's feebleness at bat is a baseball jest, and the fans howled when he combed a terrific drive on one bounce off the scoreboard and ran like a scared rabbit to second—so frantically that he overlooked the formality of tagging first.

So the day was saved for the 6-foot-3 Ehmke, who walked only one and faced just 28 batters.

The day also was saved in the eighth, when Philly's Frank Welch laced a drive to left and Mike Menosky fumbled it knee high. It was ruled a hit,

Howard Ehmke narrowly missed pitching consecutive no-hitters.

but the official scorer changed it to an error after giving it further thought and conferring with others.

So the somewhat tainted no-hitter was preserved for Ehmke, who notched his 18th victory. Tigers player-manager Ty Cobb must be growling now after trading the 29-year-old right-hander to the Sox last winter.

The official scorer would not be as obliging next time.

September 11, 1923

"Howard Ehmke was robbed!"

Those words of Joe Tinker sum up the feelings of the Red Sox and about 15,000 at Yankee Stadium today after the lanky Boston right-hander just missed becoming the first pitcher ever to toss two consecutive no-hitters. A controversial fluke single denied him that distinction.

Following his masterpiece at Philadelphia four days ago, Ehmke retired 27 batters in a row today as the last-place Red Sox downed the first-place Yankees, 3-0. The only Yankee to reach base was their first batter, Whitey Witt. He chopped a grounder to third baseman Hank Shanks, a converted outfielder. The bouncer took an unnatural hop and hit Shanks on the chest. Official scorer Fred Lieb ruled it a miserly hit. He conceded Shanks had played the ball clumsily, but based his decision on Witt being "probably the fastest runner in the league" and the "strange hop."

Midway through the game, as Ehmke continued to mow down Yankees, Boston writers asked Lieb if he might change the ruling to an error. "No," he said. "I scored it a hit then and it's a hit in the early edition of my paper."

Lieb, a respected writer for the *New York Post*, remained adamant when some of his Gotham colleagues later joined in, urging a change.

Meanwhile, the customers didn't know Witt had been given a hit and thought Ehmke was closing in on baseball history—applauding each Yankee out with rising crescendo. And when the last New York batter was retired, the fans poured onto the diamond and mobbed the Boston pitcher, congratulating him on his second "no-hitter."

Then the storm of protest erupted.

"I saw it perfectly and it was unquestionably an error," umpire Tommy Connolly said. "If that wasn't an error, I've never seen one."

Tinker, who was visiting his old sidekick Red Sox manager Frank Chance, agreed: "No question, it was an error all the way. Ehmke was robbed."

Chance wasn't so sure. "It was a close one that could have been called either way," he said. "But I sure feel sorry for Howard."

So did many, many others—and the rumpus may just be starting.

It was. The controversy spiraled nationally. Among the petitions to the American League was one circulated by then powerful Baseball Magazine, *but Ban Johnson, the league president, refused to reverse Lieb's ruling.*

Lieb later admitted that if the debated play had happened later in the no-hit bid he "might have scored it as an error," adding: "This was perhaps the saddest decision I ever made, for it prevented Ehmke from becoming the first pitcher ever to throw two successive no-hitters."

Fifteen years later, Cincinnati's Johnny Vander Meer became the only pitcher ever to accomplish it. Ehmke does have the consolation of owning the A.L. record for fewest hits permitted in two consecutive games—one.

○

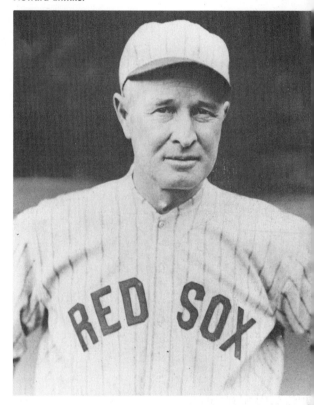

Frank Chance was among the many who felt sorry for Howard Ehmke.

There was another consolation for Ehmke. He won 20 games that season, the only Red Sox pitcher ever to reach that plateau for a last-place team. It also was the only 20-victory season of his 15-year career.

September 14, 1923

Red Sox first baseman George Burns executed the third unassisted triple play in major league history today by single-handedly retiring the Indians in the second inning at Fenway Park.

On a Cleveland hit-and-run, Burns speared Frank Brower's line drive for the first out. Burns reached out and tagged Rube Lutzke off first base for the second out. Burns then sprinted for second base trying to force Riggs Stephenson, who was scrambling back after having almost reached third. Burns and Stephenson slid into the bag from opposite directions, Burns winning the thrilling race to conclude the unasssisted triple play.

The Red Sox went on to win, 4-3, in the 11th inning.

"The lucky sons of guns!" Indians manager Tris Speaker moaned afterward.

That is the only unassisted triple play by a Red Sox player. There have been only eight in major league history.

September 27, 1923

Lou Gehrig, the Yankees' $1500 bonus boy from Columbia, smacked his first major league home run today at Fenway Park.

Recently recalled from Hartford by manager Miller Huggins, the

Despite being knocked cold a few times at Fenway, Lou Gehrig usually enjoyed playing there. For example, besides slamming his first big league home run there, 11 of the Yankee slugger's 47 homers in 1927 were hit at Fenway.

20-year-old Gehrig homered into the right-field bleachers off right-hander Bill Piercy in the first inning.

"The son of a gun is a blacksmith, isn't he?" Red Sox first baseman George Burns said to umpire Tommy Connolly as the handsome 6-foot-1, 200-pound rookie circled the bases on his homer.

Gehrig would hit 492 more home runs for the Yankees—many of them at Fenway—as he authored his legendary ironman streak of 2,130 consecutive games between 1925 and 1939.

October 2, 1927

The Red Sox served up 11 of Babe Ruth's record 60 home runs this season, including five in two days in September at Fenway Park.

Ruth hit No. 4 off Slim Harriss (April 29 at Boston), No. 13 off Deacon Danny MacFayden (May 29 at New York), Nos. 23 and 24 off Hal Wiltse (June 22 at Boston), No. 25 off Harriss (June 30 at New York), No. 43 off Tony Welzer (August 31 at New York), Nos. 45 and 46 off Welzer (opener of September 6 doubleheader at Boston), No. 47 off Jack Russell (nightcap of the September 6 doubleheader), No. 48 off MacFayden and No. 49 off Harriss (both in single game September 7 at Boston).

April 28, 1929

The Red Sox made history today, playing the first major league baseball game ever allowed on a Sunday in Boston. The game was played at Braves Field because of Fenway Park's proximity to a church.

No tongues of fire bolted from the sky, but the Sox were singed by the Athletics, 7-3, as Eddie Rommel out-pitched Red Ruffing.

The Braves were supposed to play Boston's first Sunday game last weekend against the Giants, but were rained out—which was taken as a sign by the Anti-Enjoyment of Anything League.

Weather threatened today's game, too. It was played under a gray, watery-looking sky which kept the crowd to about 22,000. A nice day undoubtedly would have lured at least 35,000 sinners to this historic event, which concludes a long, expensive legal and political bout.

Today's only untoward happening was the insistence by customers of pocketing baseballs hit into the stands. That violates the laws of most churches as well as the state. Yet the fans, many of whom had attended church a few hours earlier, sinned openly and gleefully whenever an opportunity to get a souvenir ball presented itself.

The Red Sox weren't dismayed by such thievery. They will continue playing on the Sabbath at Braves Field indefinitely.

Until July 3, 1932, when the law was sufficiently amended to allow the Sox to play seven days a week at Fenway. (Somebody Up There apparently wasn't any happier about the Sunday switch to Fenway. This time the Yankees damned the Sox, 13-2.)

May 6, 1930

The Yankees have picked the Red Sox's pocket again—this time snaring pitcher Charley "Red" Ruffing.

Bob Quinn made the deal out of financial desperation, the Sox being nearly broke. Exactly how much Ruffing brought isn't certain; guesses range between $17,500 and $50,000.

The Yankees also tossed in outfielder Cedric Durst, but that's a joke. He's almost 34, and has never played in more than 92 games in a season nor hit more than .257. Does anyone really think he'll help the Hose climb out of the cellar, where they've been entrenched the last five years and seven of the last eight seasons?

THE
THIRTIES

But Ruffing, who turned 24 this week, undoubtedly makes the Yankees even stronger. True, the 6-foot-2, 200-pound right-hander is 0-3 and has led the league in losses the last two seasons while compiling 10-25 and 9-22 records. But his support has been feeble. With a fine supporting cast in the Bronx, he should be a big winner with the Bombers.

Ruffing was—pitching himself into the Hall of Fame.
He was 231-124 in his 15 years as a Yankee, including four straight 20-victory seasons 1936–39, and had a 7-2 success in World Series games. Rubbing it in, Ruffing also was the Yankees' top right-handed pinch hitter many of those years.

○

The hard up Red Sox weren't finished peddling stars to the Yankees. Deacon Danny MacFayden, a local boy from Somerville, won 16 games for the sixth-place Sox in 1931, and the next season was dealt to the Yankees for $50,000 and two players.
"We've got a pitcher who'll win 20 games for us the next 10 years," Yankee general manager Ed Barrow gushed.
For a change, MacFayden was one Red Sox refugee who didn't help the Yankees. The bespectacled right-hander wound up back in Boston, where he became a consistent winner for the Braves in the late thirties.

September 25, 1932

Dale Alexander won the American League batting championship with a .367 average today and recorded a couple of firsts while at it.

Not only is he the first Red Soxer to wear the batting crown, but he is also the first major leaguer ever to capture the title while dividing the season between two teams.

The Red Sox obtained the right-hand-hitting first baseman, along with outfielder Roy Johnson, from Detroit on June 12 for outfielder Earl Webb.

It was a splendid trade for Boston. Not only did Alexander hit .372 in 101 games for the Sox (after batting .250 in 23 games for Detroit), but Johnson hit .299 in 94 games for Boston (after batting .251 in 49 games for the Tigers).

The Red Sox had a number of long-suffering managers during the team's drought of the twenties and early thirties. Among them were Bill Carrigan (left), Heinie Wagner (center) and Shano Collins (right).

The pair combined with another newcomer, .312-hitting Smead Jolley, to beef up the Sox batting order—making the team's losses at least exciting for the 182,150 long-suffering loyalists who clicked through Fenway's turnstiles despite the Depression economy.

The trio couldn't prevent Boston's ninth last-place finish in 11 seasons, though. Today's 8-3 victory over the Yankees at Fenway in the season finale narrowed the Hose's deficit to 64 games behind the pennant-winning New Yorkers.

The 29-year-old Alexander, a 6-foot-3, 210-pounder, beat out two other first basemen for the batting title—Philadelphia's Jimmy Foxx by three points, New York's Lou Gehrig by 18 points.

Alexander's day in the sun was brief. He hit .281 for the Red Sox the next season, his fifth and final in the majors.

Still, he retains two distinctions. He is the only American Leaguer to win a batting crown while wearing different uniforms in a season. (Harry "The Hat" Walker did it in the National League in 1947, hitting .363 for the Cardinals and Phillies.) And Alexander is the name that eludes most trivia buffs when asked to identify the seven Red Sox hitters who have won batting titles.

February 25, 1933

The Red Sox launched a new era today.

Financier-sportsman Thomas Austin Yawkey has agreed to purchase the financially barren club from broke Bob Quinn in a deal that will be sealed next month. The 30-year-old multimillionaire says he'll spend whatever is necessary to rebuild the once-proud franchise into the power it was before Harry Frazee ruined it.

"I don't intend to mess with a loser," Yawkey says. The husky onetime Yale second baseman has his work cut out with this broken-down franchise. It's been mired in the second division 14 years—ever since winning the 1918 World Series—and has been dead last nine of the past 11 seasons.

Yawkey also intends to rebuild Fenway Park and make it a showplace to lure back New England fans. Last year's attendance plummeted to almost half the previous season's—skidding to 182,150, by far the lowest figure in the club's 32 years.

The purchase price was not disclosed, but it's believed to be about a cool million. Much of that will be used to pay off Quinn's indebtedness. He's at least $350,000 in the hole and has been scrounging to keep the club afloat, even borrowing on his life insurance to get the team through spring training. The Bank Holiday was the last nail in his financial coffin.

Depression or not, Yawkey says his checkbook is at the ready, and the man who has carte blanche with it is Eddie Collins. Yawkey is bringing in the former Athletics and White Sox star to run the new operation as vice president and general manager, and he may even have a piece of the action. Collins was Yawkey's boyhood idol and is being lured from Philadelphia, where he's been Connie Mack's top lieutenant.

Yawkey, a courteous gentleman, is reluctant to gab about himself, but talks with great enthusiasm about baseball, his passion since childhood. The nephew and foster son of late Tigers owner Bill Yawkey, he has been around big league ball most of his life.

Tom has had the yen to own a team for years. So now, just four days after his 30th birthday which brought him into the bulk of his inheritance, Yawkey has a club of his own.

Red Ruffing was sold to the Yankees out of financial desperation.

Dale Alexander was the first Red Sox hitter to win the batting crown.

Bob Quinn (center) was broke when he sold the Red Sox to Tom Yawkey (right), who brought in Eddie Collins (left) as vice president and general manager.

The deal was consummated on April 20, too late to do much changing that first season. But in the next 25 years, the Red Sox would be out of the first division only five times—two of those seasons during World War II when the Sox stars were in the service.

As promised, Yawkey made the Sox contenders, building them from a failure to a rousing financial success—and into a New England institution.

December 12, 1933

Tom Yawkey took a giant step in his promised rebuilding of the Red Sox today by acquiring Robert Moses "Lefty" Grove, the top pitcher in the American League and perhaps all of baseball.

Yawkey shipped 125,000 Depression dollars, along with infielder Rabbit Warstler and right-hander Bob Kline, to Philadelphia for Grove and two other aging veterans of the great Athletics teams, second baseman Max Bishop and southpaw Rube Walberg, both 34.

Grove, the A.L.'s fastest pitcher since Walter Johnson, also will turn 34 in March, but shows no signs of slowing down. In fact, Bucky Harris, who recently succeeded Marty McManus as Sox manager and who managed Johnson four seasons at Washington, says Mose is faster than the Big Train.

Grove's temperament is as mean as his fastball, and he has made shambles of locker rooms during towering rages. Grouchy and abrasive, he often goes into moods where he speaks only to chastise teammates, reporters and photographers. No lens is safe from his wrath on days he is pitching.

Teammates tend to tolerate Grove because of his golden left arm. Mose has won 172 games (against only 54 losses) the last seven seasons—an average of almost 25 victories a season, unmatched in the lively ball era. He also has led the league in strikeouts seven times and in earned run average five times during his nine seasons in Philadelphia.

Grove won 14 straight in 1928 and a record-tying 16 in a row in 1931, when he had a 31-4 record before adding two more triumphs in the World Series for the second straight time in the Fall Classic.

While not given to overindulgence, Grove allows himself the luxury of a 25-cent cigar when he wins, a dime stogie when he loses.

Grove smoked eight of each his first season with the Red Sox. His expensive left arm became sore in spring training and he pitched only 109 innings in 22 games that year as he grimaced through an 8-8, 6.52 ERA season.

Mack wrote to Yawkey, offering to "gladly take Grove back and refund your money. We believed you were getting a sound pitcher." Yawkey declined with thanks.

The owner's patience paid off as Grove regained his touch—although no longer the league's premier pitcher. The fastball gone, he refashioned himself into a crafty pitcher, developing a forkball and improving his curve. The result was a 20-12 season the following year, which he followed with 17-12, 17-9, 14-4 and 15-4 records despite being without a fastball and approaching 40. At age 39, his 15-4 mark led the majors in winning percentage (.789) and his 2.54 ERA led the league.

Meanwhile, Grove's ill-temper was undiminished. Typical was a tantrum following a loss at Chicago. "You think Grove is going to pitch his arm off for you hitless wonders?" he roared before stomping out of the clubhouse after a game. He refused to ride with his teammates the rest of the series, preferring to walk—and fume—the five miles between Comiskey Park and the hotel.

OSCAR MELILLO: "'Grove had a temper all right—a beauty. He'd cuss out anyone.

"Joe Cronin was our player-manager, and sometimes he'd go down on his knees to field a ground ball.

"One day at Fenway, a ball went through Joe while Lefty was pitching and we lost the game. Cronin hurried into the clubhouse and went right into his office and locked the door.

"His office had a screen across the top of the wall. Grove pushed a bench against the wall, climbed up so he could look down on Cronin through the screen and yelled:

"'You sophomore so-and-so. Why don't you field the ball like a man? You couldn't even play on my high school team.'

"Joe never said a word."

TED WILLIAMS: "Grove was a moody guy, a tantrum thrower like me, but smarter.

"When he punched a locker or something, he always did it with his *right* hand. He was a *careful* tantrum thrower.

"I wasn't. Like the time I was playing for Minneapolis and punched the water cooler with my fist. I landed a beauty on that big bottle—*ker-rack!* It sounded like an explosion. I was lucky I didn't cut my hand off—there was blood and glass all over—and I just missed a nerve that could have ended my career before it started.

"Grove was too smart for that. And he was some kind of pitcher.

"They told me his arm was dead when the Sox got him, but as far as I was concerned he was the smoothest, smartest, prettiest left-handed pitcher I had ever seen, just beautiful style."

August 12, 1934

A record crowd of 46,766 jammed Fenway Park today to say goodbye to Babe Ruth as the Red Sox and Yankees divided a doubleheader.

Fans squeezed into every inch of Fenway, clogging all aisles and ramps, and some literally hanging from the rafters. The overflow spilled

Lefty Grove says goodbye to Connie Mack.

Lefty Grove cussed out teammates—even shortstop-manager Joe Cronin.

Babe Ruth loved returning to Fenway Park, even when a wheelchair was needed at Back Bay Station in 1931. That's Babe's wife Claire with him.

onto the field, herded behind ropes in left, center and right fields. Another 15,000-20,000 were turned away and milled around outside.

The prime attraction was what's expected to be the 39-year-old Bambino's last appearance at Fenway in a Yankee uniform. It was on that same Fenway soil that George Herman Ruth made his debut with the Red Sox 20 years ago, and Boston fans still claim him as "our Babe."

Today marks the first time this season that Ruth has started both ends of a twin bill, and the vast crowd shouted for a circuit smash every time he came to bat. Babe managed a single and a double in five trips during the opener. But he let in the deciding run when handcuffed by Billy Werber's liner—officially, it was ruled a triple—as the Sox won, 6-4.

In the nightcap, the crowd lustily booed the Red Sox when Ruth was walked twice, going 0-for-1 before retiring in the sixth inning as the Yanks were coasting to a 7-1 victory.

Babe was given a roaring ovation as he slowly crossed the field from the third-base dugout to the runway by the first-base dugout, frequently tipping his cap in farewell.

"It's a sight I'll never forget," Ruth told reporters. "Boston has always been kind to me, and I was a bit disappointed that I couldn't hit a homer for that big mob."

Babe had another home run left in his bat for his legion of Boston admirers, and he hit it on Opening Day the following season—at Braves Field (off Carl Hubbell). Ruth had joined the Braves as player-assistant manager-vice president before quitting in early June, thus ending his careeer where it began—in Boston.

October 26, 1934

Tom Yawkey today peeled $250,000 off his bankroll to pluck slugger-shortstop-manager Joe Cronin from the Senators.

That price dwarfs the previous high paid for a player, and the Red Sox also must send shortstop Lyn Lary to Washington in the deal.

Those were the stiff terms demanded by Senators owner Clark Griffith before he'd part with his star in-law. Cronin recently married Griffith's niece Mildred. She was virtually brought up by the Old Fox, and in recent years has been his secretary.

Yawkey pried Cronin away by making Griffith an offer "he couldn't refuse," according to Red Sox general manager Eddie Collins.

"During the World Series in Detroit, Tom asked me what could be done to add inspiration and game-winning ability to the Red Sox," Collins revealed. "I told him I knew of only one man who had Mickey Cochrane-like qualities of leadership and inspiration—Joe Cronin.

"I said that was probably out of the question, though, because Griffith wouldn't let him go. But Tom said he'd offer a sum that would at least jar Griff—an offer larger than any ever paid for a player—yes, more than the $139,000 the Yankees paid for Babe Ruth.

"It was a sum Griffith could not refuse. I also feel Griff had it in mind that he ought to give Joe a chance to better himself in the way of a long-term contract at a higher figure."

It is the latter factor that is believed to have changed Griffith's mind. He had first dismissed the offer—scowling "no player is worth a quarter of a million"—before his mind was changed by Yawkey a few days later.

The Red Sox are giving Cronin a five-year contract for substantially more than his reported $20,000 salary in Washington, terms Griffith couldn't afford.

Collins wouldn't say precisely how much more—nor the exact purchase price, the $250,000 figure disclosed by another source.

"I would prefer the talk of big money cease," Collins said. "Before

What a difference a year made. Left, Bucky Harris was Red Sox manager and Joe Cronin the Senators' skipper on Opening Day 1934, the afternoon reconstructed Fenway opened. Right, the pair had swapped uniforms in 1935, with Harris managing the Senators, Cronin the Red Sox.

Tom Yawkey (right) meets with his new manager, Joe Cronin.

long the talk will be that Tom Yawkey and the Red Sox are trying to buy their way up with big money. That isn't the case, regardless of what's transpired to date."

Ironically, Griffith wanted to ship Cronin to Boston for virtually nothing six years ago after Joe's first season in Washington, as one of the five players to be sent to the Red Sox for Buddy Myer. But then Senators manager Bucky Harris talked Griff out of it, insisting Cronin had potential. Now, ironically, Cronin is replacing Harris as Red Sox skipper.

Collins said the Sox acquired "two high-ranking men in one—a heady shortstop and manager" in trying to improve last season's 76-76 fourth-place finish.

Cronin, who turned 28 this month, is considered the league's best shortstop as well as a scrappy skipper—a sparkplug who drove the Senators to the 1933 pennant in his rookie season as "boy manager." A series of calamities helped drop the Senators to seventh last season—Cronin was one of the victims when he broke a thumb in a first-base collision with Boston's Wes Ferrell.

The 6-foot, 180-pounder is also a sturdy right-handed hitter, well-suited to Fenway's left-field porch. Cronin hit .346 in 1930, when he won the Most Valuable Player Award over Al Simmons (.381, 165 RBIs, 36 homers), Lou Gehrig (.379, 174 RBIs, 41 homers), Babe Ruth (.359, 153 RBIs, 49 homers) and Lefty Grove (28-5).

Collins said Cronin was the only man considered for the managing job—not Babe Ruth as some had guessed.

○

San Francisco—Joe Cronin is "tickled to pieces" about being the Red Sox's new shortstop-manager.

"I'm delighted," Cronin said after arriving here in his hometown with his bride Mildred after their honeymoon cruise through the Panama Canal.

"Boston is one of the greatest sports towns in the world. A fellow with an Irish name like mine ought to get along there. Remember, John L. Sullivan came from Boston.

"And I feel the team can be developed into a contender. I'm looking forward to working with Tom Yawkey and Eddie Collins. With such a setup, I don't see how we can miss out."

September 7, 1935

A dramatic last-of-the-ninth rally by the Red Sox was snuffed out by a stunning triple play today to give the Indians a 5-3 victory in the first game of a doubleheader at Fenway Park.

Trailing 5-1 entering the final inning, the Sox scored twice and had bases loaded with none out as clutch-hitting Joe Cronin came to bat against Oral Hildebrand.

Cronin pulled a scorching drive down the third-base line. The ball glanced off Odell "Bad News" Hale's glove before exploding off his forehead—caroming on the fly to Bill Knickerbocker. The shortstop flipped the ball to second baseman Roy Hughes before Billy Werber could scramble back to the bag, and the relay to first baseman Hal Trotsky tripled off Mel Almada.

"That was using your head," teammates congratulated the stunned but happy Hale in the Cleveland clubhouse.

December 10, 1935

Tom Yawkey went shopping again today and came away with Jimmy Foxx, baseball's most menacing slugger.

Yawkey sent $150,000 and two throw-ins, pitcher Gordon Rhodes and minor league catcher George Savino, to the financially strapped Athletics for Foxx and right-hander John "Footsie" Marcum.

The brawny first baseman, 28, has averaged 41 homers the last seven seasons and is expected to be awesome at Fenway Park, his raw right-handed power tailor-made for the chummy left-field wall.

"Well, we'll have some fun this summer," said manager Joe Cronin, seeking improvement of the Sox's fourth-place finishes the last two seasons. "Sure, Jimmy will bat fourth—and how!"

The deal also delighted Foxx. "Brother, I'd have to have the eloquence of a politician to express my joy at coming to Boston," he said. "My dream has come true."

So has that of Red Sox fans. They've long admired the Maryland Strong Boy with the bulging biceps (he appears bigger than his 6-feet, 195-pound statistics) and grinning moon face (he's one of baseball's friendliest guys).

Foxxie smashed 58 homers in 1932 to threaten Babe Ruth's record. He was the American League's Most Valuable Player that year and the following season, when he won a Triple Crown.

Like Ruth, Foxx strikes out a lot—leading the league in that department three straight years, 1929–31. And like Babe, Foxx thrills the crowd even when he whiffs. Significantly, while leading the A.L. in strikeouts those three seasons, Foxx also totaled 100 homers and 493 runs batted in as the Athletics captured three pennants. Besides first base, the versatile Foxx also can catch and play third base.

This latest purchase on Yawkey's long and expensive shopping list has observers around the league suggesting that the Red Sox's name be changed to "Gold Sox" or "Millionaires."

New player-manager Joe Cronin and his 1935 Red Sox were launched in style.

Unlike some of Yawkey's purchases, Foxx repaid full value.

As expected, Double X assaulted The Wall—although it cost him some homers, too. He hit far more bullets than wind-blown pop-ups that caught the screen. And so many of his whistling liners hit the tall fence while still on the rise, before being fully airborne—home runs in other parks, singles at Fenway.

Still, Foxx would total 222 homers during his little more than six Red Sox seasons, averaging 36 in those six full years. In 1938, he enjoyed his best season ever, collecting 50 homers, 175 RBIs and 398 total bases while batting .349. That earned him a third MVP award, one of few to achieve that distinction, and an honor doubly conspicuous because none were achieved as a member of a pennant winner.

Twenty years after he'd gone, Foxx's 534 homers still ranked second only to Ruth's 714. And almost 40 years later, he's seventh on the all-time list, a notch ahead of Ted Williams (521).

Foxx's 50 home runs in 1938 and the 35 he slammed at Fenway that year remain as Red Sox records—targets for another right-handed slugger named Jim Rice.

CONNIE MACK: "Jimmy Foxx could hit a home run farther than anyone else I ever saw."

LEFTY GOMEZ: "Jimmy Foxx could hit me at midnight with the lights out."

August 21, 1936

Manager Joe Cronin fined Wes Ferrell $1,000 and suspended him ten days for storming off the mound at Yankee Stadium today in a tantrum over what the talented-but-temperamental right-hander considered shabby support. It is believed to be the second largest fine in baseball history, surpassed only by the $5,000 penalty pinned on Babe Ruth by the Yankees in 1925.

Ferrell led the American League in victories last year while compiling a 25-14 record for the fourth-place Red Sox and is headed for the 20-win plateau again this season.

Ferrell fired his cap and glove into the air and marched off the field in a rage during the sixth inning without the Sox having a relief pitcher warmed up. It marked the second time in five days he has left the mound of his own volition, having done the same thing against the Senators last Sunday at Boston.

The 28-year-old veteran showered and left the stadium before yesterday's game was over, so didn't learn of the fine and suspension until late this afternoon. The news enraged him once more.

"I'm going to slug that so-and-so Irishman right on his lantern jaw," Ferrell fumed when he learned of it from John Kieran of the *New York Times.*

"If he wants to slug me," Cronin advised, "I'll be passing through the lobby at 6 o'clock on my way to dinner."

Cronin was in the lobby at 6:00 as promised, as were about 15 Sox players who wanted front-row seats for the confrontation. But Ferrell wasn't in sight.

"I'm through with him," Cronin told newsmen. "I don't care if he goes

Jimmy Foxx (left) was welcomed to Boston by Joe Cronin.

Jimmy Foxx with manager Joe Cronin (left) and general manager Eddie Collins (center).

back to Boston, home to North Carolina or to the Fiji Islands. I'm washed up with the guy."

Red Sox management has had its fill of the troublesome Ferrell's temper which has trademarked his three seasons with the team. Now he is openly embarrassing the club, as he did earlier this summer when he boldly thumbed his nose at Fenway fans.

So Cronin—with the blessing of owner Tom Yawkey who is in New York for the series—ordered the suspension and mammoth fine in desperation.

Ferrell insists he won't pay the fine. "They can suspend me or trade me," he stormed. "But they're not going to get any dough from me."

Ferrell was traded to Washington the next season. He left behind a legacy of often superb pitching, frequent outrageous behavior and the largest fine in Red Sox history—until Ted Williams and Gene Conley came along.

August 25, 1937

Fireballing Bob Feller—the 18-year-old farmboy from Van Meter, Iowa, whose high school graduation three months ago was blanketed by press, radio and newsreels—struck out a near-record 16 Red Sox today in Cleveland while notching his first victory over Boston.

Depending almost exclusively on his fastball, Feller fanned everyone in the Red Sox lineup at least once, except Ben Chapman, while easily besting Bobo Newsom, 8-1, at League Park.

Joe Cronin was twice a strikeout victim. After taking a called third strike for the second, the Boston player-manager stared out at Feller for a few seconds. Cronin then turned to umpire Lou Kolls and said, "If *I* didn't see it, how did *you* see it?"

Feller had a chance to equal the 17-strikeout major league record he shares with Dizzy Dean, but he could fan only two of the three Boston batters in the ninth inning.

The slick four-hitter avenged Feller's loss at Fenway Park last August when the Red Sox handed the then schoolboy his first big league defeat. Jimmy Foxx had three hits and as many RBIs that day as Feller survived only five innings in a 5-1 Boston victory.

"I seldom pitched well at Fenway Park," Feller once said. "I think I had a complex about it going back to that first game there when I was 17. I looked at that left-field wall and felt hemmed in. I knew Cronin and Foxx could pop it over with half a swing."

Feller was 16-16 (allowing 23 homers) at Fenway compared to 17-11 (16 homers) against the Red Sox in Cleveland. Of his 11 one-hitters, four were against the Sox. Bobby Doerr spoiled two of the no-hit bids, Johnny Pesky and Sammy White one each.

JIMMY FOXX: "Feller never bothered me. I always hit his curve. He couldn't get his fastball over consistently in those years, so I never offered at them. I just waited for the curve."

March 16, 1938

The Red Sox today farmed out Ted Williams to Minneapolis, but the temperamental rookie vows he'll be back.

Only 19, the stringbean outfielder is the highly touted slugger purchased last December from San Diego of the Pacific Coast League for

Following this meeting, Joe Cronin lifted the suspension of Wes Ferrell (right) after four days. But the $1,000 fine stuck, then the largest in Red Sox history.

Jimmy Foxx had three hits off Bob Feller (right) in the schoolboy pitcher's Fenway debut, and always did hit the Cleveland fireballer.

Nineteen-year-old Ted Williams was controversial from his first day in training camp.

The Red Sox outfield (left to right) of Ben Chapman, Doc Cramer and Joe Vosmik gave Ted Williams a riding during his first training camp. When farmed out, Ted vowed he'd be back and make more money than all three put together—and he did.

$35,000 and two players, Dom Dallessandro and Al Niemiec.

Signed by general manager Eddie Collins to a two-year contract calling for $3,000 the first season and $4,500 the second, the Red Sox are counting on Williams as a star of the future. Although a skinny 6-foot-3, 175 pounds, the Californian has a classic left-handed swing and snaps the bat like a buggy whip.

Williams's personality also has attracted attention at the team's Sarasota training camp. He's a fresh but likable kid who is alternately an introvert and extrovert. An individualist, he calls everyone "sport" (including manager Joe Cronin—*once*) and is almost always capless, often shagging flies while slapping his hip to a galloping gait and yelling, "Hi-ho, Silver!"

All of which has drawn mixed reactions from teammates. In particular Williams has been taking a riding from the outfield trio he was attempting to crack—Doc Cramer, Joe Vosmik and Ben Chapman, all .300 hitters.

"Tell them I'll be back," Williams told Johnny Orlando as the equipment manager saw him off at the bus depot. "And tell them I'm going to wind up making more money in this game than all three of them put together."

May 30, 1938

The biggest crowd in Yankee Stadium history—83,533—got something extra for their money today: a Red Sox-Yankee brawl.

Boston's Joe Cronin and New York's Jake Powell collided near the mound in the opener of the holiday doubleheader swept by the Yankees.

The Red Sox shortstop-manager intercepted Powell, who was intent upon doing bodily harm to Archie McKain, after the Sox southpaw had dusted the Yankee outfielder on two consecutive pitches, the second hitting him.

Powell never reached McKain, cut off by the charging Cronin. Several punches were exchanged as both benches emptied before the adversaries were separated. More fisticuffs would follow, but Round 2 occurred out of the howling mob's sight.

Both combatants were ejected, and Cronin headed for the Boston locker room via the runway adjoining the New York dugout. He soon was taking on half the Yankee team in the tunnel.

The crowd had no knowledge of that until umpire Cal Hubbard, who had been instrumental in breaking up the first fight, glanced at the Yankee dugout and saw it empty. Hubbard didn't have to be Dick Tracy to figure out where the Yankees had gone, and the 6-foot-4, 255-pound former Green Bay Packer star sprinted for the tunnel—quickly followed by the other umps and all the Red Sox.

The record throng—which, incidentally, would have been even bigger had not 6,000 been turned away and 511 given refunds because they couldn't find anywhere to stand—was left bewildered, viewing nothing but grass.

Cronin appeared little damaged afterward, showing only minor bruises and scratches.

"My intent was just to keep McKain out of it," he explained. "We couldn't afford to have him thrown out for fighting. We needed the pitching."

Future American League President Cronin was fined $200 by the American League office.

And it would not be the Red Sox's last brawl at Yankee Stadium.

Joe Cronin (center) intercepts Jake Powell (right) before the Yankee can get at Red Sox pitcher Archie McKain (left, No. 14) as New York shortstop Frank Crosetti (No. 1) joins the debate. *(Associated Press)*

JOE CRONIN: "Bodies were flying everywhere. It sure was good to see Cal (Hubbard) coming in there, all 255 pounds of him."

CAL HUBBARD: "I noticed later that there was nobody left on the Yankee bench. I thought, 'Oh, oh, that Irishman must be in trouble.'

"So I called time and rushed into the runway. There was Cronin, taking on half the Yankee team. They had him down, but Joe was giving a good account of himself. Well, being young and strong, I had one job to do, and that was to start pulling players apart."

June 16, 1938

Jimmy Foxx was walked a record six times in succession today as the Red Sox outlasted the last-place Browns, 12-8, at St. Louis.

The record string of walks—which set an American League record while tying the 1891 major league mark—was issued by a parade of Brownie pitchers: Les Tietje, Ed Linke, Ed Cole and Russ Van Atta.

Double X has been on a home-run tear and yesterday hit his 19th of the season. It was a colossal clout which hit the top of the huge

Jimmy Foxx (right) might as well have used an umbrella for a bat when he was walked a record six times in a game. That's Joe Cronin holding an open umbrella.

scoreboard backing the left-field bleachers, one of the longest artillery shots in Sportsman's Park history.

TED WILLIAMS: "Next to Joe DiMaggio, Jimmy Foxx was the greatest player I ever saw.

"I truly admired him. He was older, of course; he and I were a generation apart. But he was such a good-natured guy, a big farm boy from Maryland. He never badmouthed anybody. What a disposition —always a giggle. He was a real guy and a fine friend to me.

"He never made any bones about his love for Scotch. He used to say he could drink 15 of those little bottles of Scotch, those miniatures, and not be affected.

"What a hitter. With all those muscles, he hit drives that sounded like gunfire. *Ker-rack!*

"I batted behind him, and remember one road trip when Jimmy hit four balls like I had never seen hit before, including one over the left-field bleachers in Chicago and one way up in the left-center bleachers in Detroit, the longest ball I had ever seen. Just hard to believe."

BILL DICKEY: "If I were catching blindfolded, I'd always know when it was Foxx who connected. He hit the ball harder than anyone else."

June 22, 1938

An enemy pitcher finally retired Mike "Pinky" Higgins today in Detroit, but not before the Red Sox third baseman earned his way into the record books for most consecutive hits ever by a major leaguer.

Higgins was fanned in his first at-bat by Tiger right-hander Vern Kennedy, snapping Higgins's streak at 12 straight hits—bettering by one the mark set by Tris Speaker in 1920.

Higgins's streak covered four games—a doubleheader in Chicago,

The Red Sox infield of the late thirties (left to right): second baseman Bobby Doerr, shortstop Joe Cronin, third baseman Mike "Pinky" Higgins and first baseman Jimmy Foxx.

another doubleheader in Detroit—during which he collected two doubles and 10 singles.

No batter has topped Higgins's record, although Walt Dropo equaled it playing for the Tigers in 1952, the month after the Red Sox traded him to Detroit.

October 18, 1938

The frosting has been applied to Jimmy Foxx's superb season. The brawny Red Sox slugger was chosen the American League's Most Valuable Player today.

Foxx hit .349 with 50 home runs (35 at Fenway Park) and 175 runs batted in—missing the Triple Crown as Detroit's Hank Greenberg outhomered him with 58. Foxx totaled 305 points to easily win over Yankee Bill Dickey (196) and Greenberg (162).

Double X becomes the first player to win the MVP Award three times; he captured it in 1932 and 1933 with the Athletics.

Foxx also becomes the first Red Soxer to win the award, instituted in 1931, although Tris Speaker won the 1912 Chalmers Award, a comparable honor given from 1911 to 1914.

Cincinnati's Ernie Lombardi was selected MVP in the National League.

April 20, 1939

After striking out in his first two at-bats, Ted Williams rifled a double at Yankee Stadium today in his Red Sox debut. The ball smashed a foot from the top of the bleacher fence in right-center field above the 407-foot mark. It came off big Red Ruffing, the veteran right-hander who had twice fanned the lanky right fielder on high fastballs.

The brash 20-year-old rookie—nicknamed "Slugger"—has been predicting all spring that he'll make mincemeat out of big league pitching. So when he returned to the dugout after his second strikeout, teammate Jack Wilson needled: "What do you think of this league now, Bush?"

"If he puts it in the same place again," the hot-tempered Williams fumed, "I'll ride it out of here."

Ruffing did—and the Splendid Splinter almost did, his drive falling just short.

Ted Williams's first big league homer, a 400-foot-plus blast into Fenway's bleachers, came in his fourth game.

Williams notched his first Fenway hit the next day in the home opener, singling off Athletics southpaw Edgar Smith, scoring Joe Cronin for Ted's first major league RBI.

Two days later, Williams recorded his first major league home run, lining a 400-plus-foot drive into the bleachers in right-center off A's right-hander Luther Thomas. A Fenway crowd of 12,000 sat through a drizzle to see Ted nearly hit for the cycle as he added a double and two singles while going four for five.

The only time Philadelphia got Williams out was in his last trip, when he lashed a drive through a strong wind that drove Bob Johnson against the left-field scoreboard. Johnson speared what appeared to be at least a double—or, with a lucky carom off the multicontoured scoreboard, a triple that would have given him the cycle.

○

July 4, 1939

Jim Tabor celebrated the Fourth of July today by rocketing four home runs—two of them grand-slams—as the Red Sox swept a doubleheader at Philadelphia, 17-7 and 18-12.

The Boston third baseman collected 19 total bases and 11 RBIs for the day. Three of his homers, including both grand-slams, came in the nightcap. George Caster was the victim of the first slam. Lynn "Line

Jim Tabor celebrated the Fourth of July.

Joe Cronin gave Joe McCarthy (right) a headache when the 1939 Red Sox swept five games from the Yankees at New York.

Drive" Nelson confirmed his nickname by serving up the second slam, inside the park.

The day's fireworks included 65 hits—35 by the Red Sox, 30 by the Athletics.

July 9, 1939

"Who the hell are supposed to be the World Champions, us or the Red Sox?"

That's what Yankee manager Joe McCarthy asked after the Red Sox completed an unprecedented sweep of a five-game series at Yankee Stadium today by blitzing the mighty Bronx Bombers in a double-header.

The Sox are now very much in the pennant race, having whittled the Yankees' lead from a yawning 11½-game advantage to a catchable 6½ games.

More than 50,000 Sunday fans, most cheering for the underdog Bostonians, saw relief pitchers Emerson Dickman and Jack Wilson notch victories in today's 4-3 and 5-3 conquests. Joe Cronin and Jimmy Foxx hit crucial home runs, the second for each slugger in the series.

Today's twin triumphs follow reliever Dickman's 4-3 success in Friday's opener and yesterday's 3-1 and 3-2 wins behind Fritz Oster-mueller and Denny Galehouse.

The Red Sox went on to a 17-5 (including 12 straight victories) trip, one of their best ever. But come October, the Yankees had won 106 for another pennant—17 games ahead of the second-place Sox.

o

The 1959 Red Sox also would sweep a five-game set from the Yankees, that one at Fenway Park. Frank Sullivan won the opener and finale as the Sox prevailed 14-3, 8-5, 8-4 (on Don Buddin's grand-slam in the tenth inning), 7-3 and 13-3.

September 3, 1939

The Red Sox forfeited the second game of today's doubleheader with the Yankees when Fenway fans wouldn't stop littering the field to protest the farce disguised as a baseball game.

New York scored twice in the eighth to take a 7-5 lead as the clock atop the center-field bleachers approached the 6:30 Sunday curfew. Not wanting those runs to be erased by that deadline, the Yankees tried to purposely let themselves be put out so the Sox could come to bat.

George Selkirk and Joe Gordon jogged from third to the plate in burlesqued steals of home. The Red Sox responded with stalls of their own, giving time-consuming walks intentionally. Runs didn't matter. If the Sox didn't get their ups by 6:30, the score reverted to the last full inning and a 5-5 tie.

Fed up with the travesty, the customers started to let go with pop bottles and other missiles and debris—the left-field area in particular soon resembling the city dump.

After issuing warnings, umpire Cal Hubbard forfeited the game to the visitors.

Five days later, American League President Will Harridge canceled the forfeit and ordered the game replayed (it never was because of rainouts). He also fined both managers, Joe McCarthy and Joe Cronin (who would replace Harridge 20 years later).

August 24, 1940

Ted Williams pitched the last two innings today as the pennant-bound Tigers mauled the Red Sox, 12-1, at Fenway Park.

Williams allowed one run on three hits and fanned Rudy York on a sweeping, side-arm curve that the surprised Detroit slugger took for a called third strike. Pitcher Jim Bagby replaced Williams in left field during Ted's stint on the mound.

Williams, a pitcher-outfielder in high school who hurled a few innings in the minors, has been joking "what a loss it is to baseball that I haven't followed up on my pitching." He was given his chance today by manager Joe Cronin.

This marks the third straight August that a strong-armed fielder has been used as a pitcher by Cronin, who figures it saves his bull pen in a lopsided game while giving the Fenway fans something to talk about.

First baseman Jimmy Foxx pitched the ninth inning of a 10-1 rout by the Tigers on August 6, 1939. He struck out one while retiring the side in order.

Center fielder Doc Cramer pitched the last four innings in a 9-4 loss to the Browns on August 30, 1938. He allowed two runs on three hits and three walks while striking out one.

July 17, 1941

The Rex Sox were the opposition eight times during Joe DiMaggio's 56-game hitting streak—which ended tonight—including when he tied and broke Wee Willie Keeler's major league record of 44 games.

DiMaggio tied Keeler's record when he singled off Jack Wilson in the second game of a July 1 doubleheader at Yankee Stadium. Joltin' Joe broke the record there the next day when he homered off Heber "Dick" Newsome.

DiMag also hit safely against Newsome in Game 9 (May 23), Earl Johnson in Game 10 (May 24), Lefty Grove in Game 11 (May 25), Johnson in Game 15 (opener of May 30 doubleheader), Mickey Harris in Game 16 (nightcap of May 30 doubleheader), and Harris and Mike Ryba in Game 43 (opener of July 1 doubleheader) before tying the Keeler record.

◇ ◇ ◇

JOE DiMAGGIO: "The Red Sox made two great catches—one by my brother Dom—to nearly stop me the day I was trying to break Wee Willie Keeler's record of 44 straight games.

"I'd tied it against Boston the day before and knew breaking it

THE FORTIES

During Joe DiMaggio's 56-game hitting streak, Ted Williams checked on the Yankee Clipper's progress with the scoreboard operator inside Fenway's left-field wall and hollered any news over to outfield mate Dom DiMaggio.

wouldn't be a cinch when I saw Heber Newsome warming up for them. He was never a cinch for me.

"I lit into a pitch in the first inning, though, and thought it was out of Yankee Stadium. But Stan Spence went back and made a fine catch. The next time up it was Dom who got on his bike and made a terrific catch of a long drive.

"When Dom came up with it I thought it was rubbing it in to be robbed for a record by your own brother—one who was coming over for dinner that night.

"I was a little down. I'd hit Newsome hard twice, about as often as I figured to hit him under the law of averages. But in the fifth inning I tagged him for a home run—and the record.

"And Lefty Gomez said: 'Joe, you not only beat Keeler's record but used his formula, hitting 'em where the Red Sox ain't—in the stands.' "

July 8, 1941

Ted Williams electrified a crowd of 54,674 at Detroit today when he crashed a three-run homer against the facade of the third tier with two out in the last of the ninth inning to give the American League a 7-5 victory in the All-Star Game.

The Red Sox slugger was mobbed and kissed by teammates as he followed Yankees Joe Gordon and Joe DiMaggio across the plate as Briggs Stadium went wild.

Unnoticed as they walked off the field were the National League's two most disconsolate figures, pitcher Claude Passeau and second baseman Billy Herman. Passeau served up the dramatic homer on a 2-1 pitch; Herman made a wide throw to first base as the pivotman on DiMaggio's potential double-play grounder to shortstop that would have ended the game with Williams still on deck.

Of all his homers, Ted Williams says the one that won the 1941 All-Star Game at Detroit thrilled him most.

TED WILLIAMS: "That was the most thrilling hit of my life.

"Claude Passeau was always tough. A right-hander, he had a fast tailing ball that he'd jam a left-handed hitter with, right into your fists.

"He'd struck me out in the eighth inning. I was late on that one, and as I came up in the ninth I said to myself, 'Damn it, you've got to be quicker, you've got to get more in front of this guy. *You've got to be quicker.'*

"He worked the count to two and one, then came in with that sliding fastball around my belt and I swung, an all-out home run swing, probably with my eyes shut.

"My first thought was that I was late again. I had pulled it to right field, but I was afraid I hadn't got enough of the bat on the ball. But gee, it just kept going, up, up, way up into the right-field stands.

"Well, it was the kind of thing a kid dreams about and imagines himself doing when he's playing those little playground games.

"Halfway down to first, seeing that ball going out, I stopped running and started leaping and jumping and clapping my hands, and I was just so happy I laughed out loud. I've never been so happy. It was a wonderful, wonderful day for me."

July 25, 1941

Lefty Grove finally reached the summit of Everest today.

The silver-haired, 41-year-old southpaw chalked up his 300th victory as the Red Sox outslugged the Indians, 10-6, to delight a Ladies Day crowd of 16,000 at Fenway Park.

Mose staggered the distance for his hard-earned "biggest thrill," surviving 12 Cleveland hits as the Sox battled back from 4-0 and 6-4 deficits to win it for Grove on his third try for No. 300.

"It was the toughest game I ever sweated through," said Grove, who lost eight pounds during the 2½-hour struggle in the sweltering 90-degree heat.

Fittingly, it was Jimmy Foxx who won the game for his longtime Athletics and Sox mate. Double X powered a triple against the center-field bleacher wall off Al Milnar for two runs to snap a 6-6 deadlock in the eighth. And when Foxx scored via an overthrow on the play, he was hugged and kissed by Grove in the dugout.

Jim Tabor followed with his second homer of the afternoon to send Grove into the final inning with a four-run cushion, and Mose went out and mowed down the Indians in order.

When Dom DiMaggio clutched the last out, he raced in from center field to present the ball to Grove, who plans to ship it to Cooperstown.

Grove becomes only the sixth pitcher to win 300 since the turn of the century. He joins Cy Young (511), Walter Johnson (416), Christy Mathewson (373), Grover Alexander (373) and Eddie Plank (327).

It was Grove's final victory. He made six more starts without success and retired at season's end, 7-7 for the year and 300-141 for his magnificent 17-season career.

○

In the more than 35 years since, only two more pitchers have joined the selective 300-victory circle: Warren Spahn (363) and Early Wynn (300).

September 27, 1941

Ted Williams vented his pressure with a ten-mile walk and a couple of chocolate milkshakes tonight as he prepared for tomorrow's assault on .400.

Williams didn't prowl the streets of Philadelphia alone. He was

Jimmy Foxx's two-run triple gave 41-year-old Lefty Grove (left) his 300th victory.

accompanied by pal Johnny Orlando, the Red Sox equipment manager. "We must have walked ten miles easy," said Orlando.

Orlando also said they made a "couple of quick stops" along the way for some "instant energy"—Johnny ducking into a tavern or two, non-drinker Ted into a couple of malt shops.

○

September 28, 1941

The Kid has done it!

Ignoring a mountain of pressure, Ted Williams completed the season with a glittering .406 batting average, machine-gunning six hits in eight at-bats today as the Red Sox split a doubleheader at Philadelphia.

The 23-year-old stringbean is the first major leaguer to reach the select .400 circle since Bill Terry (.401) in 1930 and the first American Leaguer since Harry Heilmann (.403) in 1923. Ted is only the eighth player to hit .400 since 1900—joining Ty Cobb (three times), Rogers Hornsby (three times), George Sisler (twice), Shoeless Joe Jackson, Nap Lajoie, Heilmann and Terry.

Going into the twin bill, Williams was batting .3996—.400 rounded off—and last night Joe Cronin suggested: "Why not sit out, Ted? These two games mean nothing. You have the .400. Take it. You've earned it."

"To hell with that. I don't want it that way," Terrible Ted snapped, despite the fact he's dropped almost a point a day the last two weeks in September's cool weather. "I'll play."

Williams got a big hand from the 10,268 when he stepped to the plate for the first time at cold and damp Shibe Park, and Athletics catcher Frank Hayes greeted him: "I wish you all the luck in the world, Ted, but

YOUNG TED

Ted couldn't escape cameramen.

Ted hated neckties, rarely wore them. *(Boston Globe)*

Ted occasionally turned sports writer to do a guest column.

Ted took flight training in 1943.

Ted and John Pesky visited Fenway as air cadets.

Ted and Eddie Collins, the man who discovered him for the Sox.

we're not giving you a darn thing. Mr. Mack said he'll run us out of baseball if we let up on you."

The Splendid Splinter promptly thumped (in order) a single, a 440-foot homer and two more singles before reaching on an error as the Sox won, 12-11.

Williams now was hitting .404, and no one expected he'd play the nightcap. But when Cronin again approached him about sitting out, Ted again declined. "No," he said, "I'm going all the way."

And the colorful and often controversial Californian did exactly that. He singled and doubled in three official at-bats against a rookie he'd never seen before, Fred Caligiuri, who held the Sox to just six hits while outpitching Lefty Grove, 7-1, in what was likely Grove's farewell to baseball.

Williams's last hit was his most vicious of the day, maybe of his career. He drilled a screaming liner that hit the cluster of loud-speaker horns atop the fence in right center, smashing one of the horns. The ball caromed back onto the field, and Ted had to settle for a double.

The .406 easily gives Ted his first batting crown over runners-up Cecil Travis (.359) and Joe DiMaggio (.357). Williams also led in homers with 37. And he narrowly missed the Triple Crown by five RBIs, his 120 shy of DiMaggio's 125. Ted also led in slugging percentage (.735), runs (135) and walks (145)—while striking out just 26 times.

"Ain't I the best damn hitter you ever saw?" Ted gleefully shouted to reporters who mobbed him afterward.

No one disputed it. The only question is what Ted can possibly do for an encore this side of Cooperstown.

Cooperstown would come in July 1966.

But first there would be nearly two more decades of heroics, including five more batting crowns, the last at age 40. No one would break the .400 barrier again, but Williams would come closest with .388 in 1957 at age 39. And although Rod Carew has since equaled that .388, in nearly 40 years no one has come any closer to Ted's magnificent .406, his greatest batting achievement.

September 27, 1942

Tex Hughson lassoed his twenty-second victory today to tie the major league lead with the Cardinals' Mort Cooper as the Red Sox edged the Yankees, 7-6, in the season finale at Fenway Park. The 22-6 right-hander gives the Sox their first 20-game winner since 1936, when Wes Ferrell was 20-15.

A crowd of 26,166—including 4,293 youngsters who gained free admission by bringing 29,000 pounds of scrap metal for the war effort—watched Hughson scatter 11 hits, including a Joe DiMaggio homer, to defeat the pennant-winning Yankees for the fifth straight time.

The Red Sox solved Marius Russo, Johnny Murphy and Jim Turner for 13 hits, including a single by Ted Williams, who has won his second straight major league batting championship. Williams's average of .356 far exceeds the runners-up, rookie teammate Johnny Pesky, who hit .331, and N.L. leader Ernie Lombardi's .330. Ted also easily led the majors in homers (36), RBIs (137), runs (141) and walks (145).

Despite all that—and the fact that it was Williams's farewell for the war's duration—the Kid was razzed by boo-birds for what they considered loafing on the bases in the first inning.

Williams and Pesky soon will be wearing Navy air cadet uniforms.

Tex Hughson threw an assortment of pitches, including an occasional spitter.

Tex Hughson won 22 games in 1942.

Joe Cronin crosses the plate after hitting his second pinch homer in a doubleheader. That's Dee Miles congratulating Cronin as Athletics catcher Hal Wagner looks on.

TEX HUGHSON: "I threw several spitters, but only with two strikes. I struck out Joe DiMaggio with one at Fenway, bases full and the count 2-2. He swung right through the ball and stood there paralyzed. He didn't say a word.

"I threw another later in the game, and when it got away from catcher Johnny Peacock, Art Fletcher came running in from the third base coaching box yelling for umpire Bill Summers to look at the ball. After the game Summers told me, 'Don't embarrass me and throw that thing too often.'

"I struck out George McQuinn with one, and later, when we were together on the All-Star team, he called me a cheating bastard in the lobby of our hotel.

"Others threw the spitter then, like Dick Newsome and Charley Wagner on our team. Mike Ryba, who used to warm me up, thought I had a good spitter. If I'd pitched longer, I was planning to lean on it more and more in my late years."

June 17, 1943

Aging Joe Cronin hammered his name into the record books again today by pinch-hitting dramatic home runs in both ends of a doubleheader—the first major leaguer ever to do it.

Today's spree against the Athletics at Fenway Park gives the right-handed clutch slugger three pinch homers in his last four at-bats—all three-run wallops.

Two days ago, in another twin bill with the A's, Cronin pinch-homered to win the opener, but flied out in the nightcap. Today Cronin homered off Everett Fagan to give the Red Sox a 5-4 victory in the first game. He homered off Don Black in the second game, but it wasn't enough to save the Sox and they fell short, 8-7.

Approaching 37 and no longer playing regularly, Manager Cronin has forced Player Cronin to remain active because of losing such hitters as Ted Williams, Dom DiMaggio and Johnny Pesky to military service. And Manager Cronin doesn't hesitate to put Player Cronin squarely on the spot.

"I guess the old man showed them something today," Cronin said in the Red Sox locker room.

"What's gotten into Joe?" Connie Mack asked in the A's locker room.

Hitting .429 (18 for 42 plus seven walks) as a pinch hitter in 1943, Cronin added two more pinch homers that year for a total of five—still the American League record. Previously, the league pinch-hitting record was five in a career.

LEFTY GOMEZ: "Joe Cronin gave me fits. He was the toughest I ever went up against, particularly in the clutch."

CONNIE MACK: "Oh my, yes, Joe Cronin was the best there is in the clutch. With a man on third and one out, I'd rather have him hitting for me than anybody I've ever seen—and that includes Cobb and the rest of them."

JOE CRONIN: "I used to pull rank and wait until the wind was blowing out."

July 13, 1943

A Red Sox slugger has become the All-Star Game hero again, providing the winning home run in two of the last three Midsummer Dream games.

Bobby Doerr's three-run blast off Mort Cooper tonight at Philadelphia proved the difference as the American League prevailed, 5-3, to defeat the Nationals for the eighth time in 11 years.

Doerr's feat wasn't as spectacular as Ted Williams's electrifying blow at Detroit in 1941, but it was the game's climactic wallop—the payoff punch that erased the 1-0 N.L. lead in the second inning and gave the A.L. the two-run advantage it maintained.

"I guess that's my biggest baseball thrill," the Boston second baseman said. "But it shows how lucky you can be. I didn't hit the ball good. It barely got in the stands."

In the field, Doerr handled six balls flawlessly. But what's that to a lad who has accepted 307 chances without error since May 20?

Doerr went on to set records for errorless chances (349) and games (54). Five years later, in 1948, he would break his own marks by handling 414 chances in 73 games before erring—still the A.L. records.

Bobby Doerr (right) and Ted Williams hit home runs to win All-Star Games in the early forties.

September 3, 1944

Red Sox pennant stock plummeted today when Bobby Doerr departed for the Army.

The Sox are in fourth place, but only 1½ games behind the king-of-the-mountain Browns with the Yankees and Tigers squeezed between.

The hot race is being followed closely not only by a nation at war, but also by American servicemen in all corners of the globe. And pennant fever has Fenway attendance approaching a half-million—up almost 150,000 from last season and more than double what the Braves are drawing further up Commonwealth Avenue this season.

Doerr is leading the league with a .325 average, and his remarkable fielding has kept the Sox in the thick of the race since the losses of pitcher Tex Hughson (18-5) and catcher Hal Wagner (.332) to the service last month.

The Red Sox were in second place for four weeks through mid-season and can't be ruled out as pennant winners. But now without Doerr as well as Hughson, it's an almost impossible task.

It was. The Red Sox finished fourth, 12 games out.

September 17, 1944

George "Catfish" Metkovich's hitting streak was snapped at 25 successive games today at Washington by southpaw Mickey Haefner, but not before the first baseman-outfielder had authored a Red Sox record in that department.

Destroyed was the Sox's old mark of 23 shared by Del Pratt, George Burns and Ted Williams.

Despite hitting a heady .407 during his record streak, Metkovich finished the season at .277—only sixth best among Red Sox regulars. Bobby Doerr (.325) and Bob Johnson (.324) came in a close second and third respectively for the league batting title won by Lou Boudreau (.327). Pete Fox hit .315, Lou Finney and Jim Tabor .285. Not included among the regulars (because he played only 66 games before heading into the service) was Hal Wagner, acquired early in the season from the Athletics, with .332.

○

Joe Cronin ships Red Sox caps to Marine pilots in the South Pacific during World War II.

Yankee Joe Gordon (left) and Bobby Doerr were friendly rivals, the American League's best all-around second basemen of the forties.

How would Red Sox history have been altered if Jackie Robinson and Ted Williams had been teammates?

Metkovich set a less glamorous record in the Red Sox opener the following season—committing three errors in one inning at first base against the Yankees. Perhaps unstrung, pitcher Rex Cecil then served a grand-slam to Russ Derry. The Sox lost, 8-4, and didn't recover for their first victory until eight games later.

And while Metkovich's batting streak has long since been erased, his fielding mark has endured—still good enough for a share of the major league record.

October 1, 1944

It took the Red Sox and White Sox just two hours and 48 minutes to split a doubleheader at Chicago today and bring down the curtain on their seasons.

A "crowd" of 3,917 saw Rex Cecil outduel Joe Haynes as the Red Sox won the opener, 3-1, in 1:38 as each team managed five hits. Then Johnny Humphries bested Pinky Woods, 4-1, in just 1:10, despite Chicago collecting 11 hits and Boston seven.

The split gave the fourth-place Red Sox a split for the season, 77-77, 12 games behind the Browns, who won their first pennant today.

November 1, 1944

The *Sporting News* today selected Bobby Doerr the American League's Most Valuable Player even though the Red Sox second baseman missed the last month of the season.

Before entering the Army, Doerr was enjoying his best season —leading the league in hitting (.325) and third in RBIs (81). The 26-year-old Californian lost the batting crown by two points to Lou Boudreau of the Indians, but ended in a tie for heftiest slugging percentage (.528) with Sox teammate Bob Johnson.

And afield, Doerr was again brilliant as the debate still rages as to who is the best all-around second baseman—Bashful Bobby or the Yankees' Joe Gordon.

Joining Doerr in today's spotlight is Marty Marion, shortstop of the World Champion Cardinals, who was selected National League MVP by the *Sporting News*.

Marion's selection as N.L. MVP stood up as that league's official choice. But Doerr was beaten out for the official A.L. MVP Award by 29-game winner Hal Newhouser of the Tigers.

TOMMY HENRICH: "Bobby Doerr is one of the very few who played this game hard and came out of it with no enemies."

April 16, 1945

Are the Red Sox considering breaking baseball's color line?

They became the first big league team to give blacks a tryout today, auditioning three Negro League stars at Fenway Park as the nation mourned the death of President Franklin Delano Roosevelt, who was buried yesterday.

Jackie Robinson, Sam Jethroe and Marvin Williams worked out under the direction of Red Sox scout Hugh Duffy, who batted .438 back in 1894 for the old Boston Red Stockings and later managed the Sox.

Robinson, 26, a former UCLA football star and recently discharged Army lieutenant, is earning $400 a month playing shortstop for the Kansas City Monarchs. Jethroe, 23, is a switch-hitter and league-leading base stealer for the Cleveland Buckeyes. And Williams, 20, plays for the Philadelphia Stars.

The tryout was arranged through Wendell Smith, sports editor of the black weekly *Pittsburgh Courier*, by City Councilor Isadore Muchnick from the Roxbury section of Boston, originally a Jewish stronghold now becoming predominantly black.

Aware of votes in his changing constituency, Muchnick has been putting pressure on both the Red Sox and Braves to open their doors to black players. He is threatening to side with church groups for repeal of the city's Sunday baseball ordinance. It is believed that Muchnick has targeted the Red Sox first because they are the more popular of Boston's two major league baseball teams.

Duffy praised the players after the workout and had them fill out information cards.

None of the three heard from the Red Sox again, and four months later Robinson was summoned to Brooklyn by Dodger boss Branch Rickey. The rest is history.

"Not for one minute did we believe the Boston tryout was sincere," Robinson said later. *"We were going through the motions."*

Jethroe also made the majors—and coincidentally in Boston, but with the Braves. He originally was signed by the Dodgers, but after stealing a record 89 bases for their Montreal Royals farm in 1949, was sold to the Braves for a then high price of $150,000. Jethroe was a National League Rookie of the Year in 1950, playing three years in Boston before the Braves headed for Milwaukee and Jethroe headed back to the minors.

Today, Sam sits in Jethroe's Steak House in Erie, Pennsylvania, and recalls the Red Sox tryout with no apparent bitterness. "We did well that day, all three of us," he says. "But the time had not yet come. The time just was not yet right."

○

"They weren't ready for the majors and we would have had to send them down to Triple-A just as the Dodgers did," Joe Cronin, Red Sox manager at the time of the tryout, said years later. *"We didn't have a Montreal as the Dodgers did. Our long-time top farm was at Louisville, and we couldn't send them there. What kind of reception do you think they would have gotten? So we didn't have anywhere to send them."*

○

A gnawing question, of course, is how Red Sox history would have been altered had any of the three blacks been signed that day— particularly future Hall of Famer Robinson.

Instead of being the first, the Red Sox were the last team in the majors to field a black, when, in 1959, infielder Elijah "Pumpsie" Green joined the team, followed a week later by pitcher Earl Wilson.

April 19, 1945

Joe Cronin's 20-year playing career ended abruptly at Yankee Stadium today, his right leg fractured when he caught his spikes rounding second base in the Red Sox's third game of the season.

At age 38, Cronin would have preferred to be strictly a bench manager this season. But he pressed himself into service as a third baseman to bolster a team depleted by the war.

Cronin had three hits in eight at-bats for a .375 average in this opening series and made a brilliant play to throw out a Yankee earlier in the game. It had prompted the jovial Cronin to holler to Yankee third base coach Art Fletcher: "Hey, Art, who was that guy Jimmy Collins they used to talk about?"

An inning later, Cronin, writhing in pain, was carried off the field on a stretcher.

Joe Cronin's playing career ended when he broke a leg sliding into second base at Yankee Stadium. *(Associated Press)*

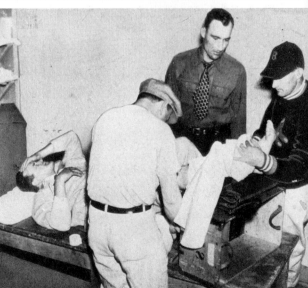

Cronin's playing career was over, but his Hall of Fame saga—from the streets of San Francisco to the halls of Cooperstown—was only half written. The onetime Washington Senators "Boy Manager" would guide the Red Sox to the 1946 pennant before moving upstairs as general manager after the 1947 season. And in 1959, he'd become President of the American League, the first former player to rise to the presidency of either major league.

April 29, 1945

A Red Sox star was born in Philadelphia today when Army Air Corps veteran David Meadow "Boo" Ferriss blanked the Athletics, 2-0.

The nervous right-hander almost didn't survive his first big league inning, nearly being yanked by manager Joe Cronin, perhaps to be shipped back to the minors. Ferriss's first ten pitches were balls. In fact, the 23-year-old former Mississippi State star threw 17 pitches wide during the inning and loaded the bases on walks.

"One more walk and he was out of there," said Cronin, managing on crutches, his broken right leg in a cast.

The 6-2, 208-pound Ferriss calmed down to pitch a five-hit masterpiece, lifting the struggling Red Sox to their second straight victory after opening the season with eight straight losses.

Ferriss was recently discharged from the service because of an asthma condition. He was summoned, even with little minor league experience, because the patchquilt Sox are desperate for manpower as the war winds to a close.

Ferriss impressed as a hitter as well as a pitcher. He stung three singles in as many trips. His third was cracked back through the pitcher's box into center field, whereupon mound opponent Bobo Newsom hollered to Ferriss: "Hell, you ought to be in the outfield, kid!"

Ferriss continued his storybook start, pitching a league-record 22 scoreless innings. He racked up ten straight victories, four by shutout, and took New England by storm. Enormously likable—quick with smile, slow with soft-spoken drawl—he was showered with gifts, including a Lincoln Zephyr in September on Dave Ferriss Day.

Despite an asthma attack that dogged him the last six weeks, Ferriss

Joe Cronin (center) huddles with his "Big Four" that would pitch the Red Sox to the 1946 pennant (left to right): Mickey Harris, Dave Ferriss, Joe Dobson and Tex Hughson. The next season, Hughson, Ferriss and Harris developed career-shortening sore arms. *(Boston Globe)*

finished 21-10 with a 2.96 ERA—the first American League freshman to win 20 since Wes Ferrell in 1929, the first Red Sox rookie since Hugh Bedient in 1912.

Ferriss did it while keeping interest alive in a seventh-place team that was treading water waiting for the war to end. He was one of the few wartime Red Sox to remain when the stars returned the following season. Ferriss was the Sox's top winner (25-6) and, with roomie Tex Hughson (20-11), pitched the 1946 team to a runaway pennant.

The combination of asthma and a sore arm then cut short Ferriss's career, although he didn't pitch his final game until 1950. He would return as the Red Sox pitching coach 1955–59.

May 11, 1946

The Red Sox victory streak came to a screeching halt at 15 today as the Hose managed only two hits off Tiny Bonham while falling to the Yankees, 2-0, at New York.

The Yankees coaxed just six hits off Tex Hughson (seven innings) and Dave Ferriss (one inning), but Tommy Henrich accounted for both runs while going 3-for-3 with a homer, double and single to delight 52,011 at Yankee Stadium.

It was only the Red Sox's fourth loss, and their 21-4 record still is good enough for a 4½-game lead over the second-place Yankees.

That 15-game win streak remains the longest in Red Sox history. And it was the springboard to a pennant.

July 9, 1946

Ted Williams stole the All-Star Game show again today.

The Red Sox slugger blasted two home runs and added two singles and a walk while knocking in five runs and scoring four more to lead the American League to a 12-0 humiliation of the Nationals at Fenway Park. The perfect performance was every bit as spectacular as when Williams won the 1941 Midsummer Dream game with his now-legendary homer—only in a different way.

Ted became the first hitter to drive in five runs in an All-Star Game, only the second to get four hits (joining Ducky Medwick) and two homers (joining Arky Vaughn), and the first hitter anytime to propel Rip Sewell's famous "eephus" ball for a home run.

Sewell's "blooper" pitch is a lob that comes to the plate on a 20-foot arc, like a pop fly. The batter must supply all the power, and it had been thought that no one could generate enough thrust to power it out of a stadium.

But in the eighth inning Williams solved it, taking a couple of steps into Sewell's floater and drilling it into the bull pen to send the hometown crowd of 34,906 into a frenzy.

"I still don't believe it," said Sewell, the veteran right-hander shrugging off suggestions the homer might have been illegal because Ted was out of the batter's box when he hit the ball.

"That's the greatest exhibition of hitting I've ever seen," raved N.L. manager Charley Grimm, also noting Williams's other homer into the center-field bleachers off Kirby Higbe and singles off Higbe and Ewell Blackwell—part of the Americans' awesome 14-hit attack.

The Red Sox, running away with the pennant, dominated the A.L. squad with eight representatives. Dom DiMaggio, Bobby Doerr and Johnny Pesky joined Williams in the starting lineup, and Rudy York and Hal Wagner were used as substitutes. Pitchers Dave Ferriss and Mickey Harris didn't see service—not needed as the N.L. managed only three hits, all singles.

Ted Williams smashed two home runs in the 1946 All-Star Game at Fenway.

RIP SEWELL: "Before the game, Ted said to me, 'Hey, Rip, you wouldn't throw that damned crazy pitch in a game like this, would you?'

" 'Sure,' I said. 'I'm gonna throw it to you.'

" 'Man,' he said, 'don't throw that ball in a game like this.'

" 'I'm gonna throw it to you, Ted,' I said. 'So look out.'

"Well, they had us beat 8-0 going into the last of the eighth. It was a lousy game and the fans were bored.

"I was pitching that inning and Ted came to bat. You know how Ted used to be up there at the plate, all business.

"I smiled at him. He must've recalled our conversation because he shook his head from side to side in quick little movements, telling me not to throw it. I nodded to him: You're gonna get it, buddy.

"He shook his head again. And I nodded to him again. He was gonna get it.

"So I wound up like I was going to throw a fastball, and here comes the blooper. He swung from Port Arthur and just fouled it on the tip of his bat.

"He stepped back in, staring out at me, and I nodded to him again: You're gonna get another one. I threw him another one, but it was outside and he let it go. Now he was looking for it.

"Well, I threw him a fastball and he didn't like that. Surprised him. Now I had him one ball, two strikes.

"I wound up and threw another blooper. It was a good one, dropping right down the shute for a strike. He took a couple of steps up on it—which was the right way to attack that pitch, incidentally—and he hit it right out of there. And I mean he *hit* it.

"Well, the fans stood up and they went crazy. I walked around the base lines with Ted, talking to him. 'Yeah,' I told him, 'the only reason you hit it is because I told you it was coming.' He was laughing all the way around. I got a standing ovation when I walked off the mound after that inning. We'd turned a dead turkey of a ball game into a real crowd pleaser.

"And he was the only man ever to hit a home run off the blooper—Ted Williams, in the '46 All-Star Game."

RUDY YORK: "Ted Williams was the greatest hitter I ever saw. And he's a good friend. But he was the only guy I ever remember raising my voice to in the clubhouse.

"That was in 1946, when we were going for the pennant. It seemed to me that Ted was slow going after a hit in the outfield and a run scored. So in the clubhouse I had a few things to say to him.

"I told him that I was about washed up and wasn't about to let a pennant slip away from me now. I told him that anyone on the team who loafed would have to answer to me.

"Ted took it in the right spirit."

Williams had great respect for York and apologized.

July 14, 1946

A "Williams Shift" was born at Fenway Park today in a desperate attempt to prevent Ted from shattering every batting record in the book.

Cleveland shortstop-manager Lou Boudreau sprung the surprise alignment in the nightcap of a doubleheader swept by the Red Sox after

"Williams Shift" designer Lou Boudreau (center) and Joe Cronin meet with Babe Ruth during the Babe's final visit to Fenway in 1947, the year before he died.

Williams had devastated the Indians with three homers and eight RBIs to win the marathon opener, 11-10.

"We had to do something," explained Boudreau, whose record four doubles and homer had been wasted in the first game.

Boudreau waited until Williams's second at-bat in the second game—after Ted had doubled home three more runs in his first trip. The Indians then shifted into their radical arrangement: packing the right side of the diamond against the pull-hitting Williams, leaving only one defender to protect the entire left side.

The first baseman and right fielder were stationed almost directly on the foul line. The second baseman moved closer to first but well back on the outfield grass. The shortstop played in the second baseman's normal position. The third baseman stood directly behind second base; the center fielder moved over to deep right-center. Only left fielder George Case remained on the left side, camping in short left-center about 30 feet behind the infield.

Williams looked at the shift and began laughing, stepping out of the batter's box and shaking his head as the big crowd buzzed in amazement.

The Splendid Splinter, who is leading the league in almost every hitting category and is a heavy favorite to win another Triple Crown, made no attempt to bunt or swing for the opposite field. Instead, he grounded out to Boudreau. Ted was walked in his next two trips, and the Indians reverted to a normal defense in his last at-bat because there were runners on base.

The shift makes sense in many ways, Boudreau daring Williams to bunt or shorten his swing and punch the ball to left. If Ted goes that route, Boudreau has taken away the long-ball threat. If Ted defies the shift and swings away, the defense will take away some hits because it is stacked in the area where 85 percent of Williams's hits go.

Either way, Boudreau has created a psychological stunt that will disturb Ted's concentration—particularly if he bullheadedly becomes determined to beat the shift.

When Williams stubbornly tried to buck the shift, most managers followed Boudreau's lead, many adding a minor modification or two to what became known as the "Boudreau Shift."

"There's no question the shift hurt me," Williams acknowledges. The only question is: how many hits did the defense cost Ted during the remaining 1600-plus games in his career?

LOU BOUDREAU: "I was so damn mad seeing my hits wasted in the first game that I came up with the cockeyed shift on the spur of the moment.

"I knew Ted could get pop-fly hits to left all day long if he wanted, but that was better than home runs into the seats in right."

TY COBB: "Ted is one of the greatest natural hitters I've ever seen. If he'd hit to left field, he'd break up that shift and break every record in the book. He'd hit .500."

July 27, 1946

Rudy York smashed two grand-slam home runs off Tex Shirley to power the Red Sox to a 13-6 victory at St. Louis today.

The Boston slugger also hit a two-run double to total 10 RBIs for the day. That gives him 15 RBIs in two days against the Browns.

The Red Sox were bolstered for their 1946 pennant drive by acquiring veterans Rudy York (left) and Mike "Pinky" Higgins from the Tigers.

Ted Williams slides across the plate with the only inside-the-park homer of his career. It gave the Red Sox a 1-0 victory at Cleveland to clinch the 1946 pennant.

September 13, 1946

Friday the 13th proved lucky for the Red Sox at Cleveland today as they finally clinched their first pennant in 28 years on the most dramatic inside-the-park home run in the team's history.

Ted Williams rapped the homer as the "Boudreau Shift" boomeranged. Ted punched the ball over the head of Pat Seerey, the left fielder camped a few steps behind the normal shortstop position. By the time the Indians chased down the rolling ball against the left-field fence nearly 400 feet away, the galloping Williams had slid across the plate with his 38th home run of the season and the first inside-the-park homer of his career.

It came in the first inning, one of only two Boston hits off Red Embree. But it was all Tex Hughson needed as he shut out Cleveland on three hits. "Get me a run and we'll win," the veteran right-hander had told Sox mates before the game. A League Park crowd of only 3,295 saw the duel which lasted only an hour and 28 minutes.

Hughson was brilliant in notching his 18th victory of the season. It was his sixth shutout, his fourth by a skinny 1-0 margin. The power-hitting Sox have managed only two hits for Hughson in three of those four 1-0 victories.

Today's triumph enabled the Red Sox to finally pop the champagne which road secretary Tom Dowd has been keeping on ice. He's had to have it carted from city to city as the team, breezing to the pennant, suddenly stuttered and lost four straight games before clinching today.

"Now that we've won on Friday the 13th," manager Joe Cronin said, "I'll never again believe in superstitions."

After 14 years of patience and spending, owner Tom Yawkey led the victory celebration tonight with a team party at the hotel. The only absentee was Williams, reportedly visiting a dying war veteran.

The press was barred from the party, fanning the flames of ill feeling between the team and writers. The writers felt insulted even though Red Sox management held a separate party for them at the hotel. And when Yawkey dropped by the press party, the mood was so nasty that he and columnist Austen Lake became embroiled in a shouting match.

That was pale in comparison to a confrontation between Cronin and writer Huck Finnegan in a hotel elevator after the game. That season-long feud nearly erupted into a fight: both men were red with rage, their fists were clenched and they were screaming obscenities at each other.

◇◇◇

TED WILLIAMS: "That was the only inside-the-park home run I ever hit. And it was the hardest. I had to run."

◇◇◇

October 6, 1946

Rudy York's tenth-inning home run powered the Red Sox to a 3-2 victory over the Cardinals today in the World Series opener at St. Louis.

York's blast off 21-game winner Howie Pollet was a rainbow shot into a refreshment stand at the top of the left-field bleachers at Sportsman's Park. It was greeted by a massive groan, then an eerie silence from the capacity crowd of 36,218 as York trotted around the bases.

The triumph confirmed the Red Sox as heavy favorites to extend their distinction of never having lost a World Series.

Earl Johnson was the winning pitcher with two perfect innings in relief of starter Tex Hughson, who was lifted for a pinch hitter during Boston's ninth-inning rally which produced a run to tie the score at 2-2—setting the scene for York's towering game-winner the next inning.

Besides providing a one-victory jump in the Series, the win also seems to have quieted two Sox worries. There was anxiety that the team might have lost its zip after coasting to the American League pennant and waiting through a four-day delay while the Cardinals and Dodgers collided in a playoff series for the National League pennant.

The other side of that coin, of course, is whether the Cardinals are dead tired or razor sharp after their furious pennant fight and two-game playoff sweep of Brooklyn.

The other major concern was how much Ted Williams would be restricted by his still-swollen and painful right elbow. The slugger was plunked by a pitch from Senators southpaw Mickey Haefner at Fenway this past week during a practice game against a group of A.L. stars— a game which was intended to keep the Sox from getting stale during the N.L. playoffs.

Williams has been taking almost round-the-clock treatment from trainer Win Green ever since, the still-blue elbow continually submerged in ice.

Encouragingly, The Kid singled (and also narrowly missed an extra-base hit on a long foul) in three official at-bats while walking twice. However, he doesn't appear to be whipping the bat with his usual picture-book snap and rhythm.

Incidentally, Cardinals manager Eddie Dyer sprung a similar version of the Boudreau Shift against Williams—moving third baseman Whitey Kurowski to the right side of second base while leaving shortstop Marty Marion on the left side but shaded nearer the bag.

○

Ever wonder what a manager and pitcher talk about during those mound conferences at a crucial moment in a baseball game?

Joe Cronin and Earl Johnson discussed World War II during a tenth-inning huddle in today's Red Sox victory over the Cardinals in the World Series opener.

Although trailing 3-2, the Cards were staging a last-ditch threat, advancing a runner to third base with two outs after reaching on an error. With always-dangerous Enos Slaughter, who had tripled earlier, coming to bat, Cronin strolled to the mound to talk with Johnson, a twice-decorated hero who won a battlefield commission.

What did the manager tell his reliever?

"Nothing much," Cronin said afterward. "We chatted a minute; then I asked Earl, 'What's the name of the battle you fought in?'

Joe Cronin gets a pennant-celebrating ride in a Cleveland hotel lobby from (left to right) Johnny Pesky, Tom McBride and Earl Johnson.

THE 1946 WORLD SERIES

The Red Sox arrive in St. Louis for the Series opener (left to right): front row, Joe Dobson, Earl Johnson, Wally Moses and Hal Wagner; back row, Rudy York, Tom Carey and Mike Ryba.

Enos Slaugh
run that wo

Rival managers Eddie Dyer (right) and Joe Cronin.

George Munger (second left) was the winning pitcher when the Cardinals raked six Red Sox hurlers for 20 hits and a 12-3 victory at Fenway to even the Series at two games apiece. Joe Garagiola (right), Whitey Kurowski (second right) and Enos Slaughter (left) had four hits apiece, each tying the World Series record.

disappointed in The Kid's .200 (five singles including a bunt in 25 at-bats) than Williams himself, and he later went into the shower room and wept.

Ted would never play in another World Series game, even though he wore a Red Sox uniform 14 more seasons.

ENOS SLAUGHTER: "As I turned second, I saw Culberson bobble the ball—not much, but I could see he didn't have control of the ball. That gave me the first idea of scoring. Then he made sort of a slow throw to Pesky, and I said to myself, 'I can score.' I knew John certainly wouldn't be expecting it.

"So I really turned it on. I still don't know to this day if Gonzalez gave the stop sign or not. I didn't look at him. It wouldn't have made a lick of difference if he had. Sometimes you just make up your mind about something and lock everything else out. So I rounded third and kept going. I knew I *had* to score.

"Man, I don't think I ever ran that fast. All I kept seeing was that World Series ring on my hand. I didn't know where the ball was, but as long as I didn't see it in the catcher's mitt I knew I was all right. Then, as

The Red Sox regained the Series lead by winning the fifth game, buoyed by the four-hit pitching of Joe Dobson (left) and the home run by Leon Culberson (right), who are congratulated by Tom Yawkey.

The Red Sox 1946 American League champions.

I went into my slide, I saw their catcher take a couple of steps in front of the plate, and I just slid across easily.

"There were a lot of 'ifs' on that play. If Dom DiMaggio and his good arm had still been in the game I wouldn't have tried to score. If Pesky had been able to hear Doerr hollering over the roar of the crowd, he probably would have nailed me by ten feet. And I also had gotten permission from Eddie Dyer to run on my own if I thought I could score after Gonzalez had held me at third earlier in the Series to cost us a big run.

"So all those things went into it. I had never done that before in my career and I never did it again. But, man, I'll never forget that once."

JOHNNY PESKY: "They said I took a snooze. Well, I've looked at those films a hundred times, but can't see where I hesitated.

"I turned around to pick up Slaughter and he's 15-20 feet from the plate. I'd have needed a shotgun to get him."

JOE GARAGIOLA: "Pesky took the rap for it, but he never hesitated. You could almost say it was a dumb play that worked. The difference between dumb and smart is the word 'safe.' "

November 14, 1946

Ted Williams was voted the American League's Most Valuable Player today while teammate Bobby Doerr placed third. Both were keys to the Red Sox pennant drive last season—particularly Williams, who hit .342 with 38 homers and 123 RBIs to rank second in all three departments.

Williams polled nine of 24 first-place votes and totaled 224 points. Doerr collected 158. And 26-game winner Hal Newhouser of the Tigers was sandwiched between with 197.

Stan Musial of the World Champion Cardinals was named the National League's MVP.

June 13, 1947

An audience of 34,510 "first nighters" sat in on history tonight —Fenway Park's first night game.

Clearly dazzled, the crowd roared its approval when the arcs were switched on before the game which was won by the Red Sox, 5-3, as Dave Ferriss bested White Sox southpaw Frank Papish.

The Red Sox thus became the 14th of the 16 major league teams to have night baseball. Only Detroit's Briggs Stadium and Chicago's Wrigley Field are without lights.

Tom Yawkey has been an outspoken opponent of big-league baseball's use of artificial light ever since it was introduced by Larry McPhail at Cincinnati in 1935. However, Yawkey has bowed to fan interest and the trend among fellow owners.

The Red Sox have been playing under lights on the road since July 13, 1939, when they made their arc debut a winning one by scoring a 6-5 victory in ten innings at Cleveland.

Both Boston major league parks now have lights, the Braves installing them last season. Unlike the Braves, however, the Red Sox have not adopted shiny sateen uniforms for night home games, preferring to stick with their usual white flannels.

September 29, 1947

The Red Sox today coaxed Joe McCarthy out of retirement to be their manager, replacing Joe Cronin who becomes general manager in place of ailing Eddie Collins.

The 60-year-old McCarthy is the winningest manager in baseball history. He's won nine pennants and seven world championships during 20 full seasons—capturing one pennant with the Cubs before becoming a legend with the Yankees, guiding them to eight pennants and seven world titles before quitting because of ill health in May 1946. He has never managed a second-division team.

"Joe McCarthy's record proves he is not only the best manager in the league but the best in baseball," said Cronin, whose first act as GM was to sign McCarthy. McCarthy agreed to a two-year contract, and his salary is probably $50,000, which is what Cronin received as skipper.

"I'm starting all over again," McCarthy said. "I've got to make good again.

"I've been itching to get back into baseball. It took me a year to find out how much baseball was a part of me. I just couldn't forget it.

"I could have gone with other clubs, but the Red Sox are my choice."

It is believed McCarthy turned down an offer to manage the Sox a year ago after they won the pennant. He has been owner Tom Yawkey's choice to succeed Cronin for some time, one lantern-jawed Irishman replacing another.

It all depended on McCarthy's health and when Cronin wanted to move into the front office to succeed Collins. Eddie's failing health made the move imperative now, although he will remain as a vice president and adviser to Cronin.

The Red Sox coaxed Joe McCarthy out of retirement.

Cronin, about to turn 41, thus ends 13 years as Red Sox manager, the club's longest tenure. During that time he won one pennant, was second four times, third once, fourth three times, fifth once, sixth once and seventh twice as the franchise was rebuilt from doormat to one of baseball's best teams.

Although the Red Sox were a disappointing third this year, 14 games off the pace, McCarthy saw a simple explanation. He pointed to the sore arms suffered by three starting pitchers—Tex Hughson (three wins), Dave Ferriss (12 wins) and Mickey Harris (five wins). Thus the trio totaled only 20 victories, compared to 62 the previous season when the Sox won the pennant.

The big question is whether the no-nonsense McCarthy can make the tempestuous Ted Williams an even greater performer. Can two such strong-willed personalities get along? McCarthy brushed aside any suggestions of potential combustion there. Instead, he bubbled over with enthusiasm about coming to Boston.

"I'm going up with the real Irish now," he said. "Although I've had some battles in Boston, I've had fun with the fans there. They've been great to me and I hope I can produce for them."

What McCarthy produced was two thrilling but heartbreaking seasons in his two full years, losing both the '48 and '49 pennants in the final game. His 1950 team was 8½ games off the pace when McCarthy resigned in June; they finally finished four games off the top in third place despite losing Williams when he shattered an elbow in the All-Star Game.

The McCarthy-Williams fireworks predicted by some never developed. "Any manager who can't get along with a .400 hitter is crazy," McCarthy maintained from the start. He also made Williams feel comfortable from the first day of spring training. Although always a stickler for coats and neckties in public, the strict manager marched into the Red Sox's hotel dining room wearing a sports shirt—Ted's costume.

And after the funereal clubhouse had cleared after the Red Sox playoff loss to the Indians that first season, Williams heard McCarthy's voice from behind: "Well, we fooled 'em, didn't we? They said you and I couldn't get along, but we got along pretty damn good."

McCarthy's .614 winning percentage still stands as the No. 1 of all time among major league managers.

◇◇◇

TED WILLIAMS: "Joe McCarthy was something special. I loved Joe McCarthy.

"You certainly couldn't blame him for us not winning in '48 and '49. He got us to the brink, to the very last day, two years in a row. One victory would have meant the pennant both times. I think it proves how much he got out of the club.

"Joe McCarthy got more out of his players than anybody. He was the complete manager."

◇◇◇

JOHNNY PESKY: "Joe Cronin was a damn good manager, but Joe McCarthy was the best."

◇◇◇

TEX HUGHSON: "The only man in baseball I completely disliked was Joe McCarthy. I asked to be traded and said I wouldn't be back in 1950. So they sold me to the Giants, then in New York. I refused to report. I

Joe McCarthy greets Babe Ruth at Sarasota in March 1948, the Babe's last visit to Red Sox training camp. He died that August.

didn't want to live in New York, and I didn't want to start pitching in a new league at my age (34).

"So the Red Sox sent Jack Kramer to the Giants instead and I retired. The same day McCarthy quit in June 1950, Bobby Doerr called me in Texas while I was buying cattle and said they wanted me to go back.

" 'No, I'm retired for good,' I told him.

"Yes, I had arm problems my last three seasons. But I'm positive I could have pitched some more. I wouldn't when McCarthy was there, though, and when he was gone it was too late."

November 18, 1947

The Red Sox have swung their second trade in as many days with the St. Louis Browns and come away with a slugging shortstop and two front-line starters to patch their sore-armed pitching staff.

Coming to Boston in the double deal are right-handers Jack Kramer and Ellis Kinder, all-star shortstop Vern Stephens and veteran utility infielder Billy Hitchcock.

In exchange, the Red Sox sent $375,000 to the financially struggling Browns along with a parade of varsity reserves and minor leaguers: infielders Eddie Pellagrini, Sam Dente and Bill Sommers; outfielder Pete Layden; catchers Roy Partee and Don Palmer; pitchers Jim Wilson, Clem Dreisewerd, Al Widmar and Joe Ostrowski.

Kramer and Kinder will bolster the mound corps that suddenly went sour last season when Tex Hughson, Dave Ferriss and Mickey Harris all developed sore arms. And Stephens has right-hand power custom-made for Fenway Park.

The only question is the identity of the Sox shortstop next season —Stephens or incumbent Johnny Pesky, averaging .330 in his three big league seasons. New manager Joe McCarthy says he will experiment in spring training and shift one to third base.

Pesky was moved to third and Stephens stayed at shortstop, becoming a slugging fool—particularly at Fenway. Featuring a wide foot-in-bucket stance, he averaged 33 homers the next three seasons—and must have hooked twice that many barely foul, so many that he was dubbed Wrongway Stephens.

Kramer was 18-5 the next season, then faded from sight. Kinder became a legend—on and off the field. During his eight memorable seasons in Boston, Kinder was first a brilliant starter (23-6 in '49) then a rubber-armed reliever (a league-leading 27 saves in '53 at age 39).

Hitchcock was a valuable utility man, probably best recalled for (1) brawling with Braves first baseman Earl Torgeson during a City Series game in 1948, and (2) stealing home to beat the Senators during the 1949 stretch run.

November 27, 1947

Amid a storm of controversy, Joe DiMaggio was named the American League's Most Valuable Player today by a single point over Ted Williams.

The Yankee Clipper received 202 points (including eight first-place votes) to the Red Sox star's 201 (including three first-place votes). One of the writers voting didn't list Williams among any of his ten choices. Even a tenth-place vote, worth two points, would have been enough to make Ted the award winner.

Williams won the Triple Crown by batting .343 with 32 homers and 114 RBIs batted in for the third-place Red Sox. DiMaggio hit .315 with 20 homers and 97 RBIs for the World Champion Yankees.

Ted Williams wasn't smiling when a Boston sports writer cost him the 1947 American League MVP Award by one point.

Interestingly, while snubbed for the American League MVP honor, Williams was selected Major League *Player of the Year by the* Sporting News.

TED WILLIAMS: "The writer's name was Mel Webb. He was a grouchy old guy, a real grump, and we didn't get along. We'd had a big argument early in the year over something he had written, and I said, 'That's a lot of crap you're writing about me,' and he got offended as hell.

"I didn't realize until much later that he hadn't even put me on his ballot. The commissioner should have gotten in on that. The Most Valuable Player award shouldn't depend on being buddy-buddy with a sports writer."

April 28, 1948

The Red Sox and Braves reached agreement today with Boston's two soon-to-be-born TV stations to televise an unspecified number of home games this season. The teams will receive no payment for the rights in a mutual effort to stimulate development of television in the area.

The baseball telecasts will begin as soon as the licensees, WBZ-TV (Channel 4) and WNAC-TV (Channel 7), go on the air some time in June. The two outlets will share the baseball telecasts 50-50.

Radio station WHDH, which broadcasts both teams' games, has waived TV rights pending their application for a TV license. It is expected the telecasts will be sponsored by the present radio advertisers, the Narragansett Brewing Company and the Atlantic Refining Company.

It also is expected that the games will be announced by the current broadcasting team of Jim Britt and Tom Hussey. The pair would shuttle between the radio and TV booths, and probably would be joined for commentary at certain times by former Yankee pitcher Bump Hadley. Britt and Hussey announce all Red Sox and Braves home games since road games generally aren't broadcast—only by telegraphic re-creation via tickertape when the team back in Boston is idle.

TV sets within a 40-mile radius of Boston should be able to pick up the telecasts, although few homes are equipped yet with the expensive sets.

Leading the cheers for today's approval are the owners of cocktail lounges and taverns. Large numbers of baseball fans are expected to be lured there by the phenomenon.

Proprietors do have a few concerns, however.

"We'll have to make sure people don't come in and die on a single glass of beer," one observed. Another confided: "We'll just shut off the draught beer—just bottles when the games are on. In New York they reserve the bar for whisky drinkers while baseball is on. But this isn't New York. Besides, I think baseball fans are more beer drinkers."

A few owners expressed concern that their bartenders and barmaids might get too wrapped up in the game and forget their mission.

Boston's first baseball telecast came on June 15, a few days after TV made its debut in Greater Boston, as the pennant-bound Braves defeated the Cubs, 6-3. Johnny Sain out-pitched Russ Meyer to give the Braves a one-game lead in the National League.

The first Fenway Park telecast came the following week, when the Red Sox returned from the road.

It was a landmark in the often-lively broadcasting history of the Red Sox. Tom Yawkey invigorated it in the mid-thirties when he hired Fred Hoey to announce the games on radio. Hoey led off a parade of memora-

Joe DiMaggio talks with Jim Britt (right), longtime Voice of the Red Sox who, along with Tom Hussey and Bump Hadley, announced Fenway Park's first telecast in 1948.

Curt Gowdy blossomed as a broadcaster when he succeeded Jim Britt as Voice of the Red Sox in 1951.

ble *Red Sox Voices over the years—a galaxy including Britt, Curt Gowdy, Ned Martin and Ken Coleman.*

Now, 30 years after giving away their product free on television, the Red Sox reap close to $2,500,000 for TV rights. Coupled with $550,000 for radio, their nearly $3,000,000 per-season local package is the second best in baseball behind the Yankees. And that doesn't include the $1,800,000 for network rights that every team receives. Thus the Red Sox harvest close to $5,000,000 in all from radio and TV—a long way from that free first telecast in 1948.

October 4, 1948

Shortstop-manager Lou Boudreau thumped two homers and two singles while rookie knuckleballer Gene Bearden pitched a five-hitter today as the Indians blew out the Red Sox, 8-3, in a one-game, winner-take-all playoff for the pennant.

Red Sox manager Joe McCarthy shocked the crowd of 33,957 that jammed Fenway Park by ignoring his rotation pitchers: Jack Kramer (18-5), Joe Dobson (16-10), Mel Parnell (15-8) and Ellis Kinder (10-7). Instead, he chose Denny Galehouse (8-7), a journeyman in the twilight of a mediocre career.

The Indians promptly jumped on the veteran right-hander while coasting to victory in the American League's first playoff ever, forced yesterday when the Sox defeated the Yankees while the Indians lost to the Tigers. The Yankees had been part of the dramatic three-team pennant chase until eliminated in Boston in the next-to-last game of the schedule.

The Indians and Red Sox swapped runs in the first inning, the visitors scoring on Boudreau's first homer, the Sox on Johnny Pesky's double and Vern Stephens's single.

But Cleveland sewed up the game in the fourth with a four-run explosion highlighted by Ken Keltner's three-run homer. Each team added two more runs apiece thereafter—Boston on Bobby Doerr's homer with Ted Williams aboard in the sixth. But the Sox couldn't muster any more off the stingy Bearden, a southpaw defying the left-field wall.

Thus the Red Sox's uphill comeback from a frightful start (14-23 at Memorial Day, 11½ games out) fell just short of its goal. And the loss spoiled New Englanders' dreams of Boston's first Subway Series against the city-rival Braves, who will host the World Series opener after winning their first National League pennant since 1914.

The playoff marked a milestone for many of its principals.

It crowned the best season for Boudreau, whose Indians went on to defeat the Braves for the World Championship in six games. He was chosen American League MVP after hitting .355, second only to Williams's .369, as Ted became just the third player to win four or more A.L. batting crowns.

It was the 20th victory (against seven losses with a league-leading 2.43 ERA) for Bearden, a 28-year-old freshman still limping with war wounds that left him wearing aluminum plates in his head and left leg. (He had been presumed dead while floating ten days in the Pacific after his battleship was torpedoed.) He would never again win more than eight games in a season.

It amounted to Galehouse's farewell. He would pitch only two more innings in the majors.

It also triggered a story by incendiary Boston columnist Dave "The Colonel" Egan that persists more than 30 years later—suggesting that McCarthy chose Galehouse out of desperation because none of the Red Sox regular starters would volunteer.

Denny Galehouse was a surprise selection as the Red Sox starting pitcher—a gamble by Joe McCarthy that didn't work.

MEL PARNELL: "That story that none of us wanted the ball is pure fiction, a terrible lie. Each of us would have given anything to pitch that game. Besides the honor of it, it would have meant a lot of money —probably between $5,000 and $10,000—in next year's contract to the guy who beat the Indians to win the pennant.

"So all of us wanted the ball. I had only one day's rest after beating the Yankees on Saturday, but was dying to pitch again. I was in bed by 9 o'clock the night before and ready to go.

"I felt McCarthy probably would pick Kramer, though. I never dreamed Galehouse. Neither did Denny. He was dumbfounded. He was shagging flies in the outfield during batting practice when McCarthy sent a clubhouse man for him. When Joe told him, Denny went white as a ghost. He took a short rest on the rubbing table and then went out to warm up.

"When Boudreau looked out of the Cleveland dugout and saw Galehouse, he thought McCarthy was trying to pull a fast one. Lou told me later he thought we had someone else warming up beneath the stands. He simply couldn't believe McCarthy would pick Galehouse.

"I don't know why he did. Maybe it was because Denny had pitched eight innings of two-hit relief against the Indians about a month earlier. But with everything riding on one game, it didn't make a lot of sense.

"All I know for certain is what McCarthy told me. During batting practice, the four rotation pitchers were waiting in the clubhouse for McCarthy's decision. Joe came out of his office, came up from behind me and put a hand on my shoulder. 'Sorry, kid,' he said. 'It's not a day for left-handers. The wind is blowing out to left. So I'm going with a right-hander.

"Still, the Indians used a left-hander, Gene Bearden. He also had only one day's rest. And he didn't have any trouble getting people out that day."

LOU BOUDREAU: "I'd have to put that playoff game at the top of my list of thrills because of the game's importance, to say nothing of the impact on my entire career.

"There was extraordinary emotional background for me. For me it was make or break.

"I had convinced myself long before that Bill Veeck, then the Indians president and by no means the country's greatest admirer of my managerial moves, would trade me or buy up my contract if I failed to produce the pennant. I believed that every move I made was a life-or-death move so far as my future with the Indians was concerned.

"Many times I have planned just as carefully and thought just as hard as I planned and thought that day, only to have my strategy look silly. But that day everything worked.

"Starting a freshman southpaw was a gamble, particularly in Fenway Park. But Gene Bearden didn't let me down.

"We went into the fourth inning tied, 1-1, and I led off with a single. Joe Gordon also singled, moving me to second. With Ken Keltner at bat I was tempted to order the orthodox sacrifice bunt. But at that stage of the game I decided to play for the big inning.

"Seldom in baseball history has a manager's judgment been so quickly or spectacularly justified. Keltner hit the ball far over the left-field fence for a 4-1 lead, and for all practical purposes, the pennant race was over."

Lou Boudreau later wore a Red Sox uniform, first as a pinch hitter and handyman, then as manager.

June 30, 1949

A biplane circled packed Fenway Park before today's game trailing a banner: *The Great DiMaggio!*

And limping Joe DiMaggio promptly lived up to it, climaxing the most dramatic series of his career by walloping his fourth home run in three days to fire the Yankees to a 6-3 victory and a three-game sweep of the Red Sox.

DiMaggio's three-run homer on a 3-2 pitch from Mel Parnell in the eighth inning was Joltin' Joe's most mammoth of the series—a soaring shot high off the light tower in left, about 80 feet above the field.

It was DiMag's third straight game-winning homer and gave him these statistics for the series: nine RBIs (nearly half the Yanks' 20-run total), five runs scored and four homers and a single for a .455 batting average.

Not bad for a guy in obvious pain playing in his first series of the season after being sidelined the first 65 games because of heel spur surgery.

"This is the greatest series of my career," the gaunt and exhausted 34-year-old said as he slipped the special heel-cushioned spike off his right foot. Asked how he could muster such an output after just eight workouts, DiMaggio shrugged: "You swing the bat and hit the ball."

And that's exactly what he did throughout the series. He won the opener, 5-4, with a two-run homer off Maury McDermott. He homered off both Ellis Kinder and Earl Johnson for last night's 9-7 win. And then came today's blast with Snuffy Stirnweiss and Tommy Henrich aboard for the deciding runs.

The sweep cools off the Red Sox, dropping them 8½ games behind the Yankees, who had been sagging before DiMaggio revitalized them with a storybook comeback that left even Fenway patrons roaring with respect.

August 9, 1949

Joe DiMaggio helped end brother Dom's batting streak at 34 tonight as the Red Sox defeated the Yankees, 6-3, at Fenway Park.

Joe grabbed a sinking liner off his shoetops in center field to rob Dom on his fifth and final bid in the eighth inning. The capacity crowd of 34,691 groaned, then gave both DiMaggios a long standing ovation.

Joe as much as called the shot before the game.

"I hope Dom does it—and with luck he could," he'd said. "But it'll be very tough. And don't think I'm going to let any ball drop in front of me for him."

Joe didn't.

The streak Dom was aiming at, of course, is Joe's 56-gamer set in 1941. While well short of that mark, Dom has set a Red Sox record, topping teammate Johnny Pesky's 26 of two years ago.

"I'm glad it's over," said Dom, who is batting .338, fourth best in the

The Red Sox finally found a way to stop—temporarily—Joe DiMaggio's historic homer binge at Boston in 1949. He got only one base here when hit by a Mel Parnell pitch that never reached catcher Birdie Tebbetts. But seven innings later, DiMaggio slammed a three-run homer off Parnell, his third game-winner in as many days at Fenway.

league and just eight points behind leader Ted Williams's .346. "There's a certain pressure in a batting streak that's distracting."

Vic Raschi was the pitcher who finally stopped DiMaggio. Coincidentally, Raschi had been the last pitcher to shut off Dom before his streak. In the 34 games between, Dom batted .357 and had 15 extra-base hits.

While DiMaggio went cold on a very hot night (temperatures reached a record 99 today), mates Birdie Tebbetts and Williams didn't. Each hit a two-run homer to power Ellis Kinder's 13th victory, offsetting two homers by Hank Bauer.

The surging Sox now have won 26 of their last 34 games to move within 5½ games of the Yankees—less than half Boston's 12½-game deficit on July Fourth.

DiMaggio's 34 is still the Red Sox record. Only three Sox hitters in the last 20 years have managed streaks of 20 or more games. Denny Doyle reached 22 in 1975, Fred Lynn 20 the same season and Ed Bressoud 20 in 1964.

September 25, 1949

The 160-day chase is over. After 148 games, the Red Sox have caught the Yankees for a first-place tie. And now it's down to a one-week season. All that came about today when the Red Sox concluded their home schedule with a 4-1 triumph over the Yankees for a two-game series sweep.

It was the McCarthymen's 21st straight victory at Fenway, where they were 61-16 for the season. Overall, home and away, the Hose have won 58 of their last 77 games to erase the 12½-game deficit of July Fourth, when their record was 35-36.

Yesterday, Ellis Kinder (15-1 at Fenway) pitched a six-hitter for his 22d victory and Ted Williams rifled his 42d homer to beat the Yankees and Ed Lopat, 2-0. Today the heroes were Mel Parnell (25th win, 16-3 at Fenway) and Williams (43d homer) in the 4-1 vanquishing of the Yankees and Allie Reynolds.

There was no Joe DiMaggio to save the Yankees this time, the Clipper confined to a New York hospital with pneumonia, not polio as whispered.

"We still think we're gonna win the pennant, we ain't quittin' now," an uncharacteristically grim Casey Stengel said before excusing himself and rushing for the Yankees train to New York, where the rivals collide again tomorrow.

Mrs. Babe Ruth was among the mob greeting the Yankees at Grand Central and told reporters: "Whoever wins tomorrow should go all the way."

The next day she was one of the 67,434 at Yankee Stadium watching the Red Sox win a 7-6 thriller as Bobby Doerr's squeeze bunt in the eighth capped a four-run comeback. The Sox moved on to Washington for a three-game series before returning to New York for the final weekend—their one-game lead intact.

They were on the threshold. A victory in either the Saturday or Sunday game at the Stadium would give them the pennant.

Claire Ruth would prove a poor forecaster.

October 2, 1949

Red Sox pennant hopes disintegrated on the season's last day for the second year in a row today.

The Sox lost the flag to the Yankees after suffering two weekend losses at New York, 5-4 yesterday and 5-3 today, to thrill the nearly 70,000 squeezed into Yankee Stadium each day. A victory in either game would have given Boston the pennant.

The Red Sox entrained for New York with high hopes—Bobby Doerr (above), Ellis Kinder and Birdie Tebbetts (below).

Although the elbow ballooned, no one had a hint of the injury's severity until Williams flew home this morning and went to Fenway so trusted trainer Jack Fadden could examine it. Fadden rushed him to a hospital for X-rays.

Williams, who signed what may be baseball's first guaranteed $100,000 contract this year, was off to perhaps his best season with 60 RBIs and 25 home runs. Yet Ted's career may now be over a month short of his thirty-second birthday.

It wasn't. The radius was saved in surgery, and Williams played another ten seasons and led the league in hitting four more times, twice officially, twice unofficially. Yet Ted labels the injury "the biggest disappointment of my career," and says he was never the same hitter again.

Fadden, the man Williams credits with rehabilitating the elbow, is now the Mr. Chips of Harvard sports medicine and recalls:

"There were seven distinct fractures in Ted's elbow, a disaster. There was a serious question he'd ever be able to swing a bat normally again. The most you could hope for was 80, maybe 85 percent normal freedom.

"That wasn't good enough for Ted. His dedication to therapy, his application, was amazing. Home or away. Morning, noon and night. He'd even exercise in the dugout between innings. And it paid.

"Williams attacked his later injuries with the same perseverance—the broken collarbone, the fractured ankle, the pinched neck nerve.

"The man was truly remarkable in every way, one of a kind. He had the greatest approach to his job of anyone I've ever seen—total dedication."

August 28, 1950

The Red Sox forged their greatest modern comeback today by overcoming 10-0 and 12-1 deficits to outlast the Indians, 15-14, at Fenway Park. In the process, the rampaging Sox chased Bob Lemon and defeated Bob Feller in his only relief appearance of the season.

Lemon, the American League's winningest pitcher, was breezing with the 12-1 lead in the fourth inning when the Red Sox rallied for eight runs to climb back into the game. The Sox won it with four runs in the eighth off Feller as Walt Dropo (triple) and Al Zarilla (homer) provided the key blows to give Willard Nixon (6-2) the victory in relief.

It was the Red Sox's second king-sized rally in as many days. Yesterday, Feller blew a 7-0 lead during Boston's 11-9 victory.

October 1, 1950

Versatile Billy Dale Goodman became the first "non-regular" ever to win a major league batting crown when he clinched the American League title today.

The Red Sox's skinny handyman led the majors with a fat .354 average while playing 110 games, never having a position to call his own, spending 45 games in the outfield and splitting the remainder of his time among every infield position.

Besides topping National League leader Stan Musial's .346, the line-drive-hitting Goodman bested A.L. runner-up George Kell of the Tigers by 14 points, while Sox teammate Dom DiMaggio was third at .328.

DiMaggio led the league in runs scored (131), stolen bases (15) and tied for most triples (11) with teammate Bobby Doerr and Detroit's Hoot Evers. DiMag also was third in hits with 193.

Red Sox rookie Walt Dropo also was among statistical leaders despite a serious beaning by Hank Wyse of the A's. The 6-5, 220-pound first baseman tied teammate Vern Stephens for the RBI crown with 144 each. Dropo led in total bases with 326, edging Stephens who had five

Ted Williams and Billy Goodman both won batting crowns.

fewer. Dropo was second in homers with 34, Stephens fourth with 30. And Dropo was second in slugging percentage, two points behind the Yankees' Joe DiMaggio.

Dropo's performance is expected to earn the 27-year-old Moosup, Connecticut, native the A.L. Rookie of the Year Award.

It did.

May 23, 1951

Johnny Pesky rates an assist on the assist record set today by Red Sox teammate Vern "Junior" Stephens.

Stephens had ten assists—the most ever by an American League third baseman—as the Sox defeated the Browns at Fenway Park.

Playing shortstop, Pesky made the record possible on the last out of the game when he scooped up a grounder and flipped the ball to Stephens, who fired it to first base for the out—and the record tenth assist.

Coincidentally, Pesky and Stephens swapped positions this season after three years of playing side by side with Stephens at shortstop and Pesky at third base.

Frank Malzone equaled Stephens's ten assists on September 24, 1957, at Washington. They shared the record for American League third basemen until it was broken in 1966 by Ken McMullen of the Senators.

July 28, 1951

Dutch the Clutch has done it again!

Clyde Vollmer added another chapter to his incredible hitting saga today when he ripped a bases-full homer in the 16th inning to give the Red Sox an 8-4 victory over the Indians at Fenway Park.

The dramatic grand-slam came off Bob Feller, summoned for a rare relief appearance by manager Al Lopez in an attempt to cool off Vollmer. Clyde had tied the game with a clutch single the previous inning as the 29-year-old slugger's heroics continue.

The quiet one-man gang now has 13 homers (including two with bases filled) in 24 games since being put in the lineup July 4, clubbing one key hit after another (30 in all) in the hottest hitting month in Red Sox history.

The 6-1, 185-pound right-handed hitter looks the part of a slugger but had only 23 career homers in six previous seasons. The journeyman outfielder was obtained from Washington a year ago for pinch-hitting and reserve duty.

Overnight, Vollmer has become a household name throughout New England as he's won one game after another in a devastating spree that's keyed the Sox surge to first place.

It was Vollmer who sparked the Red Sox to a three-game sweep of the Yankees earlier this month—tripling off Ed Lopat in the opener, hitting a bases-loaded homer off Allie Reynolds in the second game and homering off Vic Raschi in the third game. The blitz vaulted the Sox into third place ahead of New York, one game behind Chicago.

Two days ago against the White Sox, he hit three homers in one game, the last one breaking a 10-10 tie for a 13-10 triumph.

The question is how long Circuit Clyde's splurge can continue.

Not long. The Mighty Vollmer was dramatically struck out by Mike Garcia in the last of the ninth the following day, and Clyde's Month That Was was essentially over—although he did add a double on July's final day.

Red Sox infield of the early fifties (left to right): Bobby Doerr, Vern Stephens, Johnny Pesky and Walt Dropo.

Clyde Vollmer became a household name overnight in New England.

Capt. Ted Williams meets Korean elder in a village near Marine air base.

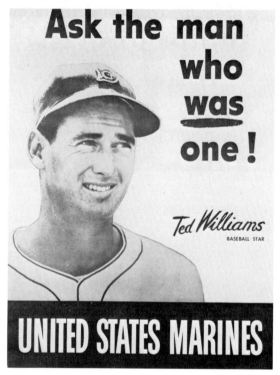

Ask the man who was one!

Ted Williams
BASEBALL STAR

UNITED STATES MARINES

Ted Williams was a Marine pilot in both World War II and Korea—and the Marines promoted it in this poster.

Below, old foe Lou Boudreau became Red Sox manager in 1952, signing aboard with general manager Joe Cronin. Boudreau promptly introduced a youth movement which included an early-season infield (left to right) of first baseman Dick Gernert, second baseman Ted Lepcio, shortstop Jimmy Piersall and third baseman Fred Hatfield. The unit didn't last long.

Ted returned late the following season after flying 39 missions, including one that nearly cost him his life when his jet was hit over North Korea. He guided his crippled jet back, radioless and streaming 30 feet of fire, and made a spectacular crash landing without wheels or brakes.

Williams would hit 197 more home runs, including one as a pinch hitter in his first at-bat back at Fenway . . . and, most dramatic of all, another on the final swing of his career in 1960.

TED WILLIAMS: "Counting injuries and service hitches, I lost six full seasons. The cost in dollars and cents is not as sad as the realization that it cost me one-fourth of my playing career."

May 24, 1952

Red Sox rookie Jimmy Piersall became embroiled in two fistfights today at Fenway Park, brawling first with Yankee second baseman Billy Martin before tangling with Sox pitcher Maury McDermott.

Piersall and Martin began swapping insults during infield practice, then moved under the stands to have it out in the tunnel connecting the Red Sox dugout and clubhouse. After exchanging a number of punches, it took three men to pry the pair apart: Yankee coach Bill Dickey, Red Sox coach Oscar Melillo and Ellis Kinder, Boston's starting pitcher.

When Piersall went to the clubhouse to cool off and change his torn and bloodied shirt, he and McDermott exchanged words, then punches. Manager Lou Boudreau then decided to sit Piersall out for the game.

The incident was just one of several involving Piersall, and he would be admitted to a mental institution by mid-July. But he'd return from his breakdown the next spring to star as a brilliant outfielder for the Red Sox for six seasons, playing 17 years in the majors in all.

June 3, 1952

The Red Sox and Tigers today pulled off one of baseball's biggest trades in recent years, a nine-player swap.

The Sox sent shortstop Johnny Pesky, first baseman Walt Dropo, outfielder Don Lenhardt, third baseman Fred Hatfield and pitcher Bill Wight to Detroit for third baseman George Kell, outfielder Hoot Evers, pitcher Dizzy Trout and shortstop Johnny Lipon.

The deal was nearly killed by the Red Sox yesterday after Lenhardt hit a tenth-inning grand-slam homer in what proved his final at-bat in a Boston uniform.

The trade helped cost Red Rolfe his job as Tiger manager. Asked if Rolfe had made a good deal with the Red Sox, Tiger owner Spike Briggs snapped: "It better be." A month later, with the Tigers headed for their first last-place finish ever, Rolfe was gone as manager.

o

And, oh yes, Lenhardt would wear a Red Sox uniform again—twice. He returned in 1954 to finish his career in Boston that season, returned a second time as a coach under Eddie Kasko in the early 1970s, and remains in the Sox family as a scout.

June 11, 1952

Two colorful rookies stole the show tonight during a zany six-run rally in the ninth inning that promoted the Red Sox to a tingling 11-9 triumph over Satchel Paige and the Browns.

Sammy White climaxed one of the noisiest innings ever heard at Fenway when he walloped a grand-slam homer—celebrating his game-winning blast by crawling the final 15 feet and kissing the plate.

It capped a daffy and often hilarious windup that left the crowd dizzy—the 14,524 fans limp from laughing and cheering almost nonstop throughout the ten-minute rally sparked by the other hero of the hour, Jimmy Piersall.

Piersall led off the inning and, as he waited for Paige to complete his warm-ups, yelled out to the mound: "Satchmo, I'm going to bunt on you. And then watch out!"

The ageless (45?) right-hander grinned with a confidence that comes with a 9-5 lead and a string of 26⅓ scoreless relief innings in a row, including the previous two frames last night.

True to his word, Piersall bunted the second pitch down the first-base line and beat it out as Paige was too late covering.

The 22-year-old Waterbury, Connecticut, product then went into Act I of his one-man clowning show. As Paige prepared to pitch to Hoot Evers, Piersall started imitating Satch's every move, then began flapping his arms like a trained seal while cupping his hands and shouting, "Oink, oink, oink!"

Piersall advanced to second on Evers's infield hit and promptly began Act II. Jimmy continued mirroring Paige's loose and lazy windup, then began jumping and whistling. Now Paige was clearly annoyed, the crowd clearly delighted as it roared its approval.

Piersall, who opened the season at shortstop in manager Lou Boudreau's youth movement but recently was shifted back to the outfield, is becoming one of the Red Sox's biggest crowd-pleasers ever.

When the distracted Paige walked George Kell, Piersall almost went berserk and danced to third base for Act III. "Oink, oink, oink," he taunted Paige, flapping his arms wildly. "You sure look funny on that mound. Oink, oink, oink!"

After Vern Stephens popped out, Paige walked Billy Goodman to force home the prancing Piersall. Another run soon scored on a clutch single by another rookie, Ted Lepcio. That left the bases filled for White, who quickly unloaded them by hooking a high drive just inches fair inside the neon foul pole in left to end the three-hour-plus marathon.

The Red Sox were still in stitches in their locker room afterward, and whenever it showed any sign of settling down, an "oink, oink, oink" would be heard from Piersall to break up everyone again.

"I've never seen a show like tonight's anywhere," said the veteran Kell, "not even in a circus."

The Browns didn't think it funny.

At first Paige wouldn't acknowledge Piersall's name. "I don't know who you're talking about, man," he said, his head in his hands. Then he finally allowed: "I didn't see any of that stuff yesterday while I was giving the Red Sox hell."

Catcher Clint Courtney, who was consoling his battery mate, was more outspoken. "Want to know something?" he said. "I believe that

The blockbuster trade with the Tigers made Red Soxers out of (left to right) Johnny Lipon, Dizzy Trout, Hoot Evers and George Kell.

Jimmy Piersall (left) and Sammy White stole the show in a six-run ninth-inning explosion that beat Satchel Paige and had Fenway fans in an uproar throughout much of the ten-minute rally.

man is plumb crazy. Yuh, he's nuts altogether. I never saw any man do those things anywhere. Is he crazy, really? Tell me, because I'll always think so unless somebody can prove otherwise."

Piersall shrugged off the Browns' remarks. "I don't care what anybody thinks about what I was doing," the right fielder said. "We won the game, right?

"Oink, oink, oink."

Piersall entered a sanitarium the following month.

To this day he has no recollection of orchestrating one of the most memorable and hilarious innings in Fenway history.

June 15, 1952

The Red Sox today signed a top catching prospect, former University of Florida quarterback Haywood Sullivan. The 21-year-old Alabaman was signed by scout Neil Mahoney for a bonus package estimated between $75,000 and $98,000 as the Sox outbid the Yankees, among other teams.

The Yankees had brought the 6-foot-4, 210-pounder to a special training camp this spring to work out under the eye of Yankee coach Bill Dickey, the former catching great.

"I think he'll make a great catcher," manager Casey Stengel said afterward. "Dickey says he's the best catching prospect he's ever seen."

Plagued by an aching back that eventually required disc surgery in 1958, Sullivan never fulfilled expectations. He played only 60 games over portions of four seasons for the Red Sox before being dealt in 1961 to Kansas City, where he was in 252 games for the A's before retiring in 1963 to manage in the minors.

By 1965, he had managed the A's for a season before leaving to rejoin the Red Sox as vice president in charge of player personnel.

Among other distinctions, Sullivan is the only person to hit .150 for the Red Sox and go on to co-own the team.

June 10, 1953

Jimmy Piersall beat out three infield hits while batting a perfect six for six, a double and five singles, as the Red Sox routed the Browns, 11-2, in the opener of a doubleheader tonight in St. Louis.

Satchel Paige knocked Piersall down in the second game as the outfielder went hitless in five trips during the Sox's 3-2 victory.

Piersall's six-for-six performance ties the American League record for most consecutive hits in a regulation game and also sets the Red Sox mark in that department.

Those two distinctions still stand more than 25 years later.

June 18, 1953

The Red Sox today set a modern major league record for most runs in an inning—17—during a 23-3 slaughter of the Tigers at Fenway Park. Following yesterday's 17-1 drubbing, it gave the Sox back-to-back routs of Detroit, outscoring the hapless Tigers, 40-4.

Adding machines were called for in the press box during the seventh inning when the Red Sox sent 23 batters to the plate against three Detroit pitchers: Steve Gromek, Dick Weik and Earl Harris.

Twenty of the 23 batters reached base, 14 by hits, six by walks. Dick Gernert and Gene Stephens drum-majored the pounding—Gernert with four RBIs, Stephens with three hits.

Catcher Haywood Sullivan went on to be a Red Sox co-owner.

How the runs scored:

Sammy White singled to right. Stephens singled to right, sending White to third. Stephens stole second. Tom Umphlett singled to left, scoring White and Stephens with runs 1 and 2. Johnny Lipon struck out.

George Kell doubled off the left-field wall, Umphlett stopping at third. Billy Goodman walked to fill the bases. Jimmy Piersall singled to right, scoring Umphlett and Kell with runs 3 and 4. Gernert homered over the left-field fence, scoring behind Goodman and Piersall for runs 5, 6 and 7. Ellis Kinder singled to right. White walked.

Detroit manager Fred Hutchinson summoned Weik to replace Gromek. Weik wild-pitched past catcher Matt Batts, advancing Kinder to third and White to second. Stephens doubled to right, scoring Kinder and White with runs 8 and 9. Umphlett walked. Lipon singled to left, scoring Stephens with run 10.

Kell lined out to right. Goodman singled to center, scoring Umphlett with run 11. Ted Lepcio ran for Goodman.

Harrist replaced Weik on the mound for Detroit.

Al Zarilla batted for Piersall and walked, loading the bases. Gernert walked, forcing home Lipon with run 12. Kinder singled to center, scoring Lepcio and Zarilla with runs 13 and 14. White singled to center, scoring Gernert with run 15. Stephens singled to right, scoring Kinder with run 16. Umphlett singled to center, scoring White with run 17. Lipon walked, loading the bases.

Kell flied to right, mercifully ending the inning.

That 17-run record still stands as the modern major league record, two more runs than the Dodgers scored against the Reds in a 1952 inning for the National League mark.

December 1, 1953

The Red Sox today obtained hard-hitting outfielder Jackie Jensen from the Washington Senators for southpaw Maury McDermott and outfielder Tom Umphlett.

Acquisition of the former University of California All-America Golden Boy and onetime bonus boy for the Yankees is expected to give the Red Sox one of baseball's best one-two punches. They'll have back-to-back sluggers from both sides of the plate, the right-hand-hitting Jensen likely batting cleanup behind the lefty-swinging Ted Williams.

The trio of Jensen, Williams and Jimmy Piersall also gives the Sox one of the best two-way outfields in the majors—and one of the most sensitive and high-strung ever.

"Jensen will be right at home at Fenway," enthused owner Tom Yawkey. "The left-field wall is tailor-made for him."

"Jackie will tattoo the wall," predicted Senators manager Bucky Harris, who has seen Jensen's 400-foot drives to left and center fields at Washington's spacious Griffith Stadium wasted as simply long outs. "Fenway will help make him a great star."

Coincidentally, Jensen's first game in the majors was at Fenway— Opening Day 1950, when he pinch-ran for Johnny Mize during a nine-run Yankee rally that erased a 9-0 Red Sox lead.

"I've wanted to play for the Red Sox since I've been in the majors," said the delighted Jensen.

March 1, 1954

Ted Williams broke his collarbone today within minutes of taking the field to start spring training at Sarasota. Cloaked in a blanket, the Red Sox superstar was rushed from Payne Field to the hospital by trainer Jack Fadden for X-rays which confirmed the break.

Jackie Jensen (right) was welcomed to the Red Sox by Billy Goodman.

Ted Williams is assisted from the Red Sox locker room by clubhousemen Don Fitzpatrick (left) and Johnny Orlando (right) en route to a Sarasota hospital where X-rays revealed a broken collarbone.

Tom Brewer (center), posing with Ted Lepcio (left) and Jimmy Piersall, was one of the Red Sox's better pitchers in the fifties.

"It's a severe blow," manager Lou Boudreau told newsmen after visiting Ted.

Doctors project the 35-year-old Williams won't be able to swing a bat for at least six weeks and will be out of the lineup until sometime in May.

Williams returned May 16 with a bang. In a doubleheader at Detroit, he went eight for nine—including two home runs—while driving in seven runs, adding another chapter to his legend.

TED WILLIAMS: "I wasn't out there 60 seconds when it happened. I had driven up (to Sarasota) from the Florida Keys that morning, a four-hour drive, and was in uniform and on the field at ten. The Red Sox were taking batting practice.

"I trotted out to where Jimmy Piersall was shagging in the field and said, 'Let's try to get together in the outfield this year, Bush, and maybe do something right,' and I had just turned around to face the infield when Hoot Evers hit a ball in my direction.

"I started for it. It was sinking fast, I speeded up, and when I realized I couldn't get it and tried to slow down, I began to stumble, then I fell. I heard the pop. Piersall came running to me. 'I broke it,' I said. 'I'm sure something's broken.'

"It was put together with a stainless steel pin about four inches long and big around as a pencil. It's still in there. You can feel it through the skin."

August 16, 1954

Jimmy Piersall hurt his rifle right arm in a throwing contest with Willie Mays tonight before a Red Sox-Giants charity game at jammed Fenway Park.

The highly publicized throwing matchup, which helped attract a record 37,710, pitted two of the best arms among major league outfielders.

On one of his five throws from right field to catcher Mickey Owen, Piersall felt a sharp twinge in his back below his right shoulder. Mays, incidentally, was declared winner of the contest.

The game followed, played in a light drizzle, with Piersall starting in right field for the Sox, but he was forced out early when he felt a sharp pain while making a routine throw.

The next morning Piersall awoke with a king-sized sore arm which plagued him the remainder of the year. He played 13 more seasons in the majors but there is a serious question whether he ever threw as well again. Still, Piersall ranks among the best defensive outfielders in Red Sox history.

June 27, 1955

The sports world was stunned today by the death of Red Sox first baseman Harry Agganis, one of the greatest athletes ever produced in New England. Barely 26, Agganis died of a "massive pulmonary embolism"—a large blood clot—at Sancta Maria Hospital, Cambridge.

Agganis was the American dream come true. The son of poor immigrant parents, he rose from the Lynn sandlots to the heights of stardom as an All-America quarterback and major league .300 hitter.

The Boston University superstar—No. 33, the "Golden Greek"—was a No. 1 draft choice of the powerhouse Cleveland Browns while still a junior. Browns boss Paul Brown frankly labeled him "the quarterback who will succeed Otto Graham."

Agganis reportedly spurned a $50,000 offer from the Browns to sign for an estimated $10,000-$15,000 less with the Red Sox, thus staying at Fenway Park, where BU played its home football games during what's known as the Agganis Era.

After a season in Triple-A in Louisville, the Marine Corps veteran unseated Dick Gernert at first base last season. Eight of the rookie's 11 home runs came at Fenway; except for Ted Williams, that's the most there by a left-handed batter in 25 years. One of those homers came on a memorable Sunday a year ago this month, a game-winner the same day he collected his diploma up Commonwealth Avenue at Braves Field, now a BU facility.

His .251 rookie average disappointed Agganis, considered a key to the Red Sox's future. He vowed before heading to training camp in Sarasota this spring: "I'm a .300 hitter. I know I'll do it."

Agganis did, despite a bout with pneumonia which hospitalized him ten days late last month. He rushed back to the lineup, too soon, doctors said later, joining the team for a western swing. He played in the trip's first two games in Chicago and got two hits in his finale June 2. But two days later he was flown back to Boston because of fever and chest pains, and was hospitalized immediately, the severe pulmonary infection complicated by phlebitis.

The Red Sox were in Pittsburgh today for an exhibition game when they learned of their teammate's death. Black bands were immediately sewn on their left uniform sleeves for 30 days of mourning.

Pitcher Frank Sullivan (left) and general manager Joe Cronin represent the Red Sox at Harry Agganis's funeral. The team was in Washington.

Agganis lay in state for a day and a half in the Greek Orthodox Church in his native Lynn, an industrial city north of Boston. Between 20,000 and 30,000 filed past his bier, including consuls, governors, educators and some of the biggest names in sports.

More than 1,000 jammed the church for the funeral, 3,000 spilling into the adjacent hall and 6,000 more standing outside. Over 20,000 lined the route to the cemetery, where Agganis was buried on a hillside overlooking Manning Bowl, which as an All-America schoolboy he had packed to 20,000-plus capacity on Friday nights for games so attractive they were televised.

○

Agganis is among a handful of players to die while members of the Red Sox.

Chick Stahl, 34-year-old outfielder-captain-manager, died after taking poison in March 1907 in Indiana while the team was barnstorming north from spring training in Little Rock, Arkansas.

Pitcher Ed Morris was stabbed to death in March 1932 at a Florida fish fry. At the time, owner Bob Quinn reportedly was mulling a Yankee offer of close to $100,000 for the 32-year-old right-hander, once a 19-game winner.

September 25, 1955

Ted Williams has led the American League in batting for the second consecutive season—and been denied the title for the second consecutive season. The reason both times: Williams has fallen short of the 400 official at-bat minimum.

The 37-year-old Red Sox star concluded the season today at .356, well ahead of Al Kaline's winning .340. But Williams batted 320 times, 80 short. Last season Ted hit .345, topping Bobby Avila's winning .341. But Williams was 14 at-bats short.

Casey Stengel is among those outraged by the injustice, pointing to all

The Boston Baseball Writers gave a Harry Agganis Memorial Award for the Red Sox's top rookie, won the first year by infielder Billy Klaus. That's teammate Mickey Vernon at right.

the walks Williams received (136 in '54, 91 in '55) that don't count as official at-bats.

"That rule is in the books to keep some Humpty-Dumpty from stealing the title with half a season," the Yankees manager says. "It ain't never going to be a disgrace to have Williams win it."

The injustice was recognized and the yardstick was changed. But not taking any chances, Williams managed more than 400 at-bats to win the '57 (.388) and '58 (.328) crowns.

July 14, 1956

Mel Parnell pitched the first Fenway Park no-hitter in 30 years today as the Red Sox defeated the White Sox, 4-0.

It also was the first no-hitter (1) by a Red Sox pitcher in 33 years, and (2) by a left-hander at Fenway in 39 years.

The 34-year-old southpaw allowed only three opponents to reach base, two on walks, one on shortstop Don Buddin's throwing error. But two were quickly wiped out, one attempting to steal, the other on a double play. So Parnell faced only 28 batters, one over minimum.

One base on balls probably preserved the no-hitter. After Sammy Esposito walked on a 3-2 pitch to lead off the ninth inning, Red Sox second baseman Billy Goodman dove behind the bag to glove Luis Aparicio's grounder and flip to Buddin for a force play. Had there been no base runner, it's doubtful Goodman could have thrown out the speedy Aparicio at first.

The Saturday afternoon crowd of 14,542 saw Parnell aided by two other nice catches of line drives—by Jimmy Piersall in center field (off Aparicio) and Billy Klaus at third base (off Minnie Minoso). Minoso also hit the hardest drive of the game, a smash that hooked foul into the left-field stands.

Parnell praised that support afterward while insisting he hadn't been nervous. "I wasn't jumpy, not a bit," said the veteran, forced to warm up twice before the game when it was delayed more than an hour by showers. "I figured I either do it or I don't."

Parnell did, and it paid an immediate $500 dividend. Owner Tom Yawkey marched into the clubhouse and presented him with a new contract containing the raise.

Even more gratifying to Parnell was the dramatic comeback from having been written off by many as "washed up" because of a rash of injuries, including a fractured wrist that has dogged him the last three years while winning only eight games.

"This makes up for a lot of times the past few years when things didn't go so good," Parnell said. "Boy, it felt good having those people cheering for me."

It was Parnell's last hurrah. Soon afterward he tore a muscle in his pitching elbow. He underwent surgery, but the career of the winningest southpaw in Red Sox history was over.

MEL PARNELL: "A no-hitter is something a pitcher dreams of and never expects. Not only does he have to be near-perfect that day, but everything must fall into place.

"That's why I truthfully wasn't nervous as I got closer and closer to the last out. I was relaxed because I didn't think it'd happen; I was sure something would happen to break it up.

"Sure I knew I had a no-hitter going. That's baloney when a pitcher

Mel Parnell (right) is congratulated for his no-hitter by battery mate Sammy White.

says he didn't know until late that he had one going. If your mind is on your work, you have to know.

"Besides, the fans remind you. I heard them that day at Fenway, and there was talk of it on the bench. The other players were more nervous than me; they were afraid they'd blow it for me. Jackie Jensen was nerved up and said, 'Whatever you do make sure they don't hit one to me.'

"I didn't believe it until the last out. Walt Dropo bounced back to me. My momentum was toward first base when I caught it, so I just kept going and beat Dropo to the bag. Mickey Vernon was our first baseman, and he laughed, 'What's the matter, Mel, don't you trust me?' Hell, I didn't trust *myself* at that point as impossibility became reality.

"I couldn't believe it had happened. I was on Cloud 9. And without a doubt it ranks as my happiest memory."

TED WILLIAMS: "If there was one guy on our '48-through-'53 teams who was going all out, it was Mel Parnell.

"With a little luck, he easily could have won 200 games. A lot of his losses were heartbreakers. And if he hadn't been plagued by all those injuries in '54, '55 and '56, he would have had 250 victories.

"Mel Parnell was a *great* pitcher."

August 7, 1956

Red Sox teammates had to restrain Jackie Jensen from climbing into the right-field stands during pregame practice today in pursuit of a heckler who had been tormenting him. The usually stolid slugger was held back by pitcher Mel Parnell and coach Paul Schreiber.

Jensen is the favorite target of Fenway boo-birds. He has had words with Fenway loudmouths before, as when he challenged one to come out of the stands during a doubleheader last September.

"I guess I was a little edgy that day," Jensen recalls. "I thought he got too personal in things he was saying about my wife."

August 7, 1956

Ted Williams has been fined $5,000 for spraying Fenway Park with saliva tonight as the Red Sox edged the Yankees, 1-0, on a bases-loaded walk to the Splendid Spitter in the 11th inning.

Fenway's largest single-game crowd ever, 36,350, witnessed Ted's series of four spitting gestures which triggered the fine, equaling Babe Ruth's 1925 penalty by the Yankees as the biggest in baseball history.

Williams learned of the fine after the game, following a telephone huddle between general manager Joe Cronin and owner Tom Yawkey. Yawkey heard about the incident on the Yankee broadcast at his New York hotel suite.

"I'm not a bit sorry for what I did," Ted seethed. "I was right and I'd spit again at the same fans who booed me today. Some of them are the worst in the world. Nobody's going to stop me from spitting."

Obviously. It was Williams's third spitting incident in as many weeks at Fenway. He spit at the press box after hitting his 400th homer in a game against the A's. And he spit at the fans in a game against the Tigers on Joe Cronin Night, a display observed by the baseball commissioner as well as the governor and mayor.

Yawkey warned Ted after those one-spitters. He had little choice but to take action on today's four-spit grand-slam.

Jackie Jensen often reacted to hecklers.

It all began with two out in the top of the 11th when Williams was booed for muffing Mickey Mantle's wind-tossed fly. Ted then retired the side with a nice over-the-shoulder catch on Yogi Berra in deep left-center, for which he was mostly cheered.

Just before Williams reached the bench he gave a hop, skip and an emphatic spit to his left, then let go with another to his right before ducking into the dugout. Then, like a ham returning for a curtain call, Ted bounced back up the steps and let go a third salvo.

A few minutes later, Williams spat a fourth time toward the Yankee dugout when he came to bat against reliever Tommy Byrne with bases full. And when he walked, Ted flipped his bat high into the air in disgust despite forcing home the winning run.

The question now is what Williams will do for an encore.

The answer came the following night against the Orioles when a Family Night crowd mobbed Fenway in such a crush the game had to be delayed.

Predictably, the fans cheered Williams's every move. Even more predictably, Ted won the game with a mammoth homer to break a tie in the sixth. After circling the bases, just before disappearing into the dugout, he clamped his right hand over his mouth in an exaggerated gesture as the crowd howled.

The press wasn't amused. Two of Boston's most respected sports writers, the Herald's *Bill Cunningham and the* Globe's *Harold Kaese, wrote strong pieces saying Williams should quit.*

○

Yawkey, who flew up for the game, wasn't doing much laughing either. He had been criticized for not fining Williams six years earlier when Ted had made obscene gestures during a game against the Tigers; instead, he had reprimanded Williams privately and Ted had apologized publicly. Now there was the series of spitting incidents.

"Why the man does those things I can't figure out," he said. "So many times I've tried to figure it out, but I can't."

Yawkey never did deduct the $5,000 from Williams's paycheck.

Nor did Ted ever spit in anger again during a Fenway game, although he did slip once in Kansas City, for which his wrists were slapped $250 worth by the league. Presumably, he paid that fine.

March 18, 1957

The Red Sox today offered the Indians $1,000,000 for fireballing southpaw Herb Score, by far the largest sum ever offered for a baseball player.

Joe Cronin made the offer to Cleveland general manager Hank Greenberg during a two-hour huddle between the two recent Hall of Fame inductees at the Sox training camp in Sarasota.

"I'll give you a million dollars for Score," Cronin said. "Shake hands on it now and I'll get Tom Yawkey on the phone."

Greenberg left town without giving an answer and Cronin is sticking close to the telephone.

"Hank didn't say yes and he didn't say no," Cronin said. "I'm expecting him to give me a call."

The 23-year-old Score has struck out 508 batters in his two big league seasons while compiling 16-10 and 20-9 records.

The answer early the next morning was no.

"I hesitated because of the size of the offer," Greenberg told reporters in Tampa. "But I must reject the offer. Score is going to become one of the greatest southpaws in history."

The Red Sox opened the 1957 season with this lineup (left to right): front, pitcher Tom Brewer and catcher Sammy White; middle row, third baseman Frank Malzone, shortstop Billy Klaus, second baseman Gene Mauch and first baseman Dick Gernert; back row, outfielders Ted Williams, Jimmy Piersall and Gene Stephens.

Two months later Score was hit in the face by a screaming drive off the bat of Gil McDougald, and the brilliant young pitcher's career was essentially over.

September 29, 1957

Ted Williams became the oldest batting champion in big league history today, concluding the season at .388, the majors' highest average since Ted's .406 in 1941.

The 39-year-old Red Sox legend was only five hits short of hitting an even .400.

Williams batted .453 the season's last half—an incredible .667 the last few weeks, when he had 12 hits in 18 at-bats. And that doesn't include 13 walks during that span. Thus Ted reached base 25 of the final 31 times he stepped to the plate.

The batting title crowns what many consider his greatest hitting accomplishment, considering his age and the predominantly night schedule.

Williams's slugging average was an incredible .731, the majors best since his .735 in 1941. He also tied the majors record and set a league mark by twice slamming three homers in a game—off Early Wynn in Cleveland and off Bob Keegan in Chicago.

Coming back from a prolonged siege with a virus in late August, Ted reached base 16 straight times, including four homers in consecutive official at-bats sandwiched among a glut of walks.

He pinch-homered off the A's Tom Morgan, then hit one-a-day homers at Yankee Stadium off Whitey Ford, Bob Turley (grand-slam) and Tom Sturdivant before ending the binge with a single. Meanwhile, the Yankees were jeered by their fans for walking Ted five times.

In all, Williams clouted 38 homers, his most since 1949 when he hit 43.

Mickey Mantle, last season's batting king, was runner-up to Ted with a .365 average.

Yet Mantle outpointed Williams for the MVP Award, surprising Mantle and angering Tom Yawkey. The Red Sox owner branded the voting "incompetent and unqualified," noting a couple of Chicago writers had voted for Ted no higher than ninth or tenth.

○

The .388 still stands as the majors' tallest average in nearly 40 years, equaled in 1977 by Rod Carew, then of the Twins.

◇◇
◇

MICKEY MANTLE: "Ted Williams was the best hitter I ever saw. He *attacked* a pitch, *exploded* at the ball."

◇◇
◇

September 21, 1958

Joe Cronin's 60-year-old housekeeper was struck in the head by a bat thrown in disgust by Ted Williams during today's Red Sox-Senators game at Fenway Park.

Williams, hitless in his last eight at-bats and trailing teammate Pete Runnels by ten points in the homestretch of the batting race, flung his bat away after taking a called third strike. The bat caught on a sticky substance on Ted's hands and flipped through the air into the box seats, where it hit the woman, Gladys Heffernan.

The horrified Williams rushed to the railing and was roundly booed as

Ted Williams beat out Mickey Mantle (right) by 23 points for the 1957 batting crown, but Mantle outpointed Williams for the American League's MVP Award.

Ted Williams is horrified when his bat, which he had flung away in disgust, flipped into the box seats and wounded a 60-year-old woman.

Ted Williams edged teammate Pete Runnels (right) for the 1958 batting title.

Jackie Jensen was the American League's MVP in 1958 and quit a year later.

the woman, blood running from her head, was escorted to the First Aid Room.

There she comforted the embarrassed Williams. "I almost died," he said later. The following Christmas he sent her a $500 diamond watch.

September 28, 1958

Ted Williams beat out Pete Runnels for the American League batting title today in a teammate-against-teammate hitting duel that has captured the interest of the baseball world the past week.

The 40-year-old Williams won his sixth batting crown and second in a row by homering and doubling in four at-bats at Washington to end the season at .328, six points higher than the 30-year-old Runnels.

The Red Sox mates were tied at .322 going into yesterday's second-last game. Williams moved ahead, .327 to .324, when he went three for four while Runnels was three for six.

Today, Runnels was blanked in four trips by Senators ace Pedro Ramos while Williams went two for four.

Bothered by an assortment of ailments early this season, Williams hit .403 in his last 55 games to overtake Runnels. Ted was seven for 11 in his last four games, a .636 pace.

"I'd have felt bad if I had been beaten out by anyone else," Runnels said. "But it's no disgrace to finish second to Ted Williams."

November 20, 1958

Jackie Jensen today was chosen the American League's Most Valuable Player.

The Red Sox outfielder led the league in RBIs with 122 while slamming 35 home runs and batting .286. Jensen collected 233 points, 42 more than 21-game winner Bob Turley of the World Champion Yankees.

Cubs shortstop Ernie Banks was selected the National League's MVP.

Unusually, Jensen was on a third-place team, Banks on a fifth-place club.

TED WILLIAMS: "Right field at Fenway is a bitch, the sun field, and few play it well. Jackie Jensen was the best I saw at it."

JACKIE JENSEN: "It was silly retiring in 1959. I was only 32, and probably had a better season that year than in '58 when I was MVP. I was at the height of my career and, looking back, it was foolish to quit.

"Maybe I wouldn't have if my head had been screwed on better. But I thought it would answer my problems (a deteriorating marriage and an extraordinary fear of flying).

"I also made a mistake coming back in 1961. I had a terrible season by my standards. No, the year away didn't throw me off. I had a great spring training. It's just that the same problems resurfaced. I thought they were solved, but they weren't."

January 31, 1959

Joe Cronin today became president of the American League, the first former baseball player to climb to the top of his league's ladder.

The Red Sox general manager was unanimously confirmed and given a seven-year contract by team owners to succeed Will Harridge, who is retiring after 27 years.

"It's a great honor," said Cronin, who is ending nearly 25 years with the Red Sox as star, manager and GM. He will be succeeded as GM by his assistant, Bucky Harris, who coincidentally was the manager Cronin replaced when he came to Boston after the 1934 season.

"Whatever makes Joe happy makes me happy," said Tom Yawkey, who has always maintained Cronin had a job with the Sox as long as Yawkey owned the team. "So I'm happy for Joe. It's quite an honor.

"No, Joe isn't breaking a contract with me. We never had one. Neither of us felt we needed one. It's that type of relationship."

Cronin will move A.L. headquarters from Chicago to Boston.

Today's appointment climaxes a Horatio Alger-type story: The son of Irish immigrants rising from the sandlots of San Francisco to the big leagues at age 19 . . . A.L. MVP at 23 . . . directing the Senators to a pennant in his rookie season as "boy manager" at 26 . . . marrying the boss's pretty niece . . . being sold to the Red Sox for the fattest price in baseball history . . . leading the Sox to a pennant . . . promoted to general manager at 40 . . . elected to the Hall of Fame at 49 . . . and now league president at 52.

August 4, 1959

Elijah Jerry "Pumpsie" Green made history at Fenway Park tonight when he stepped to the plate as the Red Sox lead-off batter in the first inning of a twi-night doubleheader against the A's. It marked the first time a black man has worn a Red Sox uniform in a game at Fenway.

The 25-year-old switch-hitter celebrated by rapping an opposite-field triple against the left-field wall off right-hander John Tsitouris, and minutes later scoring to launch the Sox toward a 4-1 victory.

"I'm glad I got off to a good start here," said the second baseman, who went 1-for-3 in each game and handled 13 chances flawlessly.

The hits weren't Green's first as a Red Soxer. He nicked Jim Perry for his first big league hit, a single, July 28 at Cleveland, added a half-dozen more during the road trip, and is now batting an even .300.

Green was beckoned from the Sox's top farm at Minneapolis July 21, and made his debut that night in Chicago as a pinch runner, officially integrating the Red Sox, the last major league team to be so. He made his first start the next night and went 0-for-3 against Early Wynn.

"Pumpsie has lots of poise," said Billy Jurges, who replaced Mike Higgins as manager a month ago.

Joe Cronin cleared out his desk at Fenway Park, leaving to become American League president.

Pumpsie Green (second right) was inserted into the lineup at second base, teaming in the infield with (from left) third baseman Frank Malzone, shortstop Don Buddin and first baseman Pete Runnels.

"He looks so much better at second base," said third baseman Frank Malzone. "He isn't rushing the ball at second the way he did at shortstop. He seems to have much more confidence at second."

After he hit well in spring training, the Red Sox sent Green back to the minors just before breaking camp to convert to second base under Gene Mauch's tutelage at Minneapolis, where Pumpsie hit .263 as a shortstop last season. The demotion caused a furor as the Boston branch of the NAACP charged the Red Sox with discrimination.

Yet Green, who hit .320 and made the all-star team at Minneapolis before being called up, says: "I wasn't ready this spring. I was in a daze all spring and played poorly defensively. I didn't do anything right. Shortstop was hard for me. I'm more relaxed and feel much more at home at second base."

While that upholds the Sox's on-the-field judgment this spring, their off-the-field judgment at camp wasn't as sound.

Green was isolated at a motel 17 miles from the team's segregated quarters in Scottsdale, Arizona, chauffeured back and forth to the ball park daily. Midway through camp, he shifted about ten miles closer, moving in with the Giants' black players at that team's hotel in Phoenix.

Green now is rooming with Earl Wilson, the black pitcher called up by the Red Sox last week. The big right-hander made his first start July 31 at Detroit.

Pitcher Earl Wilson (left) became the Red Sox's second black, summoned from the minors a week after Pumpsie Green.

Wilson's debut had been more memorable if less historic.

The converted catcher walked the first three batters, then struck out Al Kaline and Lou Berberet and made Gail Harris fly out. Wilson walked two to lead off the second and one to open the third, escaping unscathed each time. In the fourth he got the first two batters, then walked the bases loaded.

No-hitter or not, Jurges felt it was time to replace the struggling rookie, who departed with a 4-0 lead he had helped create by doubling home a run. Remarkably, Wilson walked nine in 3⅔ innings, yet escaped without a run. He wasn't involved in the decision as the Sox outlasted the Tigers, 6-5.

o

Wilson was the victim of a bias incident in 1966 when he was refused service in a Winter Haven restaurant. This time the Red Sox were quick to step in and protest along with Wilson, and the restaurant promptly apologized and changed its policy.

THE SIXTIES

September 26, 1960

Ted Williams concluded his storybook career with a punch ending today, walloping a classic home run on his final swing.

The drive, in the eighth inning of the Red Sox 5-4 victory over the Orioles at Fenway Park, was one of Ted's trademarked moonshots through heavy moist air, landing with a thud on the roof of the bench in the Red Sox bull pen more than 400 feet away.

"I let everything I had go on that one," Williams said of No. 521, ranking him third on the all-time homer list behind Babe Ruth and Jimmy Foxx. "I really wanted that one."

While the game was supposed to be Williams's Fenway finale, it wasn't until after the game that he revealed he had worn No. 9 for the last time, that he won't accompany the team to New York for its last series. Thus the 10,454 who cheered themselves hoarse weren't aware of the full dramatics involved.

That crowd braved the cold, dreary and threatening day not to watch a meaningless game between the seventh-place Sox and second-place

Bob Stanley came out of the bull pen 49 times along with three starts in 1978, compiling a 15-2 record and ten saves. He won 11 straight at one point, the fourth most in Red Sox history.

Fred Lynn is the only major leaguer ever to capture the Most Valuable Player and Rookie of the Year awards in the same season, sweeping both honors in 1975. He added the American League batting crown to his laurels in 1979. *(Dick Raphael)*

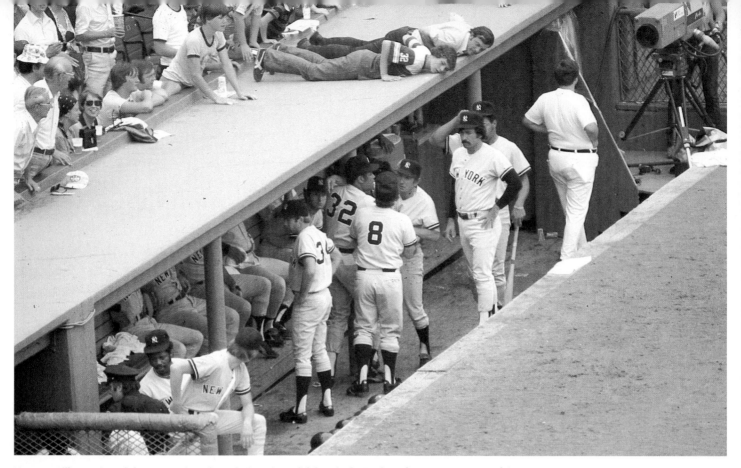

Manager Billy Martin and slugger Reggie Jackson during a heated debate in the Yankees dugout at Fenway Park in 1977 while a national television audience watched.

Dwight Evans is a Golden Glove right fielder with a rifle arm.

Yaz is the first American Leaguer to combine 400 homers and 3,000 hits in a career. *(Dick Raphael)*

Carl Yastrzemski hammered ten hits, including this one, to lead Red Sox batters in the 1967 World Series. *(Dick Raphael)*

Dennis Eckersley was 11-1 at Fenway Park and 20-8 overall in 1978, his first season with the Red Sox.

Ted Williams and Jim Rice—Red Sox sluggers of different generations—have hit some classic home runs.

Manager Don Zimmer (left) and batting professor Ted Williams observe Red Sox hitters from behind the batting cage during spring training.

Tony Conigliaro hit 32 homers in 1965 at age 20, the youngest ever to lead either major league. *(Dick Raphael)*

Luis Tiant is the third-winningest pitcher in Red Sox history and the only hurler in the club's modern history to win 20 or more games three seasons. *(Dick Raphael)*

Carlton Fisk springs for Ed Armbrister's bunt in the tenth inning of Game Three in the 1975 World Series. The pair collided before Fisk threw the ball wildly, and his vehement claim of interference was disallowed in one of the most controversial plays in World Series history. *(Dick Raphael)*

Carlton Fisk rounds third base (left) and jumps on home plate amid traffic jam on his 12th-inning home run that won Game Six of the 1975 World Series. *(Dick Raphael)*

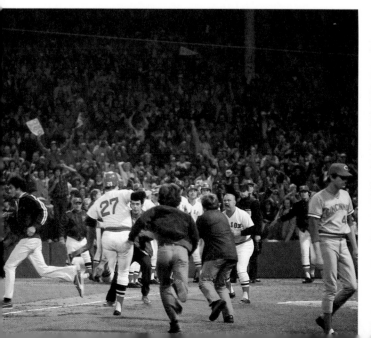

Jerry Remy was an All-Star second baseman in 1978 before being sidelined much of 1979 with a knee injury.

Butch Hobson runs bases with his old football abandon.

Rick Burleson is annually among baseball's leading shortstops, named to the All-Star team the past three seasons.

Jim Rice was the American League's Most Valuable Player in 1978, hitting 46 homers and becoming the first player since Joe DiMaggio in 1937 to collect more than 400 total bases, accumulating 406.

Mike Torrez won 16 games in 1978, his first season with the Red Sox, but he lost the crucial playoff game to his former Yankee teammates.

Bill Campbell was the American League's top relief pitcher in 1977 with 13 victories and 31 saves in 69 games.

Top left
Often-controversial Bill Lee pitched in 321 games during ten Boston seasons, the most appearances ever by a Red Sox left-hander.

Top right
Jim Lonborg was the pitching force behind the 1967 Impossible Dream, winning 22 games, including the pennant-winner, before adding a one-hitter and three-hitter in the World Series. *(Dick Raphael)*

Dick Radatz was baseball's premier reliever in the early sixties when he pitched in almost every other Red Sox game. "The Monster" averaged more than a strikeout per inning during his career. *(Dick Raphael)*

Orioles, but to join Mayor John Collins in saying goodbye to the 42-year-old Williams. Collins had proclaimed it "Ted Williams Day," and presented a check to the Jimmy Fund in the slugger's name during pregame ceremonies.

Williams, who didn't take batting or fielding practice, told a reporter before the game: "I've gone as far as I can."

Not quite.

Ted walked and flied to center on his first two trips. Then he teased the crowd with a blast to right center that appeared gone; but it suddenly died in the damp air and was caught by Al Pilarcik with his back pressed against the Sox bull pen wall 400 feet away.

"If that one didn't go out, nothing is going out today," Williams growled as he clumped down the dugout steps in disgust.

Then came the eighth, and everyone was standing and roaring for what they knew would be Williams's final Fenway at-bat (only manager Mike Higgins and a few of Ted's intimates knew it would be his last *period*).

The standing ovation prompted umpire Ed Hurley to call time, but Ted ignored it all and stepped into the batter's box. For one last time he went through his ritual of pawing the dirt with his left foot, wiggling his hips, twitching his neck and bouncing up and down to get into a comfortable stance.

A full minute later, the cheering for a man who wouldn't acknowledge it continued unabated while nine Orioles and four umpires stood almost motionless. It was an eerie tableau, bathed in the glow of lights turned on two innings earlier.

When the ovation passed two minutes, Hurley called time in and right-hander Jack Fisher pitched despite the continuing roar. Ball one.

On the next pitch, Williams unleashed an enormous cut and missed as the crowd groaned.

Fisher—born in 1939, Ted's rookie year—then tried to blow another fastball low and away past Williams. But it came in waist high and again there was a mighty swing. This time Ted connected, and even the thick air couldn't stop this one as the crowd erupted in a frenzy.

Ted galloped around the bases, no home-run trot for him this time, and disappeared into the dugout. To the end there was no tip of the cap, no handshake with the next batter (although Jim Pagliaroni managed to grab Ted's *wrist*).

The deafening roar continued more than four minutes. But Williams ignored the *"We want Ted!"* chants and refused to come out of the dugout for a bow, despite the urging of Higgins, his teammates and even first-base umpire John Rice.

Higgins managed to pry Ted out for one last hurrah, though. The manager sent him back to left field for the start of the ninth inning, then dispatched Carroll Hardy in his footsteps. When Williams got to his position, he turned, only to see the grinning Hardy shadowing him.

Ted scowled and loped back to the dugout—head down and bobbing—as the crowd once again was up and applauding wildly, one last time.

TED WILLIAMS: "They reacted like nothing I have ever heard. They cheered like hell, and as I came around the cheering grew louder and louder.

"I thought about tipping my hat, you're damn right I did, and for a moment I was torn. But by the time I got to second base I knew I couldn't do it. It just wouldn't have been me."

Ted Williams ends his Red Sox career with a dramatic home run in his final swing. (*Associated Press*)

Equipment managers Don Fitzpatrick (left) and Vince Orlando put away Ted Williams's No. 9 for the last time. Williams's No. 9 is the only number retired by the Red Sox.

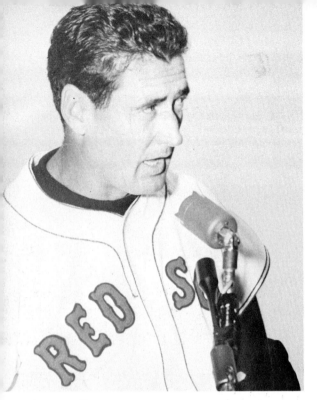

Ted says goodbye.

Pete Runnels won batting crowns in 1960 and 1962.

Ted Williams said in his farewell speech to Fenway Park fans before taking the field for his final game:

"... despite some of the terrible things written about me by the knights of the keyboard up there, and they were terrible things—I'd like to forget them but I can't—my stay in Boston has been the most wonderful part of my life. If someone should ask me the one place I'd want to play if I had it to do all over again, I would say Boston, for it has the greatest owner in baseball and the greatest fans in America...."

October 2, 1960

Pete Runnels today clinched the American League batting title that eluded him two years ago. The Red Sox handyman, playing mostly second base this season but also seeing service at first and third, batted .320, five points higher than Al Smith of the White Sox.

Red Sox hitters now have won the batting championship three of the last four years, Ted Williams capturing the '57 and '58 crowns.

Runnels would win another A.L. title in 1962, when he hit .326.

April 11, 1961

Highly touted Carl Yastrzemski singled once in five at-bats during his major league debut today as the Red Sox were 5-2 losers to the A's in the season opener at wet and frigid Fenway Park.

Yastrzemski, last year's American Association MVP who is replacing retired Ted Williams in left field, singled off right-hander Ray Herbert in his first big league at-bat. But the Notre Dame student, batting fifth in the lineup between Jackie Jensen and Pete Runnels, was retired in his last four trips, striking out twice, grounding out twice.

The 21-year-old Yastrzemski was impressive defensively, throwing out one runner and barely missing another on successive plays in the second inning. The quick-charging converted infielder threw a strike to catcher Russ Nixon to wipe out Leo Posada trying to score from second on a single; then he nearly nailed Haywood Sullivan racing from first to third on a blooper to left center.

"It's going to be awfully hard to score from second with that kid out there," A's manager Joe Gordon said. "I didn't think he could throw like that."

The shivering crowd of 10,277, the smallest for a Fenway opener since World War II, was impressed by the Sox's other highly regarded rookie, Chuck Schilling. The 23-year-old second baseman singled twice in four trips and enticed a walk in the leadoff position.

Yastrzemski got off to a slow start and didn't hit his first homer until his 17th game on May 9 at Los Angeles, off former Red Sox-turned-Angel Jerry Casale. Yaz was hitting .246 at the time and fell further to near .200—overshadowed by fellow Long Islander and roommate Schilling, who was hitting about 70 points higher and on his way to a league fielding record for least errors by a second baseman.

The dejected Yaz was consoled by Tom Yawkey, who sent an SOS to Ted Williams, reaching him by radio aboard a fishing boat off Florida. The next day Williams was tutoring Yastrzemski at Fenway, and from then on the rookie was literally on the upswing, improving his average to .266 by season's end.

Two years later Yastrzemski was American League batting champion.

1

2

3

4

5

6

YOUNG YAZ

1. Yastrzemski met manager Billy Jurges in September 1959 when the 20-year-old was a minor leaguer visiting Fenway.
2. Yaz was a second baseman at Red Sox training camp in 1960. He was sent back to the minors to be converted to an outfielder to replace retiring Ted Williams in 1961.
3. Yaz and pal Chuck Schilling, a fellow Long Islander, were prize rookies in the Sox's Opening Day lineup in 1961.
4. Carl and wife Carol brought daughter Maryann to 1961 training camp.
5. Yaz's first outfield mates were Jackie Jensen (left) and Gary Geiger.
6. When the Red Sox signed him during his sophomore year at Notre Dame, Yaz promised his father that he'd earn his college degree. He kept that promise, graduating in 1966 from Merrimack College. With the graduate are his wife and parents.

Bill Monbouquette struck out 17 batters in a game, the most ever by a Red Sox pitcher.

Tracy Stallard served up Roger Maris's record 61st home run.

May 12, 1961

Bill Monbouquette set a Red Sox strikeout record at Washington tonight when he fanned 17 Senators, eclipsing Smokey Joe Wood's 15 in 1911.

Monbouquette's total was one short of Bob Feller's modern major league record for a nine-inning game. Since strikeouts aren't Monbo's specialty, his total surprised even him.

"I didn't know I was close to any record; I thought I had 12 or 13," said the right-hander, whose 2-1 victory was saved by Jackie Jensen's sparkling catch for the final out with two Senators on base.

Coincidentally, 17 Red Sox batters struck out two days ago in Los Angeles, mowed down by three Angel pitchers.

Monbouquette struck out no more than seven in any other game that season.

His 17 that night remains the most by a Red Sox pitcher. But Sox batters have topped their 17. Eighteen were fanned by three Detroit pitchers in 1965—Denny McLain notching 14 of them in relief, including a record seven in a row.

June 18, 1961

The Red Sox erupted for their biggest last-ditch rally ever—eight runs with two out in the ninth inning—to catch the Senators, 13-12, in the opener of today's doubleheader at Fenway Park.

Catcher Jim Pagliaroni highlighted the explosion with a grand-slam homer. Pag also homered in the 13th inning of the nightcap to give the Sox another victory, 6-5. Those were Pagliaroni's only two hits of the day in 11 trips, and he grinned afterward: "My batting average is going to blazes."

Trailing 12-5 against Carl Mathias, the Sox's backs-to-the-wall ninth inning of the opener went this way:

Vic Wertz grounded out. Don Buddin singled. Billy Harrell struck out as a pinch hitter for Ted Wills (winning pitcher). Chuck Schilling singled. Carroll Hardy singled, scoring Buddin. Gary Geiger walked to load the bases.

Dave Sisler (losing pitcher) replaced Mathias. Jackie Jensen walked, forcing home Schilling. Frank Malzone walked, forcing home Hardy. Pagliaroni hit a slam to tie the score, 12-12.

Marty Kutyna replaced Sisler. Wertz walked. Buddin singled. Pete Runnels ran for Wertz and scored on Russ Nixon's pinch single.

October 1, 1961

Red Sox rookie Tracy Stallard engraved his name in baseball history today when he served up Roger Maris's record 61st home run in the season's final game.

The roar from the Sunday crowd of 23,154 at Yankee Stadium could be heard across the Harlem River at the Polo Grounds, where the Boston Patriots were losing to the New York Titans, 37-30.

Maris's blast was the only run of the game, and came on a 2-0 fastball while leading off the fourth inning after Stallard had retired him on a soft fly in the first inning. The homer was lined 360 feet into the right-field stands off the 6-foot-5 right-hander.

Stallard was cheered in his remaining at-bats because he'd had the courage to pitch to the Yankee slugger, who was down to his last game. Maris had failed to homer off the Red Sox the last two days as Bill Monbouquette shut him off Friday, Don Schwall yesterday.

"I didn't want to be remembered as the guy who gave up the big homer," said the 24-year-old Stallard, who saw his record fall to 2-7 despite a brilliant five-hitter. "Still, I have nothing to be ashamed of. Maris hit 60 other homers, didn't he?"

The game proved a high-water mark of sorts for both hitter and hittee.

Although Maris would hit many more homers against the Red Sox (including one as a Cardinal during the 1967 World Series when he batted .385), he has since noted: "The game was never really fun after hitting those 61 homers."

Stallard pitched only one more inning for the Red Sox the following season before being shipped with Pumpsie Green to the Mets for Felix Mantilla in 1963. Stallard's career record was 30-57, but his name is etched at Cooperstown and is the answer to one of America's favorite trivia questions.

○

Seven of Roger Maris's record 61 home runs came at the Red Sox's expense, including the historic 61st off Tracy Stallard.

Maris hit No. 8 off Gene Conley (May 24 at New York), No. 10 off Conley and No. 11 off Mike Fornieles (both in a single game May 30 at Boston), No. 12 off Billy Muffett (May 31 at Boston), No. 33 off Bill Monbouquette (July 9 at New York) and No. 36 off Monbouquette (July 21 at Boston), before Stallard gained immortality by serving up No. 61.

Ted Williams shares a laugh with another left-handed slugger who wore No. 9, Yankee Roger Maris.

June 26, 1962

Earl Wilson hurled the Red Sox's first no-hitter in six years tonight when he blew down the Angels, 2-0, at Fenway Park. Wilson also provided the only run he needed by walloping a solo homer in the third inning, one of only three hits allowed by loser Bo Belinsky, who tossed a no-hitter six weeks ago.

"That ball went about 420 feet," Wilson said. "To hit and pitch like that makes a big night for me. I can't believe it."

The 27-year-old right-hander, a converted catcher, walked four and fanned five while relying mostly on his fastball.

"My catcher, Bob Tillman, kept saying, 'Earl, stay with the fastball. It's hummin', man,' " said Wilson, who received Tom Yawkey's traditional new contract afterward. "So I stayed with the fastball and made it."

The victory was Wilson's sixth of the season and only the tenth of his big league career since becoming the Sox's first black pitcher in 1959.

The no-hitter is the American League's first by a black pitcher. It is also the first no-hitter by the Red Sox since Mel Parnell's at Fenway in 1956, and the first by a Sox right-hander at Fenway since Ernie Shore's in 1917.

○

More than most teams, the Red Sox have had a notorious reputation for capers off the field.

The most notorious caper of all began on a humid Thursday on the streets of New York, when Donald Eugene Conley and Elijah Jerry Green bolted and vanished from the Red Sox bus while it was stuck in traffic.

The most celebrated Lost Weekend in at least modern Red Sox history had begun. And it would intrigue a nation before it concluded.

Earl Wilson authored the first no-hitter by a Red Sox right-hander in 39 years.

July 26, 1962

Gene Conley and Pumpsie Green disappeared late this afternoon after jumping the Red Sox bus while it was snarled in New York rush-hour traffic.

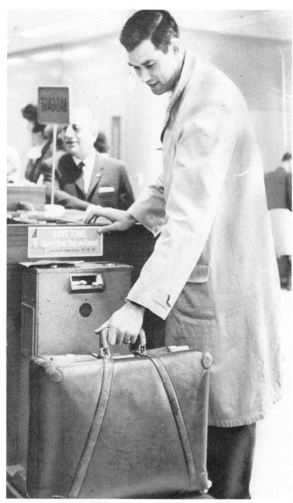

Gene Conley went AWOL and bought a plane ticket to Israel, saying he wanted to "go to Bethlehem" to get "nearer to God."

Pumpsie Green (left) was missing only half as long as Gene Conley. After 27 hours, Green rejoined the Red Sox in Washington but was too ill to play against the Senators that night. He was even more ill when tagged with a $1,000 fine by manager Mike Higgins (right).

The incident followed a 13-3 thrashing of the hapless Sox at Yankee Stadium as the luckless Conley was chased by the defending world champions in their eight-run third inning.

Pursuing his tenth victory, Conley was the victim of non-support both in the field and at bat. Teammates haven't scored a run for the big right-hander in his last 23 innings.

After the game, the Red Sox headed for Newark Airport en route to Washington for a series with the Senators. Their chartered bus was locked in a massive jam near the George Washington Bridge and didn't budge a block in 15 minutes.

In the back of the bus, Conley nudged Green. "C'mon, Pumps, let's get out of here," he said, and the pair darted for the front door, excusing themselves in pursuit of a restroom.

"We'll be right back," Conley called to manager Mike Higgins as the pair ran in one side of a garage and out the other, disappearing into Manhattan's concrete jungle.

The fun-loving Conley, a 6-foot-9, 225-pound ironman who tossed baseballs for the Red Sox and basketballs for the Celtics in a 12-months-a year grind, would be gone 68 hours. During that time he'd surface only to cash a $1,000 check and buy a plane ticket to Israel, while Boston and New York newspapers frantically tried to chase him down and headlined every development.

The New York Daily News *couldn't find Conley but tracked down a cab driver who had chauffeured Gene to Idlewild (now JFK) Airport. The cabbie quoted Conley as saying he wanted "to go to Bethlehem" to get "nearer to God." But the athlete was refused passage on a flight to Tel Aviv because he didn't have a passport.*

Instead, Conley took a plane to Providence en route to his home in Foxboro, Massachusetts, exhausted mentally and physically. "I'm tired, very tired," he told reporters waiting at his home that Sunday. "I'm worn out."

Green, a .246-hitting utility infielder and the Red Sox's first black, was missing less than half as long. He rejoined the club in Washington 27 hours after his exit, but was too ill to play in a doubleheader that night. Pumpsie was fined a reported $1,000 and the next season was wearing a Mets uniform.

Newspapers estimated Conley's fine at $2,000. But the actual figure was $1,500—less than the $5,000 assessed Ted Williams in 1956, more than the $1,000 pinned on Wes Ferrell in 1938 and the $1,000 that would be plastered on both Tony Conigliaro in 1965 and Rico Petrocelli in 1966.

GENE CONLEY: "I guess people will never forget that lost weekend. It used to bother me that people recalled me more for three off-the-field days than for playing 11 seasons of big league baseball and seven of big league basketball.

"I'd hear it all the time: 'Oh yes, Gene Conley. You're the guy who wanted to go to Israel.' I'd think, 'Hey, what is this? I break my butt in two sports and all people remember is that one mistake.'

"I'll admit it was an incident that almost went too far, though. It sure was a pip, wasn't it?

"Some people have suggested I didn't know what I was doing. I knew exactly what I was doing—at least at first.

"I'd had a terrible day at Yankee Stadium, and so had my teammates. Even Yaz mishandled a ball or two. It was one big mess, a nightmare. So I'd gotten an early start and had a pretty good glow on when I got on the bus after the game.

"When we got bogged down in traffic in all that heat, I said to heck with it. It didn't figure I'd be pitching in the Washington series and then we'd have the All-Star Game break, so I didn't think I'd be needed for a while.

"I didn't have anything specific in mind. I just figured we'd have a few drinks and felt it was worth $50 or $100 for a night in New York to rest and relax.

"So I invited Pumpsie along and we got off. Pumpsie suggested Scotch and milk for openers, but I think I got all the Scotch and Pumps got all the milk. And we went on from there.

"Going to Israel was my idea. Some guys want to lick the world when they get half loaded. Not me. I'd start thinking and get bogged down in my mind. And this time I kind of flipped out—almost.

"I was struggling as a pitcher then and had been since hurting my arm in 1955. I had been taking cortisone shots secretly ever since. Now I was hanging on. I also was tired from playing two sports year round. It was all getting to me, and I was just about ready to crack.

"I had also started reading the Bible about that time. And the more I got tanked the more an idea made sense to me. 'Hey,' I thought, 'I'm going to Bethlehem and Jerusalem and get all my problems straightened out and come back and be a big winner.'

"I tried to get Pumpsie to go with me. 'C'mon, Pumps, we'll get all squared away,' I said. 'You'll come back a .400 hitter and I'll win 20.'

"I thought I had him just about convinced. But then he said, 'Hey, man, you're crazy. I'm going back.' He did, but I was gone another two days.

"When I finally returned home, I couldn't believe all the fuss. I honestly didn't think it had been that big a thing. But when I saw all the media coverage, I thought, 'Oh, wow, what have I done?'

"The next day I was called to Fenway, the Prodigal Son with his tail between his legs. I knew I'd done wrong.

"Mr. Yawkey called me up to his office. He was shaving when I arrived and he called out of the bathroom: 'Well, Gene, you really pulled a beauty this time, didn't you?' I could see his face in the bathroom mirror—all lathered—and he was laughing. 'Sit down and make yourself comfortable,' he said. 'I'll be with you in a minute.'

"There was a pause and then he said, 'Care for a drink, Gene?'

"I darn near fell off my chair.

" 'No thanks, Mr. Yawkey,' I said. 'I never touch the stuff.'

"I really jolted him with that one. I could see him wince in the mirror. I mean, he almost pulled a Van Gogh and darn near cut his ear off.

"We talked awhile, and he fined me $1,500, not the $2,000 the newspapers estimated. And what most people don't know is that Mr. Yawkey gave it back to me at season's end. He said to me that day: 'Gene, I'm going to have to fine you. But settle down and earn it back in your own way, on the mound. If you do, you'll get the money back. I'll be watching.'

"I went out and broke my back the rest of the season, winning 15 for the year (15-14 record), my most victories in a season. My arm was hanging off, I really was in pain, but I wanted that $1,500 back. I also felt ashamed and wanted to make amends, particularly to Mr. Yawkey, who was the greatest.

"Looking back, I guess I took that 100 percent stuff a little too far. I always gave 100 percent on the field, and that's the way it should be. But I also gave 100 percent off the field, and sometimes that got me into trouble.

"Well, I haven't had a drink in more than 15 years now. My drinking was getting so bad I was afraid I wouldn't be able to hold a job. I don't think I was an alcoholic, but I had a real problem. Who knows? Maybe I

The media was camped on the doorstep of Gene Conley's trailer, awaiting his return. After being missing for 68 hours, Conley came home and made a brief statement. The next day Tom Yawkey fined him $1,500—the second biggest fine in Red Sox history—but later gave it back.

Katie and Gene Conley can laugh about it now. (Boston Globe)

Bill Monbouquette (right) pitched the Red Sox's second no-hitter in five weeks, matching Earl Wilson.

Dick Stuart loved to hit.

was an alcoholic and didn't know it. Whatever, I knew my next step would be AA, and I didn't think that would do me any good.

"I knew religion was all that could straighten me out, and it did. Religion saved me. I became a Seventh Day Adventist. I would have become a first-class drunk. I would have blown everything. I was going pretty fast for a lot of years. So I've kind of settled down, thank heaven."

August 1, 1962

Bill Monbouquette pitched the Red Sox's second no-hitter in five weeks tonight when he put down the White Sox, 1-0, at Chicago. The only Chicago batter to reach base was Al Smith, who walked in the second inning.

Monbouquette struck out seven, including two in the ninth, to dramatically nail down the no-hitter. He sandwiched strikeouts of Sherm Lollar and Luis Aparicio around Nellie Fox's groundout to seal the triumph.

"Sure it's a thrill," said the 25-year-old right-hander. "It's the best game I ever pitched."

The game's only run came in the eighth when Lu Clinton singled home Jim Pagliaroni from second base.

The hardluck loser was 42-year-old Early Wynn, seeking his 298th career victory.

Monbo's no-hitter matches that of stablemate Earl Wilson on June 26 against the Angels—the first time two Red Sox pitchers have thrown no-hitters the same season since George Foster and Dutch Leonard did it in 1916.

June 28, 1963

Man bit dog at Yankee Stadium today.

Dick Stuart, the Red Sox's power-hitting but poor-fielding "Dr. Strangeglove," authored a major league fielding record for first basemen in the first inning when he handled three grounders flawlessly, flipping the ball to pitcher Bob Heffner for putouts each time.

The Red Sox bench, aware of Stuart's six-error potential on the three plays, greeted the slugger's return to the dugout with all the glee due a game-winning grand-slam.

Stuart's record for most assists in an inning by a first baseman still stands, although it was tied by National Leaguer Andre Thornton of the Cubs in 1975.

JOHNNY PESKY: "Big Stu was 10 years ahead of his time in Boston. He would have been a great DH. He really could hit and had tremendous power. But in the field he was a menace. Nobody could hit well enough to make up for what he cost us in the field. He just waved at ground balls. If you took the bat out of Dick's hands, he wasn't even a good semi-pro player."

DICK RADATZ: "Dick wasn't a bad fielder; he'd catch most balls hit to him. He was just lazy and didn't go after many balls."

July 2, 1963

Yankees manager Ralph Houk has labeled Dick Radatz "the best relief pitcher I've ever seen" in naming the Red Sox fireman to the American League pitching staff for next week's All-Star Game at Cleveland.

The description is high praise from Houk; he's dealt with some pretty fair relief pitchers. Houk caught Joe Page of the Yankees in the late forties and was a World Series foe of the Phillies' Jim Konstanty and the Dodgers' Joe Black in the early fifties. Houk also managed against the Orioles' Stu Miller, then of the Giants, in last year's World Series.

Radatz, the 6-foot-6, 245-pounder nicknamed "The Monster," was A.L. Fireman of the Year as a rookie last season, when he had a 9-6 record with 24 saves and a 2.24 ERA in 62 games.

Radatz would appear in the All-Star Game the next year, too, because in 1963-64 he was baseball's most feared pitcher despite playing for a second-division team. The fireballer simply overpowered batters. In 1963, he was 15-6 with 25 saves and a 1.97 ERA in 66 games, including a stretch of 33 scoreless innings. In 1964, he was 16-9 with 29 saves and a 2.29 ERA in 79 games.

Those 79 appearances shattered (1) the Red Sox record of 70 set by Mike Fornieles in 1960, (2) the A.L. record of 71 set by Miller when he joined the Orioles in 1963, and (3) the major league record of 75 set by Konstanty in 1950. And of the Sox's 72 victories that season, Radatz was responsible for 45.

"God bless Dick Radatz," said manager Johnny Pesky, who had converted him from starter to reliever in the minors. "He's our franchise."

DICK RADATZ: "There's nothing like relief pitching. You come in with the bases loaded in the eighth inning, your team ahead by a run, and it's *your* game. It's what *you* do that means *everything*. It's exhilarating."

September 29, 1963

Carl Yastrzemski sewed up the American League batting championship today. His .321 average easily topped runner-up Al Kaline's .312. Yaz also led the league in hits (183), doubles (40) and walks (95) for the seventh-place Red Sox.

It is the fifth time in seven years that the batting crown has been worn by a Red Sox player, Yastrzemski joining two other pretty fair left-handed hitters: Ted Williams ('57 and '58) and Pete Runnels ('60 and '62).

Dick Radatz thrusts arms above head in a victory salute that was his trademark. *(Boston Globe)*

Carl Yastrzemski's classic swing as viewed by George Scott (5) in the on-deck circle.

A Red Sox hitter also led the league in runs batted in, Dick Stuart's 118 topping Kaline's 101. Big Stu also led in total bases with 319, and his 42 homers were second only to Harmon Killebrew's 45.

April 18, 1964

It's the stuff fantasies are made of.

Tony Conigliaro cracked a home run today on the first pitch ever served him at Fenway Park, jumping on a Joe Horlen fastball and arching a rainbow shot over the left-field wall to launch the Red Sox to a 4-1 victory over the White Sox.

The 19-year-old outfielder from nearby Swampscott hit his storybook homer not only before his parents and 20,211 other hometown fans, but also before a galaxy of celebrities attending the home opener dedicated to the memory of a longtime Red Sox fan, the late President Kennedy. The game's $36,818 proceeds went to the JFK Library Fund, and among those cheering Conigliaro on were Kennedy family members including Bobby and Teddy, Carol Channing, Fredric March, Gene Tunney and Stan Musial, along with the governor and mayor.

"It was the least I could do after they all showed up for my home debut," joked the 6-foot-3, 185-pound right-hand slugger, who played only one year in the minors after signing with the Red Sox over 13 other teams for about $20,000.

Tony C is a cocky teenager who, in his major league debut two days ago at New York, accused veteran Whitey Ford of throwing him a spitball. Conig got his first big league hit that day, a single, and robbed Tom Tresh with a nice catch in deep center field as the Red Sox spoiled Yankee Stadium's Opening Day in 11 innings, 4-3.

But Fenway Park's 1964 Opening Day is the one Conigliaro will remember most. He'll undoubtedly hit more homers, but none with more of a fairy-tale touch.

Conigliaro hit 23 more that season (while batting .290) despite missing six weeks with an assortment of injuries, including two broken bones—only the beginning of the mishaps that would haunt his career.

The next season, despite another hairline wrist fracture that sidelined him 24 games, Conig hit 32 homers to lead the American League—at 20, the youngest ever to lead either major league.

Teenager Tony Conigliaro (left) homered in his first Fenway at-bat, a feat witnessed by his family: parents Sal and Theresa, brothers Richie and Billy.

September 16, 1965

The Red Sox made double-barreled news today at Fenway Park.

Dave Morehead pitched a no-hitter in defeating the Indians, 2-0. And after the game it was announced that Mike Higgins was fired as general manager.

The firing overshadowed the no-hitter. But the ill-timing proved unavoidable after the press box had been alerted early in the game that there would be a major announcement 30 minutes after the final out.

Morehead was brilliant in disposing of the Indians on only 105 pitches and walking only one batter, Rocky Colavito. The 22-year-old right-hander avenged missing a no-hitter against the Indians two years ago in Cleveland, spoiled on Fred Whitfield's bad-hop single in the eighth inning.

The Red Sox promptly rewarded Morehead for his no-hitter with a new contract containing a $1,000 raise.

September 25, 1965

The Red Sox were put down for three innings at Kansas City tonight by a 59-year-old pitcher—old nemesis Leroy "Satchel" Paige. He thus became the oldest man by far ever to play in the major leagues, admitting to being 59 years and 78 days old.

The A's pitching tutor was activated by Charles O. Finley for one night. Paige started and was near perfect in the three innings he worked: no runs, one hit, no walks, one strikeout.

"I felt like I was batting against a chapter out of history," said Carl Yastrzemski, who doubled on a 3-0 pitch for the only hit off the legendary right-hander.

Paige's strikeout victim? Bill Monbouquette—on three pitches. But Monbo had the last laugh. He was the winning pitcher as the Red Sox jumped on reliever Don Mossi for a 5-2 victory.

June 2, 1966

The Red Sox traded Dick "The Monster" Radatz to the Indians today for pitchers Lee Stange and Don McMahon.

"A couple of years ago," McMahon said in Cleveland, "the Red Sox could have gotten a whole team for Radatz."

The darling of Fenway fans less than two years ago when he was baseball's premier relief pitcher, the 29-year-old Radatz was 0-2 with three saves and a 4.73 ERA in 16 appearances this season.

The fans and press turned on Radatz as things began going sour for him last season when he was 9-11. He apparently sealed his fate the other night in Washington when he served a grand-slam homer to Jim King.

"I'm surprised," Radatz said before enplaning for Cleveland. "I realize I haven't been going as good as I had been. But I thought they'd bear with me until I got back in the groove.

Among the galaxy of celebrities to witness Tony Conigliaro's dramatic homer were (from left) Governor Endicott "Chub" Peabody, Stan Musial, Joe Cronin, Senator Ted Kennedy, Attorney General Robert Kennedy, Jean Kennedy Smith, Pat Kennedy Lawford and Carol Channing. Making one of his first public appearances since the assassination of his brother five months earlier, Bobby Kennedy received a standing ovation before throwing out the first pitch for the JFK Library Fund game.

Dave Morehead displays his no-hit baseball.

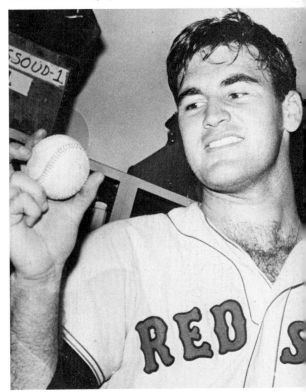

Dick Radatz says goodbye to Boston as he enplanes for Cleveland.

"Nothing is wrong with my arm. My trouble is mechanical. It's just a matter of getting back in the groove. If I pitch the way I think I can, the Indians will win the pennant."

Radatz never won a game for the Indians, who finished fifth. Dick would win only three more games against nine losses in the two and a half seasons he had left in the majors.

His meteor, and perhaps his arm, had burned out quickly. He left behind an abundance of records and achievements, but that was only part of it. More exhilarating was the type reliever he was, and the sense of drama he exuded.

Radatz was the Red Sox's greatest drawing card since Ted Williams, even though fans couldn't be sure he'd pitch. Even the most loyal Sox fans would root for the opposition to chase the Boston starter so they could see The Monster, the 6-foot-6 right-hander with the size 18 neck, size 14 shoes and weight which was often as much as 20 pounds above the advertised 245.

Their wishes came true almost every other game for a couple of seasons, including one stretch when he pitched in nine straight games. Manager Johnny Pesky would bounce up the dugout stairs with his right hand raised high, and Fenway Park would go wild. And mammoth No. 17 would strut out of the bull pen.

The baseball looked like a golf ball in Radatz's massive hands, and it seemed he threw it just as effortlessly. He challenged the hitters with a roaring fastball 85 percent of the time. Batters knew it was coming but rarely could do anything about it. Radatz simply smoked them, overpowered them, dazzled them with the blazing fastball he pumped from that slow easy motion.

Radatz could make that fastball break in or out, up or down. It paid off in a career average of more than a strikeout per inning, ranking him among baseball's all-time leaders.

Pitching half the time in a park where disaster lurked less than 315 feet away, Radatz gave the second-division Red Sox respectability and thrived on the almost daily challenge of pulling them out of one jam after another.

As he notched each of his 49 victories and 100 saves from 1962-65 (accounting for more than half his team's wins during that span), Radatz would thrust both arms high above his head in a victory salute that was his trademark.

DICK RADATZ: "No, I didn't burn myself out.

"But, yes, I was a power pitcher, a one-pitch pitcher. And my specialty pitch, the fastball, is the most perishable. Still, the fastball is the best pitch. Two hundred years from now there still won't be a better pitch than the fastball because it requires the hitter to react the quickest, the hardest thing for a batter to do.

"Still, I wish I'd been able to develop another pitch because the day comes when the fast one disappears. I tried to develop another pitch but couldn't do it and retain my fastball. In fact, that's what began my downfall.

"During 1965 spring training, Ted Williams (tutoring hitters) said to me: 'You ought to come up with another pitch. Your motion is a natural for throwing a sinker.'

"I agreed and worked hard to develop a sinker. I came up with a pretty good one and fell in love with it. The only trouble was that in doing so I lost my fastball. I'd developed a different motion for the sinker, and my fastball wasn't effective out of that motion. And before I knew it, I was

5-11 that season before getting straightened out and winning my last four decisions.

"That was the beginning of the end, though. I couldn't regain my good control, and it got to be a mental thing. I went from an excellent control pitcher to no control at all. It took hypnosis by a Detroit psychiatrist years later to regain the control. But by then I was older, and the really good fastball was gone."

April 7, 1967

Dick Williams predicts "we'll win more than we'll lose" as his Red Sox prepare to break camp at Winter Haven.

If the cocky rookie manager makes good on that prediction, it will be the first time in nine years that the Sox have reached .500 (since 1958, when they were 79-75). They haven't been higher than seventh the last five years, and have had a 62-100 record and two 72-90 marks the last three seasons.

A .500 record would be a major improvement.

The Red Sox also are captainless for the first time in awhile. Williams has relieved Carl Yastrzemski of the job this spring, a role Yaz never wanted anyway.

"I'm the only chief," Williams says. "All the rest are Indians."

The Impossible Dream was about to begin.

DICK WILLIAMS: "When I was a rookie manager in 1967, I looked at the talent I had and couldn't believe how the Red Sox had been so out of it the previous season.

"Well, it turned out that this was a team that needed shaking up. So all year long I motivated these guys by goading and criticizing them.

"Even though we won the pennant, I don't think there was a player on the team who liked me by the end of the season. But I noticed that none sent back their World Series checks."

RICO PETROCELLI: "What made 1967 so memorable was not only the pennant but that it was the beginning of what's carried over ever since. It was the start of better Red Sox teams, more excitement and of Boston being a better baseball town.

"The Red Sox hadn't been winners for years—they had some bad ball clubs—and the fans were always booing, always getting on guys. It was rough. But in 1967 we finally started winning and the fans finally had a chance to cheer and get excited about the team.

"So '67 was important as the year that changed it all around."

Dick Williams (center) was named Red Sox manager for 1967, promoted from the club's Toronto farm by General Manager Dick O'Connell (right) and Personnel Director Haywood Sullivan.

Dick Williams named Jim Lonborg (right) the Red Sox's Opening Day pitcher, launching the Impossible Dream.

Billy Rohr's cap flies off while he pitches a near no-hitter in his major league debut.

April 14, 1967

A 21-year-old Red Sox southpaw ignored an aching knee and came within a pitch of baseball immortality in his first major league game today at Yankee Stadium.

Billy Rohr's dream of a no-hitter was shattered by Elston Howard's line single to left-center on a 3-2 pitch with two out in the ninth inning.

It's the closest an American League pitcher has ever come to a no-hitter in his big league debut. Also remarkable is that Rohr's battery mate, soon-to-be-28 Russ Gibson, also was playing in the majors for the first time, but obviously steadied his pitcher and chipped in with a pair of hits.

Howard was booed by Yankee fans. Among the disappointed in the Friday afternoon crowd of 14,375 was John-John Kennedy, who sat near the Boston dugout with his mother Jackie. When Howard singled, Mrs. Kennedy hugged her six-year-old son to comfort him.

"When Howard hit it, it was like losing the game," Carl Yastrzemski said after the Red Sox 3-0 victory.

Yastrzemski had kept the no-hitter alive with a spectacular catch of Tom Tresh's smash to deep left which opened the ninth inning. Yaz had been playing shallow to guard against a single. He was off at the crack of the bat, racing with his back to the plate. He half turned in mid-stride and speared the ball with a desperate lunging catch, holding the ball as he tumbled heavily to the ground.

"I may have made better catches," Yaz said, "but I don't recall any."

Carl Yastrzemski makes a spectacular catch in the ninth inning to keep the no-hitter alive.

There was no catching Howard's clean single, though, and Rohr had to settle for the one-hitter.

"It was a curve ball," reviewed Rohr, who walked five. "I threw it because I hadn't thrown him one all day and didn't think he'd be looking for it."

Rohr pitched in pain after being struck on the left knee by a line drive off the bat of Bill Robinson in the sixth inning. Dick Williams considered taking him out, but Rohr pleaded to stay in.

"I told him he could try, but not to hurt himself or the team," said the first-year manager.

Rohr got a standing ovation when he limped off the field at inning's end, and trainer Buddy LeRoux kept the knee packed in ice between innings the remainder of the game.

"Naturally I'm disappointed I missed the no-hitter," Rohr added, "but I'm happy to win."

Ironically, Howard soon was wearing a Boston uniform, joining the Red Sox in early August for their storybook pennant drive. But by then Rohr had long since faded back to the minors after winning only one more game (against the Yankees a week later at Boston), his Red Sox career over after only 42⅓ innings and a 2-3 record.

"He has the equipment," Dick Williams said in shipping out Rohr, who later surfaced briefly with the Indians. "He needs the desire."

August 18, 1967

Tony Conigliaro was nearly killed at Fenway Park tonight when his left cheekbone was shattered by a pitch from hard-throwing right-hander Jack Hamilton of the Angels. Conigliaro was carried off the field in intense pain and rushed by ambulance to Sancta Maria Hospital in Cambridge.

While Red Sox officials won't say pending more medical evidence, it's likely Tony C is through for the season. And while that would be a blow to the team's pennant hopes, everyone is thankful. If the pitch had been an inch or two higher, Conig might have been killed.

Many angry teammates feel the pitch was a spitball that got away from Hamilton—his first pitch in the fourth inning after the game had been delayed ten minutes when a smoke bomb went off in left field. Not only does Hamilton have a reputation for moistening baseballs, but the pitch acted strangely, tailing in and seeming to follow Conig as he ducked away. Tony jerked his head so hard his helmet flipped off an instant before the ball struck the left side of his head.

The crowd shrieked in horror, then stood in stunned silence as on-deck hitter Rico Petrocelli and trainer Buddy LeRoux led the rush to the striken Conigliaro.

The 22-year-old local-boy-made-good had singled in his first at-bat, hiking his batting average to .287 with 20 homers and 67 RBIs in 95 games.

"Death was constantly on my mind," Conigliaro would recall. "I thought I was going to die."

Further examinations revealed not only the fractured cheekbone but also a dislocated jaw and, worst of all, a damaged retina. Conigliaro later was told he would never play baseball again.

Not only did he miss the remainder of 1967 but also all of the 1968 season, after failing in spring training. But while trying a comeback as a pitcher in the Florida Instructional League during the fall of 1968, there was a dramatic improvement in Conigliaro's vision, and Tony returned to his right-field job in 1969.

August 28, 1967

Tom Yawkey, who has spent millions buying stars from other teams, acquired one for free today.

The Red Sox signed free agent Ken Harrelson, who was controversially fired ten days ago by A's owner Charles O. Finley. The Sox outbid several contenders, Harrelson agreeing to an estimated $150,000 package extending through 1969. His salary with the A's was $12,000.

The 25-year-old outfielder-first baseman was obtained primarily to fill the cavity in right field left by seriously injured Tony Conigliaro.

Harrelson's .273 average is somewhat deceptive. He hit .305 in 61 games with the last place A's after being reacquired from the Senators early this season. And while he has only nine homers, the 6-foot-2, 190-pound right-hand swinger is well suited to Fenway's Wall. He used it to advantage for two game-winning hits for the A's this month, homering off Gary Bell and doubling off John Wyatt.

It was on the A's flight back to Kansas City after that series that a chain of events was ignited, triggering a team revolt against Finley—charges and countercharges, fines, and finally the firing of manager Al Dark.

Harrelson then teed off at Finley, branding his actions "detrimental to baseball." When Harrelson refused to retract the statement, he was fired by the owner, freeing Harrelson for the Sox to sign him.

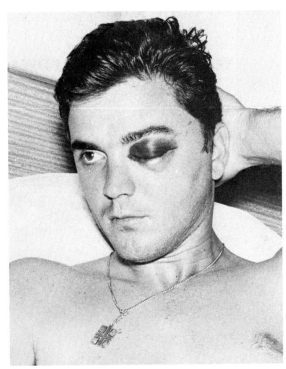

Tony Conigliaro after he was nearly killed by a pitch.

Fifteen thou
team arrive

1967:

Jim Lonborg gets the ride of his life after the final out.

An enthusiastic fan gives George Scott a scalp massage.

It was the Y
bread.

Tom Yawkey was near tears amid the celebration as he went from locker to locker congratulating his Red Sox after their pennant became official early tonight.

Someone handed Yawkey a paper cup brimming with champagne.

"I haven't had one of these in four years," Yawkey said, studying the drink.

The Red Sox owner took it into the manager's office.

"I want to have a toast with you, Dick," Yawkey said to Williams.

"Fine," said the freshman manager, borrowing a water glass filled with bubbly.

"Here's to you, sir, for giving me the opportunity," Williams saluted.

"And here's to you, Dick, for making the most of it," said Yawkey, who has waited 21 years since his only other pennant and is awaiting his first world championship. "This is the happiest moment of my life."

October 5, 1967

Julian Javier's double with two out in the eighth inning stopped Jim Lonborg on the threshold of a no-hitter today as the Red Sox surprised the Cardinals, 5-0, to even the World Series at a victory apiece.

Carl Yastrzemski provided Lonborg with more than enough runs by slamming two home runs worth four RBIs to delight 35,188 drizzle-dampened fans at Fenway Park.

"When I hit the first one," Yaz said, "I told Lonnie: 'You have enough, big guy. Go get 'em.' And he sure did."

Yastrzemski, who took batting practice after going hitless in yesterday's 2-1 opening loss, predicted one homer today—and got two. "I feel great; I bet I'll hit one today," he told manager Dick Williams, passing up batting practice and "taking a 45-minute nap instead."

His homers were the first by a Red Sox lefty in a World Series since 1915, when Harry Hooper hit two in Philadelphia.

As electrifying as Yaz's homers were, it was Lonborg's pitching that stole the show as the 6-foot-5 right-hander pitched the fourth one-hitter in World Series history. It took the Californian just 93 pitches to fashion his masterpiece, striking out four.

Lonborg was working on a perfect game as he mowed down the first 19 Cardinal batters before walking Curt Flood on a close 3-2 pitch in the sixth. Then, the next inning, Javier rammed the first pitch thrown him into the left-field corner to spoil Lonborg's dream.

"It was a hanging slider," Lonborg said. "When he hit it I just put my left hand in front of my eyes like someone seeing a car wreck. I just didn't make a good pitch and might have if I wasn't having trouble with my thumb."

Lonborg had developed a blister on his thumb during the middle innings, requiring him to limit his number of breaking pitches. He was given solid support by second baseman Jerry Adair and shortstop Rico Petrocelli, each making two sparkling plays.

Lonborg had not heard the last from Javier's bat. The wiry Cardinal second baseman broke open the seventh game by hooking a three-run homer into the Fenway screen off a tired Lonborg, who was seeking a third Series triumph with only two days' rest. The Cardinals won, 7-2, to capture the World Championship.

MIKE ANDREWS: "The World Series was sort of anticlimactic to the pennant race. I was walking around in a daze for awhile. I don't think we woke up to the fact we were really in the Series until we were halfway through it."

Fans storm the dugout.

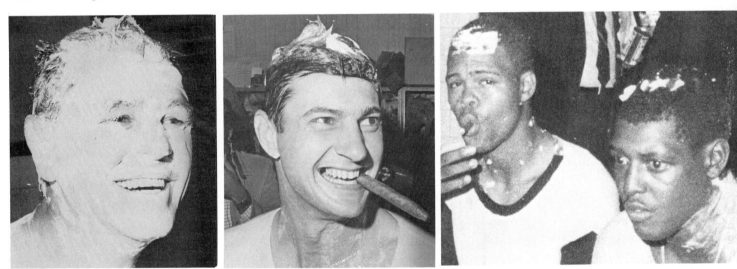

Dick Williams (left) and Carl Yastrzemski (center) get all lathered up in locker-room celebration. So do Reggie Smith and Joe Foy (far right).

Above, Tom Yawkey embraces Reggie Smith, the rookie who helped author the Impossible Dream. Left, Jose Tartabull helps give Carl Yastrzemski a shower. Before Yaz left the locker room, his salary had been nearly doubled to $100,000 by Yawkey. It was then the biggest raise in Red Sox history.

The 1967 Red Sox, American League champions.

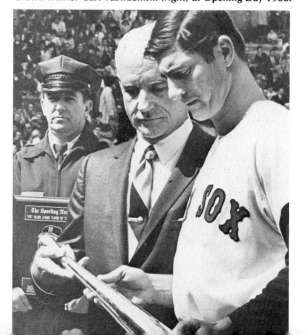

Above, baseball commissioner William Eckert presents Cy Young Award to Jim Lonborg and, below, a silver bat to Triple Crown winner Carl Yastrzemski (right) at Opening Day 1968.

November 16, 1967

The Red Sox added a postscript to their pennant today by sweeping the American League's two top honors.

Triple Crown winner Carl Yastrzemski was selected Most Valuable Player, and 22-game winner Jim Lonborg won the Cy Young Award.

Yastrzemski climaxed the Year of Yaz by polling 19 of 20 first-place votes, all but the one a Minnesota writer gave to Cesar Tovar of the Twins. Yaz received 275 overall points, 114 more than runner-up Harmon Killebrew of the Twins.

Orlando Cepeda of the World Champion Cardinals was a unanimous choice for National League MVP.

This is the first year dual Cy Young Awards have been made, one for each league. The Giants' Mike McCormick was chosen in the National League. Both Lonborg and McCormick received 18 of 20 possible votes. Joe Horlen of the White Sox got the A.L.'s other two votes.

The Red Sox are expected to also dominate the *Sporting News* awards to be announced soon.

They did, as Dick Williams and Dick O'Connell joined Yastrzemski and Lonborg in the spotlight: Williams/Major League Manager of the Year, O'Connell/Major League Executive of the Year, Yastrzemski/Major League Player of the Year and Lonborg/American League Pitcher of the Year.

December 27, 1967

Surgeons found Jim Lonborg's ski-injured left knee more damaged than they originally thought during today's operation at Sancta Maria Hospital. Two ligaments were discovered torn, not just the one anticipated, and there were complications deep in the joint.

Still, Doctors John McGillicuddy and Thomas Tierney are optimistic the 25-year-old Cy Young Award winner will be ready for the season opener April 9.

Lonborg injured the knee four days ago while skiing Heavenly Valley slope on the California side of Lake Tahoe. He hurt both knees, but luckily the right one was only bruised.

Lonborg has long enjoyed skiing, and he's explained the fascination:

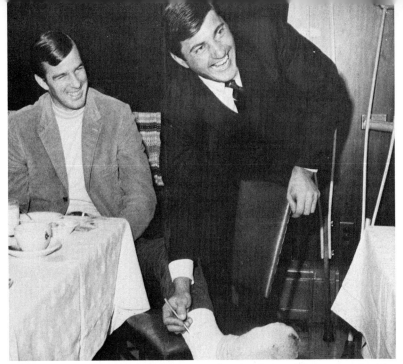

Carl Yastrzemski signs Jim Lonborg's leg cast, but the pitcher's injury was no laughing matter.

Dick Williams signs a three-year contract for a reported $55,000 per season after being voted 1967 Major League Manager of the Year. General manager Dick O'Connell (center) and president Tom Yawkey (right) clearly approve.

"When you're skiing you're fighting the mountain—and that's more exciting than anything I've ever done."

Lonborg's skiing has been a source of concern. While the Californian never attempted to cover up his participation, many fans weren't aware of it until just before the accident, when the Associated Press photographed the handsome bachelor showing actress Jill St. John how to throw snowballs at the Tahoe resort.

Red Sox general manager Dick O'Connell says he had asked Lonborg to use caution skiing. In the past, the Red Sox have stopped players from participating in some sports, such as Sammy White in basketball and Bill Monbouquette in hockey.

"It's one thing to bar a player from team sports and contact sports," says O'Connell, "but individual sports are a different matter. Skiing is a personal thing, like squash and golf."

Manager Dick Williams seems less upset, saying, "You can go out on a golf course and get hit on the head by a ball."

Lonborg disagrees with those who feel he took a foolhardy risk. "Anyone who performs athletically knows he faces a risk," shrugs the 6-foot-5, 200-pound Stanford graduate. And he won't say he'll never ski again.

Lonborg moved in with Buddy and Adelaide LeRoux for the remainder of the winter so the trainer could closely supervise the pitcher's rehabilitation (the retreat also shielding Lonborg from the press).

It would be a long way back for Lonborg. He was only 6-10 the following season, 27-29 over the next four years (not counting two quick trips back to the minors), before being traded to Milwaukee.

And while he had winning seasons with the Brewers and Phillies, Lonborg never again approached his overpowering and super year of 1967.

June 14, 1968

Ken Harrelson became the only Red Sox batter ever to hit three home runs in succession today as he drove in all seven Boston runs during the Sox's 7-2 victory at Cleveland.

Harrelson did it on three different types of pitches—off a Luis Tiant

Ken Harrelson hits a homer—one of 35 in 1968.

fastball in the fifth inning, a Tiant curve in the sixth and an Eddie Fisher knuckleball in the eighth.

The next time Tiant faced Harrelson, at Fenway Park, he struck him out three straight times.

September 29, 1968

Carl Yastrzemski today became only the fifth hitter ever to collect three American League batting crowns.

In retaining the title with a .301 average, the Red Sox veteran is the only A.L. player to hit in the .300s this season. Oakland's Danny Cater was runner-up at .290.

Yastrzemski's .301 is the lowest average ever to top either major league, and is a 25-point dip from his Triple Crown figure last season. Yaz's home run output also tumbled from 44 to 23 and RBIs from 121 to 74.

Still, Yastrzemski and Ken Harrelson, who led the majors in RBIs with 109 while belting 35 homers, have been two of the Red Sox's few bright lights in a disappointing season.

Today's 4-3 loss to the Yankees at Fenway dropped the Sox into fourth place, 17 games behind the pennant-winning Tigers. There has been an assortment of reasons for the plunge from last year's Impossible Dream pennant.

After his ski accident, Jim Lonborg's victory total fell from 22 to six. Jose Santiago and Ken Brett had arm problems, and the latter didn't pitch an inning for the varsity. Tony Conigliaro's comeback try from last year's near-fatal beaning failed in spring training and his career appears over. And George Scott's batting average plummeted from .303 to .171, and he didn't hit a single homer at Fenway.

Carl Yastrzemski was the only American League batter to hit .300 in 1968, winning his third batting crown.

November 1, 1968

Ken Harrelson was named American League Player of the Year today by the *Sporting News.* The award climaxes a year in which the colorful Hawk took New England by storm.

Harrelson blossomed as a fearsome right-hand hitter and led the majors with 109 RBIs while belting 35 home runs and hitting .275. Hawk also tied the major league record for highest fielding average for an outfielder: 1.000.

Harrelson nearly was traded by the Red Sox last March, but was retained when Tony Conigliaro was unable to return to the lineup following spring training.

Harrelson missed out on being the A.L.'s official MVP, that honor being swept along with the Cy Young Award by 31-game winner Denny McLain of the Tigers. In contrast, the *Sporting News* spread out the bouquets, naming McLain the Man of the Year while selecting Harrelson A.L. Player of the Year.

The baseball weekly picked Cincinnati's Pete Rose the National League Player of the Year.

April 8, 1969

Tony Conigliaro celebrated his return to baseball with a dramatic two-run homer in the tenth inning of the season opener at Baltimore today and scored the winning run in the 12th as the Red Sox outlasted the Orioles, 5-4.

His career apparently ended a year ago, Conigliaro started in right field today and homered on a 2-2 pitch from southpaw Pete Richert to give the Sox a 4-2 lead in the tenth. But Frank Robinson tied the game with a home run in the bottom of the same inning.

Conig wasn't to be denied the hero's mantle, though. He walked in the 12th and scored on Dalton Jones's sacrifice fly.

Among teammates congratulating Tony was a new roommate, his brother Billy, an outfielder up from Louisville seeing his first game as a big leaguer.

"It's been a long time between my 104th and 105th homers," Tony told reporters. "That's as good as I've ever hit a ball."

That was the first chapter in Tony C's Comeback of the Year story. He would hit 19 more homers, drive in 80 more runs and play 140 more games that season to win the Hutch Award, given annually to the major leaguer who "best exemplifies the fighting spirit and burning desire of the late Fred Hutchinson."

Conigliaro went on to an even better season in 1970, reaching career highs of 36 homers and 116 RBIs, only to be traded at season's end to the Angels in the Doug Griffin deal.

Eye specialists had regarded Conig's comeback as a near miracle, but the miracle wasn't complete. Tony had recurring eye problems, and retired after only half a season with California.

He tried another comeback with the 1975 Red Sox, but after 21 games quit for keeps—after 162 home runs in 802 games wearing a Boston uniform.

April 19, 1969

The Red Sox today shocked New England—and Ken Harrelson—by trading last season's American League Player of the Year to the Indians.

The deal—Harrelson, Dick Ellsworth and Juan Pizarro to Cleveland for Sonny Siebert, Vicente Romo and Joe Azcue—was announced after the scheduled Sox-Indians game at Fenway had been rained out.

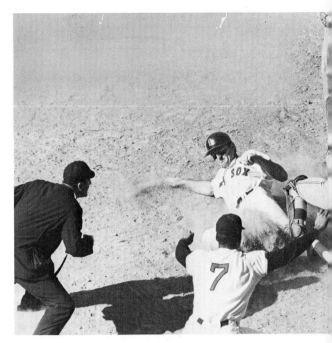

Ken Harrelson blossomed in 1969 and was named the American League Player of the Year.

A couple of heavy hitters named Henry Aaron (left) and Tony Conigliaro chat at Fenway.

Luis Aparicio fell *twice* while rounding third base during a crucial game with the Tigers at Detroit; here, he has fallen in the baseline in a game against the Yankees.

The trade lived up to Red Sox fans' worst expectations—even though the Yankees, perhaps out of a guilty conscience, shipped shortstop Mario Guerrero to Boston the following June as further compensation.

Cater's "Fenway swing" produced a total of just 14 homers in three Red Sox seasons during which he averaged .262 and 70 games per year.

Lyle, meanwhile, was the Yankees' top reliever six straight years and won the 1977 Cy Young Award with 13 victories and 26 saves.

October 2, 1972

Like Humpty Dumpty, the Red Sox took a great fall at Detroit today in more ways than one. And it probably cost them the American League East title.

Normally sure-footed Luis Aparicio *fell* twice while rounding third base, killing a Boston rally, and the Sox went on to *fall* to the Tigers, 4-1, and *fall* out of first place.

The Red Sox now trail the Tigers by a half-game with two games remaining in Detroit. The Sox must win both—highly unlikely since they have won only one of six games at Tiger Stadium this season. Instead of Boston having to sweep the last two, that burden would have been facing Detroit—*if.*

The Tigers had jumped to a 1-0 lead on Al Kaline's homer off John Duffield Curtis II in the second inning. But in the third, the Sox tied the game, and maybe lost a title.

Tommy Harper and Aparicio both singled off Mickey Lolich, and Carl Yastrzemski poled a drive over center fielder Mickey Stanley's head. Harper scored, but the 38-year-old Aparicio, who once led the league in stolen bases for ten straight years, lost his balance approaching third base and went down twice rounding the bag.

Luis finally scrambled back to the bag, only to find Yaz already there. The crowd of 51,518 howled at the sight of two on a base, and Yaz was tagged out. Reggie Smith struck out to end the threat. The Tigers went on to win on three RBIs by Aurelio Rodriguez.

The Sox were haunted by Aparicio's double tumble afterward. "We lost it right there," Yaz said. "We had Lolich on the ropes and let him off."

So this strike-shortened season may be remembered as the year the championship literally slipped away from the Red Sox—unless there's a mini-miracle and they sweep the last two games in a ball park where they've had little luck this year.

There would be no miracles. The Tigers clinched the next day as Woody Fryman outdueled Luis Tiant, 3-1. That gave Detroit a 1½-game lead and rendered Boston's 4-1 victory on the final day meaningless, except to make fans wonder forever after if the players' strike at season's start had cost the Sox first place. The resulting uneven schedule had Boston playing one less game than Detroit—a game that might have been the difference, as the Tigers won by a half-game margin, Detroit's 86-70 to Boston's 85-70.

The ending also frustrated the late-season charge by Eddie Kasko's team. The Sox were 48-48 on August 3 and took 37 of their last 59 to nearly win it. Still, two individual success stories couldn't be diminished: one by Luis Tiant, the other by Carlton Fisk.

Tiant easily won the league's Comeback of the Year award with a league-leading 1.91 ERA, the Sox's first under 2.00 since Carl Mays in 1917. An unimpressive 1-7 in 1971 after the Sox salvaged him from the minors, the 31-year-old Tiant regained his pre-injury effectiveness with a 15-6 record, 11-2 and 1.19 down the stretch.

Fisk became the first unanimous choice for A.L. Rookie of the Year. He not only established himself as a take-charge guy behind the plate and perhaps the league's best catcher, but also hit with authority. The 24-year-old New Hampshire resident batted .293 with 22 homers and a league-leading nine triples, and his .538 slugging average was second best in the league behind Chicago's Richie Allen.

CARL YASTRZEMSKI: "It's one of those things you'll always think about and always wonder about: whether we would have won the pennant if Aparicio hadn't fallen.

"Most people don't realize that Luis fell twice going around third base. I was standing on the bag when he went down the second time and remember wanting to push him to go home. I still think he would have made it."

January 18, 1973

The Red Sox became the first team to hire a player strictly as a designated hitter today when they acquired free-agent Orlando Cepeda to fill that new role.

General manager Dick O'Connell wouldn't disclose Cepeda's salary except to label the one-year contract "substantial," and added that team medics have pronounced the 35-year-old slugger fit despite gimpy knees.

While with the Giants, Cepeda was the National League's first unanimous Rookie of the Year in 1958. And he was that league's first unanimous Most Valuable Player with the Cardinals in 1967, when he opposed the Red Sox in the World Series.

"I've always wanted to play in Boston since Ted Williams was my idol," said the 15-year veteran, who has a .298 lifetime average and 358 career homers. "Now I have my chance."

Cepeda was an effective DH during his only season with the Red Sox, batting .289 with 20 homers and 86 RBIs. He led the club in winning RBIs (14) and had the team's longest hitting streak (17).

June 18, 1975

Three home runs. A triple. A single. Sixteen total bases. Ten runs batted in. Four runs scored.

That was all in a night's work for Fred Lynn tonight as he accounted for all but one Boston run in the first-place Red Sox's 15-1 taming of the Tigers at Detroit. The 16 total bases are the most ever by a Red Sox player and tie the American League record while establishing a major league rookie mark.

"I guess it pays to take extra practice," said the 23-year-old Californian, who, after a restless night, came to Tiger Stadium early to work on his hitting.

The results were awesome. One of Lynn's homers was off the upper deck's roof, the other two landing in the top deck. And the former USC football player narrowly missed a fourth homer when his triple was a few feet short of home run territory. Lynn also singled and lined out, thus stinging the ball all six times at bat.

The splurge increased the sweet-swinging lefty's batting average to .352, his slugging percentage to a league-leading .640 and his homer total to 14.

Lynn's ten RBIs and three homers tie Red Sox records. Rudy York (1946) and Norm Zauchin (1955) also had ten RBIs in a game. And seven others have hit three homers in a game, including Ted Williams three times.

Orlando Cepeda gets familiar with Fenway's left-field wall after signing as the Red Sox's first designated hitter. *(Boston Globe)*

Fred Lynn's bat accounted for 16 bases in a game—the most ever by a Red Sox batter or major league rookie.

Has a team ever had a more brilliant rookie hitting duet than Fred Lynn (left) and Jim Rice in 1975?

Winning pitcher Rick Wise pours bubbly over the head of battery mate and batting star Carlton Fisk after the Red Sox won the pennant by sweeping the A's in the playoffs. Below, Reggie Jackson congratulates Carl Yastrzemski.

That was the game that thrust Lynn into the spotlight coast to coast, and by year's end he would collect eight major national awards.

September 21, 1975

There's some good news—and some *awful* news.

The Red Sox today whipped the Tigers, 6-5, at Detroit to maintain their 3½-game lead over the Orioles in the American League East. But Jim Rice's left hand was broken by a pitch and he's lost until next year.

Rice, half the Sox's dynamic rookie duo, was struck by a Vern Ruhl fastball and will be flown back to Boston where a decision will be made on possible surgery.

The 22-year-old slugger, already named by Hank Aaron as a threat to his all-time home-run record, was hitting .309 with 102 RBIs and a team-high 22 homers, a balanced 12 at home and ten on the road. Any other season that would have made Rice a shoo-in for Rookie of the Year—except in 1975. Has a team ever had a more brilliant rookie duet than Rice and Fred Lynn?

Rice has had a solid year in the field, too. After starting the season as a designated hitter, he became the team's left fielder on July 2 and didn't make an error in his 90 games there. He combined with Lynn and Dwight Evans to give the Sox one of baseball's best young outfields.

Although the divisional title is all but assured, Rice's loss has to hinder the Red Sox as they chase their first World Championship since 1918.

The Red Sox clinched the division six days later and coasted to the pennant. But most New Englanders are convinced Rice would have made the difference in the World Series when the Sox fell two runs short of winning it all.

October 7, 1975

The Red Sox won the pennant today with a 5-3 victory at Oakland that gave them a three-game sweep of the American League Championship Series.

A crowd of 49,358 at the Coliseum saw the A's three-year reign as World Champions shattered.

The Red Sox raked three A's pitchers, including starter and loser Ken Holtzman, for 11 hits—ten singles and Rick Burleson's double. Carl Yastrzemski, Carlton Fisk, Denny Doyle and Burleson each had two hits for Boston.

Rick Wise was the winning pitcher, bolstered by 1⅔ innings of hitless relief by Dick Drago. Wise joins Luis Tiant and Roger Moret in the series' winner's circle. Tiant tossed a three-hitter in winning the opener, 7-1, and Moret was the 6-3 victor in relief of Reggie Cleveland in the second game at Fenway before the series shifted to the West Coast.

Now it's back to Boston to open the World Series against the Reds, who completed their three-game sweep of the Pirates today for the National League pennant.

October 21, 1975

Tonight's image of Carlton Fisk will long be frozen in the memories of the 35,205 who saw it at Fenway Park and the 50 million more who saw it on television.

There he was, bouncing along the first-base line in the 12th inning, frantically waving his arms and exhorting the baseball he'd just slammed toward the left-field screen to stay fair. The ball was hit high enough and far enough; the only question was whether it was fair enough.

"I was giving it every bit of body English I could muster," Fisk explained.

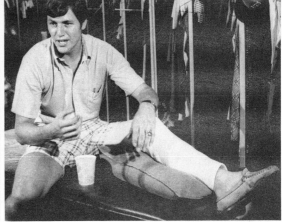

CARLTON FISK'S LIFE OF HARD KNOCKS

The life of a catcher is one of hard knocks. Carlton Fisk has been one of baseball's most durable catchers despite a litany of injuries. *(Boston Globe)*

Fisk's left knee was shattered in a June 1974 collision, sidelining him the remainder of the season.

Fisk was hit in the groin by a foul tip during a May 1974 game against the Yankees. Pitcher Bill Lee and umpire Ron Luciano come to his aid. *(Boston Globe)*

His right arm was broken during 1975 spring training.

Fisk was voted to the 1974 American League All-Star team despite the knee injury, and joined long-time Yankee foe Thurman Munson (left) and White Sox knuckleballer Wilbur Wood (center).

The ball crashed against the neon foul pole and Fisk leaped high, slapping his hands together in elation before breaking into a home-run trot that was really a victory dance.

"The fans jumped onto the field, but I made sure I touched every one of those sweet white bases," Fisk said.

New Hampshire's favorite son landed on the plate with both feet at 12:33 A.M., and it was finally over—a tingling 7-6 victory for the Red Sox that tied this World Series with the Reds at three games each.

The four-hour, one-minute marathon left everyone limp—and with a collection of goosebumps—from one of the most thrilling World Series games ever played. And the parade of images will linger awhile:

The roar of the crowd as Fred Lynn ripped a three-run homer in the first inning.

The deafening silence as Lynn lay still after crashing heavily into the

THE SIXTH GAME

Fred Lynn crashed heavily into The Wall in the fifth inning but stayed in the game.

wall in the fifth while leaping for a ball he couldn't reach—before finally getting up and staying in the game despite an aching back.

The thundering ovation and echoing *Loo-ie! Loo-ie!* as Luis Tiant departed in the eighth, running out of gas in his bid to be only the fifth pitcher in modern history to win three games in one World Series.

Then there was Bernie Carbo smashing a three-run pinch homer in the eighth against his old team to tie the game at 6-6. "I was just trying to make contact," he said of his second pinch homer in the Series. "It was the happiest moment of my life."

There was Denny Doyle apparently misinterpreting coach Don Zimmer's "no, no, no" for "go, go, go" and trying to tag up and score on an 180-foot fly in the ninth—an easy out to help kill a rally.

There was Dwight Evans robbing Joe Morgan of a homer in the 11th

Bernie Carbo smashed a three-run pinch homer in the eighth inning to tie the game.

Dwight Evans robs Joe Morgan of a homer in the 11th inning.

Carlton Fisk wallops his unforgettable home run off the Fenway foul pole in the 12th inning to tie the Series at three victories each.

with a leaping catch, snaring the ball just before it disappeared into the seats. "That was the greatest catch I've ever seen," marveled Reds manager Sparky Anderson.

And finally there was the crowning image of Fisk's gyrations and his homer kissing the foul pole.

Are there any images left for tomorrow night's Game 7 finale?

Yes, but most would be negative for Red Sox fans as an all-time sports record 75 million watched on TV, enticed by the previous night's high drama.

Red Sox fans jam City Hall Plaza the day after the World Series to pay tribute to their team—heroes in defeat.

The Sox built a 3-0 lead against Don Gullett through five. But in the sixth, Tony Perez crashed a two-run homer off a Bill Lee balloon ball, and Pete Rose singled home the tying run the next inning. And in the ninth, Joe Morgan singled home the Series winner off rookie Jim Burton, a surprise successor to more experienced Jim Willoughby.

There would be no World Championship for Tom Yawkey.

November 26, 1975

Fred Lynn today became the first major leaguer ever to capture both the Most Valuable Player and Rookie of the Year awards.

The center fielder swept those American League honors by hitting .331 with 21 homers and 105 RBIs while winning a Golden Glove and helping fire the Red Sox to the pennant.

Lynn received 22 of 24 first-place votes and totaled 326 points. Teammate Jim Rice, sidelined the remainder of the season after a pitch broke his left hand September 21, was third with 154 points, three points less than Kansas City's John Mayberry.

Joe Morgan of the World Champion Reds was named National League MVP.

Among the honors swept by Lynn were two of the highest in the sports world: United Press International selected him Athlete of the Year while the Associated Press chose him Male Athlete of the Year.

June 15, 1976

The Red Sox made the largest purchase in baseball history today when they bought relief pitcher Rollie Fingers and outfielder Joe Rudi from the A's for $2 million.

Struggling in defense of their American League crown, the Sox outbid the Yankees for the all-star pair. But George Steinbrenner didn't come away empty. He purchased A's southpaw Vida Blue for a reported $1.5 million. Thus Charles O. Finley collected a quick $3.5 million for the day.

Fingers and Rudi have not signed 1976 contracts because of major salary differences with Finley. The pair, both soon to be 30, immediately joined the Red Sox for tonight's game at Oakland, having to travel only 50 yards from the A's clubhouse to the Sox locker room at the Coliseum.

"I'm both happy and sad," Rudi said as he tugged on Boston jersey No. 25. "I'm sad to be leaving my A's teammates, happy to be joining a good club."

"Nobody likes to leave a team," Fingers added, donning jersey No. 30. "But if you've got to go somewhere, it's good to go with a fine club like the Red Sox."

Three days later the pair had to give back their new uniforms without having played an inning for the Red Sox—ordered back to Oakland (along with Blue from New York) when Baseball Commissioner Bowie Kuhn voided the sales in the "best interests of baseball."

Kuhn's action infuriated the Red Sox (not to mention Finley, who filed a $10-million damage suit against Kuhn).

"I can't understand what went through Kuhn's head," manager Darrell Johnson fumed. "What's the difference between this and, say, selling Joe Lahoud to Texas for $25,000? What's the dividing line?

"I keep thinking I could have avoided this whole thing. I mean, what would have happened if I had played them that first day (before Kuhn suspended the sale the next day pending today's hearing)? Would he have canceled the deal then?"

"It's against the American system of free enterprise," added catcher Carlton Fisk.

None summed up the bewilderment better than Rico Petrocelli, who said: "The whole game has gone completely crazy."

○

The loss of Rudi and Fingers was just one of a number of unlikely happenings that frustrated the Red Sox in their title defense. The Major League Manager of the Year the previous season, Johnson would be fired in mid-July. And the Sox had to win 15 of their last 18 games to barely beat out Cleveland for third place.

July 9, 1976

Tom Yawkey died of leukemia today, ending an era.

He was in his 44th season as Red Sox owner, operating a major league team longer than anyone in baseball history. During those years at 24 Jersey Street, he transformed the franchise from one of baseball's sickest to among the healthiest, and created a New England institution.

The 73-year-old Yawkey died at New England Baptist Hospital, Boston, and the team was told the news by general manager Dick O'Connell during a clubhouse meeting before tonight's game with the Twins.

O'Connell then informed the media in the rooftop press room before the news was announced to the fans at Fenway as the team took the field for the start of the game.

Yawkey has been ill since last fall's World Series, when the Red Sox came within two runs of giving him a World Championship. He has been

Tom Yawkey looks over the ball park he loved.

taking treatment in Boston since January, the first winter he's been away from his island retreat in South Carolina.

For the first summer since he purchased the team in 1933, Yawkey has been frequently missing from his familiar rooftop box. That's where he's watched most home games from June through September each season, with his wife Jean usually at his side.

A private person, Yawkey was friendly but aloof—and generous, some say to a fault. They claim that generosity was a key reason the team won only three pennants during his ownership, claiming his players were too content and not hungry enough.

The absence of a World Championship and more pennants undoubtedly frustrated Yawkey, but in looking back over his Red Sox years recently he said: "Oh, once or twice I felt like chucking the whole thing. But we all feel that way at one time or another. Overall, though, I've never regretted it—and have enjoyed it tremendously."

SPARKY ANDERSON: "Tom Yawkey was the greatest gentleman I've ever met in baseball.

"I had never met him before the '75 World Series. But I'd heard so many great things about him that I was eager to meet him. Just before the Series I told Eddie Kasko, who was scouting us for the Red Sox, 'Do me one favor, Eddie. Introduce me to that owner of yours.'

"So the day we got to Boston and practiced at Fenway, Eddie came and got me and brought me upstairs to Mr. Yawkey's office. There he was, wearing an old, *old* Red Sox jacket—almost moth-eaten. And I said to myself, 'This is a multi-, multimillionaire?'

"Well, we had a wonderful meeting, and I soon learned why everyone who ever worked for him or knew him thought the world of Mr. Yawkey.

"And later, the day of the seventh game, he called me and said, win or lose, he probably wouldn't be able to see me after the game because of all the end-of-Series confusion and all. But he said he wanted me to know how much he enjoyed having me and the Reds as Series opponents.

"Then, after we won, during the clubhouse celebration, I get word there's a call for me—it's Tom Yawkey to congratulate us.

"The man was all class."

November 6, 1976

The Red Sox created their first instant millionaire today when they signed Bill Campbell, their No. 1 target in baseball's historic first reentry draft this week. The right-handed reliever, last season's Fireman of the Year, is believed to have signed a five-year contract worth $1,050,000.

Campbell was paid $22,000 by the Twins last season while compiling a 17-5 record, with 20 saves and a 3.01 ERA in a league-leading 78 games and league-record 167 innings.

"I'm very, very happy to be with Boston and with a contender," said the 28-year-old screwballer. "I've always liked it here—both the ball park and the fans. I won't have any trouble pitching here."

Campbell didn't—at least not for a year. He overcame an 0-3 start in 1977 to finish with a team-high 13 victories (against nine losses) and a league-high 31 saves along with a 2.96 ERA in 69 appearances. All of which earned him the league's best reliever award for the second straight year. The 31 saves was a Red Sox record as Campbell gave the club its best relief pitcher since Dick Radatz.

But Campbell was dogged by continual arm problems the following

When Bill Campbell signed with general manager Dick O'Connell (above) and donned a Red Sox uniform, the ace reliever became the team's first instant millionaire.

Former University of Alabama quarterback Butch Hobson reverts to football habits to score against the Orioles in June 1976, knocking catcher Rick Dempsey unconscious. *(Boston Globe)*

season, jeopardizing his future and impairing the Sox's near-miss pennant bid.

July 4, 1977

The Red Sox celebrated July Fourth by skyrocketing a record eight home runs today in subduing the Blue Jays, 9-6, at Fenway Park.

The major league mark was tied when George Scott and Fred Lynn hit two homers each while Butch Hobson, Bernie Carbo, Jim Rice and Carl Yastrzemski added one apiece.

The explosion follows the Sox's record spree of 33 home runs in ten games, June 14-24, before being stopped by Mike Torrez in New York.

November 23, 1977

The Red Sox made another instant millionaire today, signing free-agent Mike Torrez to a seven-year, $2.5-million contract.

The 31-year-old right-hander was 17-13 last year with the A's and Yankees, and beat the Dodgers twice in the World Series.

Manager Don Zimmer labeled Torrez's signing "wonderful" because it strengthens the Red Sox while it weakens the rival Yankees.

General manager Haywood Sullivan added: "Obviously, we're happy we've signed Mike, even though I still don't like the free-agent principle. But we had to go out there hard because if you don't keep up in today's market, you get lost in the shuffle."

Torrez attended the press conference at Fenway Park accompanied by his wife Danielle, a Montreal model and TV personality.

"I'm looking forward to playing with a club capable of scoring runs like the Red Sox," he said.

The Red Sox got him one less run than his former Yankee playmates mustered for Ron Guidry in the rivals' winner-take-all playoff the following October. And many fans would remember the game-winning homer Torrez served Bucky Dent in that 5-4 loss more than they'd recall Mike's 16-13 record for the season.

Mike Torrez and his wife Danielle were $2.5 million richer after the free-agent pitcher signed with the Red Sox.

March 30, 1978

The Red Sox today acquired right-hander Dennis Eckersley in a six-player deal with the Indians. Pitchers Rick Wise and Mike Paxton, catcher Bo Diaz and outfielder Ted Cox were sent to Cleveland for Eckersley and catcher Fred Kendall.

Dennis Eckersley salutes his 20th victory after retiring final Blue Jay batter. *(Boston Globe)*

"Eckersley will do for us what Tom Seaver does for the Cincinnati Reds," manager Don Zimmer said.

"We now have the premier pitcher in the American League," general manager Haywood Sullivan said.

In three seasons with the second-division Indians, Eckersley had a 3.23 ERA and 40-32 record, including a no-hitter.

"This is it, I finally got out of Cleveland," said the 23-year-old right-hander. "This is what you dream about—being with a winner."

Eckersley nearly pitched the Red Sox to a pennant, the club's top pitcher with a 2.99 ERA and a 20-8 record, the only Sox pitcher besides Luis Tiant to win 20 games since 1967. Eck was 11-1 at Fenway, the best since Dave Ferriss's 13-0 there in 1946.

May 23, 1978

The American League today unanimously approved transfer of the Red Sox to a group headed by Jean Yawkey, Buddy LeRoux and Haywood Sullivan. The purchase price was $15 million, believed to be the most ever paid for a baseball team.

Approval came at a league meeting in Chicago and ends months of uncertainty regarding disposal of the club from the Yawkey estate. The A.L. owners had rejected a bid by Sullivan and LeRoux at the winter meetings in Honolulu last December.

The proposal was then rearranged, with Mrs. Yawkey taking a more prominent role. The widow of longtime Red Sox owner Tom Yawkey becomes one of three general partners along with LeRoux and Sullivan, who put the package together. There also are seven limited partners in the new ownership, which is capitalized at $23.5 million.

The approval climaxes a success story for Sullivan and LeRoux, both rising from dugout to ownership of the club. Sullivan, 47, is a onetime reserve catcher who has been the team's vice president for player personnel since late 1965. LeRoux, 44, was the team's trainer from 1966 to 1974.

Mrs. Yawkey will be club president, Sullivan and LeRoux executive vice presidents, with Sullivan heading the baseball operation, LeRoux the administration and business sides.

October 2, 1978

"Even though we won I can't say we're better. I think we're both equal," Graig Nettles said in the Yankee locker room at Fenway Park late this afternoon. "We played 162 games, then nine more innings, and it all came down to the last pitch. How close can you get?"

Ninety feet away. That's how close the Red Sox were to tying the game

At left, new Red Sox co-owners Haywood Sullivan (left) and Buddy LeRoux watch their team from the press box. At right, new president Jean Yawkey chats with team captain Carl Yastrzemski.

with two out in the last of the ninth and Rick Burleson on third base. And the Sox weren't much further away from winning it; speedy Jerry Remy was on first base.

And at bat: Carl Yastrzemski, Mr. Clutch. It was a script writer's dream.

The pitcher? Rich Gossage, the Yankees' ace reliever. So there it was: the best vs. the best, fastball pitcher vs. fastball hitter.

It was a classic match-up within a classic match-up.

"Yastrzemski is the greatest player I've ever pitched against," Gossage said. "I wasn't going to get beaten by anything but my best. Forget the breaking ball. I just wound up and threw as hard as I could."

Yaz expected the 1-0 pitch to tail away, but it tailed in. He tried to hold his swing but couldn't, and the ball popped high into foul territory off third base. When it came down into Nettles's glove, the Yankees were 5-4 victors and champions of the American League East.

It capped the greatest comeback in league history. Trailing the Red Sox by 14 games on July 19, the Yankees rallied to win 52 of their last 73 to not only catch the Sox but pass them. A disastrous August 30-September 16 stretch when the Sox lost 14 of 17 left them 3½ behind, but they won 11 of their last 13, including the pressure-packed final seven, to tie.

There were plenty of heroes in this playoff, and the biggest and most unlikely was Bucky Dent.

Mike Torrez went into the seventh inning with a two-hitter and leading, 2-0, on Yaz's homer in the second off tired and struggling Ron Guidry and Jim Rice's RBI single in the sixth.

But Chris Chambliss and Roy White singled, and then came the .243-hitting Dent, who had four homers all season. The chunky shortstop fouled a pitch off his foot. As he took a minute to shake off the pain, on-deck batter Mickey Rivers talked Bucky into using his bat.

Dent used it well, pulling a fastball to left that barely caught the screen for a 3-2 Yankee lead. "I never thought it would carry," said Torrez. "I was shocked." So were 32,925 fans who saw it but didn't quite believe it, no matter which side they were rooting for.

Both teams scored more runs—Reggie Jackson's homer into the center-field bleachers in the eighth proving the actual title-deciding run. And there were two sparkling plays in right field by sun-blinded Lou Piniella. But it was Dent's homer that was the key, as he turned the Sox's left-field-wall sword against them.

And suddenly there was Nettles, clutching Yaz's foul pop, holding it high for all the world to see, and a few feet away Gossage leaping high before the pair embraced in victory.

"It's a shame this wasn't a seven-game series and that it wasn't the World Series," Yankees owner George Steinbrenner said in the Red Sox clubhouse. "We are the best two teams in baseball. We proved that on the field today. We won, but you didn't lose."

"Both of us should be champions," Jackson said as he shook every Red Sox hand in sight.

"We have everything in the world to be proud of," Yaz allowed. "What we don't have is the ring."

MIKE TORREZ: "I thought it was a routine fly ball ending the inning. I looked over my shoulder on the way to the dugout and couldn't believe it. Yaz is back to the wall, popping his glove, looking up. I said, 'What's this? What the . . .'

" 'Goddam,' I was saying to myself. 'Goddam, how could that happen?'

"It's still hard to believe. I've seen the replays on television, Carlton

Third baseman Graig Nettles (left) and pitcher Rich Gossage jump with joy, Nettles still clutching Carl Yastrzemski's playoff-ending foul pop-up. (*Boston Globe*)

Yankees cheer teammate Mickey Rivers as he trots to first base on the seventh-inning base on balls that finished Red Sox pitcher Mike Torrez. Rivers scored the Yankees' fourth run. (*Boston Globe*)

Mike Torrez thought Bucky Dent's homer over the left-field wall was "a routine fly ball ending the inning."

Jim Rice beat out Yankee Ron Guidry as American League MVP.

calling for the fastball, inside. It wasn't exactly where I wanted it but Bucky just hit it hard enough to get out of the park with that breeze.

"I would have loved to have won that game, beating my ex-mates. I would have *loved* it. But, hey, you can't put every pitch exactly where you want it. If I could do that I'd be making $10 million a year.

"I'm sorry we didn't win it. In my heart I know I gave it all I had, 100 percent. I pitched a hell of a game—not too bad. I pitched tough.

"But I can't keep going back over it. I can't keep going back over that homer, that pitch. It's not too good a remembrance."

RON GUIDRY: "Every time the Red Sox and Yankees meet it's like a mini-World Series.

"It's just too bad we're in the same league and can't meet in the real World Series. It's that kind of match-up—pitting the best."

CARL YASTRZEMSKI: "Red Sox versus Yankees is the greatest rivalry in sports."

November 7, 1978

Ending a month of speculation and debate, Jim Rice was named the American League's Most Valuable Player today by a surprisingly comfortable margin over Yankee pitching ace Ron Guidry.

The 25-year-old Red Sox slugger received 20 of 28 first-place votes and 352 points to Guidry's eight first-place votes and 291 points.

"I'd say that being the everyday player made the difference," said Rice, who played in 163 games—114 as an outfielder, 49 as the designated hitter.

Rice led the majors in hits (213), homers (46), runs batted in (139), triples (15) and slugging percentage (.600) while batting .315 and scoring 121 runs. He became the first player since Joe DiMaggio in 1937 to amass more than 400 total bases, collecting 406.

Rice's 213 hits are the second most in Red Sox history behind Tris Speaker's 222 in 1912. And Rice's 46 homers are the second most in club annals behind Jimmy Foxx's 50 in 1938.

Pittsburgh's Dave Parker was named National League MVP.

While missing the A.L. MVP honor, Guidry won the league's Cy Young Award. The 25-3, 1.75 ERA southpaw also was named Major League Player of the Year by the Sporting News, *which named Rice A.L. Player of the Year.*

November 13, 1978

Luis Tiant—the *Loo-ie, Loo-ie* darling of Fenway fans—is now a Yankee and will next be seen wearing the hated pinstripes. The Yankees today signed the soon-to-be-38 free agent for an estimated $875,000 package. The pact guarantees Tiant two seasons as a player and, upon retirement, ten years as a Latin America scout.

"The Red Sox made me go, the way they treated me," said the third-winningest pitcher in team history. "After all I did for them it wasn't fair. But they didn't care. They would give me only one year.

"I'm looking out for No. 1," added the pitching contortionist. "And that's me."

Haywood Sullivan said the Red Sox made Tiant "one helluva offer."

"It's tough to lose Tiant," the general manager added. "And it hurts to

Luis Tiant, the man of many motions, won 20 games for the Red Sox in 1973, adding 22 in 1974 and 21 in 1976.

Luis Tiant ranks among the Red Sox's all-time pitchers—and characters.

realize that now the only thing that counts is money. The sense of loyalty no longer exists."

The Yankees were the only team to pick Tiant in the free-agent sweepstakes. Beyond Luis's abilities, owner George Steinbrenner's interest was undoubtedly further whetted by the opportunity to needle the rival Red Sox—particularly in retribution for their selection of Mike Torrez in last year's free-agent draft. Since no other team chose Tiant, Steinbrenner's offer bailed out Luis.

Tiant's age—he'll be 38 in ten days and there long have been rumors that he's older than his listed birthday—was the reason the Sox refused to offer him a longer contract. Also, his record, while still a winning one, has slipped to 12-8 in '77 and 13-8 in '78.

The cigar-chomping Cuban has totaled a 122-81 record since joining the Red Sox in mid-1971 after being released that year by both the Twins and Braves. The right-hander was 1-7 the remainder of that season, but Sox patience soon paid off. He won at least 15 games each of the next five years, including three 20-or-more-victories seasons. He also won one championship series game and two World Series games in 1975.

Tiant is one of only three pitchers in Red Sox history to be a 20-game winner three times, joining Cy Young and Bill Dinneen, who did it in the dead-ball era. Until Dennis Eckersley did it this season, Tiant was the only Red Sox pitcher to win 20 in a season since Jim Lonborg in 1967.

Tiant ranks second behind Young on the Sox's all-time list for starts (238) and innings (1774), third behind Young and Mel Parnell in victories (122) and shutouts (26).

Tiant ices his pitching arm after notching another 20-victory season.

January 8, 1979

Slugger Jim Rice today received the fattest contract ever given a Red Sox player. The American League's Most Valuable Player signed a seven-year pact estimated at $5.4 million.

"I'm extremely happy with this deal," said the 25-year-old Rice, who would have been free after the 1980 season under his old contract. "I didn't want to go through the free-agent process. I wanted to stay in Boston."

Tiant in action as a master bench jockey.

Fred Lynn (left), Jim Rice (center) and Carl Yastrzemski were voted the American League's starting outfield for the 1979 All-Star Game, the first time any club's entire outfield unit received that distinction.

3
HOSE
LINES

Jimmy Piersall had an answer for those who taunted him about his breakdown.

Sam Snead (left) had the last word in his debate with Ted Williams comparing golf and baseball. *(Associated Press)*

When Babe Ruth died in August 1948, his pallbearers included Jumping Joe Dugan and Waite Hoyt. Like Ruth, they had been traded from the Red Sox to the Yankees during the twenties.

As they carried his heavy coffin out of St. Patrick's Cathedral into the sweltering summer heat, Dugan whispered, "Lord, I'd give my right arm for an ice-cold beer."

"So would the Babe," Hoyt grunted.

o

A Cleveland loudmouth was giving Jimmy Piersall a verbal roasting during an early-1953 game when the Red Sox outfielder was coming back from his breakdown the previous season.

"Hey, screwball, look out for the man in the white suit!" the heckler bellowed from the safety of the Municipal Stadium bleachers.

Piersall didn't flinch. He turned around, cupped his hands and hollered: "How would you like to be making the dough this screwball is making?"

o

After Jimmy Dykes had lined to Joe Cronin to start a triple play, A's manager Connie Mack greeted Dykes on his return to the dugout: "James, you certainly know how to keep them off the bases."

o

Sam Snead visited the Red Sox dugout one day and was being needled about how much easier it is to be a professional golfer than a major league baseball player.

"You use a club with a flat hitting surface and hit a stationary object. What's so tough about that?" Ted Williams demanded. "I have to use a round bat to try to hit a ball traveling about 110 miles an hour—and sometimes curving."

Snead considered the comparison for a moment.

"Yeah," he drawled finally, "but you don't have to go up into the stands and play your foul balls like we do."

o

Inserted into the Red Sox lineup at Minnesota one afternoon in 1970, utilityman-humorist George Thomas responded by punching three opposite-field doubles before his home-area fans.

Thomas was waiting when the press crowded around his locker afterward.

"I'm exhausted," he said in mock disgust. "So you can just tell (Eddie) Kasko for me that he can either bench me or trade me."

o

Ellis Kinder was an irrepressible one-of-a-kind who endeared himself to Red Sox fans with his stamina on and off the field.

When he crashed his car at 2:30 one morning in 1955, the veteran pitcher said he had been trying to avoid hitting a dog.

"Can you imagine that?" Kinder asked teammates. "What respectable dog would be out at that hour?"

o

Dick "The Monster" Radatz was another who enjoyed himself off the field as well as on, a blithe spirit with a sense of humor the size of himself.

Asked in training camp at Scottsdale one spring about the Red Sox's fun-loving reputation, baseball's No. 1 relief pitcher deadpanned: "We're not going to drink any more this year."

He paused for effect.

"Of course," he added with a wink, "we're not going to drink any *less,* either."

o

Jovial Gene Conley showed up in the Red Sox clubhouse one day after a game's absence, and immediately headed for Mike Higgins's office.

"Sorry, Mike, there was sickness in my family," the pitcher told the manager.

"That's too bad," Higgins said. "Who was sick?"

"Me."

○

On an oculist's advice, witty Yankee pitcher Lefty Gomez donned glasses one day while starting at Fenway Park against the power-hitting Jimmy Foxx-Joe Cronin-Ted Williams lineup.

Gomez discarded the glasses after an inning.

"Couldn't you see with them?" a teammate asked.

"Sure, I could see out of them," Gomez replied. "That was the trouble—I could see too damn well.

"I nearly had a heart attack when that Foxx came to the plate. I never knew he was *that* big. Then I looked out at that left-field wall and almost had another cardiac. I never knew it was *that* close.

"So to hell with the glasses. What I don't know won't hurt me."

○

Another time when Foxx stepped into the batter's box against Gomez, the pitcher shook off one sign after another from catcher Bill Dickey. Finally, Dickey called time out and charged out to the mound.

"Just how the hell do *you* want to pitch this guy?" Dickey demanded.

"To tell the truth, Bill," Gomez replied, "I'd rather not throw this guy *anything*."

○

Red Sox pitcher Jim Bagby Jr. had a harelip and a sense of humor.

When Ted Williams played in Detroit for the first time in 1939, Tiger first baseman Hank Greenberg was playing the left-hand-swinging rookie near the bag.

"You'd better get back, Hank," Bagby urged from the visiting team dugout along the first-base line. "The kid can really rip a ball."

Greenberg ignored the advice.

Ball one.

"You don't know this kid, Hank," Bagby prodded. "You'd better get back."

Ball two.

"Hank, I'm not kidding, you'd better get back," Bagby persisted. "You'll . . . be . . . sor-ry."

Ball three.

"Okay, Hank," Bagby shrugged. "If you want to *look* like me and *talk* like me, stay right where you are."

Greenberg couldn't possibly have played deep enough. On the next pitch, Williams drilled a home run off the facing of the right-field stands' upper deck. And in his next at-bat, Ted lifted one over everything: the first ball hit out of Briggs Stadium (now Tiger Stadium) since it was double-decked in 1937.

○

Public address announcers can't inform the crowd of a lineup change until officially ordered to do so by the umpire-in-chief.

During a 1969 game at Fenway, Dick Williams sent in Don Lock to run for Tony Conigliaro.

Fenway p.a. veteran Sherm Feller, a Boston broadcasting institution, awaited the plate umpire's signal to announce the change.

No signal.

Lock loosened up with a couple of deep knee bends by first base.

Feller waited.

No signal.

Lefty Gomez (left) didn't relish pitching to Jimmy Foxx (right). Could that be what Lou Gehrig is pointing out?

Jim Bagby Jr. warned Hank Greenberg about Ted Williams, but Greenberg ignored him.

Rookie Ted Williams hammered the first homer out of Detroit's stadium after it was double-decked.

Richard Cardinal Cushing and Nun's Day crowd were asked to "please remove their clothing..."

Moe Berg (right) was the Red Sox's resident wit and usually had an eager audience, such as coach Herb Pennock (left) and outfielder Doc Cramer.

"Sherm, announce the runner," Red Sox public relations director Bill Crowley called across the press box.

"I can't, Bill," Feller replied. "He's not official until the umpire tells me."

Still no signal.

By now the next Red Sox hitter had stepped into the batter's box, the pitcher was toeing the rubber and the plate umpire was getting set behind the catcher.

Still no signal.

"Sherm, announce the runner!" Crowley ordered, hollering this time.

"Bill, he's not official until the umpire..."

"To hell with the umpire!" Crowley roared. "Announce the runner!"

Feller shrugged and flipped open his microphone switch.

"Your attention please... for the Red Sox... Number 18... Don Lock... *probably* running for Tony Conigliaro."

o

Feller got another laugh one day—unintentionally.

It was Nun's Day in 1967, with Richard Cardinal Cushing, as usual, wearing a Red Sox cap while leading the delegation.

Midway through the game, some front-row occupants of boxes had draped sweaters and jackets over the railing. Fearing possible obstruction on an overthrow, the plate umpire signaled Feller to announce a request to clear the railing.

"Your attention please, ladies and gentlemen, boys and girls," Feller boomed. "Would those in the front boxes please remove their clothing..."

Feller paused for a breath—unfortunate timing—and the crowd erupted in laughter, few hearing him conclude the sentence: "... from the railing?"

o

Moe Berg is one of the more remarkable figures in Red Sox history.

Educated at Princeton, Columbia Law and the Sorbonne, it was often written with affection that the back-up catcher "can speak a dozen languages flawlessly but can hit in none."

Berg was also the Red Sox's father-confessor and resident wit.

One afternoon in 1939, Moe rammed a drive off The Wall, his only double that season. He soon scored and plunked down on the bench next to rookie Ted Williams.

"That's the way you are supposed to hit them, my boy," the .243 lifetime hitter winked at the .344 lifetime hitter. "I certainly hope you were watching."

o

Berg spent most of his time in the Red Sox bull pen, warming up pitchers and counseling them on baseball and other matters. It was an event when he was summoned to catch the remainder of a game.

One afternoon, manager Joe Cronin waved Moe in from the bull pen. While snapping on his catching gear, Berg asked Cronin in an exaggerated whisper so all the dugout could hear: "Joe, it's been a while. Do the batters still get three strikes?"

o

Retiring after 15 big league seasons in 1939, Berg was a Red Sox coach 1940–41 as World War II ignited in Europe.

A player with a drinking problem asked Berg if he could move into Moe's lodgings at the Myles Standish Hotel for a few days.

A day or two later, Berg became alarmed when the player hadn't arrived at Fenway by the end of batting practice. Moe collared a couple of pitchers and headed for the hotel four blocks away, stopping traffic as they crossed busy Kenmore Square dressed in their Red Sox uniforms and street shoes.

The trio found their distressed teammate on the floor of Berg's room, snoring. Since he was clearly in no shape to play, they put him to bed and returned to Fenway just in time for the game.

Cronin asked Berg where his roommate was.

"Like France, Spain and England," Moe shrugged, "he's devastated."

○

Throughout the fifties, the give-and-take jousts in the Red Sox training room between supreme egotist Ted Williams and master ego-deflator Jack Fadden were classics.

Typical was the summer morning Williams sat on the edge of the rubbing table and asked the trainer, "Am I the greatest ball player you ever saw, Jack?"

"Theodore," Fadden responded matter-of-factly, "I could name 50 guys I'd rather have."

"*Fifty*?" roared Williams. "Name one!"

"How about Joe DiMag?" Fadden said. "Can you field like him? Can you run as well?"

"No," Ted admitted.

"And when it comes to throwing," Fadden said, "you're the world's highest-paid shot putter."

Williams was subdued—briefly.

"Well," he persisted, "I'm still the greatest hitter—and the greatest fisherman."

"Greatest fisherman?" Fadden baited. "Listen, there was a guy who produced more fish in one minute than you could in a year."

Williams squinted. "Who the hell was that?" he demanded.

"Didn't you ever hear about the Sermon on the Mount, about the loaves and fishes?" Fadden said.

"My God," Williams bellowed. "You had to go back far enough to top me, didn't you?"

○

Jimmy Piersall once was tricked by Browns shortstop Billy Hunter.

Standing next to base-runner Piersall, Hunter said, "Give the bag a kick, will you, Jim?"

Piersall took his foot off the base to kick it, and Hunter tagged him out.

"Thank you," said Hunter.

○

Joe Cronin was doubly embarrassed when victimized by Yankee shortstop Frankie Crosetti's hidden-ball trick.

"It's humiliating," Cronin said. "I taught it to him in San Francisco."

○

Veteran Virgil "Fire" Trucks kept shaking off A's catcher Tim Thompson one day in 1957 while facing the hot-hitting Billy Klaus, the scrappy little Red Sox infielder.

"Give him the knockdown pitch, for cripes sakes," Klaus said finally. "That's what he's waiting for."

Thompson gave the sign. Trucks nodded and had a sudden lapse in control. Klaus went down. The game continued.

○

During the second game of the 1912 World Series, the Giants made five errors behind Christy Mathewson, a display that had manager John McGraw frothing and 30,148 Fenway Park fans howling.

Shortstop Art Fletcher committed three of the errors and was needled by Sox shortstop Heinie Wagner: "Shall I get you a net or do you want a basket?"

Fletcher's reply is not recorded.

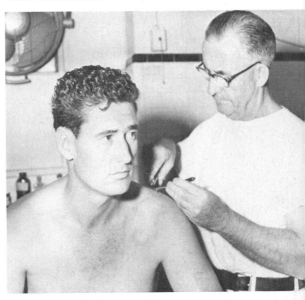

The verbal jousts between Ted Williams and trainer Jack Fadden were classics.

Billy Klaus suggested the knockdown pitch—on himself.

o

Besides leading the American League in batting in 1951 and 1952, Ferris Fain was a slick-fielding first baseman for the A's. His specialty was rushing the batter with reckless vigor when he suspected a bunt was about to come his way.

One day at Fenway, the Red Sox had runners on first and second with one out. The batter bunted toward the charging Fain, who threw the ball into the third-base grandstand trying to force the lead runner. Umpires waved that runner home and the Red Sox took the lead.

When the inning ended, A's manager Connie Mack was waiting when the exasperated Fain returned to the dugout.

"What happened, Ferris?" the elderly manager asked softly.

Still flushed, Fain snapped: "What did you want me to do with it, eat it?"

The dugout was stunned into silence. Nobody talked to Mr. Mack like that.

Mack, in his late eighties, kept his cool.

"Yes, Ferris," he said calmly, "it would have been better if you had."

o

John F. Kennedy, candidate for Congress, and Dave Powers, his Charlestown campaign manager, were watching the Red Sox and Tigers battle at Fenway Park in 1946.

Joe Cronin was coaching at third base, and Kennedy asked Powers, a first-class baseball buff, how good a hitter the Red Sox manager had been.

"He was a great clutch hitter with plenty of power who batted .302 lifetime," Powers replied. "But, unfortunately, many will remember him more for being the fifth consecutive batter struck out by Carl Hubbell in the 1934 All-Star Game—Ruth, Gehrig, Foxx, Simmons and Cronin."

Fifteen years later, Kennedy and Cronin were presidents, Kennedy of the United States, Cronin of the American League. And Powers was still with Kennedy, his confidante and probably closest friend next to his family.

Cronin visited the White House to present Kennedy with the traditional gold season's pass.

"Dave," Kennedy said, "what was that you once told me about Joe Cronin?"

Powers flinched, knowing Kennedy meant Cronin's historic strike-out, but kept his cool.

"That he was a Hall of Fame shortstop, Mr. President?" Powers said.

"No, no, no—not that, Dave," Kennedy said.

"That he was one of the great clutch hitters of all time and batted .302 lifetime?" Powers said.

"No, no—there was something else."

"That he managed the Washington Senators to a pennant at age 26?"

"No—something else, Dave."

"That he was the fifth batter in a row struck out by Hubbell in the All-Star Game?" Powers said, his face flushing.

"*That's* the one," Kennedy said, and roared. So did the press members covering the presentation in the Oval Office.

Cronin laughed, too, unembarrassed.

"Mr. President," he said, "it was a pleasure to be in such company as Ruth, Gehrig, Foxx and Simmons."

o

President Eisenhower tossed out the traditional first pitch for a Senators-Red Sox opener one year at old Griffith Stadium in Washington, and, as usual, the players on both teams clustered to scramble for the ball.

President Kennedy needled Joe Cronin about being the fifth batter in a row struck out by Carl Hubbell in the 1934 All-Star Game. (*Associated Press*)

One Red Sox player stood off to the side as Ike wound up and pitched. As the players scrambled, shrewd Jim Piersall dashed to the presidential box. He held out another ball to Eisenhower and asked: "Mr. President, would you sign this one while those clowns kill each other for the other one?"

The grinning Ike, a former five-star general who admired sound strategy, signed.

○

Dick Stuart gave Fenway fans plenty to cheer about during his 1963 and '64 seasons as the Red Sox's power-hitting, no-fielding first base-man. They cheered him for his tape-measure home runs and they cheered him when he picked up a hot-dog wrapper near first base without muffing it.

His nickname, Dr. Strangeglove, was fitting because Stuart made even the most simple ground ball to him an adventure, a thrilling will-he-or-won't-he drama. Like the time during a spring training game at Scottsdale, Arizona, when the batter tapped an easy roller to Stuart near the bag.

Stuart came up with the ball, but it squirted out of his grasp and popped up by the peak of his cap. Stuart grasped it again, and again it squirted free as though greased. Stuart grasped it a third time and hung on with both hands as he flashed out his left foot to tag the bag an instant ahead of the hitter pounding down the baseline.

The crowd roared with delight, giving Stu a standing ovation.

And upstairs, a press-box wag dryly announced: "That play went 3–3–3!"

○

Stuart had another appropriate nickname.

As he strolled across the field at Cooperstown before the 1963 Hall of Fame game between the Red Sox and Braves, a voice boomed out of the opposing dugout: "Hello, *Stonefingers!*"

The voice belonged to grinning Henry Aaron. The nickname stuck.

○

Another good-hit, no-field Red Soxer was outfielder Smead Jolley.

When infielder Marty McManus was appointed manager during the 1932 season, one of the first things he did was spend hours working on Jolley's fielding. Much of the tutoring was concentrated on how to cope with "Duffy's Cliff," the tricky ten-foot incline in front of the left-field wall.

McManus's instruction appeared to have paid a dividend one after-noon when the 6-foot-3½, 210-pound Jolley lumbered up the embank-ment and made a nice catch, only to tangle his feet coming down, tumbling on his behind and dropping the ball.

The acrobatics tickled the fans but exasperated McManus.

"I spent all that time showing you how to go up the cliff and you muff it," he scolded Jolley at inning's end.

"Yes, you showed me how to go up, all right," replied Smead. "But you didn't show me how to come *down.*"

○

When Billy Werber broke a toe in 1935 while kicking a water bucket in frustration, he was advised by teammate and bucket-kicking expert Lefty Grove: "Bill, you should kick an *empty* water bucket and you should always kick it with the *bottom* of your foot, not your toe."

○

Mickey Owen, the former Dodger catcher who gained notoriety for his passed ball in the 1941 World Series and later for jumping to the Mexican League, joined the Red Sox for his final season in 1954.

As the team barnstormed north that spring, Owen was telling team-

Dick Stuart (right) asks Russ Nixon if a catcher's mitt would help his fielding at first base. *(Boston Globe)*

Mickey Owen (arrow) ended his playing career with the Red Sox in 1954. In 32 games he hit .235 and one home run—a grand slam in the last of the ninth inning to lift the Sox to a 9-7 victory over the Orioles.

When Ted Williams hit a homer, he never tipped his cap and rarely shook hands with the next batter, habits which upset some Red Sox fans.

Manager Mike Higgins (left) kept telling general manager Bucky Harris "to go bleep himself" when Harris tried to fire Higgins. Harris fired him anyway, and Higgins later succeeded Harris as general manager.

mates about a brawl so vicious that he'd bitten off part of an opponent's ear.

"Good God," said wide-eyed Jimmy Piersall, shaking his head in horror. "And they call *me* crazy."

○

One reason vagabond pitcher Bobo Newsom changed uniforms 16 times in 20 major league seasons was his big mouth.

Exhibit A occurred one afternoon during Newsom's fraction of a season with the Red Sox in 1937. Player-manager Joe Cronin trotted from shortstop to mound with some advice.

"You play shortstop," Newsom told Cronin, "and I'll do the pitching."

Bobo did his pitching the next season for the Browns in St. Louis, then the Devil's Island of the American League.

○

Teammate Birdie Tebbetts once nearly talked Ted Williams into tipping his cap.

"The next time you hit a homer, tip your hat while looking up at the crowd and giving them a big smile," the catcher suggested. "And while they're cheering and you're smiling, you yell, '*Go to hell, you S.O.B.'s!*'

"They won't know what you're saying, but you sure as hell will."

The last-laugh idea appealed enormously to Ted, and he later said he never came closer to tipping his cap. But in a few days the temptation passed.

○

The Red Sox were foundering in early July 1959 when Tom Yawkey dispatched general manager Bucky Harris to Baltimore to fire manager Mike Higgins.

Harris found reporters milling around the Lord Baltimore in anticipation of the move, so he spirited Higgins out of the hotel to apply the ax in private. However, the pair were spotted in a tavern by a couple of writers who took seats at the opposite end of the bar. They tipped the barmaid, pointed out Higgins and Harris, and said they'd be pleased to know the gist of the two gentlemen's conversation.

The barmaid returned in a few minutes.

"Well?" said the reporters.

"Well," said the barmaid, "the little one (Harris) keeps saying, 'You gotta quit, you gotta resign,' and the big one (Higgins) keeps on telling the little one to go *bleep* himself."

Higgins was fired the next morning, replaced by Billy Jurges—a move which sent the Sox hurtling from frying pan to fire. Within a year, Higgins was back as manager.

○

Joe Cronin suspended hard-to-handle Jim Tabor at training camp one spring, installing Lou Finney in Tabor's place at third base.

A first baseman-outfielder, Finney diligently practiced at his new position until he was black and blue.

"The only one getting hurt by Tabor's suspension," he growled, "is *me.*"

○

The Red Sox were trailing the Indians by a run in the eighth inning of a crucial game during the 1949 pennant race. The Cleveland pitcher had been weakening in recent innings, and the Boston fans were demanding a rally.

Veteran Satchel Paige and rookie Mike Garcia were warming up for the Indians. The consensus in the bull pen was that if Cleveland manager Lou Boudreau made a change, he'd choose the young and overpowering right arm of Garcia.

All of which heightened the rookie's anxiety. So Paige, the 43-year-old legend, tried to soothe the youngster's nerves as they heated up side by side.

"I wouldn't worry none about them Red Sox," Satch said confidently. "There ain't a hitter among 'em."

Crack—the Boston pinch hitter singled. One on, no out.

Dom DiMaggio stepped to the plate.

"Now, this here fella is nothin' special," Paige said. "In fact, he's a mess up there."

Crack—DiMaggio singled. Two on, no out.

Johnny Pesky stepped to the plate.

"I don't know why they say this man can hit," Satch said. "Just deal him right at the knees."

Crack—Pesky singled. Bases loaded, no out.

Ted Williams gangled to the plate and Fenway was a madhouse.

"Now we're going to be all right," Paige assured Garcia.

Boudreau went to the mound and signaled to the bull pen—for *Paige*.

Paige stared in disbelief, the air suddenly out of his balloon. He recovered with a sigh, grabbing his jacket and heading toward the bull-pen gate.

"And just remember one last thing, son," Satch concluded, rolling his eyes. "When you're disputin' the Red Sox, put your trust in the power of prayer."

Whether it was prayer or superb control or both, Satch held the Sox to one run in the inning.

o

Another time, Boudreau summoned Indian sinkerballer Red Embree to face Williams.

When Embree arrived on the mound he asked if he could pitch low to Ted. "Sure you can," Boudreau said. "But as soon as you throw the ball run like hell and hide behind second base."

o

Birdie Tebbetts, an oversized leprechaun with twinkling eyes, was a chatterbox who rarely stopped talking behind the plate. He was continually barking at his pitcher (sometimes encouraging, sometimes insulting), distracting the batter and baiting the umpire.

Among his favorite distractions for batters:

(1) Suggesting what pitch was coming. Sometimes he told the truth, sometimes he didn't. The batter never knew which until it was too late, after his concentration had been destroyed.

(2) Playfully tossing a handful of dirt on the batter's spikes just as the pitch was being delivered.

It's not surprising then that Tebbetts was involved in more than one fight in the vicinity of home plate.

Birdie also infuriated umpires by needling them while still in his catcher's crouch, with his back to them. Thus, if they reacted openly to his taunts, it would appear to the crowd that the umpire was picking on the catcher.

The content of Tebbetts's comments was disturbing to umpires, too.

"Haven't you ever worn a mask before?" he asked one ump. "You're supposed to look through the open spaces *between* the bars."

Umpires found Tebbetts annoying long-distance, too. Bill McGowan once walked over to the dugout and ejected Tebbetts for no apparent reason.

"For what?" Birdie demanded.

"For nothing," the umpire said. "Your voice just gives me an awful headache."

Satchel Paige said he prayed a lot on the Fenway mound.

Birdie Tebbetts barked at opponents and umpires—and occasionally teammates.

Frank Sullivan (right) and Sammy White were a pair of free spirits who combined as a live-wire battery.

Joe Cronin imitated a fielder catching a baseball to illustrate a point.

Ultimately, Tebbetts's voice apparently gave one or more Red Sox officials a headache, too. After the team had finished a disappointing third in 1950, Birdie made a speech in which he labeled some teammates "moronic malcontents and juvenile delinquents." Within a month, the 41-year-old catcher was banished to Cleveland.

o

Dick Stuart stepped to the microphone at the Boston Baseball Writers Dinner in January 1966, invited back to town as a guest a year after being traded to the Phillies for Dennis Bennett.

Standing at the podium, Stuart punctuated his opening comments by gazing down the head table at Billy Herman, the Red Sox manager who had enthusiastically endorsed the trade.

"And, Billy, I hope you're having a good winter," Big Stu said, pausing briefly for effect, "because you sure had a horseshit summer."

o

A Red Sox-Twins game at Minnesota in the early 1970s was interrupted by a bomb scare.

"Ladies and gentlemen, we are halting this game at this point and ask that you pay attention to this announcement," veteran public address announcer Bob Casey told the crowd at Metropolitan Stadium. "We request that you remain *calm* and *do not panic,* but we have just been informed by the Bloomington Police that in 15 minutes there will be an *ex-PLO-sion!*"

"What I recall most about the bomb scare," Casey recalls, "is that when I had finished the instructions to clear the stands, I got up to leave. But the federal man there told me I had to stay because I was in charge of communications. And then he left!"

o

A charter flight carrying the seventh-place Red Sox was being buffeted by a storm one summer night in 1960, lightning crackling around the plane.

Free spirit Frank Sullivan leaned across to a writer and whispered: "This team is insured for $2,000,000. Sort of makes you wonder which way Mr. Yawkey is rooting, doesn't it?"

o

It wasn't easy to get the last word on George Thomas, resident wit of the 1967 Impossible Dream Red Sox. But manager Dick Williams did one day when he snapped: "George, you are as funny *on* the field as you are off it."

o

During Ted Williams's first season in 1939, all the rookie could think of was hitting—even when in the outfield. He'd often be taking swings at a phantom ball with an imaginary bat while in right field, then his position.

All of which had manager Joe Cronin doing double takes from his shortstop position and shouting at his prodigy to "wake up out there!"

One day Cronin had enough and called time.

"Hey, Bush, never mind this," Cronin hollered, mimicking Williams's swings. "Try more of this," he added, imitating a fielder catching a baseball.

Ted got the message—and so did the fans, who loved the sideshow.

o

Told that the tall old man smoking the pipe was a former major league pitcher, the cub reporter approached Cy Young and asked, "Did you pitch in the big leagues, sir?"

Young, never a braggart, answered matter-of-factly: "Son, I *won* more games than you'll ever see."

o

Tom Yawkey was always tickled by an incident involving Yankee owner Jake Ruppert when Yawkey bought the Red Sox in 1933.

Ruppert still held a mortgage on Fenway Park, lingering from the Babe Ruth deal in the Frazee days. Since Yawkey had spent a large sum purchasing the Sox, he went to Ruppert and asked if he would carry the mortgage until the following year.

"Of course," said Ruppert. "We're happy to have you in the league."

Later that season, the lowly Red Sox swept a series from the mighty Yankees at Fenway.

"My lawyer phoned the next morning to say it was a costly sweep, that Ruppert's lawyer had called to demand payment on the mortgage," Yawkey laughed. "So I sent the S.O.B. a check the next day."

○

Satchel Paige once said of the Williams Shift: "That thing has taken more mitts off first basemen than the end of an inning."

○

Ernie Shore's two victories, including a three-hitter, in the 1916 World Series made the Red Sox southpaw a national celebrity—except, apparently, in his North Carolina hometown.

When he came home soon after the Series, a neighbor greeted: "How are you, Ernie? Ain't see you awhile. Been away?"

○

Broadway Charley Wagner, Ted Williams's longtime roommate, had the rudest of awakenings one morning.

Williams was up before breakfast swinging a bat in front of the hotel room's mirror while Wagner slept.

A bedpost knob caught Ted's attention. So he took his stance, drew a bead on it and gave it his best home-run rip.

Bwaaaaaanngg!

The bed collapsed, landing Wagner on the floor.

"Damn, what power!" marveled Williams, his hands tingling—and Wagner's head throbbing.

Jake Ruppert (right) demanded his Fenway mortgage money in a hurry from Tom Yawkey when the Red Sox swept a series from the Yankees.

Ted Williams may be telling Fred Lynn (right) about the time he took batting practice in the hotel room and sent the bed crashing down—with roommate Charley Wagner still in it.

4
TED vs.
JOE D

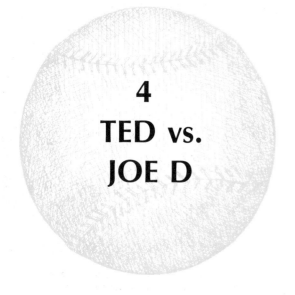

Dom DiMaggio with teammate Ted (top) and brother Joe (bottom).

Ted Williams and Joe DiMaggio.

They were from the same golden era, the two top players in their league and perhaps in all baseball.

So the comparison always will be inevitable, argued for as long as fans debate baseball.

So now, decades after both have retired, the argument not only lingers but thrives: Who was better, Ted Williams or Joe DiMaggio?

JOE DiMAGGIO: "Ted Williams was the best hitter I ever saw. There was nobody like him."

TED WILLIAMS: "In my heart I've always felt I was a better hitter than Joe, which was always my first consideration. But I have to say he was the greatest baseball player of our time. He could do it all.

"He was a better fielder. A better thrower. Everything he did was stylish. He ran gracefully, he fielded gracefully, he hit with authority and style. Even when Joe missed, he looked good.

"It is also true, of course, that in his 13 years with the Yankees they won ten pennants. That has to be a factor."

The person in the best position to compare Ted Williams and Joe DiMaggio was Joe McCarthy, the only man to manage both. But McCarthy consistently ducked the issue.

"I've been asked that question over and over, and have never answered it," he said right up until his death at age 90 in 1978. "I was very fond of both men and wouldn't want to hurt anyone's feelings."

But McCarthy once revealed his opinion to Ed Rumill of the *Christian Science Monitor* on the condition the comparison wouldn't be printed "until I'm gone."

This is what McCarthy told Rumill:

"Williams was the greatest student of hitting I've ever seen—perhaps the greatest in the history of the game.

"DiMaggio was the complete ballplayer, including the best base runner I ever saw. He could do it all."

Who was better, Joe DiMaggio or Ted Williams?

Ask Dominic DiMaggio, the brother of one who played ten seasons alongside the other in the Red Sox outfield.

Who was best, Dom?

"Joe was the best right-handed hitter," he replies with a grin, "and Ted was the best left-handed hitter."

Unquote.

o

The Yankees twice tried to put Ted Williams in pinstripes; three times if you include Ted's mother turning down Yankee scout Bill Essick's offer in 1939.

Once, in 1947, Tom Yawkey and Dan Topping chewed over a blockbuster trade in which Williams and Joe DiMaggio would swap uniforms. Yawkey, however, insisted the Yankees throw in a clumsy rookie outfielder-catcher named Larry Berra. End of discussion.

Fourteen years later, in 1961, the Yankees wanted to lure Williams out of retirement, but he wasn't interested. Ted reveals in his autobiography, *My Turn At Bat*, with John Underwood:

"Nobody knew this, but the Yankees tried to hire me to play one more year in 1961.

"Shortly after my last game, Fred Corcoran (Williams's business agent) got a call from Dan Topping, the Yankee owner, and they met at the Savoy Plaza in New York. According to Fred, Mr. Topping said, 'Would Williams play one year with the Yankees, strictly pinch-hit for us for what he's making now—$125,000?'

"Corcoran told him I was still tied up with the Red Sox on a deferred payment setup, that he ought to call Tom Yawkey about it.

" 'I don't want to call Yawkey; I want to sign him as a free agent. Can he get his release?'

"I'm sure if I had wanted him to Mr. Yawkey would have worked it out, but I wasn't interested in playing for the Yankees. What did New York have to offer? A lot of bad air and traffic jams.

"I told Fred to forget it, not to promote anything, I wasn't interested; I was never going to hit another ball in a big league park.

"There was a time, though, that a deal was actually worked out between the Red Sox and Yankees: Ted Williams for Joe DiMaggio.

"The feeling was that a right-handed power hitter like Joe was made for Fenway Park, with that short fence in left field, and I was better suited for Yankee Stadium, with right field so handy, and it was just fate that crossed us up.

"Mr. Yawkey and Mr. Topping met in a restaurant in New York, and the way Fred Corcoran tells it, they talked until 2:00 A.M. and shook hands on the deal.

"The press got to sniffing around and almost got it right. The trade was on the verge of going through. But the next morning, Mr. Yawkey asked Mr. Topping to throw in that 'little guy you've got in left field.' The little guy was Yogi Berra. The deal fell through."

Yawkey felt entitled to a two-for-one deal. Not only was Williams coming off an MVP season while DiMaggio had hit 52 points lower at .290, but Ted (28) was four years younger than DiMag (32).

The latter factor looms even bigger in retrospect. DiMaggio played only five more seasons while Williams played *14*.

o o o

There are those who feel a Williams-DiMaggio trade would have given both superstars a shot at Babe Ruth's home-run record. But Williams rejects suggestions that Yankee Stadium was an ideal park for him, advising:

"I didn't like Yankee Stadium. A bad background in center field when the crowd was big, and all that smoke hanging in there. I never saw the ball well in Yankee Stadium, although I averaged .305 there.

"There were other parks I would have preferred to play in. Like Detroit. I saw the ball better there. I hit 54 home runs in Detroit, more than any other park I played in on the road.

"I always felt jacked up in Yankee Stadium because of the crowds, but I never wanted to play there."

Tom Yawkey's two favorite players were Carl Yastrzemski and Ted Williams. Yet Yawkey nearly traded Williams to the Yankees in 1947.

Babe Ruth swapped Red Sox flannels for Yankee pinstripes in 1920, and Ted Williams nearly did the same thing in 1947. If Ted had, he might have broken Babe's record of 60 homers in a season.

Among the many who feel that way was Birdie Tebbetts, who said: "Ted Williams would have broken Babe Ruth's record if he had played his home games in Yankee Stadium, Tiger Stadium or Sportsman's Park in St. Louis, where right-field barriers were short."

5
ODD BALLS

Red Sox batters were often stood on their heads by opposing pitchers in the thirties, as Doc Cramer illustrates.

Joe Cronin tried to send mascot Donald Davidson to bat in 1938. But umpire Bill Summers ordered the 42-inch-tall Davidson back to the dugout.

During a trip to New York his second season, Ted Williams visited an uncle who was a fireman in nearby Westchester. They spent much of the off-day at the firehouse, playing checkers and gabbing about baseball and old times.

A few days later, in the agonies of a slump, Williams told a wire-service reporter: "That's the life, being a fireman. It sure beats being a ball player. I'd rather be a fireman."

The story went around the country, including Chicago, where Jimmy Dykes resided. The White Sox manager may have been baseball's all-time greatest needler, and had assembled an all-star cast of bench jockeys.

They were waiting when the Red Sox came to Comiskey Park a few days later. When Williams came to bat, half the White Sox bench broke out toy fire hats and began clanging fire bells and set off a screaming siren.

And for weeks, all Ted heard from enemy dugouts was *"Fireman, save my child!"*

It got so bad in New York, with Lefty Gomez and Red Ruffing ringing cowbells while Williams was batting, that umpire Bill Summers gave both agitators the rest of the day off.

○

And how's this for outsmarting yourself?

With the count 3-0 on Lee Thomas during a 1965 game, Oriole Stu Miller decided to put the Red Sox first baseman on base. But Thomas swung at the next two wide pitches, "hoping they'd pitch to me on 3-and-2."

They did—and Thomas fouled out.

○

When Tommy Harper stole a Red Sox record and league-leading 54 bases in 1973, two of the more spectacular thefts came in quick succession at Kansas City.

The 32-year-old outfielder went from first to home on just two pitches by future Sox teammate Dick Drago: stealing second, continuing to third on the catcher's wild throw and stealing home on the next pitch.

○

Ellis Kinder, then pitching for the Browns, had his concentration disturbed while pitching to a Red Sox batter at Fenway in 1947. A Boston seagull flying high above dropped a smelt on the mound, narrowly missing Kinder. He picked it up with right thumb and forefinger and carried it off the field at arm's length.

Unruffled, he regained his concentration and went on to defeat the Red Sox, 4-2.

Perhaps it was a sign. Or maybe Red Sox officials were impressed with Kinder's cool. Whatever the reason, Ellie was wearing a Boston uniform the next season and for more than a half-dozen seasons thereafter, most of them notable.

○

Joe Cronin beat Bill Veeck to the punch in sending a midget to the plate.

The Red Sox manager once put 42-inch-tall Donald Davidson, the team's mascot, into a 1938 exhibition game. Like Eddie Gaedel 13 years later, Davidson walked on four straight pitches and got his name in the box score.

Cronin was preparing to do the same thing in a game at Fenway Park after the Yankees had clinched the 1938 pennant. Davidson skipped out of the Red Sox dugout and headed for the plate, armed with a fungo bat to pinch-hit for Moe Berg.

But Davidson was intercepted by umpire Bill Summers, who ordered the 70-pound schoolboy back to the dugout and had a few words for Cronin about making a farce out of the game.

Davidson made it to the big leagues in a different role—as publicity chief and later traveling secretary of the Milwaukee and Atlanta Braves. He's now a Houston Astros official.

o

Most managers followed Lou Boudreau's lead and employed a shift against Ted Williams after mid-season 1946. But none of the alignments was as radical as one executed during a Red Sox exhibition game at Dallas in 1947.

When Williams came to bat for the first time, the entire Dallas defense—except pitcher and catcher—climbed into the right-field stands and took seats.

o

Probably no Fenway batter has been more embarrassed than Larry Gardner, the Red Sox's solid-hitting, steady-fielding third baseman from 1908 to 1917. He lined a hit off the left-field wall—and was thrown out at first base.

"I didn't run because I thought it was foul," he explained.

o

That lapse merely proved the shrewd Gardner was human.

"Larry was one third baseman I never could successfully bunt against," admired Ty Cobb. "He would be in there pouncing on the ball before I was ten strides down the baseline. Time and again he threw me out like I was his bowlegged sister Kate."

Years later Cobb coaxed Gardner into revealing his secret.

"You clenched your jaw and clamped your lips together when you intended to bunt," Gardner said. "The minute I saw that I came running."

o

Frustration is what Tom Wright felt when he tripled in a 1950 game at Fenway, only to learn, upon huffing and puffing into third base, that an umpire had called time out.

Wright took another swing—and was out.

o

Embarrassment is what Gary Geiger felt when he thought his 11th-inning triple had beaten the Angels at Fenway in 1961. He kept going for the clubhouse, only to be tagged out and learning the hard way that his triple had only tied the score.

Instead of having the winning run on third base and no out, the Red Sox had nobody on and one out. (And it remained a tie through the 1:00 A.M. curfew.)

In 1940, rookie Dom DiMaggio was similarly abashed when tagged out while returning to his center-field position after hitting a routine fly. He assumed the ball had been caught by Tommy Henrich for the third out. He was half right. The ball hadn't been caught, but he was the third out when tagged.

o

Johnny Pesky also was embarrassed when thrown out at the plate in a big July 4, 1949, game at Yankee Stadium.

Pesky was on third base with the tying run when Al Zarilla lined a single to right with bases loaded. But, as if on cue from the Great Yankee in the Sky, a gust of wind swirled a mini-dust storm in the infield so Pesky couldn't see if the ball would be caught by right fielder Cliff Mapes.

Pesky tagged up and was a dead duck when Mapes fielded the ball on one hop and gunned him down on a force play at the plate.

Jackie Jensen also was thrown out at the plate while trying to score

Larry Gardner (left) and Bobby Doerr both experienced embarrassing moments at Fenway. Gardner hit the ball off the left-field wall—and was thrown out at first base. Doerr doubled in his first game there—and was picked off second base.

Perhaps the massage by Charley Wagner (right) helped ease Dom DiMaggio's discomfort after the rookie had blundered.

Hawk-eyed, rabbit-eared Ted Williams could spot targets in the left-field stands from the on-deck circle.

from third on a single. That happened in 1955 at Fenway, when the A's Enos Slaughter nailed him after Billy Klaus had singled to left.

o

Lefty Grove hurt his pitching arm throwing to first base (after fielding a Charley Gehringer bunt). Frank Sullivan hurt his pitching shoulder, not by throwing a baseball, but by trying to hit one in the batter's box.

o

Of Ted Williams's 2,654 hits, one deserves an asterisk.

One afternoon at Fenway early in his career, Williams aimed three or four straight line fouls at a heckler in the left-field seats as fans scattered for cover.

Trying one more for good measure, Ted undercut a pitch and the ball blooped fair down the left-field line. He was so shocked he hardly ran, and had to settle for a single on what should have been an easy double.

It also cost Williams $250 from his next paycheck, compliments of manager Joe Cronin.

o

Nearly 25 years after the Boudreau Shift was introduced at Fenway, the Bristol Shift was unveiled there in 1970.

When the Red Sox loaded the bases with none out in the 12th inning, Milwaukee manager Dave Bristol summoned Tommy Harper from the outfield and stationed him between the shortstop and third baseman as a fifth infielder.

It was a waste of time. George Scott lifted a sacrifice fly over the packed infield to win the game.

(If it means anything, Scott and Harper swapped uniforms two years later.)

o

The Yankees beat the Dodgers in a 1941 World Series game on Mickey Owen's famed dropped third strike, but the Red Sox used a similar lever to drop the Yankees six years earlier on Opening Day 1935.

While catcher Bill Dickey was throwing out a strikeout victim after dropping the third strike, Billy Werber broke from third to the plate and beat Lou Gehrig's return throw home as the Sox won, 1-0.

o

Red Sox outfielder Lu Clinton once place-kicked a home run—for the Indians.

Vic Power slammed a drive off the wire fence in right-center field at Cleveland's Municipal Stadium during a 1960 game. The carom hit hard-charging right fielder Clinton's foot and was booted over the fence.

The Sox claimed it should be a ground-rule double, but the umpires disagreed, ruling it a homer.

o

Ted Williams once propelled a ball over the fence—with his arm.

It happened during a preseason game against the Reds in Atlanta on April Fools' Day 1939, when Williams was the Red Sox's rookie right fielder.

After running down a foul ball, Williams picked it up, dropped it, then booted it as he reached down for it. Seething, Ted grabbed the ball and threw it over the fence—and off a Sears store across the street.

Manager Joe Cronin halted the game and replaced his temperamental rookie.

o

A frustrated pitcher once threw the ball over the roof at Fenway Park after being roughed up by the Red Sox in a 1946 game.

Angry Browns pitcher Jack Kramer heaved the baseball over the first-base grandstand roof before departing for the showers. Perhaps impressed by the strength of his arm, the Red Sox purchased him two years later.

o

Arriving at Fenway Park from St. Louis with Kramer was another right-hander named Ellis Kinder, who would carve his name in Red Sox history for his remarkable pitching and thirst.

Tossed the warm-up ball in the clubhouse before a 1950 start against the White Sox, it bounced off his chest and he had difficulty finding it on the floor. He did find the practice mound, but his warm-ups were unsteady.

His first pitch of the game was a strike; his second was up against the backstop. Then he began moving on and off the mound, peering at Birdie Tebbetts's signals. They seemed to confuse him.

Finally, after walking two, he was relieved because, it was announced afterward, of a sore arm. The right-hander had wobbled off holding his *left* elbow.

o

Catcher Johnny Peacock once discarded his mitt as well as his mask while pursuing a foul pop, making the catch bare-handed.

Equally impressive, Roman Mejias took a tumble on the cinder track in right field at Yankee Stadium while chasing a long drive, and made the catch while on his back.

And Rico Petrocelli slipped at shortstop while taking a hit away from Brooks Robinson at Fenway, gunning down the Oriole with a shotgun throw from a sitting position.

o

Following a July 4 doubleheader at Fenway in 1937, the Red Sox and A's took different sleepers out of South Station around midnight.

Oscar Melillo and Eric McNair of the Red Sox found their correct berth numbers—on the wrong train.

All of which triggered a real-life "who's on first?" routine when the two Red Soxers saw their nearby bunkmates were a couple of Athletics. McNair and Melillo thought the A's players had been traded to Boston while the A's players thought the two Red Sox had been traded to the Athletics.

The mystery was solved by the time the train reached Providence where the two lost Bostonians got off, Melillo playing his accordion on the platform until the Red Sox's train arrived.

o

That wasn't the first time Melillo became confused over who was friend and who was foe.

While wearing his St. Louis Browns uniform in 1935, he dropped by the Red Sox clubhouse socially one morning when the home and visiting dressing rooms were adjacent beneath the first-base stands at Fenway.

Told to take off his uniform, he thought it was because the Sox were concerned about fraternization.

"And when you take it off, put on this one," he was told while being handed a Red Sox uniform. "You've just been traded to us for Moose Solters."

o

A's pitcher Duke Maas defeated the Red Sox at Fenway in 1958 only to be told in the locker room afterward that he'd been traded to the Yankees *before* the game.

o

Yankees first baseman Babe Dahlgren had to leave a 1940 game at Fenway when hit in the face by his own foul.

o

Catcher Johnny Peacock landed in a Cleveland hospital for skull X-rays in 1942 because of a communications breakdown with pitcher Joe Dobson.

"He switched signs and forgot to tell me," Dobson recalls. "I thought

Ellis Kinder had great difficulty throwing a baseball one night at Fenway.

Johnny Peacock didn't always need a mitt to catch a baseball.

6
THE
OLD BRAWL
GAME

"Baseball fights? They're just one of those things that happen on a hot summer's day."
— GEORGE "BIRDIE" TEBBETTS,
who ought to know. He had
three memorable ones.

The Red Sox have had more than their share of brawls.

Beneath the pileup, the reason usually can be found among these categories: (1) Dusters; (2) Hard slides and/or hard tags; (3) Jockeying which accelerates out of control; or (4) Jokes that go too far.

The result is that tempers erupt and fists start swinging. Fortunately, most baseball "brawls" are of the one- and two-punch variety. Or, in one Red Sox instance, one karate kick. It's rare that anything more than feelings get hurt.

The Red Sox have fought opponents mostly, but have also swung at each other, an occasional sportswriter, even an umpire or two.

The incidents are countless. Here are some:

Predictably, the archrival Yankees are the foe that the Red Sox have fought most often. Probably best remembered is their 1976 free-for-all at Yankee Stadium.

It began with heavyweights Carlton Fisk and Lou Piniella colliding at the plate. After Piniella was called out, Fisk was kicked in the tangle of arms and legs. So Pudge tagged Sweet Lou a second time for good measure—on the head.

As they rolled on the ground, pitcher Bill Lee was bear-hugged by Yankee Graig Nettles and both benches emptied. Mickey Rivers plowed in and took a couple of shots at Lee, and Nettles added one to the southpaw's left eye.

The donnybrook resulted in a baseball fight rarity: a serious injury. A ligament was torn in Lee's pitching shoulder and he was disabled nearly two months.

o

A home-plate smashup also triggered a Sox-Yankees misunderstanding at Fenway Park in 1973. Batter Gene Michael missed a squeeze bunt, and runner Thurman Munson tried to steamroll Fisk. Fisk took on both Yankees, his left eye bruised by Munson and his face scratched by Michael.

o

The rivals went at it in 1967 at Yankee Stadium in a bean brawl. Yankee Thad Tillotson creased the batting helmet of Joe Foy, who had hit a grand-slam the previous day. In the bottom of the inning, Jim Lonborg plunked Tillotson with a get-even pitch.

Both benches cleared. Rico Petrocelli busily engaged in a number of jousts, including a main bout with fellow Brooklyn product Joe Pepitone. Amid clusters of skirmishes, Reggie Smith picked up Tillotson and bodily slammed him to the turf.

Afterward, manager Dick Williams shrugged innocently: "Lonborg's pitch slipped." Lonnie was more to the point: "I can't let him (Tillotson) get away with hitting our guys."

o

The Red Sox and Yankees went at it in 1967 at New York. After Yankee Thad Tillotson creased Joe Foy's helmet with a pitch, Jim Lonborg responded by nicking Tillotson with a revenge pitch. As Tillotson headed for first base he exchanged words with Lonborg—and was rushed by Foy, emptying both benches. At far right, Tillotson (wearing jacket) is being lifted by Reggie Smith, who is about to body-slam the pitcher.

1

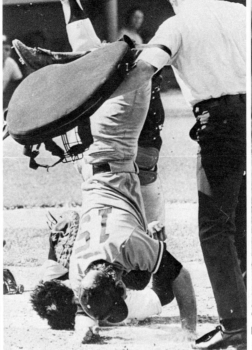

2

3

4

5

6

1. A home-plate smashup sparked a Red Sox-Yankees free-for-all that delayed a 1973 game at Boston 25 minutes. With the score tied 2-2 in the ninth inning, the Yankees tried a squeeze play. But Gene Michael (17) missed his attempted bunt and is pushed aside by catcher Carlton Fisk (27) who braces for the arrival of Thurman Munson. *(Boston Globe)*

2. Munson attempts to steamroll Fisk, producing a spectacular cartwheel. *(Boston Globe)*

3. Fisk and Munson confer after scrambling to their feet. *(Boston Globe)*

4, 5. One word leads to another, then one punch to another, and both benches clear as umpire Joe Brinkman moves in. *(Boston Globe)*

6. Fisk heads for showers after being banished. Munson was also ejected, but somehow Michael was allowed to remain in the game.

A Yankee Stadium beanball was also the spark that ignited the classic punch-out between Joe Cronin and Jake Powell in 1938. After being hit by an Archie McKain pitch, Powell was en route to the mound when he was intercepted by shortstop-manager Cronin. After both were ejected, Cronin took on half the Yankee bench in the runway en route to the locker room.

○

Cronin wasn't the only Red Sox infielder to try taking on a team. Heinie Wagner charged into the Cubs dugout in pursuit of Hippo Vaughn during the 1918 World Series, emerging bloody and bruised.

○

Rookie Jimmy Piersall had the distinction of fighting an opponent and a teammate within 15 minutes of each other before a 1952 game at Fenway. After swapping insults with Yankee Billy Martin during infield practice, the pair headed for the locker room runway where they traded a number of punches. Piersall then repaired to the Sox clubhouse, where he exchanged words and more punches with Maury McDermott.

○

McDermott also fought Jackie Jensen in 1955, the year after the southpaw fireballer had been traded to Washington for the Golden Boy. In the 12th inning, McDermott picked Jensen off first base and a rundown ensued. McDermott tagged Jensen, but the former football All-American knocked the ball out of the pitcher's hand, and McDermott resented it.

○

Birdie Tebbetts is among those who fought for and against the Red Sox.

The fiery catcher battled against them in 1938 as a Tiger, engaging similarly thin-tempered Ben Chapman. A master agitator, Tebbetts had been needling the Sox outfielder all afternoon before Ben finally blew in the ninth inning.

As Chapman stepped to the plate with two out and the tying run on base, Birdie chirped: "OK, gang, three out, three out."

Chapman bristled, and on a 3-2 pitch, he swung mightily and struck out, ending the game.

"See—ha, ha, ha—I told you so," Tebbetts roared, holding the ball aloft in triumph.

Chapman dropped his bat and engaged Birdie in combat. It took several players to pry them apart.

○

Traded to the Red Sox nine years later, Tebbetts was involved in two extraordinary punches—one he gave, one he received.

Tagged hard by Tebbetts in a 1948 plate collision, enraged Tiger George Vico bounced up and threw a haymaker at the catcher's chin. It probably would have landed on target, too, if Birdie hadn't neglected to take off his mask, and Vico howled in pain after nearly breaking his fist. The pair adjourned for early showers, but paused long enough in the runway to do some serious punching.

Tebbetts was on the throwing end of a haymaker at Fenway in 1950 when Hank Wyse struck hot-hitting rookie Walt Dropo on the head with a pitch. While the other Red Sox rushed to the fallen Dropo's side, Tebbetts charged to the mound and slugged Wyse.

Postscript: Tebbetts was sidelined 16 games with lumbago; Dropo was out of the hospital and back in the lineup in five days.

○

Birdie Tebbetts (8, at bottom) collided twice with Tiger runner George Vico one May day in 1948 at Fenway. The first time, Vico threw a punch that nearly broke his fist because Tebbetts had neglected to take off his mask. And a few minutes after this photo was taken, Vico and Tebbetts resumed their battle in the privacy of the runway to the locker rooms.

Billy Hitchcock is another who had fistfights while wearing uniforms of friend and foe. As a Red Sox player, he fought Braves first baseman Earl Torgeson during a 1948 preseason City Series game at Braves Field.

When the Braves pitcher threw wildly while trying to pick Hitchcock off first, Billy's right arm somehow got wrapped around one of Torgy's legs, thus delaying the first baseman's pursuit of the ball. Torgeson took umbrage and walked across Hitchcock's stomach, then sat on his face. It went on from there before Ted Williams subdued Torgeson while Eddie Stanky latched on to Hitchcock. The most serious damage: Torgy's broken eyeglasses.

○

Later traded to the Athletics, Hitchcock fought against the Red Sox in 1952 at Philadelphia in a brawl ignited by his smile.

When Cass Michaels smashed a bases-full double to put the A's ahead in the eighth inning, brash rookie catcher Sammy White turned to plate umpire Bill McGowan and asked, "Are you satisfied now, you so-and-so?"

Goodbye, Sammy. The heave-ho did nothing to improve White's humor, and the last straw came when he noticed next-batter Hitchcock standing by the plate smiling like a Cheshire cat (a likeness bench jockeys had been noting for years).

"What are *you* laughing about?" White demanded.

Hitchcock continued his silent treatment, but his smile broadened. White tried to wipe it off with a wild right that missed. Hitchcock retaliated, and the fun started.

Cooled off, White took the blame. "I lost my head when I saw him laughing," Sammy said. "Besides, I was out of the game anyway and had nothing to lose." Hitchcock did; he was ejected too.

Perhaps there was something about Philadelphia that set off White. He tangled there the next season with Allie Clark.

○

While Hitchcock at least smiled to get into trouble, a couple of Red Sox infielders did absolutely nothing to infuriate Tiger old-timer George

His face bruised and his left arm in a sling, **Bill Lee** was flown back to Boston after the 1976 free-for-all at Yankee Stadium. Lee was disabled nearly two months by a torn ligament in his pitching shoulder. *(Boston Globe)*

The Red Sox and A's had a couple of disagreements in 1970, including this one at Fenway. *(Boston Globe)*

missed and his fist smashed into the wall, swelling the index finger on his pitching hand to three times its normal size. Unable to grip the ball as usual, Ruth's record scoreless-inning string ended the next day.

It was Ruth, of course, who assaulted the umpire. He slugged Brick Owen on the neck when the ump called "ball four" on the leadoff batter of a 1917 game at Fenway. The runner was erased trying to steal, and reliever Ernie Shore retired the next 26 batters in order for a perfect game.

○

Jim Rice dropped a plate umpire on his backside at Fenway in 1979. But it was ruled a slip and not held against Rice, who was trying to separate ump Lester Pratt from irate Rick Burleson, who had just bumped the umpire after being ejected.

○

And, finally, Red Sox players have directed more than quotes at Boston sportswriters.

Maury McDermott threw a punch at Bob Holbrook of the *Globe*, and Stuffy McInnis aimed one at Paul Shannon of the *Post*.

○

Jim Rice (right) visits Royals pitcher Jim Colborn on the mound during a 1978 game at Fenway, but umpire Bill Haller and Kansas City catcher Darrell Porter step in to preserve peace. *(Boston Globe)*

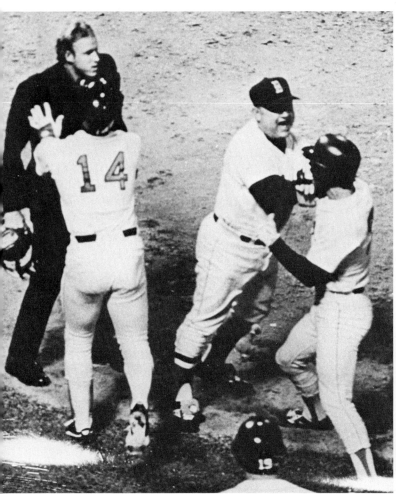 

Umpire Lester Pratt took a great fall during a 1979 discussion at Fenway. At left, manager Don Zimmer restrains Rick Burleson (right) while Jim Rice (14) fends off Pratt. Burleson had bumped the umpire, who then ejected the Red Sox shortstop, further infuriating him. At right, Rice is so zealous in holding off Pratt that the umpire lands on his backside. The ump ruled it a slip, and Rice wasn't penalized; but Burleson was slapped with a three-game suspension. (Boston Globe)

Dave "The Colonel" Egan, the most cutting writer of sports in Boston history, usually stayed away from the clubhouse, but one irate player caught up with him by chance and nearly dropped Egan head first out of the Fenway press box.

Rough-and-tumble Jim Tabor was recovering from an appendectomy when he read in Egan's *Record* column how much better off the Red Sox were without their hospitalized third baseman. Although one of Egan's milder knocks, it upset Tabor since it was the latest of many criticisms by Egan.

When the Alabaman left the hospital, Joe Cronin suggested he watch the games from the Fenway press box while regaining his strength. On his first afternoon upstairs, Tabor was chatting with witty writer Jim Bagley as Egan came by.

"James, my boy, I'd like you to meet a very big admirer of yours," Bagley said. "Say hello to Colonel Dave Egan."

Jim Tabor (left) nearly dropped a writer out of the press box less than an hour after this picture was taken with Joe Cronin.

Tabor nearly had a convulsion. He grabbed Egan by the throat and backed him toward the railing. The fall probably wouldn't have killed Egan, but it was a sizable drop to the diagonal screen behind home plate.

Nobody knows if the livid Tabor would have gone through with it because general manager Eddie Collins rushed in from an adjacent roof box and ordered his third baseman to release the writer. Collins led Tabor away, the still-livid player hurling insults and challenges at Egan till he was out of sight.

○

Cliff Keane of the *Globe* also had a close call. When he wrote that "Don Buddin should have E-6 on his license plate" because the shortstop made so many errors, Buddin went after Keane the next time their paths crossed. But the shortstop was intercepted by teammate Bobby Avila.

○

Keane didn't fare as well one day while chatting with Washington's Roy Sievers by the batting cage. Fun-loving Ted Williams bowled a baseball at Keane from his blind side, and it bounced up and broke the writer's glasses and cut his eyebrow.

○

That's one of the few times blood has flowed in Red Sox altercations. They provide little gore but a lot of writer's ink and excitement.

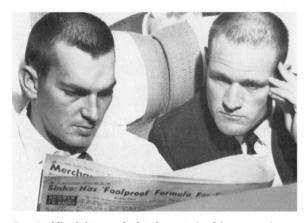

Don Buddin (left) once had to be restrained from pursuing a writer who suggested the shortstop have "E-6" on his license plate. Reading the newspaper with Buddin is Carroll Hardy, who gained trivia immortality by being the only batter ever to pinch hit for Ted Williams. He also pinch hit for Carl Yastrzemski.

Reggie Jackson, then with Oakland, goes after an umpire who had ejected him following a disputed call at second base. A's manager Dick Williams and two coaches thought they had Reggie under control until his outrage was renewed when he learned that he had been thrown out of the game.

7

FIELDER'S CHOICE

Red Sox season openers in Washington have been seen by seven presidents—Taft, Harding, Coolidge, Hoover, Roosevelt, Eisenhower and Johnson . . . but, ironically, not lifelong Red Sox fan John F. Kennedy.

Schedule makers somehow never booked the Red Sox into Washington for the then traditional season opener against the Senators during the three years of JFK's presidency. The White Sox had that honor in 1961, the Tigers in 1962 and the Orioles in 1963.

Mostly for security reasons, those three games and the 1962 All-Star Game in Washington were the only baseball games Kennedy attended while president.

"But he was a great baseball fan, a lifelong Red Sox fan," recalls Dave Powers, his aide and confidante. "And he was a great admirer of Ted Williams, even though Ted cost him $10 one day.

"That happened when we were at Fenway Park one afternoon in 1946 when the Red Sox were on that 15-game winning streak in early May that got them off and running for the pennant.

"Well, Ted came to bat against that stylish Detroit southpaw, Tommy Bridges—making it left-hander versus left-hander—and Jack asked me what the odds were against Williams hitting a home run.

" 'Fifteen to one,' I said.

"Ted fouled off the first pitch.

" 'I'll give you ten dollars to one that he doesn't hit one,' Jack said, and I took the bet.

"Ted swung at the next pitch and missed. I look at Jack and he's beaming.

"Well, Bridges didn't even waste a pitch and tried to sneak a third strike by Williams. Ted ripped it into the Tiger bull pen for a home run.

"I jumped up cheering, and so did everyone else in the park—except one. Jack just sat there and fumed.

"That's the way he was. He hated to lose in *anything* he did, even the smallest thing. He paid up, but didn't speak to me for two innings."

o

During batting practice that day, Kennedy visited the Red Sox dugout and had his picture taken with Ted Williams and Eddie Pellagrini of the Red Sox, and Tigers star Hank Greenberg.

Pellagrini, the baseball coach at Boston College for the past 20 years, recalls:

"Somebody in the dugout asked if I'd mind taking a picture with a veteran. It was the first year after the war, and I got the impression it was a disabled vet who probably wanted to have a picture to take back to the hospital. So I said, 'Sure, sure. Bring him down.'

"Well, here comes this kid around the corner and he looked *awful* —so thin, really emaciated. So I said to myself, 'This poor kid has *really* been through it!'

Top of page, Franklin Delano Roosevelt threw out the first pitch of the 1940 season as the Red Sox and Senators met at Washington. Cheering on the President are Postmaster General Jim Farley (left), Sox manager Joe Cronin (second right) and Senators manager Bucky Harris (far right).
FDR saw 40-year-old Lefty Grove pitch seven and one-third perfect innings that day en route to a two-hit, 1-0 masterpiece.

Campaigning for Congress in 1946, rookie politician John Fitzgerald Kennedy shook some hands at Fenway Park — including those of (left to right) Ted Williams, Eddie Pellagrini and Hank Greenberg. JFK made the mistake of betting $10 that Williams wouldn't hit a homer. Ted did—for a 5-4 victory.

"We shook hands and got set for the picture when I saw Williams and Greenberg coming down the runway next to the dugout. So I said to this veteran, 'Would you like a few more guys in the picture?' And he said, 'Foine, foine.'

"I heard that and thought, 'Wow, this poor bastard has a speech impediment on top of everything else.'

"Well, we take the picture, and he thanked us and left. Somebody asked if I knew who that was, and I shrugged, 'Some vet.'

" 'He's a veteran, all right, and he's also running for Congress,' I was told. 'That's the Kennedy kid and his father used to be ambassador to England.'

"I'd never heard of either the kid or the old man. Hell, I didn't know the current ambassador to England let alone a former one.

"The reason Kennedy wanted a picture with me was that I was a local boy, a Boston kid who'd made the Red Sox, and he was interested in the local vote. My name probably wouldn't hurt with the Italian vote, either.

"Well, the years went by and I found out who John Fitzgerald Kennedy was. Our paths crossed again once when he was campaigning for the Senate. And when he ran for president in 1960, he wrote me asking for my support. I didn't think the guy had a chance as an Irish Catholic, and didn't even keep the letter.

"Well, he pulled the big upset and got elected, and the next day I'm up in the attic digging out that old picture taken in the dugout. I put a frame on it and stuck it on the living room TV, where people couldn't miss it.

"And when a visitor would comment on it, I'd play it casual and say, 'Oh, yes, me and *Jack*. We go way back.' "

○

JFK also asked another former Red Sox player for help during the 1960 campaign—Jimmy Piersall, a Cape Cod neighbor who had been traded to Cleveland and was having trouble there with general manager Frank Lane and manager Joe Gordon.

Kennedy wired Piersall: "Dear Jimmy: Do you have any ideas that might be helpful in the Ohio campaign? Jack Kennedy."

Piersall replied: "Dear Jack: I'm having big problems with Lane and Gordon. Please don't bother me with your little ones."

○

Another Red Sox player received a communication from a different White House resident.

Luis Aparicio was mired in a nightmarish one-for-55 slump in 1971, and before a game at Fenway he received this message from a longtime baseball fan named Richard Milhous Nixon: "In my own career I have experienced long periods when I couldn't seem to get a hit, regardless of how hard I tried, but in the end I was able to hit a home run."

Aparicio broke out of his slump that night and drove in a couple of runs during a 10-1 rout of the Angels. It is not known if Luis returned the favor and sent the President similar encouragement three summers later when Nixon went into the greatest slump in the history of the presidency.

o

Luis Aparicio celebrated his 10,000th career trip to the plate in 1973. Two years earlier he was haunted by a different statistic—a one-for-55 slump which prompted a message of encouragement from the White House.

The Red Sox All-Tempermental Team?

Ted Williams would be captain, of course. And although their Fenway years were far fewer, Lefty Grove and Wesley Cheek Ferrell weren't far behind Terrible Ted. In fact, for one-man riots, Williams couldn't touch either one.

Both pitchers were furious competitors with tempers to match, enlivening the Sox games in the thirties, and, in Grove's case, through 1941. But whereas Grove flew into frequent rages at others, Ferrell often directed his anger at himself. Consider this reported study in self-destruction, which is part of Red Sox legend:

Ferrell was staked to a rare 10-1 lead early in a 1934 game at Philadelphia. But future Sox teammate Jimmy Foxx hit a grand-slam as the Athletics rallied for six runs in the third inning.

Returning to the bench, tall and Hollywood-idol handsome Wes not only told mates how much he loathed himself for blowing the lead, but also illustrated the point. According to legend, he doubled up his right fist and delivered an uppercut squarely to his jaw, slamming the back of his head against the dugout wall for a spectacular doubleheader. Woozy but not out, the story goes on, Ferrell then delivered a hard left to his chin before being restrained by teammates.

Fortunately, the Red Sox won, 11-9, or Ferrell might have gotten really angry at himself.

Normally, Wes wasn't quite so demonstrative. He'd bang his head against concrete walls now and then and stomp on an occasional wristwatch, but mostly restricted himself to things like shredding uniforms—and gloves, finger by finger. One glove caught blazes, literally, when he threw it into the clubhouse stove during a fit of temper.

Grove made different use of his glove during a tantrum at Chicago. When Eric McNair made a crucial mistake behind him, Lefty stood on the mound chewing—not nibbling, *chewing*—his glove in frustration.

No dugout water cooler or tunnel lightbulb, traditional targets for frustrated baseball players, was safe from Ferrell or Grove or a parade of other Red Soxers with short fuses over the decades.

Although not usually a hothead, Dick Radatz rates consideration at least as a relief pitcher here—for one act alone. He lost his best glove by scaling it into the stands in 1963 at Detroit when Rocky Colavito beat him with a game-ending homer.

As for catchers, Sammy White will do for openers. He starred in one of the costlier and more memorable tantrums in Red Sox history during a 1956 game. Incensed by an umpire's call, White heaved the ball into left-center field, but neglected to call time out, allowing Detroit's Red Wilson to circle the bases.

The Sox's most temperamental infielder? Start with Billy Werber. He broke a toe kicking a water bucket in 1935.

The outfielder with the lowest boiling point has to be Williams. Ben Chapman is among others meriting consideration. Infuriated by plate umpire John Quinn in 1937, Chapman gunned a throw at him from right

Jimmy Piersall and Ted Williams—two-thirds of the most sensitive and high-strung outfield in baseball history. The unit's other member? Jackie Jensen.

The Ferrells, catcher Rick (left) and pitcher Wes, are the only brother battery in Red Sox history.

field—and didn't miss by much. His consolation prize? A $50 fine and a three-game suspension.

And for an entire outfield, could any team in baseball history claim a more sensitive and high-strung unit than the Red Sox's 1954–58 trio of Williams, Jimmy Piersall and Jackie Jensen?

These are just a few candidates for the Red Sox All-Temperamental Team. Any nominations?

o

Some Red Sox managers have allowed card playing in the clubhouse; others have prohibited it.

A veteran utilityman and cardplayer who had recently joined the club won several hundred dollars from a teammate during a gin rummy game one night in 1963.

"Nobody has the right to win or lose this much in a locker-room card game," the winner said as he pocketed his winnings. "If I was manager, I'd fine us each a grand."

The winner was Dick Williams, and among his first moves as a rookie manager four years later was to ban high-stakes card games.

o

Pete Jablonowski was an unimpressive 0-3 for the Red Sox after being acquired from Cleveland during the 1932 season, and faded to the minors the next year.

But the right-hander was back in the majors in 1936, buoyed with a better assortment of pitches and a new name: Pete Appleton.

He promptly had a 14-9 season for the Senators, one of eight years he'd spend in the majors under the name of Appleton.

A far more famous Red Sox player changed his name, too. But John Paveskovitch became Johnny Pesky long before he arrived in Boston.

o

Befitting a hitter who played in the thirties, forties, fifties and sixties, Ted Williams homered off father and son.

White Sox southpaw Thornton Lee was a victim in 1939, Williams's first season. So was Senators right-hander Don Lee in 1960, Ted's last season.

o

It's all relative:

Three sets of fathers and sons have played for the Red Sox: catcher Ed Connolly Sr. (1929–32) and pitcher Ed Connolly Jr. (1964), pitchers Walt Ripley (1935) and Allen Ripley (1978–79), and pitchers Smokey Joe Wood (1908–15) and Joe Wood (1944).

There has been one grandfather-grandson combination: Shano Collins (1921–25) and Robert Collins Gallagher (1972), both outfielders.

Nine sets of brothers have played for the Red Sox:

Conigliaro—Outfielders Tony (1964–67, 1969–70, 1975) and Billy (1969–71).

Ferrell—Pitcher Wes (1934–37) and catcher Rick (1933–37).

Stahl—Outfielder Chick (1901–06) and catcher-first baseman Jake (1903, 1908–10, 1912–13).

Sadowski—Catcher Eddie (1960) and pitcher Bob (1966).

Johnson—Outfielders Roy (1932–35) and Bob (1944–45).

Hughes—Pitchers Long Tom (1902–03) and Ed (1905–06).

Heving—Pitcher Joe (1938–40) and catcher Johnnie (1924–25, 1928–30).

Gaston—Catcher Alex (1926, 1929) and pitcher Milt (1929, 1931).

Carlyle—Outfielders Roy (1925–26) and Cleo (1927).

The Ferrells are the only brother battery in Red Sox history.

And the Stahls are the only brothers who have managed the team, Chick in 1906, Jake in 1912 and 1913.

SPRING TRAINING

Another full house for an exhibition game at Winter Haven, the Red Sox spring training home.

There's more than one way to see a Grapefruit League game as these fans prove in 1949 at Payne Field, Sarasota, where the Red Sox trained 1933–58 except during World War II.

Tony Conigliaro gets into the heavy calisthenics of spring training.

Carl Yastrzemski says it's easy to touch your toes—when you bend your knees.

Jackie Jensen (left), Mike Higgins (center) and Ted Williams are welcomed to Arizona by the sheriff and a couple of his deputies. The Red Sox trained at Scottsdale 1959–65 before returning to Florida at Winter Haven.

Manager Eddie Kasko found this snake in the grass at Chain O' Lakes Park, Winter Haven—a discovery that cleared the practice field in record time. (Boston Globe)

Brothers-in-law have been Red Sox teammates, too: Carlton Fisk and Rick Miller. Miller married Fisk's sister Janet following the 1973 season.

o

Pitcher Gene Conley (1961–63) played for another Boston major league team in a different sport: the 1953, 1959–61 Celtics. In all, he played for *three* big league teams in Boston, breaking in with the 1952 Braves the year before they left for Milwaukee.

o

Ted Williams is the oldest player ever to win a major league batting championship. He was 40 years, 28 days when he hit .328 to win the 1958 American League crown.

Tony Conigliaro is the youngest player ever to win a major league home run championship. He was 20 years, 270 days when he hit 32 to win the 1965 American League title.

o

Deacon McGuire is the oldest player to wear a Red Sox uniform. He pinch-hit in one game (hitless) in 1908 at age 44.

Jim Pagliaroni is the youngest player to wear a Red Sox uniform. He appeared in one game in 1955 at age 17, catching a few innings and hitting a sacrifice fly in his only at-bat before going to the minors for four seasons.

o

Dave Shean is the oldest to play for the Red Sox in a World Series. He was their second baseman in all six games of the 1918 Series against the Cubs (hitting .211) three and a half months after his 40th birthday.

Ken Brett is the youngest to play for the Red Sox in a World Series. He made relief appearances in two games (fourth and seventh) in the 1967 Series three weeks after his 19th birthday, pitching hitless ball in 1⅓ innings in all.

o

As with Pearl Harbor and other electric moments in history, Red Sox fans recall exactly where they were that October Sunday when their team clinched its Impossible Dream by beating out the Twins for the 1967 pennant.

So does Vince Orlando, an equipment manager at Fenway Park for 46 years. When Rich Rollins popped up Jim Lonborg's last pitch, Orlando was in the funeral-quiet Twins dugout as the visiting-team clubhouse man.

The normally stoic Orlando couldn't hide his joy when Rico Petrocelli squeezed the final out. He vaulted onto the field and spotted American League president Joe Cronin's wife Mildred in a nearby box.

Orlando rushed to the railing and pinned a kiss on her.

"She was kind of stunned," he recalls.

"It hadn't dawned on me that her brother owned the Twins. In the thrill of victory—the biggest moment I've ever seen at Fenway—all I could think of was that she had been a member of the Red Sox family all those years through the thirties, forties and fifties. And this was a moment for the Red Sox family to celebrate.

"Then it hit me that she was a Griffith. So I felt like a fool—kissing one of the few people in the park who wasn't celebrating."

o

Ted Williams's most crucial swing may not have come in a batter's box.

Fred Corcoran, Williams's business manager and confidante, tells this story:

"Ted was living in a swamp cabin near Everglades City and was awakened by the sound of somebody—or some*thing*—prowling across the metal roof. Ted slipped out of bed and took a shotgun from the wall rack. Then he deliberated, returned it and grabbed a revolver.

Tony Conigliaro is the youngest player ever to win a major league home-run championship—at age 20 in 1965.

"But he had second thoughts about the revolver and put it aside for a lead-weighted baseball bat he used to swing every day to strengthen his wrists. With this and a flashlight, he stepped outside just as the creature leaped from the roof.

"In the beam of the flashlight, Williams found himself eye-to-eye with a snarling Florida bobcat. But that bobcat made a fatal mistake. He came in fast, high and on the inside, right down Home Run Alley. He got clobbered."

○

Williams's eyesight also enabled Ted to pick out one heckler from a sea of 35,000 faces.

"It's amazing," outfield mate Jimmy Piersall once said. "I think the guy is radar-equipped."

○

Fenway Park was always mobbed for the Great Southpaw Match-ups pitting Lefty Grove against Lefty Gomez in the late thirties and early forties.

Donald Davidson, the Red Sox clubhouse boy who went on to become a Braves and Astros official, recalls one of those Grove-Gomez confrontations that fizzled:

"The Yankees knocked out Grove in the third inning. So I got him a cup and ice and he poured himself a tall bourbon in the clubhouse as he listened to the game on radio. The next inning the Red Sox clobbered Gomez.

"So Grove asks for more ice and another cup, filling it with bourbon. 'Take this to Gomez in the Yankee clubhouse,' he said, 'and tell him that Lefty Grove said better luck next time.' "

After finishing the drink, the appreciative Gomez went to the Red Sox clubhouse to thank Grove, and the two kayoed pitchers sat side by side listening to the game they had started.

○

More trivia: The Red Sox's three greatest catchers all were from northern New England. Bill Carrigan was a Lewiston, Maine, product. Birdie Tebbetts was born in Vermont (Burlington) and grew up in New Hampshire (Nashua). Carlton Fisk also was born in Vermont (Bellows Falls) and raised in New Hampshire (Charlestown).

And all three went to college in New England: Carrigan to Holy Cross, Tebbetts to Providence College and Fisk to the University of New Hampshire.

In fact, you could assemble a pretty fair team comprised of New Englanders who went on to play for the Red Sox.

Here's a start with the catchers. Who would you pick at the other eight positions?

○

Eddie Kasko was ejected from a 1972 game at Anaheim because he swooned on the grass between home and third base, pretending to faint in surprise over a reversed decision at the plate. The sight of the Red Sox manager spread-eagled on his back with eyes closed was too much for crew chief John Rice, who revived Kasko by running him.

The normally placid Kasko wasn't through. When Phil Gagliano was ejected a half-inning later for baiting the umpires from the Boston bench, Kasko, who had been hiding in the runway, charged onto the field to protest.

"What are you doing here?" demanded Rice. "You were thrown out a long time ago!"

"How the hell would I know that?" Kasko replied. "I was out cold, remember?"

○

Ted Williams is the oldest player ever to win a major league batting championship—at age 40 in 1958.

Manager Eddie Kasko swooned on the infield grass at Anaheim, pretending to faint in surprise after an umpire's reversed decision.

In contrast to Kasko not leaving when he was supposed to, Joe McCarthy once left when he didn't have to.

During a 1950 rhubarb in Washington, umpire Bill McKinley told the Red Sox manager to "Get out of here!"

McCarthy did—retreating to the Sox's clubhouse at Griffith Stadium.

It wasn't until after the game that McCarthy learned he hadn't been banished after all. McKinley only wanted him to go back to the dugout and quit arguing.

o

Carl Yastrzemski's protest of a checked-swing third-strike call by Lou DiMuro in 1975 was eloquent. He climaxed his beef by stooping in the batter's box and scooping dirt over the plate until it was covered—and got the remainder of the afternoon off.

o

Carl Yastrzemski, disgusted over a called third strike, covers home plate—and is given the rest of the afternoon off by umpire Lou DiMuro. (Boston Globe)

Fed up with the abuse, Red Jones cleared the Chicago bench at Fenway Park during a 96-degree scorcher in mid-July 1946, banishing all 14 White Sox not needed to continue the game.

As the Chicago 14 paraded Indian file from their dugout on the third-baseline to the clubhouse runway adjoining the first-base dugout, each had something to say to the beleaguered umpire.

"Take these," said coach Bing Miller, offering his glasses to Jones. "You need 'em more than I do."

Last in line was Wally Moses, a 35-year-old outfielder nearing the end of his career.

"Red, this is my 12th season in the big leagues and I've never been thrown out of a game before," said the soft-spoken Moses. "I never said a word to you on the bench."

Jones was sympathetic. "Wally, it's like a raid on a whorehouse," the umpire said. "The good go with the bad."

There was a silver lining for Moses. Four days later he was traded by the second-division White Sox to the pennant-bound Red Sox, and hit .417 that fall in his only World Series.

o

An umpire's call once put a Red Sox batting champion out of commission.

Normally even-tempered Billy Goodman was so incensed by the ump's decision that he had to be restrained by a teammate, whose bear hug dislocated one of the skinny Goodman's ribs.

The Red Sox player doing the restraining? High-voltage Jimmy Piersall.

Now *there* was a switch in roles!

o

The Tigers had fair warning the day Ted Williams smashed two tape-measure homers at Detroit in 1939.

In Williams's first trip, the count went to 3-0, prompting catcher Rudy York to say to the rookie, "You're not hitting on the next one, are you, kid?"

"I sure as hell am," the 20-year-old Williams replied.

The Tigers didn't believe him, and grooved the "automatic" down the middle. They *did* believe him when Ted thumped the pitch off the upper-deck facing in right field.

As he crossed the plate, the stoic York said, "You weren't kidding, were you, kid?"

The next time up, Williams drilled the ball even further—over the roof.

○

The Red Sox didn't have to travel far for spring training in 1943. Under wartime demands from the government that teams train close to home, the Sox journeyed less than ten miles from Fenway Park, to the indoor cage at Tufts College in suburban Medford.

With travel restrictions apparently eased a bit, the team went further south the remaining two war years—to Baltimore in 1944, to Pleasantville, N.J., in 1945, but presumably didn't get tans there either.

○

Like every other American League team, the Red Sox competed against a one-arm hitter in 1945: Browns outfielder Pete Gray (held hitless in four trips in his Fenway debut by Dave Ferriss).

But the Red Sox were the *only* team to face a one-legged pitcher that season.

Bert Shepard, wearing an artificial limb after being shot down over Germany, pitched 5⅓ innings in relief against the Sox for the second-place Senators in his only big league appearance. The 25-year-old former P.O.W. allowed three hits and one run while striking out two, walking one and hitting a batter.

○

Like other major league teams, the Red Sox had about two dozen players serving in the Armed Forces during World War II. But only the Sox can claim a spy.

Moe Berg, the catcher-coach who could speak a dozen languages fluently, was one of the nation's premier atomic spies in the crucial A-bomb race. That intrigue was recently uncovered by Lou Kaufman, Barbara Fitzgerald and Tom Sewell in their *Moe Berg: Athlete, Scholar, Spy*.

The Princeton-, Columbia- and Sorbonne-educated Berg became involved in espionage while still in baseball. Movies of the Tokyo skyline he secretly took in 1934, while barnstorming in Japan with Ruth, Gehrig, Foxx and Gomez among others, were the chief photographs to prepare Jimmy Doolittle's pilots for the first air attack against the Japanese mainland in 1942.

And while in Red Sox uniform, Berg approached Lefty Gomez at Yankee Stadium in 1936, mysteriously asking him to send his movies of the Japan trip to a government address in Washington.

After Pearl Harbor, Berg quit baseball and led an undercover life through Europe—at times impersonating a Nazi officer—while hunting clues to Germany's atomic progress.

Berg's exploits reportedly prompted President Roosevelt to tell aides: "I see Berg is still catching pretty well."

○

Doug Griffin (left), Luis Tiant (center) and Carl Yastrzemski enjoy some bench jockeying. Their target: former and future teammate George Scott, then playing first base for the Brewers between his two tours with the Red Sox. *(Boston Globe)*

Moe Berg was a spy during World War II, reportedly prompting President Roosevelt to note: "I see Berg is still catching pretty well."

Johnny Pesky was blossoming in the Red Sox farm system in 1940, so another farmhand shortstop named PeeWee Reese was sold to the Dodgers. Pesky was the American League's top rookie in 1942, leading both leagues in hits with 205 while batting .331, second best in the majors behind pal Ted Williams's .356.

Carl Yastrzemski succeeded Ted Williams as the Red Sox left fielder. The pair gave the team decades of superstar stability at that position, a trademark of Red Sox lineups being continued by Jim Rice. *(Boston Globe)*

his two partners wanted the quick sale. Besides, the Red Sox had another promising shortstop in the system at Rocky Mount—Johnny Pesky.

Another pretty fair shortstop farmhand got away to the Angels in the 1961 expansion draft: Jim Fregosi.

Babe Herman slipped through the Red Sox's hands. Obtained with Howard Ehmke from Detroit in the fall of 1922, management was unimpressed in training camp by the slugging first baseman and packed him off to Brooklyn. Converted to an outfielder, he had a couple of lusty back-to-back seasons with the Dodgers, hitting .381 and 21 homers in 1929, .393 and 35 homers in 1930.

The Sox shipped Lefty O'Doul back to the minors as an inadequate pitcher. He returned to the majors five years later as an outfielder and won two National League batting crowns, hitting .398 for the 1929 Phillies, .368 for the 1932 Dodgers.

The Red Sox bundled good-field, little-hit third baseman Bucky Walters off to the Phillies in 1934, and he soon developed into one of baseball's premier pitchers. He had three seasons in which he won 27, 23 and 22 victories for the Reds, helping them win a couple of pennants.

Southpaw Wilbur Wood was a little-used local boy who got away. But, in fairness, he hadn't developed the knuckleball on which he later built a career.

So the Red Sox have had their share of talent misjudgments. But for years they've taken a bad rap for a mistake they *didn't* make. Supposedly, Pie Traynor, another local boy, begged the Sox to sign him but was shooed off the Fenway infield during a practice session by manager Ed Barrow.

"That story is wrong and I'm still trying to straighten it out," the Hall of Fame third baseman said before he died in 1972. "I was chased out of *Braves Field* by Braves manager George Stallings, something I liked to remind him of later when I'd come to town with the Pirates.

"So that story accusing the Red Sox is wrong—right city, wrong team."

○

Those fond of statistics should enjoy dissecting these home-and-away career batting averages of two of the more prominent hitters in Red Sox history:

TED WILLIAMS		CARL YASTRZEMSKI	
At		At	
Fenway Park	.360	Fenway Park	.310
St. Louis	.400	Seattle	.383
Kansas City	.371	Texas	.333
Philadelphia	.353	Baltimore	.301
Detroit	.332	Washington	.300
Washington	.326	Minnesota	.295
New York	.309	Detroit	.293
Cleveland	.301	Kansas City (Royals)	.293
Baltimore	.299	California	.289
Chicago	.298	Chicago	.286
		Oakland	.284
		New York	.281
		Cleveland	.278
		Milwaukee*	.274
		Toronto	.266
		Kansas City (A's)	.259

*Includes when Brewers' franchise was Seattle Pilots one season.

There was a Red Sox flavor to the Baseball Hall of Fame dedication at Cooperstown on June 12, 1939.

Of the then 11 living immortals—all attending—three were Red Sox alumni: Cy Young, Tris Speaker and Babe Ruth. And a fourth, Eddie Collins, was then Red Sox general manager and vice president.

In the dedication game at Doubleday Field that afternoon, the Honus Wagner team featured an all-Red Sox battery: Lefty Grove pitching to Moe Berg.

And the first-base stands at quaint Doubleday Field, a converted cow pasture, were donated by Red Sox owner Tom Yawkey.

○ ○ ○

There are a dozen baseball immortals in the Hall of Fame who played a significant part of their careers with the Red Sox.

They are, in order of admission:

8
HALL OF FAMERS

Player/Red Sox Years	Entered
Babe Ruth (1914–19)	1936
Tris Speaker (1907–15)	1937
Cy Young (1901–08)	1937
Jimmy Collins (1901–07)	1945
Lefty Grove (1934–41)	1947
Herb Pennock (1915–22)	1948
Jimmy Foxx (1936–42)	1951
Joe Cronin (1935–45)	1956
Ted Williams (1939–60)	1966
Red Ruffing (1924–30)	1967
Harry Hooper (1909–20)	1971

They are joined at Cooperstown by two longtime Red Sox executives:

Eddie Collins (1933–51)	1939
Tom Yawkey (1933–76)	1980

A number of other Hall of Famers have worn Red Sox uniforms.

Waite Hoyt totaled a 10-12 record while pitching two seasons for the Sox in 1919 and 1920. After wrecking the Sox for more than a decade, Lou Boudreau played his final 86 games for them 1951–52 and served as manager 1952–54. Jesse Burkett played his final big league season for the Sox in 1905. Heinie Manush played in 82 games for the 1936 team, Al Simmons 40 games for the 1943 club. And Jack Chesbro pitched one game for the Red Sox, his final major league appearance in 1909. But each in this group was selected for achievements with other teams.

The same is true of six other Hall of Famers who managed the Red Sox for relatively brief periods of time: Joe McCarthy (1948–50), Ed Barrow (1918–20), Hugh Duffy (1921–22), Frank Chance (1923), Bucky Harris (1934) and Billy Herman (1965–66).

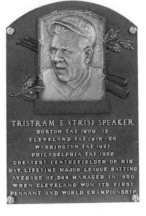

"Anyway, it gave me a reprieve and I didn't miss the second chance. I singled for a run to tie the score. Then Larry Gardner's long fly brought in the deciding run and we had the championship.

"So that single off Matty was my biggest moment.

"My first game for Boston in 1907 was quite a thrill, too. I was sent in to bat in the ninth inning against Rube Waddell, and he knocked me down a few times. That was more part of the game then, especially with recruits. Then he threw one of his blazing left-handed hooks, and I hit it back through the box. I scored the tying run, and the game went 16 innings before it was called by darkness.

"No, I never took any particular pains to develop my batting. It seemed to come naturally; from the outset I always could hit. Not like any Ted Williams, of course. I've seen them all, and he was in a class by himself.

"If he'd had the opportunity to play right through his career like Ruth and most all the other great hitters did, his record would be all the more amazing. He had to make the grade five times: when he came up, when he returned from World War II, after he broke his elbow, when he returned from Korea and after breaking his shoulder. Amazing.

"Williams was just out of this world as a hitter, the best of them all."

BABE RUTH, 1914–1919:

"I put quite a few gray hairs on Bill Carrigan, the best manager I ever had. Carrigan was nice to me when I joined the team and told me, 'I hear you like to step out, Babe. But you play fair with me and I'll play fair with you.'

"I was a kid with a healthy appetite and a zest for life who had been in reform school practically all the time since I was seven. Life looked like a great big lark to me. And the next season, free from any further legal restraint, I soon became a kid who took fun where he found it.

"They didn't have Sunday ball in Washington in those days. Once when we were in the capital for an idle Sunday, I asked Bill's permission to go home to Baltimore to spend some time with the folks. Bill said, 'Sure, Babe, run along and be back Monday.'

"I guess everything would have been all right if my dad hadn't come over from Baltimore to see the Monday game. They gave him a box near the Red Sox bench, and when he saw me he yelled, 'You're a fine son, George, down in the neighborhood and didn't even come home to see me.'

"There wasn't much for me to say, with Bill standing there eyeing me and rocking back and forth on his heels.

"Bill could get just about as tough as anybody I ever met. They didn't call him 'Rough' Carrigan for nothing. I had great respect for him as a man and as a great baseball general. It was a heavy blow to me when Carrigan quit baseball after the 1916 World Series to go back to his hometown, Lewiston, Maine, where he owned a bank.

"Bill was followed as manager by Jack Barry in 1917 and Ed Barrow in 1918. Barrow was a two-fisted, hard-boiled soul who had built a reputation as a man who not only knew how to use his fists but liked the idea. He was hot-tempered. And though it was Barrow who helped make me what I became in the game, we had our share of clashes.

"Barrow rarely went to bed until he knew all his players were in, but I figured I could outfox him.

"I sneaked into the hotel at six one morning in Washington and thought I had gotten away with it until I heard a thundering knock on the door. Ed had tipped a porter to call him the moment I came in. The light was on in the room, but I didn't answer the knock. In charged Ed,

(National Baseball Hall of Fame)

looking surprisingly mad for a guy wearing a dressing gown and slippers. He found me lying in bed, the covers over me, smoking my pipe.

" 'What in blazes are you doing smoking a pipe at this hour of the morning?' he roared.

"I took a few more puffs and replied offhandedly, 'Oh, I always smoke in the middle of the night. It's restful, and then I can go back to sleep again.'

"Suddenly, Barrow lunged forward, yanked off the covers, and found me fully dressed. He looked at me with a face full of scorn. 'You're a fine citizen, Babe. Yes, I must say you are a very fine citizen.'

"He stamped out, and after a bit my relief turned to anger. By the time I got to our clubhouse at the ball park I was shaking. I walked over to where Ed was dressing and bawled, 'If you ever come into my room like that again, you so-and-so, I'll punch you right in the nose.'

"Barrow looked me in the eye and quietly said, 'Call me that again, Babe.'

"By that time I already appreciated I'd said something for which I was sorry. I did not repeat it. Barrow turned to the players dressing all around us.

" 'As soon as you fellows are dressed, I want every man to leave this clubhouse. Ruth will stay here. Then we'll lock the door and see who is the better man. No man can call me that and get away with it.'

"Harry Hooper and Dave Shean came over to Ed. 'Don't fight him, Ed,' Hooper said. 'It won't do anybody any good.' But Barrow was still raging. 'I've just got to have it out with that young man,' he answered.

"I finished dressing when the others did and looked Ed over. I was 24; he was 50. I left the clubhouse with the others. I had sense enough to realize I couldn't win even if I beat him.

"He suspended me, but I apologized to him that night on the train back to Boston and we worked it out. We never had any further trouble during my time with the Red Sox."

(National Baseball Hall of Fame)

LEFTY GROVE, 1934–1941:

"Yes, sir, that 300th victory was a great thrill. But about all I can tell you about it was that I won it in Boston by beating Cleveland, 10-6. I don't recall whether I missed two or three times before I finally got that 300th. It's one of those things that can get on your nerves if you don't get the big one the first time you try for it. One thing I do remember, though, is that Bill McGowan umpired it behind the plate; by coincidence, he had umped my first victory 16 years before in 1925.

"Who knows, I might have won 500 games if I'd been born a little earlier. Those pitchers in the dead-ball days had a lot going for them that I didn't. There was the dead ball itself when there were few home runs. Also, a ball was hardly ever thrown out of play, and you could pitch with a discolored ball that was hard to follow and a scuffed ball that would sail. And there were all sorts of trick pitches like the shineball, the emoryball and the spitter.

"I came along right after all that. So who knows what might have been?

"Would I get sore at my teammates sometimes? Yes, sir, I did. Did I yell at Joe Cronin? Yes, sir, I did. I was out there to win. That's the only way to play this game.

"When I was with Philadelphia, Mr. Mack had a couple of bad-tempered guys to handle—myself and Al Simmons. Yes, sir, we were bad. But Mr. Mack never said a thing on the bench. The next day he'd sit you down in his office and talk to you like a father. It hurt worse that way. Mr. Mack was a great manager.

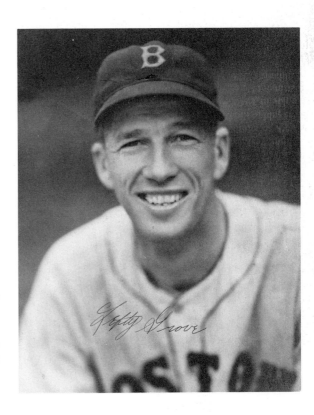

"I never threw at a batter. No, sir. If I ever hit a guy on the head with my fastball he'd be through. I knew it and the hitters knew it. Course, I was just wild enough to give 'em something to think about.

"Mostly I'd just fire the ball. One day in New York I had a 1-0 lead when Koenig led off the ninth with a triple. I struck out Ruth, Gehrig and Meusel on nine pitches. Another time I came in on relief with bases loaded and struck out Ruth, Gehrig and Lazzeri on ten pitches.

"Ruth never was any trouble for me. In ten years he only hit seven homers off me. I hit more than that myself. I remember a grand-slam I hit for the Red Sox. We were playing the Athletics, and Mr. Mack ordered the bases filled to get to me. I hit it out and told Mr. Mack, 'You shouldn't have done that.'

"Yes, I had some arm trouble my first spring with Boston in 1934. They thought it stemmed from teeth trouble, so they took a couple out when we were barnstorming north from training camp. It didn't do much good, though, and I was only 8-8 that first year with the Sox, the first time in eight years I didn't win at least 20.

"But the next year I won 20. I adjusted to the bad arm. I came up with a fork ball and improved my curve to go along with what was left of the fastball. And I made sure I kept my control. You've got to have control. When you stay ahead of the batters you can make them hit the pitch you want and probably get them out. When the batter gets you in the hole you have two choices: walk him or give him the pitch he wants. Either way you'll probably be ruined.

"Yes, sir, I loved to pitch. In my early seasons, I could pitch at my best as often as four times a week. I once got four victories in six days. Later on I required a three-day loaf between starts.

"I pitched in my forties the last two seasons in Boston, and some people marveled that a man that age retains enough to pitch a two-hit game as I did Opening Day 1940. I see nothing particularly marvelous about it. I was blessed with a strong arm, strong legs and excellent general health. Any pitcher so blessed should be a winner at 40 if he takes care of himself and trains properly.

"I did."

JOE CRONIN, 1935–1959*

"My biggest thrill and biggest disappointment while managing the Red Sox came the same year—1946. We got off to a great start and won the pennant by 12 games. But then it was terribly disappointing to lose the World Series, even though it went down to the last out of the seventh game and certainly was no disgrace.

"Even more disappointing, when I was general manager, was losing the '48 and '49 pennants on the last day. They were bigger disappointments because at least in '46 we had something to show for a great season; in '48 and '49 all we had after two terrific races was frustration. We came so close to winning pennants three out of four years—1946, '48 and '49. And we were only four games behind in '50, despite losing Ted (Williams) nearly half the season with that shattered elbow.

"There are a lot of happy memories, too. The most satisfying as a player was going into New York in '39 and beating the Yankees five straight in front of big crowds at the Stadium. That was quite an accomplishment. And we beat good pitchers—Red Ruffing, Lefty Gomez, Monte Pearson, Bump Hadley—to put ourselves back in the pennant race in a hurry. We closed the gap from something like 11 to six games. I always felt if we had come back to Boston after that series we might have closed it even more and been in a fine position. But that was just the start

*1935–45, player; 1935–47, manager; 1947–59, general manager.

of a long road trip made even longer by the All-Star Game break, and it took a lot out of us.

"Yes, Yankee Stadium is where I had that run-in with Jake Powell the year before. Jake had come out after our pitcher, Archie McKain, and that was uncalled for, so I intercepted him (Powell) to discuss it. I also didn't want my pitcher getting thrown out of the game for fighting. Well, one word led to another and Jake and I started going at it.

"Then we went to it again in the runway, and I guess half the Yankee team got in on it. I can't say for certain because I never really *saw* any of them. There were no lights in the runway, so it all happened in the dark. I just tried to hit everything that moved.

"Something else I'll always remember was one of Lefty Grove's masterpieces, Opening Day 1940. Old Mose never pitched a no-hitter in his great career, but he darn near did that day at Washington. He was just marvelous, mowing down one batter after another until the eighth inning. Then Cecil Travis bounced a ball off our third baseman's wrist, and it was ruled a hit. That snapped it, and I think the Senators got another hit before it was over. But it was a thrill just watching the old master at age 40 pitching a classic game with his head and arm.

"I'll also never forget some of the tremendous homers hit by Jimmy Foxx and Ted Williams. Foxx had awesome raw power and smashed two almost unbelievable belts in one game at Chicago, lining one into the stands in dead center, hitting the other over the roof in left. And we still lost, 4-2. Foxx's homers were the only runs we got, and Grove was the loser. You should have heard Lefty; he told us he was pitching for a one-man team consisting of Foxx.

"And, of course, Williams hit so many big homers. One that stands out came in this first Fenway at-bat after Korea. We were all wondering if he had lost his timing, and *bang!*—he smacked a tremendous pinch homer into the bleachers off big Mike Garcia. And then there was that one he hit over the roof at Detroit as a rookie.

"And who could forget Williams going for .400 on the last day of the '41 season at Philadelphia? Ted was on pins and needles the night before and we sat up gabbing in the hotel lobby until 12:30 or 1:00 o'clock in the morning. And what a show Ted put on the next afternoon—going six for eight to end up .406.

"One of my big thrills was just watching kids like Ted, Bobby Doerr and Dom DiMaggio develop into outstanding ballplayers. They were great kids and I was proud of them.

"Those pinch homers of mine? Well, they just happened. When you're managing you're playing every pitch; in fact, you're a pitch ahead, always anticipating. So that's a little different than if you're a player sitting on the bench and suddenly the manager calls you to pinch-hit. As a manager, you're more alert to what's going on and more keyed up.

"Yes, I suppose there is more pressure on the manager himself pinch-hitting, not wanting to fail in the clutch in front of his players. And that's one of the prices a player-manager has to pay. You're the leader and are expected to come through all the time. When you do, people shrug and say that's what you're supposed to do; when you don't, they wonder why not.

"That's among the reasons I'd never recommend being a player-manager. And I'd never want to do it again. It's just too tough, too much to worry about. But I'll say one thing: there's rarely a dull moment.

"And I guess you can say that about my 25 years with the Red Sox. There was a lot of excitement, a lot of thrills. And the biggest thrill of all came in '56 when I was elected to the Hall of Fame. What greater honor can there be for a baseball player?"

JIMMY FOXX, 1936–1942:

"Being traded to Boston was a dream come true. It's the most understanding baseball town in the country. So I was very glad to go there and I have some very fine memories of there.

"My greatest thrill with the Red Sox was that 1938 season. It was the best season I ever had. I hit 50 home runs, knocked in 175 runs and led the league in hitting (.349), and, yes, was voted Most Valuable Player for the third time. I fooled all those guys who kept writing that I was through.

"I just wish the Red Sox had won a pennant while I played with them. That town would have gone mad.

"Yes, sure I remember clearing the double-decker stands in Comiskey Park. I did it twice—once in left-center, once more to left. On the one to left-center, the ball soared well past the parking lot and landed in tennis courts. The groundskeeper who went out to check wanted to bet anyone the ball had traveled 600 feet. There were no takers.

"I don't remember all the homers, but I remember those two, and my first one, against the Yankees and Urban Shocker in 1927. I remember that one because I was just a baby and it meant something.

"Yes, there were some strikeouts, too, but striking out didn't bother me. Too many batters try to protect themselves on that. They'd rather ground out to the pitcher than strike out. What's the difference? Forget about striking out; swing the bat.

"And that's what I did. If I could have hit only against left-handers during my career, I would have batted .500. What did I hit, .325 and 534 homers?

"Yes, I came close to Babe Ruth's record of 60 homers in a season. I had 58 for the Athletics in 1932 and lost three more on a technicality. I used to hit a lot to right field, and I hit three balls that season that struck the wire strands at Shibe Park in Philadelphia and bounced back into play. It wasn't until two or three years later that I got out there to take a look at it. The wire was strung to brackets bolted to the outside of the fence—the *outside*.

"So, technically, the three balls I hit into them were home runs, just as a ball bouncing back onto the field from the left-field screen at Fenway Park is a home run. Those three would have given me 61.

(Editor's note: Baseball historians also point out that changes in the Cleveland and St. Louis stadiums between Ruth's record year of 1927 and Foxx's big challenge five years later cost Double X at least eight more homers.)

"It wouldn't have made any difference if I had broken Ruth's record. Oh, it might have put a few more bucks in my pocket. But there was only one Babe.

"No, I never had the distinction of being the highest-paid player in baseball, although there were seasons when I felt entitled to that honor—and to the dough." (Foxx's top salary was $32,000, raised to that figure after he was chosen American League MVP in 1938.)

"Well, I earned $275,000 playing baseball, and didn't have a dime to show for 20 years in the game. I don't feel badly for myself. The money I lost—and blew—was my own fault, 99 percent of it. I had to wonder if I wasn't born to be broke.

"Suddenly you're 51 years old and nobody wants you. So athletes have to put something away. You only stay up there so long. It's always nice to have the crowds on your side, but it doesn't last long once you stop producing."

BOBBY DOERR, 1937–1951:

"I consider myself very fortunate to have played my entire career for a team like the Red Sox, in a town like Boston and for an owner like Tom Yawkey.

"The Red Sox were always a contender and a first-class organization. There is no better baseball town than Boston. And Mr. Yawkey was a wonderful man, among the great people in baseball history. He was such a fine person and so loyal to his players, it's a great irony he wasn't rewarded with a World Championship. It was sad we couldn't win a World Series for him, and that always will be a great disappointment to me.

"That's why the biggest regrets of my career are not winning the 1946 World Series and losing the '48 and '49 pennants on the last day. Those frustrations will be with me the rest of my life.

"Our 1948, '49 and '50 teams should have won pennants, especially the '48 and '49 clubs. No, we weren't too content or not hungry enough; that's been written, but it's wrong. The reason we didn't win those pennants was that we lacked a top-flight relief pitcher.

"Our poor starts in those seasons were unbelievable for the teams we had. You'd look at our lineup and say such bad starts were impossible. We'd score plenty of runs, but the other team kept getting to us in the late innings. We'd have two- and three-run leads and couldn't hold them. We didn't have that big guy coming out of the bull pen like the Yankees had Joe Page. That was the reason we missed those pennants, and it was a great frustration.

"My biggest thrill? For a spontaneous, one-shot thing it would have to be hitting that three-run homer to win the 1943 All-Star Game. Another big thrill was just going to bat for the first time in the World Series. Playing in a World Series was my dream as a kid; it's every player's ambition. So I'll never forget walking up to the plate in the '46 Series opener at St. Louis against Howie Pollet.

"Another thrill in a different way was the 'night' the fans gave me at Fenway in 1947. They gave us a pickup truck, and Mr. Yawkey gave us a car and also a light plant to power our mountain home back in Oregon. That was something. But it wasn't the gifts that was the big thing; it was how sincere everyone was about it.

"Just going to my first spring training in '37 was quite a thrill, too. I was a green, scared 19-year-old kid, and only three years earlier I'd had my room plastered with pictures I'd cut out of newspapers and magazines—pictures of guys like Cronin, Foxx and Higgins. Now I was in the same infield. You can imagine how I felt. So there were butterflies fluttering in my stomach for quite awhile.

"We opened at Philadelphia that season, and that was the first big league game I ever saw. A fellow named Harry Kelley was pitching, I believe, and I think I got a couple of hits. We moved on to Yankee Stadium and faced Bump Hadley, Monte Pearson and Lefty Gomez, one after another. They made my head spin, and all I could think of was that old line, 'Get out the hotcakes, mother, because I'll be home for breakfast.' I thought pitching like that was beyond what I could handle.

"And when we finally got to Boston for the home opener, I made a boner that was the most embarrassing moment of my career. Fenway was jammed for the opener with the Yankees, of course, and I led off the eighth with a double off Johnny Murphy. I was either the tying or go-ahead run, and the sacrifice was on to move me over to third. So I took as big a lead as I could—and *bang-boom*, I'm out, picked off. When Frank Crosetti put the ball on me I wanted to dig a hole right there and climb in. That trip back to the dugout seemed a mile long.

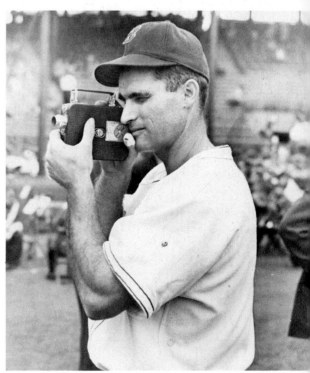

"Ted Williams, Joe DiMaggio and Bob Feller were the greatest players of my time. I didn't see the old-timers, of course, but it's hard to think any hitter could have been better than Ted. DiMag was the greatest all-around player I ever saw, but Williams was the best hitter. He helped me so much as a hitter, and now, as batting coach with the Blue Jays, I find myself often quoting Ted.

"Yes, I had pretty good luck with Feller. I broke up a couple of no-hitters on him, getting the only hit both times—in '39 at Fenway, in '46 at Cleveland. Both were singles just over the infield.

"The toughest pitchers for me were Al Benton, Bob Muncrief, Ray Scarborough and, until later years, Eddie Lopat. I finally learned not to pull Lopat, but go to the opposite field with him, and it worked. I got my 2,000th hit off him in 1951 at Yankee Stadium.

"Yes, that was my last year. My back got pretty bad that season. I'd hurt it a dozen years earlier, back in '39 while making a quick throw on a cold day in Cleveland. I had it the rest of my career, but it didn't get really bad until 1951. The doctors said if I wanted to continue playing I'd have to undergo surgery to fuse the vertebrae. But they weren't optimistic it would be successful, and Charley Keller was never the same hitter after having the same operation. So I decided to pack it in and retire at 33, cutting my career short a couple of years.

"I came back to the Sox in the late sixties as a coach under Dick Williams. And for the most part I enjoyed that, especially the thrill of being part of the '67 pennant and another seven-game World Series with the Cardinals. Yes, I was a little upset when I left Boston after the '69 season. When Dick was let go I quit. I was disappointed and thought he deserved another year. But I guess that's baseball.

"That certainly hasn't diminished my feelings about my playing career with the Red Sox. As I say, I was very fortunate to have played with the Sox, in Boston and for Mr. Yawkey. You couldn't beat that combination."

TED WILLIAMS, 1939–1960:

"I wanted to be the greatest hitter who ever lived. A man has to have goals and that was mine, to have people say, 'There goes Ted Williams, the greatest hitter who ever lived.' Certainly nobody worked harder at it. It was the center of my heart, hitting a baseball. Eddie Collins used to say I lived for my next turn at bat, and that's the way it was.

"I should have had more fun in baseball than any player who ever lived. I played in what I think was baseball's best-played era, the years just before World War II, and then the real booming years, 1946 through the early fifties. We were always fighting for a pennant; we played before big crowds. I won batting championships and home run championships and Most Valuable Player Awards, and when it was all over I made the Hall of Fame.

"I had people around who encouraged me—a real hitter's manager like Joe Cronin, who would sit around the clubhouse for hours talking hitting, and I always loved that, and Joe McCarthy, who in my mind was the best of managers.

"I played before the greatest fans in baseball, the Boston fans, and I know what you're going to say about *that*: Old Teddy Ballgame loved those fans, all right. He spat at them and made terrible gestures and threw a bat that conked a nice old lady on the head one day, and he never tipped his hat to their cheers. And you would be right.

"But there came a time when I knew, *knew*, they were for me, and how much it meant to me. As for tipping my hat, I did it my first year, but never afterward. I couldn't, not if I played another 20 years. I just couldn't. I was fed up for good with that part of the act.

"Certainly baseball doesn't owe me anything. I'm grateful for all the many things it gave me. But at the same time I've taken a lot of undue abuse. My 19 seasons as a player were enjoyable, but many times they were unhappy, too. They were unhappy because I was in a shell an awful lot. I felt a lot of people didn't like me. I did things I was ashamed of, and sorry for, and yet I know in my heart I would do them again under the circumstances, because that was me.

"I felt—I *know*—I was not treated fairly by the press. Without question, Boston had the worst bunch of writers ever in baseball, with Cleveland a close second. I hated that Boston press. I've outlived the ones who were really vicious, who wrote some of the meanest, most slanderous things you can imagine.

"I still remember the things they wrote, and they still make me mad: how I was always trying to get somebody's job—the manager's, the general manager's, the guy's in the radio booth—and I never coveted another man's job in my life.

"Or how I didn't hit in the clutch, and yet drove in more runs per time at bat than anybody who ever played except Babe Ruth, and got on base more times per at-bat than anybody *including* Babe Ruth. I was a draft dodger. I wasn't a 'team' man. I was 'jealous.' I 'alienated' the players from the press. I didn't hit to left field. I took too many bases on balls. I did this, I did that. And so on. And so unfair.

"When I came to Boston there must have been more newspapers per capita than any place in the world, with writers vying for stories, all trying to outdo each other, all trying to get a headline, all digging into places where they had no business being.

"One of them sent a private detective to San Diego in 1942 to find out if I really supported my mother. They went out into the street to take a 'public opinion' poll on my parental qualifications in 1948, when I happened to be in Florida fishing when my daughter Bobby Jo was born—*prematurely*. That type of thing.

"And certainly there were some great disappointments. The pennants we didn't win in 1948 and 1949, when we had good teams that people thought were better than they were. The 1946 World Series we lost, and in which I did so poorly. The two service hitches that took four and a half years out of the heart of my career. Shattering my elbow crashing into the wall while making that catch in the 1950 All-Star Game—the greatest disappointment of my career, because I knew I would never again be the hitter I was.

"But, as I said to the fans before my final game, my stay in Boston has been the most wonderful part of my life. If someone asked me the one place I'd want to play if I had it to do all over again, it would be Boston."

MEL PARNELL, 1947–1956:

"Yes, I take pride in being the winningest left-hander in Red Sox history while pitching half my games in a ball park that a lot of southpaws would bypass. People still talk about that, how I broke the Red Sox pitching records of Babe Ruth and Lefty Grove and how I was the last lefty to win 20 for the Red Sox. And when I hear it, I must admit it inflates me.

"No, The Wall didn't worry me. In fact, I don't think that is Fenway's biggest detriment for a pitcher. The lack of playable foul territory is. Few foul flies are caught. That means hitters get an extra swing. That's

what bothered me at Fenway, not The Wall. Instead of feeling extra pressure from the fence, I tried to use it to my advantage.

"My slider moved in on right-handed batters. It looked like a fastball before breaking sharply inside at the last moment. So I'd work the inside corner with it, breaking it a few inches inside. Right-handed hitters would see what they thought was a fastball on the inside corner. They'd see it coming and get excited—thinking Wall. So they'd usually both overswing and swing with their elbows too close to their body.

"Those were two unnatural things right there. Then there'd be a third element in my favor. All the while the hitters would be thinking fastball, because that's what it looked like. And when the pitch broke sharply at the last instant, the batter couldn't adjust and would be handcuffed, either missing the ball entirely or not getting a good piece of it.

"So The Wall never bothered me. I didn't even think about it except to use it. And I guess that worked, because I won a lot of games there. I was 16-3 there in 1949 alone. In fact, more than half my career victories (70 of 123) came there, including a no-hitter. So while Fenway has been called a graveyard for left-handers, it certainly wasn't for me. I loved pitching there. And if my career was ahead of me and I could choose where I'd play, it would still be at Fenway Park for the Red Sox.

"My only regret was that I didn't play on a pennant winner. We couldn't come any closer in '48 and '49, and those two last-day near-misses were the biggest disappointments of my career.

"The no-hitter was my greatest thrill. And there are plenty of other big victories I'll remember.

"I'll never forget going into Detroit my rookie season when Hal Newhouser was king of the mound for the Tigers, averaging something like 27 wins the previous three years. He'd won something like nine straight. So Joe Cronin didn't want to match one of his better pitchers against Hal and picked me. I won—a four-hitter, I think.

"Another game that sticks out in my memory was the following season when I was down to pitch against Satchel Paige of the Indians at Fenway. More than 17,000 were turned away—including me, almost. Even hours before the game you couldn't get near the gates. Luckily, O'Bie the mounted cop spotted me and opened a path with his horse. We won it, 3-2, on Vern Stephens's homer in the ninth.

"The following year, 1949, I had quite a duel with Virgil Trucks of the Tigers at Fenway that went 11 innings. We got two runners on, Joe McCarthy let me hit for myself, and I got the hit that won it. Getting the winning hit always tickles a pitcher, so that game was doubly memorable.

"The toughest hitters for me? Luke Appling, Lou Boudreau and Harvey Kuenn always gave me trouble. The batter who probably gave me most trouble was a fellow other pitchers got out fairly easily, Jim Hegan. Joe DiMaggio, of course, was the most dangerous hitter I faced, although overall I had pretty fair luck with him.

"The greatest hitter I ever saw, without a doubt, was a guy I never had to face in a game—Ted Williams. I pitched against him a lot in practice, though. We didn't see many left-handers at Fenway, and Ted wanted to keep his eye against lefties for when we went on the road. So I pitched a lot of game-condition batting practice to him where he wouldn't know what was coming, and I'd put everything on the pitch. It made me a better pitcher, too, because it sharpened my pitching against left-handed hitters, practicing on the best. So it was a kind of lab for both of us.

"Happily, I never had to face Ted in a game. That was one advantage I had over other pitchers."

JACKIE JENSEN, 1954–1959, 1961:

"The greatest memory, and the biggest thrill, is having played in the same outfield with two of the greatest players of all time—Joe DiMaggio during my first two years with the Yankees, Ted Williams during six of my seven years with the Red Sox. I'm grateful to have had that distinction and experience—a matter of right time, right place.

"They were opposites, each great in his own way. Ted was the greatest hitter I ever saw, Joe the most complete player. Ted could destroy you with one swing of the bat; Joe could destroy you in many ways.

"Joe was quiet and distant yet friendly. I was in awe playing next to him, a feeling I can't put into words. Joe was near the end of the trail. But even then, when he'd had a few days' rest, he played this game superbly and you could see what he had been.

"And he was simply magnetic. So was Ted, in a wholly different way.

"He was the big kid, always a lot of noise, a lot of enthusiasm. He enjoyed anything and everything, except sports writers. And when he took a bat in his hands, he was the master. Everything stopped. Every player watched, both teammate and opponent. It was like studying a great artist. There wasn't a player who didn't respect him.

"Ted knew all there was to hitting and could explain it. Everything he taught me I've spouted to every hitter I've coached, and I haven't found that advice wrong yet.

"There's only one Ted, and nobody else has come close. Yaz has had a great career, but he's no Ted. Nobody is. He's one of a kind.

"So playing with those two greats was my greatest thrill. No, there isn't any one hit during my 11 seasons that stands out. Instead, what I remember most was the great rivalry between the Red Sox and Yankees, and I saw it from both sides of the fence.

"That series was a tradition. No one game stands out, but most were wars. When we won, it was a nice warm feeling that the whole club shared—the satisfaction of a job well done. That's what the game is supposed to be all about. And that's the dream you remember most.

"I enjoyed playing for the Red Sox. Those were my happiest years in baseball.

"Playing for the Yankees was something special, too. But it was frustrating because I spent a lot of time on the bench because of Casey Stengel's platooning. Playing for the Senators was even more frustrating because, even in spring training, you knew you had no chance of winning the pennant. It was very depressing. So you had to use other means as sources of motivation, like individual goals.

"But the Red Sox were something else. Not only was it a first-class organization, but we always felt we had a chance. That was the important thing. That's why I can't say I feel frustrated that we didn't win a pennant in Boston. At least we always gave it a good try, and it was interesting, enjoyable baseball."

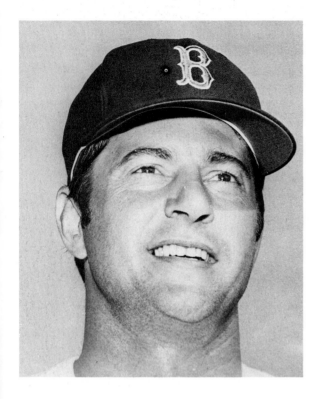

CARL YASTRZEMSKI, 1961—

"Ted Williams was my baseball hero when I was growing up, he and Stan Musial. But, no, I didn't feel extra pressure as a rookie replacing Ted in left field. Some have suggested that, but it isn't true. There was pressure enough simply trying to make the grade in the majors. That I happened to be playing Williams's old position didn't make the pressure worse.

"I was still learning a new position, too. My switch from infielder to outfielder had come the previous year. I had gone to camp with the Red Sox in 1960, but had been farmed out to Minneapolis, where Gene Mauch was manager. The day I reported to their camp he told me that Johnny Murphy (then Red Sox farm director) had called to say that Ted was going to retire after that season, so they wanted me to play left field.

"Mauch just said, 'You can do it. Just go out and do the job,' and it came naturally to me. I never modeled myself after anyone and really didn't get any special advice about playing the outfield.

"I came up the next year and got off to a horrible start at the plate. I was really struggling, and Mr. Yawkey put in an S.O.S. call to Ted, who flew to Boston from Florida and got me back in the groove.

"Yes, baseball has changed some since I came up in '61. The biggest change is relief pitching. In the early sixties there were only a couple of good relief pitchers in the league. I guess it was the arrival of Dick Radatz that started the movement toward strong bull pens. Do you know in one game when Ted was managing Washington I had to face six different left-handers in one game?

"And not only do all the teams have more pitching depth now, but most of the pitchers have good control. You don't see the fastball much now on 3-0 and 3-1 pitches. I could count on the fastball in those situations during my early years, but not now. They're throwing curves, sliders and even changeups with a 3-0 count.

"The toughest part of baseball is the mental strain. I mean, you have to be at a peak for 162 straight games. That's what makes baseball the most difficult sport—being up for that many games. How many other professions are there where you have to bear down for 162 straight days like we do, with rarely a day off to relax? And the expanded league and travel make it even tougher.

"That doesn't mean I wouldn't do it all over again, because compared to other sports this is one where an average-size guy like me can succeed. You don't need to be 6-foot-11 or weigh well over 200 pounds to have a chance. I'm just under 6 feet and weighed only about 160 when I started.

"If a young player has some ability and adds desire and a willingness to work hard, he can do it. They all don't make it, though, even those with ability.

"I'll always remember the Red Sox rookie camp in '59. There were about 40 of us there, and Johnny Murphy came in and made a little speech. 'There's about a million dollars of Red Sox money invested in the 40 of you,' he said. 'I know from experience that only a few of you will make it to the majors, even though all of you have the ability to do it. It's up to you.'

"I never forgot that because only a few did make it—Radatz, Chuck Schilling, Bob Tillman, Jim Pagliaroni, Don Schwall and me. There were guys there with more ability than me, but apparently they didn't have the desire.

"Without a doubt, the 1967 season was my most memorable year. Not only was it my first pennant, but it also was the way we won it—going from 100-to-1 underdogs to that unbelievable finish, then to the seventh game of the World Series against a team everyone thought would kill us.

"I was in a tremendous groove that year, something you can't really explain. Offensively, I thought I had an even better year in 1970. But we didn't win the pennant in '70, and people tend to overlook a year like that when you're not No. 1.

"My biggest disappointments have to be the near-miss pennants, particularly '72 and '78. In 1972 we lost by a half-game, and the Tigers won because they played one more game because of the strike. And in '78 there was that playoff game with the Yankees. No apology is needed for that one; both teams played like champions and we couldn't have come any closer without winning. But coming so close made it all the more frustrating.

"There have been far more highs than lows in my career, though. Sure, I wish there were more pennants and some World Championships. But I don't regret having signed with the Red Sox. I nearly didn't, you know. The Yankees offered $45,000 when I got out of high school, and I wanted to take it. But my father said no. Not only did he believe I was worth a lot more, but there was something the pastor of our parish on Long Island told us. The priest, Father Joe Ratkowski, was a friend of Gil Hodges, who told Father Joe that there was only one man to play for—Mr. Yawkey.

"That played a big part in our decision to sign with the Red Sox, and it was good advice. Mr. Yawkey and the ball club have taken good care of me in so many ways over the years. So I'm glad my career has been with the Red Sox. And I can't picture myself in any other uniform or playing in any other city."

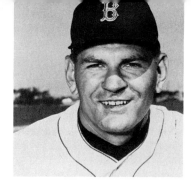

DICK RADATZ, 1962–1966:

"The game I remember above all others was one against the Yankees in Boston—in 1963, I think. It was a hot night, and more than 35,000 were squeezed into Fenway. The place was jumping.

"I was going real good at that time and was a little cocky. I was hot and knew it.

"Earl Wilson likes to tell this story, and he says he had a tendency, if he had a lead late, to look over his shoulder to the bull pen, knowing I was there.

"Well, Earl was pitching a hell of a game this night, and now it was the ninth inning. He was leading, 2-1, but the Yankees loaded the bases with no out. And the next three batters due were named Mantle, Maris and Ellie Howard.

"Johnny Pesky was our manager, and he came out and asked Wilson how he felt. As Earl tells it, they're standing there on the mound, and he could hear my fastball echoing in the bull pen—pop! pop! pop!—and he's sure Pesky is going to take him out. So Earl said, 'I feel good, skip,' and Johnny patted him on the butt and said, 'Okay, tiger, go get 'em!'

"Wilson says he nearly fell off the mound. As Pesky started back to the dugout, Earl called after him, 'Hey, wait a minute, John. Maybe I do feel a little tired at that. If the big guy is ready...'

"So in I come, and as Earl handed me the ball I said, 'Pop me a beer (in the clubhouse). I'll be right in.' And in just 10 pitches I was—three straight strikeouts. I was so elated I raised both arms over my head, the first time I ever did that; I was *that* happy.

"So I'll always remember that game. And I'll never forget the thrill of pitching in the 1963 and '64 All-Star Games, either. There's an irony there, because the '64 game was also my biggest disappointment.

"That '64 game was the one at Shea Stadium when Johnny Callison hit that three-run homer with two out in the last of the ninth to beat us, 7-4.

"I *never* had better stuff than I had that day. I was throwing blue fire.

"I'd breezed through the seventh and eighth and took a 4-3 lead into the ninth. Willie Mays was the leadoff hitter and, on a 2-2 count, I threw as good a slider as I ever threw in my life. Willie watched it go by and started walking back to the dugout. But Ed Sudol called it ball three. I couldn't believe it, and I don't think Mays could, either.

"Willie then walked, stole second and scored on Orlando Cepeda's bloop hit, Cepeda taking second on the throw to the plate. I got Ken Boyer to pop out, then intentionally passed Johnny Edwards to set up a double play.

"Hank Aaron came up to bat for Ron Hunt. I gave Henry three fastballs and he sat down. He said in the newspapers later that I was the fastest he'd ever batted against.

"Then up came Callison, the only hitter I faced twice. He'd been the first hitter when I came into the game. This time, just before he stepped into the batter's box, he turned and went back to the dugout. I heard later that he got a lighter bat, changing his usual 36 for a 32.

"Well, I gave him a fastball with good velocity. But it wasn't where I wanted it. I got it out too far, instead of in tight, and he hit the hell out of it. Ball game.

"On one pitch I went from MVP to donkey. That loss stuck with me for awhile. Usually I could go out after a loss, have a few beers and forget it. Not that one."

◇◇◇

RICO PETROCELLI, 1963, 1965–1976:

"People have never forgotten my problems with Billy Herman. Thirteen years later I'm still asked about it.

"I played 12 seasons with the Red Sox. I was lucky enough to play in two World Series and a couple of All-Star Games. And there were the 40 homers in 1966, the most ever by an American League shortstop. Yet what I'm asked about are those problems with Herman, my manager with the Sox in '65 and '66.

"Let me say I bear Billy no ill will. Instead, I'll always be grateful to him for giving me the chance to play in the majors. Yet I must say in all honesty that no person ever stung or disappointed me more than Herman.

"I've heard that Billy once said of me: 'When I played for the Cubs, my double-play partner Billy Jurges was shot by a showgirl and was out of the lineup about a week. Petrocelli is out that long with a hangnail.'

"Even more cutting and dumbfounding was what Herman said when he was fired. He told the press I'd let him down and cost him his job. Wow, that really disturbed me. I was shocked. It was inconceivable to me, and still is, how Herman could say such a thing. I guess it's easy to blame someone else for your failures—even two ninth-place finishes in a row.

"It hurt, though, and was ironic. I gave Herman everything I had, despite a bunch of ailments those two years. I played hurt and got only abuse for it. Billy did a lot of talking about this hypochondriac

baloney—to just about everyone but me. He never once mentioned it to me, the guy whose reputation was being damaged.

"Once I was dead wrong, though. That was the time I walked out during a night game at Fenway in 1966, an AWOL that cost me a $1,000 fine. My mistake was in not telling Billy I was leaving. I'm not proud of that and there's no excuse for it, merely the explanation that I was greatly upset when I did it. Frantic is a better word, because it involved the safety of my wife Elsie.

"That morning she was stricken with tremendous pains in her right side. I thought of appendicitis. I also considered postnatal complications from the birth of our first child six months before. I was really worried about Elsie's condition. I called our doctor and he said to put ice on the pained area, keep an eye on the condition and call him if it worsened.

"I wanted to call Fenway and say I couldn't make it to the game, but Elsie wouldn't let me. But her condition worried me sick throughout the game. Then, as we were heading off the field in the middle of the seventh inning, it hit me like a bolt. I guess it was something approaching extrasensory perception. It flashed through my mind: 'Elsie's in trouble and needs help—now!' It was very vivid and very frightening.

"My reaction was automatic. I had to get home immediately. I didn't think of the consequences. It was something I had to do. I never stopped running as I reached the dugout. I bounded down the steps and up the runway toward the clubhouse. As I passed Fitzie (equipment manager Don Fitzpatrick) and Buddy (LeRoux, then the trainer) on the dead run, I hollered, 'I'm going home.' Their first reaction must have been that I was joking, their second that I had flipped.

"I ripped off my uniform and grabbed a 10-second shower. As I was dressing, Buddy tried his best to dissuade me in his calm and persuasive way. But he could have saved his breath. All I could envision was Elsie collapsed in pain, and alone with our infant.

"I jumped into my car and really pushed it home. When I flung open the front door, I saw exactly what I had envisioned: there was Elsie collapsed on the stairs leading upstairs—doubled up in pain, moaning and clutching her stomach. I rushed her to the hospital, and the doctor said I'd gotten her there just in time. A cyst had burst inside her, spreading poison through her system.

"Meanwhile, back at Fenway, Herman was blowing his top. There even were reports he wanted to get rid of me on the spot. Billy had every right to be angry because I was completely wrong not telling him I was leaving.

"I met with Billy the next day. And when he said he was fining me I said, 'Okay, I deserve it.' I have no complaint with the fine. But I do have a legitimate gripe about the way he talked about me. The 'Petrocelli the Hypochondriac' image began and flourished under him. I broke my hump for the guy; yet all I got from him was a bad name that took years to live down."

◇ ◇
◇

ALL-TIME ROSTER

MANAGERS

Ed Barrow   1918-20
Jack Barry   1917
Lou Boudreau   1952-54
Bill Carrigan   1913-16, 1927-29
Frank Chance   1923
Jimmy Collins   1901-06
Shano Collins   1931-32
Joe Cronin   1935-47
Patsy Donovan   1910-11
Hugh Duffy   1921-22
Lee Fohl   1924-26
Bucky Harris   1934
Billy Herman   1954-66
Mike Higgins   1955-62
George Huff   1907
Darrell Johnson   1974-76
Billy Jurges   1959-60

Eddie Kasko   1970-73
Fred Lake   1908-09
Joe McCarthy   1948-50
Deacon McGuire   1907-08
Marty McManus   1932-33
Steve O'Neill   1950-51
Johnny Pesky   1963-64
*Eddie Popowski   1969
*Pete Runnels   1966
Chick Stahl   1906
Jake Stahl   1912-13
Bob Unglaub   1907
Heinie Wagner   1930
Dick Williams   1967-69
*Rudy York   1959
*Cy Young   1907
Don Zimmer   1976-79

*Interim manager.

11
THE RECORD

PLAYERS

A

Don Aase   1977
Jerry Adair   1967-68
Bob Adams   1925
Doc Adkins   1902
Harry Agganis   1954-55
Sam Agnew   1916-18
Dale Alexander   1932-33
Gary Allenson   1979
Mel Almada   1933-37
Nick Altrock   1902-03
Luis Alvarado   1968-70
Fred Anderson   1909
Ernie Andres   1946
Kim Andrew   1975
Ivy Andrews   1932-33
Mike Andrews   1966-70
Luis Aparicio   1971-73
Frank Arellanes   1908-10
Charley Armbruster   1905-07
Asby Asbjornson   1928-29
Ken Aspromonte   1957-58
Jim Atkins   1950
Eldon Auker   1939
Doyle Aulds   1947
Bobby Avila   1959
Ramon Aviles   1977
Joe Azcue   1969

B

Loren Bader   1917-18
Jim Bagby Jr.   1938-40, 1946
Bob Bailey   1977-78
Gene Bailey   1920
Al Baker   1938
Floyd Baker   1953-54
Jack Baker   1976-77
Tracy Baker   1911
Neal Ball   1912-13
Walter Barbare   1918
Frank Barberich   1910
Babe Barna   1943
Steve Barr   1974-75
Bill Barrett   1929-30
Bob Barrett   1929
Frank Barrett   1944-45
Jimmy Barrett   1907-08
Ed Barry   1905-07
Jack Barry   1915-17, 1919
Matt Batts   1947-51

Frank Baumann   1955-59
Bill Bayne   1929-30
Hugh Bedient   1912-14
Gary Bell   1967-68
Juan Beniquez   1971-72, 1974-75
Dennis Bennett   1965-67
Frank Bennett   1927-28
Al Benton   1952
Lou Berberet   1958
Moe Berg   1935-39
Boze Berger   1939
Charley Berry   1928-32
Hal Bevan   1952
Charley Beville   1901
Elliott Bigelow   1929
John Bischoff   1925-26
Max Bishop   1934-35
Dave Black   1923
Tim Blackwell   1974-75
Clarence Blethen   1923
Red Bluhm   1918
Larry Boerner   1932
Bob Bolin   1970-73
Milt Bolling   1952-57
Ike Boone   1923-25
Ray Boone   1960
Tom Borland   1960-61
Lou Boudreau   1951-52
Sam Bowen   1977-78
Stew Bowers   1935-37
Joe Bowman   1944-45
Ted Bowsfield   1958-60
Herb Bradley   1927-29
Hugh Bradley   1910-12
Cliff Brady   1920
King Brady   1908
Darrell Brandon   1966-68
Fred Bratchi   1926-27
Ed Bressoud   1962-65
Ken Brett   1967, 1969-71
Tom Brewer   1954-61
Ralph Brickner   1952
Jim Brillheart   1931
Dick Brodowski   1952
Jack Brohamer   1978-79
Hal Brown   1953-55
Lloyd Brown   1933
Mace Brown   1942-43, 1946
Jim Bucher   1944-45
Don Buddin   1956, 1958-61

Fred Burchell   1907-09
Bob Burda   1972
Tom Burgmeier   1978-79
Jesse Burkett   1905
Rick Burleson   1974-79
George Burns   1922-23
Jim Burton   1975, 1977
Jim Busby   1959-60
Joe Bush   1918-21
Jack Bushelman   1911-12
Frank Bushey   1927
Bill Butland   1940, 1942, 1946-47
Bud Byerly   1958

C

Hick Cady   1912-17
Earl Caldwell   1948
Ray Caldwell   1919
Dolf Camilli   1945
Bill Campbell   1977-79
Paul Campbell   1941-42, 1946
Bernie Carbo   1974-78
Tom Carey   1939-42, 1946
Walter Carlisle   1908
Swede Carlstrom   1911
Cleo Carlyle   1927
Roy Carlyle   1925-26
Bill Carrigan   1906, 1908-16
Ed Carroll   1929
Jerry Casale   1958-60
Joe Cascarella   1935-36
Danny Cater   1972-74
Rex Cecil   1944-45
Orlando Cepeda   1973
Chet Chadbourne   1906-07
Bob Chakales   1957
Estey Chaney   1913
Ed Chaplin   1920-22
Ben Chapman   1937-38
Pete Charton   1964
Ken Chase   1942-43
Charley Chech   1909
Jack Chesbro   1909
Nels Chittum   1959-60
Joe Christopher   1966
Loyd Christopher   1945
Joe Cicero   1929-30
Ed Cicotte   1908-12
Galen Cisco   1961-62, 1967

Bill Cissell   1934
Danny Clark   1924
Otie Clark   1945
Lance Clemons   1974
Reggie Cleveland   1974-78
Tex Clevenger   1954
Lu Clinton   1960-64
Bill Clowers   1926
George Cochran   1918
Jack Coffey   1918
Dave Coleman   1977
Jimmy Collins   1901-07
Ray Collins   1909-15
Rip Collins   1922
Shano Collins   1921-25
Merrill Combs   1947, 1949-50
Ralph Comstock   1915
Bunk Congalton   1907
Billy Conigliaro   1969-71
Tony Conigliaro   1964-67, 1969-70, 1975
Gene Conley   1961-63
Bud Connally   1925
Ed Connolly Sr.   1929-32
Ed Connolly Jr.   1964
Joe Connolly   1924
Bill Conroy   1942-44
Billy Consolo   1953-59
Dusty Cooke   1933-36
Jimmy Cooney   1917
Cecil Cooper   1971-76
Guy Cooper   1914-15
Vic Correll   1972
Marlan Coughtry   1960
Fritz Coombe   1914
Ted Cox   1977
Doc Cramer   1936-40
Gavvy Cravath   1908
Pat Creeden   1931
Bob Cremins   1927
Lou Criger   1901-08
Joe Cronin   1935-45
Leon Culberson   1943-47
Ray Culp   1968-73
Nig Cuppy   1901
John Curtis   1970-73

D

Babe Dahlgren   1935-36
Pete Daley   1955-59

Dom Dallessandro 1937
Babe Danzig 1909
Bobby Darwin 1976-77
Bob Daughters 1937
Cot Deal 1947-48
Pep Deininger 1902
Ike Delock 1952-53, 1955-63
Don Demeter 1966-67
Sam Dente 1947
Jim Derrick 1970
Gene Desautels 1937-40
Mel Deutsch 1946
Mickey Devine 1920
Hal Deviney 1920
Al DeVormer 1923
Bo Diaz 1977
George Dickey 1935-36
Emerson Dickman 1936, 1938-41
Bob Didier 1974
Steve Dillard 1975-77
Dom DiMaggio 1940-42, 1946-53
Bill Dinneen 1902-07
Bob DiPietro 1951
Ray Dobens 1929
Joe Dobson 1941-43, 1946-50, 1954
Sam Dodge 1921-22
Bobby Doerr 1937-44, 1946-51
John Donahue 1923
Pat Donahue 1908-10
Pete Donohue 1932
Tom Doran 1904-06
Harry Dorish 1947-49, 1956
Patsy Dougherty 1902-04
Tommy Dowd 1901
Danny Doyle 1943
Denny Doyle 1975-77
Dick Drago 1974-75, 1978-79
Clem Dreisewerd 1944-46
Walt Dropo 1949-52
Jean Dubuc 1918
Frank Duffy 1978-79
Joe Dugan 1922
Bob Duliba 1965
George Dumont 1919
Ed Durham 1929-32
Cedric Durst 1930
Jim Dwyer 1979

E

Arnold Earley 1960-65
Dennis Eckersley 1978-79
Elmer Eggert 1927
Howard Ehmke 1923-26
Hack Eibel 1920
Dick Ellsworth 1968-69
Clyde Engle 1910-14
Al Evans 1951
Bill Evans 1951
Dwight Evans 1972-79
Hoot Evers 1952-54
Homer Ezzell 1924-25

F

Carmen Fanzone 1970
Doc Farrell 1935
Duke Farrell 1903-05
Alex Ferguson 1922-25
Rick Ferrell 1933-37
Wes Ferrell 1934-37
Hobe Ferris 1901-07
Dave Ferriss 1945-50
Chick Fewster 1922-23
Joel Finch 1979
Tom Fine 1947
Lou Finney 1939-42, 1944-45
Mike Fiore 1970-71
Hank Fischer 1966-67
Carlton Fisk 1969, 1971-79
Howie Fitzgerald 1926
Ira Flagstead 1923-29
Al Flair 1941
Bill Fleming 1940-41
Ben Flowers 1951

Hank Foreman 1901
Happy Foreman 1926
Mike Fornieles 1957-63
Gary Fortune 1920
Eddie Foster 1920-22
Rube Foster 1913-17
Bob Fothergill 1933
Boob Fowler 1926
Pete Fox 1941-45
Jimmy Foxx 1936-42
Joe Foy 1966-68
Ray Francis 1925
Buck Freeman 1901-07
Hersh Freeman 1952-53, 1955
John Freeman 1927
Charley French 1909-10
Barney Friberg 1933
Owen Friend 1955
Oscar Fuhr 1924-25
Frank Fuller 1923
Curt Fullerton 1921-25, 1933

G

Fabian Gaffke 1936-39
Phil Gagliano 1971-72
Del Gainor 1914-17, 1919
Denny Galehouse 1939-40, 1947-49
Bob Gallagher 1972
Ed Gallagher 1932
Jim Galvin 1930
Bob Garbark 1945
Billy Gardner 1962-63
Larry Gardner 1908-17
Mike Garman 1969, 1971-73
Cliff Garrison 1928
Ford Garrison 1943-44
Alex Gaston 1926
Milt Gaston 1929-31
Gary Geiger 1959-65
Charley Gelbert 1940
Wally Gerber 1928-29
Dick Gernert 1952-59
Doc Gessler 1908-09
Chappie Geygan 1924-26
Joe Giannini 1911
Norwood Gibson 1903-06
Russ Gibson 1967-69
Andy Gilbert 1942, 1946
Don Gile 1959-62
Frank Gilhooley 1919
Bob Gillespie 1950
Grant Gillis 1929
Joe Ginsberg 1961
Ralph Glaze 1906-08
Harry Gleason 1901-03
Joe Glenn 1940
John Godwin 1905-06
Chuck Goggin 1974
Eusebio Gonzales 1918
Joe Gonzales 1937
Johnny Gooch 1933
Billy Goodman 1947-57
Jim Gosger 1963, 1965-66
Charley Graham 1906
Skinny Graham 1934-35
Dave Gray 1964
Lenny Green 1965-66
Pumpsie Green 1959-62
Vean Gregg 1914-16
Doug Griffin 1971-77
Marty Griffin 1928
Guido Grilli 1966
Ray Grimes 1920
Moose Grimshaw 1905-07
Marv Grissom 1953
Turkey Gross 1925
Lefty Grove 1934-41
Mike Guerra 1951
Mario Guerrero 1973-74
Bob Guindon 1964
Randy Gumpert 1952

Hy Gunning 1911
Don Gutteridge 1946-47

H

Casey Hageman 1911-12
Odell Hale 1941
Ray Haley 1915-16
Charley Hall 1909-13
Garry Hancock 1978
Fred Haney 1926-27
Carroll Hardy 1960-62
Harry Harper 1920
Tommy Harper 1972-74
Billy Harrell 1961
Ken Harrelson 1967-69
Bill Harris 1938
Joe Harris 1905-07
Joe Harris 1922-25
Mickey Harris 1940-41, 1946-49
Slim Harriss 1926-28
Jack Harshman 1959
Chuck Hartenstein 1970
Grover Hartley 1927
Charley Hartman 1908
Herb Hash 1940-41
Andy Hassler 1978-79
Fred Hatfield 1950-52
Grady Hatton 1954-56
Clem Hausmann 1944-45
John Hayden 1906
Frankie Hayes 1947
Ed Hearn 1910
Bob Heffner 1963-65
Randy Heflin 1945-46
Fred Heimach 1926
Bob Heise 1975-76
Tommy Helms 1977
Charley Hemphill 1901
Tim Hendryx 1920-21
Olaf Henriksen 1911-17
Bill Henry 1952-55
Jim Henry 1936-37
Ramon Hernandez 1977
Mike Herrera 1925-26
Tom Herrin 1954
Joe Heving 1938-40
Johnnie Heving 1924-25, 1928-30
Piano Legs Hickman 1902
Mike Higgins 1937-38, 1946
Hob Hiller 1920-21
Dave Hillman 1960-61
Gordie Hinkle 1934
Paul Hinrichs 1951
Paul Hinson 1928
Harley Hisner 1951
Billy Hitchcock 1948-49
Dick Hoblitzell 1914-18
Butch Hobson 1975-79
George Hockette 1934-35
Johnny Hodapp 1933
Mel Hoderlein 1951
Billy Hoeft 1959
John Hoey 1906-08
Fred Hofmann 1927-28
Ken Holcombe 1953
Billy Holm 1945
Harry Hooper 1909-20
Tony Horton 1964-67
Tom House 1976-77
Elston Howard 1967-68
Paul Howard 1909
Les Howe 1923-24
Waite Hoyt 1919-20
Sid Hudson 1952-54
Ed Hughes 1905-06
Long Tom Hughes 1902-03
Terry Hughes 1974
Tex Hughson 1941-44, 1946-49
Bill Humphrey 1938
Ben Hunt 1910
Buddy Hunter 1971-73, 1975
Herb Hunter 1920

Tom Hurd 1954-56
Bert Husting 1902

J

Pete Jablonowski 1932
(later known as Pete Appleton)
Ron Jackson 1960
Baby Doll Jacobson 1926-27
Beany Jacobson 1907
Charley Jamerson 1924
Bill James 1919
Hal Janvrin 1911, 1913-17
Ray Jarvis 1969-70
Ferguson Jenkins 1976-77
Tom Jenkins 1925-26
Jackie Jensen 1954-59, 1961
Adam Johnson 1914
Bob Johnson 1944-45
Deron Johnson 1974-76
Earl Johnson 1940-41, 1946-50
Hank Johnson 1933-35
Roy Johnson 1932-35
Vic Johnson 1944-45
Smead Jolley 1932-33
Charley Jones 1901
Dalton Jones 1964-69
Jake Jones 1947-48
Rick Jones 1976
Sad Sam Jones 1916-21
Eddie Joost 1955
Duane Josephson 1971-72
Oscar Judd 1941-45
Joe Judge 1933-34

K

Rudy Kallio 1925
Ed Karger 1909-11
Andy Karl 1943
Marty Karow 1927
Benn Karr 1920-22
Eddie Kasko 1966
George Kell 1952-54
Al Kellett 1924
Red Kellett 1934
Win Kellum 1901
Ed Kelly 1914
Ken Keltner 1950
Russ Kemmerer 1954-55, 1957
Fred Kendall 1978
Bill Kennedy 1953
John Kennedy 1970-74
Marty Keough 1956-60
Joe Kiefer 1925-26
Leo Kiely 1951, 1954-56, 1958-59
Jack Killilay 1911
Ellis Kinder 1948-55
Walt Kinney 1918
Billy Klaus 1955-58
Red Kleinow 1910-11
Bob Kline 1930-33
Ron Kline 1969
Bob Klinger 1946-47
John Knight 1907
Hal Kolstad 1962-63
Cal Koonce 1970-71
Andy Kosco 1972
Jack Kramer 1948-49
Lew Krausse 1972
Rube Kroh 1906-07
John Kroner 1935-36
Rick Kreuger 1975-77
Marty Krug 1912

L

Candy LaChance 1902-05
Ty LaForest 1945
Joe Lahoud 1968-71
Eddie Lake 1943-45
Jack Lamabe 1963-65
Bill Lamar 1919

Bill Landis 1967-69
Jim Landis 1967
Sam Langford 1926
Frank LaPorte 1908
John LaRose 1978
Lyn Lary 1934
Johnny Lazor 1943-46
Bill Lee 1969-78
Dud Lee 1924-26
Lefty LeFebvre 1938-39
Lou Legett 1933-35
Regis Leheny 1932
Paul Lehner 1952
Nemo Leibold 1921-23
Don Lenhardt 1952
Dutch Leonard 1913-18
Ted Lepcio 1952-59
Dutch Lerchen 1910
Louis LeRoy 1910
Duffy Lewis 1910-17
John Lewis 1911
Ted Lewis 1901
Johnny Lipon 1952-53
Hod Lisenbee 1929-32
Dick Littlefield 1950
Don Lock 1969
George Loepp 1928
Jim Lonborg 1965-71
Walt Lonergan 1911
Harry Lord 1907-10
Johnny Lucas 1931-32
Joe Lucey 1925
Lou Lucier 1943-44
Del Lundgren 1926-27
Tony Lupien 1940, 1942-43
Sparky Lyle 1967-71
Walt Lynch 1922
Fred Lynn 1974-79

M

Danny MacFayden 1926-32
Bill MacLeod 1962
Tom Madden 1909-11
Pete Magrini 1966
Chris Mahoney 1910
Jim Mahoney 1959
Jerry Mallett 1959
Paul Maloy 1913
Frank Malzone 1955-65
Felix Mantilla 1963-65
Heinie Manush 1936
Phil Marchildon 1950
Johnny Marcum 1936-38
Juan Marichal 1974
Ollie Marquardt 1931
Bill Marshall 1931
Babe Martin 1948-49
Walt Masterson 1949-52
Tommy Matchick 1970
Bill Mathews 1909
Gene Mauch 1956-57
Charley Maxwell 1950-52, 1954
Wally Mayer 1917-18
Chick Maynard 1922
Carl Mays 1915-19
Dick McAuliffe 1974-75
Tom McBride 1943-47
Dick McCabe 1918
Windy McCall 1948-49
Emmett McCann 1926
Tim McCarver 1974-75
Amby McConnell 1908-10
Maurice McDermott 1948-53
Jim McDonald 1950
Ed McFarland 1908
Ed McGah 1946-47
Lynn McGlothen 1972-73
Art McGovern 1905
Bob McGraw 1919
Deacon McGuire 1907-08
Jim McHale 1908
Marty McHale 1910-11, 1916

Stuffy McInnis 1918-21
Archie McKain 1937-38
Jud McLaughlin 1931-33
Larry McLean 1901
Doc McMahon 1908
Don McMahon 1966-67
Marty McManus 1931-33
Norm McMillan 1923
Eric McNair 1936-38
Mike McNally 1915-17, 1919-20
Gordon McNaughton 1932
Norm McNeil 1919
Bill McWilliams 1931
Roman Mejias 1963-64
Sam Mele 1947-49, 1954-55
Oscar Melillo 1935-37
Mike Menosky 1920-23
Mike Meola 1933
Andy Merchant 1975-76
Spike Merena 1934
Jack Merson 1953
George Metkovich 1943-46
Russ Meyer 1957
John Michaels 1932
Dick Midkiff 1938
Dee Miles 1943
Bing Miller 1935-36
Elmer Miller 1922
Hack Miller 1918
Otto Miller 1930-32
Rick Miller 1971-77
Buster Mills 1937
Dick Mills 1970
Rudy Minarcin 1956-57
Fred Mitchell 1901-02
Johnny Mitchell 1922-23
Herb Moford 1959
Vince Molyneaux 1918
Bill Monbouquette 1958-65
Freddie Moncewicz 1928
Bob Montgomery 1970-79
Bill Moore 1926-27
Wilcy Moore 1931-32
Dave Morehead 1963-68
Roger Moret 1970-75
Cy Morgan 1907-09
Eddie Morgan 1934
Red Morgan 1906
Ed Morris 1928-31
Deacon Morrissey 1901
Guy Morton 1954
Earl Moseley 1913
Walter Moser 1911
Gerry Moses 1965, 1968-70
Wally Moses 1946-48
Doc Moskiman 1910
Les Moss 1951
Gordy Mueller 1950
Billy Muffett 1960-62
Greg Mulleavy 1933
Freddie Muller 1933-34
Joe Mulligan 1934
Frank Mulroney 1930
Bill Mundy 1913
Johnny Murphy 1947
Tom Murphy 1976-77
Walter Murphy 1931
George Murray 1923-24
Tony Muser 1969
Paul Musser 1919
Alex Mustaikis 1940
Buddy Myer 1927-28
Elmer Myers 1920-22
Hap Myers 1910-11

N

Judge Nagle 1911
Mike Nagy 1969-72
Bill Narleski 1929-30
Ernie Neitzke 1921
Hal Neubauer 1925
Don Newhauser 1972-74
Bobo Newsom 1937

Dick Newsome 1941-43
Skeeter Newsome 1941-45
Gus Niarhos 1952-53
Chet Nichols 1960-63
Al Niemiec 1934
Harry Niles 1908-10
Merlin Nippert 1962
Russ Nixon 1960-65, 1968
Willard Nixon 1950-58
Leo Nonnenkamp 1938-40
Chet Nourse 1909
Les Nunamaker 1911-14

O

Frank Oberlin 1906-07
Mike O'Berry 1979
Buck O'Brien 1911-13
Jack O'Brien 1903
Syd O'Brien 1969
Tom O'Brien 1949-50
Lefty O'Doul 1923
Ben Oglivie 1971-73
Len Okrie 1952
Gene Oliver 1968
Tom Oliver 1930-33
Hank Olmsted 1905
Al Olsen 1943
Karl Olson 1951, 1953-55
Marv Olson 1931-33
Ted Olson 1936-38
Bill O'Neill 1904
Emmett O'Neill 1943-45
Steve O'Neill 1924
George Orme 1920
Frank O'Rourke 1922
Dan Osinski 1966-67
Harry Ostdiek 1908
Fritz Ostermueller 1934-40
John Ostrowski 1948
Marv Owen 1940
Mickey Owen 1954
Frank Owens 1905

P

Jim Pagliaroni 1955, 1960-62
Mike Palm 1948
Al Papai 1950
Larry Pape 1909, 1911-12
Stan Papi 1979
Freddy Parent 1901-07
Mel Parnell 1947-56
Roy Partee 1943-44, 1946-47
Stan Partenheimer 1944
Ben Paschal 1920
Casey Patten 1908
Hank Patterson 1932
Marty Pattin 1972-73
Don Pavletich 1970-71
Mike Paxton 1977
Johnny Peacock 1937-44
Eddie Pellagrini 1946-47
Herb Pennock 1915-17, 1919-22, 1934
Jack Perrin 1921
Bill Pertica 1918
Johnny Pesky 1942, 1946-52
Gary Peters 1970-72
Bob Peterson 1906-07
Rico Petrocelli 1963, 1965-76
Dave Philley 1962
Ed Phillips 1970
Val Picinich 1923-25
Urbane Pickering 1931-32
Bill Piercy 1922-24
Jimmy Piersall 1950, 1952-58
George Pipgras 1933-35
Pinky Pittenger 1921-23
Juan Pizarro 1968-69
Herb Plews 1959
Jennings Poindexter 1936
Dick Pole 1973-76
Nick Polly 1945
Ralph Pond 1910
Tom Poquette 1979

Dick Porter 1934
Bob Porterfield 1956-58
Nelson Potter 1941
Ken Poulsen 1967
Del Pratt 1921-22
Larry Pratt 1914
George Prentiss 1901-02
Doc Prothro 1925
Tex Pruiett 1907-08
Billy Purtell 1910-11
Frankie Pytlak 1941, 1945-46

Q

Frank Quinn 1949-50
Jack Quinn 1922-25

R

Dick Radatz 1962-66
Chuck Rainey 1979
Johnny Reder 1932
Bobby Reeves 1929-31
Bill Regan 1926-30
Wally Rehg 1913-15
Wally Rehg 1913-15
Dick Reichle 1922-23
Win Remmerswaal 1979
Jerry Remy 1978-79
Steve Renko 1979
Bill Renna 1958-59
Rip Repulski 1960-61
Carl Reynolds 1934-35
Gordon Rhodes 1932-35
Hal Rhyne 1929-32
Jim Rice 1974-79
Woody Rich 1939-41
Al Richter 1951
Joe Riggert 1911
Topper Rigney 1926-27
Allen Ripley 1978-79
Walt Ripley 1935
Pop Rising 1905
Jay Ritchie 1964-65
Aaron Robinson 1951
Floyd Robinson 1968
Jack Robinson 1949
Bill Rodgers 1915
Billy Rogell 1925, 1927-28
Lee Rogers 1938
Garry Roggenburk 1966, 1968-69
Billy Rohr 1967
Red Rollings 1927-28
Vicente Romo 1969-70
Buddy Rosar 1950-51
Si Rosenthal 1925-26
Buster Ross 1924-26
Braggo Roth 1919
Jack Rothrock 1925-32
Muddy Ruel 1921-22, 1931
Red Ruffing 1924-30
Pete Runnels 1958-62
Allan Russell 1919-22
Jack Russell 1926-32, 1936
Rip Russell 1946-47
Babe Ruth 1914-19
Jack Ryan 1909
Jack Ryan 1929
Mike Ryan 1964-67
Mike Ryba 1941-46
Gene Rye 1931

S

Bob Sadowski 1966
Ed Sadowski 1960
Ken Sanders 1966
Jose Santiago 1966-70
Tom Satriano 1969-70
Bill Sayles 1939
Ray Scarborough 1951-52
Russ Scarritt 1929-31
Wally Schang 1918-20
Charley Schanz 1950
Bob Scherbarth 1950
Chuck Schilling 1961-65
Rudy Schlesinger 1965

Biff Schlitzer 1909
George Schmees 1952
Johnny Schmitz 1956
Dick Schofield 1969-70
Ossee Schreckengost 1901
Al Schroll 1958-59
Don Schwall 1961-62
Everett Scott 1914-21
George Scott 1966-71, 1977-79
Bob Seeds 1933-34
Diego Segui 1974-75
Kip Selbach 1904-06
Merle Settlemire 1928
Wally Shaner 1926-27
Howard Shanks 1923-24
Red Shannon 1919
Al Shaw 1907
John Shea 1928
Merv Shea 1933
Dave Shean 1918-19
Rollie Sheldon 1966
Neill Sheridan 1948
Ben Shields 1930
Strick Shofner 1947
Ernie Shore 1914-17
Bill Short 1966
Chick Shorten 1915-17
Norm Siebern 1967-68
Sonny Siebert 1969-73
Al Simmons 1943
Pat Simmons 1928-29
Dave Sisler 1956-59
Ted Sizemore 1979
Camp Skinner 1923
Craig Skok 1973
Jack Slattery 1901
Steve Slayton 1928
Charley Small 1930
Al Smith 1964
Bob Smith 1955
Broadway Aleck Smith 1903
Charley Smith 1909-11
Doug Smith 1912
Eddie Smith 1947
Elmer Smith 1922
Frank Smith 1910-11
George Smith 1930
George Smith 1966
John Smith 1931
Paddy Smith 1920
Pete Smith 1962-63
Reggie Smith 1966-73
Riverboat Smith 1958
Wally Snell 1913
Moose Solters 1934-35
Rudy Sommers 1926-27
Allen Sothoron 1921
Bill Spanswick 1964
Tully Sparks 1902
Tris Speaker 1907-15
Stan Spence 1940-41, 1948-49
Tubby Spencer 1909
Andy Spognardi 1932
Jack Spring 1957

Bobby Sprowl 1978
Chick Stahl 1901-06
Jake Stahl 1903, 1908-10, 1912-13
Tracy Stallard 1960-62
Jerry Standaert 1929
Lee Stange 1966-70
Bob Stanley 1977-79
John Stansbury 1918
Jigger Statz 1920
Elmer Steele 1907-09
Ben Steiner 1945-46
Red Steiner 1945
Gene Stephens 1952-53, 1955-60
Vern Stephens 1948-52
Jerry Stephenson 1963, 1965-68
Dick Stigman 1966
Carl Stimson 1923
Chuck Stobbs 1947-51
Al Stokes 1925-26
Dean Stone 1957
George Stone 1903
Howie Stone 1931-32
Lou Stringer 1948-50
Amos Strunk 1918-19
Dick Stuart 1963-64
George Stumpf 1931-33
Tom Sturdivant 1960
Jim Suchecki 1950
Denny Sullivan 1907-08
Frank Sullivan 1953-60
Haywood Sullivan 1955, 1957, 1959-60
Carl Sumner 1928
George Susce 1955-58
Bill Swanson 1914
Bill Sweeney 1930-31
Len Swormstedt 1906

T
Jim Tabor 1938-44
Doug Taitt 1928-29
Jesse Tannehill 1904-08
Arlie Tarbert 1927-28
Jose Tartabull 1966-68
Willie Tasby 1960
Bennie Tate 1932
Ken Tatum 1971-73
Harry Taylor 1950-52
Birdie Tebbetts 1947-50
Yank Terry 1940, 1942-45
Jake Thielman 1908
Blaine Thomas 1911
Fred Thomas 1918
George Thomas 1966-71
Lee Thomas 1964-65
Pinch Thomas 1912-17
Tommy Thomas 1937
Bobby Thomson 1960
Jack Thoney 1908-09, 1911
Hank Thormahlen 1921
Faye Throneberry 1952, 1955-57
Luis Tiant 1971-78

Bob Tillman 1962-67
Jack Tobin 1926-27
Johnny Tobin 1945
Phil Todt 1924-30
Tony Tonneman 1911
Mike Torrez 1978-79
Joe Trimble 1955
Dizzy Trout 1952
Frank Truesdale 1918
John Tudor 1979
Bob Turley 1963

U
Tom Umphlett 1953
Bob Unglaub 1904-05, 1907-08

V
Tex Vache 1925
Al Van Camp 1931-32
Hy Vandenberg 1935
Ben Van Dyke 1912
Bobby Veach 1924-25
Bob Veale 1972-74
Mickey Vernon 1956-57
Sammy Vick 1921
Oscar Vitt 1919-21
Clyde Vollmer 1950-53
Jake Volz 1901
Joe Vosmik 1938-39

W
Jake Wade 1939
Charley Wagner 1938-42, 1946
Gary Wagner 1969-70
Hal Wagner 1944, 1946-47
Heinie Wagner 1906-13, 1915-16, 1918
Rube Walberg 1934-37
Tilly Walker 1916-17
Murray Wall 1957-59
Jimmy Walsh 1916-17
Bucky Walters 1933-34
Fred Walters 1945
Roxy Walters 1919-23
Bill Wambsganss 1924-25
Pee Wee Wanninger 1927
John Warner 1902
Rabbit Warstler 1930-33
Gary Waslewski 1967-68
Bob Watson 1979
Johnny Watwood 1932-33
Monte Weaver 1939
Earl Webb 1930-32
Ray Webster 1960
Bob Weiland 1932-34
Frank Welch 1927
Herb Welch 1925
Johnny Welch 1932-36
Tony Welzer 1926-27
Fred Wenz 1968-69
Bill Werber 1933-36
Bill Werle 1953-54

Vic Wertz 1959-61
Sammy White 1951-59
George Whiteman 1907, 1918
Ernie Whitt 1976
Al Widmar 1947
Bill Wight 1951-52
Del Wilber 1952-54
Joe Wilhoit 1919
Dave Williams 1902
Denny Williams 1924-25, 1928
Dib Williams 1935
Dick Williams 1963-64
Ken Williams 1928-29
Rip Williams 1911
Stan Williams 1972
Ted Williams 1939-42, 1946-60
Jim Willoughby 1975-77
Ted Wills 1959-62
Archie Wilson 1952
Duane Wilson 1958
Earl Wilson 1959-60, 1962-66
Gary Wilson 1902
Jack Wilson 1935-41
Jim Wilson 1945-46
John Wilson 1927-28
Les Wilson 1911
Squanto Wilson 1914
Hal Wiltse 1926-28
Ted Wingfield 1924-27
George Winn 1919
Tom Winsett 1930-31, 1933
George Winter 1901-08
Clarence Winters 1924
Rick Wise 1974-77
Johnny Wittig 1949
Larry Wolfe 1979
Harry Wolter 1909
Smokey Joe Wood 1908-15
Joe Wood 1944
Ken Wood 1952
Wilbur Wood 1961-64
John Woods 1924
Pinky Woods 1943-45
Hoge Workman 1924
Al Worthington 1960
Jim Wright 1978-79
Tom Wright 1948-51
John Wyatt 1966-68
John Wyckoff 1916-18

Y
Carl Yastrzemski 1961-79
Steve Yerkes 1909, 1911-14
Rudy York 1946-47
Cy Young 1901-08

Z
Paul Zahniser 1925-26
Al Zarilla 1949-50, 1952-53
Norm Zauchin 1951, 1955-57
Matt Zeiser 1914
Bill Zuber 1946-47

POSITION LEADERS YEAR BY YEAR

(Leading pitchers determined by victories and ERA;
other positions determined by most games at that position.)

Year	Pitcher	Pitcher	Pitcher	Catcher
1901	Cy Young	George Winter	Ted Lewis	Ossee Schreckengost
1902	Cy Young	Bill Dinneen	George Winter	Lou Criger
1903	Cy Young	Bill Dinneen	Long Tom Hughes	Lou Criger
1904	Cy Young	Bill Dinneen	Jesse Tannehill	Lou Criger
1905	Jesse Tannehill	Cy Young	George Winter	Lou Criger
1906	Jesse Tannehill	Cy Young	Bill Dinneen	Charley Armbruster
1907	Cy Young	George Winter	Cy Morgan	Lou Criger
1908	Cy Young	Cy Morgan	Ed Cicotte	Lou Criger
1909	Frank Arellanes	Ed Cicotte	Smokey Joe Wood	Bill Carrigan

Year	Pitcher	Pitcher	Pitcher	Catcher
1910	Ed Cicotte	Ray Collins	Smokey Joe Wood	Bill Carrigan
1911	Smokey Joe Wood	Larry Pape	Ray Collins	Bill Carrigan
1912	Smokey Joe Wood	Hugh Bedient	Buck O'Brien	Bill Carrigan
1913	Ray Collins	Hugh Bedient	Smokey Joe Wood	Bill Carrigan
1914	Dutch Leonard	Ray Collins	Rube Foster	Bill Carrigan
1915	Rube Foster	Ernie Shore	Babe Ruth	Pinch Thomas
1916	Babe Ruth	Dutch Leonard	Carl Mays	Pinch Thomas
1917	Babe Ruth	Carl Mays	Dutch Leonard	Sam Agnew
1918	Carl Mays	Sad Sam Jones	Joe Bush	Sam Agnew
1919	Herb Pennock	Sad Sam Jones	Allan Russell	Wally Schang
1920	Herb Pennock	Joe Bush	Sad Sam Jones	Roxy Walters
1921	Sad Sam Jones	Joe Bush	Herb Pennock	Muddy Ruel
1922	Rip Collins	Jack Quinn	Herb Pennock	Muddy Ruel
1923	Howard Ehmke	Jack Quinn	Bill Piercy	Val Picinich
1924	Howard Ehmke	Jack Quinn	Alex Ferguson	Steve O'Neill
1925	Ted Wingfield	Howard Ehmke	Red Ruffing	Val Picinich
1926	Ted Wingfield	Hal Wiltse	Slim Harriss	Alex Gaston
1927	Slim Harriss	Hal Wiltse	Danny MacFayden	Grover Hartley
1928	Ed Morris	Jack Russell	Red Ruffing	Fred Hofmann
1929	Ed Morris	Milt Gaston	Danny MacFayden	Charley Berry
1930	Milt Gaston	Danny MacFayden	Hod Lisenbee	Charley Berry
1931	Danny MacFayden	Wilcy Moore	Jack Russell	Charley Berry
1932	Bob Kline	Ivy Andrews	Ed Durham	Ben Tate
1933	Gordon Rhodes	George Pipgras	Bob Weiland	Rick Ferrell
1934	Wes Ferrell	Johnny Welch	Fritz Ostermueller	Rick Ferrell
1935	Wes Ferrell	Lefty Grove	Johnny Welch	Rick Ferrell
1936	Wes Ferrell	Lefty Grove	Fritz Ostermueller	Rick Ferrell
1937	Lefty Grove	Jack Wilson	Bobo Newsom	Gene Desautels
1938	Jim Bagby Jr.	Lefty Grove	Jack Wilson	Gene Desautels
1939	Lefty Grove	Joe Heving	Fritz Ostermueller	Johnny Peacock
1940	Jack Wilson	Joe Heving	Jim Bagby Jr.	Gene Desautels
1941	Dick Newsome	Charley Wagner	Joe Dobson	Frank Pytlak
1942	Tex Hughson	Charley Wagner	Joe Dobson	Bill Conroy
1943	Tex Hughson	Oscar Judd	Mike Ryba	Roy Partee
1944	Tex Hughson	Mike Ryba	Joe Bowman	Roy Partee
1945	Dave Ferriss	Mike Ryba	Emmett O'Neill	Bob Garbark
1946	Dave Ferriss	Tex Hughson	Mickey Harris	Hal Wagner
1947	Joe Dobson	Earl Johnson	Denny Galehouse	Birdie Tebbetts
1948	Jack Kramer	Mel Parnell	Joe Dobson	Birdie Tebbetts
1949	Mel Parnell	Ellis Kinder	Joe Dobson	Birdie Tebbetts
1950	Mel Parnell	Joe Dobson	Ellis Kinder	Birdie Tebbetts
1951	Mel Parnell	Ellis Kinder	Ray Scarborough	Les Moss
1952	Mel Parnell	Maurice McDermott	Dizzy Trout	Sammy White
1953	Mel Parnell	Maurice McDermott	Ellis Kinder	Sammy White
1954	Frank Sullivan	Willard Nixon	Ellis Kinder	Sammy White
1955	Frank Sullivan	Willard Nixon	George Susce	Sammy White
1956	Tom Brewer	Frank Sullivan	Ike Delock	Sammy White
1957	Tom Brewer	Frank Sullivan	Willard Nixon	Sammy White
1958	Ike Delock	Frank Sullivan	Tom Brewer	Sammy White
1959	Ike Delock	Jerry Casale	Tom Brewer	Sammy White
1960	Bill Monbouquette	Mike Fornieles	Ike Delock	Russ Nixon
1961	Don Schwall	Bill Monbouquette	Gene Conley	Jim Pagliaroni
1962	Bill Monbouquette	Gene Conley	Dick Radatz	Jim Pagliaroni
1963	Bill Monbouquette	Dick Radatz	Earl Wilson	Bob Tillman
1964	Dick Radatz	Bill Monbouquette	Earl Wilson	Bob Tillman
1965	Earl Wilson	Bill Monbouquette	Dick Radatz	Bob Tillman
1966	Jose Santiago	Jim Lonborg	Don McMahon	Mike Ryan
1967	Jim Lonborg	Jose Santiago	Gary Bell	Mike Ryan
1968	Ray Culp	Dick Ellsworth	Sparky Lyle	Russ Gibson
1969	Ray Culp	Mike Nagy	Sparky Lyle	Russ Gibson
1970	Ray Culp	Sonny Siebert	Gary Peters	Gerry Moses
1971	Sonny Siebert	Gary Peters	Ray Culp	Duane Josephson
1972	Luis Tiant	Marty Pattin	John Curtis	Carlton Fisk
1973	Luis Tiant	Bill Lee	Roger Moret	Carlton Fisk
1974	Luis Tiant	Bill Lee	Reggie Cleveland	Bob Montgomery
1975	Rick Wise	Luis Tiant	Roger Moret	Carlton Fisk
1976	Luis Tiant	Rick Wise	Ferguson Jenkins	Carlton Fisk
1977	Bill Campbell	Luis Tiant	Rick Wise	Carlton Fisk
1978	Dennis Eckersley	Bob Stanley	Luis Tiant	Carlton Fisk
1979	Dennis Eckersley	Bob Stanley	Mike Torrez	Gary Allenson

Year	First Baseman	Second Baseman	Shortstop	Third Baseman
1901	Buck Freeman	Hobe Ferris	Freddy Parent	Jimmy Collins
1902	Candy LaChance	Hobe Ferris	Freddy Parent	Jimmy Collins
1903	Candy LaChance	Hobe Ferris	Freddy Parent	Jimmy Collins
1904	Candy LaChance	Hobe Ferris	Freddy Parent	Jimmy Collins
1905	Moose Grimshaw	Hobe Ferris	Freddy Parent	Jimmy Collins
1906	Moose Grimshaw	Hobe Ferris	Freddy Parent	Red Morgan
1907	Bob Unglaub	Hobe Ferris	Heinie Wagner	John Knight
1908	Jake Stahl	Amby McConnell	Heinie Wagner	Harry Lord
1909	Jake Stahl	Amby McConnell	Heinie Wagner	Harry Lord
1910	Jake Stahl	Larry Gardner	Heinie Wagner	Harry Lord

Jimmy Foxx caught 43 games for the Red Sox.

POSITION LEADERS YEAR BY YEAR (continued)

Year	First Baseman	Second Baseman	Shortstop	Third Baseman
1911	Clyde Engle	Heinie Wagner	Steve Yerkes	Larry Gardner
1912	Jake Stahl	Steve Yerkes	Heinie Wagner	Larry Gardner
1913	Clyde Engle	Steve Yerkes	Heinie Wagner	Larry Gardner
1914	Dick Hoblitzell	Steve Yerkes	Everett Scott	Larry Gardner
1915	Dick Hoblitzell	Heinie Wagner	Everett Scott	Larry Gardner
1916	Dick Hoblitzell	Jack Barry	Everett Scott	Larry Gardner
1917	Dick Hoblitzell	Jack Barry	Everett Scott	Larry Gardner
1918	Stuffy McInnis	Dave Shean	Everett Scott	Fred Thomas
1919	Stuffy McInnis	Red Shannon	Everett Scott	Oscar Vitt
1920	Stuffy McInnis	Mike McNally	Everett Scott	Ed Foster
1921	Stuffy McInnis	Del Pratt	Everett Scott	Ed Foster
1922	George Burns	Del Pratt	Johnny Mitchell	Joe Dugan
1923	George Burns	Chick Fewster	Johnny Mitchell	Howard Shanks
1924	Joe Harris	Bill Wambsganss	Dud Lee	Dan Clark
1925	Phil Todt	Bill Wambsganss	Dud Lee	Doc Prothro
1926	Phil Todt	Bill Regan	Topper Rigney	Fred Haney
1927	Phil Todt	Bill Regan	Buddy Myer	Billy Rogell
1928	Phil Todt	Bill Regan	Wally Gerber	Buddy Myer
1929	Phil Todt	Bill Regan	Hal Rhyne	Bobby Reeves
1930	Phil Todt	Bill Regan	Hal Rhyne	Otto Miller
1931	Bill Sweeney	Rabbit Warstler	Hal Rhyne	Otto Moore
1932	Dale Alexander	Marv Olson	Rabbit Warstler	Urbane Pickering
1933	Dale Alexander	Johnny Hodapp	Rabbit Warstler	Marty McManus
1934	Ed Morgan	Bill Cissell	Lyn Lary	Bill Werber
1935	Babe Dahlgren	Oscar Melillo	Joe Cronin	Bill Werber
1936	Jimmy Foxx	Oscar Melillo	Eric McNair	Bill Werber
1937	Jimmy Foxx	Eric McNair	Joe Cronin	Mike Higgins
1938	Jimmy Foxx	Bobby Doerr	Joe Cronin	Mike Higgins
1939	Jimmy Foxx	Bobby Doerr	Joe Cronin	Jim Tabor
1940	Jimmy Foxx	Bobby Doerr	Joe Cronin	Jim Tabor
1941	Jimmy Foxx	Bobby Doerr	Joe Cronin	Jim Tabor
1942	Tony Lupien	Bobby Doerr	Johnny Pesky	Jim Tabor
1943	Tony Lupien	Bobby Doerr	Skeeter Newsome	Jim Tabor
1944	Lou Finney	Bobby Doerr	Skeeter Newsome	Jim Tabor
1945	George Metkovich	Skeeter Newsome	Eddie Lake	Johnny Tobin
1946	Rudy York	Bobby Doerr	Johnny Pesky	Rip Russell
1947	Jake Jones	Bobby Doerr	Johnny Pesky	Sam Dente
1948	Billy Goodman	Bobby Doerr	Vern Stephens	Johnny Pesky
1949	Billy Goodman	Bobby Doerr	Vern Stephens	Johnny Pesky
1950	Walt Dropo	Bobby Doerr	Vern Stephens	Johnny Pesky
1951	Walt Dropo	Bobby Doerr	Johnny Pesky	Vern Stephens
1952	Dick Gernert	Billy Goodman	Johnny Lipon	George Kell
1953	Dick Gernert	Billy Goodman	Milt Bolling	George Kell
1954	Harry Agganis	Ted Lepcio	Milt Bolling	Grady Hatton
1955	Norm Zauchin	Billy Goodman	Billy Klaus	Grady Hatton
1956	Mickey Vernon	Billy Goodman	Don Buddin	Billy Klaus
1957	Dick Gernert	Ted Lepcio	Billy Klaus	Frank Malzone
1958	Dick Gernert	Pete Runnels	Don Buddin	Frank Malzone
1959	Dick Gernert	Pete Runnells	Don Buddin	Frank Malzone
1960	Vic Wertz	Pete Runnels	Don Buddin	Frank Malzone
1961	Pete Runnels	Chuck Schilling	Don Buddin	Frank Malzone
1962	Pete Runnels	Chuck Schilling	Ed Bressoud	Frank Malzone
1963	Dick Stuart	Chuck Schilling	Ed Bressoud	Frank Malzone
1964	Dick Stuart	Dalton Jones	Ed Bressoud	Frank Malzone
1965	Lee Thomas	Felix Mantilla	Rico Petrocelli	Frank Malzone
1966	George Scott	George Smith	Rico Petrocelli	Joe Foy
1967	George Scott	Mike Andrews	Rico Petrocelli	Joe Foy
1968	George Scott	Mike Andrews	Rico Petrocelli	Joe Foy
1969	Dalton Jones	Mike Andrews	Rico Petrocelli	George Scott
1970	Carl Yastrzemski	Mike Andrews	Rico Petrocelli	George Scott
1971	George Scott	Doug Griffin	Luis Aparicio	Rico Petrocelli
1972	Danny Cater	Doug Griffin	Luis Aparicio	Rico Petrocelli
1973	Carl Yastrzemski	Doug Griffin	Luis Aparicio	Rico Petrocelli
1974	Carl Yastrzemski	Doug Griffin	Mario Guerrero	Rico Petrocelli
1975	Carl Yastrzemski	Doug Griffin	Rick Burleson	Rico Petrocelli
1976	Carl Yastrzemski	Denny Doyle	Rick Burleson	Butch Hobson
1977	George Scott	Denny Doyle	Rick Burleson	Butch Hobson
1978	George Scott	Jerry Remy	Rick Burleson	Butch Hobson
1979	Bob Watson	Jerry Remy	Rick Burleson	Butch Hobson

Year	Outfielder	Outfielder	Outfielder	Designated Hitter
1901	Charley Hemphill	Chick Stahl	Tom Dowd	_____
1902	Buck Freeman	Chick Stahl	Patsy Dougherty	_____
1903	Buck Freeman	Chick Stahl	Patsy Dougherty	_____
1904	Buck Freeman	Chick Stahl	Kip Selbach	_____
1905	Jesse Burkett	Chick Stahl	Kip Selbach	_____
1906	Jack Hayden	Chick Stahl	John Hoey	_____
1907	Bunk Congalton	Denny Sullivan	Jim Barrett	_____
1908	Doc Gessler	Denny Sullivan	Jack Thoney	_____
1909	Doc Gessler	Tris Speaker	Harry Niles	_____
1910	Harry Hooper	Tris Speaker	Duffy Lewis	_____

Year	Outfielder	Outfielder	Outfielder	Designated Hitter
1911	Harry Hooper	Tris Speaker	Duffy Lewis	
1912	Harry Hooper	Tris Speaker	Duffy Lewis	
1913	Harry Hooper	Tris Speaker	Duffy Lewis	
1914	Harry Hooper	Tris Speaker	Duffy Lewis	
1915	Harry Hooper	Tris Speaker	Duffy Lewis	
1916	Harry Hooper	Tilly Walker	Duffy Lewis	
1917	Harry Hooper	Tilly Walker	Duffy Lewis	
1918	Harry Hooper	Amos Strunk	Babe Ruth	
1919	Harry Hooper	Braggo Roth	Babe Ruth	
1920	Harry Hooper	Tim Hendryx	Mike Menosky	
1921	Shano Collins	Nemo Leibold	Mike Menosky	
1922	Shano Collins	Joe Harris	Mike Menosky	
1923	Ira Flagstead	Joe Harris	Dick Reichle	
1924	Ira Flagstead	Ike Boone	Bobby Veach	
1925	Ira Flagstead	Ike Boone	Roy Carlyle	
1926	Ira Flagstead	Bill Jacobson	Si Rosenthal	
1927	Ira Flagstead	Jack Tobin	Wally Shaner	
1928	Ira Flagstead	Doug Taitt	Ken Williams	
1929	Bill Barrett	Jack Rothrock	Russ Scarritt	
1930	Earl Webb	Tom Oliver	Russ Scarritt	
1931	Earl Webb	Tom Oliver	Jack Rothrock	
1932	Roy Johnson	Tom Oliver	Smead Jolley	
1933	Roy Johnson	Dusty Cooke	Smead Jolley	
1934	Roy Johnson	Moose Solters	Carl Reynolds	
1935	Roy Johnson	Dusty Cooke	Mel Almada	
1936	Doc Cramer	Dusty Cooke	Mel Almada	
1937	Doc Cramer	Ben Chapman	Buster Mills	
1938	Doc Cramer	Ben Chapman	Joe Vosmik	
1939	Doc Cramer	Ted Williams	Joe Vosmik	
1940	Doc Cramer	Ted Williams	Dom DiMaggio	
1941	Lou Finney	Ted Williams	Dom DiMaggio	
1942	Lou Finney	Ted Williams	Dom DiMaggio	
1943	Pete Fox	George Metkovich	Leon Culberson	
1944	Pete Fox	George Metkovich	Bob Johnson	
1945	Johnny Lazor	Leon Culberson	Bob Johnson	
1946	George Metkovich	Ted Williams	Dom DiMaggio	
1947	Sam Mele	Ted Williams	Dom DiMaggio	
1948	Stan Spence	Ted Williams	Dom DiMaggio	
1949	Al Zarilla	Ted Williams	Dom DiMaggio	
1950	Al Zarilla	Ted Williams	Dom DiMaggio	
1951	Clyde Vollmer	Ted Williams	Dom Dimaggio	
1952	Faye Throneberry	Hoot Evers	Dom DiMaggio	
1953	Jimmy Piersall	Hoot Evers	Tom Umphlett	
1954	Jimmy Piersall	Ted Williams	Jackie Jensen	
1955	Jimmy Piersall	Ted Williams	Jackie Jensen	
1956	Jimmy Piersall	Ted Williams	Jackie Jensen	
1957	Jimmy Piersall	Ted Williams	Jackie Jensen	
1958	Jimmy Piersall	Ted Williams	Jackie Jensen	
1959	Gary Geiger	Ted Williams	Jackie Jensen	
1960	Lu Clinton	Ted Williams	Willie Tasby	
1961	Gary Geiger	Carl Yastrzemski	Jackie Jensen	
1962	Gary Geiger	Carl Yastrzemski	Lu Clinton	
1963	Gary Geiger	Carl Yastrzemski	Lu Clinton	
1964	Lee Thomas	Carl Yastrzemski	Tony Conigliaro	
1965	Lenny Green	Carl Yastrzemski	Tony Conigliaro	
1966	Don Demeter	Carl Yastrzemski	Tony Conigliaro	
1967	Reggie Smith	Carl Yastrzemski	Tony Conigliaro	
1968	Reggie Smith	Carl Yastrzemski	Ken Harrelson	
1969	Reggie Smith	Carl Yastrzemski	Tony Conigliaro	
1970	Reggie Smith	Billy Conigliaro	Tony Conigliaro	
1971	Reggie Smith	Billy Conigliaro	Carl Yastrzemski	
1972	Reggie Smith	Tommy Harper	Carl Yastrzemski	
1973	Reggie Smith	Tommy Harper	Rick Miller	Orlando Cepeda
1974	Dwight Evans	Juan Beniquez	Rick Miller	Tommy Harper
1975	Dwight Evans	Fred Lynn	Jim Rice	Cecil Cooper
1976	Dwight Evans	Fred Lynn	Jim Rice	Cecil Cooper
1977	Carl Yastrzemski	Fred Lynn	Rick Miller	Jim Rice
1978	Fred Lynn	Dwight Evans	*Jim Rice	*Jim Rice
1979	Dwight Evans	Fred Lynn	Jim Rice	Carl Yastrzemski

*In 1978 Rice won both outfield and designated-hitter berths, playing in 114 games as an outfielder and 49 as a DH, while Yastrzemski was dividing his playing time among the outfield (71 games), first base (50) and DH (26).

Don Zimmer often has reason to smile.

YEAR BY YEAR

Year	Pos.	W-L	Pct.	GA/GB	Manager	Attendance	Year	Pos.	W-L	Pct.	GA/GB	Manager	Attendance
1901	2	79-57	.581	4	Jimmy Collins	289,448	1940	4	82-72	.532	8	Joe Cronin	716,234
1902	3	77-60	.562	6½	Jimmy Collins	348,567	1941	2	84-70	.545	17	Joe Cronin	718,497
1903	1	91-47	.659	14½	Jimmy Collins	379,338	1942	2	93-59	.612	9	Joe Cronin	730,340
1904	1	95-59	.617	1½	Jimmy Collins	623,295	1943	7	68-84	.447	29	Joe Cronin	358,275
1905	4	78-74	.513	16	Jimmy Collins	468,828	1944	4	77-77	.500	12	Joe Cronin	506,975
1906	8	49-105	.318	45½	J. Collins-C. Stahl	410,209	1945	7	71-83	.461	17½	Joe Cronin	603,794
1907	7	59-90	.396	32½	C. Young-G. Huff-B. Unglaub-D. McGuire	436,777	1946	1	104-50	.675	12	Joe Cronin	1,416,944
1908	5	75-79	.487	15½	D. McGuire-F. Lake	473,048	1947	3	83-71	.539	14	Joe Cronin	1,427,315
1909	3	88-63	.583	9½	Fred Lake	668,965	1948*	1T	96-58	.623	—	Joe McCarthy	1,558,798
1910	4	81-72	.529	22½	Patsy Donovan	584,619	1949	2	96-58	.623	1	Joe McCarthy	1,596,650
1911	5	78-75	.510	24	Patsy Donovan	503,961	1950	3	94-60	.610	4	J. McCarthy-S. O'Neill	1,344,080
1912	1	105-47	.691	14	Jake Stahl	597,096	1951	3	87-67	.565	11	Steve O'Neill	1,312,282
1913	4	79-71	.527	15½	J. Stahl-B. Carrigan	437,194	1952	6	76-78	.494	19	Lou Boudreau	1,115,750
1914	2	91-62	.595	8½	Bill Carrigan	481,359	1953	4	84-69	.549	16	Lou Boudreau	1,026,133
1915	1	101-50	.669	2½	Bill Carrigan	539,885	1954	4	69-85	.448	42	Lou Boudreau	931,127
1916	1	91-63	.591	2	Bill Carrigan	496,397	1955	4	84-70	.545	12	Mike Higgins	1,203,200
1917	2	90-62	.592	9	Jack Barry	387,856	1956	4	84-70	.545	13	Mike Higgins	1,137,158
1918	1	75-51	.595	2½	Ed Barrow	249,513	1957	3	82-72	.532	16	Mike Higgins	1,181,087
1919	6	66-71	.482	20½	Ed Barrow	417,291	1958	3	79-75	.513	13	Mike Higgins	1,077,047
1920	5	72-81	.471	25½	Ed Barrow	402,445	1959	5	75-79	.487	19	M. Higgins-R. York-B. Jurges	984,102
1921	5	75-79	.487	23½	Hugh Duffy	279,273	1960	7	65-89	.422	32	B. Jurges-M. Higgins	1,129,866
1922	8	61-93	.396	33	Hugh Duffy	259,184	1961	6	76-86	.469	33	Mike Higgins	850,589
1923	8	61-91	.401	37	Frank Chance	229,668	1962	8	76-84	.475	19	Mike Higgins	733,080
1924	7	67-87	.435	25	Lee Fohl	448,556	1963	7	76-85	.472	28	Johnny Pesky	942,642
1925	8	47-105	.309	49½	Lee Fohl	267,782	1964	8	72-90	.444	27	J. Pesky-B. Herman	883,276
1926	8	46-107	.301	44½	Lee Fohl	285,155	1965	9	62-100	.383	40	Billy Herman	652,201
1927	8	51-103	.331	59	Bill Carrigan	305,275	1966	9	72-90	.444	26	B. Herman-P. Runnels	811,172
1928	8	57-96	.373	43½	Bill Carrigan	396,920	1967	1	92-70	.568	1	Dick Williams	†1,727,832
1929	8	58-96	.377	48	Bill Carrigan	394,620	1968	4	86-76	.531	17	Dick Williams	1,940,788
1930	8	52-102	.338	50	Heinie Wagner	444,045	1969	3	87-75	.537	22	D. Williams-E. Popowski	†1,833,246
1931	6	62-90	.408	45	Shano Collins	350,975	1970	3	87-75	.537	21	Eddie Kasko	†1,595,278
1932	8	43-111	.279	64	S. Collins-M. McManus	182,150	1971	3	85-77	.525	18	Eddie Kasko	†1,678,732
1933	7	63-86	.423	34½	Marty McManus	268,715	1972	2	85-70	.548	½	Eddie Kasko	1,441,718
1934	4	76-76	.500	24	Bucky Harris	610,640	1973	2	89-73	.549	8	Eddie Kasko	1,481,002
1935	4	78-75	.510	16	Joe Cronin	558,568	1974	3	84-78	.519	7	Darrell Johnson	†1,556,411
1936	6	74-80	.481	28½	Joe Cronin	626,895	1975	1	95-65	.594	4½	Darrell Johnson	†1,748,587
1937	5	80-72	.526	21	Joe Cronin	559,659	1976	3	83-79	.512	15½	D. Johnson-D. Zimmer	1,895,846
1938	2	88-61	.591	9½	Joe Cronin	646,459	1977	2T	97-64	.602	2½	Don Zimmer	2,074,549
1939	2	89-62	.589	17	Joe Cronin	573,070	1978**	1T	99-63	.611	—	Don Zimmer	2,320,643
							1979	3	91-69	.569	11½	Don Zimmer	2,353,114

*Lost one-game playoff to Cleveland Indians at Fenway Park in 1948.
**Lost one-game playoff to New York Yankees at Fenway Park in 1978.
†Led league in attendance.

RED SOX FIRST-PLACE TEAMS

1903
WORLD CHAMPIONS
Manager: Jimmy Collins

Pitchers: Nick Altrock, Bill Dinneen, Norwood Gibson, Long Tom Hughes, George Winter and Cy Young. Catchers: Lou Criger, Duke Farrell, Broadway Aleck Smith and *Jake Stahl (28 games). Infielders: Jimmy Collins, Hobe Ferris, Harry Gleason, Candy LaChance, *Jack O'Brien (16 games) and Freddy Parent. Outfielders: Patsy Dougherty, Buck Freeman, *Jack O'Brien (71 games), Chick Stahl and *Jake Stahl (1 game). Pinch-hitter: George Stone.
*Played more than one position.

WORLD SERIES

	W	L	Pct.
Red Sox, A.L.	5	3	.625
Pirates, N.L.	3	5	.375

Oct. 1	Pirates (Phillippe)	7	Red Sox (Young)	3	at Boston
Oct. 2	Red Sox (Dinneen)	3	Pirates (Leever)	0	at Boston
Oct. 3	Pirates (Phillippe)	4	Red Sox (Hughes)	2	at Boston
Oct. 6	Pirates (Phillippe)	5	Red Sox (Dinneen)	4	at Pittsburgh
Oct. 7	Red Sox (Young)	11	Pirates (Kennedy)	2	at Pittsburgh
Oct. 8	Red Sox (Dinneen)	6	Pirates (Leever)	3	at Pittsburgh
Oct. 10	Red Sox (Young)	7	Pirates (Phillippe)	3	at Pittsburgh
Oct. 13	Red Sox (Dinneen)	3	Pirates (Phillippe)	0	at Boston

THURSDAY, OCTOBER 1—AT BOSTON

Pirates	AB	R	H	O	A	E
Beaumont, cf	5	1	0	3	0	0
Clarke, lf	5	0	2	4	0	0
Leach, 3b	5	1	4	0	1	1
Wagner, ss	3	1	1	1	2	1
Bransfield, 1b	5	2	1	7	0	0
Ritchey, 2b	4	1	0	1	2	0
Sebring, rf	5	1	3	1	0	0
Phelps, c	4	0	1	10	0	0
Phillippe, p	4	0	0	0	2	0
Totals	40	7	12	27	7	2

Red Sox	AB	R	H	O	A	E
Dougherty, lf	4	0	0	1	1	0
Collins, 3b	4	0	0	2	3	0
Stahl, cf	4	0	1	2	0	0
Freeman, rf	4	2	2	2	0	0
Parent, ss	4	1	2	4	4	0
LaChance, 1b	4	0	0	8	0	0
Ferris, 2b	3	0	1	2	4	2
Criger, c	3	0	0	6	1	2
aO'Brien	1	0	0	0	0	0
Young, p	3	0	0	0	1	0
bFarrell	1	0	0	0	0	0
Totals	35	3	6	27	14	4

Pirates .... 4 0 1 1 0 0 1 0 0—7
Red Sox .... 0 0 0 0 0 0 2 0 1—3

aStruck out for Criger in ninth. bGrounded out for Young in ninth. Three-base hits—Freeman, Parent, Leach 2, Bransfield. Home run—Sebring. Runs batted in—Sebring 4, Leach, Wagner, LaChance 2, Parent. Stolen bases—Wagner, Bransfield, Ritchey. Left on bases—Boston 6, Pittsburgh 9. Earned runs—Boston 2, Pittsburgh 3. Bases on balls—Off Young 3. Struck out—By Young 5, by Phillippe 10. Hit by pitcher—by Phillippe (Ferris). Passed ball—Criger. Umpires—O'Day (N.L.) and Connolly (A.L.). Time—1:55. Attendance—16,242.

FRIDAY, OCTOBER 2—AT BOSTON

Pirates	AB	R	H	O	A	E
Beaumont, cf	3	0	0	3	0	0
Clarke, lf	3	0	1	3	0	0
Leach, 3b	3	0	0	0	2	0
Wagner, ss	3	0	0	3	3	0
Bransfield, 1b	3	0	0	9	1	0
Ritchey, 2b	3	0	1	3	3	0
Sebring, rf	3	0	1	1	0	0
Smith, c	3	0	0	2	1	1
Leever, p	0	0	0	0	0	0
Veil, p	2	0	0	0	0	1
aPhelps	1	0	0	0	0	0
Totals	27	0	3	24	10	2

Red Sox	AB	R	H	O	A	E
Dougherty, lf	4	2	3	0	1	0
Collins, 3b	4	0	1	1	1	0
Stahl, cf	4	1	1	1	0	0
Freeman, rf	4	0	2	0	0	0
Parent, ss	3	0	1	3	3	0
LaChance, 1b	2	0	0	8	1	0
Ferris, 2b	4	0	0	3	0	0
Criger, c	3	0	0	11	0	0
Dinneen, p	2	0	1	0	3	0
Totals	30	3	9	27	9	0

Pirates .... 0 0 0 0 0 0 0 0 0—0
Red Sox .... 2 0 0 0 0 1 0 0 X—3

aStruck out for Veil in ninth. Two-base hit—Stahl. Home runs—Dougherty 2. Runs batted in—Dougherty 2, Freeman. Sacrifice hits—LaChance, Dinneen. Stolen bases—Collins 2. Double plays—Ferris, unassisted; Ritchey, Wagner and Bransfield; Wagner, Ritchey and Bransfield. Left on bases—Boston 11, Pittsburgh 2. Earned runs—Boston 3. Bases on balls—Off Dinneen 2, off Leever 1, off Veil 4. Struck out—By Dinneen 11, by Veil 1. Hit by pitcher— By Veil (Dougherty). Hits—Off Leever 3 in 1 inning, off Veil 6 in 7 innings. Loser—Leever. Umpires—O'Day (N.L.) and Connolly (A.L.). Time 1:47. Attendance—9,415.

SATURDAY, OCTOBER 3—AT BOSTON

Pirates	AB	R	H	O	A	E
Beaumont, cf	4	1	0	1	0	0
Clarke, lf	4	0	1	0	0	0
Leach, 3b	4	1	1	0	1	0
Wagner, ss	3	1	1	0	7	0
Bransfield, 1b	3	0	0	15	0	0
Ritchey, 2b	4	1	1	2	2	0
Sebring, rf	3	0	1	4	0	0
Phelps, c	4	0	2	5	1	0
Phillippe, p	4	0	0	0	4	0
Totals	33	4	7	27	15	0

Red Sox	AB	R	H	O	A	E
Dougherty, lf	4	0	0	1	1	0
Collins, 3b	4	2	2	2	6	1
Stahl, cf	3	0	1	2	0	0
Freeman, rf	3	0	0	1	0	0
Parent, ss	4	0	0	0	7	0
LaChance, 1b	3	0	1	15	0	0
Ferris, 2b	4	0	0	2	2	0
Criger, c	3	0	0	4	1	0
Hughes, p	0	0	0	0	0	0
Young, p	3	0	0	0	2	1
Totals	31	2	4	27	19	2

Pirates .... 0 1 2 0 0 0 0 1 0—4
Red Sox .... 0 0 0 1 0 0 0 1 0—2

Two-base hits—Collins, LaChance, Clarke, Ritchey, Wagner, Phelps 2. Runs batted in—Leach, Ritchey, Sebring, Phelps, Stahl, Parent. Sacrifice hit—Bransfield. Stolen base—Leach. Double play—Dougherty and Collins. Left on bases—Boston 5, Pittsburgh 6. Earned runs—Pittsburgh 3, Boston 2. Bases on balls—Off Hughes 2, off Phillippe 3. Struck out—By Phillippe 5, by Young 2. Hit by pitched ball—By Young (Wagner). Hits—Off Hughes 4 in 2 innings (pitched to three batters in third), off Young 3 in 7 innings. Passed ball—Criger. Loser—Hughes. Umpires—O'Day (N.L.) and Connolly (A.L.). Time—1:50. Attendance—18,801.

1903 WORLD CHAMPIONS (continued)

TUESDAY, OCTOBER 6—AT PITTSBURGH

Red Sox	AB	R	H	O	A	E
Dougherty, lf	4	0	0	3	0	1
Collins, 3b	4	1	1	1	2	0
Stahl, cf	4	1	2	3	1	0
Freeman, rf	4	0	1	0	0	0
Parent, ss	4	1	1	1	3	0
LaChance, 1b	4	1	2	6	0	0
Ferris, 2b	4	0	1	2	0	0
Criger, c	3	0	1	8	1	0
aFarrell	1	0	0	0	0	0
Dinneen, p	3	0	0	0	1	0
bO'Brien	1	0	0	0	0	0
Totals	36	4	9	24	8	1

Pirates	AB	R	H	O	A	E
Beaumont, cf	4	2	3	3	0	0
Clarke, lf	4	1	1	1	0	0
Leach, 3b	4	1	2	2	5	0
Wagner, ss	4	0	3	1	1	0
Bransfield, 1b	4	0	1	9	1	1
Ritchey, 2b	3	0	0	5	5	0
Sebring, rf	4	0	0	1	0	0
Phelps, c	4	0	1	4	0	0
Phillippe, p	3	1	1	1	1	0
Totals	34	5	12	27	13	1

```
Red Sox .......................000  010  00 3—4
Pirates .......................100  010  30 X—5
```

aFlied out for Criger in ninth, Parent scoring after the catch. bFlied out for Dinneen in ninth. Three-base hits—Beaumont, Leach. Runs batted in—Leach 3, Wagner, Bransfield, Freeman, Criger, Farrell, Parent. Stolen base—Wagner. Double plays—Ritchey and Bransfield; Criger and Parent. Left on bases—Boston 5, Pittsburgh 6. Earned runs—Pittsburgh 5, Boston 4. Struck out—By Phillippe 1, by Dinneen 7. Bases on balls—Off Dinneen 1. Umpires—O'Day (N.L.) and Connolly (A.L.). Time 1:30. Attendance—7,600.

WEDNESDAY, OCTOBER 7—AT PITTSBURGH

Red Sox	AB	R	H	O	A	E
Dougherty, lf	6	0	3	3	0	0
Collins, 3b	6	0	2	0	4	0
Stahl, cf	5	2	1	2	0	0
Freeman, rf	4	2	2	2	0	0
Parent, ss	5	1	2	1	4	1
LaChance, 1b	4	2	1	13	0	1
Ferris, 2b	5	2	1	1	3	0
Criger, c	3	1	0	5	0	0
Young, p	5	1	2	0	2	0
Totals	43	11	14	27	13	2

Pirates	AB	R	H	O	A	E
Beaumont, cf	4	1	1	0	0	0
Clarke, lf	4	1	0	3	0	1
Leach, 3b	4	0	2	2	1	1
Wagner, ss	4	0	0	1	3	2
Bransfield, 1b	4	0	0	9	1	0
Ritchey, 2b	4	0	1	1	4	0
Sebring, rf	4	0	1	2	0	0
Phelps, c	3	0	0	9	0	0
Kennedy, p	2	0	1	0	1	0
Thompson, p	1	0	0	0	1	0
Totals	34	2	6	27	11	4

```
Red Sox .....................000  006  410—11
Pirates .....................000  000  020— 2
```

Two-base hit—Kennedy. Three-base hits—Leach, Dougherty 2, Collins, Stahl, Young. Runs batted in—Leach 2, Dougherty 3, Young 3, Freeman, LaChance, Ferris 2. Sacrifice hits—Phelps, Criger. Stolen bases—Collins, Stahl. Left on bases—Boston 9, Pittsburgh 6. Earned runs—Boston 5. Struck out—By Kennedy 3, by Thompson 1, by Young 4. Bases on balls—Off Kennedy 3. Hits—Off Kennedy 11 in 7 innings, off Thompson 3 in 2 innings. Loser—Kennedy. Umpires—Connolly (A.L.) and O'Day (N.L.). Time—2:00. Attendance 12,322.

THURSDAY, OCTOBER 8—AT PITTSBURGH

Red Sox	AB	R	H	O	A	E
Dougherty, lf	3	1	1	1	0	0
Collins, 3b	5	1	1	1	2	0
Stahl, cf	5	1	2	2	0	0
Freeman, rf	5	0	0	1	0	0
Parent, ss	4	2	1	5	2	0
LaChance, 1b	4	0	1	9	2	0
Ferris, 2b	4	0	2	1	3	0
Criger, c	4	0	1	6	0	1
Dinneen, p	4	1	1	1	2	0
Totals	38	6	10	27	11	1

Pirates	AB	R	H	O	A	E
Beaumont, cf	5	1	4	5	0	0
Clarke, lf	5	0	2	2	0	0
Leach, 3b	5	0	0	1	2	2
Wagner, ss	3	0	0	2	5	1
Bransfield, 1b	3	0	1	11	0	0
Ritchey, 2b	3	0	0	1	3	0
Sebring, rf	4	1	2	2	0	0
Phelps, c	4	1	1	3	0	0
Leever, p	4	0	0	0	2	0
Totals	36	3	10	27	12	3

```
Red Sox .....................003  020  100—6
Pirates .....................000  000  300—3
```

Two base hits—Clarke, LaChance. Three-base hits—Stahl, Parent. Stolen bases—Beaumont 2, Clarke, Leach, Stahl. Runs batted in—Beaumont 2, Leach, Collins, Stahl, Freeman, LaChance, Ferris. Double plays—Ritchey, Wagner and Bransfield; Parent and LaChance. Left on bases—Boston 8, Pittsburgh 9. Earned runs—Boston 5, Pittsburgh 3. Struck out—By Leever 2, by Dinneen 3. Bases on balls—Off Leever 2, off Dinneen 3. Hit by pitched ball—By Leever (Parent). Umpires—O'Day (N.L.) and Connolly (A.L.). Time—2:02. Attendance—11,556.

SATURDAY, OCTOBER 10—AT PITTSBURGH

Red Sox	AB	R	H	O	A	E
Dougherty, lf	5	0	1	3	0	0
Collins, 3b	5	1	1	0	2	1
Stahl, cf	4	1	2	0	0	0
Freeman, rf	4	1	1	0	0	0
Parent, ss	4	2	2	3	6	1
LaChance, 1b	3	1	0	11	0	2
Ferris, 2b	3	1	2	4	4	0
Criger, c	4	0	2	6	2	0
Young, p	4	0	0	0	2	0
Totals	36	7	11	27	16	4

Pirates	AB	R	H	O	A	E
Beaumont, cf	5	0	1	2	0	0
Clarke, lf	5	1	1	1	0	0
Leach, 3b	5	0	0	0	1	0
Wagner, ss	3	0	0	2	6	1
Bransfield, 1b	4	1	3	13	2	0
Ritchey, 2b	4	0	0	5	8	0
Sebring, rf	4	1	2	1	0	0
Phelps, c	3	0	1	2	3	1
Phillippe, p	4	0	2	1	0	1
Totals	37	3	10	27	20	3

```
Red Sox .................... 2 0 0   2 0 2   0 1 0—7
Pirates .................... 0 0 0   1 0 1   0 0 1—3
```

Three-base hits—Clarke, Bransfield, Collins, Stahl, Freeman, Parent, Ferris. Runs batted in—Wagner, Ritchey, Phillippe, Criger 3, Stahl, Parent. Sacrifice hits—Wagner, LaChance, Ferris. Double plays—Ritchey, Wagner and Bransfield; Ferris and LaChance. Left on bases—Boston 4, Pittsburgh 9. Earned runs—Pittsburgh 2, Boston 5. Struck out—By Phillippe 2, by Young 6. Base on balls—Off Young 1. Wild pitch—Phillippe. Umpires—Connolly (A.L.) and O'Day (N.L.). Time—1:45. Attendance—17,038.

TUESDAY, OCTOBER 13—AT BOSTON

Pirates	AB	R	H	O	A	E
Beaumont, cf	4	0	0	5	0	0
Clarke, lf	4	0	1	3	0	0
Leach, 3b	3	0	0	0	3	0
Wagner, ss	4	0	1	3	0	1
Bransfield, 1b	3	0	0	7	1	1
Ritchey, 2b	2	0	0	2	1	0
Sebring, rf	3	0	1	1	0	0
Phelps, c	3	0	0	3	0	1
Phillippe, p	3	0	1	0	2	0
Totals	29	0	4	24	8	3

Red Sox	AB	R	H	O	A	E
Dougherty, lf	4	0	0	3	0	0
Collins, 3b	4	0	1	0	2	0
Stahl, cf	4	0	0	2	0	0
Freeman, rf	4	1	1	2	0	0
Parent, ss	4	1	0	1	1	0
LaChance, 1b	3	1	1	11	0	0
Ferris, 2b	4	0	2	0	3	0
Criger, c	3	0	2	8	3	0
Dinneen, p	3	0	1	0	3	0
Totals	33	3	8	27	12	0

```
Pirates .................... 0 0 0   0 0 0   0 0 0—0
Red Sox .................... 0 0 0   2 0 1   0 0 X—3
```

Three-base hits—Freeman, LaChance, Sebring. Runs batted in—Ferris 3. Sacrifice hit—LaChance. Stolen base—Wagner. Double play—Criger and LaChance. Left on bases—Boston 7, Pittsburgh 4. Earned runs—Boston 3. Struck out—By Dinneen 7, by Phillippe 2. Bases on balls—Off Dinneen 2. Umpires—O'Day (N.L.) and Connolly (A.L.). Time 1:35. Attendance 7,455.

COMPOSITE BATTING AVERAGES

RED SOX

Player-position	G	AB	R	H	2B	3B	HR	RBI	BA
Stahl, cf	8	33	6	10	1	3	0	3	.303
Ferris, 2b	8	31	3	9	0	1	0	6	.290
Freeman, rf	8	32	6	9	0	3	0	4	.281
Parent, ss	8	32	8	9	0	3	0	4	.281
Collins, 3b	8	36	5	9	1	2	0	1	.250
Dinneen, p	4	12	1	3	0	0	0	0	.250
Dougherty, lf	8	34	3	8	0	2	2	5	.235
Criger, c	8	26	1	6	0	0	0	4	.231
LaChance, 1b	8	27	5	6	2	1	0	4	.222
Young, p	4	15	1	2	0	1	0	3	.133
Farrell, ph	2	2	0	0	0	0	0	1	.000
O'Brien, ph	2	2	0	0	0	0	0	0	.000
Hughes, p	1	0	0	0	0	0	0	0	.000
Totals	8	282	39	71	4	16	2	35	.252

PIRATES

Player-position	G	AB	R	H	2B	3B	HR	RBI	BA
Kennedy, p	1	2	0	1	1	0	0	0	.500
Sebring, rf	8	30	3	11	0	1	1	5	.367
Leach, 3b	8	33	3	9	0	4	0	8	.273
Beaumont, cf	8	34	6	9	0	0	0	2	.265
Clarke, lf	8	34	3	9	2	1	0	0	.265
Phelps, ph-c	8	26	1	6	2	0	0	1	.231
Wagner, ss	8	27	2	6	1	0	0	3	.222
Phillippe, p	5	18	1	4	0	0	0	0	.222
Bransfield, 1b	8	29	3	6	0	2	0	1	.207
Ritchey, 2b	8	27	2	3	1	0	0	2	.111
Leever, p	2	4	0	0	0	0	0	0	.000
Smith, c	1	3	0	0	0	0	0	0	.000
Thompson, p	1	1	0	0	0	0	0	0	.000
Veil, p	1	2	0	0	0	0	0	0	.000
Totals	8	270	24	64	7	9	1	23	.237

COMPOSITE PITCHING AVERAGES

RED SOX

Pitcher	G	IP	H	R	ER	SO	BB	W	L	ERA
Young	4	34	31	13	6	17	4	2	1	1.59
Dinneen	4	35	29	8	8	28	8	3	1	2.06
Hughes	1	2	4	3	2	0	2	0	1	9.00
Totals	8	71	64	24	16	45	14	5	3	2.03

PIRATES

Pitcher	G	IP	H	R	ER	SO	BB	W	L	ERA
Veil	1	7	6	1	1	1	4	0	0	1.29
Phillippe	5	44	38	19	16	20	3	3	2	3.27
Thompson	1	2	3	1	1	1	0	0	0	4.50
Kennedy	1	7	10	4	3	3	0	1	2	5.14
Leever	2	10	13	8	7	2	3	0	2	6.30
Totals	8	70	71	39	29	27	13	3	5	3.73

Dick Williams umpired spring intra-squad games.

1904
AMERICAN LEAGUE CHAMPIONS
Claimed World Championship by Default
Manager: Jimmy Collins

Pitchers: Bill Dinneen, Norwood Gibson, Jesse Tannehill, George Winter and Cy Young. Catchers: Lou Criger, Tom Doran and Duke Farrell. Infielders: Jimmy Collins, Hobe Ferris, Candy LaChance, *Bill O'Neill (2 games), Freddy Parent and Bob Unglaub. Outfielders: Patsy Dougherty, Buck Freeman, *Bill O'Neill (9 games), Kip Selbach and Chick Stahl.
*Played more than one position.

WORLD SERIES

None.

The National League champion New York Giants refused to play. Giant president John Bush claimed the upstart American League was "minor league" and inferior despite the fact the Red Sox had defeated the Pittsburgh Pirates in the first World Series the previous year. Giants manager John McGraw also was feuding with American League president Ban Johnson at the time.

The Red Sox contended the Giants were afraid of losing as the Pirates had the previous season, and claimed the 1904 World Championship by default. And *Sporting News* confirmed that claim, making it "official" by declaring the Boston Americans "world champions by default."

1912
WORLD CHAMPIONS
Manager: Jake Stahl

Pitchers: Hugh Bedient, Jack Bushelman, Ed Cicotte, Ray Collins, Casey Hageman, Charley Hall, Buck O'Brien, Larry Pape, Doug Smith, Ben Van Dyke and Smokey Joe Wood. Catchers: *Hick Cady (43 games), Bill Carrigan, Les Nunamaker and Pinch Thomas. Infielders: Neal Ball, Hugh Bradley, *Hick Cady (4 games), *Clyde Engle (53 games), Larry Gardner, Marty Krug, Chick Stahl, Heinie Wagner and Steve Yerkes. Outfielders: *Clyde Engle (1 game), Olaf Henriksen, Harry Hooper, Duffy Lewis and Tris Speaker.
*Played more than one position.

WORLD SERIES

	W	L	T	Pct.
Red Sox, A.L.	4	3	1	.571
Giants, N.L.	3	4	1	.429

Oct. 8	Red Sox (Wood)	4	Giants (Tesreau)	3	at New York
Oct. 9*	Red Sox (tie)	6	Giants (tie)	6	at Boston
Oct. 10	Giants (Marquard)	2	Red Sox (O'Brien)	1	at Boston
Oct. 11	Red Sox (Wood)	3	Giants (Tesreau)	1	at New York
Oct. 12	Red Sox (Bedient)	2	Giants (Mathewson)	1	at Boston
Oct. 14	Giants (Marquard)	5	Red Sox (O'Brien)	2	at New York
Oct. 15	Giants (Tesreau)	11	Red Sox (Wood)	4	at Boston
Oct. 16**	Red Sox (Wood)	3	Giants (Mathewson)	2	at Boston

*11-inning tie.
**10 innings.

TUESDAY, OCTOBER 8—AT NEW YORK

Red Sox	AB	R	H	O	A	E	Giants	AB	R	H	O	A	E
Hooper, rf	3	1	1	1	0	0	Devore, lf	3	1	0	0	0	0
Yerkes, 2b	4	0	1	0	1	0	Doyle, 2b	4	1	2	2	7	0
Speaker, cf	3	1	1	0	1	0	Snodgrass, cf	4	0	1	2	0	0
Lewis, lf	4	0	0	2	0	0	Murray, rf	3	0	1	1	0	0
Gardner, 3b	4	0	0	1	1	0	Merkle, 1b	4	1	1	12	0	0
Stahl, 1b	4	0	0	6	1	0	Herzog, 3b	4	0	2	1	1	0
Wagner, ss	3	1	2	5	3	1	Meyers, c	3	0	1	6	1	0
Cady, c	3	0	1	11	1	0	bBecker	0	0	0	0	0	0
Wood, p	3	1	0	1	1	0	Fletcher, ss	4	0	0	3	1	1
							Tesreau, p	2	0	0	0	2	0
							aMcCormick	1	0	0	0	0	0
							Crandall, p	1	0	0	0	1	0
Totals	31	4	6	27	9	1	Totals	33	3	8	27	13	1

Red Sox .... 000 001 300—4
Giants .... 002 000 001—3

aFlied out for Tesreau in seventh. bRan for Meyers in ninth. Two-base hits—Hooper, Wagner, Doyle. Three-base hit—Speaker. Runs batted in—Hooper, Yerkes 2, Lewis, Murray 2, Meyers. Sacrifice hits—Hooper, Cady. Double play—Stahl and Wood. Earned runs—Boston 4, New York 3. Left on bases—Boston 6, New York 6. Struck out—By Wood 11, by Tesreau 4, by Crandall 2. Bases on balls—Off Wood 2, off Tesreau 4. Hit by pitcher—By Wood (Meyers). Hits—Off Tesreau 5 in 7 innings, off Crandall 1 in 2 innings. Losing pitcher—Tesreau. Umpires—Klem (N.L.), Evans (A.L.), Rigler (N.L.) and O'Loughlin (A.L.). Time—2:10. Attendance—35,730.

WEDNESDAY, OCTOBER 9—AT BOSTON

Giants	AB	R	H	O	A	E
Snodgrass, lf-rf	4	1	1	0	0	0
Doyle, 2b	5	0	1	2	5	0
Becker, cf	4	1	0	0	1	0
Murray, rf-lf	5	2	3	3	0	0
Merkle, 1b	5	1	1	19	0	1
Herzog, 3b	4	1	3	2	4	0
Meyers, c	4	0	2	5	0	0
aShafer, ss	0	0	0	0	3	0
Fletcher, ss	4	0	0	1	3	3
bMcCormick	0	0	0	0	0	0
Wilson, c	0	0	0	0	1	1
Mathewson, p	5	0	0	1	6	0
Totals	40	6	11	33	23	5

Red Sox	AB	R	H	O	A	E
Hooper, rf	5	1	3	3	0	0
Yerkes, 2b	5	1	1	3	4	0
Speaker, cf.............	5	2	2	2	0	0
Lewis, lf	5	2	2	2	0	1
Gardner, 3b	4	0	0	2	0	0
Stahl, 1b	5	0	2	10	0	0
Wagner, ss	5	0	0	5	5	0
Carrigan, c	5	0	0	6	4	0
Collins, p	3	0	0	0	1	0
Hall, p	1	0	0	0	0	0
Bedient, p	1	0	0	0	0	0
Totals	44	6	10	33	14	1

Giants ....010 100 030 10—6
Red Sox ....300 010 010 10—6
Stopped by darkness.

aRan for Meyers in tenth. bHit sacrifice fly for Fletcher in tenth. Two-base hits—Snodgrass, Murray. Herzog, Lewis 2, Hooper. Three-base hits—Murray, Merkle, Herzog, Yerkes, Speaker. Runs batted in—Murray 2, Herzog 2, Meyers, Mc-Cormick, Yerkes, Gardner, Stahl 2. Sacrifice hit—Gardner. Sacrifice flies—Herzog, McCormick. Stolen bases—Snodgrass, Herzog, Hooper 2, Stahl. Double play—Fletcher and Herzog. Earned runs—New York 4, Boston 2. Left on bases—New York 9, Boston 6. Struck out—By Mathewson 4, by Collins 5, by Bedient 1. Bases on balls—Off Hall 4, off Bedient 1. Hit by pitcher—By Bedient (Snodgrass). Hits—Off Collins 9 in 7⅓ innings, off Hall 2 in 2⅔ innings, off Bedient 0 in 1 inning. Umpires—O'Loughlin (A.L.), Rigler (N.L.), Klem (N.L.) and Evans (A.L.). Time—2:38. Attendance—30,148.

THURSDAY, OCTOBER 10—AT BOSTON

Giants	AB	R	H	O	A	E
Devore, lf	4	0	2	2	0	0
Doyle, 2b	3	0	0	3	1	0
Snodgrass, cf	4	0	1	0	0	0
Murray, rf	4	1	1	5	0	0
Merkle, 1b	3	0	0	5	0	1
Herzog, 3b	2	1	1	1	3	0
Meyers, c	4	0	1	8	1	0
Fletcher, ss	3	0	1	3	2	0
Marquard, p...........	1	0	0	0	2	0
Totals	28	2	7	27	9	1

Red Sox	AB	R	H	O	A	E
Hooper, rf	3	0	0	1	0	0
Yerkes, 2b	4	0	1	3	1	0
Speaker, cf.............	4	0	1	3	1	0
Lewis, lf	4	1	2	4	0	0
Gardner, 3b	3	0	1	0	2	0
Stahl, 1b	4	0	2	11	1	0
cHenriksen	0	0	0	0	0	0
Wagner, ss	4	0	0	1	3	0
Carrigan, c	2	0	0	3	1	0
aEngle	1	0	0	0	0	0
O'Brien, p	2	0	0	1	5	0
bBall	1	0	0	0	0	0
Cady, c	1	0	0	0	1	0
Bedient, p	0	0	0	0	0	0
Totals	33	1	7	27	15	0

Giants ....010 010 000—2
Red Sox ....000 000 001—1

aFlied out for Carrigan in eighth. bStruck out for O'Brien in eighth. cRan for Stahl in ninth. Two-base hits—Murray, Herzog, Stahl, Gardner. Runs batted in—Herzog, Fletcher, Gardner. Sacrifice hits—Merkle, Marquard, Gardner. Sacrifice fly—Herzog. Stolen bases—Devore, Fletcher, Wagner. Double play—Speaker and Stahl. Earned runs—New York 2, Boston 1. Left on bases—Boston 7, New York 6. Struck out—By Marquard 6, by O'Brien 3. Bases on balls—Off Marquard 1, off O'Brien 3. Hit by pitcher—By Bedient (Herzog). Hits—Off O'Brien 6 in 8 innings, off Bedient 1 in 1 inning. Losing pitcher—O'Brien. Umpires—Evans (A.L.), Klem (N.L.), O'Loughlin (A.L.) and Rigler (N.L.). Time—2:16. Attendance—34,624.

FRIDAY, OCTOBER 11—AT NEW YORK

Red Sox	AB	R	H	O	A	E
Hooper, rf	4	0	1	1	0	0
Yerkes, 2b	3	0	1	2	5	0
Speaker, cf.............	4	0	1	2	0	0
Lewis, lf	4	0	0	1	0	0
Gardner, 3b	3	2	2	0	2	0
Stahl, 1b	3	1	0	9	0	0
Wagner, ss	3	0	0	2	3	1
Cady, c	4	0	1	10	0	0
Wood, p	4	0	2	0	2	0
Totals	32	3	8	27	12	1

Giants	AB	R	H	O	A	E
Devore, lf..............	4	0	1	0	0	0
Doyle, 2b	4	0	0	4	1	0
Snodgrass, cf..........	4	0	0	2	0	0
Murray, rf	4	0	1	3	0	0
Merkle, 1b	4	0	1	8	0	0
Herzog, 3b	4	1	2	2	1	0
Meyers, c	4	0	0	5	1	1
Fletcher, ss	4	0	1	3	6	0
Tesreau, p	2	0	1	0	2	0
aMcCormick	1	0	1	0	0	0
Ames, p	0	0	0	0	1	0
Totals	35	1	9	27	12	1

Red Sox ....010 100 001—3
Giants ....000 000 100—1

aSingled for Tesreau in seventh. Two base hits—Speaker, Fletcher. Three-base hit—Gardner. Runs batted in—Cady, Wood, Fletcher. Sacrifice hits—Yerkes, Stahl. Stolen bases—Stahl, Merkle. Double play—Fletcher and Merkle. Earned runs—Boston 3, New York 1. Left on bases—New York 7, Boston 7. Struck out—By Wood 8, by Tesreau 5. Bases on balls—Off Tesreau 2, off Ames 1. Wild pitch—Tesreau. Hits—Off Tesreau 5 in 7 innings, off Ames 3 in 2 innings. Losing pitcher—Tesreau. Umpires—Rigler (N.L.), O'Loughlin (A.L.), Evans (A.L.) and Klem (N.L.). Time—2:06. Attendance—36,502.

1912 WORLD CHAMPIONS (continued)

SATURDAY, OCTOBER 12—AT BOSTON

Giants	AB	R	H	O	A	E
Devore, lf	2	0	0	0	0	0
Doyle, 2b	4	0	0	0	3	1
Snodgrass, cf	4	0	0	2	0	0
Murray, rf	3	0	0	0	1	0
Merkle, 1b	4	1	1	15	0	0
Herzog, 3b	4	0	0	2	3	0
Meyers, c	3	0	1	2	0	0
Fletcher, ss	2	0	0	2	2	0
aMcCormick	1	0	0	0	0	0
bShafer, ss	0	0	0	1	1	0
Mathewson, p	3	0	1	0	3	0
Totals	30	1	3	24	13	1

Red Sox	AB	R	H	O	A	E
Hooper, rf	4	1	2	4	0	0
Yerkes, 2b	4	1	1	3	3	0
Speaker, cf	3	0	1	3	0	0
Lewis, lf	3	0	0	1	0	0
Gardner, 3b	3	0	0	3	2	1
Stahl, 1b	3	0	0	7	0	0
Wagner, ss	3	0	1	1	1	0
Cady, c	3	0	0	5	0	0
Bedient, p	3	0	0	0	0	0
Totals	29	2	5	27	6	1

Giants ....000 000 100 0—1
Red Sox ....002 000 00X—2

aReached first on Gardner's error for Fletcher in seventh. bRan for McCormick in seventh. Two-base hit—Merkle. Three-base hits—Hooper, Yerkes. Runs batted in—Yerkes, Speaker. Double play—Wagner, Yerkes and Stahl. Earned runs—Boston 1, New York 0. Left on bases—New York 5, Boston 3. Struck out—By Mathewson 2, by Bedient 4. Bases on balls—Off Bedient 3. Umpires—O'Loughlin (A.L.), Rigler (N.L.), Klem (N.L.) and Evans (A.L.). Time—1:43. Attendance—34,683.

MONDAY, OCTOBER 14—AT NEW YORK

Red Sox	AB	R	H	O	A	E
Hooper, rf	4	0	1	2	2	0
Yerkes, 2b	4	0	2	3	1	1
Speaker, cf	3	0	0	5	0	0
Lewis, lf	4	0	0	0	0	0
Gardner, 3b	4	1	0	0	1	0
Stahl, 1b	4	1	2	8	0	0
Wagner, ss	4	0	0	3	0	0
Cady, c	3	0	1	3	2	1
O'Brien, p	0	0	0	0	1	0
aEngle	1	0	1	0	0	0
Collins, p	2	0	0	0	2	0
Totals	33	2	7	24	9	2

Giants	AB	R	H	O	A	E
Devore, lf	4	0	1	2	0	1
Doyle, 2b	4	1	1	1	1	0
Snodgrass, cf	4	0	1	6	0	0
Murray, rf	3	1	2	7	0	0
Merkle, 1b	3	1	2	4	1	0
Herzog, 3b	3	1	1	1	1	0
Meyers, c	3	1	2	6	0	0
Fletcher, ss	3	0	1	0	2	0
Marquard, p	3	0	0	0	2	1
Totals	30	5	11	27	7	2

Red Sox ....020 000 00 0—2
Giants ....500 000 00X—5

aDoubled for O'Brien in second. Two-base hits—Engle, Merkle, Herzog. Three-base hit—Meyers. Runs batted in—Engle 2, Merkle, Herzog, Fletcher. Stolen bases—Speaker, Doyle, Herzog, Meyers. Double plays—Fletcher, Doyle and Merkle; Hooper and Stahl. Earned runs—New York 3, Boston 0. Left on bases—New York 3, Boston 0. Struck out—By Marquard 3, by O'Brien 1, by Collins 1. Bases on balls—Off Marquard 1. Balk—O'Brien. Hits—Off O'Brien 6 in 1 inning, off Collins 5 in 7 innings. Losing pitcher—O'Brien. Umpires—Klem (N.L.), Evans (A.L.), O'Loughlin (A.L.) and Rigler (N.L.). Time—1:58. Attendance—30,622.

TUESDAY, OCTOBER 15—AT BOSTON

Giants	AB	R	H	O	A	E
Devore, rf	4	2	1	3	1	1
Doyle, 2b	4	3	3	2	3	2
Snodgrass, cf	5	1	2	1	0	0
Murray, lf	4	0	0	1	0	0
Merkle, 1b	5	1	2	10	0	1
Herzog, 3b	4	2	1	0	2	0
Meyers, c	4	1	3	6	0	0
Wilson, c	1	0	1	2	0	0
Fletcher, ss	5	1	1	2	4	0
Tesreau, p	4	0	2	0	6	0
Totals	40	11	16	27	16	4

Red Sox	AB	R	H	O	A	E
Hooper, rf	3	0	1	1	1	0
Yerkes, 2b	4	0	0	1	4	0
Speaker, cf	4	1	1	4	0	1
Lewis, lf	4	1	1	3	0	0
Gardner, 3b	4	1	1	2	0	1
Stahl, 1b	5	0	1	11	1	0
Wagner, ss	5	0	1	4	4	0
Cady, c	4	1	0	1	2	0
Wood, p	0	0	0	0	1	0
Hall, p	3	0	3	0	5	1
Totals	36	4	9	27	18	3

Giants ....610 002 101—11
Red Sox ....010 000 210— 4

Two-base hits—Snodgrass, Hall, Lewis. Home runs—Doyle, Gardner. Runs batted in—Doyle 2, Snodgrass 2, Merkle, Meyers, Tesreau 2, Hooper, Lewis, Gardner. Sacrifice hit—Murray. Sacrifice fly—Hooper. Stolen bases—Devore 2, Doyle. Double plays—Devore and Meyers; Speaker (unassisted). Earned runs—New York 7, Boston 2. Left on bases—Boston 12, New York 8. Struck out—By Tesreau 6, by Hall 1. Bases on balls—Off Tesreau 5, off Hall 5. Hit by pitcher—By Tesreau (Gardner). Wild pitches—Tesreau 2. Hits—Off Wood 7 in 1 inning, off Hall 9 in 8 innings. Losing pitcher—Wood. Umpires—Evans (A.L.), Klem (N.L.), O'Loughlin (A.L.) and Rigler (N.L.). Time—2:21. Attendance—32,694.

WEDNESDAY, OCTOBER 16—AT BOSTON

Giants	AB	R	H	O	A	E
Devore, rf	3	1	1	3	1	0
Doyle, 2b	5	0	0	1	5	1
Snodgrass, cf	4	0	1	4	1	1
Murray, lf	5	1	2	3	0	0
Merkle, 1b	5	0	1	10	0	0
Herzog, 3b	5	0	2	2	1	0
Meyers, c	3	0	0	4	1	0
Fletcher, ss	3	0	1	2	3	0
bMcCormick	1	0	0	0	0	0
Shafer, ss	0	0	0	0	0	0
Mathewson, p	4	0	1	0	3	0
Totals	38	2	9	*29	15	2

Red Sox	AB	R	H	O	A	E
Hooper, rf	5	0	0	3	0	0
Yerkes, 2b	4	1	1	0	3	0
Speaker, cf	4	0	2	2	0	1
Lewis, lf	4	0	0	1	0	0
Gardner, 3b	3	0	1	1	4	2
Stahl, 1b	4	1	2	15	0	1
Wagner, ss	3	0	1	3	5	1
Cady, c	4	0	0	5	3	0
Bedient, p	2	0	0	0	1	0
aHenriksen	1	0	1	0	0	0
Wood, p	0	0	0	0	2	0
cEngle	1	1	0	0	0	0
Totals	35	3	8	30	18	5

```
Giants .................... 001 000 000  1—2
Red Sox .................. 000 000 100  2—3
```

aDoubled for Bedient in seventh. bFlied out for Fletcher in ninth. cReached second on Snodgrass' error for Wood in tenth. *Two out when winning run scored. Two-base hits—Murray 2, Herzog, Gardner, Stahl, Henriksen. Runs batted in—Murray, Merkle, Speaker, Gardner, Henriksen. Sacrifice hit—Meyers. Sacrifice fly—Gardner. Stolen base—Devore. Earned runs—Boston 2, New York 2. Left on bases—New York 11, Boston 9. Struck out—By Mathewson 4, by Bedient 2, by Wood 2. Bases on balls—Off Mathewson 5, off Bedient 3, off Wood 1. Hits—Off Bedient 6 in 7 innings, off Wood 3 in 3 innings. Winning pitcher—Wood. Umpires—O'Loughlin (A.L.), Rigler (N.L.), Klem (N.L.) and Evans (A.L.). Time—2:39. Attendance—17,034.

COMPOSITE BATTING AVERAGES

RED SOX

Player-position	G	AB	R	H	2B	3B	HR	RBI	BA
Henriksen, pr-ph ..	2	1	0	1	1	0	0	1	1.000
Hall, p.............	2	4	0	3	1	0	0	2	.750
Engle, ph	3	3	1	1	1	0	0	2	.333
Speaker, cf........	8	30	4	9	1	2	0	2	.300
Hooper, rf	8	31	3	9	2	1	0	2	.290
Wood, p	4	7	1	2	0	0	0	1	.286
Stahl, 1b	8	32	3	9	2	0	0	2	.281
Yerkes, 2b	8	32	3	8	0	2	0	4	.250
Gardner, 3b	8	28	4	5	2	1	1	4	.179
Wagner, ss	8	30	1	5	1	0	0	2	.167
Lewis, lf	8	32	4	5	3	0	0	2	.156
Cady, c	7	22	1	3	0	0	0	1	.136
Carrigan, c	2	7	0	0	0	0	0	0	.000
Collins, p	2	5	0	0	0	0	0	0	.000
Bedient, p	4	6	0	0	0	0	0	0	.000
O'Brien, p	2	2	0	0	0	0	0	0	.000
Ball, ph	1	1	0	0	0	0	0	0	.000
Totals	8	273	25	60	14	6	1	21	.220

GIANTS

Player-position	G	AB	R	H	2B	3B	HR	RBI	BA
Wilson, c	2	1	0	1	0	0	0	0	1.000
Herzog, 3b	8	30	6	12	4	1	0	4	.400
Tesreau, p	3	8	0	3	0	0	0	2	.375
Meyers, c	8	28	2	10	0	1	0	3	.357
Murray, rf-lf	8	31	5	10	4	1	0	5	.323
Merkle, 1b	8	33	5	9	2	1	0	3	.273
McCormick, ph	5	4	0	1	0	0	0	1	.250
Devore, lf........	7	24	4	6	0	0	0	0	.250
Doyle, 2b	8	33	5	8	1	0	1	2	.242
Snod'ss, cf-lf-rf ...	8	33	2	7	2	0	0	2	.212
Fletcher, ss	8	28	1	5	1	0	0	3	.179
Mathewson, p	3	12	0	2	0	0	0	0	.167
Becker, pr-cf	2	4	1	0	0	0	0	0	.000
Crandall, p	1	1	0	0	0	0	0	0	.000
Shafer, pr-ss	3	0	0	0	0	0	0	0	.000
Marquard, p	2	4	0	0	0	0	0	0	.000
Ames,p	1	0	0	0	0	0	0	0	.000
Totals	8	274	31	74	14	4	1	25	.270

COMPOSITE PITCHING AVERAGES

RED SOX

Pitcher	G	IP	H	R	ER	SO	BB	W	L	ERA
Bedient	4	18	10	2	1	7	7	1	0	0.50
Collins	2	14⅓	14	5	3	6	0	0	0	1.88
Hall.........	2	10⅔	11	6	4	1	9	0	0	3.38
Wood	4	22	27	11	9	21	3	3	1	3.68
O'Brien	2	9	12	7	5	4	3	0	2	5.00
Totals	8	74	74	31	22	39	22	4	3	2.68

GIANTS

Pitcher	G	IP	H	R	ER	SO	BB	W	L	ERA
Crandall	1	2	1	0	0	2	0	0	0	0.00
Marquard	2	18	14	3	1	9	2	2	0	0.50
Mathewson ...	3	28⅔	23	11	5	10	5	0	2	1.57
Tesreau	3	23	19	10	8	15	11	1	2	3.13
Ames	1	2	3	1	1	0	1	0	0	4.50
Totals	8	73⅔	60	25	15	36	19	3	4	1.83

1915
WORLD CHAMPIONS
Manager: Bill Carrigan

Pitchers: Ray Collins, Ralph Comstock, Guy Cooper, Rube Foster, Vean Gregg, Dutch Leonard, Carl Mays, Herb Pennock, *Babe Ruth (32 games), Ernie Shore and Smokey Joe Wood. Catchers: Hick Cady, Bill Carrigan, Ray Haley and Pinch Thomas. Infielders: Jack Barry, Del Gainor, Larry Gardner, Dick Hoblitzel, Hal Janvrin, Mike McNally, Bill Rodgers, Everett Scott and Heinie Wagner. Outfielders: Olaf Henriksen, Harry Hooper, Duffy Lewis, Wally Rehg, *Babe Ruth (10 games), Chick Shorten and Tris Speaker.
*Played more than one position.

Jerry Remy goes airborne. (Boston Globe)

1915 WORLD CHAMPIONS (*continued*)

WORLD SERIES

	W	L	Pct.
Red Sox, A.L.	4	1	.800
Phillies, N.L.	1	4	.200

Oct. 8 Phillies (Alexander)	3	Red Sox (Shore)	1	at Philadelphia
Oct. 9 Red Sox (Foster)	2	Phillies (Mayer)	1	at Philadelphia
Oct. 11 Red Sox (Leonard)	2	Phillies (Alexander)	1	at Boston
Oct. 12 Red Sox (Shore)	2	Phillies (Chalmers)	1	at Boston
Oct. 13 Red Sox (Foster)	5	Phillies (Rixey)	4	at Philadelphia

FRIDAY, OCTOBER 8—AT PHILADELPHIA

Red Sox	AB	R	H	O	A	E		Phillies	AB	R	H	O	A	E
Hooper, rf	5	0	1	0	0	0		Stock, 3b	3	1	0	0	2	0
Scott, ss	3	0	1	2	2	0		Bancroft, ss	4	1	1	4	1	0
Speaker, cf	2	1	0	1	0	0		Paskert, cf	3	1	1	1	0	0
Hoblitzel, 1b	4	0	1	12	0	0		Cravath, rf	2	0	0	1	0	0
Lewis, lf	4	0	2	2	0	0		Luderus, 1b	4	0	1	10	0	1
Gardner, 3b	3	0	1	0	1	0		Whitted, lf	2	0	1	3	0	0
Barry, 2b	4	0	1	4	4	0		Niehoff, 2b	3	0	0	1	4	0
Cady, c	2	0	0	3	2	0		Burns, c	3	0	0	7	0	0
aHenriksen	1	0	0	0	0	0		Alexander, p	3	0	1	0	5	0
Shore, p	3	0	1	0	4	1								
bRuth	1	0	0	0	0	0								
Totals	32	1	8	24	13	1		Totals	27	3	5	27	12	1

```
Red Sox ......................000 000 010—1
Phillies .....................000 100 02 X—3
```

aReached first on Luderus' error for Cady in ninth. bGrounded out for Shore in ninth. Runs batted in—Lewis, Cravath, Luderus, Whitted. Sacrifice hits—Scott, Gardner, Cady, Cravath. Stolen bases—Whitted, Hoblitzel. Left on bases—Boston 9, Philadelphia 5. Earned runs—Philadelphia 3, Boston 1. Struck out—By Alexander 6, by Shore 2. Bases on balls—Off Alexander 2, off Shore 4. Umpires—Klem (N.L.), O'Loughlin (A.L.), Evans (A.L.) and Rigler (N.L.). Time—1:58. Attendance—19,343.

SATURDAY, OCTOBER 9—AT PHILADELPHIA

Red Sox	AB	R	H	O	A	E		Phillies	AB	R	H	O	A	E
Hooper, rf	3	1	1	2	0	0		Stock, 3b	4	0	0	0	2	0
Scott, ss	3	0	0	0	3	0		Bancroft, ss	4	0	1	2	2	0
aHenriksen	1	0	0	0	0	0		Paskert, cf	4	0	0	1	0	0
Cady, c	0	0	0	3	0	0		Cravath, rf	3	1	1	1	0	0
Speaker, cf	4	0	1	3	0	0		Luderus, 1b	3	0	1	9	1	0
Hoblitzel, 1b	4	0	1	8	3	0		Whitted, lf	3	0	0	3	0	0
Lewis, lf	4	0	1	1	0	0		Niehoff, 2b	3	0	0	4	1	0
Gardner, 3b	4	1	2	0	2	0		Burns, c	3	0	0	6	3	1
Barry, 2b	4	0	1	0	3	0		Mayer, p	3	0	0	1	3	0
Thomas, c	3	0	0	6	0	0								
Janvrin, ss	1	0	0	1	0	0								
Foster, p	4	0	3	3	0	0								
Totals	35	2	10	27	11	0		Totals	30	1	3	27	12	1

```
Red Sox ......................100 000 001—2
Phillies .....................000 010 000—1
```

aPopped out for Scott in seventh. Two-base hits—Foster, Cravath, Luderus. Runs batted in—Foster, Luderus. Left on bases—Boston 8, Philadelphia 2. Earned runs—Boston 1, Philadelphia 1. Struck out—By Foster 8, by Mayer 7. Bases on balls—Off Mayer 2. Umpires—Rigler (N.L.), Evans (A.L.), O'Loughlin (A.L.) and Klem (N.L.). Time—2:05. Attendance—20,306.

MONDAY, OCTOBER 11—AT BOSTON

Phillies	AB	R	H	O	A	E		Red Sox	AB	R	H	O	A	E
Stock, 3b	3	0	1	1	0	0		Hooper, rf	4	1	1	2	0	0
Bancroft, ss	3	0	1	4	1	0		Scott, ss	3	0	0	2	1	0
Paskert, cf	4	0	0	7	0	0		Speaker, cf	3	1	2	2	0	0
Cravath, rf	4	0	0	2	0	0		Hoblitzel, 1b	3	0	0	9	0	1
Luderus, 1b	3	0	0	3	1	0		Lewis, lf	4	0	3	1	0	0
Whitted, lf	3	0	0	2	0	0		Gardner, 3b	3	0	0	1	6	0
Niehoff, 2b	3	0	0	0	2	0		Barry, 2b	3	0	0	2	1	0
Burns, c	3	1	1	5	2	0		Carrigan, c	2	0	0	8	0	0
Alexander, p	2	0	0	2	0	0		Leonard, p	3	0	0	0	2	0
Totals	28	1	3	*26	6	0		Totals	28	2	6	27	10	1

```
Phillies .....................001 000 000—1
Red Sox ......................000 100 001—2
```

*Two out when winning run scored. Two-base hit—Stock. Three-base hit—Speaker. Runs batted in—Bancroft, Hoblitzel, Lewis. Sacrifice hits—Bancroft, Alexander, Stock, Scott. Sacrifice fly—Hoblitzel. Double play—Burns, Bancroft and Luderus. Left on bases—Boston 4, Philadelphia 3. Earned runs—Boston 2, Philadelphia 1. Struck out—By Leonard 6, by Alexander 4. Bases on balls—Off Alexander 2. Umpires—O'Loughlin (A.L.), Klem (N.L.), Rigler (N.L.) and Evans (A.L.). Time—1:48. Attendance—42,300.

TUESDAY, OCTOBER 12—AT BOSTON

Phillies	AB	R	H	O	A	E
Stock, 3b	4	0	1	0	3	0
Bancroft, ss	2	0	0	0	0	0
Paskert, cf	4	0	0	5	0	0
Cravath, rf	4	1	1	0	0	0
Luderus, 1b	4	0	3	5	0	0
aDugey	0	0	0	0	0	0
Becker, lf	0	0	0	0	0	0
Whitted, lf-1b	3	0	0	4	0	0
Niehoff, 2b	3	0	0	3	1	0
Burns, c	3	0	1	7	2	0
Chalmers, p	3	0	1	0	4	0
bByrne	1	0	0	0	0	0
Totals	31	1	7	24	10	0

Red Sox	AB	R	H	O	A	E
Hooper, rf	4	0	1	2	0	0
Scott, ss	4	0	0	2	4	0
Speaker, cf	3	0	1	1	0	0
Hoblitzel, 1b	4	1	3	5	2	0
Lewis, lf	2	0	1	6	1	0
Gardner, 3b	4	0	0	2	2	0
Barry, 2b	2	1	0	3	1	1
Cady, c	3	0	2	6	1	0
Shore, p	2	0	0	0	1	0
Totals	28	2	8	27	12	1

```
Phillies ..................... 000 000 010—1
Red Sox ..................... 001 001 00X—2
```

aRan for Luderus in eighth. bFlied out for Chalmers in ninth. Two-base hit—Lewis. Three-base hit—Cravath. Runs batted in—Luderus, Hooper, Lewis. Stolen base—Dugey. Sacrifice hits—Whitted, Shore, Lewis. Left on bases—Philadelphia 8, Boston 7. Earned runs—Boston 2, Philadelphia 1. Double plays—Scott, Barry, Hoblitzel and Barry; Chalmers, Burns and Whitted. Struck out—By Shore 4, by Chalmers 6. Bases on balls—Off Shore 4, off Chalmers 3. Umpires—Evans (A.L.), Rigler (N.L.), O'Loughlin (A.L.) and Klem (N.L.). Time—2:05. Attendance—41,096.

WEDNESDAY, OCTOBER 13—AT PHILADELPHIA

Red Sox	AB	R	H	O	A	E
Hooper, rf	4	2	3	2	0	1
Scott, ss	5	0	0	2	2	0
Speaker, cf	5	0	1	3	0	0
Hoblitzel, 1b	1	0	0	1	0	0
aGainor, 1b	3	1	1	9	0	0
Lewis, lf	4	1	1	0	0	0
Gardner, 3b	3	1	1	2	3	0
Barry, 2b	4	0	1	1	0	0
Thomas, c	2	0	1	4	3	0
Cady, c	1	0	0	2	1	0
Foster, p	4	0	1	1	3	0
Totals	36	5	10	27	12	1

Phillies	AB	R	H	O	A	E
Stock, 3b	3	0	0	1	1	0
Bancroft, ss	4	1	2	3	6	1
Paskert, cf	4	1	2	3	0	0
Cravath, rf	3	0	0	1	0	0
bDugey	0	0	0	0	0	0
Becker, rf	0	0	0	0	0	0
Luderus, 1b	2	1	2	13	2	0
Whitted, lf	4	0	0	2	0	0
Niehoff, 2b	4	1	1	1	2	0
Burns, c	4	0	1	2	2	0
Mayer, p	1	0	0	1	0	0
Rixey, p	2	0	1	0	1	0
cKillefer	1	0	0	0	0	0
Totals	32	4	9	27	14	1

```
Red Sox ..................... 011 000 021—5
Phillies ..................... 200 200 000—4
```

aHit into double play for Hoblitzel in third inning. bRan for Cravath in eighth. cGrounded out for Rixey in ninth. Two-base hit—Luderus. Three-base hit—Gardner. Home runs—Hooper 2, Lewis, Luderus. Runs batted in—Luderus 3, Hooper 2, Lewis 2, Barry. Double plays—Foster, Thomas and Hoblitzel; Bancroft and Luderus. Left on bases—Boston 7, Philadelphia 5. Earned runs—Boston 5, Philadelphia 3. Struck out—By Foster 5, by Rixey 2. Bases on balls—Off Foster 2, off Rixey 2. Hit by pitcher—By Foster (Stock, Luderus), by Rixey (Hooper). Hits—Off Mayer 6 in 2⅓ innings, off Rixey 4 in 6⅔ innings. Losing pitcher—Rixey. Umpires—Klem (N.L.), O'Loughlin (A.L.), Evans (A.L.) and Rigler (N.L.). Time—2:15. Attendance—20,306.

COMPOSITE BATTING AVERAGES

RED SOX

Player-position	G	AB	R	H	2B	3B	HR	RBI	BA
Foster, p	2	8	0	4	1	0	0	1	.500
Lewis, lf	5	18	1	8	1	0	1	5	.444
Hooper, rf	5	20	4	7	0	0	2	3	.350
Cady, c	4	6	0	2	0	0	0	0	.333
Gainor, 1b	1	3	1	1	0	0	0	0	.333
Hoblitzel, 1b	5	16	1	5	0	0	0	1	.313
Speaker, cf	5	17	2	5	0	1	0	0	.294
Gardner, 3b	5	17	2	4	0	1	0	0	.235
Shore, p	2	5	0	1	0	0	0	0	.200
Thomas, c	2	5	0	1	0	0	0	0	.200
Barry, 2b	5	17	1	3	0	0	0	1	.176
Scott, ss	5	18	0	1	0	0	0	0	.056
Janvrin, ss	1	1	0	0	0	0	0	0	.000
Carrigan, c	1	2	0	0	0	0	0	0	.000
Henriksen, ph	2	2	0	0	0	0	0	0	.000
Ruth, ph	1	1	0	0	0	0	0	0	.000
Leonard, p	1	3	0	0	0	0	0	0	.000
Totals	5	159	12	42	2	2	3	11	.264

PHILLIES

Player-position	G	AB	R	H	2B	3B	HR	RBI	BA
Rixey, p	1	2	0	1	0	0	0	0	.500
Luderus, 1b	5	16	1	7	2	0	1	6	.438
Chalmers, p	1	3	0	1	0	0	0	0	.333
Bancroft, ss	5	17	2	5	0	0	0	1	.294
Alexander, p	2	5	0	1	0	0	0	0	.200
Burns, c	5	16	1	3	0	0	0	0	.188
Paskert, cf	5	19	2	3	0	0	0	0	.158
Cravath, rf	5	16	2	2	1	1	0	1	.125
Stock, 3b	5	17	1	2	1	0	0	0	.118
Whitted, lf-1b	5	15	0	1	0	0	0	1	.067
Niehoff, 2b	5	16	1	1	0	0	0	0	.063
Mayer, p	2	4	0	0	0	0	0	0	.000
Dugey, pr	2	0	0	0	0	0	0	0	.000
Becker, lf	2	0	0	0	0	0	0	0	.000
Byrne, ph	1	1	0	0	0	0	0	0	.000
Killefer, ph	1	1	0	0	0	0	0	0	.000
Totals	5	148	10	27	4	1	1	9	.182

COMPOSITE PITCHING AVERAGES

RED SOX

Pitcher	G	IP	H	R	ER	SO	BB	W	L	ERA
Leonard	1	9	3	1	1	6	0	1	0	1.00
Foster	2	18	12	5	4	13	2	2	0	2.00
Shore	2	17	12	4	4	6	8	1	1	2.12
Totals	5	44	27	10	9	25	10	4	1	1.84

PHILLIES

Pitcher	G	IP	H	R	ER	SO	BB	W	L	ERA
Alexander	2	17⅔	14	3	3	10	4	1	1	1.53
Chalmers	1	8	8	2	2	6	3	0	1	2.25
Mayer	2	11⅓	16	4	3	7	2	0	1	2.38
Rixey	1	6⅔	4	3	2	2	2	0	1	2.70
Totals	5	43⅔	42	12	10	25	11	1	4	2.06

1916
WORLD CHAMPIONS
Manager: Bill Carrigan

Pitchers: Rube Foster, Vean Gregg, Sad Sam Jones, Dutch Leonard, Carl Mays, Marty McHale, Herb Pennock, *Babe Ruth (44 games), Ernie Shore and John Wyckoff. Catchers: Sam Agnew, *Hick Cady (63 games), Bill Carrigan, Ray Haley and Pinch Thomas. Infielders: Jack Barry, *Hick Cady (3 games), Del Gainor, Larry Gardner, Dick Hoblitzel, Hal Janvrin, Mike McNally, Everett Scott and Heinie Wagner. Outfielders: Olaf Henriksen, Harry Hooper, Duffy Lewis, *Babe Ruth (23 games), Chick Shorten, Tilly Walker and Jimmy Walsh.
*Played more than one position.

World Series

	W	L	Pct.
Red Sox, A.L.	4	1	.800
Dodgers, N.L.	1	4	.200

Oct. 7	Red Sox (Shore)	6	Dodgers (Marquard) 5	at Boston
Oct. 9*	Red Sox (Ruth)	2	Dodgers (Smith) 1	at Boston
Oct. 10	Dodgers (Coombs)	4	Red Sox (Mays) 3	at Brooklyn
Oct. 11	Red Sox (Leonard)	6	Dodgers (Marquard) 2	at Brooklyn
Oct. 12	Red Sox (Shore)	4	Dodgers (Pfeffer) 1	at Boston

*14 innings.

SATURDAY, OCTOBER 7—AT BOSTON

Dodgers	AB	R	H	O	A	E	Red Sox	AB	R	H	O	A	E
Myers, cf	5	0	2	1	0	0	Hooper, rf	4	2	1	1	1	0
Daubert, 1b	4	0	0	5	1	0	Janvrin, 2b	4	1	2	2	8	1
Stengel, rf	4	2	2	1	0	1	Walker, cf	4	1	2	0	0	0
Wheat, lf	4	1	2	3	0	0	Hoblitzel, 1b	5	2	1	14	0	0
Cutshaw, 2b	3	1	0	5	2	1	Lewis, lf	3	0	1	0	0	0
Mowrey, 3b	3	1	1	1	2	0	Gardner, 3b	4	0	1	1	3	0
Olson, ss	4	0	1	2	1	2	Scott, ss	2	0	0	2	4	0
Meyers, c	4	0	1	6	3	0	Cady, c	1	0	0	7	0	0
Marquard, p	2	0	0	0	0	0	Thomas, c	0	0	0	0	0	0
aJohnston	1	0	1	0	0	0	Shore, p	4	0	0	0	3	0
Pfeffer, p	0	0	0	0	0	0	Mays, p	0	0	0	0	0	0
bMerkle	0	0	0	0	0	0							
Totals	34	5	10	24	9	4	Totals	31	6	8	27	19	1

Dodgers .... 000 100 004—5
Red Sox .... 001 010 31X—6

aSingled for Marquard in eighth. bWalked for Pfeffer in ninth. Two-base hits—Lewis, Hooper, Janvrin, Wheat, Meyers. Runs batted in—Myers, Wheat, Mowrey, Merkle, Walker, Hoblitzel, Lewis, Gardner, Scott. Sacrifice hits—Scott, Janvrin, Lewis. Sacrifice fly—Scott. Double plays—Janvrin, Scott and Hoblitzel; Hooper and Cady; Gardner, Janvrin and Hoblitzel; Shore, Scott, Janvrin and Hoblitzel. Left on bases—Boston 11, Brooklyn 6. Earned runs—Boston 4, Brooklyn 3. Struck out —By Marquard 6, by Shore 5. Bases on balls—Off Marquard 4, off Pfeffer 2, off Shore 3. Hit by pitcher—By Shore (Cutshaw). Passed ball—Meyers. Hits—Off Marquard 7 in 7 innings, off Pfeffer 1 in 1 inning, off Shore 9 in 8⅔ innings, off Mays 1 in ⅓ inning. Winning pitcher—Shore. Losing pitcher—Marquard. Umpires—Connolly (A.L.), O'Day (N.L.), Quigley (N.L.) and Dinneen (A.L.). Time—2:16. Attendance—36,117.

MONDAY, OCTOBER 9—AT BOSTON

Dodgers	AB	R	H	O	A	E	Red Sox	AB	R	H	O	A	E
Johnston, rf	5	0	1	1	0	0	Hooper, rf	6	0	1	2	1	0
Daubert, 1b	5	0	0	18	1	0	Janvrin, 2b	6	0	1	4	5	0
Myers, cf	6	1	1	4	1	0	Walker, cf	3	0	0	2	1	0
Wheat, lf	5	0	0	2	0	0	Walsh, cf	3	0	0	1	0	0
Cutshaw, 2b	5	0	0	5	6	1	Hoblitzel, 1b	2	0	0	21	1	0
Mowrey, 3b	5	0	1	3	5	1	aMcNally	0	1	0	0	0	0
Olson, ss	2	0	1	2	4	0	Lewis, lf	3	0	1	1	0	0
Miller, c	5	0	1	4	1	0	Gardner, 3b	5	0	0	3	7	1
Smith, p	5	0	1	1	7	0	bGainor	1	0	1	0	0	0
							Scott, ss	4	1	2	1	8	0
							Thomas, c	4	0	1	5	4	0
							Ruth, p	5	0	0	2	4	0
Totals	43	1	6*	40	25	2	Totals	42	2	7	42	31	1

Dodgers .... 100 000 000 000 00—1
Red Sox .... 001 000 000 000 01—2

aRan for Hoblitzel in fourteenth. bSingled for Gardner in fourteenth. *One out when winning run scored. Two-base hits— Smith, Janvrin. Three-base hits—Scott, Thomas. Home run—Myers. Runs batted in—Gainor, Ruth, Myers. Sacrifice hits— Lewis, Thomas, Olson 2. Double plays—Scott, Janvrin and Hoblitzel; Mowrey, Cutshaw and Daubert; Myers and Miller. Left on bases—Boston 9, Brooklyn 5. Earned runs—Boston 2, Brooklyn 1. Struck out—By Smith 2, by Ruth 4. Bases on balls—Off Smith 6, off Ruth 3. Umpires—Dinneen (A.L.), Quigley (N.L.), O'Day (N.L.) and Connolly (A.L.). Time—2:32. Attendance—41,373.

TUESDAY, OCTOBER 10—AT BROOKLYN

Red Sox	AB	R	H	O	A	E		Dodgers	AB	R	H	O	A	E
Hooper, rf	4	1	2	1	0	0		Myers, cf	3	0	0	3	0	0
Janvrin, 2b	4	0	0	1	0	0		Daubert, 1b	4	1	3	7	0	0
Shorten, cf	4	0	3	0	0	0		Stengel, rf	3	0	1	2	1	0
Hoblitzel, 1b	4	0	1	12	2	0		Wheat, lf	2	1	1	4	0	0
Lewis, lf	4	0	0	1	1	0		Cutshaw, 2b	4	0	1	4	0	0
Gardner, 3b	3	1	1	2	0	1		Mowrey, 3b	3	1	0	2	1	0
Scott, ss	3	0	0	1	7	0		Olson, ss	4	1	2	1	2	0
Thomas, c	3	0	0	5	0	0		Miller, c	3	0	0	4	2	0
Mays, p	1	0	0	0	4	0		Coombs, p	3	0	1	0	2	0
aHenriksen	0	1	0	0	0	0		Pfeffer, p	1	0	1	0	1	0
Foster, p	1	0	0	1	2	0								
Totals	31	3	7	24	16	1		Totals	30	4	10	27	9	0

```
Red Sox ..................... 000 002 100—3
Dodgers ..................... 001 120 00x—4
```

aWalked for Mays in sixth. Three-base hits—Olson, Daubert, Hooper. Home run—Gardner. Runs batted in—Cutshaw, Olson 2, Coombs, Hooper, Shorten, Gardner. Sacrifice hits—Stengel, Miller, Myers. Stolen base—Wheat. Left on bases—Brooklyn 9, Boston 2. Earned runs—Brooklyn 3, Boston 3. Struck out—By Mays 2, by Foster 1, by Coombs 1, by Pfeffer 3. Bases on balls—Off Mays 3, off Coombs 1. Hit by pitcher—By Mays (Myers). Wild pitch—Foster. Hits—Off Mays 7 in 5 innings, off Foster 3 in 3 innings, off Coombs 7 in 6⅓ innings, off Pfeffer 0 in 2⅔ innings. Winning pitcher—Coombs. Losing pitcher—Mays. Umpires—O'Day (N.L.), Connolly (A.L.), Quigley (N.L.) and Dinneen (A.L.). Time—2:01. Attendance—21,087.

WEDNESDAY, OCTOBER 11—AT BROOKLYN

Red Sox	AB	R	H	O	A	E		Dodgers	AB	R	H	O	A	E
Hooper, rf	4	1	2	3	0	0		Johnston, rf	4	1	1	0	0	1
Janvrin, 2b	5	1	0	1	2	1		Myers, cf	4	1	1	1	0	0
Walker, cf	4	0	1	2	0	0		Merkle, 1b	3	0	1	9	1	1
Hoblitzel, 1b	3	1	2	8	0	0		Wheat, lf	4	0	1	0	0	1
Lewis, lf	4	2	2	6	0	0		Cutshaw, 2b	4	0	1	3	2	0
Gardner, 3b	3	1	1	1	3	0		Mowrey, 3b	3	0	0	1	4	0
Scott, ss	4	0	0	3	3	0		Olson, ss	3	0	0	2	2	0
Carrigan, c	3	0	2	3	1	0		Meyers, c	3	0	0	11	3	0
Leonard, p	3	0	0	0	1	0		cStengel	0	0	0	0	0	0
								Marquard, p	1	0	0	0	2	0
								aPfeffer	1	0	0	0	0	0
								Cheney, p	0	0	0	0	0	1
								bO'Mara	1	0	0	0	0	0
								Rucker, p	0	0	0	0	0	0
								dGetz	1	0	0	0	0	0
Totals	33	6	10	27	10	1		Totals	32	2	5	27	14	4

```
Red Sox ..................... 030 110 100—6
Dodgers ..................... 200 000 000—2
```

aFanned for Marquard in fourth. bStruck out for Cheney in seventh. cRan for Meyers in ninth. dGrounded out for Rucker in ninth. Two-base hits—Lewis, Cutshaw, Hoblitzel. Three-base hit—Johnston. Home run—Gardner. Runs batted in—Myers, Cutshaw, Hoblitzel, Gardner 3, Carrigan. Sacrifice hits—Carrigan, Gardner. Stolen base—Hooper. Left on bases—Brooklyn 7, Boston 5. Earned runs—Boston 5, Brooklyn 1. Struck out—By Leonard 3, by Marquard 3, by Cheney 5, by Rucker 3. Bases on balls—off Leonard 4, off Marquard 2, off Cheney 1. Wild pitch—Leonard. Passed ball—Meyers. Hits—Off Marquard 5 in 4 innings, off Cheney 4 in 3 innings, off Rucker 1 in 2 innings. Losing pitcher—Marquard. Umpires—Quigley (N.L.), Dinneen (A.L.), O'Day (N.L.) and Connolly (A.L.). Time—2:30. Attendance—21,662.

THURSDAY, OCTOBER 12—AT BOSTON

Dodgers	AB	R	H	O	A	E		Red Sox	AB	R	H	O	A	E
Myers, cf	4	0	0	0	0	0		Hooper, rf	3	2	1	1	0	0
Daubert, 1b	4	0	0	10	1	0		Janvrin, 2b	4	0	2	0	1	0
Stengel, rf	4	0	1	0	0	0		Shorten, cf	3	0	1	3	0	0
Wheat, lf	4	0	0	5	0	0		Hoblitzel, 1b	3	0	0	14	1	0
Cutshaw, 2b	3	1	0	2	3	0		Lewis, lf	3	1	2	1	0	0
Mowrey, 3b	3	0	1	1	3	1		Gardner, 3b	2	0	0	5	0	0
Olson, ss	3	0	0	2	3	2		Scott, ss	3	0	0	2	3	2
Meyers, c	3	0	1	4	2	0		Cady, c	3	1	1	4	1	0
Pfeffer, p	2	0	0	0	1	0		Shore, p	3	0	0	2	3	0
aMerkle	1	0	0	0	0	0								
Dell, p	0	0	0	0	0	0								
Totals	31	1	3	24	13	3		Totals	27	4	7	27	14	2

```
Dodgers ..................... 010 000 00 0—1
Red Sox ..................... 012 010 00 X—4
```

aFlied out for Pfeffer in eighth. Two-base hit—Janvrin. Three-base hit—Lewis. Runs batted in—Janvrin, Shorten, Gardner. Sacrifice hits—Mowrey, Lewis, Shorten. Sacrifice fly—Gardner. Left on bases—Brooklyn 5, Boston 4. Earned runs—Boston 2, Brooklyn 0. Struck out—By Pfeffer 2, by Shore 4. Bases on balls—Off Pfeffer 2, off Shore 1. Wild pitches—Pfeffer 2. Passed ball—Cady. Hits—Off Pfeffer 6 in 7 innings, off Dell 1 in 1 inning. Losing pitcher—Pfeffer. Umpires—Connolly (A.L.), O'Day (N.L.), Quigley (N.L.) and Dinneen (A.L.). Time—1:43. Attendance—42,620.

1918 WORLD CHAMPIONS (*continued*)

MONDAY, SEPTEMBER 9—AT BOSTON

Cubs	AB	R	H	O	A	E
Flack, rf	4	0	1	3	0	0
Hollocher, ss	4	0	0	2	0	0
Mann, lf	4	0	1	2	0	0
Paskert, cf	4	0	0	3	0	0
Merkle, 1b	3	0	1	9	1	0
Pick, 2b	2	0	2	0	2	0
aZeider, 3b	0	0	0	1	2	0
Deal, 3b	2	0	1	1	3	0
bO'Farrell	1	0	0	0	0	0
Wortman, 2b	1	0	0	1	0	0
Killefer, c	2	1	0	1	0	0
eBarber	1	0	0	0	0	0
Tyler, p	0	0	0	1	4	0
cHendrix	1	0	1	0	0	0
dMcCabe	0	1	0	0	0	0
Douglas, p	0	0	0	0	0	1
Totals	29	2	7	24	12	1

Red Sox	AB	R	H	O	A	E
Hooper, rf	3	0	0	1	0	0
Shean, 2b	3	0	1	4	4	0
Strunk, cf	4	0	0	0	0	0
Whiteman, lf	3	1	0	1	0	0
Bush, p	0	0	0	0	0	0
McInnis, 1b	3	1	1	16	1	0
Ruth, p-lf	2	0	1	0	4	0
Scott, ss	3	0	0	3	8	0
Thomas, 3b	3	0	0	2	3	0
Agnew, c	2	0	0	0	1	0
Schang, c	1	1	1	0	0	0
Totals	27	3	4	27	21	0

```
Cubs ....................... 000  000  02 0—2
Red Sox .................... 000  200  01 X—3
```

aWalked for Pick in seventh. bHit into double play for Deal in seventh. cSingled for Tyler in eighth. dRan for Hendrix in eighth. eHit into double play for Killefer in ninth. Runs batted in—Ruth 2, Hollocher, Mann. Two-base hit—Shean. Three-base hit—Ruth. Sacrifice hits—Hooper, Ruth. Stolen base—Shean. Double plays—Ruth, Scott and McInnis; Scott, Shean and McInnis 2. Left on bases—Chicago 6, Boston 4. Earned runs—Chicago 2, Boston 2. Struck out—By Tyler 1. Bases on balls—Off Tyler 2, off Ruth 6. Wild pitch—Ruth. Hits—Off Tyler 3 in 7 innings, off Douglas 1 in 1 inning, off Ruth 7 in 8 innings (pitched to two batters in ninth), off Bush 0 in 1 inning. Passed balls—Killefer 2. Winning pitcher—Ruth. Losing pitcher—Douglas. Umpires—Owens (A.L.), O'Day (N.L.), Hildebrand (A.L.) and Klem (N.L.). Time—1:50. Attendance—22,183.

TUESDAY, SEPTEMBER 10—AT BOSTON

Cubs	AB	R	H	O	A	E
Flack, rf	2	1	0	1	0	0
Hollocher, ss	3	2	3	2	5	0
Mann, lf	3	0	1	2	0	0
Paskert, cf	3	0	1	3	0	0
Merkle, 1b	3	0	1	11	1	0
Pick, 2b	4	0	1	4	3	0
Deal, 3b	4	0	0	0	0	0
Killefer, c	4	0	0	4	0	0
Vaughn, p	4	0	0	0	3	0
Totals	30	3	7	27	12	0

Red Sox	AB	R	H	O	A	E
Hooper, rf	4	0	1	1	0	0
Shean, 2b	3	0	1	3	2	0
Strunk, cf	4	0	1	4	0	0
Whiteman, lf	3	0	1	1	2	0
McInnis, 1b	3	0	0	9	0	0
Scott, ss	3	0	0	1	4	0
Thomas, 3b	3	0	1	1	1	0
Agnew, c	2	0	0	5	1	0
aSchang, c	1	0	0	1	0	0
Jones, p	1	0	0	1	3	0
bMiller	1	0	0	0	0	0
Totals	28	0	5	27	13	0

```
Cubs ....................... 001  000  020—3
Red Sox .................... 000  000  000—0
```

aStruck out for Agnew in eighth. bFlied out for Jones in ninth. Runs batted in—Mann, Paskert 2. Two-base hits—Mann, Paskert, Strunk. Sacrifice hits—Mann, Shean. Stolen base—Hollocher. Double plays—Merkle and Hollocher; Hollocher, Pick and Merkle 2; Whiteman and Shean. Left on bases—Chicago 6, Boston 4. Earned runs—Chicago 3. Struck out—By Vaughn 4, by Jones 5. Bases on balls—Off Vaughn 1, off Jones 5. Umpires—O'Day (N.L.), Hildebrand (A.L.), Klem (N.L.) and Owens (A.L.). Time—1:42. Attendance—24,694.

WEDNESDAY, SEPTEMBER 11—AT BOSTON

Cubs	AB	R	H	O	A	E
Flack, rf	3	1	1	2	0	1
Hollocher, ss	4	0	0	0	4	0
Mann, lf	3	0	0	2	0	0
Paskert, cf	2	0	0	5	0	0
Merkle, 1b	3	0	1	8	2	0
Pick, 2b	3	0	1	3	1	0
Deal, 3b	2	0	0	2	1	0
aBarber	1	0	0	0	0	0
Zeider, 3b	0	0	0	0	0	0
Killefer, c	2	0	0	2	2	0
bO'Farrell, c	1	0	0	0	0	0
Tyler, p	2	0	0	0	3	1
cMcCabe	1	0	0	0	0	0
Hendrix, p	0	0	0	0	0	0
Totals	27	1	3	24	13	2

Red Sox	AB	R	H	O	A	E
Hooper, rf	3	0	0	1	0	0
Shean, 2b	3	1	0	2	4	0
Strunk, cf	4	0	2	0	0	0
Whiteman, lf	4	0	0	2	0	0
Ruth, lf	0	0	0	1	0	0
McInnis, 1b	4	0	1	16	1	0
Scott, ss	4	0	1	3	3	0
Thomas, 3b	2	0	0	1	2	0
Schang, c	1	0	0	1	2	0
Mays, p	2	1	1	0	6	0
Totals	27	2	5	27	18	0

```
Cubs ....................... 000  100  00 0—1
Red Sox .................... 002  000  00 X—2
```

aLined out for Deal in eighth. bPopped out for Killefer in eighth. cFouled out for Tyler in eighth. Run batted in—Merkle. Sacrifice hits—Hooper, Thomas. Stolen base—Flack. Left on bases—Boston 8, Chicago 2. Earned runs—Boston 0, Chicago 1. Struck out—By Tyler 1, by Mays 1. Bases on balls—Off Tyler 5, off Mays 2. Hit by pitcher—By Mays (Mann). Hits—Off Tyler 5 in 7 innings, off Hendrix 0 in 1 inning. Losing pitcher—Tyler. Umpires—Hildebrand (A.L.), Klem (N.L.), Owens (A.L.) and O'Day (N.L.). Time—1:46. Attendance—15,238.

COMPOSITE BATTING AVERAGES

RED SOX

Player-position	G	AB	R	H	2B	3B	HR	RBI	BA
Schang, ph-c	5	9	1	4	0	0	0	1	.444
Whiteman, lf	6	20	2	5	0	1	0	1	.250
McInnis, 1b	6	20	2	5	0	0	0	1	.250
Shean, 2b	6	19	2	4	1	0	0	0	.211
Hooper, rf	6	20	0	4	0	0	0	0	.200
Ruth, p-lf	3	5	0	1	0	1	0	2	.200
Mays, p	2	5	1	1	0	0	0	0	.200
Strunk, cf	6	23	1	4	1	1	0	0	.174
Thomas, 3b	6	16	0	2	0	0	0	0	.125
Scott, ss	6	21	0	2	0	0	0	1	.095
Agnew, c	4	9	0	0	0	0	0	0	.000
Dubuc, ph	1	1	0	0	0	0	0	0	.000
Bush, p	2	2	0	0	0	0	0	0	.000
Jones, p	1	1	0	0	0	0	0	0	.000
Miller, ph	1	1	0	0	0	0	0	0	.000
Totals	6	172	9	32	2	3	0	6	.186

CUBS

Player-position	G	AB	R	H	2B	3B	HR	RBI	BA
Hendrix, ph	2	1	0	1	0	0	0	0	1.000
Pick, 2b	6	18	2	7	1	0	0	0	.389
Merkle, 1b	6	18	1	5	0	0	0	1	.278
Flack, rf	6	19	2	5	0	0	0	0	.263
Mann, lf	6	22	0	5	2	0	0	2	.227
Tyler, p	3	5	0	1	0	0	0	2	.200
Hollocher, ss	6	21	2	4	0	1	0	1	.190
Paskert, cf	6	21	0	4	1	0	0	2	.190
Deal, 3b	6	17	0	3	0	0	0	0	.176
Killefer, c	6	17	2	2	1	0	0	2	.118
Zeider, ph-3b	2	0	0	0	0	0	0	0	.000
Wortman, 2b	1	1	0	0	0	0	0	0	.000
O'Farrell, ph-c ...	3	3	0	0	0	0	0	0	.000
McCabe, pr-ph ...	3	1	1	0	0	0	0	0	.000
Barber, ph	2	2	0	0	0	0	0	0	.000
Vaughn, p	3	10	0	0	0	0	0	0	.000
Douglas, p	1	0	0	0	0	0	0	0	.000
Totals	6	176	10	37	5	1	0	10	.210

COMPOSITE PITCHING AVERAGES

RED SOX

Pitcher	G	IP	H	R	ER	SO	BB	W	L	ERA
Mays	2	18	10	2	2	5	3	2	0	1.00
Ruth	2	17	13	2	2	4	7	2	0	1.06
Jones	1	9	7	3	3	5	5	0	1	3.00
Bush	2	9	7	3	3	0	3	0	1	3.00
Totals	6	53	37	10	10	14	18	4	2	1.70

CUBS

Pitcher	G	IP	H	R	ER	SO	BB	W	L	ERA
Douglas	1	1	1	1	0	0	0	0	1	0.00
Hendrix	1	1	0	0	0	0	0	0	0	0.00
Vaughn	3	27	17	3	3	17	5	1	2	1.00
Tyler	3	23	14	5	3	4	11	1	1	1.17
Totals	6	52	32	9	6	21	16	2	4	1.04

1946
AMERICAN LEAGUE CHAMPIONS
Manager: Joe Cronin

Pitchers: Jim Bagby Jr., Mace Brown, Bill Butland, Mel Deutsch, Joe Dobson, Clem Dreisewerd, Dave Ferriss, Mickey Harris, Randy Heflin, Tex Hughson, Earl Johnson, Bob Klinger, Mike Ryba, Charley Wagner, Jim Wilson and Bill Zuber. Catchers: Ed McGah, Roy Partee, Frank Pytlak and Hal Wagner. Infielders: Ernie Andres, Paul Campbell, Tom Carey, *Leon Culberson (4 games), Bobby Doerr, Don Gutteridge, Mike Higgins, Eddie Pellagrini, Johnny Pesky, Rip Russell, Ben Steiner and Rudy York. Outfielders: *Leon Culberson (49 games), Dom DiMaggio, Andy Gilbert, Johnny Lazor, George Metkovich, Wally Moses, Tom McBride and Ted Williams.

Trainer: Win Green. Bat boys: Frankie Kelley (home) and Don Fitzpatrick (visitors). Equipment managers: Johnny Orlando (home) and Vince Orlando (visitors).

*Played more than one position.

World Series

	W	L	Pct.
Cardinals	4	3	.571
Red Sox	3	4	.429

Oct. 6*	Red Sox (Johnson)	3	Cardinals (Pollet)	2	at St. Louis
Oct. 7	Cardinals (Brecheen)	3	Red Sox (Harris)	0	at St. Louis
Oct. 9	Red Sox (Ferriss)	4	Cardinals (Dickson)	0	at Boston
Oct. 10	Cardinals (Munger)	12	Red Sox (Hughson)	3	at Boston
Oct. 11	Red Sox (Dobson)	6	Cardinals (Brazle)	3	at Boston
Oct. 13	Cardinals (Brecheen)	4	Red Sox (Harris)	1	at St. Louis
Oct. 15	Cardinals (Brecheen)	4	Red Sox (Klinger)	3	at St. Louis

*10 innings.

Rick Burleson and ump don't see eye-to-eye. *(Boston Globe)*

1946 AMERICAN LEAGUE CHAMPIONS (*continued*)

SUNDAY, OCTOBER 6—AT ST. LOUIS

Red Sox	AB	R	H	O	A	E		Cardinals	AB	R	H	O	A	E
McBride, rf	5	0	1	1	0	1		Schoendienst, 2b	5	1	2	2	5	0
Moses, rf	0	0	0	1	0	0		Moore, cf	4	0	0	3	1	0
Pesky, ss	5	0	0	0	3	1		Musial, 1b	5	0	1	13	0	0
DiMaggio, cf	5	0	2	1	1	0		Slaughter, rf	4	0	1	3	0	0
Williams, lf	3	0	1	4	0	0		Kurowski, 3b	3	1	1	1	4	0
York, 1b	4	2	1	10	0	0		Garagiola, c	4	0	1	4	0	0
Doerr, 2b	4	0	1	4	4	0		Walker, lf	2	0	1	3	0	0
Higgins, 3b	4	0	2	2	0	0		dDusak, lf	1	0	0	0	0	0
aGutteridge	0	1	0	0	0	0		Marion, ss	3	0	0	1	3	0
Johnson, p	1	0	0	0	2	0		Pollet, p	4	0	0	0	0	0
H. Wagner, c	3	0	0	6	1	0								
bRussell, 3b	1	0	1	0	0	0								
Hughson, p	2	0	0	0	1	0								
cPartee, c	1	0	0	1	0	0								
Totals	38	3	9	30	12	2		Totals	35	2	7	30	13	0

```
Red Sox ................... 010  000  001  1—3
Cardinals ................. 000  001  010  0—2
```

aRan for Higgins in ninth and scored. bSingled for H. Wagner in ninth. cFanned for Hughson in ninth. dFlied out for Walker in ninth. Two-base hits—Musial, Garagiola. Three-base hit—Slaughter. Home run—York. Sacrifice hits—Marion, Moore. Runs batted in—Higgins, McBride, York, Musial, Garagiola. Stolen base—Schoendienst. Bases on balls—Off Pollet 4; off Hughson 2. Struck out—By Pollet 3; by Hughson 5; by Johnson 1. Hit by pitcher—By Pollet (York); by Hughson (Kurowski). Pitching record—Off Hughson, 7 hits, 2 runs in 8 innings; off Johnson, 0 hits, 0 runs in 2 innings. Earned runs—Boston 3, St. Louis 2. Left on bases—Boston 10, St. Louis 8. Winning pitcher—Johnson. Umpires—Ballanfant (N.L.), Hubbard (A.L.), Barlick (N.L.), Berry (A.L.). Time—2:39. Attendance—36,218.

MONDAY, OCTOBER 7—AT ST. LOUIS

Red Sox	AB	R	H	O	A	E		Cardinals	AB	R	H	O	A	E
McBride, rf	4	0	1	3	0	0		Schoendienst, 2b	3	0	0	2	3	0
Pesky, ss	4	0	0	3	2	0		Moore, cf	3	0	1	3	0	0
DiMaggio, cf	4	0	1	3	0	0		Musial, 1b	4	0	0	11	0	0
Williams, lf	4	0	0	1	0	0		Kurowski, 3b	4	0	1	1	1	0
York, 1b	2	0	0	6	2	0		Slaughter, rf	4	0	0	2	0	0
Doerr, 2b	4	0	1	4	5	0		Dusak, lf	2	0	1	1	0	0
Higgins, 3b	2	0	0	0	2	1		bSisler	1	0	0	0	0	0
Partee, c	2	0	0	1	0	0		Walker, lf	0	0	0	1	0	0
H. Wagner, c	1	0	0	2	0	0		Marion, ss	4	0	0	2	6	0
Harris, p	2	0	1	1	0	0		Rice, c	2	2	2	4	0	0
aCulberson	1	0	0	0	0	0		Brecheen, p	3	1	1	0	0	0
Dobson, p	0	0	0	0	0	0								
Totals	30	0	4	24	11	1		Totals	30	3	6	27	10	0

```
Red Sox ..................... 000  000  00  0—0
Cardinals ................... 001  020  00  X—3
```

aFlied out for Harris in eighth. bGrounded out for Dusak in eighth. Two-base hits—Rice, Dusak. Sacrifice hit—Schoendienst. Runs batted in—Brecheen, Moore, Musial. Double play—Marion and Musial. Bases on balls—Off Harris 3; off Brecheen 3. Struck out—By Harris 3; by Brecheen 4. Pitching record—Off Harris, 6 hits, 3 runs in 7 innings; off Dobson, 0 hits, 0 runs in 1 inning. Earned runs—St. Louis 2. Left on bases—Boston 6, St. Louis 7. Losing pitcher—Harris. Umpires—Hubbard (A.L.), Barlick (N.L.), Berry (A.L.), Ballanfant (N.L.). Time—1:56. Attendance—35,815.

WEDNESDAY, OCTOBER 9—AT BOSTON

Cardinals	AB	R	H	O	A	E		Red Sox	AB	R	H	O	A	E
Schoendienst, 2b	4	0	0	3	2	0		Moses, rf	3	0	0	2	0	0
Moore, cf	4	0	0	1	0	0		Pesky, ss	4	1	2	1	3	0
Musial, 1b	3	0	1	8	1	0		DiMaggio, cf	4	0	1	4	1	0
Slaughter, rf	4	0	1	4	0	0		Williams, lf	3	1	1	2	0	0
Kurowski, 3b	3	0	0	1	0	0		York, 1b	4	2	2	12	0	0
Garagiola, c	3	0	1	3	1	0		Doerr, 2b	4	0	2	2	8	0
Walker, lf	3	0	1	2	0	0		Higgins, 3b	3	0	0	1	0	0
Marion, ss	3	0	1	2	3	0		H. Wagner, c	3	0	0	3	0	0
Dickson, p	2	0	1	0	2	0		Ferriss, p	4	0	0	0	3	0
aSisler	1	0	0	0	0	0								
Wilks, p	0	0	0	0	1	0								
Totals	30	0	6	24	10	1		Totals	32	4	8	27	15	0

```
Cardinals ..................... 000  000  00  0—0
Red Sox ...................... 300  000  01  X—4
```

aForced Walker while batting for Dickson in eighth. Two-base hits—DiMaggio, Dickson, Doerr. Three-base hit—Musial. Home run—York. Sacrifice hit—H. Wagner. Runs batted in—York 3. Stolen base—Musial. Double plays—DiMaggio and Pesky; Pesky, Doerr and York. Bases on balls—Off Ferriss 1; off Dickson 3. Struck out—By Dickson 4; by Ferriss 2. Pitching record—Off Dickson, 6 hits, 3 runs in 7 innings; off Wilks, 2 hits, 1 run in one inning. Passed ball—Garagiola. Earned runs—Boston 3. Left on bases—St. Louis 4, Boston 8. Losing pitcher—Dickson. Umpires—Barlick (N.L.), Berry (A.L.), Ballanfant (N.L.), Hubbard (A.L.). Time—1:54. Attendance—34,500.

THURSDAY, OCTOBER 10—AT BOSTON

Cardinals	AB	R	H	O	A	E	Red Sox	AB	R	H	O	A	E
Schoendienst, 2b	6	1	1	1	4	0	Moses, rf	5	0	4	1	0	0
Moore, cf	4	1	1	3	0	0	Pesky, ss	5	0	0	3	2	1
Musial, 1b	5	1	1	6	1	0	DiMaggio, cf	4	1	0	3	1	0
Slaughter, rf.............	6	4	4	5	1	0	Williams, lf	3	1	1	0	1	0
Kurowski, 3b	5	2	4	2	0	0	York, 1b	3	0	1	9	1	0
Garagiola, c	5	1	4	4	4	0	Doerr, 2b	3	1	2	4	6	0
Walker, lf	2	1	1	3	0	0	Gutteridge, 2b	0	0	0	0	0	0
Marion, ss	4	1	3	2	1	1	Higgins, 3b	4	0	1	2	1	1
Munger, p	4	0	1	1	0	0	H. Wagner, c	4	0	0	5	1	0
							Hughson, p	0	0	0	0	0	1
							Bagby, p	1	0	0	0	1	0
							aMetkovich	1	0	0	0	0	0
							Zuber, p	0	0	0	0	0	0
							bMcBride	1	0	0	0	0	0
							Brown, p	0	0	0	0	0	0
							Ryba, p................	0	0	0	0	0	1
							Dreisewerd, p	0	0	0	0	0	0
							cCulberson	1	0	0	0	0	0
Totals	41	12	20	27	7	1	Totals	35	3	9	27	14	4

```
Cardinals .....................0 3 3   0 1 0   1 0 4—12
Red Sox .....................0 0 0   1 0 0   0 2 0— 3
```

aFlied out for Bagby in fifth. bBounced out for Zuber in seventh. cLined out for Dreisewerd in ninth. Two-base hits—Kurowski 2, Musial, York, Slaughter, Garagiola, Marion. Home runs—Slaughter, Doerr. Sacrifice hits—Marion, Moore, Munger, Walker. Runs batted in—Slaughter, Walker, Marion 3, Musial 2, Garagiola 3, York, Kurowski, Doerr 2. Double plays—Slaughter and Garagiola; Doerr, Pesky and York; Schoendienst and Musial; Pesky and Doerr. Bases on balls—Off Munger 3; off Bagby 1; off Zuber 1; off Brown 1; off Ryba 1. Struck out—By Hughson 1; by Bagby 1; by Zuber 1; by Munger 2. Pitching record—Off Hughson, 5 hits, 6 runs in 2 innings (pitched to three batters in third); off Bagby, 6 hits, 1 run in 3 innings; off Zuber, 3 hits, 1 run in 2 innings; off Brown, 4 hits, 3 runs in 1 inning (pitched to three batters in ninth); off Ryba 2 hits, 1 run in ⅔ inning; off DreiseWerd, 0 hits, 0 runs in ⅓ inning. Earned runs—St. Louis 8, Boston 1. Left on bases—St. Louis 10, Boston 8. Losing pitcher—Hughson. Umpires—Berry (A.L.), Ballanfant (N.L.), Hubbard (A.L.) and Barlick (N.L.). Time 2:31. Attendance—35,645.

FRIDAY, OCTOBER 11—AT BOSTON

Cardinals	AB	R	H	O	A	E	Red Sox	AB	R	H	O	A	E
Schoendienst, 2b	4	0	1	3	1	0	Gutteridge, 2b	5	0	2	0	2	0
Moore, cf	4	0	0	2	0	0	Pesky, ss	5	1	3	2	2	2
Musial, 1b	3	1	1	7	0	0	DiMaggio, cf	3	1	1	3	0	0
Slaughter, rf	2	0	0	0	0	0	Williams, lf	5	0	1	4	0	0
Dusak, lf	1	0	0	0	0	0	York, 1b	2	1	0	8	0	1
Kurowski, 3b	4	1	0	3	1	0	Higgins, 3b	4	1	1	0	1	0
Garagiola, c	4	1	0	7	1	0	Culberson, rf	3	1	2	2	0	0
Walker, lf-rf	4	0	2	1	0	0	Partee, c	3	1	1	8	1	0
Marion, ss	4	0	0	1	7	1	Dobson, p	3	0	0	0	1	0
Pollet, p	0	0	0	0	0	0							
Brazle, p	2	0	0	0	1	0							
aJones	1	0	0	0	0	0							
Beazley, p	0	0	0	0	1	0							
Totals	33	3	4	24	12	1	Totals	33	6	11	27	7	3

```
Cardinals .....................0 1 0   0 0 0   0 0 2—3
Red Sox .....................1 1 0   0 0 1   3 0 X—6
```

aFanned for Brazle in eighth. Two-base hits—Walker, Musial, DiMaggio, Higgins. Home run—Culberson. Sacrifice hits—Dobson, DiMaggio. Runs batted in—Walker 3, Williams, Gutteridge, Culberson, Higgins, Partee. Stolen bases—Slaughter, Culberson, Pesky. Double plays—Partee and Pesky; Marion, Schoendienst and Musial. Bases on balls—Off Brazle 6; off Dobson 1. Struck out—By Brazle 4; by Beazley 1; by Dobson 8. Hit by pitcher—By Dobson (Slaughter). Pitching record—Off Pollet, 3 hits, 1 run in ⅓ inning; off Brazle, 7 hits, 5 runs in 6⅔ innings; off Beazley, 1 hit, 0 runs in 1 inning. Earned runs—Boston 5, St. Louis 0. Left on bases—St. Louis 5, Boston 11. Wild pitch—Beazley. Losing pitcher—Brazle. Umpires—Ballanfant (N.L.), Hubbard (A.L.), Barlick (N.L.) and Berry (A.L.). Time—2:23. Attendance—35,982.

Yaz can bunt, too.

1946 AMERICAN LEAGUE CHAMPIONS (*continued*)

SUNDAY, OCTOBER 13—AT ST. LOUIS

Red Sox	AB	R	H	O	A	E		Cardinals	AB	R	H	O	A	E
Culberson, rf	4	0	0	5	0	0		Schoendienst, 2b	4	1	1	4	3	0
Pesky, ss	3	0	1	2	3	0		Moore, cf	4	0	1	2	0	0
DiMaggio, cf	4	0	1	5	0	0		Musial, 1b	4	1	1	9	0	0
Williams, lf	3	0	1	2	0	0		Kurowski, 3b	4	0	1	2	2	0
York, 1b	4	1	1	4	0	0		Slaughter, rf............	2	0	1	2	0	0
Doerr, 2b	3	0	1	1	1	0		Dusak, lf	0	0	0	0	0	1
Higgins, 3b	3	0	1	1	1	0		bWalker, lf	3	1	0	1	0	0
Partee, c	3	0	0	4	0	0		Marion, ss	4	0	2	2	1	0
Harris, p	1	0	0	0	0	0		Rice, c	3	0	1	5	1	0
Hughson, p	1	0	1	0	0	0		Brecheen, p	4	1	0	0	2	0
aMcBride	1	0	0	0	0	0								
Johnson, p	0	0	0	0	0	0								
Totals	30	1	7	24	5	0		Totals	32	4	8	27	10	0

```
Red Sox ......................000 000 1 0 0—1
Cardinals ....................003 000 0 1 X—4
```

aFouled out for Hughson in eighth. bLined out for Dusak in third and then played left field. Two-base hits—Schoendienst, Marion. Three-base hit—York. Runs batted in—Moore, Kurowski, Slaughter, Doerr, Marion. Double plays—Kurowski, Schoendienst and Musial 2; Brecheen, Schoendienst, Marion and Musial. Bases on balls—Off Brecheen 2; off Harris 1; off Hughson 1; off Johnson 2. Struck out—By Brecheen 6; by Harris 2; by Hughson 2. Pitching record—Off Harris, 5 hits, 3 runs in 2⅔ innings; off Hughson, 2 hits, 0 runs in 4⅓ innings; off Johnson, 1 hit, 1 run in 1 inning. Earned runs—Boston 1, St. Louis 4. Left on bases—Boston 4, St. Louis 8. Losing pitcher—Harris. Umpires—Hubbard (A.L.), Barlick (N.L.), Berry (A.L.) and Ballanfant (N.L.). Time—1:56. Attendance—35,768.

TUESDAY, OCTOBER 15—AT ST. LOUIS

Red Sox	AB	R	H	O	A	E		Cardinals	AB	R	H	O	A	E
Moses, rf	4	1	1	1	0	0		Schoendienst, 2b	4	0	2	2	3	0
Pesky, ss	4	0	1	2	1	0		Moore, cf	4	0	1	3	0	0
DiMaggio, cf	3	0	1	0	0	0		Musial, 1b	3	0	1	6	0	0
cCulberson, cf..........	0	0	0	0	0	0		Slaughter, rf............	3	1	1	4	0	0
Williams, lf	4	0	0	3	1	0		Kurowski, 3b	4	1	1	3	1	1
York, 1b	4	0	1	10	1	0		Garagiola, c	3	0	0	4	0	0
dCampbell	0	0	0	0	0	0		Rice, c	1	0	0	0	0	0
Doerr, 2b	4	0	2	3	7	0		Walker, lf	3	1	2	3	0	0
Higgins, 3b............	4	0	0	0	1	0		Marion, ss	2	0	0	2	1	0
H. Wagner, c	2	0	0	4	0	0		Dickson, p	3	1	1	0	1	0
aRussell	1	1	1	0	0	0		Brecheen, p	1	0	0	0	0	0
Partee, c	1	0	0	0	0	0								
Ferriss, p	2	0	0	0	0	0								
Dobson, p	0	0	0	0	1	0								
bMetkovich	1	1	1	0	0	0								
Klinger, p	0	0	0	1	0	0								
Johnson, p	0	0	0	0	0	0								
eMcBride	1	0	0	0	0	0								
Totals	35	3	8	24	12	0		Totals	31	4	9	27	6	1

```
Red Sox ......................100 000 0 2 0—3
Cardinals ....................010 020 0 1 X—4
```

aSingled for H. Wagner in eighth. bDoubled for Dobson in eighth. cRan for DiMaggio in eighth. dRan for York in ninth. eRolled out for Johnson in ninth. Two-base hits—Musial, Kurowski, Dickson, DiMaggio, Metkovich, Walker. Sacrifice hit—Marion. Runs batted in—DiMaggio 3, Walker 2, Dickson, Schoendienst. Bases on balls—Off Ferriss 1; off Dobson 2; off Klinger 1; off Dickson 1. Struck out—By Ferriss 1; by Dobson 2; by Dickson 3; by Brecheen 1. Pitching record—Off Ferriss, 7 hits, 4 runs in 4⅓ innings; off Dobson, 0 hits, 0 runs in 2⅔ innings; off Klinger, 2 hits, 1 run in ⅔ inning; off Johnson, 0 hits, 0 runs in ⅓ inning; off Dickson, 5 hits, 3 runs in 7 innings (pitched to two batters in eighth); off Brecheen, 3 hits, 0 runs in 2 innings. Earned runs—Boston 3, St. Louis 4. Left on bases—Boston 6, St. Louis 8. Winning pitcher—Brecheen. Losing pitcher—Klinger. Umpires—Barlick (N.L.), Berry (A.L.), Ballanfant (N.L.) and Hubbard (A.L.). Time—2:17. Attendance—36,143.

Curt Gowdy (left), Mel Parnell (center) and Ned Martin broadcast a 1965 game from bleachers for different perspective.

COMPOSITE BATTING AVERAGES

RED SOX

Player-position	G	AB	R	H	2B	3B	HR	RBI	BA
Russell, ph-3b	2	2	1	2	0	0	0	0	1.000
Metkovitch, ph	2	2	1	1	1	0	0	0	.500
Moses, rf	4	12	1	5	0	0	0	0	.417
Doerr, 2b	6	22	1	9	1	0	1	3	.409
Gutteridge, pr-2b ..	3	5	1	2	0	0	0	1	.400
Harris, p	3	3	0	1	0	0	0	0	.333
Hughson, p	3	3	0	1	0	0	0	0	.333
York, 1b	7	23	6	6	1	1	2	5	.261
DiMaggio, cf	7	27	2	7	3	0	0	3	.259
Pesky, ss	7	30	2	7	0	0	0	0	.233
C'son, ph-rf-cf-pr ..	5	9	1	2	0	0	1	1	.222
Higgins, 3b	7	24	1	5	1	0	0	2	.208
Williams, lf	7	25	2	5	0	0	0	1	.200
McBride, rf-ph	5	12	0	2	0	0	0	1	.167
Partee, ph-c	5	10	1	1	0	0	0	1	.100
H. Wagner, c	5	13	0	0	0	0	0	0	.000
Johnson, p	3	1	0	0	0	0	0	0	.000
Dobson, p	3	3	0	0	0	0	0	0	.000
Ferriss, p	2	6	0	0	0	0	0	0	.000
Bagby, p	1	1	0	0	0	0	0	0	.000
Zuber, p	1	0	0	0	0	0	0	0	.000
Brown, p	1	0	0	0	0	0	0	0	.000
Ryba, p	1	0	0	0	0	0	0	0	.000
Dreisewerd, p	1	0	0	0	0	0	0	0	.000
Klinger, p	1	0	0	0	0	0	0	0	.000
Campbell, pr	1	0	0	0	0	0	0	0	.000
Totals	7	233	20	56	7	1	4	18	.240

CARDINALS

Player-position	G	AB	R	H	2B	3B	HR	RBI	BA
Rice, c	3	6	2	3	1	0	0	0	.500
Walker, lf-rf-ph ...	7	17	3	7	2	0	0	6	.412
Dickson, p	2	5	1	2	2	0	0	1	.400
Slaughter, rf	7	25	5	8	1	1	1	2	.320
Garagiola, c	5	19	2	6	2	0	0	4	.316
Kurowski, 3b	7	27	5	8	3	0	0	2	.296
Dusak, ph-lf	4	4	0	1	1	0	0	0	.250
Marion, ss	7	24	1	6	2	0	0	4	.250
Munger, p	1	4	0	1	0	0	0	0	.250
Schoendienst, 2b ..	7	30	3	7	1	0	0	1	.233
Musial, 1b	7	27	3	6	4	1	0	4	.222
Moore, cf	7	27	1	4	0	0	0	2	.148
Brecheen, p	3	8	2	1	0	0	0	1	.125
Pollet, p	2	4	0	0	0	0	0	0	.000
Wilks, p	1	0	0	0	0	0	0	0	.000
Brazle, p	1	2	0	0	0	0	0	0	.000
Beazley, p	1	0	0	0	0	0	0	0	.000
Jones, ph	1	1	0	0	0	0	0	0	.000
Sisler, ph	2	2	0	0	0	0	0	0	.000
Totals	7	232	28	60	19	2	1	27	.259

COMPOSITE PITCHING AVERAGES

RED SOX

Pitcher	G	IP	H	R	ER	SO	BB	W	L	ERA
Dobson	3	12⅔	4	3	0	10	3	1	0	0.00
Ryba	1	⅔	2	1	0	0	1	0	0	0.00
Dreisewerd ...	1	⅓	0	0	0	0	0	0	0	0.00
Ferriss	2	13⅓	13	3	3	4	2	1	0	2.03
Johnson	3	3⅓	1	1	1	1	2	1	0	2.75
Bagby	1	3	6	1	1	1	1	0	0	3.00
Hughson	3	14⅓	14	8	5	8	3	0	1	3.14
Zuber	1	2	3	1	1	1	1	0	0	4.50
Harris	2	9⅔	11	6	5	5	4	0	2	4.66
Klinger	1	⅔	2	1	1	0	1	0	1	13.50
Brown	1	1	4	3	3	0	1	0	0	27.00
Totals	7	61	60	28	20	30	19	3	4	2.95

CARDINALS

Pitcher	G	IP	H	R	ER	SO	BB	W	L	ERA
Wilks	1	1	2	1	0	0	0	0	0	0.00
Beazley	1	1	1	0	0	1	0	0	0	0.00
Brecheen	3	20	14	1	1	11	5	3	0	0.45
Munger	1	9	9	3	1	2	3	1	0	1.00
Pollet	2	10⅓	12	4	4	3	4	0	1	3.48
Dickson	2	14	11	6	6	7	4	0	1	3.86
Brazle	1	6⅔	7	5	4	4	6	0	1	5.40
Totals	7	62	56	20	16	28	22	4	3	2.32

1948
TIED FOR FIRST PLACE
WITH CLEVELAND INDIANS
Manager: Joe McCarthy

Pitchers: Earl Caldwell, Cot Deal, Joe Dobson, Harry Dorish, Dave Ferriss, Denny Galehouse, Mickey Harris, Tex Hughson, Earl Johnson, Ellis Kinder, Jack Kramer, Windy McCall, Maurice McDermott, Mike Palm, Mel Parnell and Chuck Stobbs. Catchers: Babe Martin, Matt Batts and Birdie Tebbetts. Infielders: Bobby Doerr, Billy Goodman, Billy Hitchcock, Jake Jones, Johnny Pesky, *Stan Spence (14 games), Vern Stephens and Lou Stringer. Outfielders: Dom DiMaggio, Sam Mele, Wally Moses, *Stan Spence (92 games) and Ted Williams. Pinch-hitters: John Ostrowski, Neill Sheridan and Tom Wright.

Trainer: Ed Froelich. Bat Boys: Frankie Kelley (home) and Don Fitzpatrick (visitors). Equipment managers: Johnny Orlando (home) and Vince Orlando (visitors).

*Played more than one position.

1948 TIED FOR FIRST PLACE (*continued*)

One-Game Playoff
(to decide American League pennant)
MONDAY, OCTOBER 4 AT BOSTON

Indians	AB	R	H	O	A	E		Red Sox	AB	R	H	O	A	E
Mitchell, lf	5	0	1	1	0	0		DiMaggio, cf	4	0	0	3	0	0
Clark, 1b	2	0	0	5	0	0		Pesky, 3b	4	1	1	3	4	0
Robinson, 1b	2	1	1	9	0	0		Williams, lf	4	1	1	3	0	1
Boudreau, ss	4	3	4	3	5	0		Stephens, ss	4	0	1	2	4	0
Gordon, 2b	4	1	1	2	3	1		Doerr, 2b	4	1	1	5	2	0
Keltner, 3b	5	1	3	0	6	0		Spence, rf	1	0	0	1	0	0
Doby, cf	5	1	2	1	0	0		aHitchcock	0	0	0	0	0	0
Kennedy, rf	2	0	0	0	0	0		bWright	0	0	0	0	0	0
Hegan, c	3	1	0	6	1	0		Goodman, 1b	3	0	0	7	1	0
Bearden, p	3	0	1	0	2	0		Tebbetts, c	4	0	1	3	1	0
								Galehouse, p	0	0	0	0	1	0
								Kinder, p	2	0	0	0	1	0
Totals	35	8	13	27	17	1		Totals	30	3	5	27	14	1

```
Indians ................... 1 0 0   4 1 0   0 1 1—8**
Red Sox ................... 1 0 0   0 0 2   0 0 0—3
```

Red Sox	IP	H	R	ER	BB	SO
Galehouse* (L)	3	5	4	4	1	1
Kinder	6	8	4	3	3	2

*Pitched to three batters in fourth.

Indians	IP	H	R	ER	BB	SO
Bearden (W)	9	5	3	1	5	6

aWalked for Spence in ninth. bRan for Hitchcock in ninth. Runs batted in—Keltner 3, Boudreau 2, Doerr 2, Stephens, Hegan. Two-base hits—Doby 2, Keltner, Pesky. Home runs—Boudreau 2, Keltner, Doerr. Sacrifices—Kennedy 2, Robinson. Double plays—Hegan and Boudreau; Gordon, Boudreau and Robinson; Bearden, Gordon and Robinson; Stephens, Doerr and Goodman, 2. Left on base—Indians 7, Red Sox 5. Wild pitch—Kinder. Umpires—McGowen, Summers, Rommel and Berry. Time—2:24. Attendance—33,957.

**Indians thus won the American League pennant and went on to win the World Championship by defeating the Boston Braves in the World Series, four games to two.

1967
AMERICAN LEAGUE CHAMPIONS
Manager: Dick Williams

Pitchers: Gary Bell, Dennis Bennett, Darrell Brandon, Ken Brett, Galen Cisco, Hank Fischer, Bill Landis, Jim Lonborg, Sparky Lyle, Don McMahon, Dave Morehead, Dan Osinski, Billy Rohr, Jose Santiago, Lee Stange, Jerry Stephenson, Gary Waslewski and John Wyatt. Catchers: Russ Gibson, Elston Howard, Mike Ryan, *George Thomas (1 game) and Bob Tillman. Infielders: Jerry Adair, Mike Andrews, *Don Demeter (1 game), *Joe Foy (118 games), *Ken Harrelson (1 game), Dalton Jones, Rico Petrocelli, Ken Poulsen, George Scott, *Norm Siebern (13 games), *Reggie Smith (6 games) and *George Thomas (3 games). Outfielders: Tony Conigliaro, *Don Demeter (12 games), *Joe Foy (1 game), *Ken Harrelson (23 games), Jim Landis, *Norm Siebern (1 game), *Reggie Smith (144 games), Jose Tartabull, *George Thomas (43 games) and Carl Yastrzemski.

Trainer: Buddy LeRoux. Bat boys: Keith Rosenfield and Jimmy Jackson. Equipment managers: Don Fitzpatrick (home) and Vince Orlando (visitors).

*Played more than one position.

WORLD SERIES

	W	L	Pct.
Cardinals, N.L.	4	3	.571
Red Sox, A.L.	3	4	.429

Oct. 4	Cardinals (Gibson)	2	Red Sox (Santiago)	1	at Boston
Oct. 5	Red Sox (Lonborg)	5	Cardinals (Hughes)	0	at Boston
Oct. 7	Cardinals (Briles)	5	Red Sox (Bell)	2	at St. Louis
Oct. 8	Cardinals (Gibson)	6	Red Sox (Santiago)	0	at St. Louis
Oct. 9	Red Sox (Lonborg)	3	Cardinals (Carlton)	1	at St. Louis
Oct. 11	Red Sox (Wyatt)	8	Cardinals (Lamabe)	4	at Boston
Oct. 12	Cardinals (Gibson)	7	Red Sox (Lonborg)	2	at Boston

WEDNESDAY, OCTOBER 4—AT BOSTON

Cardinals	AB	R	H	O	A	E	Red Sox	AB	R	H	O	A	E
Brock, lf	4	2	4	2	0	0	Adair, 2b	4	0	0	2	3	0
Flood, cf	5	0	1	2	0	0	Jones, 3b	4	0	1	2	2	0
Maris, rf	4	0	1	3	0	0	Yastrzemski, lf	4	0	0	4	1	0
Cepeda, 1b	4	0	0	6	0	0	Harrelson, rf	3	0	0	0	0	0
McCarver, c	3	0	0	11	2	0	Wyatt, p	0	0	0	0	0	0
Shannon, 3b	4	0	2	0	1	0	cFoy	1	0	0	0	0	0
Javier, 2b	4	0	2	1	1	0	Scott, 1b	3	0	2	8	0	0
Maxvill, ss	2	0	0	2	2	0	Petrocelli, ss	3	0	0	0	0	0
B. Gibson, p	4	0	0	0	0	0	dAndrews	1	0	0	0	0	0
							Smith, cf	3	0	1	1	0	0
							R. Gibson, c	2	0	0	8	0	0
							aSiebern, rf	1	0	1	0	0	0
							bTartabull, rf	0	0	0	1	0	0
							Santiago, p	2	1	1	0	0	0
							Howard, c	0	0	0	1	0	0
Totals	34	2	10	27	6	0	Totals	31	1	6	27	6	0

```
Cardinals .................... 001 000 100—2
Red Sox ..................... 001 000 000—1
```

aAt bat for R. Gibson when side was retired in seventh. bRan for Siebern in eighth. cGrounded out for Wyatt in ninth. dFlied out for Petrocelli in ninth. Runs batted in—Maris 2, Santiago. Two-base hits—Flood, Scott. Home run—Santiago. Stolen bases—Brock 2. Sacrifice hit—Howard. Double plays—Jones and Scott; Jones, Adair and Scott. Left on bases—St. Louis 10, Boston 5. Earned runs—St. Louis 2, Boston 1. Bases on balls—Off B. Gibson 1, off Santiago 3, off Wyatt 2. Struck out—By B. Gibson 10, by Santiago 5, by Wyatt 1. Pitching records—Off Santiago 10 hits and 2 runs in 7 innings; off Wyatt 0 hits and 0 runs in 2 innings. Balk—Wyatt. Passed ball—R. Gibson. Winning pitcher—B. Gibson. Losing pitcher—Santiago. Umpires—Stevens (A.L.), Barlick (N.L.), Umont (A.L.), Donatelli (N.L.), Runge (A.L.) and Pryor (N.L.). Time 2:22. Attendance—34,796.

THURSDAY, OCTOBER 5—AT BOSTON

Cardinals	AB	R	H	O	A	E	Red Sox	AB	R	H	O	A	E
Brock, lf	4	0	0	4	0	0	Tartabull, rf	4	1	0	2	0	0
Flood, cf	3	0	0	3	0	0	Jones, 3b	5	1	2	0	3	0
Maris, rf	3	0	0	4	0	0	Yastrzemski, lf	4	2	3	3	0	0
Cepeda, 1b	3	0	0	1	1	0	Scott, 1b	4	1	1	12	1	0
McCarver, c	3	0	0	9	0	0	Smith, cf	3	0	0	1	0	0
Shannon, 3b	3	0	0	1	1	1	Adair, 2b	4	0	2	1	4	0
Javier, 2b	3	0	1	0	1	0	Petrocelli, ss	2	0	1	3	5	0
Maxvill, ss	2	0	0	1	0	0	Howard, c	3	0	0	4	0	0
aTolan	1	0	0	0	0	0	Lonborg, p	4	0	0	1	0	0
Bressoud, ss	0	0	0	0	0	0							
Hughes, p	2	0	0	1	0	0							
Willis, p	0	0	0	0	0	0							
Hoerner, p	0	0	0	0	0	0							
Lamabe, p	0	0	0	0	0	0							
bRicketts	1	0	0	0	0	0							
Totals	28	0	1	24	3	1	Totals	33	5	9	27	13	0

```
Cardinals ..................... 000 000 00 0—0
Red Sox ..................... 000 101 30 X—5
```

aGrounded out for Maxvill in eighth. bPopped out for Lamabe in ninth. Runs batted in—Yastrzemski 4, Petrocelli. Two-base hit—Javier. Home runs—Yastrzemski 2. Stolen base—Adair. Sacrifice fly—Petrocelli. Left on bases—St. Louis 2, Boston 11. Earned runs—Boston 4. Bases on balls—Off Hughes 3, off Willis 2, off Hoerner 1, off Lonborg 1. Struck out—By Hughes 5, by Willis 1, by Lamabe 2, by Lonborg 4. Pitching records—Off Hughes 4 hits and 2 runs in 5⅓ innings; off Willis 1 hit and 2 runs in ⅔ inning (pitched to two batters in seventh); off Hoerner 2 hits and 1 run in ⅔ inning; off Lamabe 2 hits and 0 runs in 1⅓ innings. Winning pitcher—Lonborg. Losing pitcher—Hughes. Umpires—Barlick (N.L.), Umont (A.L.), Donatelli (N.L.), Runge (A.L.), Pryor (N.L.) and Stevens (A.L.). Time—2:24. Attendance—35,188.

Dwight Evans fields ball after George Scott (on bottom) and Jerry Remy collide. (Boston Globe)

1967 AMERICAN LEAGUE CHAMPIONS (*continued*)

SATURDAY, OCTOBER 7—AT ST. LOUIS

Red Sox	AB	R	H	O	A	E		Cardinals	AB	R	H	O	A	E
Tartabull, rf	4	0	0	3	0	0		Brock, lf	4	2	2	2	0	0
Jones, 3b	4	0	3	2	1	0		Flood, cf	4	0	1	3	0	0
Yastrzemski, lf	3	0	0	0	1	0		Maris, rf	4	1	2	0	0	0
Scott, 1b	4	0	0	8	1	0		Cepeda, 1b	4	0	1	13	0	0
Smith, cf	4	1	2	2	0	0		McCarver, c	4	1	1	5	1	0
Adair, 2b	4	0	0	2	2	0		Shannon, 3b	3	1	2	2	2	0
Petrocelli, ss	3	0	0	1	5	0		Javier, 2b	3	0	1	0	6	0
Howard, c	3	0	1	5	0	0		Maxvill, ss	3	0	0	2	4	0
Bell, p	0	0	0	0	1	0		Briles, p	3	0	0	0	2	0
aThomas	1	0	0	0	0	0								
Waslewski, p	0	0	0	1	0	0								
bAndrews	1	1	1	0	0	0								
Stange, p	0	0	0	0	0	1								
cFoy	1	0	0	0	0	0								
Osinski, p	0	0	0	0	0	0								
Totals	32	2	7	24	11	1		Totals	32	5	10	27	15	0

```
Red Sox .....................000  001  10 0—2
Cardinals ...................120  001  01 X—5
```

aStruck out for Bell in third. bSingled for Waslewski in sixth. cGrounded out for Stange in eighth. Runs batted in—Jones, Smith, Flood, Maris, Cepeda, Shannon 2. Two-base hit—Cepeda. Three-base hit—Brock. Home runs—Shannon, Smith. Double plays—Bell, Petrocelli and Scott; Javier, Maxvill and Cepeda. Left on bases—Boston 4, St. Louis 3. Earned runs—Boston 2, St. Louis 4. Bases on balls—None. Struck out—By Bell 1, by Waslewski 3, by Briles 4. Pitching record—Off Bell 5 hits and 3 runs in 2 innings; off Waslewski 0 hits and 0 runs in 3 innings; off Stange 3 hits and 1 run in 2 innings; off Osinski 2 hits and 1 run in 1 inning. Hit by pitcher—By Briles (Yastrzemski). Winning pitcher—Briles. Losing pitcher—Bell. Umpires—Umont (A.L.), Donatelli (N.L.), Runge (A.L.), Pryor (N.L.), Stevens (A.L.), Barlick (N.L.). Time 2:15. Attendance—54,575.

SUNDAY, OCTOBER 8—AT ST. LOUIS

Red Sox	AB	R	H	O	A	E		Cardinals	AB	R	H	O	A	E
Tartabull, rf	4	0	2	1	0	0		Brock, lf	4	1	2	2	0	0
Jones, 3b	4	0	0	0	2	0		Flood, cf	4	1	1	3	0	0
Yastrzemski, lf	4	0	2	3	0	0		Maris, rf	4	1	1	2	0	0
Scott, 1b	4	0	1	9	0	0		Cepeda, 1b	4	1	1	11	1	0
Smith, cf	3	0	0	3	0	0		McCarver, c	3	1	1	7	0	0
Adair, 2b	4	0	0	2	2	0		Shannon, 3b	3	1	0	0	2	0
Petrocelli, ss	3	0	0	2	4	0		Javier, 2b	4	0	2	0	2	0
Howard, c	2	0	0	0	0	0		Maxvill, ss	3	0	1	0	2	0
Morehead, p	0	0	0	0	0	0		Gibson, p	3	0	0	2	2	0
bSiebern	1	0	0	0	0	0								
Brett, p	0	0	0	0	0	0								
Santiago, p	0	0	0	0	0	0								
Bell, p	0	0	0	0	0	0								
aFoy	1	0	0	0	0	0								
Stephenson, p	0	0	0	0	0	0								
Ryan, c	2	0	0	4	0	0								
Totals	32	0	5	24	8	0		Totals	32	6	9	27	9	0

```
Red Sox .....................000  000  00 0—0
Cardinals ...................402  000  00 X—6
```

aStruck out for Bell in third. bFlied out for Morehead in eighth. Runs batted in—Maris 2, McCarver 2, Javier, Maxvill. Two-base hits—Maris, Cepeda, Brock, Javier, Yastrzemski. Stolen base—Brock. Sacrifice fly—McCarver. Left on bases—Boston 6, St. Louis 6. Bases on balls—Off Stephenson 1, off Morehead 1, off Brett 1, off Gibson 1. Struck out—By Morehead 2, by Brett 1, by Gibson 6. Pitching record—Off Santiago 6 hits and 4 runs in ⅔ inning, off Bell 0 hits and 0 runs in 1⅓ innings, off Stephenson 3 hits and 2 runs in 2 innings, off Morehead 0 hits and 0 runs in 3 innings, off Brett 0 hits and 0 runs in 1 inning. Wild pitch—Stephenson. Winning pitcher—Gibson. Losing pitcher—Santiago. Umpires—Donatelli (N.L.), Runge (A.L.), Pryor (N.L.), Stevens (A.L.), Barlick (N.L.), Umont (A.L.). Time—2:05. Attendance—54,575.

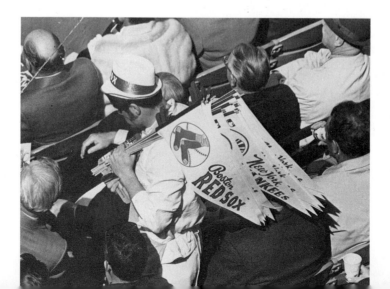

Tom Yawkey loved to talk baseball.

MONDAY, OCTOBER 9—AT ST. LOUIS

Red Sox	AB	R	H	O	A	E
Foy, 3b	5	1	1	2	4	0
Andrews, 2b	3	0	1	1	2	0
Yastrzemski, lf	3	0	1	2	0	0
Harrelson, rf	3	0	1	1	0	0
Tartabull, rf	0	0	0	0	0	0
Scott, 1b	3	1	0	14	0	0
Smith, cf	4	1	1	1	0	0
Petrocelli, ss	3	0	0	1	2	1
Howard, c	4	0	1	5	0	0
Lonborg, p	4	0	0	0	2	0
Totals	32	3	6	27	10	1

Cardinals	AB	R	H	O	A	E
Brock, lf	4	0	0	0	0	0
Flood, cf	4	0	0	2	0	0
Maris, rf	4	1	2	3	0	1
Cepeda, 1b	4	0	0	5	0	0
McCarver, c	3	0	0	9	1	0
Shannon, 3b	3	0	0	1	3	1
Javier, 2b	3	0	0	4	3	0
Maxvill, ss	2	0	1	3	4	0
bRicketts	1	0	0	0	0	0
Willis, p	0	0	0	0	0	0
Lamabe, p	0	0	0	0	1	0
Carlton, p	1	0	0	0	0	0
aTolan	1	0	0	0	0	0
Washburn, p	0	0	0	0	1	0
cGagliano	1	0	0	0	0	0
Bressoud, ss	0	0	0	0	0	0
Totals	31	1	3	27	13	2

```
Red Sox .......................001  000  002—3
Cardinals .....................000  000  001—1
```

aStruck out for Carlton in sixth. bGrounded out for Maxvill in eighth. cPopped out for Washburn in eighth. Runs batted in—Harrelson, Howard, Maris. Two-base hits—Yastrzemski, Smith. Home run—Maris. Sacrifice hit—Andrews. Double plays—Javier, Maxvill and Cepeda; McCarver, Javier, McCarver, Shannon, Lamabe and McCarver. Left on bases—Boston 7, St. Louis 3. Earned runs—Boston 1, St. Louis 1. Bases on balls—Off Carlton 2, off Willis 2. Struck out—By Lonborg 4, by Carlton 5, by Washburn 2, by Lamabe 2. Pitching record—Off Carlton 3 hits and 1 run in 6 innings, off Washburn 1 hit and 0 runs in 2 innings, off Willis 1 hit and 2 runs in 0 inning (pitched to three batters in ninth), off Lamabe 1 hit and 0 runs in 1 inning. Wild pitch—Carlton. Winning pitcher—Lonborg. Losing pitcher—Carlton. Umpires—Runge (A.L.), Pryor (N.L.), Stevens (A.L.), Barlick (N.L.), Umont (A.L.), Donatelli (N.L.). Time—2:20. Attendance—54,575.

WEDNESDAY, OCTOBER 11—AT BOSTON

Cardinals	AB	R	H	O	A	E
Brock, lf	5	2	2	2	0	0
Flood, cf	5	0	1	2	0	0
Maris, rf	4	0	2	2	0	0
Cepeda, 1b	5	0	1	10	0	0
McCarver, c	3	0	0	2	0	0
Shannon, 3b	4	0	1	1	4	0
Javier, 2b	4	1	1	3	3	0
Maxvill, ss	3	0	0	2	2	0
Hughes, p	1	0	0	0	0	0
Willis, p	0	0	0	0	0	0
aSpiezio	1	0	0	0	0	0
Briles, p	0	0	0	0	2	0
bTolan	0	1	0	0	0	0
Lamabe, p	0	0	0	0	0	0
Hoerner, p	0	0	0	0	0	0
Jaster, p	0	0	0	0	0	0
Washburn, p	0	0	0	0	0	0
eRicketts	1	0	0	0	0	0
Woodeshick, p	0	0	0	0	1	0
Totals	36	4	8	24	12	0

Red Sox	AB	R	H	O	A	E
Foy, 3b	4	1	1	3	3	0
Andrews, 2b	5	1	2	0	2	0
Yastrzemski, lf	4	2	3	2	0	0
Harrelson, rf	3	0	0	1	0	0
Tartabull, rf	0	0	0	0	0	0
dAdair	0	0	0	0	0	0
Bell, p	0	0	0	0	1	0
Scott, 1b	4	0	1	10	1	0
Smith, cf	4	1	2	4	0	0
Petrocelli, ss	3	2	2	1	3	1
Howard, c	4	0	0	4	0	0
Waslewski, p	1	0	0	1	0	0
Wyatt, p	0	0	0	0	0	0
cJones	1	1	1	0	0	0
Thomas, rf	1	0	0	1	0	0
Totals	34	8	12	27	10	1

```
Cardinals .....................002  000  20 0—4
Red Sox .......................010  300  40 X—8
```

aGrounded out for Willis in fifth. bWalked for Briles in seventh. cSingled for Wyatt in seventh. dHit sacrifice fly for Tartabull in seventh. eFlied out for Washburn in eighth. Runs batted in—Brock 3, Flood, Foy, Andrews, Yastrzemski, Adair, Smith 2, Petrocelli 2. Two-base hits—Javier, Foy, Shannon. Home runs—Petrocelli 2, Yastrzemski, Smith, Brock. Stolen base—Brock. Sacrifice hit—Foy. Sacrifice fly—Adair. Left on bases—St. Louis 9, Boston 7. Earned runs—St. Louis 4, Boston 8. Bases on balls—Off Briles 1, off Washburn 1, off Waslewski 2, off Wyatt 1, off Bell 1. Struck out—By Hughes 2, by Waslewski 4. Pitching record—Off Hughes 5 hits and 4 runs in 3⅔ innings, off Willis 0 hits and 0 runs in ⅓ inning, off Briles 0 hits and 0 runs in 2 innings, off Lamabe 2 hits and 2 runs in ⅓ inning, off Hoerner 2 hits and 0 runs in 0 inning (pitched to two batters in seventh), off Jaster 2 hits and 0 runs in ⅓ inning, off Washburn 0 hits and 0 runs in ⅓ inning, off Woodeshick 1 hit and 0 runs in 1 inning, off Waslewski 4 hits and 2 runs in 5⅓ innings, off Wyatt 1 hit and 2 runs in 1⅔ innings, off Bell 3 hits and 0 runs in 2 innings. Hit by pitcher—By Briles (Waslewski). Winning pitcher—Wyatt. Losing pitcher—Lamabe. Umpires—Pryor (N.L.), Stevens (A.L.), Barlick (N.L.), Umont (A.L.), Donatelli (N.L.), Runge (A.L.). Time—2:48. Attendance—35,188.

1975 AMERICAN LEAGUE CHAMPIONS (*continued*)

SUNDAY, OCTOBER 5—AT BOSTON

A's	AB	R	H	O	A	E
North, cf	4	0	0	0	0	0
Campaneris, ss	3	0	0	1	6	0
Bando, 3b	4	1	4	0	3	0
Jackson, rf	4	1	2	1	1	0
Tenace, 1b-c	4	0	0	11	1	0
Rudi, lf	4	1	2	1	0	0
Washington, dh	4	0	2	0	0	0
Garner, 2b	2	0	0	4	2	0
Harper, ph	0	0	0	0	0	0
Holt, 1b	1	0	0	1	2	0
Fosse, c	2	0	0	3	0	0
Williams, ph	1	0	0	0	0	0
Martinez, 2b	0	0	0	1	0	0
Tovar, ph	1	0	0	0	0	0
Blue, p	0	0	0	0	0	0
Todd, p	0	0	0	0	0	0
Fingers, p	0	0	0	1	0	0
Totals	34	3	10	24	15	0

Red Sox	AB	R	H	O	A	E
Beniquez, dh	4	1	1	0	0	0
Doyle, 2b	3	1	1	2	1	0
Yastrzemski, lf	3	2	2	2	1	0
Fisk, c	4	1	2	4	0	0
Lynn, cf	4	0	2	4	1	0
Petrocelli, 3b	4	1	1	2	3	0
Evans, rf	3	0	0	1	0	0
Cooper, 1b	3	0	2	11	0	0
Burleson, ss	2	0	1	1	6	0
Cleveland, p	0	0	0	0	1	0
Moret, p	0	0	0	0	0	0
Drago, p	0	0	0	0	0	0
Totals	30	6	12	27	13	0

```
A's ...................... 200 100 00 0—3
Red Sox .................. 000 301 11 X—6
```

A's	IP	H	R	ER	BB	SO
Blue*	3	6	3	3	0	2
Todd**	1	1	0	0	0	0
Fingers (L)	4	5	3	3	1	3

*Pitched to four batters in fourth.
**Pitched to one batter in fifth.

Red Sox	IP	H	R	ER	BB	SO
Cleveland*	5	7	3	3	1	2
Moret** (W)	1	1	0	0	1	0
Drago (S)	3	2	0	0	0	2

*Pitched to one batter in sixth.
**Pitched to one batter in seventh.

Runs batted in—Yastrzemski 2, Jackson 2, Fisk, Lynn, Petrocelli, Washington. Two-base hits—Bando 2, Rudi 2, Cooper 2, Fisk, Yastrzemski, Washington. Home runs—Jackson, Yastrzemski, Petrocelli. Sacrifice hits—Burleson, Doyle. Double plays—A's 4, Red Sox 2. Left on base—A's 6, Red Sox 3. Wild pitch—Drago. Umpires—DiMuro, Kunkel, Luciano, Evans. Morgenweck and Denkinger. Time—2:27. Attendance—35,578.

TUESDAY, OCTOBER 7—AT OAKLAND

Red Sox	AB	R	H	O	A	E
Beniquez, dh	4	0	0	0	0	0
Doyle, 2b	5	1	2	3	6	1
Yastrzemski, lf	4	1	2	2	1	0
Fisk, c	4	1	2	2	0	0
Lynn, cf	3	1	1	1	6	0
Petrocelli, 3b	4	0	1	1	0	0
Evans, rf	3	0	0	2	0	0
Cooper, 1b	1	0	1	11	1	0
Burleson, ss	4	1	2	2	6	0
Wise, p	0	0	0	2	3	0
Drago, p	0	0	0	1	1	0
Totals	35	5	11	27	18	1

A's	AB	R	H	O	A	E
Campaneris, ss	4	0	0	0	2	0
Washington, lf	4	1	1	0	0	1
Bando, 3b	4	0	2	2	4	0
Jackson, rf	4	0	2	2	0	0
Rudi, 1b	4	0	0	11	1	0
Williams, dh	4	0	0	0	0	0
Tenace, c	2	0	0	4	0	0
North, cf	3	0	0	4	1	0
Garner, 2b	1	0	0	1	1	0
Tovar, ph-2b	1	2	1	2	2	1
Martinez, 2b	0	0	0	0	0	0
Holt, ph	1	0	0	0	0	0
Holtzman, p	0	0	0	0	0	0
Todd, p	0	0	0	0	0	0
Lindblad, p	0	0	0	1	4	0
Totals	32	3	6	27	15	2

```
Red Sox .................... 000 130 010—5
A's ........................ 000 001 020—3
```

Red Sox	IP	H	R	ER	BB	SO
Wise (W)	7⅓	6	3	2	3	2
Drago (S)	1⅔	0	0	0	1	0

A's	IP	H	R	ER	BB	SO
Holtzman (L)	4⅔	7	4	3	0	3
Todd*	0	1	0	0	0	0
Lindblad	4⅓	3	1	0	1	0

*Pitched to one batter in fifth.

Runs batted in—Bando, 2, Fisk, Petrocelli, Cooper, Doyle, Jackson. Two-base hit—Burleson. Sacrifice hits—Beniquez, Lynn. Stolen base—Fisk. Double plays—Red Sox 1, A's 0. Left on base—Red Sox 6, A's 6. Wild pitch—Lindblad. Umpires—Kunkel, Luciano, Evans, Morgenweck, Denkinger and DiMuro. Time—2:30. Attendance—49,358.

COMPOSITE BATTING AVERAGES

RED SOX

Player-position	G	AB	R	H	2B	3B	HR	RBI	BA
Yastrzemski, lf	3	11	4	5	1	0	1	2	.455
Burleson, ss	3	9	2	4	2	0	0	1	.444
Fisk, c	3	12	4	5	1	0	0	2	.417
Cooper, 1b	3	10	0	4	2	0	0	1	.400
Lynn, cf	3	11	1	4	1	0	0	3	.364
Doyle, 2b	3	11	3	3	0	0	0	2	.273
Beniquez, dh	3	12	2	3	0	0	0	1	.250
Petrocelli, 3b	3	12	1	2	0	0	1	2	.167
Evans, rf	3	10	1	1	1	0	0	0	.100
Cleveland, p	1	0	0	0	0	0	0	0	.000
Drago, p	2	0	0	0	0	0	0	0	.000
Moret, p	1	0	0	0	0	0	0	0	.000
Tiant, p	1	0	0	0	0	0	0	0	.000
Wise, p	1	0	0	0	0	0	0	0	.000
Totals	3	98	18	31	8	0	2	14	.316

A's

Player-position	G	AB	R	H	2B	3B	HR	RBI	BA
Bando, 3b	3	12	1	6	2	0	0	2	.500
Tovar, ph-2b	2	2	2	1	0	0	0	0	.500
Jackson, rf	3	12	1	5	0	0	1	3	.417
Holt, ph-1b	3	3	0	1	1	0	0	0	.333
Rudi, 1b-lf	3	12	1	3	2	0	0	0	.250
Washington, lf-dh ..	3	12	1	3	1	0	0	1	.250
Fosse, c	1	2	0	0	0	0	0	0	.000
Garner, 2b	3	5	0	0	0	0	0	0	.000
Williams, dh-ph....	3	8	0	0	0	0	0	0	.000
Tenace, c-1b	3	9	0	0	0	0	0	0	.000
North cf	3	10	0	0	0	0	0	1	.000
Campaneris, ss	3	11	1	0	0	0	0	0	.000
Abbott, p	1	0	0	0	0	0	0	0	.000
Blue, p	1	0	0	0	0	0	0	0	.000
Bosman, p	1	0	0	0	0	0	0	0	.000
Fingers, p	1	0	0	0	0	0	0	0	.000
Harper, ph	1	0	0	0	0	0	0	0	.000
Holtzman, p	2	0	0	0	0	0	0	0	.000
Hopkins, pr-dh	1	0	0	0	0	0	0	0	.000
Lindblad, p	2	0	0	0	0	0	0	0	.000
Martinez, pr-2b	3	0	0	0	0	0	0	0	.000
Todd, p	3	0	0	0	0	0	0	0	.000
Totals	3	98	7	19	6	0	1	7	.194

COMPOSITE PITCHING AVERAGES

RED SOX

Pitcher	G	IP	H	R	ER	SO	BB	W	L	ERA
Tiant	1	9	3	1	0	8	3	1	0	0.00
Drago	2	4⅔	2	0	0	2	1	0	0	0.00
Moret	1	1	1	0	0	1	1	0	0	0.00
Wise	1	7⅓	6	3	2	2	3	1	0	2.45
Cleveland	1	5	7	3	3	2	1	0	0	5.40
Totals	3	27	19	7	5	14	9	3	0	1.67

Saves—Drago 2.

A's

Pitcher	G	IP	H	R	ER	SO	BB	W	L	ERA
Lindblad	2	4⅔	5	3	0	1	0	0	0	0.00
Abbott	1	1	0	0	0	0	0	0	0	0.00
Bosman	1	⅓	0	0	0	0	0	0	0	0.00
Holtzman	2	11	12	8	5	7	1	0	2	4.09
Fingers	1	4	5	3	3	3	1	0	1	6.75
Blue	1	3	6	3	3	2	0	0	0	9.00
Todd	3	1	3	1	1	0	0	0	0	9.00
Totals	3	25	31	18	12	12	3	0	3	4.32

WORLD SERIES

	W	L	Pct.
Reds	4	3	.571
Red Sox	3	4	.429

Oct. 11	Red Sox (Tiant)	6	Reds (Gullett)	0	at Boston
Oct. 12	Reds (Eastwick)	3	Red Sox (Drago)	2	at Boston
Oct. 14*	Reds (Eastwick)	6	Red Sox (Willoughby)	5	at Cincinnati (N)
Oct. 15	Red Sox (Tiant)	5	Reds (Norman)	4	at Cincinnati (N)
Oct. 16	Reds (Gullett)	6	Red Sox (Cleveland)	2	at Cincinnati (N)
Oct. 21**	Red Sox (Wise)	7	Reds (Darcy)	6	at Boston (N)
Oct. 22	Reds (Carroll)	4	Red Sox (Burton)	3	at Boston (N)

*10 innings.
**12 innings.

(NOTE: There was a four-day delay between Games 5 and 6. One was for travel, three were caused by rainstorms raking the New England coast.)

Heavyweights Butch Hobson and Buddy Bell collide at third base.

1975 AMERICAN LEAGUE CHAMPIONS (*continued*)

SATURDAY, OCTOBER 11—AT BOSTON

Reds	AB	R	H	O	A	E
Rose, 3b	4	0	0	0	0	0
Morgan, 2b	4	0	2	2	2	0
Bench, c	4	0	0	6	1	0
Perez, 1b	4	0	0	9	0	0
Foster, lf	4	0	2	1	0	0
Concepcion, ss	4	0	0	2	3	0
Griffey, rf	3	0	1	2	0	0
Geronimo, cf	1	0	0	2	1	0
Gullett, p	3	0	0	0	0	0
Carroll, p	0	0	0	0	0	0
McEnaney, p	0	0	0	0	0	0
Totals	31	0	5	24	7	0

Red Sox	AB	R	H	O	A	E
Evans, rf	4	1	1	4	0	0
Doyle, 2b	3	1	2	3	3	0
Yastrzemski, lf	4	1	1	3	0	0
Fisk, c	3	1	0	4	1	0
Lynn, cf	4	0	2	3	0	0
Petrocelli, 3b	3	1	2	1	3	0
Burleson, ss	3	0	3	1	1	0
Cooper, 1b	3	0	0	8	0	0
Tiant, p	3	1	1	0	0	0
Totals	30	6	12	27	8	0

```
Reds .......................... 000  000  00 0—0
Red Sox ....................... 000  000  60 X—6
```

Reds	IP	H	R	ER	BB	SO
Gullett (L)	6*	10	4	4	4	3
Carroll	0**	0	1	1	1	0
McEnaney	2	2	1	1	1	1

Red Sox	IP	H	R	ER	BB	SO
Tiant (W)	9	5	0	0	2	3

*Pitched to four batters in seventh. **Pitched to one batter in seventh. Bases on balls—Off Gullett 4 (Yastrzemski, Petrocelli, Tiant, Burleson), off Carroll 1 (Fisk), off McEnaney 1 (Doyle), off Tiant 2 (Geronimo 2). Strikeouts—By Gullett 3 (Cooper 2, Tiant), by McEnaney 1 (Lynn), by Tiant 3 (Perez 2, Concepcion). Runs batted in—Yastrzemski, Fisk, Petrocelli 2, Burleson, Cooper. Two-base hits—Morgan, Petrocelli, Griffey. Sacrifice hits—Doyle, Evans. Sacrifice fly—Cooper. Caught stealing—Burleson, Foster. Double plays—Geronimo and Bench; Perez unassisted. Balk—Tiant. Left on bases—Cincinnati 6, Boston 9. Umpires—Frantz (A.L.) plate, Colosi (N.L.) first base, Barnett (A.L.) second base, Stello (N.L.) third base, Maloney (A.L.) left field, Davidson (N.L.) right field. Time—2:27. Attendance—35,205.

SUNDAY, OCTOBER 12—AT BOSTON

Reds	AB	R	H	O	A	E
Rose, 3b	4	0	2	1	1	0
Morgan, 2b	3	1	0	0	4	0
Bench, c	4	1	2	9	3	0
Perez, 1b	3	0	0	8	0	0
Foster, lf	4	0	1	2	0	0
Concepcion, ss	4	1	1	2	4	1
Griffey, rf	4	0	1	2	0	0
Geronimo, cf	3	0	0	3	0	0
Billingham, p	2	0	0	0	2	0
Borbon, p	0	0	0	0	0	0
McEnaney, p	0	0	0	0	0	0
aRettenmund	1	0	0	0	0	0
Eastwick, p	1	0	0	0	0	0
Totals	33	3	7	27	14	1

Red Sox	AB	R	H	O	A	E
Cooper, 1b	5	0	1	10	1	0
Doyle, 2b	4	0	1	2	5	0
Yastrzemski, lf	3	2	1	1	0	0
Fisk, c	3	0	1	5	1	0
Lynn, cf	4	0	0	5	0	0
Petrocelli, 3b	4	0	2	0	0	0
Evans, rf	2	0	0	2	0	0
Burleson, ss	4	0	1	2	4	0
Lee, p	3	0	0	0	0	0
Drago, p	0	0	0	0	0	0
bCarbo	1	0	0	0	0	0
Totals	33	2	7	27	11	0

```
Reds .......................... 000  100  002—3
Red Sox ....................... 100  001  000—2
```

Reds	IP	H	R	ER	BB	SO
Billingham	5⅔	6	2	1	2	5
Borbon	⅓	0	0	0	0	0
McEnaney	1	0	0	0	0	2
Eastwick (W)	2	1	0	0	1	1

Red Sox	IP	H	R	ER	BB	SO
Lee	8*	5	2	2	2	5
Drago (L)	1	2	1	1	1	0

*Pitched to one batter in ninth. Bases on balls—Off Billingham 2 (Yastrzemski, Evans), off Eastwick 1 (Fisk), off Lee 2 (Morgan, Perez), off Drago 1 (Geronimo). Strikeouts—By Billingham 5 (Petrocelli, Lee, Fisk, Evans, Burleson), by McEnaney 2 (Lee, Doyle), by Eastwick 1 (Evans), by Lee 5 (Rose, Perez, Foster, Geronimo, Griffey). aFouled out for McEnaney in eighth. bLined out for Drago in ninth. Runs batted in—Perez, Concepcion, Griffey, Fisk, Petrocelli. Two-base hits—Cooper, Bench, Griffey. Stolen base—Concepcion. Caught stealing—Evans, Morgan. Double play—Billingham, Concepcion, Bench, Rose and Bench. Hit by pitcher—By Billingham (Evans). Left on bases—Cincinnati 6, Boston 8. Umpires—Colosi (N.L.) plate, Barnett (A.L.) first base, Stello (N.L.) second base, Maloney (A.L.) third base, Davidson (N.L.) left field, Frantz (A.L.) right field. Time—2:38. Attendance—35,205.

Billy Conigliaro slams against The Wall.

TUESDAY, OCTOBER 14—AT CINCINNATI

Red Sox	AB	R	H	O	A	E
Cooper, 1b	5	0	0	14	0	0
Doyle, 2b	5	0	1	0	6	0
Yastrzemski, lf	4	1	0	1	0	0
Fisk, c	3	1	1	5	0	2
Lynn, cf	3	0	1	6	0	0
Petrocelli, 3b	4	1	2	1	5	0
Evans, rf	4	1	2	1	0	0
Burleson, ss	4	0	2	0	1	0
Wise, p	2	0	0	0	0	0
Burton, p	0	0	0	0	0	0
Cleveland, p	0	0	0	0	0	0
aCarbo	1	1	1	0	0	0
Willoughby, p	0	0	0	0	0	0
Moret, p	0	0	0	0	0	0
Totals	35	5	10	28*	12	2

Reds	AB	R	H	O	A	E
Rose, 3b	4	1	1	2	1	0
Griffey, rf	3	0	0	1	1	0
cRettenmund	1	0	0	0	0	0
Morgan, 2b	4	0	1	4	5	0
Perez, 1b	3	1	0	13	1	0
Bench, c	4	1	1	2	1	0
Foster, lf	3	0	0	3	0	0
Concepcion, ss	4	1	1	2	5	0
Geronimo, cf	4	2	2	3	0	0
Nolan, p	1	0	0	0	0	0
Darcy, p	1	0	0	0	0	0
Carroll, p	0	0	0	0	0	0
McEnaney, p	1	0	1	0	0	0
Eastwick, p	0	0	0	0	0	0
bArmbrister	1	0	0	0	0	0
Totals	34	6	7	30	14	0

```
Red Sox ...................  010 001 102 0—5
Reds ......................  000 230 000 1—6
```
*One out when winning run scored.

Red Sox	IP	H	R	ER	BB	SO
Wise	4⅓	4	5	5	2	1
Burton	⅓	0	0	0	1	0
Cleveland	1⅓	0	0	0	0	2
Willoughby (L)	3†	2	1	0	0	1
Moret	⅓	1	0	0	1	1

Reds	IP	H	R	ER	BB	SO
Nolan	4	3	1	1	1	0
Darcy	2**	2	1	1	2	0
Carroll	⅔	1	1	1	0	0
McEnaney	1⅔	1	1	1	0	2
Eastwick (W)	1⅔	3	1	1	0	0

**Pitched to one batter in seventh. †Pitched to two batters in tenth.
Bases on balls—Off Wise 2 (Foster, Perez), off Burton 1 (Griffey), off Moret 1 (Rose), off Nolan 1 (Fisk), off Darcy 2 (Yastrzemski, Fisk). Strikeouts—By Wise 1 (Darcy), by Cleveland 2 (Perez, Bench), by Willoughby 1 (Perez), by Moret 1 (Rettenmund), by McEnaney 2 (Yastrzemski, Lynn). aHomered for Cleveland in seventh. bSafe on error for Eastwick in tenth. cCalled out on strikes for Griffey in tenth. Runs batted in—Fisk, Lynn, Carbo, Evans 2, Bench 2, Concepcion, Geronimo, Morgan 2. Three-base hit—Rose. Home runs—Fisk, Bench, Carbo, Evans. Stolen bases —Foster, Perez, Griffey. Sacrifice hit—Willoughby. Sacrifice flies—Morgan, Lynn. Double plays—Morgan, Concepcion and Perez; Petrocelli and Cooper; Morgan and Perez. Wild pitch—Darcy. Left on bases—Boston 5, Cincinnati 5. Umpires— Barnett (A.L.) plate, Stello (N.L.) first base, Maloney (A.L.) second base, Davidson (N.L.) third base, Frantz (A.L.) left field, Colosi (N.L.) right field. Time—3:03. Attendance—55,392.

WEDNESDAY, OCTOBER 15—AT CINCINNATI

Red Sox	AB	R	H	O	A	E
Beniquez, lf	4	0	1	4	0	0
Miller, lf	1	0	0	1	0	0
Doyle, 2b	5	0	1	2	3	1
Yastrzemski, 1b	4	0	2	8	0	0
Fisk, c	5	1	1	4	0	0
Lynn, cf	4	1	1	4	1	0
Petrocelli, 3b	4	0	1	1	2	0
Evans, rf	4	1	2	3	0	0
Burleson, ss	4	1	1	0	2	0
Tiant, p	3	1	1	0	2	0
Totals	38	5	11	27	10	1

Reds	AB	R	H	O	A	E
Rose, 3b	3	1	1	1	3	0
Griffey, rf	5	0	1	0	0	0
Morgan, 2b	3	1	0	2	7	0
Perez, 1b	4	0	0	12	1	1
Bench, c	4	0	1	4	0	0
Foster, lf	4	1	2	0	0	0
Concepcion, ss	4	1	1	3	4	0
Geronimo, cf	4	0	3	4	0	0
Norman, p	1	0	0	0	0	0
Borbon, p	0	0	0	0	0	0
aCrowley	1	0	0	0	0	0
Carroll, p	0	0	0	1	0	0
bChaney	1	0	0	0	0	0
Eastwick, p	0	0	0	0	0	0
cArmbrister	0	0	0	0	0	0
Totals	34	4	9	27	15	1

```
Red Sox ...................  000 500 000—5
Reds ......................  200 200 000—4
```

Red Sox	IP	H	R	ER	BB	SO
Tiant (W)	9	9	4	4	4	4

Reds	IP	H	R	ER	BB	SO
Norman (L)	3⅓	7	4	4	1	2
Borbon	⅔	2	1	0	0	0
Carroll	2	2	0	0	0	2
Eastwick	3	0	0	0	1	0

Bases on balls—Off Tiant 4 (Morgan 2, Rose 2), off Norman 1 (Tiant), off Eastwick 1 (Yastrzemski). Strikeouts—By Tiant 4 (Perez, Crowley, Chaney, Bench), by Norman 2 (Fisk, Lynn), by Carroll 2 (Petrocelli, Tiant). aStruck out for Borbon in fourth. bStruck out for Carroll in sixth. cSacrificed for Eastwick in ninth. Runs batted in—Evans 2, Burleson, Beniquez, Yastrzemski, Griffey, Bench, Concepcion, Geronimo. Two-base hits—Griffey, Bench, Burleson, Concepcion. Three-base hits—Evans, Geronimo. Sacrifice hit—Armbrister. Double play—Morgan, Concepcion and Perez. Wild pitch—Norman. Left on bases—Boston 8, Cincinnati 8. Umpires—Stello (N.L.) plate, Maloney (A.L.) first base, Davidson (N.L.) second base, Frantz (A.L.) third base, Colosi (N.L.) left field, Barnett (A.L.) right field. Time—2:52. Attendance—55,667.

1975 AMERICAN LEAGUE CHAMPIONS (continued)

THURSDAY, OCTOBER 16—AT CINCINNATI

Red Sox	AB	R	H	O	A	E		Reds	AB	R	H	O	A	E
Beniquez, lf	3	0	0	2	1	0		Rose, 3b	3	0	2	1	0	0
Doyle, 2b	4	1	1	1	1	0		Griffey, rf	4	0	1	2	0	0
Yastrzemski, 1b	3	1	1	6	0	0		Morgan, 2b	3	1	1	3	2	0
Fisk, c	4	0	1	6	0	0		Bench, c	3	2	1	8	1	0
Lynn, cf	4	0	1	2	0	0		Perez, 1b	3	2	2	5	0	0
Petrocelli, 3b	4	0	0	2	1	0		Foster, lf	4	0	0	2	0	0
Evans, rf	3	0	1	3	0	0		Concepcion, ss	2	0	0	0	0	0
Burleson, ss	3	0	0	1	2	0		Geronimo, cf	4	0	0	6	0	0
Cleveland, p	2	0	0	0	0	0		Gullett, p	3	1	1	0	0	0
Willoughby, p	0	0	0	1	0	0		Eastwick, p	0	0	0	0	0	0
aGriffin	1	0	0	0	0	0								
Pole, p	0	0	0	0	0	0								
Segui, p	0	0	0	0	0	0								
Totals	31	2	5	24	5	0		Totals	29	6	8	27	3	0

```
Red Sox .................. 100 000 001—2
Reds ..................... 000 113 01X—6
```

Red Sox	IP	H	R	ER	BB	SO		Reds	IP	H	R	ER	BB	SO
Cleveland (L)	5*	7	5	5	2	3		Gullett (W)	8⅔	5	2	2	1	7
Willoughby	2	1	0	0	0	1		Eastwick (S)	⅓	0	0	0	0	1
Pole	0**	0	1	1	2	0								
Segui	1	0	0	0	0	0								

*Pitched to three batters in sixth. **Pitched to two batters in eighth. Bases on balls—Off Cleveland 2 (Rose, Morgan), off Pole 2 (Bench, Perez), off Gullett 1 (Beniquez). Strikeouts—By Cleveland 3 (Griffey, Perez, Gullett), by Willoughby 1 (Gullett), by Gullett 7 (Fisk 2, Petrocelli, Cleveland 2, Lynn, Beniquez), by Eastwick 1 (Petrocelli). aLined out for Willoughby in eighth. Runs batted in—Yastrzemski, Lynn, Perez 4, Rose, Concepcion. Two-base hits—Rose, Lynn. Three-base hit—Doyle. Home runs—Perez 2. Stolen bases—Morgan, Concepcion. Sacrifice flies—Yastrzemski, Concepcion. Double plays—Beniquez and Fisk; Burleson and Yastrzemski. Hit by pitcher—By Willoughby (Concepcion). Left on bases—Boston 4, Cincinnati 5. Umpires—Maloney (A.L.) plate, Davidson (N.L.) first base, Frantz (A.L.) second base, Colosi (N.L.) third base, Barnett (A.L.) left field, Stello (N.L.) right field. Time—2:23. Attendance—56,393.

TUESDAY, OCTOBER 21—AT BOSTON

Reds	AB	R	H	O	A	E		Red Sox	AB	R	H	O	A	E
Rose, 3b	5	1	2	0	2	0		Cooper, 1b	5	0	0	8	0	0
Griffey, rf	5	2	2	0	0	0		Drago, p	0	0	0	0	0	0
Morgan, 2b	6	1	1	4	4	0		fMiller	1	0	0	0	0	0
Bench, c	6	0	1	8	0	0		Wise, p	0	0	0	0	0	0
Perez, 1b	6	0	2	11	2	0		Doyle, 2b	5	0	1	0	2	0
Foster, lf	6	0	2	4	1	0		Yastrzemski, lf, 1b	6	1	3	7	1	0
Concepcion, ss	6	0	1	3	4	0		Fisk, c	4	2	2	9	1	0
Geronimo, cf	6	1	2	2	0	0		Lynn, cf	4	2	2	2	0	0
Nolan, p	0	0	0	1	0	0		Petrocelli, 3b	4	1	0	1	1	0
aChaney	1	0	0	0	0	0		Evans, rf	5	0	1	5	1	0
Norman, p	0	0	0	0	0	0		Burleson, ss	3	0	0	3	2	1
Billingham, p	0	0	0	0	0	0		Tiant, p	2	0	0	0	2	0
bArmbrister	0	1	0	0	0	0		Moret, p	0	0	0	0	1	0
Carroll, p	0	0	0	0	0	0		dCarbo, lf	2	1	1	1	0	0
cCrowley	1	0	1	0	0	0								
Borbon, p	1	0	0	0	0	0								
Eastwick, p	0	0	0	0	0	0								
McEnaney, p	0	0	0	0	0	0								
eDriessen	1	0	0	0	0	0								
Darcy, p	0	0	0	0	1	0								
Totals	50	6	14	33	14	0		Totals	41	7	10	36	11	1

```
Reds .................. 000 030 210 000—6
Red Sox ............... 300 000 030 001—7
```
None out when winning run scored.

Reds	IP	H	R	ER	BB	SO		Red Sox	IP	H	R	ER	BB	SO
Nolan	2	3	3	3	0	2		Tiant	7*	11	6	6	2	5
Norman	⅔	1	0	0	2	0		Moret	1	0	0	0	0	0
Billingham	1⅓	1	0	0	1	1		Drago	3	1	0	0	0	1
Carroll	1	1	1	0	0	0		Wise (W)	1	2	0	0	0	1
Borbon	2**	1	2	2	2	0								
Eastwick	1†	2	1	1	1	2								
McEnaney	1	0	0	0	1	0								
Darcy (L)	2‡	1	1	1	0	1								

*Pitched to one batter in eighth. **Pitched to two batters in eighth. †Pitched to two batters in ninth. ‡Pitched to one batter in twelfth. Bases on balls—Off Norman 2 (Fisk, Lynn), off Billingham 1 (Burleson), off Borbon 2 (Burleson, Petrocelli), off Eastwick 1 (Doyle), off McEnaney 1 (Fisk), off Tiant 2 (Griffey, Armbrister). Strikeouts—By Nolan 2 (Evans, Tiant), by Billingham 1 (Petrocelli), by Eastwick 2 (Evans, Cooper), by Darcy 1 (Carbo), by Tiant 5 (Bench 2, Perez 2, Geronimo), by Drago 1 (Geronimo), by Wise 1 (Geronimo). aFlied out for Nolan in third. bWalked for Billingham in fifth. cSingled for Carroll in sixth. dHomered for Moret in eighth. eFlied out for McEnaney in tenth. fFlied out for Drago in eleventh. Runs batted in—Griffey 2, Bench, Foster 2, Geronimo, Lynn 3, Carbo 3, Fisk. Two-base hits—Doyle, Evans, Foster. Three-base hit—Griffey. Home runs—Lynn, Geronimo, Carbo, Fisk. Stolen base—Concepcion. Sacrifice hit—Tiant. Double plays—Foster and Bench; Evans, Yastrzemski and Burleson. Hit by pitcher—By Drago (Rose). Left on bases—Cincinnati 11, Boston 9. Umpires—Davidson (N.L.) plate, Frantz (A.L.) first base, Colosi (N.L.) second base, Barnett (A.L.) third base, Stello (N.L.) left field, Maloney (A.L.) right field. Time—4:01. Attendance—35,205.

WEDNESDAY, OCTOBER 22—AT BOSTON

Reds	AB	R	H	O	A	E
Rose, 3b	4	0	2	2	2	0
Morgan, 2b	4	0	2	2	4	0
Bench, c	4	1	0	7	0	0
Perez, 1b	5	1	1	8	1	0
Foster, lf	4	0	1	1	0	0
Concepcion, ss	4	0	1	0	2	0
Griffey, rf	2	2	1	3	0	0
Geronimo, cf	3	0	0	3	0	0
Gullett, p	1	0	1	0	0	0
aRettenmund	1	0	0	0	0	0
Billingham, p	0	0	0	0	0	0
bArmbrister	0	0	0	0	0	0
Carroll, p	0	0	0	1	0	0
dDriessen	1	0	0	0	0	0
McEnaney, p	0	0	0	0	0	0
Totals	33	4	9	27	9	0

Red Sox	AB	R	H	O	A	E
Carbo, lf	3	1	1	0	1	0
Miller, lf	0	0	0	0	0	0
eBeniquez	1	0	0	0	0	0
Doyle, 2b	4	1	1	5	3	2
fMontgomery	1	0	0	0	0	0
Yastrzemski, 1b	5	1	1	9	0	0
Fisk, c	3	0	0	4	0	0
Lynn, cf	2	0	0	1	0	0
Petrocelli, 3b	3	0	1	1	3	0
Evans, rf	2	0	0	5	0	0
Burleson, ss	3	0	0	2	7	0
Lee, p	3	0	1	0	1	0
Moret, p	0	0	0	0	0	0
Willoughby, p	0	0	0	0	0	0
cCooper	1	0	0	0	0	0
Burton, p	0	0	0	0	0	0
Cleveland, p	0	0	0	0	0	0
Totals	31	3	5	27	15	2

```
Reds ....................... 0 0 0  0 0 2  1 0 1—4
Red Sox .................... 0 0 3  0 0 0  0 0 0—3
```

Reds	IP	H	R	ER	BB	SO
Gullett	4	4	3	3	5	5
Billingham	2	1	0	0	2	1
Carroll (W)	2	0	0	0	1	1
McEnaney (S)	1	0	0	0	0	0

Red Sox	IP	H	R	ER	BB	SO
Lee	6⅓	7	3	3	1	2
Moret	⅓	1	0	0	2	0
Willoughby	1⅓	0	0	0	0	0
Burton (L)	⅔	1	1	1	2	0
Cleveland	⅓	0	0	0	1	0

Bases on balls—Off Gullett 5 (Lynn, Carbo, Fisk, Petrocelli, Evans), off Billingham 2 (Lynn, Burleson), off Carroll 1 (Evans), off Lee 1 (Griffey), off Moret 2 (Armbrister, Morgan), off Burton 2 (Griffey, Rose), off Cleveland 1 (Bench). Strikeouts—By Gullett 5 (Fisk, Petrocelli, Lee, Lynn, Burleson), by Billingham 1 (Fisk), by Carroll 1 (Fisk), by Lee 2 (Morgan, Geronimo. aHit into double play for Gullett in fifth. bWalked for Billingham in seventh. cFouled out for Willoughby in eighth. dGrounded out for Carroll in ninth. eFlied out for Miller in ninth. fGrounded out for Doyle in ninth. Runs batted in —Perez 2, Rose, Morgan, Yastrzemski, Petrocelli, Evans. Two-base hit—Carbo. Home run—Perez. Stolen bases—Morgan, Griffey. Sacrifice hit—Geronimo. Double plays—Doyle, Burleson and Yastrzemski; Burleson, Doyle and Yastrzemski; Rose, Morgan and Perez. Wild pitch—Gullett. Left on bases—Cincinnati 9, Boston 9. Umpires—Frantz (A.L.) plate, Colosi (N.L.) first base, Barnett (A.L.) second base, Stello (N.L.) third base, Maloney (A.L.) left field, Davidson (N.L.) right field. Time— 2:52. Attendance—35,205.

COMPOSITE BATTING AVERAGES

RED SOX

Player-position	G	AB	R	H	2B	3B	HR	RBI	BA
Carbo, ph-lf	4	7	3	3	1	0	2	4	.429
Yastrzemski, lf-1b	7	29	7	9	0	0	0	4	.310
Petrocelli, 3b	7	26	3	8	1	0	0	4	.308
Burleson, ss	7	24	1	7	1	0	0	2	.292
Evans, rf	7	24	3	7	1	1	1	5	.292
Lynn, cf	7	25	3	7	1	0	1	5	.280
Doyle, 2b	7	30	3	8	1	1	0	0	.267
Tiant, p	3	8	2	2	0	0	0	0	.250
Fisk, c	7	25	5	6	0	0	2	4	.240
Lee, p	2	6	0	1	0	0	0	0	.167
Beniquez, lf-ph	3	8	1	1	0	0	0	1	.125
Cooper, 1b-ph	5	19	0	1	1	0	0	1	.053
Griffin, ph	1	1	0	0	0	0	0	0	.000
Montgomery, ph	1	1	0	0	0	0	0	0	.000
Cleveland, p	3	2	0	0	0	0	0	0	.000
Miller, lf-ph	3	2	0	0	0	0	0	0	.000
Wise, p	2	2	0	0	0	0	0	0	.000
Moret, p	3	0	0	0	0	0	0	0	.000
Willoughby, p	3	0	0	0	0	0	0	0	.000
Burton, p	2	0	0	0	0	0	0	0	.000
Drago, p	2	0	0	0	0	0	0	0	.000
Pole, p	1	0	0	0	0	0	0	0	.000
Segui, p	1	0	0	0	0	0	0	0	.000
Totals	7	239	30	60	7	2	6	30	.251

REDS

Player-position	G	AB	R	H	2B	3B	HR	RBI	BA
McEnaney, p	5	1	0	1	0	0	0	0	1.000
Crowley, ph	2	2	0	1	0	0	0	0	.500
Rose, 3b	7	27	3	10	1	1	0	2	.370
Gullett, p	3	7	1	2	0	0	0	0	.286
Geronimo, cf	7	25	3	7	0	1	2	3	.280
Foster, lf	7	29	1	8	1	0	0	2	.276
Griffey, rf	7	26	4	7	3	1	0	4	.269
Morgan, 2b	7	27	4	7	1	0	0	3	.259
Bench, c	7	29	5	6	2	0	1	4	.207
Concepcion, ss	7	28	3	5	1	0	1	4	.179
Perez, 1b	7	28	4	5	0	0	3	7	.179
Armbrister, ph	4	1	1	0	0	0	0	0	.000
Eastwick, p	5	1	0	0	0	0	0	0	.000
Borbon, p	3	1	0	0	0	0	0	0	.000
Darcy, p	2	1	0	0	0	0	0	0	.000
Nolan, p	2	1	0	0	0	0	0	0	.000
Norman, p	2	1	0	0	0	0	0	0	.000
Billingham, p	3	2	0	0	0	0	0	0	.000
Chaney, ph	2	2	0	0	0	0	0	0	.000
Driessen, ph	2	2	0	0	0	0	0	0	.000
Rettenmund, ph	3	3	0	0	0	0	0	0	.000
Carroll, p	5	0	0	0	0	0	0	0	.000
Totals	7	244	29	59	9	3	7	29	.242

COMPOSITE PITCHING AVERAGES

RED SOX

Pitcher	G	IP	H	R	ER	SO	BB	W	L	ERA
Willoughby	3	6⅓	3	1	0	2	0	0	1	0.00
Moret	3	1⅔	2	0	0	1	3	0	0	0.00
Segui	1	1	0	0	0	0	0	0	0	0.00
Drago	2	4	3	1	1	1	1	0	1	2.25
Lee	2	14⅓	12	5	5	7	3	0	1	3.14
Tiant	3	25	25	10	10	12	8	2	0	3.60
Cleveland	3	6⅔	7	5	5	5	3	0	1	6.75
Wise	2	5⅓	6	5	5	2	2	1	0	8.44
Burton	2	1	1	1	1	0	3	0	1	9.00
Pole	1	0	0	1	1	0	2	0	0	.....
Totals	7	65⅓	59	29	28	30	25	3	4	3.86

Shutout—Tiant.

REDS

Pitcher	G	IP	H	R	ER	SO	BB	W	L	ERA
Billingham	3	9	8	2	1	7	5	0	0	1.00
Eastwick	5	8	6	2	2	4	3	2	0	2.25
McEnaney	5	6⅔	3	2	2	5	2	0	0	2.70
Carroll	5	5⅔	4	2	2	3	2	1	0	3.18
Gullett	3	18⅔	19	9	9	15	10	1	1	4.34
Darcy	2	4	3	2	2	1	2	0	1	4.50
Nolan	2	6	6	4	4	2	1	0	0	6.00
Borbon	3	3	3	3	2	0	2	0	0	6.00
Norman	2	4	8	4	4	2	3	0	1	9.00
Totals	7	65	60	30	28	39	30	4	3	3.88

Saves—Eastwick, McEnaney.

1978
TIED FOR FIRST PLACE
WITH NEW YORK YANKEES
Manager: Don Zimmer

Pitchers: Tom Burgmeier, Bill Campbell, Reggie Cleveland, Dick Drago, Dennis Eckersley, Andy Hassler, John LaRose, Bill Lee, Allen Ripley, Bobby Sprowl, Bob Stanley, Luis Tiant, Mike Torrez and Jim Wright. Catchers: Carlton Fisk, *Fred Kendall (5 games) and Bob Montgomery. Infielders: *Bob Bailey (1 game), Jack Brohamer, Rick Burleson, Frank Duffy, Butch Hobson, *Fred Kendall (13 games), Jerry Remy, George Scott and *Carl Yastrzemski (50 games). Outfielders: *Bob Bailey (3 games), Sam Bowen, Bernie Carbo, Dwight Evans, Garry Hancock, Fred Lynn, Jim Rice and *Carl Yastrzemski (71 games). Designated hitters: Bailey (34 games), Brohamer (25 games), Carbo (8 games), Duffy (6 games), Evans (4 games), Fisk (1 game), Hancock (13 games), Hobson (14 games), Kendall (1 game), Remy (5 games), Rice (49 games), Scott (7 games) and Yastrzemski (26 games).

Trainer: Charley Moss. Batboys Tom Cremens (home) and Steve Woods (visitors). Equipment managers: Vince Orlando (home) and Don Fitzpatrick (visitors).

*Played more than one position.

ONE-GAME PLAYOFF
(to decide American League East champion)
MONDAY, OCTOBER 2 AT BOSTON

Yankees	AB	R	H	O	A	E	Red Sox	AB	R	H	O	A	E
Rivers, cf	2	1	1	2	0	0	Burleson, ss	4	1	1	4	2	0
Blair, cf	1	0	1	0	0	0	Remy, 2b	4	1	2	2	5	0
Munson, c	5	0	1	7	1	0	Rice, rf	5	0	1	4	0	0
Piniella, rf	4	0	1	4	0	0	Yastrzemski, lf	5	2	2	2	0	0
Jackson, dh	4	1	1	0	0	0	Fisk, c	3	0	1	5	1	0
Nettles, 3b	4	0	0	1	3	0	Lynn, cf	4	0	1	1	0	0
Chambliss, 1b	4	1	1	8	0	0	Hobson, dh	4	0	1	0	0	0
White, lf	3	1	1	4	0	0	Scott, 1b	4	0	2	8	0	0
Thomasson, lf	0	0	0	1	0	0	Brohamer, 3b	1	0	0	1	1	0
Doyle, 2b	2	0	0	0	0	0	bBailey	1	0	0	0	0	0
aSpencer	1	0	0	0	0	0	Duffy, 3b	0	0	0	0	0	0
Stanley, 2b	1	0	0	0	0	0	cEvans	1	0	0	0	0	0
Dent, ss	4	1	1	0	2	0	Torrez, p	0	0	0	0	0	0
Guidry, p	0	0	0	0	1	0	Stanley, p	0	0	0	0	0	0
Gossage, p	0	0	0	0	0	0	Hassler, p	0	0	0	0	0	0
							Drago, p	0	0	0	0	0	0
Totals	35	5	8	27	7	0	Totals	36	4	11	27	9	0

```
Yankees ................. 0 0 0   0 0 0   4 1 0—5**
Red Sox ................. 0 1 0   0 0 1   0 2 0—4
```

Yankees	IP	H	R	ER	BB	SO	Red Sox	IP	H	R	ER	BB	SO
Guidry (W)	6⅔	6	2	2	1	5	Torrez (L)	6⅔	5	4	4	3	4
Gossage (S)	2⅓	5	2	2	1	2	Stanley*	⅓	2	1	1	0	0
							Hassler	1⅔	1	0	0	0	2
							Drago	⅓	0	0	0	0	0

*Pitched to one batter in eighth.

aFlied out for Doyle in seventh. bCalled out for Brohamer in seventh. cFlied out for Duffy in ninth. Runs batted in—Dent 3, Yastrzemski 2, Lynn, Rice, Jackson, Munson. Two-base hits—Burleson, Remy, Scott, Munson, Rivers. Home runs—Yastrzemski, Dent, Jackson. Sacrifices—Brohamer, Remy. Stolen base—Rivers. Left on base—Red Sox 9, Yankees 8. Passed ball—Munson. Time—2:52. Attendance—32,925.

**Yankees thus won the American League East title and went on to defeat the Kansas City Royals, three games to one, for the pennant. The Yankees then won the World Championship by defeating the Los Angeles Dodgers in the World Series, four games to two.

RED SOX
WORLD SERIES SHARES

1903:	$ 1,182.00	(W)
1912:	$ 4,024.68	(W)
1915:	$ 3,780.25	(W)
1916:	$ 3,910.26	(W)
1918:	$ 1,102.51	(W)
1946:	$ 2,140.89	(L)
1967:	$ 5,115.23	(L)
1975:	$13,325.87	(L)

(W) Winner's share; (L) Loser's share.

Yaz with his pants down—horsing around in his bathing suit before Fenway gates open.
(Boston Globe)

MAJOR LEAGUE AND
AMERICAN LEAGUE RECORDS
BY RED SOX PLAYERS

TRIPLE CROWN WINNERS

Year	Player	Pos.	Ave.	HR	RBI
1942	Ted Williams	LF	.356	36	137
1947	Ted Williams	LF	.343	32	114
1967	Carl Yastrzemski	LF	.326	44*	121

*Tied for home-run leadership with Harmon Killebrew.
NOTE: There have been only nine Triple Crown winners in major league history, and the last three have been Red Sox. Another long-time Red Sox player, Jimmy Foxx, won the Triple Crown, but as a member of the 1933 A's.

AMERICAN LEAGUE MOST VALUABLE PLAYER
(Inaugurated in 1922)

Year	Player	Pos.	Ave.	HR	RBI
1938	Jimmy Foxx	1B	.349	50	175
1946	Ted Williams	LF	.342	38	123
1949	Ted Williams	LF	.343	43	159
1958	Jackie Jensen	RF	.286	35	122
1967	Carl Yastrzemski	LF	.326	44	121
1975*	Fred Lynn	CF	.331	21	105
1978	Jim Rice	LF-DH	.315	46	139

*Won both MVP and Rookie of the Year awards.
NOTE: In 1912, Tris Speaker was A.L. winner of the Chalmers Award, a citation voted by the Baseball Writers Association of America between 1911 and 1914, which is comparable to today's MVP Award.

AMERICAN LEAGUE'S CY YOUNG AWARD
(Inaugurated in 1956)

Year	Player	W-L	Pct.	ERA	Innings	SO	BB
1967	Jim Lonborg	22-9	.710	3.16	273⅓	246	83

AMERICAN LEAGUE ROOKIE OF THE YEAR
(Inaugurated in 1947)

Year	Player	Pos.	Ave.	HR	RBI
1950	Walt Dropo	1B	.322	34	144
1961	Don Schwall	P	W-15	L-7	3.22 ERA
1972	Carlton Fisk	C	.293	22	61
1975*	Fred Lynn	CF	.331	21	105

*Won both Rookie of the Year and MVP awards.

AMERICAN LEAGUE JOE CRONIN AWARD
For Special Achievement
(Inaugurated in 1973)

Year	Player	Position
1978	*Jim Rice	OF-DH
1979	Carl Yastrzemski	1B-OF-DH

*Shared with Ron Guidry of Yankees.

SPORTING NEWS AWARDS

MAJOR LEAGUE
EXECUTIVE OF THE YEAR
(originated 1936)

1946—Tom Yawkey
1967—Dick O'Connell
1975—Dick O'Connell

MAJOR LEAGUE
MANAGER OF THE YEAR
(originated 1936)

1967—Dick Williams
1975—Darrell Johnson

MAJOR LEAGUE
PLAYER OF THE YEAR

1941—Ted Williams
1942—Ted Williams
1947—Ted Williams
1949—Ted Williams
1957—Ted Williams
1967—Carl Yastrzemski

AMERICAN LEAGUE
MOST VALUABLE PLAYER
(1929-45)

1938—Jimmy Foxx
1944—Bobby Doerr

AMERICAN LEAGUE
PITCHER OF THE YEAR
(originated 1948)

1949—Ellis Kinder
1967—Jim Lonborg

AMERICAN LEAGUE
PLAYER OF THE YEAR
(originated 1948)

1949—Ted Williams
1957—Ted Williams
1958—Jackie Jensen
1967—Carl Yastrzemski
1968—Ken Harrelson
1975—Fred Lynn
1978—Jim Rice

AMERICAN LEAGUE
FIREMAN OF THE YEAR
(originated 1960)

1960—Mike Fornieles
1962—Dick Radatz
1964—Dick Radatz
1977—Bill Campbell

AMERICAN LEAGUE
ROOKIE OF THE YEAR
(originated 1946)

(Two rookies usually chosen—
one pitcher, one non-pitcher)

1961—Don Schwall
1969—Mike Nagy
1972—Carlton Fisk
1975—Fred Lynn

AMERICAN LEAGUE BATTING CHAMPIONS

Year	Player	Pos.	Ave.
1932	Dale Alexander (a)	1B	.367
1938	Jimmy Foxx	1B	.349*
1941	Ted Williams	LF	.406**
1942	Ted Williams	LF	.356*
1947	Ted Williams	LF	.343
1948	Ted Williams	LF	.369
1950	Billy Goodman	IF-OF	.354*
1957	Ted Williams	LF	.388*
1958	Ted Williams	LF	.328
1960	Pete Runnels	IF	.320
1962	Pete Runnels	1B	.326
1963	Carl Yastrzemski	LF	.321
1967	Carl Yastrzemski	LF	.326
1968	Carl Yastrzemski	LF	.301
1979	Fred Lynn	CF	.333

*Led both major leagues.
**Only batter in either league to hit over .400 since Bill Terry in 1930, the first in the American League since Harry Heilmann in 1923.
(a) Played 23 games with the Tigers.

AMERICAN LEAGUE HOME RUN CHAMPIONS

Year	Player	Pos.	HR
1903	Buck Freeman	RF	13*
1910	Jake Stahl	1B	10**
1912	Tris Speaker***	CF	10
1918	Babe Ruth***	P-OF	11**
1919	Babe Ruth	P-OF	29*
1939	Jimmy Foxx	1B	35*
1941	Ted Williams	LF	37*
1942	Ted Williams	LF	36*
1947	Ted Williams	LF	32
1949	Ted Williams	LF	43
1965	Tony Conigliaro	RF	32
1967	Carl Yastrzemski***	LF	44**
1977	Jim Rice	OF-DH	39
1978	Jim Rice	OF-DH	46*

*Led both major leagues.
**Shared major-league lead.
***Shared league lead.

AMERICAN LEAGUE RUNS-BATTED-IN CHAMPIONS

Year	Player	Pos.	RBI
1902	Buck Freeman	RF	121
1903	Buck Freeman	RF	104
1919	Babe Ruth	P-OF	112*
1938	Jimmy Foxx	1B	175
1939	Ted Williams	RF	145*
1942	Ted Williams	LF	137*
1947	Ted Williams	LF	114
1949	Ted Williams	LF	159**
1949	Vern Stephens	SS	159**
1950	Vern Stephens	SS	144**
1950	Walt Dropo	1B	144**
1955	Jackie Jensen	RF	116***
1958	Jackie Jensen	RF	122
1959	Jackie Jensen	RF	112
1963	Dick Stuart	1B	118
1967	Carl Yastrzemski	LF	121*
1968	Ken Harrelson	RF	109*
1978	Jim Rice	OF-DH	139*

*Led both major leagues.
**Shared major-league lead.
***Shared league lead.

AMERICAN LEAGUE STOLEN BASE CHAMPIONS

Year	Player	Pos.	SB
1928	Buddy Myer	3B	30
1934	Billy Werber	3B	40*
1935	Billy Werber	3B	29*
1973	Tommy Harper	LF	54

*Led both major leagues.

MOST VICTORIES (LEAGUE)

1901	Cy Young	*33	(10 losses)
1902	Cy Young	*32	(10 losses)
1903	Cy Young	.28	(3 losses)
1912	Joe Wood	.34	(5 losses)
1935	Wes Ferrell	.25	(14 losses)
1942	Tex Hughson	**22	(6 losses)
1949	Mel Parnell	*25	(7 losses)
1955	Frank Sullivan	***18	(13 losses)
1967	Jim Lonborg	**22	(9 losses)

*Led both major leagues.
**Shared major-league leadership.
***Shared league leadership.

MOST SAVES (LEAGUE)

1907	Bill Dinneen (a)	4
1909	Frank Arellanes	7**
1914	Dutch Leonard	4***
1915	Carl Mays	5**
1919	Allan Russell (b)	5*
1931	Wilcy Moore	10
1946	Bob Klinger	9*
1951	Ellis Kinder	14*
1953	Ellis Kinder	27*
1960	Mike Fornieles	14***
1962	Dick Radatz	24
1964	Dick Radatz	29*
1977	Bill Campbell	31

*Led both major leagues.
**Shared major-league leadership.
***Shared league leadership.
(a)Played part of season with Browns.
(b)Played part of season with Yankees.

BEST E.R.A. (LEAGUE)

1901	Cy Young	1.63*
1914	Dutch Leonard	101**
1915	Joe Wood	1.49
1916	Babe Ruth	1.75
1935	Lefty Grove	2.70
1936	Lefty Grove	2.81
1938	Lefty Grove	3.07
1939	Lefty Grove	2.54
1949	Mel Parnell	2.78
1972	Luis Tiant	1.91*

*Led both major leagues.
**All-time major league record.

MOST SHUTOUTS (LEAGUE)

1901	Cy Young	5***
1903	Cy Young	7**
1904	Cy Young	10*
1912	Joe Wood	10*
1916	Babe Ruth	9
1918	Carl Mays	8**
1921	Sad Sam Jones	5*
1929	Danny MacFayden	4***
1936	Lefty Grove	6*
1938	Jack Wilson	3***
1949	Ellis Kinder	6**
1974	Luis Tiant	7**

*Led both major leagues.
**Shared major-league leadership.
***Shared league leadership.

MOST INNINGS PITCHED (LEAGUE)

1902	Cy Young	.385
1903	Cy Young	.342
1924	Howard Ehmke	.315*
1935	Wes Ferrell	.322
1936	Wes Ferrell	.301
1937	Wes Ferrell (a)	.281
1942	Tex Hughson	.281
1949	Mel Parnell	.295
1955	Frank Sullivan	.260

*Led both major leagues.
(a)Played part of season with Senators.

MOST GAMES PITCHED (LEAGUE)

1902	Cy Young	.45
1943	Mace Brown	.49
1951	Ellis Kinder	.63
1953	Ellis Kinder	.69*
1960	Mike Fornieles	.70*
1962	Dick Radatz	.62

*Led both major leagues.

MOST STRIKEOUTS (LEAGUE)

1901	Cy Young	.159
1942	Tex Hughson	.113*
1967	Jim Lonborg	.246

*Tied for league lead.

GOLDEN GLOVE WINNERS

Year	Player	Position
1957	Frank Malzone	Third base
1958	Frank Malzone	Third base
	Jimmy Piersall	Outfield
1959	Jackie Jensen	Outfield
	Frank Malzone	Third base
1963	Carl Yastrzemski	Outfield
1965	Carl Yastrzemski	Outfield
1967	George Scott	First base
	Carl Yastrzemski	Outfield
1968	George Scott	First base
	Reggie Smith	Outfield
	Carl Yastrzemski	Outfield
1969	Carl Yastrzemski	Outfield
1971	George Scott	First Base
	Carl Yastrzemski	Outfield
1972	Carlton Fisk	Catcher
	Doug Griffin	Second base
1975	Fred Lynn	Outfield
1976	Dwight Evans	Outfield
1977	Carl Yastrzemski	Outfield
1978	Dwight Evans	Outfield
	Fred Lynn	Outfield
1979	Rick Burleson	Shortstop
	Dwight Evans	Outfield
	Fred Lynn	Outfield

NOTE: The Red Sox have had Golden Glove winners at every position since the award was born in the mid-1950s.

RED SOX CLUB RECORDS

INDIVIDUAL SEASON RECORDS

Batting

AT BATS
  Left-handed, most .... 661, Doc Cramer, 1940
  Right-handed, most .... 677, Jim Rice, 1978
BASES ON BALLS, most .... 162, Ted Williams, 1947 & 1949
BATTING AVERAGE
  Left-handed, highest ....406, Ted Williams, 1941
  Right-handed, highest .... .360, Jimmy Foxx, 1939
DOUBLES, most ....67‡, Earl Webb, 1931
EXTRA BASES ON LONG HITS .... 201, Jimmy Foxx, 1938
GAMES, most .... 163, Jim Rice, 1978
GROUNDED INTO DOUBLE PLAYS
  Left-handed, most ....30‡, Carl Yastrzemski, 1964
  Right-handed, most .... 32‡, Jackie Jensen, 1954
  Fewest ....3, Tony Lupien, 1943
HIT BY PITCHER, most .... 17, Jack Barry, 1916
HITS, most ....222, Tris Speaker, 1912
HITTING STREAKS, longest ....34, Dom DiMaggio, 1949
  longest start of season ....20, Ed Bressoud, 1964
HOME RUNS, most right-handed .... 50, Jimmy Foxx, 1938
  Most left-handed ....44, Carl Yastrzemski, 1967
  Most at home right-handed .... 35, Jimmy Foxx, 1938
  Most at home left-handed ....28, Fred Lynn, 1979
  Most on road .... 26, Ted Williams, 1957
  by position
    1b .... 50, Jimmy Foxx, 1938
    2b ....27, Bobby Doerr, 1948 & 1950
    3b .... 30, Butch Hobson, 1977
    ss ....40*, Rico Petrocelli, 1969
    lf ....44, Carl Yastrzemski, 1967
    cf ....38, Fred Lynn, 1979
    (also 1 homer as DH)
    rf ....36, Tony Conigliaro, 1970
    catcher .... 26, Carlton Fisk, 1973 & 1977
    designated hitter .... 31, Jim Rice, 1977
    pitcher ....7, Wes Ferrell, 1935
    grand slams ....4, Babe Ruth, 1919
    one month .... 14, Jackie Jensen, 1958
LONG HITS, most .... 92, Jimmy Foxx, 1938
RUNS, most .... 150, Ted Williams, 1949

RUNS BATTED IN, most .... 175, Jimmy Foxx, 1938
SACRIFICES
  most, including flies .... 54, Jack Barry, 1917
  most, no flies ....35, Fred Parent, 1905
  most, flies .... 12, Jackie Jensen, 1955 & 1959
                      12, Jimmy Piersall, 1956
SINGLES, most ....172, Johnny Pesky, 1947
SLUGGING PERCENTAGE
  left-handed, highest ....735, Ted Williams, 1941
  right-handed, highest .... .704, Jimmy Foxx, 1938
STOLEN BASES, most .... 54, Tommy Harper, 1973
  most caught stealing .... 19, Mike Menosky, 1920
STRIKEOUTS
  left-handed, most ....96, Carl Yastrzemski, 1961
  right-handed, most ....162, Butch Hobson, 1977
  fewest ....9, Stuffy McInnis, 1921
TOTAL BASES, most .... 406, Jim Rice, 1978
TRIPLES, most .... 22, Tris Speaker, 1913; Chick Stahl, 1904

Rookie

BASES ON BALLS .... 107‡, Ted Williams, 1939
BATTING AVERAGE .... .342, Patsy Dougherty, 1902
DOUBLES ....47*, Fred Lynn, 1975
GAMES .... 162‡‡, George Scott, 1966
HITS ....205, Johnny Pesky, 1942
HOME RUNS .... 34, Walt Dropo, 1950
LEAST STRIKEOUTS ....25*, Tom Oliver, 1930
MOST INTENTIONAL WALKS .... 13*, George Scott, 1966
RUNS .... 131, Ted Williams, 1939
RUNS BATTED IN .... 145‡, Ted Williams, 1939
SLUGGING PERCENTAGE .... .609*, Ted Williams, 1939
STRIKEOUTS .... 152‡‡, George Scott, 1966
TOTAL BASES .... 344, Ted Williams, 1939

Pitching

BASES ON BALLS
  Left-hander, most ....134, Mel Parnell, 1949
  Right-hander, most .... 121, Don Schwall, 1962

RED SOX CLUB RECORDS (continued)

Pitching (continued)
BATTERS
Most retired without a hit .... 76, Cy Young, 1904
EARNED RUNS, most .... 139, Jack Russell, 1930
EARNED RUN AVERAGE, lowest .... 1.01‡, Dutch Leonard
(223 innings), 1914
GAMES, most .... 79, Dick Radatz, 1964
complete, most .... 41, Cy Young, 1902 & 1904
finished, most .... 67, Dick Radatz, 1964
lost, most .... 25, Red Ruffing, 1928
lost consecutively, most .... 14, Joe Harris, 1906
started, most .... 43, Cy Young, 1902
winning percentage, highest .... .882, Bob Stanley (15-2), 1978
won, most .... 34, Smokey Joe Wood, 1912
won, most in relief .... 16, Dick Radatz, 1964
won consecutively, most .... 16**, Smokey Joe Wood, 1912
HIT BATSMEN, most .... 20, Howard Ehmke, 1923
HITS, most .... 350, Cy Young, 1902
HOME RUNS, most .... 37, Earl Wilson, 1964
INNINGS, most .... 385, Cy Young, 1902
consecutive hitless, most .... 25⅓, Cy Young, 1904
consecutive scoreless, most .... 45⅔, Cy Young, 1904
RUNS, most .... 162, Red Ruffing, 1929; Jack Russell, 1930
SAVES, most .... 31, Bill Campbell, 1977
SHUTOUTS
Left-hander, most won .... 9*, Babe Ruth, 1916
Right-hander, most won .... 10, Cy Young, 1904; Smokey Joe Wood, 1912
Most lost .... 8, Joe Harris, 1906
Won by 1-0, most .... 5**, Joe Bush, 1918
STRIKEOUTS, most .... 258, Smokey Joe Wood, 1912
WILD PITCHES, most .... 21**, Earl Wilson, 1963

INDIVIDUAL GAME, INNING RECORDS

Batting, Game

Most times faced pitcher .... 8‡‡, Clyde Vollmer, June 8, 1950
Most times faced pitcher, no at bats:
6‡‡, Jimmy Foxx, June 16, 1938 (6 walks)
Most runs .... 6‡‡, Johnny Pesky, May 8, 1946
Most hits .... 6**, Jimmy Piersall, June 10, 1953 (1 double, 5 singles)
Pete Runnels, Aug. 30, 1960 (1 double, 5 singles) 15 innings
Most singles .... 5, Billy Goodman, June 4, 1952
Jimmy Piersall, June 10, 1953
Most doubles .... 4‡‡, Billy Werber, July 17, 1935;
Al Zarilla, June 8, 1950; Orlando Cepeda, August 8, 1973
Most consecutive doubles .... 4‡‡, Billy Werber, July 17, 1935
Most triples .... 3‡‡, Patsy Dougherty, September 5, 1903
Most home runs .... 3, Jim Tabor, July 4, 1939; Ted Williams, July 14, 1946;
Bobby Doerr, June 8, 1950; Clyde Vollmer, July 26, 1951; Norm Zauchin,
May 27, 1955; Ted Williams, May 8, 1957; Ted Williams, June 13, 1957;
Ken Harrelson, June 14, 1968; Joe Lahoud, June 11, 1969; Fred Lynn,
June 18, 1975; Carl Yastrzemski, May 19, 1976; Jim Rice, Aug. 29, 1977
Most consecutive home runs .... 3, Ken Harrelson, June 14, 1968
Most grand slam home runs .... 2‡‡, Jim Tabor, July 4, 1939;
Rudy York, July 27, 1946
Most total bases .... 16**, Fred Lynn, June 18, 1975
Most RBI .... 10, Rudy York, July 27, 1946;
Norm Zauchin, May 27, 1955; Fred Lynn, June 18, 1975
Batting in all club's runs (most) .... 7, Ken Harrelson, June 14, 1968
Most walks .... 6‡‡, Jimmy Foxx, June 16, 1938
Most intentional walks .... 3, Carl Yastrzemski, April 17, 1968
Most strikeouts (9 innings) .... 5‡‡, Ray Jarvis, April 20, 1969
Most strikeouts (extra innings) .... 6‡‡, Cecil Cooper, June 14, 1974
Most sacrifices .... 4‡‡, Jack Barry, August 21, 1916
Most sacrifice flies for RBIs .... 3‡‡, Russ Nixon, August 31, 1965

Pitching, Game

Shutout in first major league game .... Done 9 times, last 3:
Billy Rohr at New York, April 14, 1967
Dave Morehead at Washington, April 13, 1963
Dave Ferriss at Philadelphia, April 29, 1945
Least Hits allowed first game .. 1‡‡, Billy Rohr vs. New York, April 14, 1967
Most strikeouts .... 17, Bill Monbouquette, May 12, 1961 (N)
Most consecutive strikeouts .... 6, Buck O'Brien, April 25, 1913
6, Ray Culp, May 11, 1970 (N)
Most innings .... 24**, Joe Harris, Sept. 1, 1906 (L, 4-1)
20, Cy Young, July 4, 1905 (L, 4-2)
17, Maurice McDermott, July 13, 1951 (ND)

Batting, Inning

Most times faced pitcher .... 3‡‡, Ted Williams, July 4, 1948 (7th);
Sammy White, Gene Stephens, Tom Umphlett, Johnny Lipon
and George Kell, all on June 18, 1953 (7th)
Most runs .... 3‡‡, Sammy White, June 18, 1953 (7th)
Most hits .... 3‡‡, Gene Stephens, June 18, 1953 (7th)
Most pinch hits .... 2‡‡, Russ Nixon, May 4, 1962 (4th)
Most home runs .... 2‡‡, Bill Regan, June 16, 1928 (4th)
Most RBI .... 6‡‡, Tom McBride, August 4, 1945 (4th)
Home run, first major league at-bat .... Lefty LeFevre, June 10, 1938
Eddie Pellagrini, April 22, 1946
*Bob Tillman, May 19, 1962
*First official at-bat. (Was walked twice before.)

Pitching, Inning

Most batters faced .... 16‡‡, Doc Adkins, July 8, 1902 (6th);
Lefty O'Doul, July 7, 1923 (6th);
Howard Ehmke, September 28, 1923 (6th)
Most hits allowed .... 12‡, Doc Adkins, July 8, 1902 (6th)
Most runs allowed .... 13‡, Lefty O'Doul, July 7, 1923 (6th)
Most walks allowed .... 6, Lefty O'Doul, July 7, 1923 (6th)

TEAM GAME, INNING RECORDS

Batting, Game

Most times faced pitcher .... 64*, vs. St. Louis, June 8, 1950
Most runs, one club .... Boston 29**, St. Louis 4, June 8, 1950
Most runs, both clubs .... 36*, Boston 22, Philadelphia 14, June 29, 1950
Most runs, shutout .... Boston 19, Philadelphia 0, April 30, 1950
Most runs by opposition .... Cleveland 27, Boston 3, July 7, 1923
Most runs, shutout by opposition ..... Cleveland 19, Boston 0, May 18, 1955
Most innings scored, 9-inning game
8**, vs. Cleveland, September 16, 1903, did not bat in 9th
Most runs to overcome and win
11, down 1-12 vs. Cleveland, August 28, 1950, won 15-14
Most spectacular rally to win .... down 5-12 vs. Washington.
one on and one out in 9th, June 18, 1961, won 13-12
Most hits, one club .... 28, vs. St. Louis, June 8, 1950
Most hits, both clubs .... 45**, Philadelphia 27, Boston 18, July 8, 1902
Most consecutive hits, one club .... 10*, vs. Milwaukee, June 2, 1901,
9th inning
Most players 4 or more hits .... 4**, vs. St. Louis, June 8, 1950
Most singles, one club .... 24‡‡, vs. Detroit, June 18, 1953
Most singles, both clubs ...... 36‡‡, Chicago 21, Boston 15, August 15, 1922
Most home runs .... 8‡‡, vs. Toronto, July 4, 1977
Most HR, season opener, one club ..... 5‡‡, vs. Washington, April 12, 1965
Most HR, season opener, both clubs .... 7‡‡, Boston 5, Washington 2,
April 12, 1965
Most players 2 or more HR, one club .... 3‡‡, vs. St. Louis, June 8, 1950
Most players 1 or more HR, both clubs
9‡‡, Minnesota 5, Boston 4, May 25, 1965
Baltimore 7, Boston 2, May 17, 1967
Boston 5, Milwaukee 4, May 22, 1977
Most HR, start of game ..2‡‡, vs. Minnesota, May 1, 1971 (Aparicio, Smith)
at Milwaukee, June 20, 1973 (Miller, Smith)
vs. N.Y., June 17, 1977 (Burleson, Lynn)
Most HR, 9 innings, none on .... ‡7, vs. Toronto, July 4, 1977
Most grand slams, one club
2‡‡, vs. Chicago May 13, 1934 (Bucky Walters, Ed Morgan)
vs. Philadelphia, June 4, 1939 (Jim Tabor 2)
vs. St. Louis, July 27, 1946 (Rudy York 2)
vs. Chicago, May 10, 1960 (Vic Wertz, Rip Repulski)
Most total bases .... 60‡, vs. St. Louis, June 8, 1950
Most extra base hits .... 17‡, vs. St. Louis, June 8, 1950
Most RBI .... 29‡, vs. St. Louis, June 8, 1950
Most strikeouts (nine innings) .... 19‡‡, vs. California, August 12, 1974

Batting, Inning

Most batters facing pitcher .... 23‡, vs. Detroit, June 18, 1953 (7th)
Most runs .... 17*, vs. Detroit, June 18, 1953 (7th)
Most runs with 2 out .... 10, vs. Detroit, September 21, 1937 (5th)
Most runs with 2 out, none on .... 9, vs. Milwaukee, June 2, 1901 (9th)
Most hits .... 14‡‡, vs. Detroit, June 18, 1953 (7th)
Most consecutive hits .... 10‡‡, vs. Milwaukee, June 2, 1901 (9th)
Most batters reaching first base, consecutive
12, vs. Detroit, June 23, 1952 (4th)

Most batters reaching first base .... 20, vs. Detroit, June 18, 1953 (7th)
Most triples .... 4, vs. Detroit, May 6, 1934 (4th)
Most home runs .... 4, vs. Philadelphia, September 24, 1940 (6th)
                                    vs. Cleveland, May 22, 1957 (6th)
                                    vs. Kansas City, August 26, 1957 (7th)
                                    vs. N.Y., June 17, 1977 (1st)
                                    vs. Toronto, July 4, 1977 (8th)
Most consecutive home runs ... 3, vs. Philadelphia, September 24, 1940 (6th)
                                    vs. Philadelphia, April 19, 1948 (1st)
                                    vs. Detroit, June 6, 1948 (6th)
                                    vs. New York, September 7, 1959 (7th)
                                    vs. Toronto, July 4, 1977 (8th)
                                    vs. Seattle, August 13, 1977 (6th)
Most total bases .... 25*, vs. Philadelphia, September 24, 1940 (6th)
Most extra base hits .... 7‡‡, vs. Philadelphia, September 24, 1940 (6th)

TEAM SEASON RECORDS

Most players .... 48 in 1952
Fewest players .... 18 in 1904
Most games .... 163 in 1961 and 1978
Most at-bats .... 5587 in 1978 (163 games)
Most runs .... 1027 in 1950 (154 games)
Fewest runs .... 463 in 1906 (154 games)
Most hits .... 1665 in 1950 (154 games)
Fewest hits .... 1175 in 1905 (153 games)
Most singles .... 1156 in 1950 (154 games)
Most doubles .... 310 in 1979 (160 games)
Most triples .... 113 in 1903 (141 games)
Most homers .... 213 in 1977 (161 games)
Most home runs with bases filled .... 9 in 1941, 1950
Most home runs by pinch-hitters, season ...... 6 in 1953
Most times 5 or more HR, one game .... ‡8 in 1977 (161 games)
Most times 2 or more consecutive HR .... ‡16 in 1977 (161 games)
Most long hits .... 538 in 1979 (160 games)
                        527 in 1977 (161 games)
Most extra bases on long hits .... 1009 in 1977 (161 games)
Most total bases .... 2560 in 1977 (161 games)
                        2557 in 1950 (154 games)
Most sacrifices .... (including sacrifice flies) 310 in 1917 (157 games)
                    (no sacrifice flies) 142 in 1906 (155 games)
Most stolen bases .... 215 in 1909 (151 games)
Most bases on balls .... 835 in 1949 (155 games)
Most strikeouts .... 1020 in 1966 (162 games)
                        1020 in 1967 (162 games)
Fewest strikeouts .... 329 in 1921 (154 games)
Most hit by pitcher .... 46 in 1920 (154 games)
                        46 in 1924 (156 games)

‡Major-league record
‡‡Tied for major-league record
*League record
**Tied for league record

Fewest hit by pitcher .... 11 in 1934 (153 games)
Most runs batted in .... 974 in 1950 (154 games)
Highest batting average .... .302 in 1950 (154 games)
Lowest batting average .... .234 in 1905 (153 games)
                        .234 in 1907 (155 games)
Highest slugging average .... .465 in 1977 (161 games)
Lowest slugging average .... .318 in 1916 (156 games)
                        .318 in 1917 (157 games)
Most grounded into double play .... 169 in 1949 (155 games)
                        169 in 1951 (154 games)
Fewest grounded into double play .... 94 in 1942 (152 games)
Most left on bases .... 1304 in 1948 (155 games)
Fewest left on bases .... 1015 in 1929 (155 games)
Most .300 hitters .... 9 in 1950
Most putouts .... 4418 in 1978 (163 games)
Fewest putouts .... 3939 in 1938 (150 games)
Most assists .... 2195 in 1907 (155 games)
Fewest assists .... 1555 in 1964 (162 games)
Most chances accepted .... 6425 in 1907 (155 games)
Fewest chances accepted .... 5667 in 1938 (150 games)
Most errors .... 373 in 1901 (137 games)
Fewest errors .... 111 in 1950 (154 games)
Most errorless games .... 86 in 1971 (162 games)
Most consecutive errorless games .... 9 in 1951, 1961
Most double plays .... 207 in 1949 (155 games)
Fewest double plays .... 74 in 1913 (151 games)
Most consecutive games, one or more double plays
                        ‡‡25 (38 double plays), 1951
Most double plays in consecutive games in which double plays were made—
                        ‡‡38 (25 games), 1951
Most triple plays .... ‡‡3 in 1979 (160 games)
Most passed balls .... 24 in 1913 (151 games)
Fewest passed balls .... 3 in 1975 (160 G) and in 1933 (149 G)
Highest fielding average .... .981 in 1948, 1950 and 1971
Lowest fielding average .... .942 in 1901 (137 games)
Most games won .... 105 in 1912
Most games lost .... 111 in 1932
Highest percentage games won .... .691 in 1912 (Won 105, Lost 47)
Lowest percentage games won .... .279 in 1932 (Won 43, Lost 111)
Games won, league .... 6175 in 79 years
Games lost, league .... 5978 in 79 years
Most shutouts won, season .... 26 in 1918
Most shutouts lost, season .... 28 in 1906
Most 1-0 games won .... 8 in 1918
Most 1-0 games lost .... 7 in 1909, 1914
Most consecutive games won, season .... 15 in 1946
Most consecutive games lost, season ... 20 in 1906
Most times finished first 9
Most times finished second 10
Most times finished last 10
Most consecutive games, one or more home runs ..... 13 (21 homers), 1962
                        13 (26 homers), 1963
Most home runs in consecutive games in which home runs were made
                        33 (10 games), 1977

WINNING STREAKS

Fifteen Games, 1946
Thirteen Games, 1948
Twelve Games, 1937, '39, '46
Eleven Games, 1903, '09, '49, '50, '77
Ten Games, 1912, '17, '51, '67, '75
Nine Games, 1901, '10, '12, '19, '42(2),
   '44, '48, '78

BEST MONTHLY RECORDS

	Most Wins		Best Pct.
April	13-7 —1979		.846—1918—11-2
May	23-7 —1978		.778—1946—21-6
June	21-8 —1912		.800—1901—20-5
	21-13—1961		
July	25-9 —1948		.735—1948—25-9
August	24-6 —1950		.800—1950—24-6
	24-8 —1949		
September	22-8 —1977		.741—1915—20-7
October	8-2 —1904		1.000—1905— 7-0

20-VICTORY MONTHS

25-9	July 1948	21-6	May 1946	20-7	Aug. 1912
24-6	Aug. 1950	21-6	Aug. 1915	20-7	Sept. 1915
24-8	Aug. 1949	21-8	July 1955	20-8	June 1979
23-7	May 1978	21-8	June 1912	20-9	Sept. 1972
23-9	Aug. 1942	21-9	July 1912	20-9	June 1955
23-10	July 1910	21-9	Sept. 1914	20-9	July 1918
23-10	July 1939	21-11	Aug. 1946	20-10	July 1916
22-8	Sept. 1977	21-13	June 1961	20-10	July 1946
22-10	July 1915	20-5	June 1901	20-12	July 1972
22-11	July 1975			20-15	Aug. 1967
				20-16	Aug. 1968

PITCHING LEADERS YEAR BY YEAR

Year Wins	Earned Run Average (min. 150 innings)	Innings Pitched	Year Wins	Earned Run Average (min. 150 innings)	Innings Pitched
1979 D. Eckersley, 17-10	D. Eckersley, 2.99	M. Torrez, 252	1971 S. Siebert, 16-10		
1978 D. Eckersley, 20-8	D. Eckersley, 2.99	D. Eckersley, 268	1970 R. Culp, 17-14	S. Siebert, 2.91	R. Culp, 242
1977 B. Campbell, 13-9	F. Jenkins, 3.68	F. Jenkins, 193		R. Culp, 3.04	R. Culp, 251
1976 L. Tiant, 21-12	L. Tiant, 3.06	L. Tiant, 279	1969 R. Culp, 17-8		R. Culp, 227
1975 R. Wise, 19-12	B. Lee, R. Wise, 3.95	Lee, Tiant, 260	1968 R. Culp, 16-6	M. Nagy, 3.11	R. Culp, 216
1974 L. Tiant, 22-13	L. Tiant, 2.92	L. Tiant, 311	D. Ellsworth, 16-7	R. Culp, 2.91	
1973 L. Tiant, 20-13	B. Lee, 2.75	B. Lee, 285			
1972 M. Pattin, 17-13	L. Tiant, 1.91*	M. Pattin, 253	1967 J. Lonborg, 22**-9	L. Stange, 2.77	J. Lonborg, 273

PITCHING LEADERS YEAR BY YEAR (continued)

Year	Wins	Earned Run Average (min. 150 innings)	Innings Pitched
1966	J. Santiago, 12-13	D. Brandon, 3.31	J. Lonborg, 182
1965	E. Wilson, 13-14	B. Monbouquette, 3.70	E. Wilson, 231
1964	D. Radatz, 16-9	D. Radatz, 2.29	B. Monbouquette, 2.34
1963	B. Monbouquette, 20-10	J. Lamabe, 3.15	B. Monbouquette, 267
1962	B. Monbouquette, 15-13 G. Conley, 15-14	B. Monbouquette, 3.33	G. Conley, 242
1961	D. Schwall, 15-7	D. Schwall, 3.22	B. Monbouquette, 236
1960	B. Monbouquette, 14-11	B. Monbouquette, 3.64	B. Monbouquette, 215
1959	J. Casale, 13-8	T. Brewer, 3.76	T. Brewer, 215
1958	I. Delock, 14-8	I. Delock, 3.38	T. Brewer, 227
1957	T. Brewer, 16-13	F. Sullivan, 2.73	F. Sullivan, 241
1956	T. Brewer, 19-9	F. Sullivan, 3.42	T. Brewer, 244
1955	F. Sullivan, 18**-13	F. Sullivan, 2.91	F. Sullivan, 260*
1954	F. Sullivan, 15-12	F. Sullivan, 3.14	F. Sullivan, 206
1953	M. Parnell, 21-8	M. McDermott, 3.01	M. Parnell, 241
1952	M. Parnell, 12-12	M. Parnell, 3.62	M. Parnell, 214
1951	M. Parnell, 18-11	M. Parnell, 3.26	M. Parnell, 221
1950	M. Parnell, 18-10	M. Parnell, 3.61	M. Parnell, 249
1949	M. Parnell, 25*-7	M. Parnell, 2.78*	M. Parnell, 295*
1948	J. Kramer, 18-5	M. Parnell, 3.14	J. Dobson, 245
1947	J. Dobson, 18-8	J. Dobson, 2.95	J. Dobson, 229
1946	D. Ferriss, 25-6	T. Hughson, 2.75	T. Hughson, 278
1945	D. Ferriss, 21-10	D. Ferriss, 2.96	D. Ferriss, 265
1944	T. Hughson, 18-5	T. Hughson, 2.26	T. Hughson, 203
1943	T. Hughson, 12-15	T. Hughson, 2.64	T. Hughson, 266
1942	T. Hughson, 22*-6	T. Hughson, 2.59	T. Hughson, 281*
1941	D. Newsome, 19-10	C. Wagner, 3.07	D. Newsome, 214
1940	J. Wilson, 12-6 J. Heving, 12-7	L. Grove, 3.99	J. Bagby, 183
1939	L. Grove, 15-4	L. Grove, 2.54*	L. Grove, 191
1938	J. Bagby, 15-11 J. Wilson, 15-15	L. Grove, 3.07*	J. Bagby, 199

Year	Wins	Earned Run Average (min. 150 innings)	Innings Pitched
1937	L. Grove, 17-9	L. Grove, 3.02	L. Grove, 262
1936	W. Ferrell, 20-15	L. Grove, 2.81*	W. Ferrell, 301*
1935	W. Ferrell, 25*-14	L. Grove, 2.70*	W. Ferrell, 322*
1934	W. Ferrell, 14-5	F. Ostermueller, 3.49	G. Rhodes, 219
1933	G. Rhodes, 12-15	B. Weiland, 3.87	G. Rhodes, 232
1932	B. Kline, 11-13	E. Durham, 3.80	B. Weiland, 196
1931	D. MacFayden, 16-12	W. Moore, 3.88	J. Russell, 232
1930	M. Gaston, 13-20*	M. Gaston, 3.92	M. Gaston, 273
1929	E. Morris, 14-14	D. MacFayden, 3.62	Ruffing, Gaston, 244
1928	E. Morris, 19-15	E. Morris, 3.53	R. Ruffing, 289
1927	S. Harriss, 14-21*	S. Harriss, 4.18	H. Wiltse, 219
1926	T. Wingfield, 11-16	H. Wiltse, 4.22	H. Wiltse, 196
1925	T. Wingfield, 12-19	H. Ehmke, 3.73	H. Ehmke, 261
1924	H. Ehmke, 19-17	J. Quinn, 3.20	H. Ehmke, 315*
1923	H. Ehmke, 20-17	B. Piercy, 3.41	H. Ehmke, 317
1922	R. Collins, 14-11	J. Quinn, 3.48	J. Quinn, 256
1921	S. Jones, 23-16	S. Jones, 3.22	S. Jones, 299
1920	H. Pennock, 16-13	H. Harper, 3.04	S. Jones, 274
1919	H. Pennock, 16-8	H. Pennock, 2.71	S. Jones, 245
1918	C. Mays, 21-13	J. Bush, 2.11	C. Mays, 293
1917	B. Ruth, 24-13	C. Mays, 1.74	B. Ruth, 326
1916	B. Ruth, 23-12	B. Ruth, 1.75*	B. Ruth, 324
1915	J. Foster, 19-8	J. Wood, 1.49*	G. Foster, 255
1914	R. Collins, 20-13	D. Leonard, 1.01‡	R. Collins, 272
1913	R. Collins, 19-8	D. Leonard, 2.39	D. Leonard, 259 H. Bedient, 259
1912	J. Wood, 34*-5	J. Wood, 1.91	J. Wood, 344
1911	J. Wood, 23-17	J. Wood, 2.02	J. Wood, 277
1910	E. Cicotte, 15-11	R. Collins, 1.62	E. Cicotte, 250
1909	F. Arellanes, 16-12	E. Cicotte, 1.97	F. Arellanes, 231
1908	C. Young, 21-11	C. Young, 1.26	C. Young, 299
1907	C. Young, 22-15	C. Young, 1.99	C. Young, 343
1906	C. Young, 13-21*	B. Dinneen, 2.92	C. Young, 288
1905	J. Tannehill, 22-9	C. Young, 1.82	C. Young, 321
1904	C. Young, 26-16	C. Young, 1.97	C. Young, 380
1903	C. Young, 28*-9	C. Young, 2.08	C. Young, 342*
1902	C. Young, 32*-11	C. Young, 2.15	C. Young, 385*
1901	C. Young, 33*-10	C. Young, 1.62*	C. Young, 372

*Led league **Tied for league lead ‡All-time major league record

ALL-TIME PITCHING LEADERS

Games	Innings	Games Started	Wins	Shutouts	Complete Games
Kinder 365	Young 2728	Young 298	Young 193	Young 39	Young 276
Young 327	Tiant 1774	Tiant 238	Parnell* 123	Wood 28	Dinneen 156
Delock 322	Parnell* 1753	Parnell* 232	Tiant 122	Tiant 26	Winter 141
Lee* 321	Monbouquette ...1622	Monbouquette 228	Wood 115	Leonard* 24	Wood 121
Parnell* 289	Winter 1600	Brewer 217	Dobson 106	Collins* 20	Grove* 119
Fornieles 286	Dobson 1544	Dobson 202	Grove* 105	Parnell* 20	Parnell* 113
Radatz 286	Grove* 1540	Sullivan 201	Hughson 96	Jones 18	Tiant 113
Tiant 274	Brewer 1509	Grove* 189	Monbouquette 96	Dobson 17	Ruth 105
Lyle* 260	Sullivan 1505	Nixon 177	Lee* 94	Ruth* 17	Hughson 99
Dobson 259	Lee* 1503	Dinneen 175	Brewer 91	Dinneen 16	Leonard* 96
Jack Wilson 258	Dinneen 1501	Winter 175	Sullivan 90	Foster 16	Collins* 90
Sullivan 252	Wood 1416	Lee* 167	Leonard* 89	Monbouquette 16	Dobson 90
	Hughson 1376		Ruth* 89	Hughson 16	
			Kinder 86		

Losses	Saves	Strikeouts	Winning Pct. 100 Decisions	Walks
Young 112	Radatz 104	Young 1347	Wood (115-56) 673	Parnell* 758
Winter 96	Kinder 91	Tiant 1075	Ruth* (89-46) 659	Brewer 669
Ruffing 96	Lyle* 69	Wood 986	Hughson (96-54) 640	Dobson 604
Russell 94	Fornieles 48	Monbouquette 969	Young (193-112) 633	Jack Wilson 564
Monbouquette 91	Campbell 44	Sullivan 821	Grove* (105-62) 629	Nixon 530
Dinneen 86	Drago 38	Culp 794	Kinder (86-52) 623	Delock 514
Brewer 82	Delock 31	Lonborg 784	Parnell* (123-75) 621	McDermott* 504
Tiant 81	Bolin 28	Leonard* 769	Tannehill* (62-38) 620	Tiant 501
Sullivan 80	Kiely* 28	Grove* 743	Ferrell (62-40) 608	Ostermueller* 491
MacFayden 78	Wyatt 28	Brewer 733	Tiant (122-81) 601	Earl Wilson 481
Parnell* 75		Parnell* 732	Dobson (106-72) 596	Sullivan 475
		Earl Wilson 714	Leonard* (89-64) 582	
			Collins* (85-62) 578	

*Lefthanders

NO-HIT GAMES BY RED SOX

			Sox-Opp.
1904—Cy Young vs. Philadelphia, May 5	(H)	*3-0
Jesse Tannehill vs. Chicago, Aug. 17	(A)	6-0
1905—Bill Dinneen vs. Chicago, Sept. 27 (1st game)	(H)	2-0
1908—Cy Young vs. New York, June 30	(A)	8-0
1911—Smokey Joe Wood vs. St. Louis, July 29 (1st game)	(H)	5-0
1916—Rube Foster vs. New York, June 21	(H)	2-0
Dutch Leonard vs. St. Louis, August 30	(H)	4-0
1917—Ernie Shore vs. Washington, June 23 (1st game)	(H)	*4-0
1918—Dutch Leonard vs. Detroit, June 3	(A)	5-0
1923—Howard Ehmke vs. Philadelphia, Sept. 7	(A)	4-0
1956—Mel Parnell vs. Chicago, July 14	(H)	4-0
1962—Earl Wilson vs. Los Angeles, June 26 (night)	(H)	2-0
Bill Monbouquette vs. Chicago, Aug. 1 (night)	(A)	1-0
1965—Dave Morehead vs. Cleveland, Sept. 16	(H)	2-0

*Perfect Game

NO-HIT GAMES AGAINST RED SOX

			Sox-Opp.
1908—Dusty Rhoades, Cleveland, Sept. 18	(A)	1-2
1911—Ed Walsh, Chicago, August 27	(A)	0-5
1917—George Mogridge, New York, April 24	(H)	1-2
1920—Walter Johnson, Washington, July 1	(H)	0-1
1926—Ted Lyons, Chicago, August 21	(H)	0-6
1931—Bob Burke, Washington, August 8	(A)	0-5
1934—Bobo Newsom, St. Louis, Sept. 18	(A)	2-1
(pitched 9 hitless innings, allowed hit in 10th)		
1951—Allie Reynolds, New York, Sept. 28 (1st game)	(A)	0-8
1958—Jim Bunning, Detroit, July 20 (1st game)	(H)	0-3
1968—Tom Phoebus, Baltimore, April 27	(A)	0-6

ONE-HITTERS SINCE 1950

Pitcher	Date	Opp.	Hitter	Hit	Inn.	Out	Score
M. McDermott	5-29-52	Wash.	M. Hoderlein	Single	4	1	1-0
*M. McDermott	7-19-53	at Clev.	A. Smith	Single	4	0	2-0
& E. Kinder							
R. Kemmerer	7-18-54	Balt.	S. Mele	Single	7	0	4-0
G. Susce	7-20-55	at K.C.	V. Power	Single	1	0	6-0
B. Monbouquette	5-7-60	Det.	N. Chrisley	Double	1	1	5-0
D. Morehead	5-12-63	Wash.	C. Hinton	Homer	1	2	4-1
**B. Monbouquette	9-6-64	at Minn.	Z. Versalles	Homer	6	2	1-2
B. Rohr	4-14-67	at N.Y.	E. Howard	Single	9	2	3-0
R. Culp	9-21-68	at N.Y.	R. White	Single	7	2	2-0
S. Siebert	7-31-70	at Calif.	J. Johnstone	Single	3	0	2-0
M. Pattin	7-11-72	at Oak.	R. Jackson	Single	9	1	4-0
R. Moret	8-21-74	Chi.	D. Allen	Single	7	1	4-0
R. Wise	6-14-76	at Minn.	J. Terrell	Single	3	1	5-0
R. Wise	6-29-76	Balt.	P. Blair	Single	6	0	2-0
***S. Renko	7-13-79	at Oak.	R. Henderson	Single	9	1	2-0
& B. Campbell							

*McDermott pitched 8 innings, relieved by Kinder in 9th, no outs, 2-0 count on batter.
**Versalles hit 2-run HR.
***Campbell relieved with 2 on, 2 out in 9th and struck out Revering.
(NOTE: Wise had no-hitter with 2 out in the 9th in Milw., 7-2-75, when Scott & Darwin hit consecutive homers. Wise ended with a 2-hit, 6-3 win.)

BEST SAVE MARKS

31 Bill Campbell, 1977	25 Dick Radatz, 1963
29 Dick Radatz, 1964	24 Dick Radatz, 1962
27 Ellis Kinder, 1953	22 Dick Radatz, 1965

VICTORY STREAKS WITHIN A SEASON

16 Smokey Joe Wood, 1912	*11 Roger Moret, 1973	9 Smokey Joe Wood, 1915
13 Ellis Kinder, 1949	11 Bob Stanley, 1978	9 Rube Foster, 1916
12 Cy Young, 1901	10 Cy Young, 1902	9 Elmer Myers, 1920
12 Dutch Leonard, 1914	*10 Dave Ferriss, 1946	9 Joe Bush, 1921
12 Dave Ferriss, 1946	*10 Ike Delock, 1958	9 Mel Parnell, 1950
11 Tex Hughson, 1942	10 Dick Radatz, 1963	9 Bill Monbouquette, 1963
11 Jack Kramer, 1948	9 Cy Young, 1903	*9 Sonny Siebert, 1971
	9 Jesse Tannehill, 1905	9 Rick Wise, 1975

*From the start of the season.

ONE-GAME STRIKEOUT LEADERS

17 Bill Monbouquette	5/12/61	14 Ellis Kinder	8/13/49
15 Joe Wood	7/7/11	13 Joe Wood	10/3/11
*15 Mickey McDermott	7/28/51	13 Joe Bush	8/27/18
**14 Joe Harris	9/1/06	13 Harry Harper	9/27/20
***14 Joe Wood	8/31/14	13 Earl Wilson	8/25/65
14 Dutch Leonard	8/22/15	13 Jim Lonborg	4/28/67

*16 innings
**24 innings
***11 innings

20-GAME WINNERS
(Final Standing of Team in Parentheses)

1901—Cy Young (2)	33-10	1912—Smokey Joe Wood (1)	34-5	1945—Dave Ferriss (7)	21-10
1902—Cy Young (3)	32-10	—Hugh Bedient (1)	20-9	1946—Dave Ferriss (1)	25-6
—Bill Dinneen (3)	21-21	1914—Ray Collins (2)	20-13	—Tex Hughson (1)	20-11
1903—Cy Young (1)	28-9	1916—Babe Ruth (1)	23-12	1949—Mel Parnell (2)	25-7
—Long Tom Hughes (1)	20-7	1917—Carl Mays (2)	22-9	—Ellis Kinder (2)	23-6
—Bill Dinneen (1)	21-13	—Babe Ruth (2)	24-13	1953—Mel Parnell (4)	21-8
1904—Cy Young (1)	26-16	1918—Carl Mays (1)	21-13	1963—Bill Monbouquette (7)	20-10
—Bill Dinneen (1)	23-14	1921—Sad Sam Jones (5)	23-16	1967—Jim Lonborg (1)	22-9
—Jesse Tannehill (1)	21-11	1923—Howard Ehmke (8)	20-17	1973—Luis Tiant (2E)	20-13
1905—Jesse Tannehill (4)	22-9	1935—Wes Ferrell (4)	25-14	1974—Luis Tiant (3E)	22-13
1907—Cy Young (7)	22-15	—Lefty Grove (4)	20-12	1976—Luis Tiant (3E)	21-12
1908—Cy Young (5)	21-11	1936—Wes Ferrell (6)	20-15	1978—Dennis Eckersley (2E)	20-8
1911—Smokey Joe Wood (5)	23-17	1942—Tex Hughson (2)	22-6		

BATTING LEADERS YEAR-BY-YEAR

Year	Batting Average (min. 400 ABs)	Home Runs	Runs Batted In
1979	F. Lynn, .333*	F. Lynn, 39	J. Rice, 130
		J. Rice, 39	
1978	J. Rice, .315	J. Rice, 46*	J. Rice, 139*
1977	J. Rice, .320	J. Rice, 39*	J. Rice, 114
1976	F. Lynn, .314	J. Rice, 25	C. Yastrzemski, 102
1975	F. Lynn, .331	J. Rice, 22	F. Lynn, 105
1974	C. Yastrzemski, .301	R. Petrocelli, 15	C. Yastrzemski, 79
		C. Yastrzemski, 15	
1973	R. Smith, .303	C. Fisk, 26	C. Yastrzemski, 95
1972	C. Fisk, .293	C. Fisk, 22	R. Petrocelli, 75
1971	R. Smith, .283	R. Smith, 30	R. Smith, 96
1970	C. Yastrzemski, .329	C. Yastrzemski, 40	T. Conigliaro, 116
1969	R. Smith, .309	R. Petrocelli, 40	C. Yastrzemski, 111
		C. Yastrzemski, 40	
1968	C. Yastrzemski, .301*	K. Harrelson, 35	K. Harrelson, 109*
1967	C. Yastrzemski, .326*	C. Yastrzemski, 44**	C. Yastrzemski, 121*
1966	C. Yastrzemski, .278	T. Conigliaro, 28	T. Conigliaro, 93
1965	C. Yastrzemski, .312	T. Conigliaro, 32*	F. Mantilla, 92
1964	E. Bressoud, .293	D. Stuart, 33	D. Stuart, 114
1963	C. Yastrzemski, .321*	D. Stuart, 42	D. Stuart, 118*
1962	P. Runnels, .326*	F. Malzone, 21	F. Malzone, 95
1961	F. Malzone, .266	G. Geiger, 18	F. Malzone, 87
	C. Yastrzemski, .266		
1960	P. Runnels, .320*	T. Williams, 29	V. Wertz, 103
1959	P. Runnels, .314	J. Jensen, 28	J. Jensen, 112*
1958	T. Williams, .328*	J. Jensen, 35	J. Jensen, 122*
1957	T. Williams, .388*	T. Williams, 38	Jensen, F. Malzone, 103
1956	T. Williams, .345	T. Williams, 24	J. Jensen, 97
1955	B. Goodman, .294	T. Williams, 28	J. Jensen, 116**
1954	T. Williams, .345†	T. Williams, 29	J. Jensen, 117
1953	B. Goodman, .313	D. Gernert, 21	G. Kell, 73
1952	B. Goodman, .306	D. Gernert, 19	D. Gernert, 67
1951	T. Williams, .318	T. Williams, 30	T. Williams, 126
1950	B. Goodman, .354*	W. Dropo, 34	Dropo, Stephens, 144*
1949	T. Williams, .343	T. Williams, 43*	V. Stephens, 159**
			T. Williams, 159**
1948	T. Williams, .369*	V. Stephens, 29	V. Stephens, 137
1947	T. Williams, .343*	T. Williams, 32*	T. Williams, 114*
1946	T. Williams, .342	T. Williams, 38	T. Williams, 123
1945	S. Newsome, .290	B. Johnson, 12	B. Johnson, 74
1944	B. Doerr, .325	B. Johnson, 17	B. Johnson, 106
1943	P. Fox, .288	B. Doerr, 16	J. Tabor, 85
1942	T. Williams, .356*	T. Williams, 36*	T. Williams, 137*
1941	T. Williams, .406*	T. Williams, 37*	T. Williams, 120
1940	T. Williams, .344	J. Foxx, 36	J. Foxx, 119
1939	J. Foxx, .360	J. Foxx, 35*	T. Williams, 145*
1938	J. Foxx, .349*	J. Foxx, 50	J. Foxx, 175*
1937	J. Cronin, .307	J. Foxx, 36	J. Foxx, 127
1936	J. Foxx, .338	J. Foxx, 41	J. Foxx, 143
1935	R. Johnson, .315	B. Werber, 14	J. Cronin, 95
1934	B. Werber, .321	B. Werber, 11	R. Johnson, 119
1933	R. Johnson, .313	R. Johnson, 10	R. Johnson, 95
1932	D. Alexander, .372‡	S. Jolley, 18	S. Jolley, 99
1931	E. Webb, .333	E. Webb, 14	E. Webb, 103
1930	E. Webb, .323	E. Webb, 16	E. Webb, 66
1929	J. Rothrock, .300	J. Rothrock, 6	R. Scarritt, 71
1928	B. Myer, .313	P. Todt, 12	B. Regan, 75
1927	B. Myer, .288	P. Todt, 6	I. Flagstead, 69
1926	I. Flagstead, .299	P. Todt, 7	B. Jacobson, Todt, 69
1925	I. Boone, .330	P. Todt, 11	P. Todt, 75
1924	I. Boone, .333	I. Boone, 13	B. Veach, 99
1923	J. Harris, .335	J. Harris, 13	G. Burns, 82
1922	J. Harris, .316	G. Burns, 12	D. Pratt, 86
1921	D. Pratt, .324	D. Pratt, 5	D. Pratt, 100
1920	H. Hooper, .312	H. Hooper, 7	H. Hendryx, 73
1919	B. Ruth, .322	B. Ruth, 29*	B. Ruth, 112*
1918	H. Hooper, .289	B. Ruth, 11**	B. Ruth, 66
1917	D. Lewis, .302	H. Hooper, 3	D. Lewis, 65
1916	L. Gardner, .308	T. Walker, Ruth, D. Gainor, 3	L. Gardner, 62
1915	T. Speaker, .322	B. Ruth, 4	D. Lewis, 76
1914	T. Speaker, .338	T. Speaker, 4	T. Speaker, 90
1913	T. Speaker, .365	H. Hooper, 4	D. Lewis, 90
1912	T. Speaker, .383	T. Speaker, 10**	D. Lewis, 109
1911	T. Speaker, .327	T. Speaker, 8	D. Lewis, 86
1910	T. Speaker, .340	J. Stahl, 10*	J. Stahl, 77
1909	H. Lord, .311	T. Speaker, 7	T. Speaker, 77
1908	D. Gessler, .308	D. Gessler, 3	D. Gessler, 63
1907	B. Congalton, .286	H. Ferris, 4	B. Unglaub, 61
1906	M. Grimshaw, .290	C. Stahl, 4	C. Stahl, 51
1905	J. Collins, .276	H. Ferris, 6	J. Collins, 65
1904	C. Stahl, .297	B. Freeman, 7	B. Freeman, 84
1903	P. Dougherty, .331	B. Freeman, 13*	B. Freeman, 104*
1902	P. Dougherty, .342	B. Freeman, 11	B. Freeman, 121*
1901	B. Freeman, .346	B. Freeman, 12	B. Freeman, 114

Year	Hits	Doubles
1979	J. Rice, 201	F. Lynn, 42
1978	J. Rice, 213*	C. Fisk, 39
1977	J. Rice, 206	R. Burleson, 36
1976	J. Rice, 164	D. Evans, 34
1975	F. Lynn, 175	F. Lynn, 47*
1974	C. Yastrzemski, 155	C. Yastrzemski, 25
1973	C. Yastrzemski, 160	O. Cepeda, 25
		C. Yastrzemski, 25
1972	T. Harper, 141	T. Harper, 29
1971	R. Smith, 175	R. Smith, 33*
1970	C. Yastrzemski, 186	R. Smith, 32
1969	R. Smith, 168	R. Petrocelli, 32
1968	C. Yastrzemski, 162	R. Smith, 37*
1967	C. Yastrzemski, 189*	C. Yastrzemski, 31
1966	C. Yastrzemski, 165	C. Yastrzemski, 39*
1965	C. Yastrzemski, 154	C. Yastrzemski, 45**
1964	D. Stuart, 168	E. Bressoud, 41
1963	C. Yastrzemski, 183*	C. Yastrzemski, 40*
1962	C. Yastrzemski, 191	C. Yastrzemski, 43
1961	C. Schilling, 167	C. Yastrzemski, 31
1960	P. Runnels, 169	F. Malzone, 30
1959	P. Runnels, 176	F. Malzone, 34
1958	F. Malzone, 185	P. Runnels, 32
1957	F. Malzone, 185	F. Malzone, 31
1956	J. Jensen, 182	J. Piersall, 40*
1955	B. Goodman, 176	B. Goodman, 31
1954	J. Jensen, 160	B. Goodman, 25
		Jensen, S. White, 25
1953	B. Goodman, 161	G. Kell, 41
1952	B. Goodman, 157	B. Goodman, 27
1951	D. DiMaggio, 189	D. DiMaggio, 34
		B. Goodman, 34
1950	D. DiMaggio, 193	V. Stephens, 34
1949	T. Williams, 194	T. Williams, 39*
1948	T. Williams, 188	T. Williams, 44*
1947	J. Pesky, 207*	T. Williams, 40
1946	J. Pesky, 208*	J. Pesky, 43
1945	B. Johnson, 148	S. Newsome, 30
1944	B. Johnson, 170	B. Johnson, 40
1943	B. Doerr, 163	B. Doerr, 32
1942	J. Pesky, 205*	D. DiMaggio, 36
1941	T. Williams, 185	J. Cronin, 38
1940	D. Cramer, 200**	T. Williams, 43
1939	T. Williams, 185	T. Williams, 44
1938	J. Vosmik, 201*	J. Cronin, 51*
1937	J. Cronin, 175	J. Cronin, 40
1936	J. Foxx, 198	E. McNair, 36
1935	M. Almada, 176	J. Cronin, 37
1934	B. Werber, 200	R. Johnson, 43
1933	R. Johnson, 151	A. Cooke, 35
1932	S. Jolley, 164	U. Pickering, 28
1931	E. Webb, 196	E. Webb, 67‡
1930	T. Oliver, 189	W. Regan, 35
1929	R. Scarritt, 159	P. Todt, 38
1928	B. Myer, 168	I. Flagstead, 41
1927	B. Myer, 135	W. Regan, 37
1926	P. Todt, 153	B. Jacobson, 36
1925	I. Flagstead, 160	I. Flagstead, 38
1924	B. Wambsganss, 174	B. Wambsganss, 41
1923	G. Burns, 181	G. Burns, 47
1922	D. Pratt, 183	D. Pratt, 44
1921	J. McInnis, 179	D. Pratt, 36
1920	H. Hooper, 167	H. Hooper, 30
		W. Schang, 30
1919	E. Scott, 141	B. Ruth, 34
1918	H. Hooper, 137	H. Hooper, Ruth, 26
1917	D. Lewis, 167	D. Lewis, 29
1916	H. Hooper, 156	C. Walker, Lewis, 29
1915	T. Speaker, 176	D. Lewis, 31
1914	T. Speaker, 193*	T. Speaker, 46*
1913	T. Speaker, 190	T. Speaker, 35
1912	T. Speaker, 222	T. Speaker, 53*
1911	T. Speaker, 167	T. Speaker, 34
1910	T. Speaker, 183	D. Lewis, 29
1909	T. Speaker, 168	T. Speaker, 26
1908	H. Lord, 145	H. Lord, 15
1907	B. Congalton, 142	H. Ferris, 25
1906	C. Stahl, 173	H. Ferris, 25
1905	J. Burkett, 147	J. Collins, 25
1904	C. Stahl, 173	J. Collins, 32
1903	P. Dougherty, 195*	B. Freeman, 39
1902	B. Freeman, 177	B. Freeman, 37
1901	J. Collins. 187	J. Collins, 42

*Led league. **Tied for league lead.

*Led league
**Tied for league lead
†Qualified for title
‡Led league at .367 with Boston, Detroit
   (376 AB for Boston)

Triples

B. Hobson, 7
J. Rice, 15*
J. Rice, 15
Lynn, Rice, 8
F. Lynn, 7
D. Evans, 8
R. Miller, 7

C. Fisk, 9**
J. Kennedy, 5
R. Smith, 7
R. Smith, 7
R. Smith, 5
G. Scott, 7
J. Foy, 8
L. Green, 6
C. Yastrzemski, 9
L. Clinton, 7
L. Clinton, 10
G. Geiger, Yastrzemski, 6
D. Buddin, L. Clinton, 5
P. Runnels, 6
Piersall, Runnels, 5
Malzone, Piersall, 5
J. Jensen, 11**
J. Jensen, 6
H. Agganis, 8

J. Piersall, 9
W. Evers, C. Vollmer, 4
J. Pesky, 6

D. DiMaggio, Doerr, 11**
B. Doerr, 9
V. Stephens, 8
B. Doerr, 10
B. Johnson, T. McBride, 7
B. Doerr, 10
T. Lupien, 9
J. Pesky, 9
L. Finney, 10
L. Finney, 15
T. Williams, 11
J. Foxx, 9
R. Cramer, B. Chapman, 11
J. Foxx, J. Kroner, 8
J. Cronin, 14
R. Johnson, B. Werber, 10
A. Cooke, 10
M. Olson, 6
T. Oliver, 5
W. Regan, 10
R. Scarritt, 17
D. Taitt, 14
B. Myer, 11
P. Todt, 12
P. Todt, 13
Harris, Veach, 9
J. Harris, 11
J. Harris, 9
S. Collins, 12
H. Hooper, 17

B. Ruth, 12
H. Hooper, 13
H. Hooper, 11
H. Hooper, C. Walker, 11
H. Hooper, 13
L. Gardner, 19
T. Speaker, 22
L. Gardner, 18
T. Speaker, 13
J. Stahl, 16
T. Speaker, 13
H. Gessler, 14
B. Unglaub, 13
H. Ferris, 13
H. Ferris, 16
C. Stahl, 22*
B. Freeman, 21
B. Freeman, 20
J. Collins, C. Stahl, 16

‡Major league record

Year	Walks	Runs	Stolen Bases
1979	F. Lynn, 82	J. Rice, 117	J. Remy, 14
1978	C. Yastrzemski, 76	J. Rice, 121	J. Remy, 30
1977	C. Fisk, 75	C. Fisk, 106	R. Burleson, 13
1976	C. Yastrzemski, 80	Fisk, Lynn, 76	R. Burleson, Lynn, 14
1975	C. Yastrzemski, 87	F. Lynn, 103*	F. Lynn, J. Rice, 10
1974	C. Yastrzemski, 104	C. Yastrzemski, 93*	T. Harper, 28
1973	C. Yastrzemski, 105	T. Harper, 92	T. Harper, 54*
1972	R. Petrocelli, 78	T. Harper, 92	T. Harper, 25
1971	C. Yastrzemski, 106	R. Smith, 85	D. Griffin, R. Smith, 11
1970	C. Yastrzemski, 128	C. Yastrzemski, 125*	C. Yastrzemski, 23
1969	C. Yastrzemski, 101	C. Yastrzemski, 96	C. Yastrzemski, 15
1968	C. Yastrzemski, 119*	C. Yastrzemski, 90	J. Foy, 26
1967	C. Yastrzemski, 91	C. Yastrzemski, 112*	R. Smith, 16
1966	J. Foy, 91	J. Foy, 97	J. Tartabull, 11
1965	F. Mantilla, 79	T. Conigliaro, 82	L. Green, D. Jones, 8
1964	C. Yastrzemski, 75	E. Bressoud, 86	D. Jones, Yastrzemski, 6
1963	C. Yastrzemski, 95*	C. Yastrzemski, 91	G. Geiger, 9
1962	P. Runnels, 79	C. Yastrzemski, 99	G. Geiger, 18
1961	G. Geiger, 87	C. Schilling, 87	G. Geiger, 16
1960	T. Williams, 75	P. Runnels, 80	Runnels, G. Stephens, 5
1959	P. Runnels, 95	J. Jensen, 101	J. Jensen, 20
1958	J. Jensen, 99	P. Runnels, 103	J. Piersall, 12
1957	T. Williams, 119	J. Piersall, 103	J. Piersall, 14
1956	T. Williams, 102	B. Klaus, Piersall, 91	J. Jensen, 11
1955	B. Goodman, 99	B. Goodman, 100	J. Jensen, 16
1954	T. Williams, 136*	T. Williams, 93	J. Jensen, 22*
1953	D. Gernert, 88	J. Piersall, 76	J. Piersall, 11
1952	D. DiMaggio, 57	D. DiMaggio, 81	F. Throneberry, 16
1951	T. Williams, 143*	D. DiMaggio, 113*	B. Goodman, 7
1950	J. Pesky, 104	D. DiMaggio, 131*	D. DiMaggio, 15*
1949	T. Williams, 162*	T. Williams, 150*	D. DiMaggio, 9
1948	T. Williams, 126*	D. DiMaggio, 127	D. DiMaggio, 10
1947	T. Williams, 162*	T. Williams, 125*	J. Pesky, 12
1946	T. Williams, 156*	T. Williams, 142*	D. DiMaggio, 10
1945	E. Lake, 106	E. Lake, 81	G. Metkovich, 19
1944	B. Johnson, 95	B. Johnson, 106	G. Metkovich, 13
1943	B. Doerr, 62	B. Doerr, 78	P. Fox, 22
1942	T. Williams, 145*	T. Williams, 141*	D. DiMaggio, 16
1941	T. Williams, 145*	T. Williams, 135*	J. Tabor, 17
1940	J. Foxx, 101	T. Williams, 134*	J. Tabor, 14
1939	T. Williams, 107	T. Williams, 131	J. Tabor, 16
1938	J. Foxx, 119**	J. Foxx, 139	B. Chapman, 13
1937	J. Foxx, 99	J. Foxx, 111	B. Chapman, 27†
1936	J. Foxx, 105	J. Foxx, 130	B. Werber, 23
1935	R. Johnson, 74	M. Almada, 85	B. Werber, 29*
1934	M. Bishop, 82	B. Werber, 129	B. Werber, 40*
1933	A. Cooke, 67	R. Johnson, 88	B. Werber, 15
1932	M. Olson, 61	R. Johnson, 70	R. Johnson, 13
1931	E. Webb, 70	E. Webb, 96	J. Rothrock, 13
1930	R. Reeves, 50	T. Oliver, 86	T. Oliver, R. Reeves, 6
1929	R. Reeves, 60	J. Rothrock, 70	J. Rothrock, 23
1928	I. Flagstead, 60	I. Flagstead, 84	C. Myer, 30*
1927	I. Flagstead, 57	I. Flagstead, 63	I. Flagstead, 12
1926	E. Rigney, 108	E. Rigney, 71	F. Haney, 13
1925	I. Flagstead, 63	I. Flagstead, 84	H. Ezzell, D. Prothro, 9
1924	J. Harris, 81	I. Flagstead, 106	B. Wambsganss, 14
1923	J. Harris, 52	G. Burns, 91	N. McMillan, 13
1922	D. Pratt, 53	D. Pratt, 73	M. Menosky, 9
1921	M. Menosky, 60	H. Leibold, 88	S. Collins, 15
1920	H. Hooper, 88	H. Hooper, 91	M. Menosky, 23
1919	B. Ruth, 101	B. Ruth, 103*	H. Hooper, 23
1918	H. Hooper, 75	H. Hooper, 81	H. Hooper, 24
1917	H. Hooper, 80	H. Hooper, 89	H. Hooper, 21
1916	H. Hooper, 80	H. Hooper, 75	H. Hooper, 27
1915	H. Hooper, 89	T. Speaker, 108	T. Speaker, 29
1914	T. Speaker, 77	T. Speaker, 100	T. Speaker, 42
1913	T. Speaker, 65	H. Hooper, 100	T. Speaker, 46
1912	T. Speaker, 82	T. Speaker, 136	T. Speaker, 52
1911	H. Hooper, 73	H. Hooper, 93	H. Hooper, 38
1910	H. Hooper, 62	T. Speaker, 92	H. Hooper, 40
1909	J. Stahl, 43	H. Lord, 85	H. Lord, 36
1908	D. Gessler, 51	A. McConnell, 77	A. McConnell, 31
1907	D. Sullivan, 42	D. Sullivan, 73	H. Wagner, 20
1906	C. Stahl, 47	F. Parent, 67	F. Parent, 16
1905	J. Burkett, 67 K. Selbach, 67	J. Burkett, 78	F. Parent, 25
1904	C. Stahl, 64	Collins, Parent, 85	F. Parent, 20
1903	P. Dougherty, 33	P. Dougherty, 106*	P. Dougherty, 35
1902	P. Dougherty, 42	C. Stahl, 92	P. Dougherty, 20
1901	C. Stahl, 54	J. Collins, 109	T. Dowd, 33

*Led league.   **Tied for league lead.   †Plus 8 with Washington to lead A.L.

Dick Stuart once tried eyeglasses to improve his hitting.

CAREER BATTING LEADERS

Home Runs		Runs Batted In		Batting Ave.		Games		At-Bats		Runs	
T. Williams	521	T. Williams	1,839	T. Williams	.344	Yastrzemski	2,862	Yastrzemski	10,447	T. Williams	1,798
Yastrzemski	404	Yastrzemski	1,613	Speaker	.337	T. Williams	2,292	T. Williams	7,706	Yastrzemski	1,640
Doerr	223	Doerr	1,247	Foxx	.320	Doerr	1,865	Doerr	7,093	Doerr	1,094
Foxx	222	Foxx	788	Runnels	.320	Hooper	1,646	Hooper	6,269	DiMaggio	1,046
Petrocelli	210	Petrocelli	773	Roy Johnson	.313	Petrocelli	1,553	DiMaggio	5,640	Hooper	988
Rice	172	Cronin	737	Pesky	.313	DiMaggio	1,399	Petrocelli	5,390	Pesky	776
Jensen	170	Jensen	733	Rice	.310	Malzone	1,359	Malzone	5,273	Foxx	721
T. Conigliaro	162	Malzone	716	Lynn	.309	G. Scott	1,192	Goodman	4,339	Speaker	703
G. Scott	154	Lewis	643	Goodman	.306	Lewis	1,184	Lewis	4,325	Goodman	688
Smith	149	DiMaggio	618	Cramer	.302	Goodman	1,177	G. Scott	4,234	Petrocelli	653
Fisk	144			R. Ferrell	.302	Cronin	1,134	Pesky	4,085	Cronin	645
Malzone	131			Cronin	.300						
Stephens	122			DiMaggio	.298						

Hits		Doubles		Triples		Total Bases		Extra-Base Hits		Slugging Pct.	
Yastrzemski	3,009	Yastrzemski	565	Hooper	130	Yastrzemski	4,898	T. Williams	1,717	T. Williams	.634
T. Williams	2,654	T. Williams	525	Speaker	106	T. Williams	4,884	Yastrzemski	1,025	Foxx	.605
Doerr	2,042	Doerr	381	Freeman	91	Doerr	3,270	Doerr	693	Rice	.552
Hooper	1,707	DiMaggio	308	Doerr	89	DiMaggio	2,363	Petrocelli	469	Lynn	.526
DiMaggio	1,680	Cronin	270	Gardner	87	Hooper	2,303	DiMaggio	452	Stephens	.492
Malzone	1,454	Lewis	254	Ferris	78	Petrocelli	2,263	Foxx	448	T. Conigliaro	.488
Petrocelli	1,352	Goodman	248	T. Williams	71	Malzone	2,123	Cronin	433	Cronin	.484
Goodman	1,344	Hooper	246	J. Collins	65	Foxx	1,988	Hooper	406	Fisk	.483
Speaker	1,328	Speaker	241	Parent	65	Speaker	1,898	Speaker	386	Speaker	.482
Pesky	1,277	Petrocelli	237	C. Stahl	64	Cronin	1,883	Malzone	386	Jensen	.478
		Malzone	234					Smith	386	Smith	.471
										Yastrzemski	.469
										Doerr	.461

.300 SEASON HITTERS (minimum 400 at-bats)

Rank	Player	Ave.	Year	Rank	Player	Ave.	Year	Rank	Player	Ave.	Year
1.	T. Williams	.406*	1941	46.	J. Pesky	.324	1947		B. Goodman	.310	1948
2.	T. Williams	.388*	1957		B. Johnson	.324	1944	92.	J. Rice	.309	1975
3.	T. Speaker	.383	1912		J. Vosmik	.324	1938		R. Smith	.309	1969
4.	T. Williams	.369*	1948		D. Pratt	.324	1921		B. Doerr	.309	1949
5.	D. Alexander	.367**	1932	50.	E. Webb	.323	1930		S. Jolley	.309	1932
6.	T. Speaker	.363	1913	51.	P. Runnels	.322	1958		T. Speaker	.309	1909
7.	J. Foxx	.360	1939		W. Dropo	.322	1950	97.	J. Cronin	.308	1939
8.	T. Williams	.356*	1942		B. Ruth	.322	1919		L. Gardner	.308	1916
9.	B. Goodman	.354*	1950		T. Speaker	.322	1915		G. Gessler	.308	1908
10.	J. Foxx	.349*	1938	55.	C. Yastrzemski	.321*	1963	100.	G. Kell	.307	1953
11.	B. Freeman	.346	1901		B. Werber	.321	1934		D. DiMaggio	.307	1949
12.	T. Williams	.345	1956	57.	J. Rice	.320	1977		J. Cronin	.308	1937
	T. Williams	.345	1954		P. Runnels	.320*	1960		B. Chapman	.307	1937
14.	T. Williams	.344	1940		L. Finney	.320	1940		S. McInnis	.307	1921
15.	T. Williams	.343	1949		R. Johnson	.320	1934		D. Lewis	.307	1911
	T. Williams	.343*	1947	61.	T. Williams	.318	1951	106.	B. Goodman	.306	1952
17.	T. Williams	.342	1946		B. Doerr	.318	1939		J. Pesky	.306	1949
	P. Dougherty	.342	1902		C. Stahl	.318	1902		G. Burns	.306	1922
19.	B. Chapman	.340	1938	64.	D. DiMaggio	.316	1946		N. Leibold	.306	1921
	T. Speaker	.340	1910		J. Harris	.316	1922		F. Parent	.306	1901
21.	J. Foxx	.338	1936	66.	J. Rice	.315	1978	111.	D. Cramer	.305	1937
	T. Speaker	.338	1914		C. Fisk	.315	1977		I. Flagstead	.305	1924
23.	J. Pesky	.335	1946		J. Jensen	.315	1956		S. McInnis	.305	1919
	J. Harris	.335	1923		P. Fox	.315	1944	114.	F. Parent	.304	1903
25.	T. Speaker	.334	1911		R. Johnson	.315	1935	115.	R. Smith	.303	1973
26.	F. Lynn	.333*	1979		L. Gardner	.315	1912		R. Smith	.303	1970
	E. Webb	.333	1931	72.	F. Lynn	.314	1976		G. Scott	.303	1967
	I. Boone	.333	1924		R. Runnels	.314	1959		B. Goodman	.303	1954
29.	F. Lynn	.331	1975	74.	B. Goodman	.313	1953		D. Cramer	.303	1940
	J. Pesky	.331	1942		J. Pesky	.313	1951		M. Higgins	.303	1938
	P. Dougherty	.331	1903		R. Johnson	.313	1933		C. Reynolds	.303	1934
32.	I. Boone	.330	1925		B. Myer	.313	1928		K. Williams	.303	1928
33.	C. Yastrzemski	.329	1970		D. Prothro	.313	1925	123.	S. Mele	.302	1947
	J. Collins	.329	1901	79.	C. Yastrzemski	.312	1965		M. Higgins	.302	1937
35.	T. Williams	.328*	1958		J. Pesky	.312	1950		D. Lewis	.302	1917
	D. DiMaggio	.328	1950		R. Ferrell	.312	1936	126.	C. Yastrzemski	.301	1974
	G. Burns	.328	1923		J. Hodapp	.312	1933		C. Yastrzemski	.301*	1968
38.	T. Williams	.327	1939		H. Hooper	.312	1920		D. DiMaggio	.301	1940
39.	C. Yastrzemski	.326*	1967	84.	J. Cronin	.311	1941		D. Cramer	.301	1938
	P. Runnels	.326*	1962		D. Cramer	.311	1939		R. Ferrell	.301	1935
41.	J. Rice	.325	1979		H. Hooper	.311	1911		J. Harris	.301	1924
	A. Zarilla	.325	1950		H. Lord	.311	1909		D. Pratt	.301	1922
	B. Doerr	.325	1944		B. Freeman	.311	1902	133.	J. Foxx	.300	1941
	J. Cronin	.325	1938		C. Stahl	.311	1901		J. Rothrock	.300	1929
	J. Collins	.325	1902	90.	M. Vernon	.310	1956		M. Menosky	.300	1921

*American League batting champion.
**Batted .372 in 101 games for Boston after hitting .250 in 23 games for Detroit to lead league with .367 average.

CONSECUTIVE GAME HITTING STREAKS

34 Dom DiMaggio, 1949
30 Tris Speaker, 1912
27 Dom DiMaggio, 1951
26 Buck Freeman, 1902
26 Johnny Pesky, 1949
25 George Metkovich, 1944
23 Del Pratt, 1922
23 George Burns, 1922
23 Ted Williams, 1941
22 Dom DiMaggio, 1942
22 Denny Doyle, 1975
22 Tris Speaker, 1913
20 Fred Lynn, 1975, 1979
20 Ed Bressoud, 1964

GAME-WINNING RBI LEADERS
(Since 1970)

Year	Player	
1970	Carl Yastrzemski	16
1971	Rico Petrocelli	12
1972	C. Fisk, T. Harper	10
1973	Orlando Cepeda	14
1974	Carl Yastrzemski	11
1975	Jim Rice	13
1976	C. Cooper, J. Rice	12
1977	J. Rice, C. Yastrzemski	13
1978	Jim Rice	16
1979	Fred Lynn	13

BEST HITTING STREAKS SINCE 1949
(Year by Year)

Year	Player	Games
1949	Dom DiMaggio	34
1950	Bobby Doerr	17
1951	Dom DiMaggio	27
1952	Billy Goodman	18
1953	Billy Goodman	15
1954	Karl Olson	14
1955	Billy Goodman	18
1956	Sammy White	12
1957	Ted Williams	17
1958	Jackie Jensen	17
1959	Pete Runnels	17
1960	Vic Wertz	13
1961	Frank Malzone	13
1962	Ed Bressoud	14
1963	Carl Yastrzemski	16
1964	Ed Bressoud	20
1965	Rico Petrocelli & Lee Thomas	12
1966	George Scott	14
1967	Carl Yastrzemski	13
1968	Reggie Smith	15
1969	Reggie Smith	19
1970	Reggie Smith & Carl Yastrzemski	15
1971	John Kennedy	13
1972	Carlton Fisk & Rico Petrocelli	12
1973	Orlando Cepeda	17
1974	Doug Griffin	15
1975	Denny Doyle	22
1976	Carlton Fisk & Jim Rice	18
1977	Butch Hobson	18
1978	Jerry Remy	19
1979	Fred Lynn	20

HITTING FOR THE CYCLE

Twelve Red Sox players have hit for the cycle (Single, Double, Triple, Home Run in the same game).

Player	Date	
Buck Freeman	6/21/03	(A)
Pat Dougherty	7/29/03	(H)
Tris Speaker	6/9/12	(A)
Julius Solters	8/19/34	(H)
Joe Cronin	8/2/40	(A)
Leon Culberson	7/3/43	(H)
Bobby Doerr	5/17/44(H); 5/13/47	(H)
Bob Johnson	6/6/44	(H)
Ted Williams	7/21/46	(H)
Lu Clinton	7/13/62*	(A)
Carl Yastrzemski	5/14/65**	(H)
Bob Watson	9/15/79	(A)

*15-inning game
**10-inning game

MONTHLY HOMER RECORDS

Month	No.	Name	Year
April	8	Fred Lynn	1979
May	13	Jim Rice	1978
June	14	Jackie Jensen	1958
July	13	Clyde Vollmer	1951
	13	Jimmy Foxx	1939
August	13	Jimmy Foxx	1940
September	12	Jimmy Foxx	1938

20 OR MORE HOME RUNS IN A SEASON

Homers	Player	Year	Homers	Player	Year	Homers	Player	Year
50	Jimmy Foxx	1938		Felix Mantilla	1964		Joe Cronin	1940
46	JIM RICE	1978		Ted Williams	1951	23	Carl Yastrzemski	1968
44	*CARL YASTRZEMSKI	1967		Vern Stephens	1950		Jackie Jensen	1957
43	TED WILLIAMS	1949	29	Babe Ruth	1919		Ted Williams	1940
42	Dick Stuart	1963		Rico Petrocelli	1970	22	Fred Lynn	1978
41	Jimmy Foxx	1936		Ted Williams	1960		Jim Rice	1975
40	Carl Yastrzemski	1970		Ted Williams	1954		Carlton Fisk	1972
	Carl Yastrzemski	1969		Vern Stephens	1948		Reggie Smith	1970
	Rico Petrocelli	1969	28	Butch Hobson	1979		Lee Thomas	1965
39	JIM RICE	1977		Carl Yastrzemski	1977		Lu Clinton	1963
	Fred Lynn	1979		Rico Petrocelli	1971		Clyde Vollmer	1951
	Jim Rice	1979		Tony Conigliaro	1966		Bobby Doerr	1940
	Vern Stephens	1949		Jackie Jensen	1959	21	Carl Yastrzemski	1979
38	Ted Williams	1957		Ted Williams	1955		Dwight Evans	1979
	Ted Williams	1946		Ted Williams	1950		Carl Yastrzemski	1976
37	TED WILLIAMS	1941	27	George Scott	1966		Fred Lynn	1975
36	TED WILLIAMS	1942		Norm Zauchin	1955		Reggie Smith	1973
	Tony Conigliaro	1970		Bobby Doerr	1950		Reggie Smith	1972
	Jimmy Foxx	1940		Bobby Doerr	1948		Frank Malzone	1962
	Jimmy Foxx	1937	26	Carlton Fisk	1977		Dick Gernert	1953
35	JIMMY FOXX	1939		Carlton Fisk	1973		Jim Tabor	1940
	Ken Harrelson	1968		Ted Williams	1958	20	Carlton Fisk	1978
	Jackie Jensen	1958		Jackie Jensen	1955		Orlando Cepeda	1973
34	Walt Dropo	1950	25	Jim Rice	1976		Tony Conigliaro	1969
33	George Scott	1977		Reggie Smith	1969		Tony Conigliaro	1967
	Dick Stuart	1964		Jackie Jensen	1954		Carl Yastrzemski	1965
32	TONY CONIGLIARO	1965		Ted Williams	1948		Ed Bressoud	1963
	TED WILLIAMS	1947	24	Dwight Evans	1978		Dick Gernert	1958
31	Ted Williams	1939		George Scott	1971		Jackie Jensen	1956
30	Butch Hobson	1977		Tony Conigliaro	1964			
	Reggie Smith	1971		Ted Williams	1956			

Player's name in CAPS means league leader.
*Tied for league lead.

CAREER STOLEN BASE LEADERS

Hooper	300
Speaker	266
Yastrzemski	168
Heinie Wagner	141
Gardner	134
Parent	129
Harper	107
Werber	107
C. Stahl	105
J. Collins	102
Lewis	102
DiMaggio	100

25 OR MORE STOLEN BASES IN A SEASON

SB	Player	Year
54	*Tommy Harper	1973
52	Tris Speaker	1912
46	Tris Speaker	1913
42	Tris Speaker	1914
40	*Bill Werber	1934
	Harry Hooper	1910
38	Harry Hooper	1911
36	Harry Lord	1909
35	Tris Speaker	1910
	Tris Speaker	1909
	Patsy Dougherty	1903
33	Tommy Dowd	1901
31	Amby McConnell	1908
30	Jerry Remy	1978
	*Buddy Myer	1928
29	*Bill Werber	1935
	Tris Speaker	1915

SB	Player	Year
29	Hal Janvrin	1914
	Harry Hooper	1912
	Chick Stahl	1901
28	Tommy Harper	1974
	Clyde Engle	1913
27	Ben Chapman	1937
	Harry Hooper	1916
	Larry Gardner	1911
	Harry Niles	1909
26	Joe Foy	1968
	Harry Hooper	1913
	Heinie Wagner	1910
	Amby McConnell	1909
25	Tommy Harper	1972
	Laffy Gardner	1912
	Tris Speaker	1911
	Freddy Parent	1905

*Led league

ALL-STAR GAME PARTICIPANTS
(Inaugurated in 1933)

Mike Andrews, second base (1) ...1969
Luis Aparicio, shortstop (2) ...1971, 72
Del Baker, coach (1) ...1947
Gary Bell, pitcher (1) ...1968
Lou Boudreau, coach (1) ...1953
Ed Bressoud, shortstop (1) ...1964
Tom Brewer, pitcher (1) ...1956
Don Bryant, coach (1) ...1976
Rick Burleson, shortstop (3) ...1977, 78, 79
Bill Campbell, pitcher (1) ...1977
Eddie Collins, coach (1) ...1933
Tony Conigliaro, outfielder (1) ...1967
Doc Cramer, outfielder (4) ...1937, 38, 39, 40
Joe Cronin, manager, coach, shortstop (9) ...1935, 36, 37, 38, 39, 40*, 41, 44, 47*
Ray Culp, pitcher (1) ...1969
Tom Daley, coach (1) ...1940
Dom DiMaggio, outfielder (7) ...1941, 42, 46, 49, 50, 51, 52
Joe Dobson, pitcher (1) ...1948
Bobby Doerr, second base (9) ...1941, 42, 43, 44, 46, 47, 48, 50, 51
Walt Dropo, first base (1) ...1950
Dwight Evans, outfielder (1) ...1978
Rick Ferrell, catcher (4) ...1933, 34, 35, 36
Dave Ferriss, pitcher (1) ...1946
Lou Finney, outfielder (1) ...1940
Carlton Fisk, catcher (6) ...1972, 73, 74, 76, 77, 78
Mike Fornieles, pitcher (1) ...1961
Pete Fox, outfielder (1) ...1944
Jimmy Foxx, third base, first base, outfielder (6) ...1936, 37, 38, 39, 40, 41
Billy Goodman, first base, second base (2) ...1949, 53
Lefty Grove, pitcher (5) ...1935, 36, 37, 38, 39
Ken Harrelson, outfielder (1) ...1968
Mickey Harris, pitcher (1) ...1946
Mike Higgins, coach (1) ...(second game) 1961
Tex Hughson, pitcher (3) ...1942, 43, 44
Jackie Jensen, outfielder (2) ...1955, 58
Bob Johnson, outfielder (1) ...1944

*Manager, American League Team

Darrell Johnson, manager (1) ...*1976
Oscar Judd, pitcher (1) ...1943
George Kell, third base (2) ...1952, 53
Bill Lee, pitcher (1) ...1973
Jim Lonborg, pitcher (1) ...1967
Fred Lynn, outfielder (5) ...1975, 76, 77, 78, 79
Frank Malzone, third base (8) ...1957, 58, 59, 60, 60, 63, 64
Felix Mantilla, second base (1) ...1965
Bill Monbouquette, pitcher (4) ...1960, 60, 62, 63
Gerry Moses, catcher (1) ...1970
Mel Parnell, pitcher (2) ...1949, 51
Johnny Pesky, shortstop, coach (2) ...1946, 63
Rico Petrocelli, shortstop (2) ...1967, 69
Jimmy Piersall, outfielder (2) ...1954, 56
Dick Radatz, pitcher (2) ...1963, 64
Jerry Remy, second base (1) ...1978
Jim Rice, outfielder (3) ...1977, 78, 79
Pete Runnels, first base, second base (5) ...1959, 59, 60, 60, 62
Jose Santiago, pitcher (1) ...1968
Don Schwall, pitcher (1) ...1961
George Scott, first base (2) ...1966, 77
Sonny Siebert, pitcher (1) ...1971
Reggie Smith, outfielder (2) ...1969, 72
Bob Stanley, pitcher (1) ...1979
Vern Stephens, shortstop, third base (4) ...1948, 49, 50, 51
Frank Sullivan, pitcher (2) ...1955, 56
Birdie Tebbetts, catcher (2) ...1948, 49
Luis Tiant, pitcher (2) ...1974, 76
Mickey Vernon, first base (1) ...1956
Hal Wagner, catcher (1) ...1946
Sammy White, catcher (1) ...1953
Dick Williams, manager (1) ...*1968
Ted Williams, outfielder (18) ...1940, 41, 42, 46, 47, 48, 49, 50, 51, 54, 55, 56, 57, 58, 59, 59, 60, 60
Carl Yastrzemski, outfielder, first base (16) ...1963, 65, 66, 67, 68, 69, 70, 71, 72, 73, 74, 75, 76, 77, 78, 79
Rudy York, first base (1) ...1946
Don Zimmer, coach (1) ...1978

LONGEST GAMES

Innings	Date	Opponent	Score Sox-Foe
24	9/1/06	Philadelphia	1-4
20	7/27/69	at Seattle Pilots	5-3
20	8/29/67	at New York	3-4
20	7/4/05	Philadelphia	2-4
19	7/13/51	at Chicago	4-5

RED SOX 20-RUN GAMES

Score Sox-Foe	Date	Opponent	Winning Pitcher
29-4	6/8/50	St. Louis	C. Stobbs
24-4	9/27/40	Washington	F. Ostermueller
23-3	6/18/53	Detroit	E. Kinder
23-12	5/2/01	at Philadelphia	P. Lewis
22-14	6/29/50	at Philadelphia	A. Papai
21-11	8/30/70	at Chicago	K. Brett
21-2	6/24/49	St. Louis	E. Kinder
21-8	5/29/12	Washington	J. Wood
20-6	9/6/75	at Milwaukee	R. Moret
20-10	5/31/54	Philadelphia	T. Herrin
20-4	6/7/50	St. Louis	J. Dobson

ALL-STAR GAMES AT FENWAY PARK

JULY 9, 1946

National League	AB	R	H	O	A	E
Schoendienst (Cards)	2	0	0	0	2	0
cGustine (Pirates), 2b	1	0	0	1	1	0
Musial (Cards), lf	2	0	0	0	0	0
dEnnis (Phillies), lf	2	0	0	0	0	0
Hopp (Braves), cf ..	2	0	1	0	0	0
eLowery (Cubs), cf	2	0	1	3	0	0
F. Walker (Dodgers), rf ...	3	0	0	1	0	0
Slaughter (Cards), rf	1	0	0	0	0	0
Kurowski (Cards), 3b	3	0	0	2	1	0
iVerban (Phillies)	1	0	0	0	0	0
Mize (Giants), 1b	1	0	0	7	0	0
bMcCormick (Phils), 1b ..	1	0	0	1	1	0
gCavarretta (Cubs), 1b ..	1	0	0	1	0	0
W. Cooper (Giants), c	1	0	1	0	0	0
Masi (Braves), c	2	0	0	4	1	0
Marion (Cards), ss	3	0	0	4	6	0
Passeau (Cubs), p	1	0	0	0	1	0
Higbe (Dodgers), p	1	0	0	0	0	0
Blackwell (Reds), p	0	0	0	0	0	0
hLamanno (Reds)	1	0	0	0	0	0
Sewell (Pirates), p	0	0	0	0	0	0
Totals	31	0	3	24	13	0

American League	AB	R	H	O	A	E
D. DiMaggio (R. Sox), cf .	2	0	1	1	0	0
Spence (Senators), cf	0	1	0	1	0	0
Chapman (Athletics) cf ...	2	0	0	1	0	0
Pesky (Red Sox), ss	2	0	0	1	0	1
Stephens (Browns), ss	3	1	2	0	4	0
Williams (Red Sox), lf	4	4	4	1	0	0
Keller (Yankees), rf	4	2	1	1	0	0
Doerr (Red Sox), 2b	2	0	0	1	1	0
Gordon (Yankees), 2b	2	0	1	0	1	0
Vernon (Senators), 1b	2	0	0	2	1	0
York (Red Sox), 1b	2	0	1	5	0	0
Keltner (Indians), 3b	0	0	0	0	0	0
Stirnweiss (Yanks), 3b....	3	1	1	0	0	0
Hayes (Indians), c	1	0	0	3	0	0
Rosar (Athletics), c	2	0	1	5	0	0
Wagner (Red Sox), c	1	0	0	4	0	0
Feller (Indians), p........	0	0	0	0	0	0
aAppling (White Sox)	1	0	0	0	0	0
Newhouser (Tigers), p....	1	1	1	1	0	0
fDickey (Yankees)	1	0	0	0	0	0
Kramer (Browns), p	1	1	1	0	0	0
Totals	36	12	14	27	7	1

```
National League .............. 000 000 000— 0
American League ............. 200 130 24 X—12
```

National League	IP	H	R	ER	BB	SO
Passeau (Cubs) (L) ...	3	2	2	2	2	0
Higbe (Dodgers)	1⅓	5	4	4	1	2
Blackwell (Reds)	2⅔	3	2	2	1	1
Sewell (Pirates)	1	4	4	4	0	0

American League	IP	H	R	ER	BB	SO
Feller (Indians) (W) ...	3	2	0	0	0	3
Newhouser (Tigers) ...	3	1	0	0	0	4
Kramer (Browns)	3	0	0	0	1	3

aGrounded out for Feller in third. bFlied out for Mize in fourth. cStruck out for Schoendienst in sixth. dStruck out for Musial in sixth. eSingled for Hopp in sixth. fStruck out for Newhouser in sixth. gStruck out for McCormick in seventh. hGrounded out for Blackwell in eighth. iFouled out for Kurowski in ninth. Runs batted in—Williams 5, Stephens 2, Keller 2, Gordon 2, Chapman. Two-base hits—Stephens, Gordon. Home runs—Williams 2, Keller. Double plays—Marion and Mize; Schoendienst, Marion and Mize. Left on base—N.L. 5, A.L. 4. Wild pitch—Blackwell. Umpires—Summers and Rommel A.L., Goetz and Boggess N.L. Time—2:19. Attendance—34,906.

JULY 31, 1961

National League	AB	R	H	O	A	E
Wills (Dodgers), ss	2	0	1	1	1	0
Aaron (Braves), rf	2	0	0	1	0	0
Miller (Giants), p	0	0	0	0	0	0
Mathews (Braves), 3b	3	1	0	0	2	0
Mays (Giants), cf	3	0	1	1	0	0
Cepeda (Giants), lf	3	0	0	0	0	0
Clemente (Pirates), rf.....	2	0	0	0	0	0
Kasko (Reds), ss.........	1	0	1	2	4	0
eBanks (Cubs), ss	1	0	0	0	0	0
White (Cards), 1b	4	0	2	11	1	0
Bolling (Braves) 2b	4	0	0	3	2	1
Burgess (Pirates), c	1	0	0	3	2	0
Roseboro (Dodgers), c	3	0	0	6	0	0
Purkey (Reds), p	0	0	0	0	1	0
aStuart (Pirates)	1	0	0	0	0	0
Mahaffey (Phillies), p.....	0	0	0	0	0	0
cMusial (Cards)..........	1	0	0	0	0	0
Koufax (Dodgers), p	0	0	0	0	0	0
dAltman (Cubs), rf	1	0	0	0	0	0
Totals	32	1	5	27	11	1

American League	AB	R	H	O	A	E
Cash (Tigers), 1b	4	0	0	11	0	0
Colavito (Tigers), lf	4	1	1	3	0	0
Kaline (Tigers), rf........	4	0	2	1	0	0
Mantle (Yankees), cf	3	0	0	2	0	0
Romano (Indians), c	1	0	0	1	0	0
bMaris (Yankees)	1	0	0	0	0	0
Howard (Yankees), c	2	0	0	6	0	0
Aparicio (White Sox), ss ..	2	0	0	1	3	0
fSievers (White Sox)	1	0	0	0	0	0
Temple (Indians), 2b	2	0	0	2	3	0
B. Robinson (Orioles), 2b .	3	0	1	0	3	0
Bunning (Tigers), p	1	0	0	0	0	0
Schwall (Red Sox), p	1	0	0	0	0	0
Pascual (Twins), p	1	0	0	0	0	0
Totals	30	1	4	27	9	0

```
National League .............. 000 001 000—1
American League ............. 100 000 000—1
```

(Game called after nine innings because of rain, the only tie in All-Star Game history.)

National League	IP	H	R	ER	BB	SO
Purkey (Reds)........	2	1	1	1	2	2
Mahaffey (Phillies) ...	2	0	0	0	1	0
Koufax (Dodgers)	2	2	0	0	0	1
Miller (Giants)	3	1	0	0	0	5

American League	IP	H	R	ER	BB	SO
Bunning (Tigers)	3	0	0	0	0	1
Schwall (Red Sox)	3	5	1	1	1	4
Pascual (Twins)	3	0	0	0	1	4

aGrounded out for Purkey in third. bPopped out for Romano in fourth. cStruck out for Mahaffey in fifth. dFlied out for Koufax in seventh. eStruck out for Kasko in eighth. fStruck out for Aparicio in ninth. Runs batted in—Colavito, White. Two-base hit—White. Home run—Colavito. Stolen base—Kaline. Double plays—Bolling, Kasko and White; White, Kasko and Bolling. Left on base—N.L. 7, A.L. 5. Hit by pitch—Cepeda (by Schwall). Passed ball—Burgess. Umpires—Flaherty, Napp and Smith A.L., Pelekoudas, Secory and Sudol, N.L. Time—2:27. Attendance—31,851.

RED SOX PRESIDENTS

Charles W. Somers 1901-02
Henry J. Killilea 1903-04
John I. Taylor...1904-11
James R. McAleer 1912-13
Joseph J. Lannin 1913-16

Harry H. Frazee 1917-23
John A. Quinn 1923-32
Thomas A. Yawkey 1933-76
Jean R. Yawkey...*1977-

*In 1978, Edward G. LeRoux and Haywood C. Sullivan joined Mrs. Yawkey as general partners in ownership of the team. She remained president and they are vice presidents in the new ownership.

MANAGERS' RECORDS

	G*	W	L	Pct.	Years		G*	W	L	Pct.	Years
Barrow, Ed	418	213	203	.512	1918-20	Lake, Fred	192	110	80	.579	1908-09
Barry, Jack	157	90	62	.592	1917	McCarthy, Joe	372	224	147	.604	1948-50
Boudreau, Lou	463	229	232	.497	1952-54	McGuire, Deacon	226	98	123	.443	1907-08
Carrigan, Bill	1004	489	500	.494	1913-16; '27-29	McManus, Marty	246	95	151	.386	1932-33
Chance, Frank	154	61	91	.401	1923	O'Neill, Steve	246	149	97	.606	1950-51
Collins, Jimmy	864	464	389	.544	1901-06	Pesky, Johnny	321	146	175	.455	1963-64
Collins, Shano	210	73	136	.349	1931-32	Popowski, Eddie	9	5	4	.556	1969
Cronin, Joe	2007	1071	916	.539	1935-47	Runnels, Pete	16	8	8	.500	1966
Donovan, Patsy	311	159	147	.520	1910-11	Stahl, Chick	18	5	13	.278	1906
Duffy, Hugh	308	136	172	.442	1921-22	Stahl, Jake	235	144	88	.621	1912-13
Fohl, Lee	462	160	299	.349	1924-26	Unglaub, Bob	29	8	20	.286	1907
Harris, Bucky	153	76	76	.500	1934	Wagner, Heinie	154	52	102	.338	1930
Herman, Billy	310	128	182	.413	1964-66	Williams, Dick	477	260	217	.545	1967-69
Higgins, Mike	1087	543	541	.501	1955-59; '60-62	York, Rudy	1	0	1	.000	1959
Huff, George	8	3	5	.375	1907	Young, Cy	7	3	4	.429	1907
Johnson, Darrell	408	220	188	.539	1974-76	Zimmer, Don	560	329	231	.588	1976-79
Jurges, Billy	161	78	83	.484	1959-60						
Kasko, Eddie	641	346	295	.540	1970-73	*Includes tie games					

SCOUTS

Ed Kenney
VP, Director of Player Development

*Milt Bolling
  Mobile, Alabama
*Ray Boone
  El Cajon, California
Wayne Britton
  Staunton, Virginia
George Digby
  Inverness, Florida
Howard Doyle
  Stillwater, Oklahoma
Bill Enos
  Cohasset, Massachusetts
*Earl Johnson
  Seattle, Washington
Chuck Koney
  Calumet City, Illinois

*Eddie Kasko
Director of Scouting

*Lefty Lefebvre
  Largo, Florida
*Don Lenhardt
  St. Louis, Missouri
Tommy McDonald
  Quincy, Massachusetts
Felix Maldonado
  Ponce, Puerto Rico
*Frank Malzone
  Needham, Massachusetts
*Sam Mele
  Quincy, Massachusetts
Ramon Naranjo
  Santo Domingo, Dominican Republic

William Paffen
  Caracas, Venezuela
Edward Scott
  Mobile, Alabama
Matthew Sczesny
  Long Island, New York
**Joe Stephenson
  Anaheim, California
Paul Tavares
  San Lorenzo, California
Larry Lee Thomas
  Grove City, Ohio
*Charley Wagner
  Reading, Pennsylvania

*Played for Red Sox.

**Stephenson's son Jerry pitched for Red Sox in 1960's.

NOTE: Ted Williams is a consultant and batting instructor.

SPRING TRAINING SITES

1901	Charlottesville, Virginia	1919	Tampa, Florida	1933-42	Sarasota, Florida
1902	Augusta, Georgia	1920-23	Hot Springs, Arkansas	*1943	Medford, Massachusetts
1903-06	Macon, Georgia	1924	San Antonio, Texas	*1944	Baltimore, Maryland
1907-08	Little Rock, Arkansas	1925-27	New Orleans, Louisiana	*1945	Pleasantville, New Jersey
1909-10	Hot Springs, Arkansas	1928-29	Bradenton, Florida	1946-58	Sarasota, Florida
1911	Redondo Beach, California	1930-31	Pensacola, Florida	1959-65	Scottsdale, Arizona
1912-18	Hot Springs, Arkansas	1932	Savannah, Georgia	1966-80	Winter Haven, Florida

*World War II years.

June 13, 1979

The Red Sox said goodbye to a longtime family member tonight and welcomed an aging-but-younger replacement who could prove a pennant key if he can still hit.

Enter Bob Watson, 33. The .299 lifetime hitter was obtained as a first baseman-designated hitter from the Astros for an undisclosed sum, farmhand reliever Peter Ladd of Portland, Maine, and a player to be named later.

Exit George Scott, 35. The man who has played the most games at first base in Red Sox history was traded to the Royals for reserve outfielder Tom Poquette.

The deals beating the June 15 trading deadline were announced before the Red Sox's 11-3 victory at Kansas City that kept Boston within one game of first-place Baltimore, and represent a major bid for a pennant run.

Scott's departure ends a colorful and often controversial chapter in Sox history. The Boomer came to Boston from Greenville, Mississippi, in 1966 as a refreshing 22-year-old who called home runs "taters," and now departs in the twilight of an up-and-down career. He leaves behind a legacy of fancy fielding and some power-hitting. His mighty swings may have been his undoing, but he connected often enough to rank ninth on the Sox's all-time homer parade with 154.

Scott is eighth on the club's games-played list, playing 1,192 (including 988 at first base and nearly 200 at third base) during nine seasons sandwiched in two segments around a five-year exile in Milwaukee.

Scott's return to Boston in 1977 (in the lamented Cecil Cooper trade) never worked out. Although George hit .269 and 33 homers in his first season back, he tumbled to .233/12 homers last year and .224/4 homers this season — mired in a 0-for-25 slump when benched a few weeks ago.

The unhappy veteran has been asking to be traded and now gets his wish. In return, the Red Sox get reserve strength they need. The 27-year-old Poquette plays right and left fields well, can run, and is a little left-handed hitter who makes contact—batting .302 (1976) and .292 (1977) in his only seasons as a regular.

Watson is another contact batter, but with a lot more power. Generally considered one of baseball's strongest men, he says he's not a home-run slugger but instead a line-drive hitter who stings the ball to all fields, particularly the power alleys. Despite playing his entire career in a ball park not suited to his power, Houston's Astrodome, the two-time All-Star has averaged 15 homers and 83 RBIs in his nine full-time seasons.

"I feel I can best help the Red Sox by swinging the bat as I have in the past," says the 6-foot-2, 208-pound right-handed batter, who has never seen Fenway's left-field wall. "I try to hit the ball hard instead of far."

Watson hit .289 with 14 homers and 79 RBIs last season, but slipped to .239 with three homers and 18 RBIs when benched three weeks ago. So the question lingers: Can he still hit?

"When the leaves turn brown," Watson promises, "I will have my stats in order."

Watson did. He doubled and singled in his Red Sox debut June 15 at Chicago and never stopped hitting. At season's end, appreciative fans voted the popular Watson an automobile awarded by WSBK-TV, the station that televises Red Sox games.

He had batted .337 (13 homers, 19 doubles, 53 RBIs) in 84 games, and became only the twelfth batter in Red Sox history to hit for the cycle (at Baltimore, September 15). His .548 slugging percentage was third best

12
EXTRA
INNINGS

[CONTINUED FROM PAGE 169]

George Scott, a superb glove man, said goodbye in 1979.

Carl Yastrzemski and A's catcher Jeff Newman watch Yaz's 400th home run soar toward visitors' bull pen at Fenway. Yaz then pauses to admire the blast and savor the historic moment. *(Boston Globe)*

on the team, behind league-leaders Fred Lynn (.637) and Jim Rice (.596). And despite playing little more than half a season, his 11 game-winning RBIs were a close third on the club behind Lynn's 13 and Rice's 12.

So Watson's statistics indeed were in order by the time New England's leaves had turned brown. Unfortunately, by the time those brown leaves were being raked, Bob Watson was a Yankee and an estimated $2,100,000 richer—lost in the free-agent re-entry draft amid a chorus of howls from Red Sox fans.

July 24, 1979

Carl Yastrzemski scaled another plateau tonight at Fenway Park when he smashed his 400th career home run.

Homerless in his last 16 games and admittedly pressing a little, Yastrzemski rocketed a Mike Morgan fastball 390 feet into the visitors' bull pen in the seventh inning for a two-run homer that gave the Red Sox a 5-3 lead en route to a 7-3 victory over the A's.

Oakland reliever Craig Minetto caught the historic ball and flipped it to Bill Campbell in the Red Sox bull pen for Yastrzemski.

Yaz was mobbed at the plate by teammates, and twice had to return to the field to acknowledge the hurrahs of the 30,395 fans who shared the sweet milestone—a homer they had been waiting for since June 30, when Yastrzemski hit No. 399.

"I knew I hit it pretty well and said to myself, 'If this one doesn't go out I'm in trouble,' " said Yaz, who took a step or two out of the batter's box before stopping to watch the blast and savor the moment.

"I didn't feel pressure until the last few days. I knew how many people were pulling for me, and that added a little pressure because I wanted to hit it here for them."

The Red Sox have only two more games on this home stand before leaving on a 12-game trip, so Yastrzemski knew time was getting short.

While relishing the home run, which makes him the seventeenth major leaguer to hit 400, Yaz shrugged off its importance.

"The most important thing is the pennant race," he said with an eye on the standings, where the Red Sox trail the Orioles by five games. "In the middle of a pennant fight you really don't think about milestones. My most important goal is another pennant — and to win a World Series."

Yastrzemski admits his next personal milestone is a big one, though. He's only 39 hits away from the 3,000-hit club, and he'll be the first American Leaguer to parlay 3,000 hits and 400 homers.

"Only three (National Leaguers Aaron, Mays and Musial) have done that," said Yaz, who'll turn 40 next month, "so it will mean something to be included with them."

Among the cheers, Yastrzemski nearly got some less-than-complimentary words—from Morgan, the 19-year-old right-hander who was born the year Yaz broke into pro baseball. The rookie didn't realize it was a milestone homer, and the crowd's reaction both amazed and irritated him.

"I didn't know why Yastrzemski kept coming out of the dugout," Morgan said. "The second time he came out I was about to tell him to sit down."

September 12, 1979

The Yaz Watch concluded at 9:37 tonight at Fenway Park, ending three days and a dozen at-bats of waiting and suspense.

That's when Carl Yastrzemski inscribed his name twice in baseball history with one swipe of his bat: (1) joining the exclusive 3,000-hit club, and (2) becoming the first American Leaguer to achieve the rare parlay of 3,000 hits and 400 home runs.

The elusive hit that finally elevated the 40-year-old Yastrzemski to those lofty plateaus was a bouncing single that skipped just out of second baseman Willie Randolph's reach in the eighth inning of the Red Sox's 9-2 victory over the Yankees.

The 34,337 at Fenway erupted; the fans, whose standing ovations had gone unanswered in Yastrzemski's previous 12 at-bats (10 outs, two walks), were finally rewarded. In the stands, hundreds of flashbulbs from drugstore cameras exploded one last time, a practice that had accompanied each Yaz swing the last three games as fans had tried to capture the historic hit on film.

As the crowd chanted "Yaz! Yaz! Yaz!" and the electronic scoreboard repeatedly flashed "3,000" in 15-foot digits, Yastrzemski was mobbed by teammates, umpires, team and league officials, security people, some stray fans—and old foes. Reggie Jackson scooped up the ball in right field and dashed in to hand it to Carl, and the other Yankees, led by manager Billy Martin, poured from their dugout to add their congratulations.

As the roar began to subside, the sounds of blaring automobile horns could be heard from nearby Kenmore Square as drivers learned of the historic hit on their car radios.

A microphone was set up between home and first base, and Yastrzemski stepped up to it flanked by his father, Carl Sr., and 18-year-old son Mike, who had been the first to reach him.

With his left arm wrapped around his son and waving his right arm, Yaz was clearly drained — not only by his three-day trial, but also by two aching Achilles tendons that have tormented him since June.

"I know one thing: this was the hardest of the 3,000," he told the crowd. "I took so long to do it because I've enjoyed all those standing ovations you've given me the last three days."

Yastrzemski went on to thank God, his family and the Red Sox family.

"Finally," he said, his voice cracking with emotion, "I'd like to remember probably my two biggest boosters, my mother and Mr. Yawkey. Both deserve to be here."

Mrs. Yastrzemski died in 1978, the Red Sox owner in 1976.

In tears behind the home-plate screen were 26 Yastrzemski relatives, including wife Carol and daughters Maryann, 19, Susie, 13, and Cara, 10. Ironically, Carol missed seeing her husband's milestone hit.

"I had my eyes shut," she said. "I had tried everything else, so I decided not to look this time."

"I've been telling him for three days to get this over with. I told him this was a plot to kill me. And now when he finally gets the hit, I don't see it."

The long wait had Yaz pressing, too.

"I was almost embarrassed not getting the hit the last couple of days," he later told the assembled media, which numbered about 100, including the national press and networks keeping the Yaz Watch night after night.

"I've been in pennant pressure, playoff pressure and World Series pressure situations, but nothing like this. I think it was how the fans reacted the last three days. I wanted to get that hit for the fans, and I came out of my realm of hitting and thinking. I was chasing pitchers' pitches. I was anxious. Normally I wouldn't have swung at some pitches that I have the last three days."

Then came a first-pitch fastball with two out in the eighth inning from

(Boston Globe)

Yaz shares his emotion with Fenway's capacity crowd minutes after getting his historic 3,000th hit in a game against the Yankees. *(Boston Globe)*

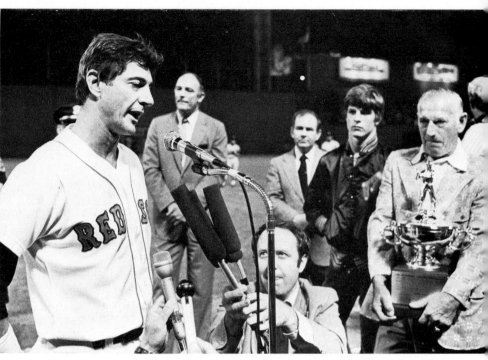

Accompanied by his father (far right) and son (second right), Yaz recalls "probably my two biggest boosters, my mother and Mr. Yawkey." In the background are Red Sox co-owners Haywood Sullivan (left) and Buddy LeRoux. *(Boston Globe)*

25-year-old Yankee right-hander Jim Beattie, who said he idolized Yaz when he was a youngster in Portland, Maine, and later while starring at Dartmouth.

"That doesn't mean I wasn't trying to get him out," Beattie said. "I threw him a good fastball down and in. I got a ground ball out of it, but it found a hole."

Yastrzemski had hit the ball much harder at least a half-dozen times during his 0-for-10 drought, including a blast that sent Jackson back to the warning track earlier last night.

While acknowledging the thrill, Yaz said it didn't compare with winning the 1967 and 1975 pennants, or the 1972 and 1978 near-misses.

Yastrzemski becomes the fifteenth major leaguer to collect 3,000 hits, only the second American Leaguer since 1925. He joins, in order of most hits, the heady lineup of Ty Cobb, Henry Aaron, Stan Musial, Tris Speaker, Honus Wagner, Pete Rose, Eddie Collins, Willie Mays, Nap Lajoie, Paul Waner, Cap Anson, Lou Brock, Al Kaline and Roberto Clemente. And Yaz is among only five to get all his hits for one team, along with Anson (Cubs), Clemente (Pirates), Kaline (Tigers), and Musial (Cardinals).

Yastrzemski is the fourth big leaguer to parlay 3,000 hits and 400 homers, joining National Leaguers Aaron, Mays and Musial.

His next milestone?

"Your next milestone," American League secretary Bob Holbrook told Yaz in front of the capacity crowd, "is Cooperstown."

The next afternoon more than 5,000 admirers jammed Faneuil Hall Marketplace for a "Carl Yastrzemski Day" celebration.

"Every time I put on a Red Sox uniform, I put it on with pride," Yaz told the cheering crowd. "I just hope I've always put it on with class and dignity."

Yastrzemski was invited to the White House after achieving his twin milestones. Here he presents a Yaz sweatshirt and Red Sox jacket to President Carter. *(White House)*

YAZ: 3,000 HITS & 400 HOME RUNS

HITS

No.	Date	Opposition & Place	Type	Pitcher
1	4/11/61 (opening day)	K.C.A's at Fenway	Single	Ray Herbert
1000	9/15/66	White Sox at Fenway	Single	Jack Lamabe
2000	6/9/73	At Texas	RBI Single	Steve Foucault
2500	7/26/76	Indians at Fenway	RBI Double	Stan Thomas
3000	9/12/79	Yankees at Fenway	Single	Jim Beattie

HOME RUNS

No.	Date	Opposition & Place		Pitcher
1	5/9/61	Angels at L.A. (Wrigley Field)		Jerry Casale
100	5/16/67	Orioles at Fenway		Eddie Fisher
200	9/23/69	Yankees at Fenway		Mel Stottlemyre
300	7/25/74	At Detroit		Mickey Lolich
400	7/24/79	Oakland A's at Fenway		Mike Morgan

His ordeal of the past week finally over, Yastrzemski was obviously relaxed as he joked and shook hands with spectators pressing up against the police barriers. He was enjoying himself so much that he never sampled the ten-foot cake shaped like a baseball bat.

CARL YASTRZEMSKI: "I've never thought of myself as a great hitter, even though I've wanted to be a great hitter all my life.

"God gave me tremendous incentive to excel and blessed me with a good body; I've been on the disabled list only once in my career. Still, I'm not a big strong guy and don't have the greatest ability in the world. I've made nine million adjustments, nine million changes.

"But one thing I can say about the 3,000 hits is that I earned every damn one of them. I worked for them and paid the price. I don't know about how the others (who have 3,000 hits) worked at hitting, but I'll bet none put more time into it than I have. Ask all the guys who have pitched batting practice to me over the years."

Yastrzemski rewarded one with a gold watch—Walt Hriniak, the tireless bull pen coach and close friend for three seasons. The watch was inscribed: "To Walt: Thanks. Wouldn't Have Made 400-3,000 Without You."

More than 5,000 admirers jam Faneuil Hall Marketplace to honor Yastrzemski. *(Boston Globe)*

September 30, 1979

Fred Lynn won the American League batting championship today, crowning his best all-around season.

Lynn hit .333, four points more than runner-up George Brett of the Royals. Jim Rice was fourth with a career-high .325.

It marks the fifteenth time a Red Sox batter has won the title, Lynn joining Ted Williams (six times), Carl Yastrzemski (three), Pete Runnels (two), Jimmy Foxx, Billy Goodman and Dale Alexander. Lynn is the first to do it since Yaz in 1968.

The 27-year-old Californian also led the league in slugging percentage (.637), the first A. L. hitter to top both categories since Minnesota's Tony Oliva in 1971. Rice was second at .596.

Lynn and Rice each swatted 39 home runs to tie for second most in the league. Fred's total is 17 more than his previous high of 22 last year, new power he attributes to a strength program last winter.

Twenty-eight of Lynn's homers came at Fenway, the most ever by a left-handed hitter there, topping the old highs of Williams and Yastrzemski. And Lynn had the most home runs and RBIs in a season by a Red Sox center fielder—38 homers (one more as a DH) and 120 RBIs (two more as a DH).

The former USC baseball All-American also won his second straight Golden Glove, the third in his five-year career. And he was the A.L.'s starting center fielder in the All-Star Game, hitting a two-run homer.

For awhile this season it appeared that Lynn and Rice might be the first A.L. teammates since Lou Gehrig and Babe Ruth of the 1927 Yankees to place 1-2 in the three Triple Crown categories. They fell short. Besides a tie with Lynn for second in homers and finishing a close fourth in batting, Rice was second in RBIs (130, nine off the pace), while Lynn's 122 were fourth most.

Rice also had 369 total bases to lead the league for the third straight year to tie Williams and Ty Cobb for the A.L. record.

The Lynn-Rice heroics helped brighten a disappointing season for the Red Sox, whose pennant hopes were wrecked by thin pitching and a rash of injuries, especially those which sidelined Carlton Fisk and Jerry Remy much of the season.

The Red Sox lost today's finale at Detroit, 5-1, to finish third, 11½ games behind Baltimore and 3½ behind Milwaukee. But by winning four of their last five games, the Sox have the small consolation of finishing 2 games ahead of the archrival Yankees, who suffered an even worse season while failing to defend their world championship.

November 20, 1979

The Red Sox today signed the man who helped defeat them in the seventh game of the 1975 World Series.

Tony Perez, who in his last Fenway appearance ripped Bill Lee's balloon ball for a crucial two-run homer, signed a three-year contract believed to exceed $1,000,000—reportedly $275,000 per season plus a $250,000 bonus.

The 37-year-old first baseman-designated hitter was signed to fill the void—on the field, in the clubhouse and in public relations—left by the defection of Bob Watson to the Yankees in the same free-agent re-entry draft this month in which Perez became available.

"I think you'll find there's a lot of Tony Perez left in this body," said the Cuba native, now a Puerto Rico resident. "Tony Perez can still hit, you can bet on that. I feel the same now as I did five years ago."

Perez played for Montreal the past three seasons after a dozen years as a vital cog in Cincinnati's "Big Red Machine" that won four pennants.

Above, a familiar sight at Fenway Park in 1979: Jim Rice following Fred Lynn around the bases. They were among league leaders in a variety of batting categories all season and finished 1-2 in slugging percentage. *(Boston Globe)*

Below, an unusual sight around Fenway was the usually placid Lynn losing his cool, restrained by Jim Rice in his attempt to debate umpire Dave Phillips. *(Boston Globe)*

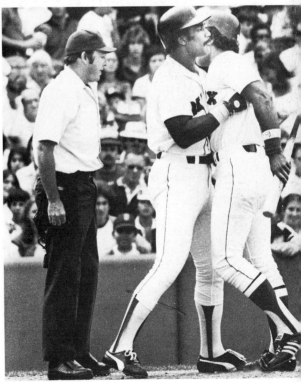

The 6-foot-2, 210-pounder is known as a clubhouse leader and clutch RBI hitter (1,357 lifetime), averaging 99 RBIs a season since becoming a regular in 1967—the year, incidentally, he won the All-Star Game at Anaheim with a 15th-inning home run.

During the decade of the seventies, Perez ranked second in the majors in RBIs (954), seventh in hits (1,560) and ninth in homers (226). His best season was 1970: .317, 40 homers and 129 RBIs. A .283 lifetime hitter, he slipped to .270 and 73 RBIs last season while being platooned by the Expos.

Perez didn't like part-time play and figures to play more for the Red Sox because of the American League's DH rule—if age (he'll be 38 in May) hasn't caught up with him.

"Don't worry about his age," advised manager Don Zimmer, who says Perez will DH and alternate at first base with Carl Yastrzemski. "The man will hit."

Especially at Fenway, presumably.

"I watched a lot of Boston's games on a Vermont station when I was with Montreal and really hoped I'd get to play at Fenway," Perez said. "I've had my eyes on Boston ever since I knew I was going to be a free agent—partly because of the city, but mostly because I like the runners that will be on base in front of me and also because the ball park is geared to my style of hitting."

Ask Bill Lee.

"Do Boston fans still remember that homer?" Perez asked. "That may have been the hardest ball I ever hit."

A week later the Red Sox shopped in the free-agent market again and came away with Skip Lockwood, signing the 33-year-old reliever for a reported $775,000 guarantee for two years with options for two more seasons.

The Sox gambled on the hard-throwing right-hander, a local product from suburban Norwood, who was a $100,000-bonus infielder with the A's in the mid-sixties before converting to pitching. He had a 1.50 ERA, a strikeout per inning, nine saves and two victories in 1979 for the Mets before a sore shoulder sidelined him the last half of the season.

Tony Perez signed a million-dollar-plus contract at Fenway, then he and wife Pituka met the Boston press. *(Boston Globe)*

SMOKEY JOE WOOD, 1908–1915:

"Baseball is all I ever wanted. I could eat, sleep and dream baseball.

"Yes, 1912 was my greatest season: 34 wins, 16 in a row, three more in the World Series, lost only six all year, struck out 279 in days when the boys didn't strike out much, and I'd beaten Walter Johnson and Christy Mathewson one after the other.

"And do you know how old I was? Well, I was 22 years old, that's all. The brightest future ahead of me that anybody could imagine in their wildest dreams.

"And do you know something else? That was *it*. That was it, right then and there. My arm went bad the next year and all my dreams came tumbling down around my ears like a damn house of cards. The next five years, seems like it was nothing but one long, terrible nightmare.

"In the spring of 1913 I went to field a ground ball on wet grass and I slipped and fell on my thumb. Broke it. The thumb on my pitching hand. It was in a cast for two or three weeks. I don't know if I tried to pitch too soon after that or whether maybe something happened to my shoulder at the same time. But whatever it was, I never pitched again without a terrible amount of pain in my right shoulder. Never again.

"I expected to have such a great year in 1913. Well, I did manage to win 11 games, with only five losses, and I struck out an average of ten a game. But it wasn't the same. The old zip was gone from that fastball. It didn't hop anymore like it used to.

"The season after that I won nine and lost three, and in 1915 I won 14 and lost five. But my arm was getting worse and worse. The pain was getting almost unbearable. After each game I pitched I'd have to lay off for a couple of weeks before I could even lift my arm. Still, in 1915 I led the league with an earned run average of 1.49.

"In the winter of 1915 I was desperate. I must have gone to hundreds of doctors over the previous three years, and nobody was able to help me. Nowadays a shot of cortisone would probably do the job in a flash, but that was 65 years ago, you know. Hell, they didn't even know about insulin back then, not to mention cortisone.

"Finally, somebody told me about a chiropractor in New York, so every week that winter I took the train to New York and this fellow worked on my back and arm. All very hush-hush—an unmarked office behind locked doors—because in those days it wasn't legal for a chiropractor to practice.

"After each treatment this chiropractor wanted me to throw as long and as hard as I possibly could. He said it would hurt, but that's what he wanted me to do. So after he was through working on me I'd go up to Columbia University, and I'd go into a corner of the gym and throw a baseball as hard as I could. I'd do that until I just wasn't able to stand the pain anymore.

"And I do mean pain. After about an hour I couldn't lift my arm as high as my belt. Had to use my left hand to put my right into my coat pocket. And if I'd go to a movie in the evening, I couldn't get my right arm up high enough to put it on the armrest.

"So in 1916 I didn't play at all. I retired. I stayed on the farm, fed the chickens, and just thought and thought about the whole situation. Only 26 years old and all washed up. A has-been. I put up a trapeze in the attic and I'd hang on that for hours to stretch my arm out. Maybe that would help—who could say? But it didn't.

"I stayed on the farm through the 1916 season. That fall, though, I began to get restless. Well, that's putting it mildly. What it was, I was starting to gnaw on the woodwork, I was getting so frustrated. Maybe I *could* come back. So what if I couldn't pitch anymore. Damn it, in 1912 I'd hit .290 in addition to winning 34 games. I could hit and I could run

13
MORE
MEMORIES

[CONTINUED FROM PAGE 234]

and I could field, and if I couldn't pitch why couldn't I do something else? Doggone, I was a *ballplayer*, not just a pitcher.

"I phoned my best friend, Tris Speaker, and told him I wanted to try again. All the years I was in the American League my roommate was Spoke. He had been traded from the Red Sox to Cleveland just before the 1916 season. Tris said he'd see what he could do.

"Meanwhile, the Red Sox had given me permission to make any deal for myself I wanted, provided it was satisfactory to them. So on February 24, 1917, I was sold to the Indians for $15,000, and once again I went to spring training, this time with Cleveland, all of 27 years old and a relic from the distant past. I'd hear fathers tell their kids, 'See that guy? That's Smokey Joe Wood. Used to be a great pitcher long ago.'

"Lee Fohl was managing Cleveland, and he encouraged me every way he could. And for my part I tried to show him that I could do more than pitch. I played the infield during fielding practice, I shagged flies in the outfield, I was ready to pinch-run, to pinch-hit—I'd have carried the water bucket if they had water boys in baseball.

"The hell with pride. I wasn't Invincible Joe Wood anymore. I was just another ball player who wanted a job and wanted it bad.

"And it paid off. My arm never did come back, but the next year, 1918, they got short of players because of the war and I was given a shot at an outfield job. Well, I *made* it. I hit .296 that season, and for *five* years I played the outfield for Cleveland, and we won the 1920 World Series. In 1921 I hit .366.

"I played in 142 games in 1922. Could have played longer, too, but I was satisfied. I figured I'd proven something to myself. To me there is great satisfaction in fooling the fates, especially when they seem dead set against you."

FRANK MALZONE, 1955–1965

"I'll never forget my first game with the Red Sox after they brought me up for a look at the end of the 1955 season. I went six for ten in a doubleheader with the Orioles at Fenway. That was a nice way to break in, but just as memorable was the embarrassment of getting picked off that day.

"One of my hits was a single off Bill Wight, a left-hander with a slick move to first base. First base coach Del Baker warned me, 'Be careful. Don't take too big a lead on this guy. He's quick over here.' No sooner were the words out of his mouth than *bang*—I'm out, picked off. All I could say was, 'You're right, coach. He's got a helluva move.'

"I don't recall who my first big league hit was off, but I do remember my first homer. It came early the next season at old Griffith Stadium in Washington off Pedro Ramos. He was a good right-hander, but I always had pretty good luck with him—a fastball hitter versus a fastball pitcher. Anyway, I hit one pretty well to left-center that must have gone 400 feet or more. It didn't just scrape the top of the wall, it was well up into the bleachers in that big ball park.

"That was a big thrill. So was an 11th-inning homer I hit into the net at Fenway off Ryne Duren to beat the Yankees. Duren was another guy I hit pretty good. He had that blazing fastball, but I knew that's all he had and so it was just a matter of waiting for a strike, another match-up of fastball hitter versus fastball pitcher.

"No, that wasn't the homer I hit during that five-game sweep of the

Yankees at Fenway in '59; that one came off Ralph Terry. That sweep was tremendous, of course. Any win over the Yankees was a thrill—especially for an old Bronx boy—but sweeping them all five in a series had to be super special.

"Not playing on a championship ball club had to be my biggest disappointment. And since we had no pennant-winners during my years as the Red Sox third baseman, I had to settle for the All-Star Games for my biggest thrills. I played in eight of them during my nine full seasons with the Sox, and each was exciting—being chosen as one of baseball's best.

"Especially the first one. It came in 1957, my first full season in the majors, and the only two Boston players chosen were me and Ted Williams, quite an honor in itself. We flew to St. Louis, and Ted filled me in on what to expect in an All-Star Game. I was George Kell's backup at third base in that game and went one-for-three. I got a single but can't recall who it was off—maybe Larry Jackson, the Cardinal right-hander.

"I do remember who I hit my only All-Star Game homer off—Don Drysdale. That was the only time I ever faced him anywhere, even counting spring training. It was the second 1959 All-Star Game—they played two a season for a few years, remember?—at the Los Angeles Coliseum, the Dodgers' temporary home while their new stadium was being built at Chavez Ravine.

"The Coliseum had that short left-field wall—what was it, 250 feet? —with that high screen in front of the bleachers, about as tall as Fenway's wall and netting put together. I was used to Fenway's short, high wall so felt right at home in the Coliseum.

"So when Drysdale hung a high curve to me, I wasn't about to let it get away, even though it wouldn't have been a strike. I jumped on it and rammed the ball up and over the screen. Yogi Berra and Rocky Colavito also homered—all the American League homers by Italians—and everyone was joking about an Italian Connection.

"The All-Star Games were great thrills, probably more so for me than for guys who played in a World Series, where there is so much more at stake.

"The closest I came to a World Series was 13 games out. We finished third in my first few seasons, then dropped to the second division in 1959 for my last seven seasons in Boston. We always lacked depth.

"Our pitching was light—one or two good ones, then we struggled beyond that. Bill Monbouquette was the best over the long span during my Red Sox years. And for a three-year period (1962-64), Dick Radatz was, well, the greatest pitcher I ever saw, barring none. Just unbelievable. When he came into a game, which was just about every other day, I felt I could sit down on the bag. *Nobody* pulled Dick Radatz. Even a left-handed hitter who managed to get wood on the ball against him never seemed to hit it my way.

"But, again, we didn't have the depth to win a pennant. And that was a big disappointment to me. So was not being able to finish my playing career with the Red Sox. I thought they'd let me, but . . . well, there's so many conflicting stories I still don't know the real one. I was 36, but felt I was still of value as a backup, a fill-in, a pinch hitter.

"Whatever, I spent my final season with the Angels, and that short-ened my career. Since it was an expansion club, I felt I had to help as a full-time player. As a part-time player with Red Sox I could have played another two or three years.

"Yes, it was a shock when the end in Boston came, although I had been expecting it in a way. In 1965 I had been alternating at third base with Dalton Jones—Jones against right-handers, Malzone against left-handers. Well, one day at Fenway the other team brought in a right-

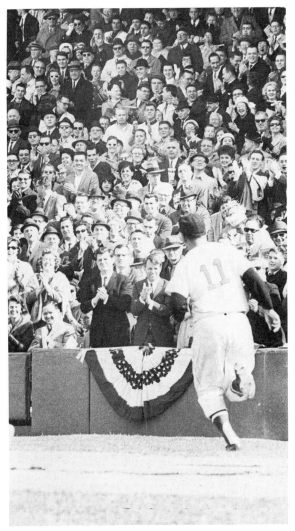

(Boston Globe)

hander to face me. When I saw Dalton coming out of the dugout to hit for me, I couldn't believe it — the first time I'd ever been pinch-hit for. It was a long walk back to the dugout.

"After the game, sportswriters asked (manager) Billy Herman about it and he said: 'Malzone's a pro. He understands.' But Malzone *didn't* understand. I was hurt. I really felt bad, especially having it happen in front of Boston fans who always had been so good to me.

"It was the biggest letdown of my career—until a few months later, when I found myself released and no longer a Red Sox. While I was sort of expecting that, it was still a shock.

"But once a Red Sox always a Red Sox, and I was delighted to rejoin the organization in 1967 as a scout, evaluating at the major league level. It was good to be back home."

JIM LONBORG, 1965–1971

"It won't come as a surprise that my biggest thrill was that magnificent moment on Sunday, October 1, 1967, when the Red Sox won the 'Impossible Dream' pennant. And to have been a central figure makes it extra special. It just as easily could have been Jose Santiago or someone else, but whether it was the fates or whatever, it was my turn in the rotation that day.

"I don't think the world's greatest screenwriter could have created a more perfect script for the Red Sox, for their fans and for baseball in general. It was a thriller that captured the imagination of baseball fans everywhere, not just in New England.

"Yes, it got a lot of attention that I pulled out of my apartment and stayed at a Boston hotel the night before the biggest game of my life. I was a bachelor then, and my family and some friends came into town and were staying at my place, and others were popping in and out. And the phone never stopped ringing. It was a party atmosphere—a wonderful atmosphere, but not one conducive to heavy concentration. So I checked into a hotel mainly for peace and quiet.

"I also did it for a secondary reason: I'd had good success on the road that season, better than at Fenway; so by staying in a hotel, I thought I might fool my body into thinking it was a road game.

"Yes, I was confident we'd beat the Twins that final day. I was just hoping for a few runs early. But the wrong team got the early runs. Yaz and Scotty made errors—and that was ironic, two guys with golden gloves—and we were down 2-0 going into the sixth inning. It was getting late.

"That's when I led off with a bunt for a hit. It wasn't a planned thing. I don't even recall when it flashed through my mind to try it, probably when Dean Chance went into his windup. No, it wasn't because I felt I couldn't hit Chance any other way; oddly enough, I'd hit Dean very well in the past, not bothered by his turn-around motion. Instead, I tried it because I had successfully bunted for hits before and thought I could do it again, particularly since a bunt was probably the last thing they were expecting.

"And it worked. It was the first of four Red Sox hits on four consecutive pitches. Dalton Jones, Jerry Adair and Yaz followed with singles on first pitches—*boom, boom, boom, boom*—and the game was tied at 2-2. So in no time we went from almost dead silence at Fenway to a madhouse. Before the inning was over we had five runs—and a pennant.

"When the last batter popped to Rico, what a *thrill*—the greatest of my career. Fenway exploded as the crowd went absolutely mad. It was

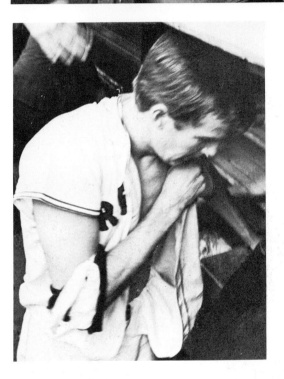

fun for a moment—getting lifted onto shoulders, just like in the movies. But it quickly got scary. I was being swept in a direction I didn't want to go, and people were just clawing at you. It was all joyous, of course, but even so the crowd was getting out of hand, in such a high state of emotion it bordered on mania.

"You can't believe the feeling of being swept up in a crowd like that. It's frightening. Fortunately, the police were tremendous and were able to get me free, but not before my uniform had been shredded. And somehow even a shoelace was pulled out of one of my spikes.

"So that game was my greatest thrill by far. Nothing I did before or after came close to producing the same emotional peak. No, not my one-hitter in the World Series; no, not *both* my Series victories. The Series didn't carry the real top-shelf emotion for us because we had already experienced that on Sunday. The climax was beating Minnesota for the pennant.

"Still, we came close to winning the Series. No, I didn't feel tired pitching the seventh game. I was loose and comfortable. But my pitches didn't have their usual velocity.

"I felt I could win anyway. Even I didn't have my best stuff, I always felt I could compensate with pinpoint location and by tricking the batters. That's the difference between a pitcher who wins 15 and a pitcher who wins 20—being able to compensate to get by when he has poor stuff.

"So I thought I could get by in that seventh game. What beat me was that I didn't have the good location I needed. I was 'wild' *over* the plate. Instead of being on the corners, or a little inside or outside to get the batter to bite for a bad pitch, I was coming over the plate too often with pitches that lacked velocity. The Cardinals caught on to that, realizing that if they waited I'd eventually come in with a fat pitch. It was one of those bad pitches that Javier jacked out for the big home run in the sixth inning.

"Yes, winning the Cy Young Award was gratifying. It's a magnificent thing, and I was proud of the honor. But it's for individual achievement, and what was far more important and stands out much more in my mind was being part of that 'Impossible Dream' *team*. That was far more of a thrill.

"That wasn't just *any* pennant story, it was one of the most unique in baseball history. How many teams have won the pennant after finishing a half-game out of last place the previous season and not finishing higher than seventh place in five years? It was a success story that endeared a team to the nation, and added to the Red Sox tradition.

"There's a special feeling for the Red Sox across the country. I saw it not only while playing for Boston, but also later while pitching for Milwaukee and Philadelphia. People always brought up that I had pitched for the Red Sox, like 'Oh, yes, you pitched for the *Red Sox*.' Almost with a reverence.

"Yes, people always seem to remember my skiing accident, too. Of course I wish it never happened; if I had *known* it was going to happen I never would have done it. Sure I realized there was a certain amount of danger involved, but there's a danger in everything, including stepping off the sidewalk. I didn't think the risk was excessive.

"I certainly wasn't doing it to defy danger and it certainly wasn't a lark. I enjoy skiing, but more important it's a *great* conditioner and I'd been doing it a few years for exactly that reason; it had been part of the reason for my success. And how many ways can you think of to have fun while doing something that's a serious conditioner?

"The knee injury led to my pitching shoulder problems. I never hurt the arm; it was the shoulder. The knee itself mended well; the recovery was excellent. But *while* it was mending I was unknowingly compensating in my motion, and that did it. I disrupted my pitching rhythm and hurt muscles and tendons in the back of my right shoulder.

"I had rushed the arm. I have aggressive tendencies, and they were magnified by an eagerness to get back pitching quickly, to help the team and, well, there had been all that flak about my skiing. Maybe it was just in my own mind, but I felt that the press and management were breathing down my neck, although management had never said anything.

"Whatever, I felt it was important to pitch as soon as I could, though unfamiliar with the precautions I had to take. I rushed it and hurt the shoulder, and kept trying and made things worse. It all snowballed. Tendons don't regenerate well, and I built up tremendous adhesions.

"I never had the same pitching strength again, never could throw as hard. But I became a better *pitcher*, as opposed to a *thrower*. I changed from a guy who blew batters away to one who had command of the corners, one who gained more and more knowledge of what *total* pitching is.

"And I had some more good seasons. Despite a lot of pain in '72 as I kept breaking down all those adhesions, I won 14 for a last-place Milwaukee team. I gave up three runs or less in 21 of 25 games, two runs or less in 15 games. And I won 18 for the Phillies in '75, probably my best season as a *pitcher*.

"My biggest disappointment? Being traded by the Red Sox after the '71 season. I had finished up with five or six victories in a row and felt everything was coming together again. I felt I was on the verge of proving something and, I suppose, of making up for the disappointments since hurting my shoulder. I had my heart set on that, and then not getting the chance was, well, it was very, very disappointing to me.

"Also, Rosemary and I had just been married and were very happy in Boston. And anyone who has the chance to play baseball in Boston—with its unique fans, its history, its New England setting and all—becomes a part of that scene that's so special. You don't want to leave all that.

"No, I wasn't glad to get away from Fenway. Pitching there didn't bother me. Although mistakes can hurt you quicker there than anywhere else, Fenway also can help you. The Wall reduces a lot of line drives to singles and doubles that would be homers elsewhere. And I'd much prefer to pitch there than in all those artificial-turf stadiums where the ball moves like lightning on the ground, especially for a sinker ball pitcher like me who kept the ball down to force grounders. The time

Fenway becomes a farce is when the wind is blowing out and carrying pop-ups into the net for cheap homers.

"Even then, pitchers are at least partly at fault. They should be making the batter beat the ball into the ground. I always insisted on having the area in front of the plate watered down and the infield grass grown a little taller to take some sting out of those grounders, and Red Sox management and the ground crew were very cooperative.

"No, our hitters didn't complain much about it that I recall. If anyone mentioned it, I just told them to hit the ball where they were supposed to hit it—on a line, not on the ground. You've got to keep those hitters in their place, don't you?"

(Boston Globe)

ABOUT THE AUTHOR

A former sports columnist for the *Boston Herald Traveler*, George Sullivan has been a contributing writer for the *Boston Globe* since 1972 when he joined the faculty of Boston University, his alma mater, as a journalism professor.

Sullivan, a onetime visiting team bat boy at Fenway Park, has been writing about the Red Sox for more than 25 years. He by-lined his first story out of Fenway for the *Boston Traveler* at age 20 in 1954, and made his first road trip two summers later.

Sullivan, wife Betty and their three children divide their time between homes in the Boston suburb of Belmont, Massachusetts, and the seaside town of Little Compton, Rhode Island.

Color photograph on front cover by Dick Raphael
Jacket design by William L. Verrill, Jr.